Analysis of Changes
NEC-2017

Analysis of Changes
NEC-2017

International Association of Electrical Inspectors
Richardson, Texas

ISBN-10: 1-890659-72-X
ISBN-13: 978-1-890659-72-1

Library of Congress Control Number: 2010930805

Photos used in this book were shot *in situ* or at tradeshows. Use of the photos does not imply endorsement by IAEI of the manufacturers or the products. Photos without a credit line are from IAEI Archives.

Notice to the Reader

This book has not been processed in accordance with NFPA Regulations Governing Committee Projects. Therefore, the text and commentary in it shall not be considered the official position of the NFPA or any of its committees and shall not be considered to be, nor relied upon as a formal interpretation of the meaning or intent of any specific provision or provisions of the 2017 edition of NFPA 70, *National Electrical Code.*[1]

Publishers do not warrant or guarantee any of the products described herein or perform any independent analysis in connection with any of the product information contained herein. Publisher does not assume, and expressly disclaims, any obligation to obtain and include information referenced in this work.

The reader is expressly warned to consider carefully and adopt all safety precautions that might be indicated by the activities described herein and to avoid all potential hazards. By following the instructions contained herein, the reader willingly assumes all risks in connection with such instructions.

THE PUBLISHERS MAKE NO REPRESENTATIONS OR WARRANTIES OF ANY KIND, INCLUDING, BUT NOT LIMITED TO, THE IMPLIED WARRANTIES OF FITNESS FOR PARTICULAR PURPOSE, MERCHANTABILITY OR NON-INFRINGEMENT, NOR ARE ANY SUCH REPRESENTATIONS IMPLIED WITH RESPECT TO SUCH MATERIAL. THE PUBLISHERS SHALL NOT BE LIABLE FOR ANY SPECIAL, INCIDENTAL, CONSEQUENTIAL OR EXEMPLARY DAMAGES RESULTING, IN WHOLE OR IN PART, FROM THE READER'S USES OF OR RELIANCE UPON THIS MATERIAL.

[1]*National Electrical Code* and *NEC* are registered trademarks of the National Fire Protection Association, Inc., Quincy, MA 02169

This book conveys the information related to each change as of July 1, 2016, but does not reflect any subsequent appeal or action taken by the NFPA Standards Council.

Table of Contents

6

◼ Chapter 7: Special Conditions, Articles 700 – 770

◼ Chapter 8: Communications Systems, Articles 810 – 840

◼ Chapter 9: Tables and Annex D

Colophon

Preface

The *National Electrical Code* is updated on a three-year *Code* cycle. The International Association of Electrical Inspectors publishes its *Analysis of Changes* every three years on the same publishing schedule as the *NEC*. This publication is based on the revisions to the 2017 *NEC*.

The 2017 *NEC* experienced a change in the revision process. In the past, the first public meeting for the *NEC* revision process was known as the Report on Proposals. This was replaced with the 2017 *NEC* First Draft meeting. Suggested changes to the *NEC*, which were known as Proposals, were replaced with Public Inputs. The PIs that were acted upon favorably resulted in a First Revision to the First Draft of the 2017 *NEC*.

The second public meeting for the *NEC* revision process was known as the Report on Comments meeting, which was replaced with the 2017 *NEC* Second Draft meeting. Submitted Comments were replaced with Public Comments. Successful PCs resulted in Second Revisions to the Second Draft of 2017 *NEC*. Appeals will be heard and voting for acceptance of the 2017 *NEC* will take place at the NFPA Annual Conference in June 2016. The NFPA Standards Council will issue the 2017 *NEC* in August 2016 with a publication date of September of 2016.

There were 4102 Public Inputs submitted from interested participants, which resulted in 1233 First Revisions to the First Draft of the 2017 *NEC*. A total of 1513 Public Comments resulted in 559 Second Revisions to the Second Draft of the *NEC*.

In this book, IAEI has reported on the most significant changes to the 2017 *NEC*. The revisions reported on in this publication were based on the Second Draft of the 2017 *NEC*. While IAEI takes every precaution to deliver the most accurate account of the changes to the latest edition of the *NEC*, these revisions are subject to alterations from the time of publication of the *Analysis of Changes* to the deliverance of the final version of the 2017 *NEC*.

Key terms and abbreviations that are used in the *Analysis of Changes*:

NEC National Electrical Code
FD First Draft (*NEC*)
SD Second Draft (*NEC*)
PI Public Input
PC Public Comment
FR First Revision
FCR First Committee Revision
SR Second Revision
SCR Second Committee Revision
CMP Code Making Panel
CI CMP Committee Input
NEC CC *NEC* Correlating Committee
NITMAM Notice of Intent to Make a Motion
CAM Certified Ammending Motion
TIA Tentative Interim Amendment
AHJ Authority Having Jurisdiction. An organization, office, or individual responsible for enforcing the requirements of a code or standard, or for approving equipment, materials, an installation, or a procedure (*NEC* Article 100). This AHJ could be the Building Official, Electrical Inspector, Fire Marshal, etc.

Analysis Introduction

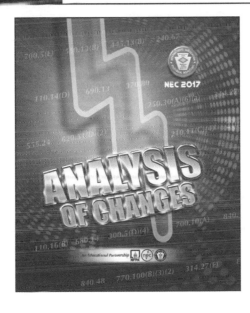

Code-Wide Changes

New Articles

Article 90

National Electrical Code

Code-Wide Changes

Definitions Relocated to Article 100

Limited Access Working Space

600 Volts Threshold to 1000 Volts

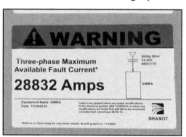

Available Short-Circuit Current

Entire NEC

- **Type of Change:** New and Revised

Analysis of the Change:

- **Definitions Relocated to Article 100.** Several existing definitions that appeared in particular articles have been relocated to Article 100 because these terms are also found in other articles, not just the article where the previous definition was located. An example of this would be the definition of "coaxial cable" relocated from 820.2 to Article 100 since this term appears in four articles of the *NEC*. The *NEC Style Manual* (see section 2.2.2.1) requires that Article 100 contain definitions of terms that appear in two or more articles of the *NEC*. Another example would be the relocation of fourteen existing definitions from 500.2 to Article 100. These "hazardous location" definitions also appear in two or more articles.

- **Limited Access Working Space in Article 110.** Electrical equipment is often installed in spaces with limited access, such as above a lay in suspended ceiling or in a crawl space. The working space rules in 110.26(A) apply to all equipment that is likely to require examination, adjustment, servicing, or maintenance while energized. Strict compliance with all of the working space rules in these ceiling spaces and crawl spaces is not always possible. The electrical industry has been installing and accepting equipment in such spaces for decades. Prescriptive requirements for equipment installed in those spaces has been sorely lacking for that same time period. This limited access provision is an attempt to provide relief for both the installer/maintainer and the enforcement community. Since it is located in Article 110, this limited access provision will have an impact on all electrical equipment across the *Code,* provides clarity and usability, and eliminates potential conflict and confusion from one article to another.

■ **Continued Migration Throughout the** *NEC* **from the 600 Volt Threshold to 1000 Volts.** The journey to raise the voltage threshold in the *NEC* from 600 volts to 1000 volts continued in the 2017 *NEC*. These changes are implemented from Public Inputs and Public Comments from a High Voltage Task Group (HVTG). The *NEC* Correlating Committee appointed the HVTG to address issues with installations over 600 volts. This task group began work at the end of the 2008 *NEC* cycle. The HVTG was charged with reviewing all *NEC* requirements and/or the lack of requirements for circuits and systems operating at over 600 volts.

This review resulted in numerous changes throughout the 2014 *NEC* from 600 volts to 1000 volts. Not all locations where 600 volts was referenced were changed in the 2014 *NEC*. Eighty-two percent of the proposals submitted to raise the voltage threshold during the 2014 *NEC* Code cycle were accepted in some form. Where a code-making panel felt there was a safety issue or where manufacturers did not want to pursue having their products evaluated at 1000 volts, the 600-volt threshold was left intact. For the 2017 *NEC*, 600 volts was raised to 1000 volts in about thirty different locations as a result of the work of the HVTG.

For the 2017 *NEC*, the HVTG was charged with the task of resolving issues with actions taken by Code Making Panels 1 and 8 on proposals and comments in the 2014 *NEC Code* cycle relative to changing the voltage threshold in articles under their purview from 600 volts to 1000 volts, addressing indoor and outdoor electrical substations, and evaluating other higher voltage threshold requirements to be included relative to present trends.

■ **Documentation of Available Short-Circuit Current.** There were several new requirements added throughout the *NEC* involving the documentation of the available short-circuit current (fault current) at specific types of equipment and the date the short-circuit current calculation was performed, with this documentation made available to the AHJ. While the earlier *NEC* editions required this documentation in many places, this requirement was added in nine locations throughout the 2017 *NEC*. The requirement for available short-circuit current documentation was added for such things as industrial control panels, motor control centers, air-conditioning equipment, elevators and industrial machinery.

NEC

Also included in these requirements is emergency system transfer equipment for emergency systems, legally required standby systems, optional standby systems, and critical operations power systems (COPS). Inspectors have a difficult time enforcing proper short-circuit current ratings on such equipment as industrial control panels (which is required by 409.22). The equipment is usually properly marked with the short-circuit current rating by the manufacturer, but typically there is no information on the job site as to the available short-circuit current at the equipment. These new requirements for documentation of the available short-circuit current will make it much easier to assure that the equipment is being properly protected.

National Electrical Code

New Articles for the 2017 NEC

NEC

> **Article 425 Fixed Resistance and Electrode Industrial Process Heating Equipment.** This article covers fixed industrial process heating employing electric resistance or electrode heating technology (boilers, electrode boilers, duct heaters, strip heaters, immersion heaters, process air heaters, or other approved fixed electric equipment used for industrial process heating).
>
> **Article 691 Large-Scale Photovoltaic (PV) Electric Power Production Facility.** This article covers the installation of large-scale PV electric power production facilities operated for the sole purpose of providing electric supply to a system operated by a regulated utility for the transfer of electrical energy with a generating capacity of no less than 5,000 kW (generating stations, substations, associated generator, storage battery, transformer, and switchgear areas).
>
> **Article 706 Energy Storage Systems .** This article applies to all permanently installed energy storage systems (ESS) operating at over 50 volts ac or 60 volts dc that may be stand-alone or interactive with other electric power production sources.
>
> **Article 710 Stand-Alone Systems.** This article covers electric power production sources operating in stand-alone mode.
>
> **Article 712 Direct Current Microgrids (DC Microgrids).** This article applies to direct current microgrids, which is a power distribution system consisting of more than one interconnected dc power sources, supplying dc-dc converters(s), dc loads(s), and/or ac loads(s) powered by dc-ac inverters(s).

Entire Code

- **Type of Change:** New

Analysis of the Change:

- **Article 425 Fixed Resistance and Electrode Industrial Process Heating Equipment.** In previous editions, the *NEC* did not adequately address requirements for industrial process heating equipment. Article 422 for appliances had some requirements for infrared heat lamps, but those requirements have been relocated to the new Article 425 for Fixed Resistance and Electrode Industrial Process Heating Equipment. This new article applies to such things as boilers, electrode boilers, duct heaters, strip heaters, immersion heaters, process air heaters, or other approved fixed electric equipment used for industrial process heating.

This article will not apply to heating and room air conditioning for personal spaces covered by Article 424, fixed heating equipment for pipelines and vessels covered by Article 427, induction and dielectric heating equipment covered by Article 665, and industrial furnaces incorporating silicon carbide, molybdenum, or graphite process heating elements.

This new article will provide clear requirements for installation and enforcement for industrial process heating equipment, including working space, listing requirements, marking of equipment, overcurrent protection, protection from physical damage, installation in damp or wet locations, and spacing from combustible materials.

■ **Article 691 Large-Scale Photovoltaic (PV) Electric Power Production Facility.** In the last few years, large-scale PV systems producing in excess of 5 megawatts have become commonplace in the United States. Some pf these systems can produce upwards of 50 megawatts. A 50 megawatt PV system produces the equivalent energy of roughly 25,000 residential PV systems. While the number of large-scale PV systems is relatively small, the volume of electricity generated by these systems is greater than the combined output of all residential and commercial PV systems addressed by Article 690.

The rapid increase in the number of large-scale PV electric power production facilities presents new challenges to the AHJ when facing inspection and approval of a PV power plant within his or her jurisdiction. These large-scale PV systems are difficult, if not impossible, to fit under the current umbrella of Article 690. With this in mind, a new article has emerged in the 2017 *NEC* for these larger-scaled PV systems. This article covers the installation of large-scale PV electric power production facilities operated for the sole purpose of providing electric supply to the utility transmission or distribution system with a generating capacity of no less than 5,000 kW. Facilities covered by this article have specific design and safety features unique to large-scale PV facilities.

Photovoltaic technology has experienced rapid changes over the last decade. The pace of change has created challenges for laboratories responsible for listing electrical equipment and for the organizations responsible for writing standards and for the *NEC*. One of the key determinants of whether a PV system is covered by Article 690 is that the PV system is connected on the customer's side of the meter and the electricity generated is primarily used to offset the local facility's normal electrical loads. Backfeeding the electrical grid is allowed but is incidental to the purpose of the system. Large-scale PV systems connect to the grid on the utility side of the metering system rather than on the customer side. Typically, they are connected at medium voltages (4.16 kV to 34.5 kV) or even

NEC

transmission voltages (69 kV or higher) rather than at 480 volts or lower. This article will help the AHJ when assessing compliance of large-scale PV electric supply stations and will enable system engineers to use engineering best practices in the design of large-scale PV electric power production facilities.

- **Article 706 Energy Storage Systems.** Added to Chapter 7 was an article addressing permanently installed energy storage systems (ESS) that may be stand-alone or interactive with other electric power production sources. An ESS is defined as a device, or more than one device together, capable of storing energy for use at a future time. An ESS could include but is not limited to electrochemical storage devices (e.g., batteries), flow batteries, capacitors, and kinetic energy devices (e.g., flywheels and compressed air). These systems can have ac or dc output for utilization and can include inverters and converters to change stored energy into electrical energy. This article is primarily the result of the work developed by a DC Task Group formed by the *NEC* Correlating Committee.

- **Article 710 Stand-Alone Systems.** This article covers electric power production sources operating in stand-alone mode. Stand-alone systems are defined as a microgrid that operates independently of a primary power source. Stand-alone systems are also known as *isolated microgrids*, *islands*, and *prime power systems*. Microgrids are getting recognition as a way to add resiliency against loss of power in premises wiring systems. These requirements were initially proposed and accepted as part of Article 705 (Interconnected Electric Power Production Sources). However, the requirements for stand-alone systems do not fit well in Article 705. For stand-alone systems to remain in Article 705, the scope and title of Article 705 would have had to be changed to encompass both interconnected and non-interconnected systems.

Creating new Article 710 was logical and is supported by the original submitter, which was the DC Task Group created by the *NEC* Correlating Committee. Currently, stand-alone system requirements exist in Articles 690, 692 and 694 of the 2014 *NEC*. Creating a new article for stand-alone systems is important to other power sources, such as engine generators. The need for regulations for stand-alone systems is the same whether the source is a generator or an inverter.

- **Article 712 Direct Current Microgrids (DC Microgrids).** A new article has been developed for direct current microgrids. A dc microgrid is defined as a power distribution system consisting of more than one interconnected dc power source, supplying dc-dc converters(s), dc loads(s), and/or ac loads(s) powered by dc-ac inverters(s). A dc microgrid is typically not directly connected to an ac primary source of electricity, but some dc microgrids interconnect via one or more dc-ac bidirectional converters or dc–ac inverters.

DC microgrids allow the direct utilization of power from dc sources to dc loads such as LED lighting, communications equipment, computers, variable-speed motor drives, etc. Direct utilization of dc, whether generated by PV systems, fuel cells, or other means (without intervening dc-ac and ac-dc conversion steps) leads to higher efficiencies and potentially smaller and lower-cost equipment than ac-coupled methods. DC microgrids with energy storage also offer inherent resilience and security from the failure of primary power sources. They also allow significantly simpler interconnection of power sources than ac microgrids, as no synchronization equipment is needed with dc. The need for higher efficiency in telecom and data centers has driven these industries to implement dc microgrids in hundreds of data centers around the world. It is a trend that will likely continue to grow. In addition to use in data centers, dc microgrids are being demonstrated in governmental, academic and commercial facilities.

As with Articles 706 (Energy Storage Systems) and 710 (Stand-Alone Systems), this new article was the result of the work of the DC Task Group of the *NEC* Correlating Committee. While the basic requirements for wiring methods, overcurrent protection, and grounding are specified in other articles of the *NEC*, they do not cover all of the issues involved when dc multiple sources and dc loads are interconnected. This lack of coverage alone would justify the need for this new article. This DC microgrid article is an important first step and a place-holder for future requirements in this rapidly developing arena.

NEC

First Revisions: See FRs and SRs with associated new articles
Public Inputs: See PIs and PCs with associated new articles

90.3

Code Arrangement

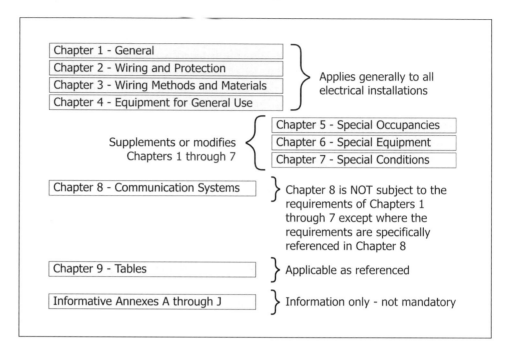

90.3 Code Arrangement

- **Type of Change:** Revision

- **Change at a Glance:** Chapters 5 –7 may supplement or modify the general requirements in Chapters 1 through 7 (not just Chapters 1 – 4).

- **Code Language: 90.3 Code Arrangement.**

    This Code is divided into the introduction and nine chapters, as shown in Figure 90.3. Chapters 1, 2, 3, and 4 apply generally; Chapters 5, 6, and 7 apply to special occupancies, special equipment, or other special conditions. ~~These latter chapters~~ and may supplement or modify the ~~general rules.~~ requirements in Chapters 1 through 7. ~~4 apply except as amended by Chapters 5, 6, and 7 for the particular conditions.~~

    Chapter 8 covers communications systems and is not subject to the requirements of Chapters 1 through 7 except where the requirements are specifically referenced in Chapter 8.

    Chapter 9 consists of tables that are applicable as referenced. Informative annexes are not part of the requirements of this Code but are included for informational purposes only.

- **2014 *NEC* Requirement**
    Section 90.3 and Figure 90.3 indicated that Chapters 1 through 4

applied generally, except as amended by Chapters 5, 6, and 7 for the particular conditions, and that the later chapters only modified Chapters 1 through 4.

- **2017 *NEC* Change**
  Revision to 90.3 and Figure 90.3 will now indicate that Chapters 5, 6, and 7 can supplement or modify Chapters 1 through 7.

Analysis of the Change:

To know and understand the *NEC*, the first place to start is 90.3 and Figure 90.3. This section and the accompanying figure give a "roadmap" of the *NEC*. Without a clear understanding of 90.3, it is common for a novice of the *Code* to interpret that conflicts exist from one chapter to another in the *NEC*. An example of this can be found by comparing the location of a service disconnect for a fire pump described at 695.4(B)(3)(4) with the grouping requirement for service disconnects found at 230.72(A). The rule in Article 695 (Chapter 6) for fire pumps requires the disconnect to be located "sufficiently remote" from other disconnecting means while the rules in Article 230 (Chapter 2) demand that all service disconnecting means be "grouped" in one location. A understanding of 90.3 would clear up this seeming conflict as this section explains that the rule in Chapter 6 would supplement or modify the grouping rule in Chapter 2.

NEC

Previous *Code* text at 90.3 indicated that Chapters 5, 6, and 7 modified only Chapters 1 through 4. There are requirements in Chapter 5, 6, and 7 that modify requirements in other articles within Chapters 5, 6, and 7 as well as the first four chapters of the *Code*. A good example of this is found at 645.4, which explicitly states that Article 645 (Information Technology Equipment) is permitted to provide alternate wiring methods to Articles 708, 725 and 770. For this reason, 90.3 was revised to permit the rules in these latter chapters to not only modify Chapters 1 through 4 but to modify each other as well.

First Revisions: FR 3
Public Inputs: PI 2590, PI 684

Chapter 1 General

Article 100 — Definitions
Accessible, Readily (Readily Accessible)

100 Accessible, Readily (Readily Accessible)

- **Type of Change:** Revision

- **Change at a Glance:** The use of a key is not considered taking an action such as the use of a "tool" to gain ready access. Crawling under something is not considered readily accessible.

- **Code Language:** Article 100 Definitions

  Accessible, Readily (Readily Accessible). Capable of being reached quickly for operation, renewal, or inspections without requiring those to whom ready access is requisite to take actions such as to use tools (other than keys), to climb over or under, to remove obstacles, or to resort to portable ladders, and so forth.

  Informational Note: Use of keys is a common practice under controlled or supervised conditions and a common alternative to the ready access requirements under such supervised conditions as provided elsewhere in the *NEC.*

- **2014 *NEC* Requirement**
  To have to resort to the use of a "tool" to gain access to something to be "readily accessible" does not meet the definition of *readily accessible.*

Equipment that can only be reached by "climbing over" an obstacle would also not meet the definition of readily accessible.

Accessible, Readily (Readily Accessible). Capable of being reached quickly for operation, renewal, or inspections without requiring those to whom ready access is requisite to actions such as to use tools, to climb over or remove obstacles, or to resort to portable ladders, and so forth.

■ **2017 *NEC* Change**
Revisions were made to indicate that the use of a key does not fall under the "use of tools." Having to resort to "crawling under" (as well as "climbing over") an obstacle was added to actions that do not meet the definition. This change aligns with the language in 110.26(F), which indicates that electrical rooms or enclosures controlled by a lock are considered accessible to qualified persons.

Analysis of the Change:

The definition of *readily accessible* has once again been revised for clarity. The phrase "to actions such as to use tools" was added in the 2014 *NEC* revision cycle. This added phrase concerning tools was interpreted by some *Code* users as a prohibition against the use of a key to gain access to an object needing ready access. CMP-1 clarified that locks do not prevent equipment from being readily accessible by adding the phrase "other than keys" follow the word "tools" in this definition for the 2017 *NEC*. This revision will continue to allow a panelboard cover to be locked with a key while recognizing that the overcurrent devices located behind the panelboard's operable lid or door are still "readily accessible."

This definition also described having "to climb over or remove obstacles, or to resort to portable ladders, and so forth" as actions that would prohibit meeting the definition of "readily accessible." For the 2017 *NEC*, having to crawl "under" obstacles was added to the definition. It is not unusual for equipment such as panelboards and disconnects (which are required to be readily accessible) to be installed between rows of conveyor belts and similar obstacles. This installation method often requires maintenance workers to have to crawl under the conveyor belt or other obstacles to access such equipment. Crawling under an obstacle is no better than climbing over an obstacle to reach a piece of electrical equipment.

It is interesting to note that in the Committee Statement for FR 8, CMP-1 indicated that the list items included in the definition of Readily Accessible are "not intended to be an all-inclusive list."

First Revisions: FR 8
Second Revisions: SR 6
Public Inputs: PI 3361, PI 2892, PI 2317
Public Comments: PC 300, PC 199, PC 1039, PC 1731

100

Article 100 — Definitions
Associated Apparatus

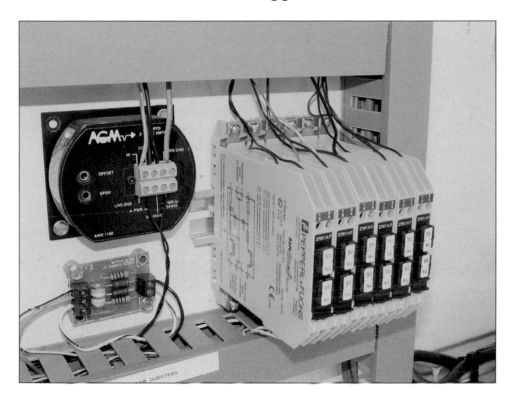

100

100 Associated Apparatus

- **Type of Change:** Relocation

- **Change at a Glance:** The definition of *Associated Apparatus* was relocated to Article 100.

- **Code Language:** Article 100 Definitions

   Associated Apparatus [as applied to Hazardous (Classified) Locations]. Apparatus in which the circuits are not necessarily intrinsically safe themselves but that affects the energy in the intrinsically safe circuits and is relied on to maintain intrinsic safety. Such apparatus is one of the following:
   (1) Electrical apparatus that has an alternative type of protection for use in the appropriate hazardous (classified) location
   (2) Electrical apparatus not so protected that shall not be used within a hazardous (classified) location

   Informational Note No. 1: Associated apparatus has identified intrinsically safe connections for intrinsically safe apparatus and also may have connections for non-intrinsically safe apparatus.

Informational Note No. 2: An example of associated apparatus is an intrinsic safety barrier, which is a network designed to limit the energy (voltage and current) available to the protected circuit in the hazardous (classified) location, under specified fault conditions.

- **2014 *NEC* Requirement**
  The definition of *Associated Apparatus* was located in Article 504 (Intrinsically Safe Systems), in Section 504.2.

- **2017 *NEC* Change**
  The definition of "Associated Apparatus" was relocated to Article 100 for application across the hazardous location *NEC* articles.

Analysis of the Change:

Whenever a definition is included in an Article other than Article 100, it is required to be located in the ".2" section. The term *Associated Apparatus* appears in Articles 500, 504, 505, and 506. For the 2014 *NEC*, this definition was located in Article 504 (Intrinsically Safe Systems) at 504.2. This location was not in compliance with the *NEC Style Manual* as Section 2.2.2.1 states that in general, definitions of terms that appear in two or more articles shall be located in Article 100. The addition of the words "[as applied to Hazardous (Classified) Locations]" will make it clear that the definition pertains to Articles 500 through 516 as applicable.

This relocation coincides with the relocation of 14 existing definitions that were located at 500.2 that will now be located in Article 100. These multiple definition relocations will be reported on in more detail in Chapter 5 of this publication.

First Revisions: FR 3919
Public Inputs: PI: PI 1756, PI 1821

100

Article 100 — Definitions
Building, Structure

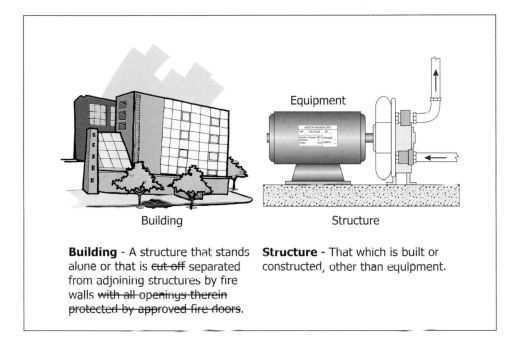

Building

Structure

Building - A structure that stands alone or that is ~~cut off~~ separated from adjoining structures by fire walls ~~with all openings therein protected by approved fire doors~~.

Structure - That which is built or constructed, other than equipment.

100 Building, Structure

- **Type of Change:** Revision

- **Change at a Glance:** The definitions for *building* and *structure* were revised to align with current Building Code terms.

- **Code Language: Article 100 Definitions**

  Building. A structure that stands alone or that is ~~cut off~~ separated from adjoining structures by fire walls ~~with all openings therein protected by approved fire doors~~.

  Structure. That which is built or constructed, other than equipment.

- **2014 *NEC* Requirement**
  Building was defined in Article 100. The definition included unnecessary text that was better suited for the Building Code. *Structure* was defined as "that which was built or constructed" and could be interpreted as including equipment.

- **2017 *NEC* Change**
  These terms were revised to eliminate Building Code provisions and to clarify that a structure is something other than equipment.

Analysis of the Change:

These two related definitions were revised for the 2017 *NEC*. The revisions were based on the work of the Task Group assigned by the *NEC* Correlating Committee to address structures, including recreational vehicle (RV) pedestals, and to resolve issues with actions taken by CMP-19 on proposals and comments during the 2014 *NEC Code* cycle relative to comparing the definitions of "Structure" and "Building."

The addition of the phrase "other than equipment" at the end of the definition of *Structure* provides clarification that structures do not include equipment. Part of the recommendation of the Task Group was to establish a difference between a "structure" and "equipment" for the purpose of establishing a grounding electrode system as compared to installing optional or auxiliary electrodes at something like an RV pedestal. Among CMP members, as well as users of the *Code*, there seemed to be confusion about what is considered equipment versus what is considered a structure. Based on the previous definition of a structure, everything built or constructed is a structure, including equipment. With the revised definition of "Structure," equipment can be mounted on a structure, but the equipment itself is not a structure. An electric vehicle (EV) charging station is a good example of equipment that is not a structure, but which could be mounted to a structure. Another example would be a motor or an air-conditioner compressor mounted on a concrete pad. The electrical equipment is mounted to the structure (concrete pad or footing). The motor or AC unit is manufactured equipment; the concrete pad or footing is the structure.

The definition of *building* was revised to replace "cut off" with "separated." This change makes the definition more consistent with building code terminology. The reference to "fire doors" was deleted as well; the term could be misleading as not all openings in firewalls are doors. Building codes determine openings permitted in firewalls, and these openings are not limited to fire doors. When such openings are included within a firewall, the building code should dictate the level of protection required for the opening (*not the NEC*).

First Revisions: FR 9, FR 13
Public Inputs: PI 2894, PI 2109

100

Article 100 — Definitions
Coaxial Cable

100 | **100 Coaxial Cable**

- **Type of Change:** Relocation

- **Change at a Glance:** The definition for *Coaxial Cable* was relocated to Article 100.

- **Code Language:** Article 100 Definitions

  Coaxial Cable. A cylindrical assembly composed of a conductor centered inside a metallic tube or shield, separated by a dielectric material, and usually covered by an insulating jacket.

- **2014 *NEC* Requirement**
  The definition of *Coaxial Cable* was found in Article 820 at 820.2.

- **2017 *NEC* Change**
  The definition of *Coaxial Cable* was relocated to Article 100 to have an application to other articles across the *NEC*.

Analysis of the Change:

Whenever a definition is included in an article other than Article 100, it is required to be located in the ".2" section. The term *Coaxial Cable* appears in Articles 400, 620, 680, 725, 760, 800, 820, 830 and 840. For the 2014 NEC, this definition was located in Article 820 (Community Antenna Television and Radio Distribution Systems) at 820.2. Since Chapter 8 is essentially a "stand-alone" chapter in the *NEC*, moving the definition to Article 100 makes it clear that the definition applies to all uses of the term throughout the *Code*.

First Revisions: FR 4501

Public Inputs: PI 1650, PI 209, PI 1649

Article 100 — Definitions
Field Evaluation Body (FEB) and Field Labeled

Field Evaluation Body (FEB). An organization or part of an organization that performs field evaluations of electrical or other equipment. [NFPA 790, 2012]

Field Labeled (as applied to evaluated products). Equipment or materials to which has been attached a label, symbol, or other identifying mark of an FEB indicating the equipment or materials were evaluated and found to comply with requirements as described in an accompanying field evaluation report.

100

100 Field Evaluation Body (FEB) and Field Labeled

- **Type of Change:** New

- **Change at a Glance:** Two new definitions pertaining to field evaluations of electrical equipment were added to Article 100

- **Code Language:** Article 100 Definitions

Field Evaluation Body (FEB). An organization or part of an organization that performs field evaluations of electrical or other equipment. [NFPA 790, 2012]

Field Labeled (as applied to evaluated products). Equipment or materials to which has been attached a label, symbol, or other identifying mark of an FEB indicating the equipment or materials were evaluated and found to comply with requirements as described in an accompanying field evaluation report.

- **2014 *NEC* Requirement**
  These two terms were not defined in the 2014 *NEC*.

- **2017 *NEC* Change**
  Two new terms —*Field Evaluation Body (FEB)* and *Field Labeled*— were added to the 2017 *NEC*.

Analysis of the Change:

Field evaluations of electrical products are a recognized process in the electrical community. For the *NEC* to use terms related to a field evaluation, these terms need to be defined.

A field evaluation is a process whereby products that do not have a certification acceptable to the authority having jurisdiction (AHJ), the owner, or another regulatory body can be evaluated to the applicable product safety standard(s) for the specific application and location where the product is being utilized. The process includes construction inspection for the use of components, assembly, and limited nondestructive testing to complete the assessment. The majority of the national, regional, city and other municipality jurisdictions typically require electrical products to be certified or evaluated by a recognized third party before they can be approved by the AHJ for use.

For products that do not have a certification or that have been modified in the field, a field evaluation accomplishes this required evaluation. This process is typically reserved for electrical products that are already installed at a designated end-use site. Installed electrical equipment that has not been previously certified, listed, recognized, or classified can be field evaluated to ensure compliance. NFPA 790 provides qualifications and competencies for third parties performing field evaluations, and NFPA 791 specifies how equipment is to be evaluated.

These two new definitions are necessary to recognize a process of field evaluation of equipment as these terms are used in two or more *NEC* articles, specifically in the photovoltaic articles in Chapter 6. These definitions are extracted material from NFPA 790 (Standard for Competency of Third-Party Field Evaluation Bodies).

First Revisions: FR 1041
Second Revisions: SR 918
Public Comment: PC 917

100

Article 100 — Definitions

Receptacle

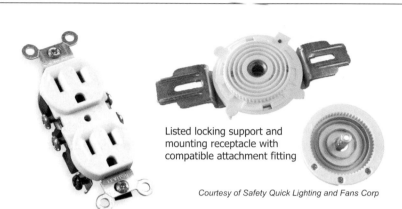

Listed locking support and mounting receptacle with compatible attachment fitting

Courtesy of Safety Quick Lighting and Fans Corp

Receptacle. A contact device installed at the outlet for the connection of an attachment plug, or for the direct connection of listed and labeled electrical utilization equipment designed to mate with the corresponding contact device. A single receptacle is a single contact device with no other contact device on the same yoke. A multiple receptacle is two or more contact devices on the same yoke.

100 Receptacle

- **Type of Change:** Revision

- **Change at a Glance:** The definition of a *receptacle* has been revised to recognize mating devices used to install luminaires and ceiling-suspended (paddle) fans.

- **Code Language:** Article 100 Definitions

  Receptacle. A ~~receptacle is a~~ contact device installed at the outlet for the connection of an attachment plug, or for the direct connection of listed and labeled electrical utilization equipment designed to mate with the corresponding contact device. A single receptacle is a single contact device with no other contact device on the same yoke. A multiple receptacle is two or more contact devices on the same yoke.

- **2014 *NEC* Requirement**
  A *receptacle* was defined as a contact device installed at the outlet for the connection of an attachment plug.

- **2017 *NEC* Change**
  The definition was modified to accommodate electrical utilization equipment employing a means, other than a traditional attachment plug cap, to connect directly to the corresponding contact device.

Analysis of the Change:

The previous definition of a *Receptacle* has been in the *Code* since the 1962 edition of the *NEC* and has not changed a whole lot since then. The definition will change significantly with the 2017 *NEC*. New technology was developed for attaching electrical apparatus using means other than the classical attachment plug. This required changing the definition of receptacle to recognize the new methodology. This revision was necessary to correlate with new provisions added by CMP-9 at 314.27(E) and to recognize the existence of equipment such as direct plug-in transformers, and other devices that do not employ a traditional attachment plug cap.

The new text accepted at 314.27(E) permits an outlet box to support listed locking support and mounting receptacles used in combination with compatible attachment fittings designed for the support of equipment covered within and subject to all weight and orientation limits contemplated by its listing. CMP 9 appropriately used the word "receptacle" in the context of accepting an attachment fitting resulting in the need to modify the definition of "receptacle" to coordinate with this new text. These locking supports and mounting receptacles are third-party certified (listed) as a combination that includes the use of a receptacle and an attachment fitting to supply, support, and connect ceiling- or wall-luminaires, ceiling suspended luminaires, and ceiling-suspended (paddle) fans. The attachment fitting is a recognized component used as part of a listed product, and is inserted in a listed receptacle.

100

First Revisions: FR 5114
Second Revisions: SR 5128
Public Inputs: PI 3139
Public Comments: PC 660

110.3(A)(1), Informational Note No. 1

Examination, Identification, Installation, and Use of Equipment

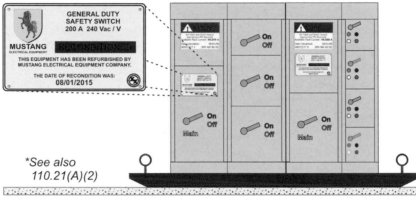

In judging equipment, considerations of such things as suitability for installation and use in conformity with the NEC shall be part of the evaluation process

GENERAL DUTY SAFETY SWITCH
200 A 240 Vac / V

MUSTANG
ELECTRICAL EQUIPMENT

RECONDITIONED

THIS EQUIPMENT HAS BEEN REFURBISHED BY MUSTANG ELECTRICAL EQUIPMENT COMPANY.

THE DATE OF RECONDITION WAS:
08/01/2015

See also 110.21(A)(2)

Informational Note No. 1: Equipment may be new, reconditioned, refurbished, or remanufactured

110.3(A)(1) , Informational Note No. 1 Examination, Identification, Installation, and Use of Equipment

- **Type of Change:** New

- **Change at a Glance:** New I-Note was added indicating equipment may be new, reconditioned, refurbished or remanufactured.

- **Code Language: 110.3 Examination, Identification, Installation, and Use of Equipment**

  (A) Examination. In judging equipment, considerations such as the following shall be evaluated:
  (1) Suitability for installation and use in conformity with the provisions of this *Code*

  Informational Note No. 1: Equipment may be new, reconditioned, refurbished, or remanufactured.

- **2014 *NEC* Requirement**
  There was no information in the previous *Code* to indicate to inspectors, building owners, installers, etc., that the equipment installed was new or refurbished.

■ **2017 *NEC* Change**
A new informational note has been added at 110.3(A)(1) indicating that electrical equipment could be either new, reconditioned, refurbished or remanufactured when installed and inspected and examined.

Analysis of the Change:

When it comes to judging electrical equipment for such things as the inspection assessment or installation suitability, inspectors and installers alike rely on the rules of 110.3 and, in particular, 110.3(A) as a basis for this evaluation. Section 110.3(A) includes a list for evaluating conformity with items such as suitability for installations, mechanical strength and durability, wire-bending and connection space, electrical insulation, heating and arcing effects, and classification of such things as size, voltage, current capacity, etc.

In the past, this "examination" judgment was typically thought to be reserved for "new" equipment. A new Informational Note No. 1 following 110.3(A) has been added to alert users of the *Code* that the general term "equipment" can apply to new equipment as well as to used, refurbished, reconditioned, or remanufactured equipment. In today's electrical environment, reconditioned, refurbished, and remanufactured electrical equipment is widely used in all types of industry to replace, upgrade, or extend the life of existing equipment. In some cases, the existing electrical equipment is no longer being produced, or the manufacturer is no longer in business. Often in these cases, the use of reconditioned, refurbished, and remanufactured equipment must be used. New equipment may not physically fit in the existing facility or equipment location so extending the life of the existing equipment is sometimes critical. When existing electrical equipment is reconditioned, refurbished or remanufactured to current industry standards, it allows the existing electrical equipment to be upgraded with modern electrical protection systems such as arc-flash protection system, solid state relays and protection systems that provide an overall safer electrical system and compliance with the current *NEC*. A good example of this would be compliance with 240.87 for arc energy reduction.

This new informational note lends itself to the new requirement 110.21(A)(2) that provides additional guidance for refurbished, reconditioned, or remanufactured equipment markings and nameplate requirements.

First Revisions: FR 31
Public Inputs: PI 3491

110.3(A)(1)

110.3(C)

Examination, Identification, Installation, Use, and Listing (Product Certification) of Equipment

OSHA's Current List of Recognized NRTLs

- Canadian Standards Association (CSA)
- Curtis-Straus LLC (CSL)
- FM Approvals LLC (FM)
- International Association of Plumbing and Mechanical Officials EGS (IAPMO)
- Intertek Testing Services NA, Inc. (ITSNA)
- MET Laboratories, Inc. (MET)
- Nemko-CCL (CCL)
- NSF International (NSF)

- QAI Laboratories, LTD (QAI)
- QPS Evaluation Services Inc.
- SGS North America, Inc.
- Southwest Research Institute
- TUV Rheinland of North America, Inc.
- TUV Rheinland PTL, LLC
- TÜV SÜD America Inc.
- TÜV SÜD Product Services GmbH
- Underwriters Laboratories Inc. (UL)

Product testing, evaluation, and listing to be performed by recognized qualified electrical testing laboratories and must comply with applicable product standards

110.3(C) Examination, Identification, Installation, Use, and Listing (Product Certification) of Equipment

- **Type of Change:** New

- **Change at a Glance:** New text and Informational Note were added to provide clarification concerning requirements for listing (product certification).

- **Code Language:** 110.3 Examination, Identification, Installation, ~~and~~ Use, **and Listing (Product Certification)** of Equipment

  (C) Listing. Product testing, evaluation, and listing (product certification) shall be performed by recognized qualified electrical testing laboratories and shall be in accordance with applicable product standards recognized as achieving equivalent and effective safety for equipment installed to comply with this *Code*.

  Informational Note: The Occupational Safety and Health Administration (OSHA) recognizes qualified electrical testing laboratories that perform evaluations, testing, and certification of certain products to ensure that they meet the requirements of both the construction and general industry OSHA electrical standards. If the listing (product certification) is done under a qualified electrical testing laboratory program, this listing mark signifies that the tested and certified product complies with the requirements of one or more appropriate product safety test standards.

- **2014 *NEC* Requirement**
  There are several specific listing requirements for particular products throughout the 2014 *NEC*. No details existed concerning who was to perform the evaluation process and to what standard.

- **2017 *NEC* Change**
  A new List Item (C) was added at 110.3 requiring the listing process be executed by a qualified third-party electrical testing laboratory and that the product testing and certification process be in accordance with appropriate product standards.

Analysis of the Change:

In exercising their approving authority (see 90.4), the authority having jurisdiction (AHJ) depends on listing requirements and product certification as the most common basis for approvals of electrical installations in accordance with the *NEC*. The *NEC* currently has many individual listing requirements for specific products. When these listed products are required, it is important that they are properly evaluated by a qualified testing organization, and that they are listed to product standards that are compatible with this *Code*. New language was added at 110.3(C) providing clarification about requirements for listing (product certification) being accomplished by qualified third-party electrical testing laboratories. This new requirement further demands that the product testing and certification process is in accordance with appropriate product standards. The product listing, based on these product standards, must meet or exceed the minimum product safety requirements developed by recognized standards development organizations. In conjunction with this new listing requirement, a new informational note provides users of the *Code* with direction to the Occupational Safety and Health Administration (OSHA) website which provides a list of nationally recognized testing laboratories (NRTL) that meet or exceed OSHA criteria. The current list of OSHA recognized NRTLs can be found at www.osha.gov/dts/otpca/nrtl/nrtllist.html.

110.3(C)

The electrical industry and the AHJ have seen increased requests to accept "CE" marked equipment, which merely indicates a one-time, "self-certified" declaration by the manufacturer to European regulations which have not been evaluated to meet the requirements of NEC or American product standards. These requests to accept "CE" marked equipment put a tremendous burden upon the AHJ to judge and determine its applicability. This new product listing requirement will give the AHJ much needed clarity to assure that listed equipment is evaluated by a qualified third-party electrical testing laboratory and judged in accordance with requirements aligned to the *NEC*.

The North American electrical evaluation system is easily one of the safest in the world. This new provision will strengthen the evaluation system, which is built on the coordination of three equal parts:

1. A comprehensive "installation code" that is practical, easy to read, and enforceable.
2. Robust "product standards" for equipment required in the "installation code."
3. Comprehensive electrical inspections that enforce the "installation code" and the applicable "product standards."

Second Revisions: SR 2
Public Inputs: PI 2839
Public Comments: PC 814, PC 938, PC 949

110.14(D)

Electrical Connection Torque Tools

110.14(D)

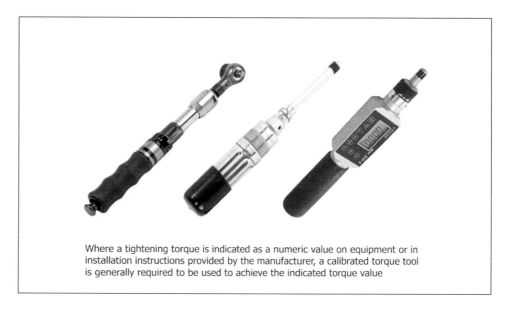

Where a tightening torque is indicated as a numeric value on equipment or in installation instructions provided by the manufacturer, a calibrated torque tool is generally required to be used to achieve the indicated torque value

110.14(D) Electrical Connections

- **Type of Change:** New

- **Change at a Glance:** New requirements were added for the use of tightening torque tools where torquing is indicated.

- **Code Language: 110.14 Electrical Connections**

  (D) Installation. Where a tightening torque is indicated as a numeric value on equipment or in installation instructions provided by the manufacturer, a calibrated torque tool shall be used to achieve the indicated torque value, unless the equipment manufacturer has provided installation instructions for an alternative method of achieving the required torque.

- **2014 *NEC* Requirement**
  The 2014 *NEC* contained an Informational Note at 110.14 alerting users of the *Code* that terminations and equipment are often either marked with tightening torque or are identified as to tightening torque in the installation instructions provided.

- **2017 *NEC* Change**
  The Informational Note that was located after the parent text of 110.14 has been deleted and replaced with enforceable *Code* text at new 110.14(D). This new requirement calls for the implementation of tightening torque tools where torquing is specified on the equipment or in installation instructions provided by the manufacturer.

Analysis of the Change:

Use of proper torque tools is essential to verify that terminations are properly made, and the equipment will function properly throughout its expected service life. Without the use of the proper torquing tools, it has been shown that even experienced electricians cannot consistently tighten the connector to the recommended torque value. For electrical connections, the adage "hand tight plus a quarter turn" is not sufficient to produce a proper mechanical connection. In articles published by IAEI in the July-August 2010 and January-February 2015 *IAEI* magazine, research indicated that only about 25% of connections performed without a torque wrench were within +/- 20% of the manufacturer's recommended torque value. That means 75% of the connections were wrong!

The mechanical interface between the connector and the conductor is an integral part of a safe and reliable electrical connection. For an electrical connection to achieve its objective of providing a low-resistance conductive path between two conductive elements, tightening the connector must create as many points of contact with the conductor as possible during initial installation. Every set-screw termination has an optimum value of tightening torque that produces the most reliable, low-resistance joint. Torque (a force applied to a lever arm multiplied by the distance measured from the pivot point) on the set-screw creates pressure between the connector and the conductor. If too little torque is applied, the connection may not have sufficient pressure to create enough contact points to maintain a low-resistance conductive path over the life of the installation. This added language will make it clear to installers that using the proper torquing tools is required when a torque value is indicated on the equipment or in the manufacturer's instructions.

First Revisions: FR 40
Public Inputs: PI 1323

110.14(D)

110.16(B)

Arc-Flash Hazard Warning, Service Equipment

In other than dwelling units, in addition to the requirements in 110.16(A), a permanent label shall be field or factory applied to service equipment rated 1200 amperes or more

> **⚠ WARNING**
>
> **Arc Flash and Shock Hazard**
> Failure to comply can result in death or serious injury.
> Refer to NFPA 70E. Appropriate PPE Required.
>
> Nominal System Voltage: _____ 480 VAC
>
> Available Fault Current: _____ 23.3 kA
>
> Clearing Time of Service OCPD: 0.03 sec (2 cycles)
>
> Date Label Applied: _____ 08/01/16
>
> Equipment ID: ___ Panel XYZ
> Sidewinder Electrical Contractors   Celina, TX   800-444-1212

Exception: Label not required if arc flash label is applied in accordance with "acceptable industry practice" (NFPA 70E)

110.16(B)

110.16(B) Arc-Flash Hazard Warning, Service Equipment

- **Type of Change:** New

- **Change at a Glance:** Non-dwelling unit service equipment rated 1200 amperes or more is required to be labeled with the normal system voltage, available fault current, clearing times, and date the label was applied.

- **Code Language: 110.16 Arc-Flash Hazard Warning**
  (B) Service Equipment. In other than dwelling units, in addition to the requirements in (A), a permanent label shall be field or factory applied to service equipment rated 1200 amps or more. The label shall meet the requirements of 110.21(B) and contain the following information:
  (1) Nominal system voltage
  (2) Available fault current at the service overcurrent protective devices
  (3) The clearing time of service overcurrent protective devices based on the available fault current at the service equipment
  (4) The date the label was applied

  Exception: Service equipment labeling shall not be required if an arc flash label is applied in accordance with acceptable industry practice.

  Informational Note No. 1: NFPA 70E-2012 2015, *Standard for Electrical Safety in the Workplace*, provides guidance, such as determining the severity of potential exposure, planning safe work practices, arc flash labeling, and selecting personal protective equipment.

Informational Note No. 2: ANSI Z535.4-~~1998~~ 2011, *Product Safety Signs and Labels*, provides guidelines for the design of safety signs and labels for application to products.

Informational Note No. 3: Acceptable industry practices for equipment labeling are described in NFPA 70E-2015 *Standard for Electrical Safety in the Workplace*. This standard provides specific criteria for developing arc-flash labels for equipment that provides nominal system voltage, incident energy levels, arc-flash boundaries, minimum required levels of personal protective equipment, and so forth.

■ **2014 *NEC* Requirement**

Section 110.16 required an arc-flash warning label; warning of potential electric arc flash hazards, to be field or factory applied to non-dwelling unit electrical equipment that is likely to require examination, adjustment, servicing, or maintenance while energized.

■ **2017 *NEC* Change**

A new List Item (B) was added requiring non-dwelling unit service equipment rated 1200 amperes or more to be labeled with the normal system voltage, available fault current, clearing times, and date the label was applied.

110.16(B)

Analysis of the Change:

The basic warning label requirements of 110.16 have been expanded to require additional information for service equipment (other than dwelling units) rated 1200 amperes or more. Part of what this new requirement will call for at service equipment is the available fault current and clearing times at the service overcurrent protective devices (OCPD). The available fault current must be known at the time the service equipment is installed to ensure compliance with the interrupting requirements of 110.9 and 110.10. This information is also needed to determine such things as the incident energy, minimum arc rating of clothing and personal protective equipment (PPE), and working distance from NFPA 70E, *Standard for Electrical Safety in the Workplace*. Some in the electrical industry would argue that this is an NFPA 70E issue. Substantiation for the new label requirement indicated that the requirement is properly located in the *NEC* to address the necessary installation requirements to identify incident energy and the working distance. Adding a requirement to label equipment with the available fault current and clearing times is an installation requirement and is properly located in NFPA 70 (*NEC*). The date the label was applied to the electrical service equipment is necessary as the posted available fault current can fluctuate and be affected by events beyond the control of the property owner.

Several attempts have been made in past *Code* cycles to mandate such labeling at the time of installation in both the *NEC* and NFPA 70E. According to the substantiation, these previous attempts were rejected in NFPA 70E because the *NEC* has purview over installation requirements. Past attempts to add such a requirement in the *NEC* have not been successful because there was no limit to the required labeling. Limiting this new requirement to a label on service equipment only and a further limit of 1200 amperes or greater helped this requirement be accepted in this *Code* cycle. The First Draft language would have applied at any equipment rating; including those below 1,200 amperes (see FR 55). This label is permitted to be either field or factory applied.

An exception to this service equipment labeling requirement was added which states that labeling would not be required if an arc flash label is applied in accordance with "acceptable industry practice." Informational Note No. 3 was added to provide direction to NFPA 70E and guidance on "acceptable industry practices" for developing arc-flash labels, incident energy levels, arc-flash boundaries, and minimum required levels of personal protective equipment and so forth. Acceptance of this public input will provide the available fault current and corresponding working distance necessary where justified energized work is performed in service equipment.

First Revisions: FR 55
Second Revisions: SR 11
Public Inputs: PI 626, PI 4789, PI 551, PI 1491
Public Comments: PC 1747, PC 327, PC 86, PC 356, PC 266, PC 951, PC 1058, PC 937

110.21(A)(2)

110.21(A)(2)

Marking, Reconditioned Equipment

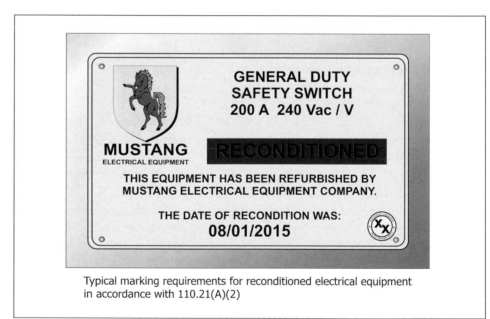

Typical marking requirements for reconditioned electrical equipment in accordance with 110.21(A)(2)

110.21(A)(2) Marking, Equipment Markings

- **Type of Change:** New

- **Change at a Glance:** New rules provide traceability and other additional information to manufacturers, owners, installers, and AHJs related to reconditioned equipment.

- **Code Language: 110.21 Marking.**
  (A) ~~Manufacturer's~~ **Equipment Markings.**
  (2) Reconditioned Equipment. Reconditioned equipment shall be marked with the name, trademark, or other descriptive marking by which the organization responsible for reconditioning the electrical equipment can be identified, along with the date of the reconditioning. Reconditioned equipment shall be identified as "reconditioned" and approval of the reconditioned equipment shall not be based solely on the equipment's original listing.

  Exception: In industrial occupancies, where conditions of maintenance and supervision ensure that only qualified persons service the equipment, the markings indicated in 110.21(A)(2) shall not be required.

  Informational Note: Industry standards are available for application of reconditioned and refurbished equipment. Normal servicing of equipment that remains within a facility should not be considered reconditioning or refurbishing.

- **2014 *NEC* Requirement**
  No rules existed in the 2014 *NEC* for identifying refurbished, reconditioned, or remanufactured electrical equipment.

  110.21(A)(2)

- **2017 *NEC* Change**
  New requirements were added at 110.21(A)(2) to require refurbished, reconditioned, or remanufactured equipment to be marked with the name, trademark, or other descriptive marking by which the organization responsible for reconditioning the electrical equipment can be identified. The date of the reconditioning must also be established on the nameplate or marking.

Analysis of the Change:

Section 110.21 contains specific requirements for markings on electrical equipment. This marking includes information from the manufacturer of the equipment such as the manufacturer's name and trademark, voltage, current, wattage, etc. This section also included field-applied hazard markings to include specific requirements for warning labels and similar markings where required or specified elsewhere in the *Code*. The *NEC* contains several requirements for hazard markings to be installed on wiring methods and equipment. For the 2017 *Code* cycle, marking requirements for reconditioned, refurbished or remanufactured electrical equipment has been added to this section as well. This type of "reconditioned" electrical equipment is starting to be more commonplace in all types of industry to replace or extend the life cycle of aging electrical equipment. Industrial facilities maintain and refurbish electrical equipment as part of a regular maintenance cycle for safety and reliability. Marking the equipment with the name of the organization responsible for the reconditioning and the date of the reconditioning will give traceability of the reconditioned equipment and necessary information to the owner, installer, inspector, and the operator.

When a listed product is reconditioned (such as being rebuilt, refurbished or remanufactured) after it leaves the original manufacturer where the original listing mark was applied, the organization responsible for the testing and inspection (as detailed at 90.7) does not know if the product continues to meet the applicable certification requirements. This new requirement will go a long way in assuring the reconditioned equipment has been specifically evaluated by an organization properly equipped and qualified for accomplishing this reconditioning process. When reconditioned electrical equipment is encountered, the authority having jurisdiction (AHJ) should never rely solely on the equipment's original listing mark as the basis of approval of such equipment.

First Revisions: FR 42
Second Revisions: SR 9
Public Inputs: PI 2369, PI 3489
Public Comments: PC 582, PC 707, PC 1550

110.26(A)(4)

Spaces About Electrical Equipment, Working Space

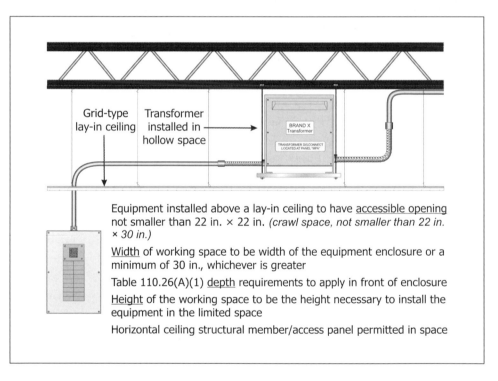

Equipment installed above a lay-in ceiling to have <u>accessible opening</u> not smaller than 22 in. × 22 in. *(crawl space, not smaller than 22 in. × 30 in.)*

<u>Width</u> of working space to be width of the equipment enclosure or a minimum of 30 in., whichever is greater

Table 110.26(A)(1) <u>depth</u> requirements to apply in front of enclosure

<u>Height</u> of the working space to be the height necessary to install the equipment in the limited space

Horizontal ceiling structural member/access panel permitted in space

110.26(A)(4) Spaces About Electrical Equipment, Working Space

- **Type of Change:** New

- **Change at a Glance:** New requirements were added concerning working space for equipment located in a space with limited access (above suspended ceiling, crawl spaces, etc.).

- **Code Language: 110.26 Spaces About Electrical Equipment**
  (A) Working Space. Working space for equipment operating at ~~600~~ 1000 volts, nominal, or less to ground and likely to require examination, adjustment, servicing, or maintenance while energized shall comply with the dimensions of 110.26(A) (1), (A)(2), ~~and~~ (A)(3), and (A)(4) or as required or permitted elsewhere in this *Code*.

  Informational Note: NFPA 70E-2015, *Standard for Electrical Safety in the Workplace*, provides guidance, such as determining severity of potential exposure, planning safe work practices, arc flash labeling, and selecting personal protective equipment.

  (4) Limited Access. Where equipment operating at 1000 volts, nominal, or less to ground and likely to require examination, adjustment, servicing, or maintenance while energized is required by installation instructions or function to be located in a space with limited access, all of the following shall apply:
  (a) Where equipment is installed above a lay-in ceiling, there shall be an opening not smaller than 559 mm × 559 mm (22 in. × 22 in.), or in a crawl space, there shall be an accessible opening not smaller than 559 mm × 762 mm (22 in. × 30 in.).
  (b) The width of the working space shall be the width of the equipment enclosure or a minimum of 762 mm (30 in.), whichever is greater.
  (c) All enclosure doors or hinged panels shall be capable of opening a minimum of 90 degrees.
  (d) The space in front of the enclosure shall comply with the depth requirements of Table 110.26(A)(1). The maximum height of the working space shall be the height necessary to install the equipment in the limited space. A horizontal ceiling structural member or access panel shall be permitted in this space.

110.26(A)(4)

- **2014 *NEC* Requirement**
  NEC 2014 contained limited access working space requirements at 424.66(B) for duct heaters installed above a lay-in ceiling.

- **2017 *NEC* Change**
  The same basic limited access working space requirements at 424.66(B) were relocated to 110.26(A)(4) to broaden this requirement to more than just duct heaters. Provisions for limited access to crawl spaces were added to this requirement as well.

Analysis of the Change:

During the 2014 *NEC* Code cycle, CMP-17 incorporated a new requirement at 424.66(B) dealing with working space with limited access for duct heaters. While this was a necessary provision for this one component of the electrical system, the *NEC* Correlating Committee quickly realized that this limited access working space requirement was also needed for more items than just duct heaters. The *NEC* Correlating Committee appointed a Working Space Task Group to review requirements for working space of electrical equipment often installed

110.26(A)(4)

in spaces with limited access such as transformers, motors, air-handling equipment, etc. The task group was charged with reviewing the new requirements at 424.66(B) and exploring the feasibility of a new general requirement for the 2017 *NEC* in Article 110 for clarity and usability.

Requirements for adequate working space for equipment (with limited access or not) that is likely to require examination, adjustment, servicing, or maintenance while energized are general requirements for all electrical equipment. The user of the *Code* is better served with this requirement located in Article 110 for a broader application. To prevent similar requirements from being implemented in other articles and sections of the *Code*, a single general requirement in Article 110 to address all impacted electrical equipment provides clarity, usability and eliminates potential conflict and confusion. This new provision in Article 110 is necessary for correlation throughout the *NEC*, as well as providing the relief necessary for other installations with limited access.

The working space rules in 110.26(A) apply to all equipment that is likely to require examination, adjustment, servicing, or maintenance while energized. Strict compliance with 110.26(A)(1), (A)(2) and (A)(3) in ceiling spaces and crawl spaces is not feasible in most cases. The electrical industry has been installing and accepting equipment in such spaces for decades. Prescriptive requirements for such limited access spaces have been sorely lacking for that same period. This limited access requirement provides guidance for both the installer/maintainer and the enforcement community.

As for the specific requirements, electrical equipment installed above a lay-in ceiling must have access through an opening not smaller than 559 mm x 559 mm (22 in. x 22 in.), which recognizes a standard 2 ft x 2 ft lay-in ceiling grid opening. The dimensions for a crawl space opening of 559 mm x by 762 mm (22 in. x by 30 in.) are similar to the access requirements for components of a sign at 600.21(E) with dimensions that correlate with the applicable building codes and spaces between standard framing members. The width of the limited access working space has to be the width of the enclosure, or a minimum of 762 mm (30 in.), whichever is greater. All doors or hinged panels must be capable of opening a minimum of 90 degrees and space in front of the enclosure must comply with the depth requirements of Table 110.26(A)(1). Notice that the last list item here provides relief from the general height requirement and permits the height of the limited access working space to be the maximum height necessary to install the equipment in the limited space. Horizontal ceiling grid structural members or removable access panels are permitted in this space as well.

A companion public input (PI 1066) was sent to CMP-17 to delete the limited access working space requirements in 424.66(B) as this Article 110 provision would apply to duct heaters as well as other types of electrical equipment installed with limited access.

First Revisions: FR 15, FR 18
Second Revisions: SR 12
Public Inputs: PI 1065
Public Comments: PC 708

110.41(A) and (B)
Inspections and Tests

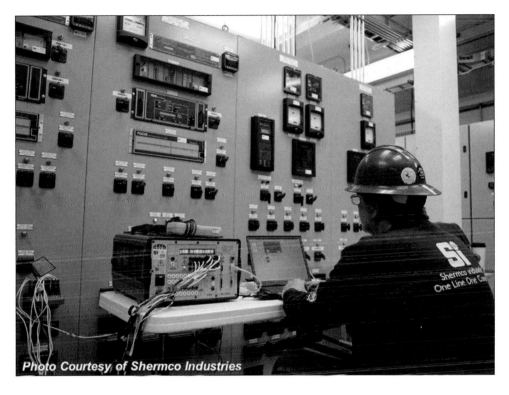

Photo Courtesy of Shermco Industries

110.41

110.41(A) and (B) Inspections and Tests

- **Type of Change:** New

- **Change at a Glance:** New requirements were added for the performance and reporting of pre-energization testing of electrical equipment rated over 1000 volts upon request by the AHJ.

- **Code Language: 110.41 Inspections and Tests**
  (A) Pre-energization and Operating Tests. Where required elsewhere in this *Code*, the complete electrical system design, including settings for protective, switching, and control circuits, shall be prepared in advance and made available on request to the authority having jurisdiction and shall be tested when first installed on-site.

  (B) Test Report. A test report covering the results of the tests required in 110.41(A) shall be available to the authority having jurisdiction prior to energization and made available to those authorized to install, operate, test, and maintain the system.

- **2014 *NEC* Requirement**
  Pre-energization testing of electrical equipment rated over 1000 volts was required at 225.56, but this requirement was limited to outdoor feeders

and branch circuits greater than 1000 volts. Section 230.95(C) calls for ground-fault protection system to be performance tested when first installed on site with a written record of this test made available to the authority having jurisdiction (AHJ).

■ **2017 *NEC* Change**
New requirements were added at 110.41 for pre-energization testing and reporting of electrical equipment (over 1000 volts) upon request by the AHJ. Since it is located in Article 110, this will apply to all equipment rated over 1000 volts regardless of its location.

Analysis of the Change:

A new requirement was added to Article 110 necessitating pre-energization testing of electrical equipment rated over 1000 volts upon request by the authority having jurisdiction (AHJ), along with reporting requirements. The testing could include performance and/or safety testing. This requirement was strategically placed at the end of Part III (Over 1000 Volts, Nominal) to ensure that this requirement applied only to equipment rated greater than 1000 volts. This added text was an attempt to ensure that electrical system installations of over 1000 volts perform to their design specifications and that a record for verifying the proper settings and test data would be available to the AHJ as well as the installers, operators, testers, and maintainers after the equipment is put into service. This pre-energization testing requirement aligns with other *NEC* provisions calling for test procedures to be performed, such as 230.95(C) for testing of ground-fault protection systems.

This added text in Article 110 is very similar to and is modeled after the language at 225.56 for outdoor feeders and branch circuits greater than 1000 volts. When accepted during the 2011 *NEC Code* cycle, 225.56 was included to increase safety by ensuring that the initial installation of high-voltage outside feeders and branch circuits was performed properly, the protective switching and control schemes were set properly, and all acceptance testing completed. Most would argue that circuits of greater than 1000 volts installed inside a building present even greater hazards and higher life safety risks than their counterparts installed outdoors. These indoor feeders and branch circuits arguably have an even greater need for assurance that the initial installation is as designed, and the equipment will operate as intended by the original design team. Having the test data available from the initial installation provides essential information to evaluate the condition of maintenance for the life of the equipment to those who must operate, test, or maintain that same equipment.

First Revisions: FR 36
Public Inputs: PI 4117

110.41

Wiring & Protection

Chapter 2

Articles 210 – 250

210.5(C)(1), Exception
Identification for Ungrounded Conductors

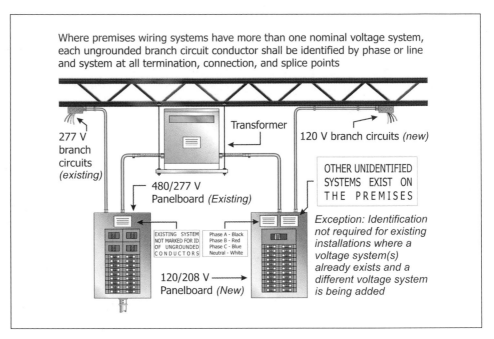

Where premises wiring systems have more than one nominal voltage system, each ungrounded branch circuit conductor shall be identified by phase or line and system at all termination, connection, and splice points

277 V branch circuits *(existing)*

Transformer

120 V branch circuits *(new)*

480/277 V Panelboard *(Existing)*

OTHER UNIDENTIFIED SYSTEMS EXIST ON THE PREMISES

Exception: Identification not required for existing installations where a voltage system(s) already exists and a different voltage system is being added

EXISTING SYSTEM NOT MARKED FOR ID OF UNGROUNDED CONDUCTORS

Phase A - Black
Phase B - Red
Phase C - Blue
Neutral - White

120/208 V Panelboard *(New)*

210.5(C)(1)

210.5(C)(1), Exception Identification for Branch Circuits

- **Type of Change:** New

- **Change at a Glance:** A new exception was added for identifying each ungrounded conductor for existing installations where a voltage system(s) already exists and a different voltage system is being added.

- **Code Language: 210.5 Identification for Branch Circuits.**

  (C) Identification of Ungrounded Conductors. Ungrounded conductors shall be identified in accordance with 210.5(C)(1) or (2), as applicable.

  (1) Branch Circuits Supplied from More Than One Nominal Voltage System. Where the premises wiring system has branch circuits supplied from more than one nominal voltage system, each ungrounded conductor of a branch circuit shall be identified by phase or line and system at all termination, connection, and splice points in compliance with 210.5(C)(1)(a) and (b).

  (a) Means of Identification. The means of identification shall be permitted to be by separate color coding, marking tape, tagging, or other approved means.

  (b) Posting of Identification Means. The method utilized for conductors originating within each branch-circuit panelboard or similar branch-circuit distribution equipment shall be documented in a manner that is readily available or shall be permanently posted at each branch-circuit panelboard or similar branch-circuit distribution equipment. The label shall be of sufficient durability to withstand the environment involved and shall not be handwritten.

Exception: *In existing installations where a voltage system(s) already exists and a different voltage system is being added, it shall be permissible to mark only the new system voltage. Existing unidentified systems shall not be required to be identified at each termination, connection, and splice point in compliance with 210.5(C)(1)(a) and (b). Labeling shall be required at each voltage system distribution equipment to identify that only one voltage system has been marked for a new system(s). The new system label(s) shall include the words "other unidentified systems exist on the premises."*

- **2014 *NEC* Requirement**

  Where the premises wiring system has branch circuits supplied from more than one nominal voltage system, each ungrounded conductor of a branch circuit be identified by phase or line and system at all termination, connection, and splice points. The means of identification for these different voltage systems can be by separate color coding, marking tape, tagging, or other approved means. These identification means must be documented in a manner that is readily available or permanently posted at each branch-circuit panelboard or similar branch-circuit distribution equipment.

- **2017 *NEC* Change**

  The previous identification requirements for branch circuits supplied from more than one nominal voltage system moved forward for the 2017 *NEC* with a new exception added for relief from identifying each ungrounded conductor for existing installations where a voltage system(s) already exists and a different voltage system is being added. A new requirement was also added concerning the durability and makeup of the labels.

Analysis of the Change:

In the 2002 edition of the *NEC*, 210.4(D) addressed the identification of multi-wire branch circuits where more than one nominal voltage system existed in the same building or premise. For the 2005 *NEC*, these requirements were shifted to 210.5(C), and revisions made this identification requirement mandatory for all branch circuits (not just multiwire branch circuits). For the 2017 *NEC*, a new exception was added for 210.5(C) that would make these branch circuit identification rules applicable only to the new system(s) of existing installations where a voltage system(s) already exists and a different voltage system is being added. Existing unidentified systems will not be required to be identified at each termination, connection, and splice point in compliance with 210.5(C)(1)(a) and (b) under this new exception.

210.5(C)(1)

In existing and older buildings, numerous systems exist that are supplied by more than one nominal voltage system and were installed prior to the adoption of the 2005 *NEC* [when 210.5(C) was first mandated]. These older systems were and are not identified at each termination, connection, and splice point. This new exception will allow existing unidentified installations to remain in place without requiring the addition of identification in compliance with 210.5. It is not practical to remove every existing device, luminaire, connection point, or to open every junction box cover of the old existing system to mark the existing branch circuit conductors. The majority of the enforcement community might have already offered this relief for these existing systems as the *Code* is not retroactive, but this new exception will make this allowance very clear.

This new exception also includes some labeling requirements for older existing unidentified installations that would require a label at each voltage system distribution equipment point to identify that only the added voltage system(s) have been marked or identified at each termination, connection, and splice point for a new system(s). This new label(s) will be required to include the words "Other Unidentified Systems Exist on the Premises."

210.5(C)(1)

One other change that occurred was to add a requirement that the label for 210.5(C)(1)(b) be "sufficiently durable" and able to withstand the environment in which it is installed. This added text will also require that the marking on the label be legible and not handwritten. This text is very similar to existing language found at 110.21(B) for field-applied hazard markings and other locations throughout the *Code*.

First Revisions: FR 302
Second Revisions: 304, SCR 68
Public Inputs: PI 4496, PI 2712
Public Comments: PC 877

210.8

Measurements for GFCI Protection

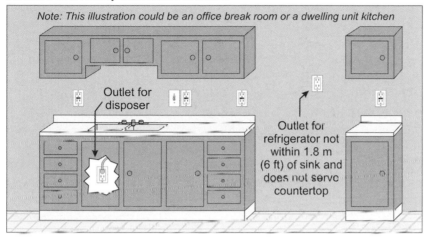

GFCI protection shall be provided as required in 210.8(A) through (E) and installed in a readily accessible location

Note: This illustration could be an office break room or a dwelling unit kitchen

Outlet for disposer

Outlet for refrigerator not within 1.8 m (6 ft) of sink and does not serve countertop

When determining distance from receptacles, distance shall be measured as the "shortest path" the cord of an appliance connected to the receptacle would follow without piercing a floor, wall, ceiling, or fixed barrier, or passing through a door, doorway, or window

210.8

210.8 Ground-Fault Circuit-Interrupter Protection for Personnel

- **Type of Change:** New

- **Change at a Glance:** New language added to clarify how measurements are to be determined for GFCI receptacle.

- **Code Language: 210.8   Ground-Fault Circuit-Interrupter Protection for Personnel**. Ground-fault circuit-interrupter protection for personnel shall be provided as required in 210.8(A) through (D) (E). The ground-fault circuit interrupter shall be installed in a readily accessible location.

  Informational Note No. 1: See 215.9 for ground-fault circuit-interrupter protection for personnel

  Informational Note No. 2: See 422.5(A) for GFCI requirements for appliances.

  For the purposes of this section, when determining distance from receptacles the distance shall be measured as the shortest path the cord of an appliance connected to the receptacle would follow without piercing a floor, wall, ceiling, or fixed barrier, or passing through a door, doorway, or window.

■ **2014 *NEC* Requirement**

No *Code* provisions existed at 210.8 giving clear-cut direction on the proper measurement technique to employ when determining the necessity of GFCI protection.

■ **2017 *NEC* Change**

A new provision was added to the parent text of 210.8 to indicate that measurements from receptacles to objects (such as a sink) that would qualify for GFCI protection should be measured as the "shortest path" a cord of an appliance connected to a receptacle would take without piercing a floor, wall, ceiling, or fixed barrier, or passing through a door, doorway, or window.

210.8

Analysis of the Change:

How is the measurement supposed to be made when the *Code* gives a measurable dimension such as where receptacles are installed within 1.8 m (6 ft) of the outside edge of a sink they require GFCI protection? What path should the installer or enforcer take to determine this distance? Various interpretations have been offered for accomplishing these measurements for as long as they have existed in the *Code*. New language added at 210.8 clarifies how these measurements are determined, and it applies to dwelling units and non-dwelling units alike. This "shortest path" measurement language is very similar to the existing text at 680.22(A)(5) for receptacle measurements around permanently installed swimming pools, which was the inspiration for this new text at 210.8.

During the 2014 *NEC* revision process, CMP-2 deliberated at length on how these GFCI measurements were to be made, but no clear guidance was mandated in the form of enforceable text. In a Panel Statement (see 2014 ROC 2-22), CMP 2 stated that the distance should be "the shortest path the cord of an appliance could take without penetrating a doorway, floor, etc.," but no prescriptive requirements were brought forth. This deliberation was the genesis for several Public Inputs (PI), which resulted in this new requirement for the 2017 *NEC*.

Strict interpretation, along with commentary from CMP-2 during the 2017 *NEC Code* development process, indicate that this added text would alleviate the need for GFCI protection for receptacles installed inside a cabinet as the measurement to the sink would constitute "penetrating a cabinet door" to achieve this measurement. An example of this situation would be a receptacle for a cord-and-plug connected, under-the-counter garbage disposal installed under a kitchen sink. For further confirmation on this point, see the revisions at 210.8(A)(7) (dwelling units) and 210.8(B)(5) (non-dwelling units).

First Revision: FR 333
Second Revision: SR 318
Public Inputs: PI 2806, PI 2991, PI 2541, PI 1915, PI 1436

210.8(A)(7)

GFCI Protection at Sinks

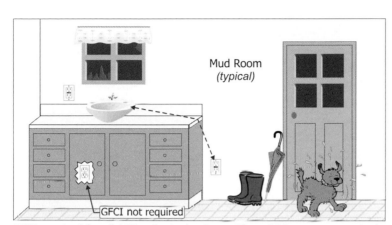

GFCI required for all 125-volt, single-phase, 15- and 20-ampere receptacles installed within 1.8 m (6 ft) from the top inside edge of a dwelling unit sink *(laundry, utility, mud room, kitchen, wet bar, etc.)* without the measurement piercing a floor, wall, ceiling, or fixed barrier, or passing through a door, doorway, or window

Note: Same requirement at 210.8(B)(5) for non-dwelling unit sinks

210.8(A)(7) Ground-Fault Circuit-Interrupter Protection for Personnel

- **Type of Change:** Revision

- **Change at a Glance:** Measurement criteria at dwelling unit sinks were revised for clarity in determination of which receptacles around these sinks would and would not require GFCI protection.

- **Code Language: 210.8 Ground-Fault Circuit-Interrupter Protection for Personnel.**

Ground-fault circuit-interrupter protection for personnel shall be provided as required in 210.8(A) through ~~(D)~~ (E). The ground-fault circuit-interrupter shall be installed in a readily accessible location.

Informational Note No. 1: See 215.9 for ground-fault circuit-interrupter protection for personnel on feeders.

Informational Note No. 2: See 422.5(A) for GFCI requirements for appliances.

For the purposes of this section, when determining distance from receptacles, the distance shall be measured as the shortest path the cord of an appliance connected to the receptacle would follow without piercing a floor, wall, ceiling, or fixed barrier, or passing through a door, doorway, or window.

(A) Dwelling Units. All 125-volt, single-phase, 15- and 20-ampere receptacles installed in the locations specified in 210.8(A)(1) through (10) shall have ground-fault circuit-interrupter protection for personnel.

(7) Sinks — where receptacles are installed within 1.8 m (6 ft) ~~of~~ from the ~~outside~~ top inside edge of the ~~sink~~ bowl

- **2014 *NEC* Requirement**
  All 125-volt, single-phase, 15- and 20-ampere receptacles installed within 1.8 m (6 ft) of the "outside edge" of any dwelling unit sink (including the kitchen sink) required GFCI protection.

- **2017 *NEC* Change**
  All 125-volt, single-phase, 15- and 20-ampere receptacles installed within 1.8 m (6 ft) of the "top inside edge of the bowl" of any dwelling unit sink (including the kitchen sink) requires GFCI protection without the measurement piercing a floor, wall, ceiling, or fixed barrier, or passing through a door, doorway, or window.

210.8(A)(7)

Analysis of the Change:

For the sixth straight *Code* cycle, the provisions of 210.8(A)(7) for GFCI protection within 1.8 m (6 ft) of dwelling unit sinks has experienced some form of revision to its content. Back in the 2002 *NEC*, this list item (7) only pertained to GFCI protection for receptacles located within 1.8 m (6 ft) of a wet bar sink and "intended to serve the countertop." The 2005 *NEC* saw this requirement expanded to "Laundry, Utility, and Wet Bar Sinks" with the previous provision that the receptacle be "intended to serve the countertop" removed. For the 2011 *NEC*, the title was simplified to just "Sinks", but excluded kitchen sinks as the GFCI provisions for kitchen sinks was covered at 210.8(A)(6) and this list item only required GFCI protection for receptacles that served a kitchen countertop and did not extend GFCI protection for such things as a receptacle under the kitchen sink for a garbage/waste disposer even though that disposer receptacle might be within 1.8 m (6 ft) of the outside edge of dwelling unit kitchen sink. Last *Code* cycle, this provision was expanded to all dwelling unit sinks (*including the kitchen sink*) by eliminating the phrase "located in areas other than kitchens" at 210.8(A)(7). This meant that all 125-volt, single-phase, 15- and 20-ampere receptacles installed within 1.8 m (6 ft) of any dwelling unit sink required GFCI protection. With literal interpretation, this 2014 *NEC* modification brought about some unintended circumstances such as mandated GFCI protection for a receptacle under the kitchen sink for a garbage/waste disposer.

For the 2017 *NEC*, revisions to this list item (7), along with an addition to the parent text of 210.8 will eliminate the necessity for GFCI protection for receptacles installed inside a cabinet (such as a receptacle for the garbage disposer) as the measurement to the sink would constitute "penetrating a cabinet door" in order to achieve this required 1.8 m (6 ft) measurement. This revision makes it clear that the measurement from the receptacle to the sink ends or begins at the "top inside edge of the bowl" of the sink rather than the "outside edge" of the sink. The outside edge of a sink is three dimensional and could include the bottom of the bowl, which apparently was an unintended interpretation. In today's modern dwelling units, it is not difficult to find some unconventional sinks. This would include such things as a free-standing bowl that sits atop a countertop with no recess into the countertop at all. This revised text will help with consistent interpretation as to the method of measurement for these types of sinks. Again, literal interpretation of the previous text could have resulted in the 1.8 m (6 ft) measurement being addressed at the bottom of such a sink when only the "outside edge" of the sink was the driving factor.

This same revision occurred at 210.8(B)(5) for GFCI protection and measurements at a non-dwelling unit sink (see SR 322 and PC 599). Nothing previously stated concerning the measurement methodology at a dwelling unit sink would change for a sink at a commercial office break room or any other non-dwelling unit sink location.

Second Revision: SR 316
Public Inputs: PI 2991, PI 4178
Public Comments: PC 598

210.8(B)

Three-Phase GFCI Protection

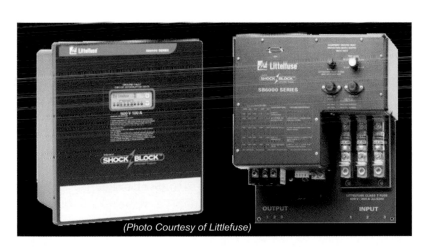

(Photo Courtesy of Littlefuse)

(Other Than Dwelling Units) All single-phase receptacles rated 150 volts to ground or less, 50 amperes or less; and three-phase receptacles rated 150 volts to ground or less, 100 amperes or less, installed in specified locations shall have ground-fault circuit-interrupter protection for personnel

210.8(B) Ground-Fault Circuit-Interrupter Protection for Personnel

- **Type of Change:** Revision

■ **Change at a Glance:** The GFCI requirements for receptacles at commercial/industrial applications have been expanded to recognize ground faults other than 15 and 20A 125-volt applications only.

■ **Code Language: 210.8 Ground-Fault Circuit-Interrupter Protection for Personnel.**

Ground-fault circuit-interrupter protection for personnel shall be provided as required in 210.8(A) through (D) (E). The ground-fault circuit-interrupter shall be installed in a readily accessible location.

Informational Note No. 1: See 215.9 for ground-fault circuit-interrupter protection for personnel on feeders.

Informational Note No. 2: See 422.5(A) for GFCI requirements for appliances.

For the purposes of this section, when determining distance from receptacles, the distance shall be measured as the shortest path the cord of an appliance connected to the receptacle would follow without piercing a floor, wall, ceiling, or fixed barrier, or passing through a door, doorway, or window.

(B) Other Than Dwelling Units. All 125-volt, single-phase, 15- and 20-ampere receptacles rated 150 volts to ground or less, 50 amperes or less; and three-phase receptacles rated 150 volts to ground or less, 100 amperes or less, installed in the locations specified in 210.8(B)(1) through (8) (10) shall have ground-fault circuit-interrupter protection for personnel.

■ **2014 *NEC* Requirement**
The GFCI requirements at "Other Than Dwelling Units" were limited to 125-volt, single-phase, 15- and 20-ampere receptacles.

■ **2017 *NEC* Change**
The GFCI requirements at "Other Than Dwelling Units" still include coverage of 125-volt, single-phase, 15- and 20-ampere receptacles. These requirements have been expanded to include all single-phase receptacles rated 150 volts to ground or less, 50 amperes or less; and three-phase receptacles rated 150 volts to ground or less, 100 amperes or less.

Analysis of the Change:
Class A GCFI devices, which are designed to trip when the current to ground exceeds 4 to 6 mA (see UL 943, Standard for Ground-Fault Circuit Interrupters), have proven to be a reliable resource in reducing the number of injuries and fatalities due to electrical shock. They have saved numerous lives over the years, and they were introduced into the *Code* in the 1968 *NEC*. Class A GFCI devices have typically been associated with 125-volt, single-phase, 15- and 20-ampere applications, but what about the shock hazards and electrocutions involving higher currents and voltages, particularly in the workplace? Class A

210.8(B)

GFCI devices cannot be used where the electrical equipment employs 480 or 600 volts or is a three-phase system, yet the shock hazards of exist for these applications as well.

Revisions in the 2017 *NEC* at 210.8(B) have resulted in the expansion of GFCI protection for non-dwelling unit receptacles to include all single-phase receptacles rated 150 volts to ground or less, 50 amperes or less; and three-phase receptacles rated 150 volts to ground or less, 100 amperes or less. These requirements have been expanded in recognition of the fact that shock hazards are not limited to 15- and 20-ampere, 125-volt receptacles alone at commercial/industrial applications. Receptacles of the higher voltage and current ratings in the locations identified in 210.8(B) present similar shock hazards as those of lower voltage and current ratings.

According to information published in IAEI magazine, from 2003 to 2009 there were 801 fatal workplace accidents caused by worker contact with electrical current. These figures do not include construction industry fatalities (see, Now That Industrial GFCIs are Here, Inspectors Have a Proactive Option for Shock Protections in the January-February 2014 issue). Statistics continue to show electrocutions as a significant cause of death in other than dwelling units. NFPA 70E (Standard for Electrical Safety in the Workplace), Annex K states that electrocutions are the fourth leading cause of industrial fatalities.

210.8(B)

UL Standard 943C (Outline of Investigation for Special Purpose Ground-Fault Circuit-Interrupters) identifies protective devices designated as GFCI devices other than Class A GFCI devices. GFCI devices addressed by UL 943C are divided into three classes, Class C, D and F, based on voltage rating and the characteristics of the grounding circuit. Such devices operate at 20 mA or less to prevent fibrillation and require an equipment grounding conductor in the protected circuit with an internal means to monitor equipment grounding conductor continuity. Although the new classes of GFCI devices trip at higher current levels (20 mA instead of 6 mA), UL 943C calls these devices GFCIs and defines them as "a device intended for the protection of personnel." The increase in personnel protection trip level of these new GFCI classes is based upon the availability of a reliable equipment grounding conductor in parallel with the body. During a ground fault condition, the equipment grounding conductor will shunt the fault current around the body and cause the device to trip. This action provides the "let-go" protection while the 20 mA threshold provides protection against fibrillation. These so-called "Industrial" GFCIs provide workers with vital protection against shock hazards and electrocution at a cost that is trivial compared to the enormous costs involved with a serious injury or a fatality.

It should be noted that provisions for an Equipment Ground-Fault Protective Device (EGFPD) and Special Purpose Ground-Fault Circuit Interrupter (SPGFCI) devices were proposed for the 2017 *NEC* but did not receive the necessary support from CMP-2 for inclusion in the requirements at 210.8(B). An EGFPD is a device that operates to disconnect the electric circuit from the source of supply when ground-fault current exceeds the ground-fault pickup level marked on the device. An SPGFCI is a device intended for the protection of personnel that de-energizes a circuit or portion of a circuit within an established period when a current to ground exceeds the values established for a Class C, D, and E GFCI device.

First Revision: FR 347

Second Revision: SR 321

Public Inputs: PI 2192

Public Comments: PC 642, PC 819

210.8(B)(9)

Non-Dwelling Unit Crawl Space

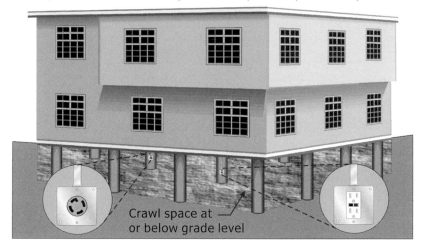

All single-phase receptacles (150 volts to ground or less, 50 amperes or less) and three-phase receptacles (150 volts to ground or less, 100 amperes or less) installed in non-dwelling unit crawl spaces requires GFCI protection

Crawl space at or below grade level

210.8(B)(9) Ground-Fault Circuit-Interrupter Protection for Personnel.

- **Type of Change:** New

- **Change at a Glance:** GFCI protection for receptacles in non-dwelling unit crawl spaces has been added.

- **Code Language: 210.8 Ground-Fault Circuit-Interrupter Protection for Personnel.**

Ground-fault circuit-interrupter protection for personnel shall be provided as required in 210.8(A) through (D) (E). The ground-fault circuit-interrupter shall be installed in a readily accessible location.

Informational Note No. 1: See 215.9 for ground-fault circuit-interrupter protection for personnel on feeders.

Informational Note No. 2: See 422.5(A) for GFCI requirements for appliances.

For the purposes of this section, when determining distance from receptacles, the distance shall be measured as the shortest path the cord of an appliance connected to the receptacle would follow without piercing a floor, wall, ceiling, or fixed barrier, or passing through a door, doorway, or window.

(B) Other Than Dwelling Units. All ~~125-volt~~, single-phase, ~~15- and 20-ampere~~ receptacles rated 150 volts to ground or less, 50 amperes or less; and three-phase receptacles rated 150 volts to ground or less, 100 amperes or less, installed in the locations specified in 210.8(B)(1) through ~~(8)~~ (10) shall have ground-fault circuit-interrupter protection for personnel.

(9) Crawl spaces — at or below grade level

- **2014 *NEC* Requirement**
  GFCI protection for personnel is required for all 125-volt, single phase, 15- and 20-ampere receptacles installed in dwelling unit crawl spaces when that crawl space is at or below grade level. This requirement is located at 210.8(A)(4), which pertains to dwelling units only. No such requirement existed for receptacles installed in a non-dwelling unit crawl space.

- **2017 *NEC* Change**
  GFCI protection is now required for all single-phase receptacles rated 150 volts to ground or less, 50 amperes or less; and three-phase receptacles rated 150 volts to ground or less, 100 amperes or less installed in non dwelling unit crawl spaces.

210.8(B)(9)

Analysis of the Change:

The *Code* has mandated GFCI protection for all 125-volt, single-phase, 15- and 20-ampere receptacles installed in dwelling unit crawl spaces since the 1990 *NEC*. From that time until the present, no similar requirement existed for similar receptacles installed in a non-dwelling unit crawl space. That will change for the 2017 *NEC* with all single-phase receptacles rated 150 volts to ground or less, 50 amperes or less; and three-phase receptacles rated 150 volts to ground or less, 100 amperes or less installed in non-dwelling unit crawl spaces now requiring GFCI protection.

It could be argued with a high degree of certainty that a receptacle outlet is not intelligent enough to know whether it is installed in a dwelling unit or a non-dwelling unit. If a hazard from a ground-fault condition exists, it would seem that both locations would need and warrant GFCI protection. It is interesting to look back at the substantiation for GFCI protection for dwelling unit crawl spaces. Part of this substantiation stated, "In its analysis of over 3,000 electric shock incidents for the period from 1976 and mid-1984, the Consumer Product Safety Commission (CPSC) had found approximately 312 deaths and 192 injuries involving consumer products in residential basements. In this study, 330 in-depth investigative reports were examined to determine what products were involved and the location. Of the basement fatalities, 61.5% occurred in crawl spaces involving portable power tools, extension lights, and extension cords. Furthermore, the death rate in crawl spaces was very significant compared to the injury rate, accounting for 86.7% of the electric shock incidents" (see 1990 ROP 2-53 and 1990 ROC 2-649).

If a crawl space exists at a non-dwelling unit facility and that crawl space is at or below grade level, these same electrical shock hazards would exist. It is interesting to note that this non-dwelling unit crawl space GFCI requirement is not limited to 125-volt receptacles. Revisions of the parent text of 210.8(B) have resulted in the expansion of GFCI protection for non-dwelling unit receptacles that now will include all single-phase receptacles rated 150 volts to ground or less, 50 amperes or less; and three-phase receptacles rated 150 volts to ground or less, 100 amperes or less. These requirements have been expanded to recognize the fact that shock hazards are not limited to 15- and 20-ampere, 125-volt receptacles alone at commercial/industrial applications.

First Revisions: FR 347
Second Revisions: SR 322, SCR 117
Public Inputs: PI 564
Public Comments: PC 2702, PC 988

210.8(B)(10)

210.8(B)(10)

GFCI Protection for Receptacles in Non-Dwelling Unit Unfinished Basements

210.8(B)(10) Ground-Fault Circuit-Interrupter Protection for Personnel.

- **Type of Change:** New

- **Change at a Glance:** GFCI protection has been added for receptacles installed in non-dwelling unit unfinished basements.

- **Code Language: 210.8 Ground-Fault Circuit-Interrupter Protection for Personnel.**

  Ground-fault circuit-interrupter protection for personnel shall be provided as required in 210.8(A) through ~~(D)~~ (E). The ground-fault circuit-interrupter shall be installed in a readily accessible location.

  Informational Note No. 1: See 215.9 for ground-fault circuit-interrupter protection for personnel on feeders.

  Informational Note No. 2: See 422.5(A) for GFCI requirements for appliances.

  For the purposes of this section, when determining distance from receptacles, the distance shall be measured as the shortest path the cord of an appliance connected to the receptacle would follow without piercing a floor, wall, ceiling, or fixed barrier, or passing through a door, doorway, or window.

  (B) Other Than Dwelling Units. All ~~125-volt~~, single-phase~~, 15- and 20-ampere~~ receptacles rated 150 volts to ground or less, 50 amperes or less; and three-phase receptacles rated 150 volts to ground or less, 100 amperes or less, installed in the locations specified in 210.8(B)(1) through ~~(8)~~ (10) shall have ground-fault circuit-interrupter protection for personnel. (10) Unfinished portions or areas of the basement not intended as habitable rooms

- **2014 *NEC* Requirement**
  125-volt, single-phase, 15- and 20-ampere receptacles installed in dwelling unit unfinished basements require GFCI protection. An exception exists for a receptacle supplying only a permanently installed burglar or fire alarm system installed in a dwelling unit unfinished basement. This GFCI requirement for unfinished basements did not apply to non-dwelling unit unfinished basements.

- **2017 *NEC* Change**
  GFCI protection for receptacles installed in unfinished basements has been expanded to include commercial applications as well as dwelling units. Revisions to the parent text at 210.8(B) has expanded the receptacles involved to those that are rated 150 volts to ground or less, 50 amperes or less; and three-phase receptacles rated 150 volts to ground or less, 100 amperes or less.

210.8(B)(10)

Analysis of the Change:

If GFCI protection is warranted for receptacles installed in a dwelling unit unfinished basement, why would anyone not want that same protection for a receptacle located in a non-dwelling unit facility? The same shock hazards exist in an unfinished basement of a commercial building as they do in an unfinished basement of a dwelling unit. GFCI protection for unfinished basements was first introduced in the 1987 *NEC*. This GFCI requirement was only applicable to dwelling unit unfinished basements and remained related to dwelling units only until this change in the 2017 *NEC*.

It should be noted that the text at 210.8(A)(5) for GFCI requirement for receptacles in dwelling unit unfinished basements has been revised to match this new text for non-dwelling unit unfinished basements in such a way as to eliminate the need for a definition of an unfinished basement. Also worth noting is the change to the voltage and ampere ratings of the receptacles covered by the GFCI requirements of 210.8(B). In previous editions of the *Code*, these GFCI requirements only applied to 125-volt, single-phase, 15- and 20-ampere receptacles. Revisions to the parent text at 210.8(B) has expanded the receptacles covered to those that are rated 150 volts to ground or less, 50 amperes or less; and three-phase receptacles rated 150 volts to ground or less, 100 amperes or less.

210.8(B)(10)

First Revisions: FR 347
Second Revisions: SR 322
Public Inputs: PI 564
Public Comments: PC 358, PC 988

210.8(E)

GFCI Protection for Lighting Outlets in Crawl Spaces

210.8(E)

210.8(E) Ground-Fault Circuit-Interrupter Protection for Personnel

- **Type of Change:** New

- **Change at a Glance:** GFCI protection for lighting outlets in crawl spaces has been added.

- **Code Language: 210.8 Ground-Fault Circuit-Interrupter Protection for Personnel.**

  Ground-fault circuit-interrupter protection for personnel shall be provided as required in 210.8(A) through (D) (E). The ground-fault circuit-interrupter shall be installed in a readily accessible location.

  Informational Note No. 1: See 215.9 for ground-fault circuit-interrupter protection for personnel on feeders.

  Informational Note No. 2: See 422.5(A) for GFCI requirements for appliances.

  For the purposes of this section, when determining distance from receptacles, the distance shall be measured as the shortest path the cord of an appliance connected to the receptacle would follow without piercing a floor, wall, ceiling, or fixed barrier, or passing through a door, doorway, or window.

(E) Crawl Space Lighting Outlets. GFCI protection shall be provided for lighting outlets not exceeding 120 volts installed in crawl spaces.

■ **2014 *NEC* Requirement**
GFCI protection for lighting outlets is mandated for luminaires in shower stalls of recreational vehicles (RVs) [551.53(B)] and for park trailers [552.54(B)]. If temporary lighting outlets at construction sites are powered through a receptacle outlet, 590.6(A) would require GFCI protection. There are seven specific requirements for GFCI protection of lighting outlets and luminaires in Article 680 for swimming pools and similar installations. Receptacle outlets are required to be GFCI-protected by provisions at 210.8(A)(4).

■ **2017 *NEC* Change**
In addition to the GFCI requirements for lighting outlets of the previous *Code*, GFCI protection is now required for lighting outlets not exceeding 120 volts in crawl spaces where space is at or below grade level.

Analysis of the Change:

210.8(E)

A new requirement was added at 210.8(E) establishing GFCI protection for lighting outlets not exceeding 120 volts installed in crawl spaces where that space is located at or below grade level. This new GFCI requirement for lighting outlets was justified due to the fatality of a worker in a crawl space. The incandescent light bulb of a keyless lampholder was accidently broken, and the worker was electrocuted upon unintentional contact with the live, exposed parts of the broken light bulb. The number of open-bulb keyless or pull chain lampholders installed in crawl spaces is countless, and they are frequently damaged in this same manner.

This crawl space lighting outlet GFCI provision was originally proposed for 210.70(C), which deals with required lighting outlets in attics and underfloor spaces, utility rooms, and basements. The original public input called for the crawl space lighting outlet to be "protected from physical damage" or be GFCI-protected. CMP-2 indicated that "physical protection does not provide the appropriate shock protection" and decided to place the requirement for GFCI protection in 210.8(E). While this crawl space lighting outlet GFCI requirement has merit, this requirement might be relocated in a future *Code* cycle to Article 410 where protection of luminaires, lampholders, and lamps are addressed. Regardless of its location, GFCI protection for these typically bare, exposed, open bulbs is a small price to pay compared to the cost of an injury or fatality to a human being.

Since this new GFCI requirement for crawl space lighting outlets is located at 210.8(E), it will apply to all crawl spaces, dwelling unit and non-dwelling units alike.

First Revision: FR 347
Second Revision: SR 317
Public Input: PI 564
Public Comments: PC 2702, PC 988

210.11(C)(4)

Garage Branch Circuit(s)

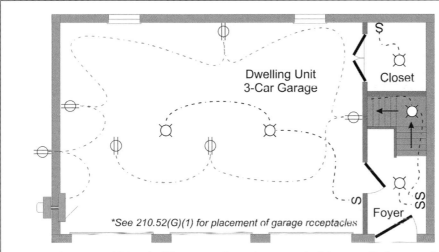

Dwelling Unit
3-Car Garage

S

Closet

Foyer

See 210.52(G)(1) for placement of garage receptacles

At least one 120-volt, 20-ampere branch circuit shall be installed to supply receptacle outlets in dwelling unit garages (no other outlets)

Exception permits supply of readily accessible outdoor receptacle outlets

210.11(C)(4)

210.11(C)(4) Garage Branch Circuits

- **Type of Change:** New

- **Change at a Glance:** New requirement added for minimum rated 120-volt, 20-ampere branch circuit for dwelling unit garage receptacles.

- **Code Language: 210.11 Branch Circuits Required.**
  Branch circuits for lighting and for appliances, including motor-operated appliances, shall be provided to supply the loads calculated in accordance with 220.10. In addition, branch circuits shall be provided for specific loads not covered by 220.10 where required elsewhere in this *Code* and for dwelling unit loads as specified in 210.11(C).

  (C) Dwelling Units.
  (4) Garage Branch Circuits. In addition to the number of branch circuits required by other parts of this section, at least one 120-volt, 20-ampere branch circuit shall be installed to supply receptacle outlets in attached garages and in detached garages with electric power. This circuit shall have no other outlets.

  Exception: This circuit shall be permitted to supply readily accessible outdoor receptacle outlets.

- **2014 *NEC* Requirement**
  The branch circuit supplying receptacle outlets in dwelling unit garages could be a 120-volt, 15- or 20-ampere rated branch circuit. The branch circuit supplying this receptacle(s) could not supply outlets outside of the garage as indicated by 210.52(G)(1).

- **2017 *NEC* Change**
  The branch circuit supplying receptacle outlets in dwelling unit garages is now required to be a 120-volt, 20-ampere rated branch circuit. The garage receptacle outlet branch circuit is still prohibited from serving other outlets with the exception of readily accessible receptacles located outdoors.

Analysis of the Change:

A new requirement, which was added to the required branch circuits for dwelling units, calls for at least one dedicated branch circuit for garage receptacle outlets only. This 120-volt branch circuit must have a minimum rating of 20 amperes. An exception was also added to allow readily accessible outdoor receptacle outlets to be supplied from the branch circuit as well. Many of the appliances and tools used in today's dwelling unit garages are rated at 12 to 16 amperes or higher and demand, at least, a 20-ampere rated branch circuit. A 15-ampere rated branch circuit in the modern dwelling unit garage is typically not sufficient for these loads. While most residential electricians might already be installing 20-ampere rated branch circuits in dwelling unit garages, the *NEC* did not require or demand this 20-ampere rated branch circuit previous to this 2017 *NEC* change. A small, portable, 120-volt, 1 horsepower air compressor drawing 16 amperes would be an example of a tool requiring 20-ampere rated branch circuit.

This requirement was originally proposed at 210.52(G)(1) for dwelling unit garage receptacle outlets, not the branch circuit supplying these receptacle outlets. 210.11(C)(4) is a more appropriate location for this requirement as 210.11(C) deals with required branch circuits for dwelling units. Lighting outlets in the dwelling unit garage are still required to be supplied by general lighting circuits and are not allowed to be supplied from this newly required 20-ampere rated receptacle outlet branch circuit. The thought process here is to protect the illumination of the garage area in the event of an outage on the 20-ampere rated receptacle outlet branch circuit. The added exception will allow readily accessible receptacles located outdoors to be supplied from this garage branch circuit.

First Revision: FR 330
Second Revision: SR 324
Public Input: PI 1010, PI 2722
Public Comments: PC 952, PC 954

210.11(C)(4)

210.12(C)

AFCI Protection in Guest Rooms and Guest Suites

210.12(C)

210.12(C) Arc-Fault Circuit-Interrupter Protection

- **Type of Change:** New

- **Change at a Glance:** New provisions added requiring AFCI protection for guest rooms/guest suites of hotels/motels.

- **Code Language: 210.12 Arc-Fault Circuit-Interrupter Protection.**
  Arc-fault circuit-interrupter protection shall be provided as required in 210.12(A) (B), ~~and~~ (C), and (D). The arc-fault circuit interrupter shall be installed in a readily accessible location.

  (C) Guest Rooms and Guest Suites. All 120-volt, single-phase, 15- and 20-ampere branch circuits supplying outlets and devices installed in guest rooms and guest suites of hotels and motels shall be protected by any of the means described in 210.12(A)(1) through (6).

- **2014 *NEC* Requirement**
  Rules exist at 210.18 requiring guest rooms and guest suites that are provided with "permanent provisions for cooking" to have branch circuits installed to meet the rules for dwelling units. This provision would mean that the AFCI requirements of 210.12 would apply to a hotel and motel guest room/guest suite if this room/suite were furnished with "permanent provisions for cooking." No AFCI requirements existed for guest rooms and guest suites of hotels and motels lacking "permanent provisions for cooking."

■ **2017 *NEC* Change**

New provisions were added at 210.12(C) requiring AFCI protection for all 120-volt, single-phase, 15- and 20-ampere branch circuits supplying outlets and devices installed in guest rooms and guest suites of hotels and motels, regardless of the existence of "permanent provisions for cooking" or not.

Analysis of the Change:

AFCI technology that can help save lives and avoid property damage from fire-related events has been expanded to include guest rooms and guest suites of hotels and motels. Previous editions of the *Code* would extend AFCI protection to these guest quarters with a qualifying condition that "permanent provisions for cooking" must be a part of these accommodations (see 210.17, was 210.18). This new AFCI requirement does not depend on cooking provisions in order to be enforceable. The same or similar threats imposed by arcing events exist in hotel or motel guest occupancies as exist in dwelling units. In numerous cases, guest rooms and guest suites are used in the same basic fashion as school dormitories, and dormitories are already afforded the safety measures of AFCI protection.

210.12(C)

The evolution and expansion of AFCI protection play a major role in protecting the lives and property of homeowners and their families. These families deserve the same protection while occupying a hotel room away from their home. AFCI technology is the next generation of product safety in the protection of electrical circuits. While working smoke detectors, fire extinguishers, and other safety measures provide some life-saving help, these measures are only useful after a fire has already ignited. An AFCI circuit breaker or device detects dangerous electrical conditions (arcing events) and shuts the branch circuit off before an electrical fire can ignite.

The previous requirements of 210.12 were rearranged to accommodate this new requirement for guest rooms and guest suites. Requirements at 210.12(C) for AFCI protection for dormitory units were moved to 210.12(B), and the requirements at 210.12(B) for branch circuit extensions and modifications were moved to new 210.12(D).

First Revision: FR 352
Second Revision: SR 328
Public Inputs: PI 1453
Public Comments: PC 683, PC 818

210.17
Electric Vehicle Branch Circuit

210.17

210.17 Electric Vehicle Branch Circuit

- **Type of Change:** Deletion and Relocation

- **Change at a Glance:** The requirement for an individual branch circuit for electric vehicle outlets has been relocated from 210.17 to 625.40.

- **Code Language:** ~~210.17 Electric Vehicle Branch Circuit. An outlet(s) installed for the purpose of charging electric vehicles shall be supplied by a separate branch circuit. This circuit shall have no other outlets.~~
  ~~**Informational Note:** See 625.2 for the definition of Electric Vehicle.~~

  625.40 Electric Vehicle Branch Circuit. ~~An outlet(s)~~ Each outlet installed for the purpose of charging electric vehicles shall be supplied by ~~a separate~~ an individual branch circuit. ~~This~~ Each circuit shall have no other outlets.

- **2014 *NEC* Requirement**
  There was no requirement for an outlet to be installed for charging of an electric vehicle. If an outlet(s) for the purpose of charging electric vehicles was installed, the requirements of 210.17 would require the outlet(s) to be supplied by a "separate" branch circuit. This circuit may have no other outlets.

- **2017 *NEC* Change**
  The requirement for a separate branch circuit for electric vehicle outlets was relocated to 625.40, the article for electric vehicle charging systems.

During this relocation, the requirement for a "separate" branch circuit was changed to an "individual" branch circuit. There is still no requirement for an outlet to be installed specifically for the purpose of charging of an electric vehicle.

Analysis of the Change:

During the 2014 *NEC Code* revision process, a new requirement was added at 210.17 providing for a "separate" branch circuit for circuits that supply electric vehicle charging (EV) systems. Without this "separate" branch circuit with no other outlets, combining an EV charging load with older and traditional wiring methods (particularly at dwelling units) was challenging at best. Charging an electric vehicle by simply plugging into an existing 120-volt receptacle outlet that is more than likely supplied from a general lighting circuit can and will overload the existing general purpose branch circuit. In relocating this EV branch circuit requirement to Article 625 (Electric Vehicle Charging Systems), it was noted by the submitter that this requirement did not belong in *NEC* Chapter 2 as Article 210 deals with general provisions for branch circuits, and it more appropriately belongs in *NEC* Chapter 6, which is specific to special equipment.

210.17

At its previous location at 210.17, the *Code* language used referred to the need for a "separate" branch circuit. This term is not defined anywhere in the *Code* and, in particular, not in Article 100. The one and only *Code* cycle that this term was used, it caused confusion among installers and inspectors alike as to what constituted a "separate" branch circuit. At its present location at 625.40, this branch circuit was renamed as an "individual" branch circuit. This term that is defined in Article 100 and is intended to supply only one piece of utilization equipment, which fits with the last sentence of the requirement ("...circuit shall have no other outlets"). The previous 210.17 text was also unclear as to whether multiple outlets on one branch circuit could be installed, as long as the outlets are only intended for EV charging systems, or if each EV charging outlet had to have a single (individual) branch circuit supplying it and no other outlets. The new text at 625.40 makes it clear that the latter is intended.

It should be noted that neither the previous 210.17 requirement or this relocated requirement demand that an outlet for the specific and sole purpose of charging EV equipment must be installed. This requirement simply states that where such EV charging outlets are installed (by choice), each of these EV charging outlets must be supplied by an individual branch circuit with no other outlets. This new provision for EV charging will go a long way to ensuring that EV charging can be performed safely and effectively without overloading an existing branch circuit.

First Revisions: FR 353, FR 3371
Public Inputs: PI 3601, PI 3604, PI 810, PI 3307

210.52(A)(2)(1)
Receptacle Wall Space

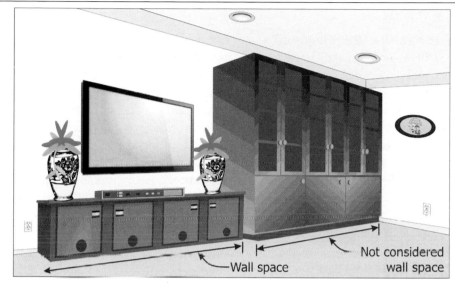

Any space 600 mm (2 ft) or more in width and unbroken along the floor line by doorways and similar openings, fireplaces, and fixed cabinets that do not have countertops or similar work surfaces

210.52(A)(2)(1)

210.52(A)(2)(1) Dwelling Unit Receptacle Outlets

- **Type of Change:** Revision

- **Change at a Glance:** Fixed cabinets "that do not have countertops or similar work surfaces" was added as an item that will constitute a break in a wall space for receptacle spacing requirements at dwelling units.

- **Code Language: 210.52 Dwelling Unit Receptacle Outlets**
  This section provides requirements for 125-volt, 15- and 20-ampere receptacle outlets.
  (Remainder of text unchanged.)

  (A) General Provisions. In every kitchen, family room, dining room, living room, parlor, library, den, sunroom, bedroom, recreation room, or similar room or area of dwelling units, receptacle outlets shall be installed in accordance with the general provisions specified in 210.52(A)(1) through (A)(4).

  (2) Wall Space. As used in this section, a wall space shall include the following:
  (1) Any space 600 mm (2 ft) or more in width (including space measured around corners) and unbroken along the floor line by doorways and similar openings, fireplaces, and fixed cabinets that do not have countertops or similar work surfaces

(2) The space occupied by fixed panels in ~~exterior~~ walls, excluding sliding panels

(3) The space afforded by fixed room dividers, such as freestanding bar-type counters or railings

■ **2014 *NEC* Requirement**
All "fixed cabinets," regardless of their dimension or size, with or without countertop or work surfaces were considered as items (along with doorways and fireplaces) that would not be counted as "wall space" and would establish a break in that wall space as far as receptacle spacing and location were concerned.

■ **2017 *NEC* Change**
Only "fixed cabinets that do not have countertops or similar work surfaces" are now considered as an item (along with doorways and fireplaces) that would not be counted as "wall space" concerning receptacle spacing and location requirements.

Analysis of the Change:

210.52(A)(2)(1)

When it comes to determining just how many general-use wall receptacle outlets are needed in a dwelling unit, the *Code* language found at 210.52(A)(1) through (A)(4) provides requirements and guidance. For spacing of these required receptacles, 210.52(A)(1) states that receptacles are to be located so that "no point measured horizontally along the floor line of any *wall space* is more than 1.8 m (6 ft) from a receptacle outlet." What is considered "wall space" and what is not? To answer that question, the provisions of 210.52(A)(2) step forward. During the 2011 *NEC* revision process, 210.52(A)(2)(1) was revised by adding the term "fixed cabinets" to a list of things that actually would break up a "wall space" that was 600 mm (2 ft) or more in width. These items also include doorways and fireplaces. In reading the substantiation for adding the term "fixed cabinets," it was quite clear that the cabinets referred to were large cabinets, such as kitchen cabinets. Receptacle placement and spacing for kitchen cabinets and countertops have their set of rules at 210.52(C). The term "fixed cabinets" was added to ensure that the requirements for "1.8 m (6 ft) from a receptacle outlet" wall spacing were not applied to large pantry-type cabinets occupying the space from the floor to the ceiling (with no countertop) in a kitchen area.

In a literal reading or interpretation of this 2011 *NEC* revision, any and all "fixed cabinets" (not just kitchen cabinets) were now subject to having no receptacle outlets required in, on, or above them. This requirement would include any fixed cabinet at any height in any room not counting as "wall space." This rule presented a problem for enforcement at such things as cabinets in a home office, library, or family room where the cabinets may be only 900 mm (36 in.) tall. In some of these areas, these cabinets are installed around the majority of the room. As previously written, there was no *Code* requirement the AHJ could fall back on to require any receptacle outlets for the "wall space" these cabinets consumed. This situation resulted in rooms, other than kitchens, with fixed cabinets and cabinet countertops occupying a substantial length of wall space with no required receptacle outlets serving these countertop areas.

This revision for the 2017 *NEC* at 210.52(A)(2)(1) will eliminate this problem by separating "fixed cabinets," such as kitchen pantry-type cabinets (but not limited to kitchen cabinets), that do not have countertops or similar work surfaces from short desk-type cabinets with countertops that are clearly intended as work surfaces. This change will ensure that receptacle outlets are required and installed along with these desk-type fixed cabinets that need receptacle outlets for such things as laptop computers, printers, televisions, etc. These fixed desk-type cabinets will be under the same "no point more than 1.8 m (6 ft) from a receptacle outlet" rules as the other walls of that particular room.

First Revisions: FR 324
Second Revisions: SR 307
Public Inputs: PI 1438, PI 2650, PI 2651
Public Comments: PC 54

210.52(B)(1)

210.52(B)(1), Ex. No. 2

Appliance Branch Circuit

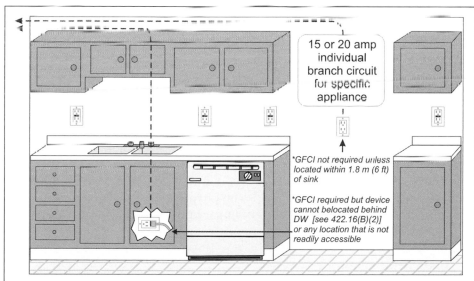

15 or 20 amp individual branch circuit for specific appliance

*GFCI not required unless located within 1.8 m (6 ft) of sink

*GFCI required but device cannot belocated behind DW [see 422.16(B)(2)] or any location that is not readily accessible

Refrigeration equipment generally required to be served by one of the two or more 20-ampere small-appliance branch circuits

The receptacle outlet for any specific appliance is permitted to be supplied from an individual branch circuit rated 15 amperes or greater

210.52 Dwelling Unit Receptacle Outlets

- **Type of Change:** Revision

■ **Change at a Glance:** An individual branch circuit supplying a receptacle outlet for any specific appliance (not just the refrigerator) at a dwelling unit is allowed to be rated 15-ampere or greater.

■ **Code Language: 210.52 Dwelling Unit Receptacle Outlets**
This section provides requirements for 125-volt, 15- and 20-ampere receptacle outlets.
(Remainder of text unchanged.)

(B) Small Appliances
(1) Receptacle Outlets Served. In the kitchen, pantry, breakfast room, dining room, or similar area of a dwelling unit, the two or more 20-ampere small-appliance branch circuits required by 210.11(C)(1) shall serve all wall and floor receptacle outlets covered by 210.52(A), all countertop outlets covered by 210.52(C), and receptacle outlets for refrigeration equipment.

Exception No. 1: In addition to the required receptacles specified by 210.52, switched receptacles supplied from a general-purpose branch circuit as defined in 210.70(A)(1), Exception No. 1, shall be permitted.

Exception No. 2: ~~The receptacle outlet for refrigeration equipment~~ *In addition to the required receptacles specified by 210.52, a receptacle outlet to serve a specific appliance shall be permitted to be supplied from an individual branch circuit rated 15 amperes or greater.*

■ **2014 *NEC* Requirement**
Dwelling unit refrigeration equipment was permitted by exception to be supplied from an individual branch circuit rated 15 amperes or greater rather than from one of the 20-ampere rated small-appliance branch circuits. This "smaller than 20 amperes" permission was not afforded to any other kitchen appliance.

■ **2017 *NEC* Change**
Any specific dwelling unit kitchen appliance is permitted by exception to be supplied from an individual branch circuit rated 15 amperes or greater rather than from one of the 20-ampere rated small-appliance branch circuits.

Analysis of the Change:
The receptacle outlets in dwelling unit kitchens, pantries, breakfast rooms, dining rooms, or similar areas are required to be supplied by the required 20-ampere small-appliance branch circuits. It comes as a surprise for many individuals that 210.52(B)(1) also demands that the receptacle outlet serving the refrigeration equipment be supplied from one of the two or more 20-ampere small-appliance branch circuits as well.

Beginning with the 1996 *NEC*, an exception to this main rule has allowed the refrigeration equipment to be supplied by its own individual branch circuit rated

210.52(B)(1)

15 amperes or greater rather than one of the 20-ampere small-appliance branch circuits. Some users of the *Code* have recently begun to ask why this exception is exclusive to just the refrigerator. Why can't this exception be applied to other dwelling unit kitchen appliances such as the garbage disposal, dishwasher, and permanently installed microwave? Currently, these appliances are installed on individual branch circuits and cord-and-plug connected in the kitchen area routinely, with the refrigerator being the only permitted non-small appliance permitted to be supplied by a branch circuit smaller than a 20-ampere branch circuit.

This exception was originally instituted for the refrigeration equipment to allow an individual branch circuit (rated as small as 15 amperes) and to allow this appliance load to be removed from the small appliance branch circuits, as the refrigeration is not a small appliance. It is interesting to note that the original proposal (see NFPA 70 A95 ROP 2-257) was seeking an individual branch circuit used to supply "a specific appliance such as a refrigerator or freezer" not the refrigerator alone.

For the 2017 *NEC*, a revision to Exception No. 2 of 210.52(B)(1) will recognize that an individual branch circuit supplied specifically for any single appliance is allowed to be rated at 15-ampere or greater. Apparently, this was happening on a fairly regular basis with the seeming permission coming from 210.22, which states that an individual branch circuit is permitted to supply any load for which it is rated, but in no case shall the load exceed the branch-circuit ampere rating. This revision will help weave these two rules together.

210.52(B)(1)

Second Revisions: SR 308
Public Input: PI 3807
PC: PC 1031

210.52(C)(3)

Peninsular Countertop Spaces

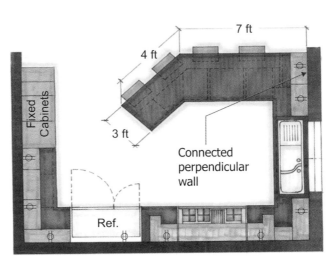

At least one receptacle outlet to be installed at each peninsular countertop with a long dimension of 600 mm (24 in.) or greater and a short dimension of 300 mm (12 in.) or greater

Measurements to be measured from the "connected perpendicular wall"

210.52(C)(3)

210.52(C)(3) Dwelling Unit Receptacle Outlets

- **Type of Change:** Revision

- **Change at a Glance:** The measurement point for peninsular countertops has been changed from the "connecting edge" to the "connected perpendicular wall."

- **Code Language: 210.52 Dwelling Unit Receptacle Outlets**
  This section provides requirements for 125-volt, 15- and 20-ampere receptacle outlets.
  (*Remainder of text unchanged.*)

  (C) Countertops and Work Surfaces. In kitchens, pantries, breakfast rooms, dining rooms, and similar areas of dwelling units, receptacle outlets for countertop and work surface spaces shall be installed in accordance with 210.52(C)(1) through (C)(5).

  (3) Peninsular Countertop Spaces. At least one receptacle outlet shall be installed at each peninsular countertop long dimension space with a long dimension of 600 mm (24 in.) or greater and a short dimension of 300 mm (12 in.) or greater. A peninsular countertop is measured from the ~~connecting edge~~ connected perpendicular wall.

- **2014 *NEC* Requirement**

  At least one receptacle outlet must be installed at each peninsular counter-top with a long dimension of 600 mm (24 in.) or greater and a short dimension of 300 mm (12 in.) or greater. These measurements were measured from the "connecting edge."

- **2017 *NEC* Change**

  At least one receptacle outlet is still required at each peninsular countertop with a long dimension of 600 mm (24 in.) or greater and a short dimension of 300 mm (12 in.) or greater, but the measurement is now measured from the "connected perpendicular wall."

Analysis of the Change:

The requirements at 210.52(C)(3) speak to the placement and measurement for required receptacle outlet(s) at dwelling unit kitchen peninsular counter-top spaces. At least one receptacle outlet is required to be installed at each peninsular countertop with a long dimension of 600 mm (24 in.) or greater and a short dimension of 300 mm (12 in.) or greater. Since its inception in the 1993 edition of the *NEC*, this measurement has always been measured from the "connecting edge" where the peninsular countertop mates with the base kitchen countertop. This will no longer be true beginning with the 2017 *NEC* as these measurements will now be measured from the "connected perpendicular wall."

The change was not intended to create language that reduces the coverage of receptacle outlets serving these peninsular countertops, but rather to better define how the long dimension of the peninsular countertop is measured. The final language at 210.52(C)(3) allows a receptacle outlet at the connecting wall (which serves the base countertop) to serve the peninsular countertop as well. When measured from the connecting edge rather than the wall, this require-ment previously demanded at least one receptacle outlets be placed somewhere at or on the peninsular countertop itself. This revision will allow relief from the burden of trying to figure out a solution to the placement of the required recep-tacle outlet at a peninsular countertop without any supporting cabinets installed under the peninsular countertop. Some peninsular countertops are installed and resemble a permanently installed kitchen table more than the traditional cabinet-style countertops.

In the original proposed language accepted at the 2017 *NEC* First Draft stage, a receptacle outlet in a wall countertop space was only permitted to serve as the receptacle for a peninsular countertop space where the spaces were continuous and the wall receptacle was located within 1.8 m (6 ft) of the outside edge of the peninsular countertop. This 1.8 m (6 ft) restriction was removed at the 2017 *NEC* Second Draft stage allowing the wall receptacle outlet to serve the base countertop as well as all of the peninsular countertop, regardless of the length of the peninsular countertop.

Some will argue that this revision achieved the opposite effect than was intended as the number of required receptacle outlets to serve kitchen peninsular counter-

210.52(C)(3)

tops has been reduced rather than maintained. No doubt this issue will be revisited again in future *Code* revision cycles.

First Revisions: FR 356
Second Revisions: SR 309
Pubic Inputs: PI 3605
Public Comments: PC 572

210.52(G)

*Receptacle for Basements, Garages,
and Accessory Buildings*

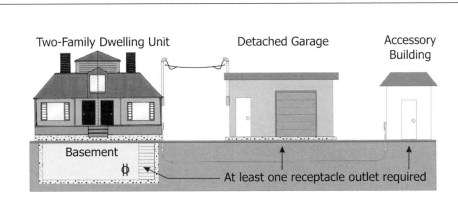

At one- and two-family dwellings, at least one 125-volt, 15- or 20-ampere receptacle outlet, in addition to those for specific equipment, shall be installed in areas specified below:

- Attached garages and in each detached garage with electric power

- Accessory buildings with electric power

- Unfinished basements - each seperate portion of the basement

210.52(G) Dwelling Unit Receptacle Outlets

- **Type of Change:** Revision

- **Change at a Glance:** Receptacle requirements for dwelling unit garages, basements, and accessory buildings expanded to two-family dwellings (not just one-family dwellings).

- **Code Language: 210.52 Dwelling Unit Receptacle Outlets**
This section provides requirements for 125-volt, 15- and 20-ampere receptacle outlets.
(*Remainder of text unchanged.*)

(G) Basements, Garages, and Accessory Buildings. For a one- and two-family dwellings, at least one receptacle outlet shall be installed in the areas specified in 210.52(G)(1) through (3). These receptacles shall be in addition to receptacles required for specific equipment.

- **2014 *NEC* Requirement**
  At least one receptacle outlet is required to be installed in each attached garage and detached garage with electric power, each separate unfinished portion of a basement, and each accessory building with electric power. This requirement applied to one-family dwellings only.

- **2017 *NEC* Change**
  The same one receptacle outlet requirement still applies to qualifying basements, garages, and accessory buildings, but this requirement has been extended to two-family dwellings as well as one-family dwellings.

Analysis of the Change:

At least one 125-volt, 15- or 20-ampere receptacle outlet has been required to be installed in each garage and unfinished basement since the 1978 *NEC*. Detached garages were added to this provision in the 1987 *NEC* and accessory buildings with electric power were added in the 2011 *NEC*. Historically, this requirement has applied to one-family dwellings. Without a close look at the text at 210.52(G), some users of the *Code* would assume that this receptacle outlet rule would and has applied to both one- and two-family dwellings alike.

For the 2017 *NEC*, this same level of electrical safety has been extended to two-family dwellings as it has been for one-family dwellings for the past 10 *Code* cycles. The purpose of this rule is to help prevent the use of extension cords as a substitute for permanent wiring, which often occurs when receptacle outlets are not readily available. When extension cords are used as a substitute for permanent wiring, they are often stretched through doorways, windows, and similar openings. This frequently leads to damaged cords and the creation of an electrical hazard. The same potential for creating a hazard occurs at a two-family dwelling as it does for a one-family dwelling.

First Revisions: FR 310
Public Inputs: PI 96

210.52(G)

210.52(G)(1)

Dwelling Unit Garages

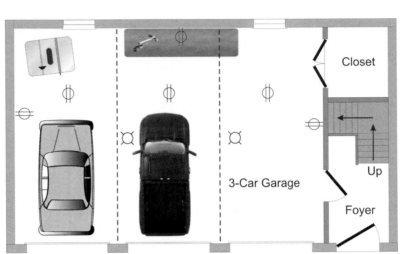

In each attached garage and in each detached garage with electric power, at least one receptacle outlet is required to be installed "in each vehicle bay and not more than 1.7 m (5½ ft) above the floor"

Note: *See 210.11(C)(4) for garage branch circuit requirements*

210.52(G)(1)

210.52(G)(1) Dwelling Unit Receptacle Outlets

- **Type of Change:** Revision

- **Change at a Glance:** At least one receptacle outlet is required to be installed "in each vehicle bay" and not more than 1.7 m (5½ ft) above the floor in dwelling unit garages.

- **Code Language: 210.52 Dwelling Unit Receptacle Outlets**
  This section provides requirements for 125-volt, 15- and 20-ampere receptacle outlets.
  (Remainder of text unchanged.)

  (G) Basements, Garages, and Accessory Buildings. For ~~a~~ one- and two-family dwellings, at least one receptacle outlet shall be installed in the areas specified in 210.52(G)(1) through (3). These receptacles shall be in addition to receptacles required for specific equipment.

  (1) Garages. In each attached garage and in each detached garage with electric power~~,. The branch circuit supplying this receptacle(s) shall not supply outlets outside of the garage. At~~ at least one receptacle outlet shall be installed ~~for~~ in each ~~car space~~ vehicle bay and not more than 1.7 m (5½ ft) above the floor.

- **2014 *NEC* Requirement**
  In each attached garage and in each detached garage with electric power, at least one receptacle outlet was required to be installed "for each car space." The branch circuit supplying these receptacle(s) could not supply outlets outside of the garage.

- **2017 *NEC* Change**
  In each attached garage and in each detached garage with electric power, at least one receptacle outlet is required to be installed "in each vehicle bay and not more than 1.7 m (5½ ft) above the floor." The branch circuit supplying these receptacle(s) cannot serve outlets outside of the garage with the exception of readily accessible receptacles located outdoors. This latter requirement concerning the branch circuit supplying the garage is now located at 210.11(C)(4).

Analysis of the Change:

When it comes to the required number of receptacle outlets required in a dwelling unit garage, at least one 125-volt, 15- or 20-ampere receptacle outlet has been required to be installed in each garage beginning in the 1978 *NEC*. To ensure that both attached and detached type garages were covered by this requirement, detached garages were specifically added to this provision in the 1987 *NEC*. This minimum of one required receptacle outlet remained in place until the 2014 *NEC* when the *Code* language was revised to require at least one receptacle outlet to be installed "for each car space."

This 2014 *NEC* revision was created due to the increased activities in dwelling unit garages as well as the possibility of the existence of electric vehicle (EV) charging equipment in a modern day garage. This 2014 *NEC* change was also intended to require a minimum of three receptacle outlets in a three-car garage, four receptacle outlets in a four-car garage, etc. The verbatim language "for each car space" brought about a wide variety of interpretations. With a literal interpretation, it was not a stretch to determine that one receptacle outlet placed between two "car spaces" could be "for each car space." Some would argue that a receptacle outlet in the ceiling for a garage door opener could be "for" that particular "car space." The parent text at 210.52(G) which states that "these receptacles shall be in addition to receptacles required for specific equipment" would eliminate receptacle outlets specific to such things as a garage door opener from serving as this required receptacle outlet "for" or in each vehicle space.

For these and other reasons, the 2017 *NEC* text at 210.52(G)(1) was further revised by changing the requirement for at least one receptacle outlet to be installed "for each car space" to "in each vehicle bay and not more than 1.7 m (5½ ft) above the floor." The change from "for" to "in" each vehicle bay will eliminate the interpretation of one receptacle outlet being shared by two adjacent spaces. The term "car space" was changed to "vehicle bay" to recognize the fact that other vehicles such as pickup trucks, sports utility vehicles, tractors, and so forth could be parked in a dwelling unit garage as well as a car. The "not more than 1.7 m (5½ ft) above the floor" requirement removes all doubt concerning the receptacle outlet installed in the ceiling specifically for a garage door opener

210.52(G)(1)

serving double-duty and also serving as the required receptacle outlet "in each vehicle bay." This requirement and the revision as a whole is intended to ensure that a receptacle outlet is reasonably close to where it is needed in the garage area and to diminish or eliminate the use of an extension cord in a garage as fixed or permanent wiring, which of course is a violation of previous 400.8(1) [now 400.12(1)].

This revision also included the relocation of the requirement that the "branch circuit supplying these receptacle(s) shall not supply outlets outside of the garage" from this section of the *Code*. This branch circuit requirement was relocated to new 210.11(C)(4) which pertains to required branch circuits for dwelling units. The requirement under discussion here at 210.52(G)(1) relates to dwelling unit garage receptacle outlets, not the branch circuit supplying these receptacle outlets. Closer examination of the new requirements for the branch circuit supplying the garage at 210.11(C)(4) will still find a requirement that this branch circuit serve no other outlets, but with an exception allowing readily accessible receptacles located outdoors to be supplied by this garage branch circuit.

As a side note, lighting outlets in the dwelling unit garage are still required to be supplied by general lighting circuits and not allowed to be supplied from this newly required 20 ampere rated receptacle outlet branch circuit of 210.11(C)((4) to protect the illumination of the garage area in the event of an outage on the 20-ampere rated receptacle outlet branch circuit.

210.52(G)(1)

First Revisions: FR 317
Second Revisions: SR 326
Public Inputs: PI 1431, PI 1572, PI 705, PI 839, PI 4303, PI 3608, PI 4691, PI 2655, PI 2905, PI 365, PI 366
Public Comments: PC 929, PC 954, PC 1549

210.64

Receptacle at Electrical Service Areas

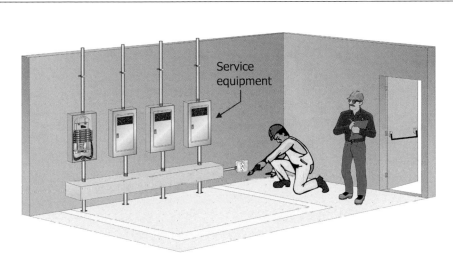

At least one 125-volt, single-phase, 15- or 20-ampere-rated receptacle outlet shall be installed in an accessible location within 7.5 m (25 ft) of all indoor electrical service equipment and located within the same room or area as the service equipment *(other than one- and two-family dwellings)*

Exception added for service areas covered in Articles 675 and 682

210.64

210.64 Electrical Service Areas

- **Type of Change:** Revision

- **Change at a Glance:** The required receptacle outlets at electrical service equipment must be installed in an accessible location within 7.5 m (25 ft) of indoor electrical service equipment.

- **Code Language: 210.64 Electrical Service Areas.**
  At least one 125-volt, single-phase, 15- or 20-ampere-rated receptacle outlet shall be installed in an accessible location within ~~15 m (50 ft)~~ 7.5 m (25 ft) of the indoor electrical service equipment. The required receptacle outlet shall be located within the same room or area as the service equipment.

  Exception No. 1: The receptacle outlet shall not be required to be installed in one-and-two-family dwellings.
  Exception No. 2: Where the service voltage is greater than 120 volts to ground, a receptacle outlet shall not be required for services dedicated to equipment covered in Articles 675 and 682.

- **2014 *NEC* Requirement**
  At least one 125-volt, single-phase, 15-or 20-ampere receptacle outlet was required to be installed within 15 m (50 ft) of the electrical service area.

This service area receptacle outlet is not required at one- and two-family dwellings by exception.

- **2017 *NEC* Change**
  At least one 125-volt, single-phase, 15- or 20-ampere-rated receptacle outlet is still required to be installed at the electrical service equipment. The maximum distance this receptacle outlet can be located from the electrical service has been shortened to 7.5 m (25 ft) and limited to indoor service equipment only. This required receptacle outlet is now required to be installed in an accessible location and must be located within the same room or area as the service equipment. This requirement is still not applicable to one- and two-family dwellings. A new exception was also added allowing services dedicated to equipment covered in Articles 675 and 682 to be exempt from this requirement when the service voltage is greater than 120 volts to ground.

210.64

Analysis of the Change:

For the 2014 *NEC Code* cycle, a new provision was added in Article 210 requiring, at least one 125-volt, single-phase, 15-or 20-ampere receptacle outlet to be installed within 15 m (50 ft) of all electrical service areas (*other than one- and two-family dwellings*). The substantiation for this change indicated that there is sometimes a need for connecting portable electrical data acquisition equipment for the qualitative analysis of the electrical service system, and test equipment is frequently needed for monitoring and servicing electrical equipment in service areas as well. This service area receptacle outlet requirement was revised for the 2017 *NEC*.

The first revision requires this service area receptacle outlet to be installed in an accessible location, within the same room or area as the service equipment. Part of the rationale for requiring this receptacle outlet in the first place was to eliminate extension cords from being run across the floor of the electrical equipment room, and down a hallway into an adjoining room when a receptacle was not provided in the electrical service area. With the previous text at 210.64, the rules for a service area receptacle outlet could be literally accomplished with a receptacle outlet located in the next room, down and across the hallway from the electrical service area by employing an extension cord as long as the receptacle outlet was "installed within 15 m (50 ft) of the electrical service equipment."

The second revision was to reduce the maximum distance between the required receptacle outlet and the electrical service equipment to 7.5 m (25 ft) rather than the previous 15 m (50 ft). This 7.5 m (25 ft) distance is consistent with 210.63, which is a similar receptacle outlet requirement for heating, air-conditioning, and refrigeration equipment. The measurement of 15 m (50 ft) is typically associated with visibility, such as "within sight", while this requirement (like 210.63) pertains to servicing of equipment. Part of the substantiation for this 2017 *NEC* revision indicated that the typical length of an electrical worker's service truck extension cord is 7.5 m (25 ft) versus 15 m (50 ft).

The third revision was to limit this service area receptacle outlet requirement to only "indoor" service equipment (other than one- and two-family dwellings). Revising the text to specify only indoor locations provides a reasonable solution to unintended consequences from the language introduced in the 2014 *NEC*. Much of the discussion during the 2014 *NEC* revision cycle was related to indoor locations where monitoring equipment would be used and with the proliferation of cordless tools, vehicle power inverters, and mobile generators; the need for this outlet seems marginal in outdoor locations.

The final revision to 210.64 added a second exception pertaining to service equipment that is dedicated to equipment covered in Articles 675 (Electrically Driven or Controlled Irrigation Machines) and 682 (Natural and Artificially Made Bodies of Water) where the service voltage is greater than 120 volts to ground. These unique and mostly discrete, stand-alone pumping facilities often receive their power source from metered utility distribution systems of 480 or 600 volts grounded or ungrounded systems. These remote services typically serve only these irrigation loads. These loads could be items such as an irrigation pump or center pivot irrigation machine for a farm or ranch, or equipment for an industrial facility settling pond pumping system. Without this exception, these 480- or 600-volt services would require something like the installation of a step-down transformer for the sole purpose of supporting a 120-volt receptacle outlet, which seems excessive. These installations are normally installed and serviced by qualified persons using portable power generators, or battery powered electrical tools. Once again, remember that the service area receptacle outlet is now required for indoor installations only. The exempted services are often mounted on poles in fields, where they are unsupervised for long stretches of time.

210.64

As requested by one public input, CMP-2 chose not to include agricultural buildings in this exception as these buildings are normally associated with 120/240 volt services and GFCI protected receptacle outlets are required by 547.5(G).

First Revisions: FR 323
Public Inputs: PI 437, PI 1439, PI 840, PI 3344, PI 3611, PI 443, PI 483, PI 653, PI 1309, PI 4750, PI 4038

210.70(C)
Lighting Outlet(s) All Occupancies

At non-dwelling unit attics, underfloor spaces, utility rooms, and basements, at least one <u>lighting outlet</u> containing a switch or controlled by a wall switch must be installed where these spaces are used for storage or contain equipment requiring servicing *[See 210.70(A)(3) for dwelling units]*

At least one switch to be located at the "usual point of entry" to space with lighting outlet(s) located "at or near the equipment requiring servicing"

210.70(C) (sidebar)

210.70(C) Lighting Outlets Required

- **Type of Change:** Revision

- **Change at a Glance:** Lighting outlet requirements for storage or equipment spaces added for non-dwelling unit utility rooms and basements.

- **Code Language: 210.70 Lighting Outlets Required.**
  Lighting outlets shall be installed where specified in 210.70(A), (B), and (C).

  (C) ~~Other Than Dwelling Units~~ **All Occupancies.** For attics and underfloor spaces, ~~containing equipment requiring servicing, such as heating, air-conditioning, and refrigeration equipment~~ utility rooms, and basements, at least one lighting outlet containing a switch or controlled by a wall switch shall be installed ~~in such~~ where these spaces are used for storage or contain equipment requiring servicing. At least one point of control shall be at the usual point of entry to these spaces. The lighting outlet shall be provided at or near the equipment requiring servicing.

- **2014 *NEC* Requirement**
  For dwelling unit attics, underfloor spaces, utility rooms, and basements, at least one lighting outlet containing a switch or controlled by a wall switch must be installed where these spaces are used for storage or contain equipment requiring servicing. This requirement is found

at 210.70(A)(3). For other than dwelling units, this lighting requirement only applied to attics and underfloor spaces (not utility rooms and
basements). This non-dwelling unit lighting requirement is located at
210.70(C). Both of these *Code* sections require at least one point of control
to be located at the "usual point of entry" to these spaces with the lighting
outlet(s) itself located "at or near the equipment requiring servicing."

- **2017 *NEC* Change**
  The title of 210.70(C) was changed from "Other Than Dwelling Units" to
  "All Occupancies" and the text at this provision was revised to mirror the
  Code text at 210.70(A)(3) for dwelling units. This lighting outlet requirement
  for storage or equipment spaces now applies to dwelling units as well as
  non-dwelling unit attics, underfloor spaces, utility rooms, and basements.

Analysis of the Change:

A switched lighting outlet has been required to be installed in dwelling unit
attics, underfloor spaces, utility rooms, and basements beginning with the 1975
NEC. A switched lighting outlet has been a requirement for non-dwelling unit
attics and underfloor spaces since the 1990 edition of the *Code*. Non-dwelling
unit utility rooms and basements have not been subject to a required lighting
outlet until a revision to 210.70(C) for the 2017 *NEC*.

A utility room or basement located at other than a dwelling unit often contains
or has the ability to contain the very same electrical equipment as non-dwelling
unit attics or an underfloor space. However, the non-dwelling unit utility room
or basement was not required to have any lighting outlet provided for servicing
of the equipment until this revision. The same types of hazards that can exist
due to the lack of illumination exist in all attics, underfloor spaces, utility rooms,
and basements whether these areas are located in a dwelling unit or other than
a dwelling unit. Illumination is needed for the safety of a homeowner as well as
for service personnel in all locations where there is storage or electrical equipment requiring servicing. The revised wording at 210.70(C) for all occupancies is
the same as the text found in 210.70(A)(3) for dwelling units.

In the revised text in the First Draft of 2017 *NEC*, 210.70(C) contained language
calling for a lighting outlet installed in a crawl space to be protected from physical damage or be provided with GFCI protection. This requirement for GFCI
protection was more appropriate for the GFCI requirements found at 210.8 and
was moved to new 210.8(E). This location at 210.70 is for required lighting outlets and, therefore, addresses the luminaire itself or GFCI protection. The option
of protection from physical damage was removed from 210.8(E) since physical
protection does not provide the appropriate shock protection.

210.70(C)

First Revisions: FR 315
Second Revisions: SR 311
Public Inputs: PI 150, PI 3099
Public Comments: PC 985

210.71

Receptacle Outlets in Meeting Rooms

210.71

210.71 **Meeting Rooms**

- **Type of Change:** New

- **Change at a Glance:** Receptacle outlet requirements were added for non-dwelling unit meeting rooms.

- **Code Language: 210.71 Meeting Rooms.**

  (A) General. Each meeting room of not more than 93 m² (1000 ft²) in other than dwelling units shall have outlets for nonlocking-type, 125-volt, 15- or 20-ampere receptacles. The outlets shall be installed in accordance with 210.71(B). Where a room or space is provided with movable partition(s), each room size shall be determined with the partition in the position that results in the smallest size meeting room.

  Informational Note No. 1: For the purposes of this section, meeting rooms are typically designed or intended for the gathering of seated occupants for such purposes as conferences, deliberations, or similar purposes, where portable electronic equipment such as computers, projectors, or similar equipment is likely to be used.

  Informational Note No. 2: Examples of rooms that are not meeting rooms include auditoriums, schoolrooms, and coffee shops.

(B) Receptacle Outlets Required. The total number of receptacle outlets, including floor outlets and receptacle outlets in fixed furniture, shall not be less than as determined in (1) and (2). These receptacle outlets shall be permitted to be located as determined by the designer or building owner.

(1) Receptacle Outlets in Fixed Walls. Receptacle outlets shall be installed in accordance with 210.52(A)(1) through (A)(4).

(2) Floor Receptacle Outlets. A meeting room that is at least 3.7 m (12 ft) wide and that has a floor area of at least 20 m² (215 ft²) shall have at least one receptacle outlet located in the floor at a distance not less than 1.8 m (6 ft) from any fixed wall for each 20 m2 (215 ft²) or major portion of floor space.

Informational Note No. 1: See Section 314.27(B) for floor boxes used for receptacles located in the floor.

Informational Note No. 2: See Article 518 for assembly occupancies designed for 100 or more persons.

■ **2014 *NEC* Requirement**
The 2014 *NEC* and previous editions of the *Code* have provisions for the location and wall spacing of nonlocking-type, 125-volt, 15- or 20-ampere receptacles, but these provisions were only binding at dwelling units [see 210.52(A)(1) through (A)(4)]. There were no such receptacle outlet spacing requirements at "other than a dwelling unit."

■ **2017 *NEC* Change**
New provisions were added at 210.71 with minimum provisions for receptacle outlets placement and wall spacing requirements in non-dwelling unit meeting rooms such as those found at hotels and convention centers. See *NEC* text for complete requirements and specifics.

Analysis of the Change:

To emphasize the receptacle outlet spacing requirements specific to dwelling units, the instructor conducting a residential electrical training class will often ask the attendees, "How many receptacle outlets does the *Code* require us to supply for this beautiful meeting room of this fine-looking hotel facility that we are meeting in today?" The answer, of course, was "Zero!"

The answer to that question is about to change with the new requirements introduced at 210.71 for the 2017 *NEC*. For certain sized non-dwelling unit meeting rooms, receptacle outlets will be required to be provided and spaced apart similar to a dwelling unit and the wall spacing rules of 210.52(A)(1) through (A)(4) [see complete *Code* text at 210.71 for specifics]. Meeting rooms with a floor area greater than 93 m2 (1000 ft2) will not be subject to these rules, unless they can be partitioned into smaller rooms meeting that threshold.

210.71

In some cases, floor receptacles will be required to be installed to meet the needs of the present and future meeting room occupants. A meeting room that is at least 3.7 m (12 ft) wide and has a floor area of 20 m2 (215 ft²) must be provided with one floor receptacle outlet located not less than 1.8 m (6 ft) from any fixed wall for each 20 m² (215 ft²) or major portion of floor space. These required floor receptacle outlet(s), located away from fixed walls, will minimize the need for extension cords and multi-outlet devices to facilitate the use of equipment (such as a projector) in the middle of the meeting room. We have all witnessed the current practice of providing an extension cord—usually plugged into a wall receptacle outlet and taped to the carpet—to provide power for such things as laptops, phone chargers, and projectors that are used in areas several feet away from the available wall receptacles.

Without this new requirement, there was previously no *Code* requirement to provide receptacle outlets in meeting rooms of commercial or non-dwelling occupancies. The fact that 125-volt, 15- or 20-ampere receptacle outlets are installed in meeting rooms at all is due, in part, to building owners and designers recognizing the need for access to electrical power for a multitude of different types of portable equipment. From a design standpoint, you rarely encounter a meeting room with no receptacle outlets; but, under previous editions of the *Code*, a *Code*-compliant project could have resulted in a hotel meeting room with no receptacle outlets whatsoever.

210.71

A close look at 210.50(B) reveals that a receptacle outlet is to be installed wherever flexible cords with attachment plugs are used. Since it would be virtually impossible to use these meeting rooms in the fashion that they are typically used and not resort to some form of flexible cords with an attachment plug, it would follow that there is a need for some minimum requirement for receptacle outlets in these gathering places. Receptacle outlets are needed in meeting rooms to provide electrical power for such things as booth displays, coffee pots, heating of catered food, and other electrical/electronic equipment such as laptop computers, phone chargers, and projectors. There is also a great need to provide electrical power at moveable partitions in the form of floor receptacle outlets to help prevent the use of portable extension cords in these areas.

It should be noted that in a meeting room or space provided with movable partition(s), each room size will be determined by the partition in the position that results in the "smallest size meeting room." If a meeting area were equipped with a movable partition and that partition (when opened or in place) would divide the space into two equal spaces, this would result in two separate meeting rooms. Each side would be treated as a separate meeting room. If each side of these two spaces is each at least 3.7 m (12 ft) wide and have a floor area of at least 20 m² (215 ft²), this would require at least one floor-receptacle outlet located on both sides of this partition.

While the placement of receptacle outlets may be best left to the designer, the decision on whether or not to provide receptacle outlets is a safety issue and belongs in the *NEC*. These new provisions have language that will leave the placement of receptacle outlets up to the designer or building owner while also including minimum provisions for receptacle outlets in meeting rooms, in the same way that 210.60 does for guest rooms or guest suites in hotels, motels, sleeping rooms in dormitories, and similar occupancies.

First Revisions: FR 7517
Second Revisions: SR 329
Public Inputs: PI 2872
Public Comments: PC 762, PC 1188, PC 1761, PC 828

215.2(A)(1)(a), Ex. No. 2
Feeder Rating and Size

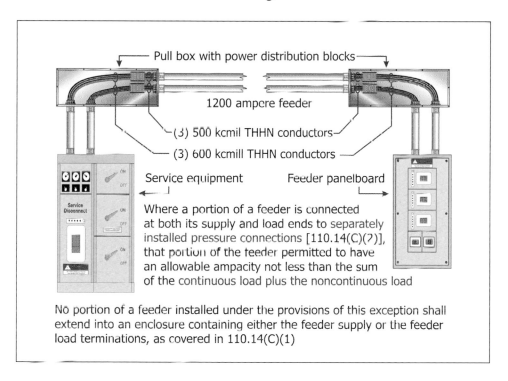

215.2(A)(1)(a)

Pull box with power distribution blocks

1200 ampere feeder

(3) 500 kcmil THHN conductors

(3) 600 kcmill THHN conductors

Service equipment   Feeder panelboard

Where a portion of a feeder is connected at both its supply and load ends to separately installed pressure connections [110.14(C)(?)], that portion of the feeder permitted to have an allowable ampacity not less than the sum of the continuous load plus the noncontinuous load

No portion of a feeder installed under the provisions of this exception shall extend into an enclosure containing either the feeder supply or the feeder load terminations, as covered in 110.14(C)(1)

210.7 Minimum Rating and Size

- **Type of Change:** New

- **Change at a Glance:** A new exception allows a portion of a feeder that is not connected directly to load terminations to have an allowable ampacity not less than the sum of the continuous load plus the noncontinuous load (rather than the noncontinuous load plus 125 percent of the continuous load). It also clarifies when correction factors are to be applied.

- **Code Language: 215.2 Minimum Rating and Size.**

  (A) Feeders Not More Than 600 Volts.
  (1) General. Feeder conductors shall have an ampacity not less than required to supply the load as calculated in Parts III, IV, and V of Article

220. Conductors shall be sized to carry not less than the larger of 215.2(A)(1)(a) or (b).

(a) Where a feeder supplies continuous loads or any combination of continuous and noncontinuous loads, the minimum feeder conductor size shall have an allowable ampacity not less than the noncontinuous load plus 125 percent of the continuous load.

Exception No. 1: If the assembly, including the overcurrent devices protecting the feeder(s), is listed for operation at 100 percent of its rating, the allowable ampacity of the feeder conductors shall be permitted to be not less than the sum of the continuous load plus the noncontinuous load.

Exception No. 2: Where a portion of a feeder is connected at both its supply and load ends to separately installed pressure connections as covered in 110.14(C)(2), it shall be permitted to have an allowable ampacity not less than the sum of the continuous load plus the noncontinuous load. No portion of a feeder installed under the provisions of this exception shall extend into an enclosure containing either the feeder supply or the feeder load terminations, as covered in 110.14(C)(1).

215.2(A)(1)(a)

Exception No. 3: Grounded conductors that are not connected to an overcurrent device shall be permitted to be sized at 100 percent of the continuous and noncontinuous load.

(b) The minimum feeder conductor size shall have an allowable ampacity not less than the maximum load to be served after the application of any adjustment or correction factors.

[(3) Informational Notes unchanged]

~~*Exception No. 1: If the assembly, including the overcurrent devices protecting the feeder(s), is listed for operation at 100 percent of its rating, the allowable ampacity of the feeder conductors shall be permitted to be not less than the sum of the continuous load plus the noncontinuous load.*~~

~~*Exception No. 2: Grounded conductors that are not connected to an overcurrent device shall be permitted to be sized at 100 percent of the continuous and noncontinuous load.*~~

■ **2014 *NEC* Requirement**

215.2(A)(1) stated that a feeder had to be sized based on the larger of two separately required calculations or conditions. 215.2(A)(1)(a) requires the feeder conductors to have an allowable ampacity of not less than the noncontinuous load plus 125 percent of the continuous load. The conditions described at 215.2(A)(1)(b) requires the feeder conductors to have an allowable ampacity not less than the maximum load to be served after the application of any adjustment or correction factors. Two exceptions existed allowing the feeder conductors to be sized at not less than the sum of the continuous load plus the noncontinuous load, but these exceptions appeared after 215.2(A)(1)(b), which created confusion as to their application.

■ **2017 *NEC* Change**
The previous exceptions to 215.2(A)(1)(b) have been relocated after
215.2(A)(1)(a). This relocation clarifies that these exceptions apply to the
main rule that the feeder conductors must have an allowable ampacity of
not less than the noncontinuous load plus 125 percent of the continuous
load. A new exception was also added that allows a portion of a feeder that
is connected at both its supply and load ends to separately installed pressure connections to have an allowable ampacity not less than the sum of
the continuous load plus the noncontinuous load (rather than the noncontinuous load plus 125 percent of the continuous load).

Analysis of the Change:

For the 2017 *NEC*, the previous exceptions that appeared after 215.2(A)(1)(b)
have been moved to follow 215.2(A)(1)(a) to clarify that these exceptions apply
to the requirement that the feeder conductors must have an allowable ampacity
of not less than the noncontinuous load plus 125 percent of the continuous load.
In a literal reading of 2014 *NEC*, the location of the exceptions after 215.2(A)(1)
(b) could have implied that the user did not have to consider ampacity adjustment or temperature correction factors when using these exceptions. By placing
the existing exceptions after 215.2(A)(1)(a), it clarified that these are exceptions
to the requirements found in item (a), not item (b).

A new 215.2(A)(1)(a), Ex. No. 2 allows a portion of a feeder that is connected
at both its supply and load ends to separately installed pressure connections to
have an allowable ampacity not less than the sum of the continuous load plus
the noncontinuous load. This is allowable since the 125% rule for continuous
loads is necessary for temperature-sensitive equipment like circuit breakers,
not for separately installed connectors. This provision is technically appropriate and has been done in the past, but was inadvertently prohibited due to the
recent restructuring of the requirements at 215.2(A)(1). This new exception
also includes language that omits that portion of the feeder that extends into an
enclosure containing either the feeder supply or the feeder load terminations, as
covered in 110.14(C)(1). Without this new exception, 215.2(A)(1)(a) would seem
to be in conflict with 110.14(C)(2), which states that separately installed pressure
connectors must be used with conductors at the ampacities not exceeding the
ampacity at the listed and identified temperature rating of the connector.

215.2(A)(1)(a)

The key to making correct conductor selection decisions is to remember that
the end of a conductor is different from its middle. Special rules apply to calculating conductor sizes based on how the terminations are expected to function.
Entirely different rules aim at assuring that conductors, over their length, do
not overheat under current loading and conditions of use. Sometimes it is the
termination requirements that produce the largest conductor, and sometimes
the adjustment and correction factor requirements prevent conductor overheating. These two separate calculations must be performed, and then one makes
a comparison to determine the proper size of a conductor. In a cost-saving
effort, it has become relatively commonplace for installers to place pull boxes
at both ends of long feeder-conductor installations and reduce the size of the
feeder conductors in the middle of this run. This procedure leaves and arrives

at overcurrent devices with feeder conductors sized to accommodate the effects of continuous loading on those devices while complying with the provisions of 110.14(C)(1). This method leaves the middle of this run of feeders sized in accordance with the ampacity requirements for the conductor and to provide wiring that will accommodate the maximum current in amperes, whether or not any portion of that current is continuous, that will not exceed its temperature rating under the conditions of use. Splicing devices rated for full conductor temperatures are readily available and clearly permitted in the middle of runs by 110.14(C)(2). This new exception will encompass this type of installation and allow it to be *Code*-compliant.

This concept has a precendent in the *Code* in the form of previous Ex. No 2 [now 215.2(A)(1)(a), Ex. No. 3], which allows grounded conductors to use this procedure provided they do not arrive at or depart from an overcurrent device.

First Revisions: FR 337
Public Inputs: PI 3612, PI 4680

Article 220 and 220.1

Branch-Circuit, Feeder, and Service Load Calculations

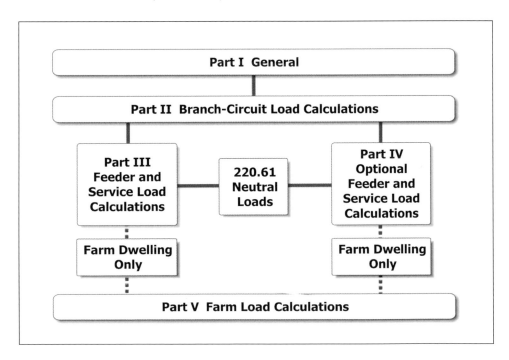

Article 220 and 220.1 Branch-Circuit, Feeder, and Service Load Calculations

- **Type of Change:** Revision

- **Change at a Glance:** The Title and Scope of Article 220 were revised to enhance clarity of what is covered by the article.

- **Code Language: Article 220 Branch-Circuit, Feeder, and Service Load Calculations**
  220.1 Scope. This article provides requirements for calculating branch-circuit, feeder, and service loads. Part I provides for general requirements for calculation methods. Part II provides calculation methods for branch-circuit loads. Parts III and IV provide calculation methods for feeders feeder and services service loads. Part V provides calculation methods for farms farm loads.

  Informational Note No. 1: See examples in Informative Annex D.

  Informational Note No. 2: See Figure 220.1 for information on the organization of Article 220.

- **2014 *NEC* Requirement**
  The title of Article 220 was "Branch Circuit, Feeder, and Service Calculations." The scope of the article indicated that Parts III and IV provide calculation methods for "feeders and services." The scope went on to state that Part V provided calculation methods for "farms."

- **2017 *NEC* Change**
  The title of Article 220 was changed to "Branch Circuit, Feeder, and Service 'Load' Calculations." Parts of the scope of the article were changed to clarify that Parts III and IV provide calculation methods for "feeder and service loads." Text concerning Part V was revised to clarify that this part of the article covers calculation methods for "farm loads."

Analysis of the Change:

The title and scope statement for Article 220 have been revised to enhance the clarity of the article. The word "Load" was added to the title of the article and the word "loads" was added a couple of times in the scope. These revisions will help make it clear that the place for calculating loads is Article 220 and the place for determining branch circuit and feeder conductor sizes is Articles 210 and 215. Titles and scope statements for all articles should clearly describe in general terms what the article covers and include sufficient details to indicate the range or limits of what is covered by the article.

The title of Article 220 is now "Branch Circuit, Feeder, and Service 'Load' Calculations." What differentiates Article 220 from Articles 210, 215, and 230 is the fact that Article 220 substantially addresses loads. This is confirmed by the titles of Parts II, III, and IV of Article 220, all of which contain the word "load."

First Revisions: FR 343, FR 342
Public Inputs: PI 695

220 & 220.1

225.30(F)

Multiple Feeders in One- or Two-Family Dwellings

225.30(F)

Feeders are generally limited to one feeder on the load side of the service equipment per building or structure *[see permissive conditions at 225.30]*

Service point

Service drop

225.31 and 225.32 Disconnecting Means

Dwelling Unit

Feeders

Multiple feeders are now allowed to enter a one- or two-family dwellings under certain restrictions that include the feeder disconnects at the building served must be grouped

225.30(F) Number of Supplies. (Outside Branch Circuits and Feeders)

- **Type of Change:** New

- **Change at a Glance:** Multiple feeders are now allowed to enter a one- or two-family dwelling under certain restrictions, which include that the feeder disconnects at the building served must be grouped.

- **Code Language: 225.30 Number of Supplies. (Outside Branch Circuits and Feeders)**
  A building or other structure that is served by a branch circuit or feeder on the load side of a service disconnecting means shall be supplied by only one feeder or branch circuit unless permitted in 225.30(A) through (E) (F). For the purpose of this section, a multiwire branch circuit shall be considered a single circuit.

  Where a branch circuit or feeder originates in these additional buildings or other structures, only one feeder or branch circuit shall be permitted to supply power back to the original building or structure, unless permitted in 225.30(A) through (E)(F).

(F) One- or Two-Family Dwelling Unit(s). For a one- or two-family dwelling unit(s) with multiple feeders, it shall be permissible to install not more than six disconnects grouped at one location where the feeders enter the building, provided the feeder conductors originate at the same switchboard, panelboard, or overcurrent protective device location.

- **2014 *NEC* Requirement**

  A building or structure is generally required to be served by only one feeder or branch circuit on the load side of the service equipment in accordance with the parent text of 225.30. Several "conditions" are described at 225.30(A) through (E) that would allow more than one feeder or branch circuit to serve a building or structure.

- **2017 *NEC* Change**

  A new first level subdivision (F) was added to 225.30 that will allow multiple feeders at one- or two-family dwelling unit(s) with not more than six grouped disconnecting means. These feeder conductor(s) are to originate at the same switchboard, panelboard, or overcurrent protective device location.

Analysis of the Change:

Similar to the service requirements of 230.2, feeders are generally limited to one feeder on the load side of the service equipment per building or structure. As with services, several "conditions" exist at the subsections of 225.30 that will allow more than one feeder or branch circuit in a particular building or structure as long as the multiple feeders (or branch circuits) meet the described conditions. Some of these conditions for allowing an additional feeder or branch circuit would include such things as additional feeders or branch circuits for a fire pump, emergency systems, legally required standby systems, optional standby systems, buildings that are "sufficiently large" making two or more supplies necessary, and feeders of different characteristics (different voltages, phases, etc.).

In order to permit more than one feeder to a one- or two-family dwelling unit(s), a new 225.30(F) was added to the 2017 *NEC*. This new first level subdivision allows multiple feeders at one- or two-family dwelling unit(s) with not more than six disconnects grouped at one location where the feeders enter the building. These feeder conductor(s) are to originate at the same switchboard, panelboard, or overcurrent protective device location.

Custom dwelling units are getting larger and larger. The increased size of services and feeders to one- or two-family dwelling unit(s) has made the necessity of permitting more than one feeder to supply a dwelling unit a must. The well-established requirement to group the disconnects for these feeders in one location and limit the number of disconnects to a maximum of six will address any safety concerns involved. This new multiple feeder allowance for dwelling units will incorporate a provision for feeders that is already a common installation method used for services.

An example of a situation where this new multiple feeder provision for dwelling units will apply is a common installation of pedestal-type meterbases with service

225.30(F)

disconnects mounted on a built structure away for the main building. The service disconnects are either an integral part of the meterbase assembly or located directly adjacent to the meterbase assembly. Multiple individual feeders are then installed from these service disconnects to a large dwelling unit directly to panelboards that includes a single main disconnect. Under the previous requirements at 225.30(A) through (E) and the 2014 *NEC*, this installation would not be allowed even though this would be a *Code*-compliant installation if this installation involved service conductors rather than feeders. The new provisions of 225.30(F) will make this situation described above a *Code*-compliant installation for feeders as well.

First Revisions: FR 921
Second Revisions: SR 902
Public Inputs: PI PI 4318, PI 3487, PI 4315
Public Comments: PC 1755, CAM 70-3

230.24(B)(5)

230.24(B)(5)

Clearance for Overhead Service Conductors

Overhead service conductors (not over 600 volts) shall have a minimum clearance from track rails of a railroad of not less than 7.5 m (24.5 ft)

230.24(B)(5) Clearances

- **Type of Change:** New

- **Change at a Glance:** New vertical clearance of 7.5 m (24.5 ft) added for overhead service conductors installed over railroad tracks.

■ **Code Language: 230.24 Clearances.**
Overhead service conductors shall not be readily accessible and shall comply with 230.24(A) through (E) for services not over 1000 volts, nominal.

(B) Vertical Clearance for Overhead Service Conductors. Overhead service conductors, where not in excess of 600 volts, nominal, shall have the following minimum clearance from final grade:

(1) 3.0 m (10 ft) — at the electrical service entrance to buildings, also at the lowest point of the drip loop of the building electrical entrance, and above areas or sidewalks accessible only to pedestrians, measured from final grade or other accessible surface only for overhead service conductors supported on and cabled together with a grounded bare messenger where the voltage does not exceed 150 volts to ground

(2) 3.7 m (12 ft) — over residential property and driveways, and those commercial areas not subject to truck traffic where the voltage does not exceed 300 volts to ground

(3) 4.5 m (15 ft) — for those areas listed in the 3.7 m (12 ft) classification where the voltage exceeds 300 volts to ground

(4) 5.5 m (18 ft) — over public streets, alleys, roads, parking areas subject to truck traffic, driveways on other than residential property, and other land such as cultivated, grazing, forest, and orchard

(5) 7.5 m (24.5 ft) over tracks of railroads

■ **2014 *NEC* Requirement**
Article 230 for services had no requirements pertaining to vertical clearances for overhead service conductors installed above the tracks of a railroad. Similar requirements did and still exist at 225.18(5) for a clearance of 7.5 m (24.5 ft) for outside overhead branch circuits and feeders installed over railroad tracks.

■ **2017 *NEC* Change**
A new vertical clearance of 7.5 m (24.5 ft) was added at 230.24(B)(5) for overhead service conductors installed over the tracks of a railroad. This will coordinate with the same requirement for outside overhead branch circuits and feeders in Article 225.

Analysis of the Change:

Overhead service conductors (not exceeding 600 volts) must be installed with a minimum vertical clearance from final grade as prescribed at 230.24(B). This subsection describes vertical clearances above such things as sidewalks accessible to pedestrians, residential property and driveways, commercial areas not subject to truck traffic, and public streets, alleys, roads, and parking areas subject to truck traffic. For the 2017 *NEC*, a vertical clearance for overhead service conductors of 7.5 m (24.5 ft) above the tracks of a railroad was added to 230.42(B).

230.24(B)(5)

This will bring this vertical clearance requirement for overhead service conductors in line with the existing clearance requirements for outside overhead branch circuits and feeders found at 225.18. This same railroad track clearance requirement was added at 225.18 for outside overhead branch circuits and feeders during the 2011 *NEC* revision cycle. The vertical clearance requirements for overhead service conductors should be at least equal to the same requirements for outside overhead branch circuits and feeders. At a minimum, it seemed strange to have specified height requirements for outside overhead branch circuits and feeders above a railroad track and not have any such requirement for overhead service conductors in the *NEC*.

This new provision for overhead service conductors will bring some enforceability for a minimum clearance where these service conductors are installed over rail track spurs or other railway systems on private property areas that are under the control of the *NEC*. The 7.5 m (24.5 ft) clearance requirement is derived from and matches vertical clearance requirements found in ANSI Standard C2, *National Electrical Safety Code* (*NESC*) published by the Institute of Electrical and Electronics Engineers (IEEE).

First Revisions: FR 929
Public Inputs: PI 2974

230.29

230.29

Supports over Buildings

Metal support structures supporting overhead service conductors passing over a roof required to be bonded to grounded overhead service conductor

230.29 Branch-Circuit Receptacle Requirements

■ **Type of Change:** New

- **Change at a Glance:** New requirement added for bonding of metal overhead service support structures over buildings.

- **Code Language: 230.29 Supports over Buildings.**
  Service conductors passing over a roof shall be securely supported by substantial structures. For a grounded system, where the substantial structure is metal, it shall be bonded by means of a bonding jumper and listed connector to the grounded overhead service conductor. ~~The bonding jumper shall be of the same conductor size and material as the grounded overhead service conductor, and in no case smaller than mandated in 250.102(C)(1) based on the size of the ungrounded service conductors.~~ Where practicable, such supports shall be independent of the building.

- **2014 *NEC* Requirement**
  Bonding of equipment for services (raceways, cable trays, auxiliary gutters, etc.) is found at 250.92(A). This bonding requirement did not include substantial support structures for overhead service conductors installed over a roof of a building.

- **2017 *NEC* Change**
  Metal support structures that support overhead service conductors installed over a roof are now required to be bonded to the grounded overhead service conductor.

230.29

Analysis of the Change:

New requirements were added to 230.29 requiring metal support structures that support overhead service conductors passing over a roof to be bonded to the grounded overhead service conductor. These metal structurers; sometimes referred to as a "roof jack" in the field, should be adequately bonded to limit a potential shock hazard.

The *Code* contains bonding requirements pertaining to "equipment for services" at 250.92(A), but this provision covers "normally non-current-carrying metal parts of equipment" such as "all raceways, cable trays, cablebus framework, auxiliary gutters, or service cable armor or sheath that enclose, contain, or support service conductors." This subsection goes on to require "all enclosures containing service conductors, including meter fittings, boxes, or the like, interposed in the service raceway or armor" to be bonded together. As thorough as this list of service related items required to be bonded is, the "substantial metal structures" described here at 230.29 does not seem to fit into any of these categories. These substantial support structures are not a raceway, as it does not act as a channel for conductors; it is simply an auxiliary or supplemental support for the overhead service conductors. This new requirement will add clear direction to installers and enforcers alike for the bonding of these structural metal supports.

The bonding jumper used to accomplish this bonding is based on the size of the ungrounded service conductors. This bonding and sizing requirement is very similar to the bonding requirements for bonding of a ferrous metallic raceway used to chase or enclose a grounding electrode conductor found at 250.64(E).

First Revisions: FR 936
Second Revisions: SR 909
Public Inputs: PI 2976
Public Comments: PC 967

Table 240.6(A)

Standard Ampere Ratings for Fuses and Inverse Time Circuit Breakers

The standard ampere ratings for fuses and inverse time circuit breakers shall be considered as shown in Table 240.6(A)

15	20	25	30	35
40	45	50	60	70
80	90	100	110	125
150	175	200	225	250
300	350	400	450	500
600	700	800	1000	1200
1600	2000	2500	3000	4000
5000	6000			

Additional standard ampere ratings for fuses shall be 1, 3, 6, 10, and 601

The use of fuses and inverse time circuit breakers with nonstandard ampere ratings shall be permitted

240.6(A)

Table 240.6(A) Standard Ampere Ratings

■ **Type of Change:** New

■ **Change at a Glance:** New Table 240.6(A) added for "Standard Ampacity Ratings for Fuses and Inverse Time Circuit Breakers."

■ **Code Language: 240.6 Standard Ampere Ratings.**

(A) Fuses and Fixed-Trip Circuit Breakers. The standard ampere ratings for fuses and inverse time circuit breakers shall be considered 15, 20, 25, 30, 35, 40, 45, 50, 60, 70, 80, 90, 100, 110, 125, 150, 175, 200, 225, 250, 300, 350, 400, 450, 500, 600, 700, 800, 1000, 1200, 1600, 2000, 2500, 3000, 4000, 5000, and 6000 amperes as shown in Table 240.6(A). Additional standard ampere ratings for fuses shall be 1, 3, 6, 10, and 601. The use of fuses and inverse time circuit breakers with nonstandard ampere ratings shall be permitted.

Table 240.6(A) Standard Ampere Ratings for Fuses and Inverse Time Circuit Breakers

(See *NEC* and illustration provided for complete table)

- **2014 *NEC* Requirement**
  The standard ampere ratings for fuses and inverse time circuit breakers were contained at 240.6(A) in a sentence format.

- **2017 *NEC* Change**
  The standard ampere ratings for fuses and inverse time circuit breakers have been revised to be included in a list format located at new Table 240.6(A).

Analysis of the Change:

The information pertaining to the standard ampere ratings for fuses and inverse time circuit breakers has been reformatted into a table format for clarity and usability. A new Table 240.6(A) was formed from the list of standard ampere ratings that have appeared in a single sentence for decades in previous editions of the *NEC*.

This continues a concentrated effort by many of the Code Making Panels to streamline and make the *Code* more "user friendly" whenever possible. Converting a long list of items previously addressed in long sentences or paragraphs is one way to accomplish this goal. This revision to "list format" style has a long precedence in the *NEC*. An example would be the revisions that occurred at 250.8(A) for permitted connection methods for equipment grounding conductors, grounding electrode conductors, and bonding jumpers to metal enclosures. Another example would be the list format at 404.2(C) for locations where a grounded conductor would not be required at switch locations.

This revision to the text at 240.6(A) and the accompanying new Table 240.6(A) will be another step in the direction toward a more "user friendly" *NEC* format.

First Revisions: FR 2703
Public Inputs: PI 1056, PI 1441

240.6(A)

240.67

Arc Energy Reduction

Where fuses rated 1200 amperes or higher are installed, 240.67(A) and (B) shall apply

This requirement shall become effective January 1, 2020

A fuse shall have a clearing time of 0.07 seconds or less at the available arcing current, or one of the following shall be provided:

(1) Differential relaying

(2) Energy-reducing maintenance switching with local status indicator

(3) Energy-reducing active arc flash mitigation system

(4) An approved equivalent means

Courtesy of Eaton Corporation

240.67

240.67 Arc Energy Reduction

- **Type of Change:** New

- **Change at a Glance:** New arc energy reduction requirements have been added for fuses rated 1200 amperes or higher.

- **Code Language: 240.67 Arc Energy Reduction.**
  Where fuses rated 1200 amperes or higher are installed, 240.67(A) and (B) shall apply. This requirement shall become effective January 1, 2020.
  (A) Documentation. Documentation shall be available to those authorized to design, install, operate, or inspect the installation as to the location of the fuses.

  (B) Method to Reduce Clearing Time. A fuse shall have a clearing time of 0.07 seconds or less at the available arcing current, or one of the following shall be provided:
  (1) Differential relaying
  (2) Energy-reducing maintenance switching with local status indicator
  (3) Energy-reducing active arc flash mitigation system
  (4) An approved equivalent means

  Informational Note No. 1: An energy-reducing maintenance switch allows a worker to set a disconnect switch to reduce the clearing time while the worker is working within an arc-flash boundary as defined in NFPA

70E-2015, *Standard for Electrical Safety in the Workplace*, and then to set the disconnect switch back to a normal setting after the potentially hazardous work is complete.

Informational Note No. 2: An energy-reducing active arc flash mitigation system helps in reducing arcing duration in the electrical distribution system. No change in the disconnect switch or the settings of other devices is required during maintenance when a worker is working within an arc flash boundary as defined in NFPA 70E-2015, *Standard for Electrical Safety in the Workplace*.

Informational Note No. 3: IEEE 1584, *IEEE Guide for Performing Arc Flash Hazard Calculations*, is one of the available methods that provides guidance in determining arcing current.

- **2014 *NEC* Requirement**
  Arc energy reduction requirements for circuit breakers rated 1200 amperes or greater are located at 240.87. There are five methods to reduce clearing times to achieve the goal of arc energy reduction identified at this location; these requirements are only related to circuit breaker overcurrent protective devices. The 2014 *NEC* has no similar arc energy reduction requirements for fuse-type overcurrent devices.

- **2017 *NEC* Change**
  Comparable methods of incident energy reduction as that of 240.87 have been introduced into the 2017 *NEC* at 240.67 for fuses rated at 1200 amperes and greater.

240.67

Analysis of the Change:

The benefits of arc energy reduction of incident energy for circuit breakers rated 1200 amperes and greater have been recognized and implemented by the requirements at 240.87, which were incorporated into the *Code* in the 2011 *NEC*. Those same methods of incident energy reduction have been introduced into the 2017 *NEC* at 240.67 for fuses rated at 1200 amperes and greater.

Arc energy reduction is designed to limit the arc-flash energy to which an electrical worker or maintenance personnel could be exposed when working on the load side of an overcurrent device that is rated or can be adjusted to 1200 amperes or higher. These industry-proven methods reduce arc-flash injuries by reducing the amount of time a fault will be permitted to persist in the electrical system. The incident energy in an arcing event is directly proportional to the time frame for such an event. The installation requirements of 240.87 for circuit breakers and the new requirements at 240.67 for fuses provide a means to reduce the level of incident energy.

The new requirements added at 240.67 were patterned after the requirements in 240.87, but modified to accommodate their application with fuses. This new arc energy reduction requirement for fuses has been properly located in Part VI of Article 240, which is titled, "Cartridge Fuses and Fuseholders." The numbering sequence of 240.67 was selected to parallel the numbering of 240.87. Circuit breakers utilizing zone-selective interlocking (ZSI) applications to meet the requirements of 240.87 can take up to 0.07 seconds to open the circuit. With that in mind, a maximum fuse opening time of 0.07 seconds was also selected in the parent text of 240.67(B) to provide equivalent protection for a fuse as that provided by a circuit breaker with zone selective interlocking.

This new requirement has a future effective date of January 1, 2020, due in part to the contained requirements for "energy-reducing maintenance switching with local status indicator." A maintenance-type switch for fusible switches is not readily available at this time, and this future effective date will allow the manufacturers time to develop such a device. This future date is also needed to allow manufacturers time to get equipment listed and to allow the electrical industry to respond with feasible solutions, and to ensure there is ample availability of devices from multiple manufacturers that meet this requirement.

First Revisions: FR 2707
Second Revisions: SR 2702
Public Input: PI 3293
Public Comments: PC 1365, PC 575, PC 614

250.22(6)

250.22(6)

Circuits Not to Be Grounded

The following circuits shall not be grounded:

(1) Circuits for electric cranes operating over combustible fibers in Class III locations, as provided in 503.155

(2) Circuits in health care facilities as provided in 517.61 and 517.160

(3) Circuits for equipment within electrolytic cell working zone as provided in Article 668

(4) Secondary circuits of lighting systems as provided in 411.6(A)

(5) Secondary circuits of lighting systems as provided in 680.23(A)(2)

(6) Class 2 load side circuits for suspended ceiling low-voltage power grid distribution systems as provided in 393.60(B)

250.22(6) Circuits Not to Be Grounded

- **Type of Change:** New

- **Change at a Glance:** Class 2 load-side circuits for suspended ceiling low-voltage power grid distribution systems were added to the list of circuits not to be grounded.

- **Code Language: 250.22 Circuits Not to Be Grounded.**
  The following circuits shall not be grounded:
  (1) Circuits for electric cranes operating over combustible fibers in Class III locations, as provided in 503.155
  (2) Circuits in health care facilities as provided in 517.61 and 517.160
  (3) Circuits for equipment within electrolytic cell working zone as provided in Article 668
  (4) Secondary circuits of lighting systems as provided in 411.6(A)
  (5) Secondary circuits of lighting systems as provided in 680.23(A)(2)
  (6) Class 2 load-side circuits for suspended ceiling low-voltage power grid distribution systems as provided in 393.60(B).

- **2014 *NEC* Requirement**
  There were five circuits that were not to be grounded identified at 250.22(1) through (5). Included in new Article 393 was a requirement that stated Class 2 load-side circuits for suspended ceiling low-voltage power grid distribution systems were not to be grounded, which is stipulated at 393.60(B).

- **2017 *NEC* Change**
  A new List Item (6) was added to 250.22 for circuits not to be grounded with the addition of Class 2 load-side circuits for suspended ceiling low-voltage power grid distribution systems as provided in 393.60(B).

250.22(6)

Analysis of the Change:

In Article 250, alternating-current (ac) systems are divided into three categories: (1) ac systems that are required to be grounded (see 250.20), (2) ac systems (50 volts to 1000 volts) that are not required to be grounded (see 250.21), and (3) ac systems that are prohibited from being grounded (see 250.22). The previous edition of the *Code* identified five circuits that were not to be grounded at 250.22(1) through (5). For the 2017 *NEC*, a new List Item (6) was added to the list of circuits not to be grounded with the addition of Class 2 load-side circuits for suspended ceiling low-voltage power grid distribution systems.

Low-voltage suspended ceiling power distribution systems are defined as "a system that serves as a support for a finished ceiling surface and consists of a busbar and busbar support system to distribute power to utilization equipment supplied by a Class 2 power supply" (see 393.2). These systems were added to the 2014 *NEC* at Article 393 to address low-voltage Class 2 supplied equipment (lighting and power) connected to ceiling grids, floors, and walls built for this purpose. The article addresses equipment with characteristics similar to track lighting, but that also includes the wiring and power supply requirements while providing the specific requirements for the safe installation of low-voltage, power-limited power distribution that provides power to lighting and non-lighting loads.

Adding these low-voltage systems to the list of circuits not to be grounded was a natural step since the relevant article stipulates that the "Class 2 load-side circuits for suspended ceiling low-voltage power grid distribution systems shall not be grounded." This requirement is located at 393.60(B). The supply side of these Class 2 power sources is to be grounded by connection to an equipment grounding conductor in accordance with the applicable requirements in Part IV of Article 250 [see 393.60(A)]. The ungrounded nature of the load side of this low-voltage system helps ensure safety similar to other identified low-voltage systems not to be grounded at 250.22.

First Revisions: FR 1208
Second Revisions: SR 1203
Public Inputs: PI 1444
Public Comments: PC 1558, PC 1767

250.30(A)(4)&(5)

250.30(A)(4) and (A)(5)

Grounding Separately Derived Systems

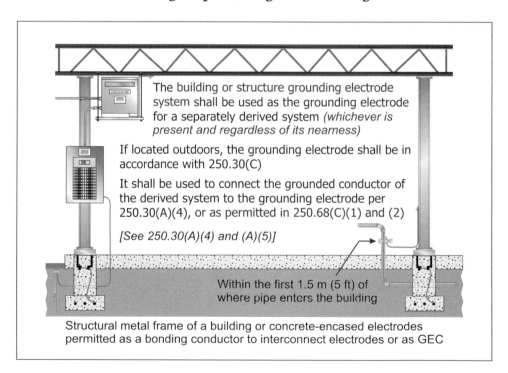

The building or structure grounding electrode system shall be used as the grounding electrode for a separately derived system *(whichever is present and regardless of its nearness)*

If located outdoors, the grounding electrode shall be in accordance with 250.30(C)

It shall be used to connect the grounded conductor of the derived system to the grounding electrode per 250.30(A)(4), or as permitted in 250.68(C)(1) and (2)

[See 250.30(A)(4) and (A)(5)]

Within the first 1.5 m (5 ft) of where pipe enters the building

Structural metal frame of a building or concrete-encased electrodes permitted as a bonding conductor to interconnect electrodes or as GEC

250.30(A)(4) and (A)(5) Grounding Separately Derived Alternating-Current Systems

- **Type of Change:** Revision

■ **Change at a Glance:** The use of metal water piping or building steel as the first options as a grounding electrode system for a separately derived system has been removed.

■ **Code Language: 250.30 Grounding Separately Derived Alternating-Current Systems.**
In addition to complying with 250.30(A) for grounded systems, or as provided in 250.30(B) for ungrounded systems, separately derived systems shall comply with 250.20, 250.21, 250.22, or 250.26, as applicable. Multiple separately derived systems that are connected in parallel shall be installed in accordance with 250.30.

(A) Grounded Systems. A separately derived ac system that is grounded shall comply with 250.30(A)(1) through (A)(8). Except as otherwise permitted in this article, a grounded conductor shall not be connected to normally non–current-carrying metal parts of equipment, be connected to equipment grounding conductors, or be reconnected to ground on the load side of the system bonding jumper.

Informational Note: See 250.32 for connections at separate buildings or structures and 250.142 for use of the grounded circuit conductor for grounding equipment.

Exception: *Impedance grounded neutral system grounding connections shall be made as specified in 250.36 or 250.187, as applicable.*

(4) Grounding Electrode. The building or structure grounding electrode system shall be used as the grounding electrode for the separately derived system. If located outdoors, the grounding electrode shall be in accordance with 250.30(C). ~~as near as practicable to, and preferably in the same area as, the grounding electrode conductor connection to the system. The grounding electrode shall be the nearest of one of the following:~~
~~(1) Metal water pipe grounding electrode as specified in 250.52(A)(1)~~
~~(2) Structural metal grounding electrode as specified in 250.52(A)(2)~~
~~**Exception No. 1:** Any of the other electrodes identified in 250.52(A) shall be used if the electrodes specified by 250.30(A)(4) are not available.~~

Exception ~~No. 2 to (1) and (2)~~: *If a separately derived system originates in equipment that is listed and identified ~~equipment~~ as suitable for use as service equipment, the grounding electrode used for the service or feeder equipment shall be permitted to be used as the grounding electrode for the separately derived system.*

Informational Note No. 1: See 250.104(D) for bonding requirements for interior metal water piping in the area served by separately derived systems.

Informational Note No. 2: See 250.50 and 250.58 for requirements for bonding all electrodes together if located at the same building or structure.

250.30(A)(4)&(5)

(5) Grounding Electrode Conductor, Single Separately Derived System. A grounding electrode conductor for a single separately derived system shall be sized in accordance with 250.66 for the derived ungrounded conductors. It shall be used to connect the grounded conductor of the derived system to the grounding electrode as specified in accordance with 250.30(A)(4), or as permitted in 250.68(C)(1) and (2). This connection shall be made at the same point on the separately derived system where the system bonding jumper is connected.

[*See NEC text for Exception No. 1, 2, and 3 to 250.30(A)(5)*]

■ **2014 *NEC* Requirement**

In order to establish a grounding electrode system for a separately derived system, the 2014 *NEC* called for the nearest of either a metal water pipe grounding electrode as identified at 250.52(A)(1) or a structural metal frame of the building or structure as described at 250.52(A)(2) to be utilized. If these two grounding electrodes were not available, 250.30(A)(4), Ex. No. 1 allowed "any of the other electrodes specified in 250.52(A)" to be used as a grounding electrode for a separately derived system. These grounding electrodes had to be located "as near as practicable and preferably in the same area" as the grounding electrode conductor connection to the separately derived system.

250.30(A)(4)&(5)

■ **2017 *NEC* Change**

For the 2017 *NEC*, any of the building or structure grounding electrode(s) that are present can now be used as the grounding electrode(s) for a separately derived system. The grounding electrode(s) for the separately derived system do not have to be located near the grounding electrode conductor connection. The metal water piping and the structural metal frame as covered in 250.68(C)(1) and (2) have been recognized as conductors to extend the grounding electrode connection at 250.30(A)(5).

Analysis of the Change:

Since the 1971 edition of the *NEC*, specific requirements have applied to the allowable choices regarding which grounding electrode(s) must be used for a separately derived system. The first requirement concerned the grounding electrode's *location* as it had to be "as near as practicable and preferably in the same area" as the grounding electrode conductor connection to the separately derived system. The second requirement was with the *type* of grounding electrode utilized, which had to be the nearest of either a metal water pipe grounding electrode [within 1.5 m (5 ft) from the point of entry to the building] as specified in 250.52(A)(1), or a structural metal frame grounding electrode of the building or structure as specified in 250.52(A)(2). Whichever of these two grounding electrodes was closest to the grounding electrode conductor connection to the separately derived system would determine which grounding electrode must be used. If neither of the two grounding electrodes described at 250.30(A)(4)(1) or (2) (*metal water pipe or structural metal*) was "available" for use, an exception would allow any of the other electrodes specified in 250.52(A) to be used as a grounding electrode for a separately derived system.

For the 2017 *NEC*, the hierarchy of preferences as to which grounding electrodes to use for a separately derived system has been removed. The building or structure grounding electrode system (whatever is present and regardless of its nearness) can now be used as the grounding electrode(s) for the separately derived system. The revisions to 250.30(A)(4) better describe a grounding electrode system for a separately derived system and don't limit the grounding electrode choices. The revisions to 250.30(A)(5) include the conductors that are suitable to extend the grounding electrode connection and recognize the fact that the metal water piping and the structural metal frame as covered in 250.68(C)(1) and (2) are not grounding electrodes but are conductors extending the grounding electrode connection.

These revisions also allowed previous 250.30(A)(4), Exception No. 1 to be deleted as those previous options allowing any of the grounding electrodes described at 250.52(A) to be used "if metal water piping and the structural metal framing are not available" to be used were incorporated into the main text of 250.30(A)(4). Editorial changes were made to the former Exception No. 2 of 250.30(A)(4) (now the only exception) to make it more technically accurate.

First Revisions: FR 1219, FR 1214
Second Revisions: SR 1210, SR 1205
Public Inputs: PI 572, PI 347/1
PC: PC 1561, PC 1768, PC 1571, PC 1769

250.30(A)(6)(a)

250.30(A)(6)(a)

Common GE Conductor

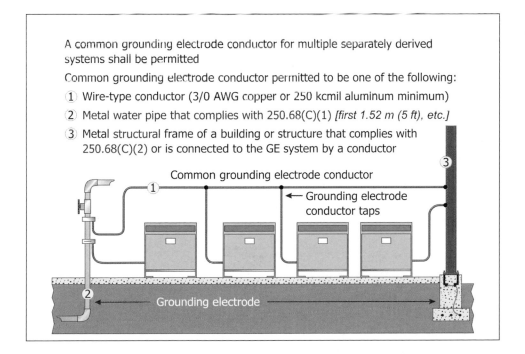

A common grounding electrode conductor for multiple separately derived systems shall be permitted

Common grounding electrode conductor permitted to be one of the following:

1. Wire-type conductor (3/0 AWG copper or 250 kcmil aluminum minimum)
2. Metal water pipe that complies with 250.68(C)(1) [first 1.52 m (5 ft), etc.]
3. Metal structural frame of a building or structure that complies with 250.68(C)(2) or is connected to the GE system by a conductor

Common grounding electrode conductor

← Grounding electrode conductor taps

Grounding electrode

250.30(A)(6)(a) Grounding Separately Derived Alternating-Current Systems

- **Type of Change:** New and Revision

- **Change at a Glance:** A metal water pipe was added to the methods of achieving a common grounding electrode conductor permitted for multiple separately derived systems.

- **Code Language: 250.30 Grounding Separately Derived Alternating-Current Systems**
  In addition to complying with 250.30(A) for grounded systems, or as provided in 250.30(B) for ungrounded systems, separately derived systems shall comply with 250.20, 250.21, 250.22, or 250.26, as applicable. Multiple separately derived systems that are connected in parallel shall be installed in accordance with 250.30.

  (A) Grounded Systems. A separately derived ac system that is grounded shall comply with 250.30(A)(1) through (A)(8). Except as otherwise permitted in this article, a grounded conductor shall not be connected to normally non–current-carrying metal parts of equipment, be connected to equipment grounding conductors, or be reconnected to ground on the load side of the system bonding jumper.

  Informational Note: See 250.32 for connections at separate buildings or structures and 250.142 for use of the grounded circuit conductor for grounding equipment.

  Exception: Impedance grounded neutral system grounding connections shall be made as specified in 250.36 or 250.187, as applicable.

  (6) Grounding Electrode Conductor, Multiple Separately Derived Systems. A common grounding electrode conductor for multiple separately derived systems shall be permitted. If installed, the common grounding electrode conductor shall be used to connect the grounded conductor of the separately derived systems to the grounding electrode as specified in 250.30(A)(4). A grounding electrode conductor tap shall then be installed from each separately derived system to the common grounding electrode conductor. Each tap conductor shall connect the grounded conductor of the separately derived system to the common grounding electrode conductor. This connection shall be made at the same point on the separately derived system where the system bonding jumper is connected.

  Exception No. 1: (No change-see *NEC* for complete text)

  Exception No. 2: (No change-see *NEC* for complete text)
  (a) Common Grounding Electrode Conductor. The common grounding electrode conductor shall be permitted to be one of the following:

250.30(A)(6)(a)

(1) A conductor of the wire type not smaller than 3/0 AWG copper or 250 kcmil aluminum

(2) A metal water pipe that complies with 250.68(C)(1)

(3) The metal structural frame of the building or structure that complies with ~~250.52(A)(2)~~ 250.68(C)(2) or is connected to the grounding electrode system by a conductor ~~that shall~~ not ~~be~~ smaller than 3/0 AWG copper or 250 kcmil aluminum

- **2014 *NEC* Requirement**
  A common grounding electrode conductor for multiple separately derived systems was permitted to be either one of the following: (1) a wire-type conductor (*not smaller than 3/0 AWG copper or 250 kcmil aluminum*) or (2) the metal frame of a building or structure that conforms to 250.52(A)(2) or the metal frame of a building or structure that is connected by a bonding jumper (*not smaller than 3/0 AWG copper or 250 kcmil aluminum*) to the grounding electrode system.

- **2017 *NEC* Change**
  A metal water pipe that complies with 250.68(C)(1) was added to the allowable methods for a common grounding electrode conductor for multiple separately derived systems. Revisions were also made to the provisions of a metal structural frame of a building or structure qualifying as a common grounding electrode conductor for multiple separately derived systems.

Analysis of the Change:

Whenever a building or structure employs multiple separately derived systems, a common grounding electrode conductor is permitted to be utilized for connection of the grounded conductor of the separately derived systems to the grounding electrode(s) described at 250.30(A)(4). If installed, a grounding electrode conductor tap would be installed from each separately derived system to the common grounding electrode conductor. The tap conductors, in turn, would connect the grounded conductor of each of the separately derived systems to the common grounding electrode conductor with the connection required to be made at the same point on the separately derived system where the system bonding jumper is connected.

This "common grounding electrode conductor" approach for multiple separately derived systems has been allowed by the *Code* since the 2002 edition of the *NEC*. For the previous edition of the *Code*, this common grounding electrode conductor was permitted to be either a wire-type conductor (not smaller than 3/0 AWG copper or 250 kcmil aluminum), the metal frame of a building or structure that qualified as a grounding electrode in conjunction with 250.52(A)(2), or the metal frame of a building or structure that is connected by a bonding jumper (not smaller than 3/0 AWG copper or 250 kcmil aluminum) to the grounding electrode system.

For the 2017 *NEC*, along with revisions to the metal structural frame of a building or structure provisions, a metal water pipe was added to the allowable methods of achieving the "common grounding electrode conductor" for multiple separately derived systems. For this metal water pipe to qualify as a common

250.30(A)(6)(a)

grounding electrode conductor, it must meet the conditions of 250.68(C)(1). This section of the *Code* allows a metal water pipe to be used as a conductor to interconnect electrodes that are part of the grounding electrode system as long as the connection is made to an interior metal water pipe that is electrically continuous with a metal underground water pipe electrode and is within the first 1.52 m (5 ft) from the point of entrance to the building (see exception for industrial, commercial, and institutional buildings with only qualified persons servicing the installation).

The use of a metal structural frame of a building or structure as a common grounding electrode conductor for multiple separately derived systems was revised by adding the word "structural" to the reference to give a better description to this method. The *Code* reference of 250.52(A)(2) was changed to 250.68(C)(2) as 250.52(A)(2) pertains to the conditions a metal structural framing member must meet to qualify as a grounding electrode. The revised *Code* reference of 250.68(C)(2) relates to a metal structural frame of a building or structure being used as a conductor to interconnect electrodes that are part of the grounding electrode system, which is what is being discussed here at 250.30(A)(6).

250.30(A)(6)(a)

First Revisions: FR 1218
Second Revisions: SR 1206
Public Inputs: PI 3472
Public Comments: PC 364, PC 740, PC 1574, PC 1770, PC 321

250.52(A)(2)

Metal In-Ground Support Structures

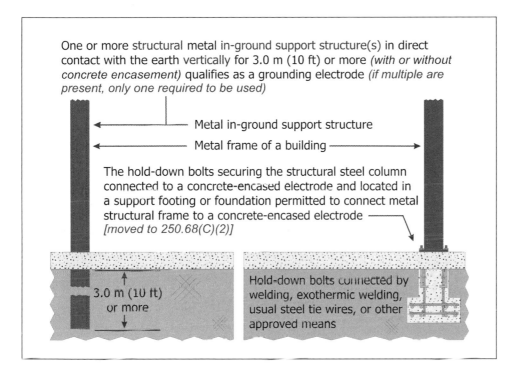

One or more structural metal in-ground support structure(s) in direct contact with the earth vertically for 3.0 m (10 ft) or more *(with or without concrete encasement)* qualifies as a grounding electrode *(if multiple are present, only one required to be used)*

Metal in-ground support structure

Metal frame of a building

The hold-down bolts securing the structural steel column connected to a concrete-encased electrode and located in a support footing or foundation permitted to connect metal structural frame to a concrete-encased electrode
[moved to 250.68(C)(2)]

3.0 m (10 ft)
or more

Hold-down bolts connected by welding, exothermic welding, usual steel tie wires, or other approved means

250.52(A)(2) Grounding Electrodes

- **Type of Change:** Revision

- **Change at a Glance:** The title of a "Metal Frame of a Building" grounding electrode renamed "Metal In-Ground Support Structure." Conditions for this grounding electrode revised.

- **Code Language: 250.52 Grounding Electrodes.**

(A) Electrodes Permitted for Grounding.
(2) Metal ~~Frame of the Building or~~ In-Ground Support Structure(s). ~~The metal frame of the building or structure that is connected to the earth by one or more of the following methods:~~
~~(1) At least~~ One or more structural metal in-ground support structure(s) ~~member that is~~ in direct contact with the earth vertically for 3.0 m (10 ft) or more, with or without concrete encasement. If multiple metal in-ground support structures are present at a building or a structure, it shall be permissible to bond only one into the grounding electrode system.
~~(2) Hold-down bolts securing the structural steel column that are connected to a concrete-encased electrode that complies with 250.52(A)(3) and is located in the support footing or foundation. The hold-down bolts shall be connected to the concrete-encased electrode by welding, exothermic welding, the usual steel tie wires, or other approved means.~~

Informational Note: Metal in-ground support structures include, but are not limited to, pilings, casings, and other structural metal.

- **2014 *NEC* Requirement**
  Two items or objects were identified at 250.52(A)(2) as meeting the requirements or conditions necessary to qualify as a metal frame of a building or structure-type grounding electrode. Those two items were (1) at least one structural metal member in direct contact with the earth for 3.0 m (10 ft) or more, with or without concrete encasement, and (2) a structural metal member connected to a concrete-encased electrode by hold-down bolts securing the structural steel column to the concrete-encased electrode. The hold-down bolts had to be connected to the concrete-encased electrode by welding, exothermic welding, the usual steel tie wires, or other approved means.

- **2017 *NEC* Change**
  The title of 250.52(A)(2) was changed from "Metal Frame of a Building" to "Metal In-Ground Support Structure." Only one item remains that would qualify as a "metal in-ground support structure" grounding electrode: an in-ground support structure that is in direct contact with the earth vertically for 3.0 m (10 ft) or more, with or without concrete encasement.

250.52(A)(2)

Analysis of the Change:

Grounding electrodes must "qualify" or meet specific conditions to be considered a grounding electrode. These "qualifications" or conditions for grounding electrodes can be found at 250.52(A). For the fourth time in the last five *Code* cycles, revisions, and/or deletions, were made to the descriptive language of 250.52(A)(2) pertaining to a metal frame of a building or structure as a permitted grounding electrode.

For this *Code* cycle, the title of 250.52(A)(2) was even changed from "Metal Frame of a Building" to "Metal In-Ground Support Structure." This new title is more in line with the definition of a grounding electrode in Article 100, which is "a conducting object through which a direct connection to earth is established." A "metal frame of building or structure" typically does not extend into the ground making a "direct connection to earth." Metal or concrete reinforced pilings or similar objects are driven into the earth, or a hole is bored, and the structural support placed into the hole. Often, concrete is poured around the metal piling at or near the surface of the earth. Typically, the metal or concrete piling is capped where a transition is made from the piling to the metal frame of the building. For correct application of this definition, the structural metal members of a building or structure need to be the conducting object with a direct connection to the earth.

Theoretically, a "metal frame of a building or structure" that is above ground in the manner specified above cannot be a grounding electrode by the pure definition of a grounding electrode. Even if a metal structural member is driven into the ground and extends above the ground for any length, technically, a transition from grounding electrode to grounding electrode conductor is made at the point of emergence from the earth. This metal structural member may function as a grounding electrode conductor by providing a conductive path to the grounding electrode as recognized by 250.68(C)(2).

It should also be noted that the previous condition of a metal structural member connected to a concrete-encased electrode through the hold-down bolts, etc., qualifying as a grounding electrode has not been deleted. Rather, it has been relocated to 250.68(C)(2) (Grounding Electrode Connections) as it is no longer appropriate for 250.52(A)(2) (Electrodes Permitted for Grounding) but adds clarity to 250.68(C)(2) and should be preserved as a permitted connection method.

Included in the 2005 *NEC* at 250.52(A)(2) were four items (*with specific conditions*) that were considered to qualify as a "metal frame of the building or structure" grounding electrode. With this 2017 *NEC* revision, there is only one object that would qualify as a "metal in-ground support structure" grounding electrode. An in-ground support structure that is in direct contact with the earth vertically for 3.0 m (10 ft) or more, with or without concrete encasement, is the lone qualifying survivor at 250.52(A)(2).

First Revisions: FR 1217
Public Inputs: PI 3311

250.52(B)(3)

250.52(B)(3)

Not Permitted for Use as Grounding Electrodes

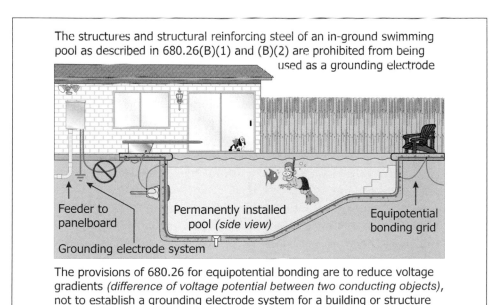

The structures and structural reinforcing steel of an in-ground swimming pool as described in 680.26(B)(1) and (B)(2) are prohibited from being used as a grounding electrode

Feeder to panelboard

Permanently installed pool *(side view)*

Equipotential bonding grid

Grounding electrode system

The provisions of 680.26 for equipotential bonding are to reduce voltage gradients *(difference of voltage potential between two conducting objects)*, not to establish a grounding electrode system for a building or structure

250.52(B)(3) Grounding Electrodes

■ **Type of Change:** New

■ **Change at a Glance:** In-ground swimming pool structures are not permitted to be used as a grounding electrode.

■ **Code Language: 250.52 Grounding Electrodes.**
(B) Not Permitted for Use as Grounding Electrodes. The following systems and materials shall not be used as grounding electrodes:
(1) Metal underground gas piping systems
(2) Aluminum
(3) The structures and structural reinforcing steel described in 680.26(B)(1) and (B)(2)

Informational Note: See 250.104(B) for bonding requirements of gas piping.

■ **2014 *NEC* Requirement**
There were two items described at 250.52(B) that were prohibited from being used as a grounding electrode. The first item is a metal underground gas piping system, and the second item is an aluminum electrode.

■ **2017 *NEC* Change**
A third item was added to the list of objects that are prohibited from being used as a grounding electrode defined at 250.52(B). The structures and structural reinforcing steel of an in-ground swimming pool as described in 680.26(B)(1) and (B)(2) are now prohibited from being used as a grounding electrode, as well as the two items identified in the previous edition of the *Code*.

Analysis of the Change:

Detached buildings or structures with electrical power from a feeder—such as detached garages, workshops, etc.—require that a grounding electrode system be established and installed in accordance with the requirements of 250.32(A). Occasionally, these detached structures are located near in-ground permanently installed swimming pools. When this situation occurs, it has been documented that the electrical installer will sometimes run a grounding electrode conductor from the electrical subpanel at the detached structure to the reinforcing steel of the conductive pool shell (belly steel) or to the structural steel of the perimeter surfaces (deck steel) with the intent to identify the pool reinforcing steel as an "other local metal underground system or structure" as described at 250.52(A)(8). Unfortunately, this action is sometimes at the request of the local AHJ. This action would make the swimming pool in question (and its inhabitants) a "super-target" for any stray currents or ground-fault current introduced on this grounding electrode system, and could potentially introduce safety hazards to the occupants of the pool during events such as lightning-induced stray currents.

For the 2017 *NEC*, language was added at 250.52(B) to prohibit the use of the structures and structural reinforcing steel of an in-ground swimming pool as described in 680.26(B)(1) and (B)(2) from being used as a grounding electrode in the manner described above. CMP-5 determined that it was never the intent of the *NEC* to use a pool bonding grid as a grounding electrode. Adding the additional requirement to prohibit the use of the metal components of an in-ground swimming pool is an important clarification to point out the difference between grounding and bonding. The equipotential bonding requirements of 680.26 are to reduce voltage gradients (difference of voltage potential between two conducting objects), and not to create a grounding electrode system for a building or structure.

This point is further illustrated in the current language at 680.26(B), which states in part that "an 8 AWG or larger solid copper bonding conductor provided to reduce voltage gradients in the pool area shall not be required to be extended or attached to remote panelboards, service equipment, or electrodes."

First Revisions: FR 1220
Second Revisions: SR 1209
Public Inputs: PI 4809
Public Comments: PC 1587

250.66

250.66(A), (B), and (C)
Size of GECs

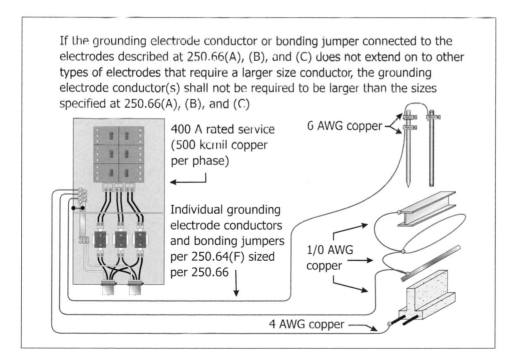

If the grounding electrode conductor or bonding jumper connected to the electrodes described at 250.66(A), (B), and (C) does not extend on to other types of electrodes that require a larger size conductor, the grounding electrode conductor(s) shall not be required to be larger than the sizes specified at 250.66(A), (B), and (C).

400 A rated service (500 kcmil copper per phase)

6 AWG copper

Individual grounding electrode conductors and bonding jumpers per 250.64(F) sized per 250.66

1/0 AWG copper

4 AWG copper

250.66(A), (B), and (C) Size of Alternating-Current Grounding Electrode Conductor

250.66

■ **Type of Change:** Revision

■ **Change at a Glance:** The "sole connection" language for sizing of grounding electrode conductors for connection to specific grounding electrodes has been removed and revised.

■ **Code Language: 250.66 Size of Alternating-Current Grounding Electrode Conductor.**
The size of the grounding electrode conductor at the service, at each building or structure where supplied by a feeder(s) or branch circuit(s), or at a separately derived system of a grounded or ungrounded ac system shall not be less than given in Table 250.66, except as permitted in 250.66(A) through (C).

(A) Connections to a Rod, Pipe, or Plate Electrode(s). ~~Where~~ If the grounding electrode conductor or bonding jumper ~~is~~ connected to a single or multiple rod, pipe, or plate electrode(s), or any combination thereof, as ~~permitted~~ described in 250.52(A)(5) or (A)(7)~~, that portion of the conductor that is the sole connection to the grounding electrode(s)~~ does not extend on to other types of electrodes that require a larger size conductor, the grounding electrode conductor shall not be required to be larger than 6 AWG copper wire or 4 AWG aluminum wire.

(B) Connections to Concrete-Encased Electrodes. ~~Where~~ If the grounding electrode conductor or bonding jumper ~~is~~ connected to a single or multiple concrete-encased electrode(s) as ~~permitted~~ described in 250.52(A)(3)~~, that portion of the conductor that is the sole connection to the grounding electrode(s)~~ does not extend on to other types of electrodes that require a larger size conductor, the grounding electrode conductor shall not be required to be larger than 4 AWG copper wire.

(C) Connections to Ground Rings. ~~Where~~ If the grounding electrode conductor or bonding jumper ~~is~~ connected to a ground ring as ~~permitted~~ described in 250.52(A)(4)~~, that portion of the conductor that is the sole connection to the grounding electrode~~ does not extend on to other types of electrodes that require a larger size conductor, the grounding electrode conductor shall not be required to be larger than the conductor used for the ground ring.

■ **2014 *NEC* Requirement**
Grounding electrode conductors are required to be sized using Table 250.66 based on the size of the largest ungrounded service-entrance conductor or equivalent area for parallel conductors. A grounding electrode conductor with its sole connection to a rod, pipe, or plate electrode never had to be larger than a 6 AWG copper conductor or a 4 AWG aluminum conductor, regardless of the size of the ungrounded service-entrance conductors. A grounding electrode conductor with its sole connection to a concrete-encased electrode never had to be larger than a 4 AWG copper

conductor. A grounding electrode conductor with its sole connection to a ground ring never had to be larger than the conductor used for the ground ring (2 AWG copper). Language was added to 250.66(A) and (B) to clarify that the "sole connection" provisions of these subsections pertain to the types of electrodes in these subsections, and the "sole connection" sizing provisions are still relevant even if more than one of the specified types of electrodes involved were present.

■ **2017 *NEC* Change**
The sizing requirements of 250.66(A), (B), and (C) are still the same as the previous edition of the *Code*, but the "sole connection" requirement in all three subsections was replaced with language indicating that a grounding electrode conductor that does not extend to other types of electrodes requiring a larger size conductor still qualifies for the smaller size conductors (instead of the size spelled out in Table 250.66).

Analysis of the Change:

To size a grounding electrode conductor properly, a visit to Table 250.66 is in order. Grounding electrode conductors are required to be a minimum size of 8 AWG copper (6 AWG aluminum or copper-clad aluminum) and need not be larger than 3/0 AWG copper (250 kcmil aluminum or copper-clad aluminum). The size of the grounding electrode conductor is typically based upon the size of the largest ungrounded service-entrance conductors; or if installed in parallel, the circular mil area of one set of parallel conductors added together and treated as a single conductor for sizing purposes.

250.66

What amounts to a three-part exception to the general rule for sizing grounding electrode conductors from Table 250.66 is provided in the text at 250.66(A) through (C). In the past, this *Code* language has permitted a grounding electrode conductor to be sized not larger than 6 AWG copper or 4 AWG aluminum when connected to a rod, pipe or plate electrode, and not larger than 4 AWG copper when connected to a concrete-encased grounding electrode as long as it was the "sole connection" to that grounding electrode. This section went on to permit a grounding electrode conductor connected to a ground ring to be sized no larger than the ground ring conductor, where that portion of the grounding electrode conductor is the "sole connection" to the ground ring.

This "sole connection" language has been in the *Code* since the 1965 *NEC*. Last *Code* cycle, explanatory-type language and plural text were added to 250.66(A) and (B) to clarify that the "sole connection" provisions of these subsections pertained to the types of electrodes in these subsections. The "sole connection" sizing provisions were not forfeited if more than one of the specified types of electrodes involved are present. The term "sole connection" apparently caused confusion in the electrical community as to the intended application of these provisions, even after the clarifications in the 2014 *NEC*.

For the 2017 *NEC*, the term *sole connection* was completely removed from 250.66(A), (B), and (C). The term was replaced with text that makes it clear that the action of "daisy chaining" grounding electrodes with properly sized bonding jumpers to form a grounding electrode system is an acceptable practice, as long as any downstream grounding electrode would not require a larger grounding electrode conductor or bonding jumper. The phrase "or bonding jumper" was added to subdivisions A, B, and C to use the correct terminology when "daisy chaining" occurs past the first grounding electrode in the chain of multiple electrodes.

First Revisions: FR 1227
Second Revisions: SR 1215
Public Inputs: PI 4196, PI 1407
Public Comments: PC 489, PC 1600, PC 1774

250.94

250.94(A) and (B)

Intersystem Bonding Terminations

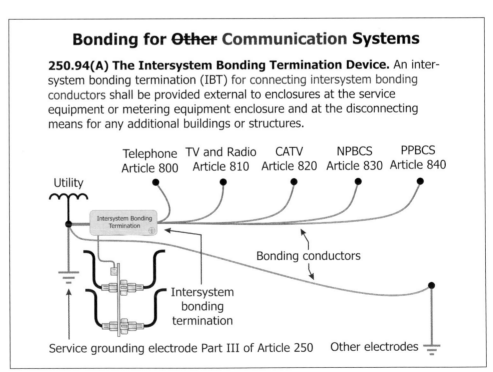

Bonding for ~~Other~~ Communication Systems

250.94(A) The Intersystem Bonding Termination Device. An intersystem bonding termination (IBT) for connecting intersystem bonding conductors shall be provided external to enclosures at the service equipment or metering equipment enclosure and at the disconnecting means for any additional buildings or structures.

Bonding for ~~Other~~ Communication Systems

250.94(B) Other Means. Connections to an aluminum or copper busbar not less than 6 mm thick × 50 mm wide (¼ in. thick × 2 in. wide) and of sufficient length to accommodate at least three terminations for communication systems in addition to other connections.

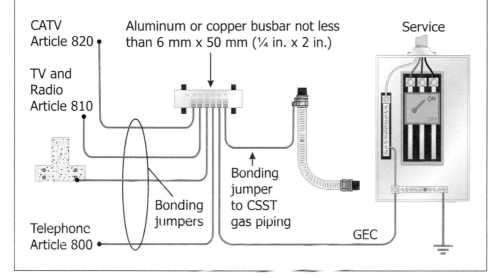

CATV
Article 820

Aluminum or copper busbar not less than 6 mm x 50 mm (¼ in. x 2 in.)

Service

TV and
Radio
Article 810

Bonding
jumper
to CSST
gas piping

Bonding
jumpers

Telephone
Article 800

GEC

250.94

250.94(A) and (B) Bonding for Communication Systems

- **Type of Change:** Revision and New

- **Change at a Glance:** The title of this section was renamed "Bonding for Communication Systems" and a new 250.94(B) was added titled "Other Means" allowing an alternate connection option to be made on a common bus bar.

- **Code Language: 250.94 Bonding for ~~Other~~ Communication Systems.**
  Communications system bonding terminations shall be connected in accordance with (A) or (B).
  (A) The Intersystem Bonding Termination Device. An intersystem bonding termination (IBT) for connecting intersystem bonding conductors ~~required for other systems~~ shall be provided external to enclosures at the service equipment or metering equipment enclosure and at the disconnecting means for any additional buildings or structures. ~~The intersystem bonding termination~~ If an IBT is used, it shall comply with the following: (Remainder of 250.94(A) unchanged. See *NEC* for complete text.)

  (B) Other Means. Connections to an aluminum or copper busbar not less than 6 mm thick × 50 mm wide (¼ in. thick × 2 in. wide) and of sufficient length to accommodate at least three terminations for communication systems in addition to other connections. The busbar shall be securely fastened and shall be installed in an accessible location. Connections shall be made by a listed connector. If aluminum busbars are used, the installation shall also comply with 250.64(A).

Exception to (A) and (B): Means for connecting intersystem bonding conductors are not required where communications systems are not likely to be used.

Informational Note: The use of an IBT can reduce electrical noise on communication systems.

250.94

- **2014 *NEC* Requirement**
  The section was titled, "Bonding for Other Systems." An intersystem bonding termination for connecting only intersystem bonding conductors was required to be provided external to enclosures at the service equipment or metering equipment enclosure and at the disconnecting means for any additional buildings or structures. The intersystem bonding termination has six conditions that must be met to qualify as an intersystem bonding termination. This rule has one exception for existing buildings or structures.

- **2017 *NEC* Change**
  The title of the section was changed to "Bonding for Communication Systems." The existing text for the intersystem bonding termination was placed under List Item (A) and titled, "The Intersystem Bonding Termination Device." The six conditions that must be met to qualify as an intersystem bonding termination have not changed, and the one exception for existing buildings or structures remains the same. A new 250.94(B) was added titled, "Other Means," which permits intersystem bonding connections to an aluminum or copper busbar that will accommodate at least three terminations for communication systems as well as "other connections." A new exception was added for 250.94(A) and (B) offering relief from an intersystem bonding connection means "where communications systems are not likely to be used."

Analysis of the Change:
An accessible point for bonding of intersystem bonding conductors for "other systems" such as telephone and cable television has been required for dwelling units since the 1981 *NEC*. The bonding of these intersystem bonding conductors was required for all types of occupancies beginning with the 1990 *NEC*. Part of the substantiation for this change in the 1990 *NEC*, which was simply to delete "for dwelling units," indicated that "The accessibility for intersystem bonding is needed at all services. Small business buildings and multi-unit commercial buildings should not be exempted from this requirement." An intersystem bonding termination point has been required since the 2008 *NEC*.

Intersystem bonding—which is accomplished by connection of a communication grounding conductor to the power system grounding electrode system—is an important safety measure to prevent occurrences of difference of voltages potentials between the communication system and power system. The intersystem bonding termination is for bonding of intersystem bonding conductors only. Previous proposals that also sought to allow other bonding conductors, such as a bonding jumper for bonding of metal gas piping, to terminate on the intersystem bonding termination have been rejected in past *Code* cycles. For the 2017 *NEC*, to further emphasize the fact that the intersystem bonding termination is for bonding of intersystem bonding conductors only, CMP-5 chose to change the title of 250.94 from "Bonding for Other Systems" to "Bonding for Communication Systems."

A new subsection (B) titled, "Other Means," was also added to 250.94. The alternate connection option allows connections to be made on a common bus bar with other bonding jumpers. This method is often used in commercial or multi-family mixed-use buildings. Even though the previous language was not restricted to just dwelling units and worked well for a dwelling unit, it did not take into account how a commercial or industrial building may bond the communication systems and other systems. Many commercial buildings commonly utilize a common grounding terminal bar for the connection of multiple electrodes and bonding of other systems, such as water piping systems, building steel, and internal antenna systems—to name a few. These common bus bars also allow easy connection of the other systems, such as communication, satellite dish systems, and network-powered broadband systems. This new "other means" of terminating other systems allows the installer to terminate other bonding conductors for bonding all systems, including such things as corrugated stainless steel tubing (CSST) gas piping, which is still prohibited to be terminated on the intersystem bonding termination device.

A new exception to 250.94(A) and (B) was also added to give relief from providing a means for connecting intersystem bonding conductors where communications systems are not likely to be used. This exception would include such things as outhouses, chicken coops or garden sheds.

First Revisions: FR 1215

Public Input: PI 702, PI 2889

250.94

250.102

Grounded Conductors, Bonding Conductors, and Jumpers

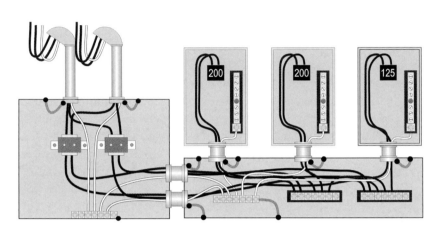

Grounded conductors, bonding conductors, and bonding jumpers of copper, aluminum, copper-clad aluminum, or other corrosion-resistant material are to be sized in accordance with 250.102 and Table 250.102(C)(1)

Supply-side bonding jumpers installed in parallel in two or more raceways or cables to comply with 250.102(C)(2)

250.102

250.102 Grounded Conductors, Bonding Conductors, and Jumpers

- **Type of Change:** Revision

- **Change at a Glance:** Title changed to "*Grounded Conductors*, Bonding Conductors, and Jumpers" which more clearly reflects what this section covers.

- **Code Language: 250.102 Grounded Conductors, Bonding Conductors, and Jumpers.**
  (A) Material. Bonding jumpers shall be of copper, aluminum, copper-clad aluminum, or other corrosion-resistant material. A bonding jumper shall be a wire, bus, screw, or similar suitable conductor.

  (B) Attachment. (Text unchanged, see *NEC* for complete text.)

  (C) Size — Supply-Side Bonding Jumper.
  (1) Size for Supply Conductors in a Single Raceway or Cable. The supply-side bonding jumper shall not be smaller than specified in Table 250.102(C)(1).
  (2) Size for Parallel Conductor Installations in Two or More Raceways or Cables. (Text unchanged, see *NEC* for complete text.)

(D) Size — Equipment Bonding Jumper on Load Side of an Overcurrent Device. (Text unchanged, see *NEC* for complete text.)

(E) Installation.
(1) Inside a Raceway or an Enclosure. (Text unchanged, see *NEC* for complete text.)
(2) Outside a Raceway or an Enclosure. (Text unchanged, see *NEC* for complete text.)
(3) Protection. (Text unchanged, see *NEC* for complete text.)

■ **2014 *NEC* Requirement**
To size a grounded conductor, the main bonding jumper, a system bonding jumper or a supply-side bonding jumper for an alternating-current (ac) systems, use 250.102 and Table 205.102(C)(1). The title of 250.102 previously referenced bonding conductors and jumpers. No mention of sizing of a grounded conductor existed other than in the title of Table 250.102(C)(1).

■ **2017 *NEC* Change**
"Grounded Conductor" was added to the title of 250.102 to reflect more accurately what the section addresses.

250.102

Analysis of the Change:
The *Code* requires that the provisions of 250.102 and Table 205.102(C)(1) be utilized for proper sizing of a grounded conductor, main bonding jumper, system bonding jumper, or a supply-side bonding jumper for an alternating-current (ac) systems. Table 250.102(C)(1) was new for the 2014 *NEC*. Before this table, the correct table to use for sizing a grounded conductor or a bonding jumper was Table 250.66.

For the 2017 *NEC*, 250.102 added "Grounded Conductor" to the title of this section, which was "Bonding Conductors and Jumpers," to more accurately reflect the items covered in this section. This change harmonizes the title with the content of the section.

Another clarification to this section was to explicitly add "aluminum and copper-clad aluminum" to the choices of material acceptable for bonding jumpers. This harmonized the language with that found in 250.62 and other locations recognizing aluminum and copper-clad aluminum as corrosion-resistant materials. Previously, users of the *Code* were sometimes left wondering whether aluminum and copper-clad aluminum were considered corrosion-resistant materials.

The previous title of 250.102(C)(2) was "Size for Parallel Conductor Installations in Two or More Raceways." This heading was revised by adding "or Cables" at the end of the title. Two or more raceways or cables are clearly referenced in the body of this text for sizing supply-side bonding jumpers, and the rules contained within apply to both raceways and cables. This addition to the title helps avoid any misinterpretation, as a cable is not the same as a raceway.

First Revisions: FR 7509
Second Revisions: SR 1219
Public Inputs: PI 4186, PI 1236, PI 2778, PI 1390, PI 4540
Public Comments: PC 1778, PC 1634

250.122(F)

EGCs Installed in Parallel

Rules for equipment grounding conductors installed in parallel in single or multiple raceways or cables and in cable tray, have been expanded to cover EGCs installed in auxiliary gutters and as part of a multiconductor cable

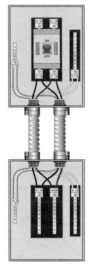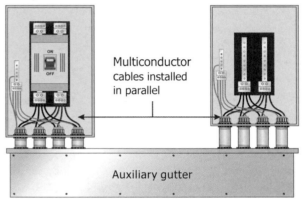

Multiconductor cables installed in parallel

Auxiliary gutter

If multiconductor cables are installed in parallel in the same raceway, auxiliary gutter, or cable tray, a single EGC is permitted in combination with the EGCs provided within the multiconductor cables *(must be connected together)*

250.122(F)

250.122(F) Size of Equipment Grounding Conductors

- **Type of Change:** Revision and New

- **Change at a Glance:** Revision and new text added to clarify how to size and install equipment grounding conductors when installed in parallel in a single or multiple raceways, multiconductor cable, auxiliary gutter, or cable tray.

- **Code Language: 250.122 Size of Equipment Grounding Conductors. (F) Conductors in Parallel.** ~~Where conductors are installed in~~ For circuits of parallel conductors ~~in multiple raceways or cables~~ as permitted in 310.10(H), the equipment grounding conductors, ~~where used,~~ shall be installed in parallel in accordance with (1) or (2): ~~each raceway or cable.~~

  (1) Conductor Installations in Raceways, Auxiliary Gutters, or Cable Trays.
  (a) Single Raceway or Cable Tray. If ~~Where~~ conductors are installed in parallel in the same raceway, ~~cable,~~ or cable tray ~~as permitted~~

in 310.10(H), a single wire-type conductor shall be permitted as the equipment grounding conductor shall be permitted. Each The wire-type equipment grounding conductor shall be sized in accordance compliance with 250.122, based on the overcurrent protective device for the feeder or branch circuit. Wire-type equipment grounding conductors installed in cable trays shall meet the minimum requirements of 392.10(B)(1)(c). Metal raceways or auxiliary gutters in accordance with 250.118 or cable trays complying with 392.60(B) shall be permitted as the equipment grounding conductor.

(b) Multiple Raceways. If conductors are installed in parallel in multiple raceways, wire-type equipment grounding conductors, where used, shall be installed in parallel in each raceway. The equipment grounding conductor installed in each raceway shall be sized in compliance with 250.122 based on the overcurrent protective device for the feeder or branch circuit. Metal raceways or auxiliary gutters in accordance with 250.118 or cable trays complying with 392.60(B) shall be permitted as the equipment grounding conductor.

(2) Multiconductor Cables
(a) If multiconductor cables are installed in parallel, the equipment grounding conductor(s) in each cable shall be connected in parallel. Except as provided in 250.122(F)(2)(b) for raceway or cable tray installations, the equipment grounding conductor in each multiconductor cable shall be sized in accordance with 250.122 based on the overcurrent protective device for the feeder or branch circuit.
(b) If multiconductor cables are installed in parallel in the same raceway, auxiliary gutter, or cable tray, a single equipment grounding conductor that is sized in accordance with 250.122 shall be permitted in combination with the equipment grounding conductors provided within the multiconductor cables and shall all be connected together. Equipment grounding conductors installed in cable trays shall meet the minimum requirements of 392.10(B)(1)(c). Cable trays complying with 392.60(B), metal raceways in accordance with 250.118, or auxiliary gutters, shall be permitted as the equipment grounding conductor.

■ **2014 *NEC* Requirement**
The requirements for installing equipment grounding conductors in parallel were (and are) covered by 250.122(F). These requirements were combined into one paragraph and addressed where equipment grounding conductors were installed in parallel in multiple raceways or cables and the same raceway, cable, or cable tray. These equipment grounding conductors were to be sized in compliance with 250.122.

■ **2017 *NEC* Change**
In addition to the existing rules for equipment grounding conductors installed in parallel in multiple raceways or cables and the same raceway, cable, or cable tray, these rules for parallel installations were revised to allow equipment grounding conductors installed as part of a multiconduc-

250.122(F)

tor cable to be used in combination with a separate equipment grounding conductor in a raceway, cable tray or auxiliary gutter. The requirements for 250.122(F) have been expanded into two separate Second Level Subdivisions (1) and (2) with third level subdivisions for each.

Analysis of the Change:

Conductors are permitted to be installed in parallel according to the rules of 310.10(H). When conductors are installed in parallel in separate raceways or cables, the equipment grounding conductor must be in parallel as well. Section 250.122(F) covers the requirements for installing equipment grounding conductors in parallel. For the 2017 *NEC*, these rules for parallel installations were expanded to cover equipment grounding conductors installed as part of a multiconductor cable in combination with a separate equipment grounding conductor when installed in raceways, auxiliary gutters, or cable trays. While the previous text of 250.122(F) was a single, long paragraph, it has now been expanded into two separate second-level subdivisions with third-level subdivisions for each.

This revised text separates individual equipment grounding conductors installed in raceways or cable trays from multiconductor cables. The requirements are further separated for single or multiple raceways. The revisions also recognize standard multiconductor cables installed in a raceway, auxiliary gutter, or cable tray, and permits them to be installed even though the internal equipment grounding conductors of the multiconductor cable may or may not be sized less than that required by Table 250.122 for the entire raceway, auxiliary gutter, or cable tray. This can occur if the raceway, auxiliary gutter, or cable tray is suitable as the equipment grounding conductor or where a fully sized wire-type equipment grounding conductor is provided in the raceway, auxiliary gutter, or cable tray.

It is now permissible to provide an additional equipment grounding conductor in the same raceway, auxiliary gutter, or cable tray as long as all equipment grounding conductors are bonded together to create a safe condition. A ground fault in a single cable would then not create an unsafe condition as the additional equipment grounding conductor is installed. A safe installation is still maintained by the presence of a full-sized equipment grounding conductor for the raceway, auxiliary gutter, or cable tray. Running a separate equipment grounding conductor in the raceway, auxiliary gutter, or cable tray will provide an adequate fault-current path while allowing the use of commercially available cable wiring methods.

First Revisions: FR 1246
Second Revisions: SR 1225, SR 1226, SR 1224
Public Input: PI 1315, PI 330, PI 3521, PI 3329, PI 4103
Public Comments: PC 901, PC 1783

250.122(F)

250.148

Continuity and Attachment of EGC to Boxes

If circuit conductors are spliced within a box, or terminated on equipment within or supported by a box, all equipment grounding conductor(s) (EGC) associated with any of those circuit conductors shall be connected within the box or to the box with devices suitable for the use

EGC from branch circuit
(all conductors not shown)

Bonding jumper for connection to metal box

Bonding jumper to receptacle

Metal box

See exception for isolated ground receptacles at 250.146(D)

250.148

250.148 Continuity and Attachment of Equipment Grounding Conductors to Boxes

- **Type of Change:** Revision

- **Change at a Glance:** Revision to clarify that all equipment grounding conductors associated with any and all circuits in the box must be connected together and to the box and not just each equipment grounding conductors of each associated circuit.

- **Code Language: 250.148 Continuity and Attachment of Equipment Grounding Conductors to Boxes.**

  ~~Where~~ If circuit conductors are spliced within a box, or terminated on equipment within or supported by a box, ~~any~~ all equipment grounding conductor(s) associated with any of those circuit conductors shall be connected within the box or to the box with devices suitable for the use in accordance with 250.8 and 250.148(A) through (E).

  Exception: The equipment grounding conductor permitted in 250.146(D) shall not be required to be connected to the other equipment grounding conductors or to the box.

- **2014 *NEC* Requirement**
  Direction was given at 250.148 for the splicing together or connection of

equipment grounding conductors for continuity within a box or enclosure. It was unclear if this meant splicing together all of the present equipment grounding conductors regardless of the circuit conductors they were associated with or just the equipment grounding conductors for the same circuit with which the equipment grounding conductors are associated.

- **2017 *NEC* Change**
  Clear directions in 250.148 specify that all of the equipment grounding conductors present in a box or enclosure are required to be connected, regardless of the circuit with which they are associated. The existing exception to 250.148 still applies, giving relief to the equipment grounding conductor of an isolated ground circuit for an isolated ground receptacle not being required to be connected to the other equipment grounding conductors or the box.

Analysis of the Change:

An equipment bonding jumper is typically required to connect the grounding terminal of a grounding-type receptacle to both a grounded metal box and the supply equipment grounding conductor(s) (EGC). Where one or more EGCs enters a box, they are typically required to be spliced or joined inside the box with suitable devices (listed grounding screws, listed grounding clips, etc.) to bond the box and to connect to the device with a bonding jumper [see 250.146(A) through (D) for exceptions to this general rule].

In situations where the circuit conductors (ungrounded branch-circuit conductors, feeder conductors, etc.) are spliced or terminated on devices or equipment in a metal box, the EGCs installed with these circuit conductors are required to be connected to the metal box by listed devices. The removal of a receptacle or other devices or equipment installed in or on the metal box is not permitted to interrupt or break the continuity of the EGC connections to other equipment or devices that are supplied from the same box where EGCs are connected, or to interrupt or break the continuity of the EGC connections downstream. EGCs installed in nonmetallic boxes are required to provide a means of connecting EGCs to receptacles, switches, luminaires, and other equipment installed in or supplied from the nonmetallic box.

If these boxes happen to contain two or more different branch circuits of feeders, it has been argued whether or not it is required to splice or join all the EGCs together in the box, or just the EGCs from each circuit being required to be spliced or joined. In other words, are we allowed to co-mingle EGCs from different circuits together? Changes to 250.148 in the 2017 *NEC* went a long way in answering these question. The revised language at 250.148 clearly indicates that all of the EGCs present in a box are required to be connected regardless of the circuit with which they are associated.

The requirements of 250.148 are frequently misunderstood and misinterpreted to mean that where multiple circuits are present in a box, the EGCs *for each circuit* are to be connected, but not connected to the EGCs *of other circuits* that are present. The word "any" was changed to "all" as in "...all equipment grounding conductor(s) associated with "any of" those circuit conductors shall be connect-

250.148

ed within the box..." in the *Code* text. This change makes it definite that all of the EGCs present in the box are required to be connected together.

A reference to 250.8 was also added to provide guidance on terminating an EGC or bonding jumper to a metal box or enclosure. Section 250.8 is titled, "Connection of Grounding and Bonding Equipment" and gives eight specific list items on permitted methods to properly connect grounding and bonding conductors to metal enclosures.

First Revisions: FR 1237
Public Inputs: PI 1331
Second Revisions: SR 1227
Public Comments: PC 1667, PC 1784

250.187(B)
Impedance Grounded Neutral Systems

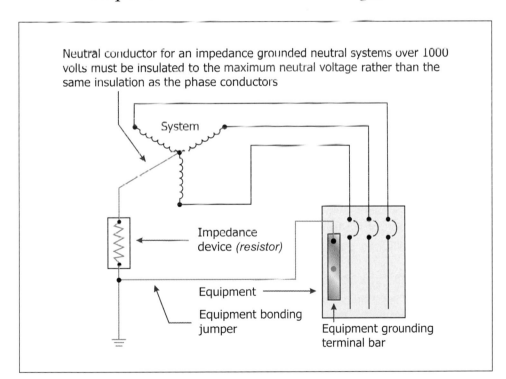

250.187(B)

250.187(B) Impedance Grounded Neutral Systems

■ **Type of Change:** Revision

■ **Change at a Glance:** Neutral conductor for an impedance grounded neutral system over 1000 volts must be insulated to the maximum neutral voltage rather than the same insulation as the phase conductors.

- **Code Language: 250.187 Impedance Grounded Neutral Systems.**
Impedance grounded neutral systems in which a grounding impedance, usually a resistor, limits the ground-fault current shall be permitted where all of the following conditions are met:
(1) The conditions of maintenance and supervision ensure that only qualified persons service the installation.
(2) Ground detectors are installed on the system.
(3) Line-to-neutral loads are not served.
Impedance grounded neutral systems shall comply with the provisions of 250.187(A) through (D).

(B) Identified and Insulated. The neutral conductor ~~of an impedance grounded neutral system shall be identified, as well as fully insulated with the same insulation as the phase conductors.~~ shall comply with both of the following:

(1) The neutral conductor shall be identified.

(2) The neutral conductor shall be insulated for the maximum neutral voltage.

Informational Note: The maximum neutral voltage in a three-phase wye system is 57.7 percent of the phase-to-phase voltage.

250.187(B)

- **2014 *NEC* Requirement**
The neutral conductor of an impedance grounded neutral system was to be identified, as well as fully insulated with the same insulation as the phase conductors.

- **2017 *NEC* Change**
The neutral conductor of an impedance grounded neutral system still must be identified, but it must be insulated to the maximum neutral voltage rather than fully insulated with the same insulation as the phase conductors.

Analysis of the Change:

NEC 250.180 indicates that where systems or circuits of over 1000 volts are grounded, they must comply with Article 250, but specifically the rules in Part X of Article 250 (Grounding of Systems and Circuits of Over 1000 Volts). The requirements of Part X of Article 250 supplement or modify other rules in Article 250. Many medium-voltage systems in the 2.4 to 15 kV range are either low-resistance grounded or are high-resistance grounded. The only difference between low- and high-resistance grounding is the value of the resistor that, in turn, controls the amount of ground-fault current permitted during a ground-fault event. The other common method is to solidly ground the system, especially if it is exposed to lightning.

Medium voltage systems above 15 kV are typically either solidly grounded or ungrounded. For the ungrounded system, even though there is not an effective ground provided, there is still a relationship to earth through the surge (lightning) arresters installed where outdoor lines are open and commonly subjected to lightning surges and transient over-voltages.

Grounding may be achieved through solid connections to earth or connection through a grounding impedance, typically a resistor, purposely installed in the equipment-grounding path at the source. The choice depends on available ground-fault current, the size of the system, tolerance for outages, and tolerance for damage from ground faults. It is common in industrial systems to ground the neutral of systems rated 2400 volts and above through a resistor. Impedance grounded neutral systems must be installed in accordance with 250.187. Impedance grounded neutral systems can be accomplished by reactance grounding, low-resistance grounding, or high-resistance grounding.

For the 2017 *NEC*, revisions to 250.187 call for the neutral conductor for impedance grounded neutral systems to be insulated to the maximum neutral voltage. Prior to this change, this neutral conductor had to be "fully insulated with the same insulation as the phase conductors." According to the substantiation for this revision to the neutral conductor insulation, it is not necessary to provide the same insulation for the neutral conductor as for the phase conductors. The maximum voltage on the neutral conductor in a three-phase impedance grounded neutral system is 57.7% of the phase-to-phase voltage or 2400 volts for a 4160-volt system. The 57.7% of the phase-to-phase voltage is true for a three-phase wye system only. The 57.7% would not hold true for a system such as a three-phase delta system operated with an impedance grounded neutral system.

250.187(B)

There is no hazard or disadvantage from a different insulation rating on the neutral conductor. The requirements of 300.3(C) prevent routing conductors with different insulation ratings in the same raceway or cable tray section. This revision will allow proper use of system components, such as 2400-volt grounding transformers, that are designed for use with unshielded conductors.

Revisions also reformatted 250.187 into a list format to provide a clearer statement for enforcement and improved clarity. A new informational note was added to clarify the magnitude of the neutral voltage.

First Revision: FR 7525
Second Revision: SR 1229
Public Inputs: PI 1798
Public Comments: PC 1404

Wiring Methods & Materials

Chapter 3

Articles 300 – 370

Table 300.5, Footnotes a and b

Minimum Cover Requirements

Minimum Cover Requirements, 0 to 1000 Volts, Nominal, Burial to Millimeters (Inches)

Location of Wiring Method or Circuit	Column (1) Direct-Buried Cables or Conductors		Column (2) Rigid Metal Conduit or Intermediate Metal Conduit		Column (3) Nonmetallic Raceways Listed for Direct Burial (No Concrete Encasement)		Column (4) Residential BC (120 Volts or Less, GFCI, Max. OCPD of 20 Amperes)		Column (5) Irrigation and Landscape Ltg (30 Volts Max., Type UF or Other Identified Cable or Raceway)	
	mm	in.	mm	in.	mm	in.	mm	in.	mm	in.
All locations not specified below	600	24	150	6	450	18	300	12	150[a,b]	6[a,b]
In trench below 50 mm (2 in.) thick concrete or equivalent	450	18	150	6	300	12	150	6	150	6
Under a building *(see NEC text)*	0	0	0	0	0	0	0	0	0	0
Under min.102 mm (4 in.) thick concrete exterior slab with no vehicular traffic [slab extending not less than 152 mm (6 in.)]	450	18	100	4	100	4	150 *(direct burial)* 100 *(in raceway)*	6 1	150 *(direct burial)* 100 *(in raceway)*	6 4
Under streets, highways, roads, alleys, driveways, parking lots	600	24	600	24	600	24	600	24	600	24
One- and two-family dwelling driveways/parking areas, (dwelling related purposes only)	450	18	450	18	450	18	300	12	450	18
In or under airport runways	450	18	450	18	450	18	450	18	450	18

Reproduction of NEC Table 300.5 (in part)(see next slide for Footnotes and Notes to table)

Table 300.5

Table 300.5 Underground Installations

- **Type of Change:** New

- **Change at a Glance:** Two new footnotes were added to Table 300.5 allowing lesser depths for listed low-voltage lighting system and pool, spa, and fountain lighting where they are part of a listed low-voltage lighting system.

- **Code Language:** Table 300.5 Minimum Cover Requirements, 0 to 1000 Volts, Nominal, Burial in Millimeters (Inches) (See *NEC* text for complete table.)(See below for notes to table.)

[a]A lesser depth shall be permitted where specified in the installation instructions of a listed low-voltage lighting system.

[b]A depth of 150 mm (6 in.) shall be permitted for pool, spa, and fountain lighting, installed in a nonmetallic raceway, limited to not more than 30 volts where part of a listed low-voltage lighting system.

Notes:
1. Cover is defined as the shortest distance in ~~millimeters~~ mm (~~inches~~ in.) measured between a point on the top surface of any direct-buried conduc-

tor, cable, conduit, or other raceway and the top surface of finished grade, concrete, or similar cover.

2. Raceways approved for burial only where concrete encased shall require concrete envelope not less than 50 mm (2 in.) thick.

3. Lesser depths shall be permitted where cables and conductors rise for terminations or splices or where access is otherwise required.

4. Where one of the wiring method types listed in Columns 1 through 3 is used for one of the circuit types in Columns 4 and 5, the shallowest depth of burial shall be permitted.

5. Where solid rock prevents compliance with the cover depths specified in this table, the wiring shall be installed in a metal raceway, or a nonmetallic raceway permitted for direct burial. The raceways shall be covered by a minimum of 50 mm (2 in.) of concrete extending down to rock.

■ **2014 *NEC* Requirement**
Burial depth requirements for underground wiring methods are located in Table 300.5. Column 5 covers "Circuits for Control of Irrigation and Landscape Lighting Limited to Not More Than 30 Volts and Installed with Type UF or in Other Identified Cable or Raceway." Table 300.5 would call for these irrigation and landscape circuits to have a minimum depth of 150 mm (6 in.).

■ **2017 *NEC* Change**
Two new footnotes were added below Table 300.5. These notes address a reduction of burial depth of 150 mm (6 in.) for pool, spa, and fountain lighting that is limited to not more than 30 volts. The installation is required to be within a nonmetallic raceway and part of a listed low-voltage lighting system.

Analysis of the Change:
Minimum burial depth requirements for conductors and wiring methods installed underground are typically addressed at Table 300.5. Column 5, which is titled, "Circuits for Control of Irrigation and Landscape Lighting Limited to Not More Than 30 Volts and Installed with Type UF or in Other Identified Cable or Raceway" requires low-voltage landscape lighting cable to be buried a minimum of 150 mm (6 in.) below grade. However, UL 1838 (*Standard for Safety for Low Voltage Landscape Lighting Systems*) requires the installation instructions for junior and hard service cords (that are not rated for direct burial) of low-voltage lighting systems to inform the installer that the main secondary wiring is "intended for shallow burial" [less than 6 inches (152 mm)], unless the manufacturer has provided wiring intended for direct burial.

This requirement appears to create a conflict between the product standard UL 1838 and Table 300.5. *NEC* 110.3(B) requires installers and inspectors to comply with the manufacturer's installation instructions for listed equipment. This situation has caused confusion regarding requirements found in Table 300.5, Column 5.

Table 300.5

Another issue of misperception with Table 300.5 involved listed low-voltage lighting systems installed around swimming pools, spas, and hot tubs. Since the actual text covering swimming pools, spas, etc., is not located in Column 5 of Table 300.5, there appeared to be some inspectors who require the nonmetallic raceway containing these low-voltage lighting conductors to be installed at a 450 mm (18 in.) depth. This depth apparently was being taken from Column 3 of Table 300.5, which includes nonmetallic raceways in its title. These listed low-voltage landscape lighting cables (with a voltage less than 30 volts) for a swimming pool environment installed in a nonmetallic raceway or similar installation should not be required to be installed at any depth other than the Table 300.5, Column 5 burial depths.

Two new footnotes have been added in the first row of Table 300.5 at Column 5 with an explanation of the footnotes added directly below the table. The first footnote "a" explains that a lesser depth is permitted where specified in the installation instructions of a listed low-voltage lighting system. The second added footnote "b" allows for a depth of 150 mm (6 in.) for pool, spa, and fountain lighting (installed in a nonmetallic raceway) where the lighting is limited to not more than 30 volts and where part of a listed low-voltage lighting system.

These additional footnotes help clarify any perceived conflicts between the burial depth requirements of Table 300.5 and the product standard for listed low-voltage lighting systems.

Table 300.5

First Revisions: FR 604
Second Revisions: SR 623
Public Input: PI 1294

300.5(D)(4)

Protection from Physical Damage

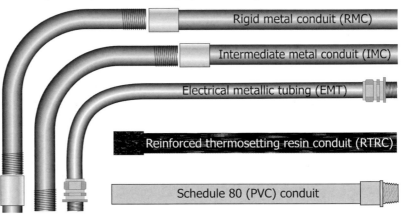

Where direct-buried conductors and cables are installed in enclosures or raceways and are subject to physical damage, electrical metallic tubing (EMT), rigid metal conduit (RMC), intermediate metal conduit (IMC), reinforced thermosetting resin conduit (RTRC) (Type RTRC-XW), Schedule 80 rigid polyvinyl chloride (PVC) conduit, or equivalent is allowed to be used to provide protection from physical damage

Rigid metal conduit (RMC)

Intermediate metal conduit (IMC)

Electrical metallic tubing (EMT)

Reinforced thermosetting resin conduit (RTRC)

Schedule 80 (PVC) conduit

300.5(D)(4)

300.5(D)(4) Underground Installations

- **Type of Change:** New

- **Change at a Glance:** Electrical metallic tubing (EMT) was added as an acceptable wiring method to afford protection from physical damage for conductors installed underground and subject to physical damage.

- **Code Language: 300.5 Underground Installations.**
  (D) Protection from Damage. Direct-buried conductors and cables shall be protected from damage in accordance with 300.5(D)(1) through (D)(4).
  (4) Enclosure or Raceway Damage. Where the enclosure or raceway is subject to physical damage, the conductors shall be installed in electrical metallic tubing, rigid metal conduit, intermediate metal conduit, RTRC-XW, Schedule 80 PVC conduit, or equivalent.

- **2014 *NEC* Requirement**
  Where direct-buried conductors and cables are installed in enclosures or raceways and are subject to physical damage, an installation in rigid metal conduit (RMC), intermediate metal conduit (IMC), reinforced thermosetting resin conduit (RTRC) (Type RTRC-XW), Schedule 80 rigid polyvinyl chloride (PVC) conduit, or equivalent was allowed to be used to provide protection from physical damage. RTRC-XW was added to this list of wiring methods in the 2014 *NEC* revision cycle.

- **2017 *NEC* Change**

  Electrical metallic tubing (EMT) was added to the list of acceptable wiring methods that can be used to provide protection from physical damage for conductors installed underground and subject to physical damage.

Analysis of the Change:

Revisions are being made to 300.5(D)(4) that will allow electrical metallic tubing (EMT) to be used to provide protection from physical damage where direct-buried conductors and cables installed in enclosures or raceways is subject to physical damage. The previous provisions for this application allowed an installation in rigid metal conduit (RMC), intermediate metal conduit (IMC), reinforced thermosetting resin conduit (RTRC) (Type RTRC-XW), Schedule 80 rigid polyvinyl chloride (PVC) conduit, or equivalent, but not EMT.

EMT is permitted to be installed in concrete, in direct contact with the earth, or in areas subject to severe corrosive influences where protected by corrosion protection and approved as suitable for the condition [*see 358.10(B)*]. As with RMC and IMC, EMT is protected from corrosion by its zinc (typical) coating. Galvanized steel conduit and EMT have excellent corrosion protection coatings and can be depended upon for a long service life. For severely corrosive environments, supplementary corrosion protection should be applied to further extend the life expectancy of its installation.

Corrosion protection is a requirement for listed EMT per UL 797 (Electrical Metallic Tubing – Steel) and in accordance with 300.6, which requires raceways to be made of materials suitable for the environment in which they are to be installed. This section goes on to require ferrous metal raceways, such as EMT that are to be installed in concrete, in direct contact with the earth, or in areas subject to severe corrosive influences to be made of material approved for the condition, or "provided with corrosion protection approved for the condition."

Adding EMT to this list of acceptable wiring methods to provide protection from physical damage where direct-buried conductors and cables are installed is a natural step in the maturation of this requirement which has appeared in the *Code* since the 1981 *NEC*.

First Revisions: FR 606

Public Inputs: PI 1328

300.5(D)(4)

Table 310.15(B)(3)(c)
Raceways and Cables on Rooftops

Where raceways or cables are exposed to direct sunlight on or above rooftops, they shall be installed 23 mm (7/8 in.) above the roof or be subject to a rooftop temperature adder of 33°C (60°F) *(see exception for Type XHHW-2 conductors)*

Electrical metallic tubing (EMT) installed on or above rooftop

At least 23 mm (7/8 in.)

Previous temperature adders and Table 310.15(B)(3)(c) deleted

310.15(B)(3)(c)

Table 310.15(B)(3)(c) Ampacities for Conductors Rated 0–2000 Volts

- **Type of Change:** Deletion and Revision

- **Change at a Glance:** Raceways or cables installed on rooftops are now required to be installed 23 mm (7/8 in.) above the rooftop to avoid a temperature adder of 33°C (60°F). Previous Table 310.15(B)(3)(c) was deleted.

- **Code Language: 310.15 Ampacities for Conductors Rated 0–2000 Volts.**

  (B) Tables. Ampacities for conductors rated 0 to 2000 volts shall be as specified in the Allowable Ampacity Table 310.15(B)(16) through Table 310.15(B)(19), and Ampacity Table 310.15(B)(20) and Table 310.15(B)(21) as modified by 310.15(B)(1) through (B)(7). The temperature correction and adjustment factors shall be permitted to be applied to the ampacity for the temperature rating of the conductor, if the corrected and adjusted ampacity does not exceed the ampacity for the temperature.

  (3) Adjustment Factors.
  (c) Raceways and Cables Exposed to Sunlight on Rooftops. Where raceways or cables are exposed to direct sunlight on or above rooftops, the adjustments shown in Table 310.15(B)(3)(c) raceways or cables

shall be installed a minimum distance above the roof to the bottom of the raceway or cable of 23 mm (7⁄8 in.). Where the distance above the roof to the bottom of the raceway is less than 23 mm (7⁄8 in.), a temperature adder of 33°C (60°F) shall be added to the outdoor temperature to determine the applicable ambient temperature for application of the correction factors in Table 310.15(B)(2)(a) or Table 310.15(B)(2)(b).

Exception: *Type XHHW-2 insulated conductors shall not be subject to this ampacity adjustment.*

Informational Note: One source for the ambient temperatures in various locations is the ASHRAE Handbook — Fundamentals.
~~**Informational Note to Table 310.15(B)(3)(c):** The temperature adders in Table 310.15(B)(3)(c) are based on the measured temperature rise above the local climatic ambient temperatures due to sunlight heating.~~
~~**Table 310.15(B)(3)(c) Ambient Temperature Adjustment for Raceways or Cables Exposed to Sunlight on or Above Rooftops**~~
(see 2014 *NEC* for complete content of deleted table).

- **2014 *NEC* Requirement**
  Where raceways and cables are installed on rooftops exposed to the direct rays of the sun, these rooftop raceways and cables were required to comply with the temperature adders of Table 310.15(B)(3)(c). This table required a temperature adder to be added to the anticipated maximum ambient temperature in which the raceway or cable was installed based on the height the raceway of cable was installed above the rooftop.

- **2017 *NEC* Change**
  Table 310.15(B)(3)(c) was deleted and replaced with text added at 310.15(B)(3)(c). This new text requires a temperature adder of 33°C (60°F) only when a raceway or cable is installed directly on or less than 23 mm (7⁄8 in.) above a rooftop.

Analysis of the Change:

In conditions where raceways and cables are installed on a rooftop and exposed to the direct rays of the sun, care must be taken for the enclosed conductors and their insulation due to the potential of exposure to excessive heat. Not only are these raceways and enclosed conductors subject to exposure to the radiant heat of the direct sunlight, but they are also subject to absorb the "bounce back" heat from the roof material as well.

Beginning with the 2008 *NEC*, these rooftop raceways and cables were required to comply with the temperature adders of Table 310.15(B)(3)(c) [this was Table 310.15(B)(2)(c) when it first appeared in the 2008 *NEC*]. Depending on how high above the rooftop the raceway of cable was installed, this table required a temperature adder to be added to the anticipated maximum ambient temperature in which the raceway or cable was installed. For example, Table 310.15(B)(3)(c) called for a raceway installed 50 mm (2 in.) above a rooftop in 106°F temperatures to add 40°F to the actual temperature to create a 146°F value to be

310.15(B)(3)(c)

used for a temperature correction adjustment factor from Table 310.15(B)(2)(a).

For the 2017 *NEC*, Table 310.15(B)(3)(c) has been deleted and replaced with text added to the parent text of 310.15(B)(3)(c). This new text will require a temperature adder of 33°C (60°F) only when a raceway or cable is installed directly on or less than 23 mm (⅞ in.) above a rooftop. The issue of ambient temperature and temperature correction factor adders for raceways and cable assemblies installed on rooftops has been vigorously debated by CMP-6 since the inception of this requirement in the 2008 *NEC Code* cycle.

The deleted rooftop temperature adder table was originally supported by collected data from a test report entitled *Effects of Rooftop Exposure on Ambient Temperatures Inside Conduits, November 2005*. This original testing and a UL fact-finding report to verify those test results were found to be accurate based upon how the tests were performed and the parameters of the testing. However, there are numerous heat transfer methods by which a rooftop raceway or cable assembly can and will dissipate heat. This original testing took into consideration only two of these heat dissipation methods.

310.15(B)(3)(c)

During the later stages of 2014 *NEC*, CMP-6 requested that an independent task group be formed to review the ambient temperature correction factors for raceways and cable assemblies exposed to sunlight on rooftops (*see 2014 ROC 6-16*). The *NEC* Correlating Committee appointed such a task group and Public Input 3373 was submitted for the 2017 *NEC* as a result of this task group's work. The task group researched this rooftop temperature issue and solicited third party investigations by subject matter experts that did not have a vested interest in the outcome of the issue. The task group's investigation concluded that as long as raceways or cable assemblies are supported, conductors are properly terminated, and the raceway is not in direct contact with the rooftop surface, no rooftop temperature adder is necessary. It was also noted that this determination was made without consideration of the cooling effects of natural convection, which would result in further cooling inside the conduit. Additional findings proved that the heat inside a raceway insulates it from solar radiation; therefore, the thermal effects of rooftop installations are not additive. The research also indicated that wiring methods placed directly on the rooftop will have higher internal temperatures. Finally, the task group concluded that no documented evidence of actual field-installed conductor failures due to exposure to direct sunlight had ever been reported to CMP-6.

Part of the research that the task group considered was a test study of temperature factors on rooftop raceways and cables sponsored by the Southern Nevada Chapter of IAEI and the Las Vegas Section of IEEE. This experimental test data was gathered and analyzed by the University of Las Vegas, Nevada (UNLV). The conclusions of the study state that: "Based on the data gathered in this experiment, it is unlikely that wiring methods sized appropriately for the load and located on rooftops anywhere in the United States will ever exceed their rated insulation temperature, even if sized without using the adders in Table 310.15(B)(3)(c). There is a definite temperature rise inside wiring methods due to sunlight exposure; however, the pre-existing allowable ampacity and temperature correction factors adequately size the conductors to ensure that the conductors operate within a comfortable safety zone."

First Revisions: FR 1503
Public Inputs: PI 3373, PI 2809, PI 1947, PI 3232, PI 1

Table 310.15(B)(7)

120/240 Volt or 208Y-120 Volt, Single-Phase Dwelling Services and Feeders

Single-phase, 120/240-volt services or feeders (100 - 400 ampere) and single-phase, 208Y/120-volt feeders (100 - 400 ampere), supplying the entire dwelling unit load permitted to have an ampacity not less than 83% of the service or feeder rating

Correction or adjustment factors required by 310.15(B)(2) or (3) permitted to be applied to the ampacity associated with the temperature rating of these conductors

Service/feeder ratings addressed by this section are based on the standard ampacity ratings from 240.6(A)

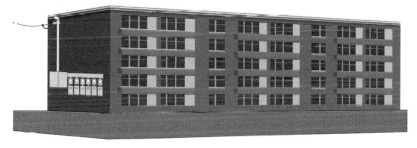

310.15(B)(7)

Table 310.15(B)(7) Ampacities for Conductors Rated 0–2000 Volts

- **Type of Change:** Revision

- **Change at a Glance:** 120/208 volts were added to allowable voltages for dwelling unit service conductor ampacity rating requirements. A new informational note was added indicating service rating based on standard ampacity ratings of 240.6(A). Correction or adjustment factors required by 310.15(B)(2) or (3) are permitted to be applied to the ampacity associated with the temperature rating of the conductor.

- **Code Language: 310.15 Ampacities for Conductors Rated 0–2000 Volts.**

  (B) Tables. Ampacities for conductors rated 0 to 2000 volts shall be as specified in the Allowable Ampacity Table 310.15(B)(16) through Table 310.15(B)(19), and Ampacity Table 310.15(B)(20) and Table 310.15(B)(21) as modified by 310.15(B)(1) through (B)(7). The temperature correction and adjustment factors shall be permitted to be applied to the ampacity for the temperature rating of the conductor if the corrected and adjusted ampacity does not exceed the ampacity for the temperature.

(7) ~~120/240-Volt,~~ **Single-Phase Dwelling Services and Feeders.** For one-family dwellings and the individual dwelling units of two-family and multifamily dwellings, service and feeder conductors supplied by a single-phase, 120/240-volt system shall be permitted to be sized in accordance with 310.15(B)(7)(1) through (4). For one-family dwellings and the individual dwelling units of two-family and multifamily dwellings, single-phase feeder conductors consisting of 2 ungrounded conductors and the neutral conductor from a 208Y/120-volt system shall be permitted to be sized in accordance with 310.15(B)(7)(1) through (3).

(1) For a service rated 100 through 400 ~~A~~ amperes, the service conductors supplying the entire load associated with a one-family dwelling, or the service conductors supplying the entire load associated with an individual dwelling unit in a two-family or multifamily dwelling, shall be permitted to have an ampacity not less than 83 percent of the service rating.
(2) For a feeder rated 100 through 400 ~~A~~ amperes, the feeder conductors supplying the entire load associated with a one-family dwelling, or the feeder conductors supplying the entire load associated with an individual dwelling unit in a two-family or multifamily dwelling, shall be permitted to have an ampacity not less than 83 percent of the feeder rating.
(3) In no case shall a feeder for an individual dwelling unit be required to have an ampacity greater than that specified in 310.15(B)(7)(1) or (2).
(4) Grounded conductors shall be permitted to be sized smaller than the ungrounded conductors, ~~provided that~~ if the requirements of 220.61 and 230.42 for service conductors or the requirements of 215.2 and 220.61 for feeder conductors are met.

Where correction or adjustment factors are required by 310.15(B)(2) or (3), they shall be permitted to be applied to the ampacity associated with the temperature rating of the conductor.

Informational Note No. 1: ~~The conductor ampacity may require other correction or adjustment factors applicable to the conductor installation.~~ The service or feeder ratings addressed by this section are based on the standard ampacity ratings from 240.6(A).

Informational Note No. 2: See Example D7 in Annex D.

■ **2014 *NEC* Requirement**
The provisions of 310.15(B)(7) for sizing dwelling unit service and certain feeder conductors were permitted for single-phase, 120/240-volt systems only. The previous Table 310.15(B)(7) was deleted entirely. For sizing service conductors and the "main power feeder" for dwelling units, the user of the *Code* can use a conductor sized from Table 310.15(B)(16) at no less than 83% of the service or feeder rating. An informational note takes users of the *Code* to Example D7 in Annex D for an example of how to perform this dwelling unit service and feeder calculation.

310.15(B)(7)

- **2017 *NEC* Change**

  The provisions of 310.15(B)(7) for sizing dwelling unit service and certain feeder conductors was expanded to single-phase, 208Y/120-volt systems as well as single-phase, 120/240-volt systems. Explanatory language was added to address the permitted application of correction or adjustment factors required by 310.15(B)(2) or (3) applied to the ampacity associated with the temperature rating of the conductors. A new informational note directs the user of the *Code* to 240.6(A) for service ratings based on standard ampacity ratings for application of 310.15(B)(7). Previous Table 310.15(B)(7) was added back into the *Code* as part of Example D7 in Informational Annex D.

Analysis of the Change:

The sizing requirements of 310.15(B)(7) for residential service and certain feeder conductors have been part of the *Code* in some form or fashion since the 1956 *NEC*. These provisions allow residential service-entrance conductors and a feeder supplying the entire load to be sized at a marginally higher ampacity value than the normal ampacity values found in the standard ampacity table, Table 310.15(B)(16). This higher ampacity allowance is permitted primarily due to the diversity of loads used within dwelling units. These requirements were first introduced as a note at the bottom of Table 1a of Chapter 10 of the 1956 *NEC*. In the 1975 *NEC*, this residential service ampacity provision became "Note 3 to Tables 310-16 through 310-19" titled, "Three-Wire Single-Phase Residential Services." The residential ampacity values first appeared in a table format in the 1978 *NEC* under Note 3 to Tables 310-16 through 310-19. The 1978 *NEC* was also where feeder conductors first were introduced to this residential ampacity value provision. The 1999 *NEC* witnessed this residential ampacity provision moved to its own subsection at 310-15(b)(6) and Table 310-15(b)(6) [later renumbered 310.15(B)(7) and Table 310.15(B)(7)].

310.15(B)(7)

Table 310.15(B)(7) was removed from the 2014 *NEC* and replaced with an ampacity requirement of not less than 83 percent of the service or feeder rating of the ampacity values of Table 310.15(B)(16). This table will now resides in Informative Annex D at the end of Example D7 and serves as a useful guide for users of the *Code* for sizing service conductors and the "main-power feeder" at dwelling units.

Multiple changes occurred at 310.15(B)(7) for the 2017 *NEC*. The first of these changes occurred with the voltage rating that can qualify for the allowable dwelling unit service ratings of 310.15(B)(7). From its inception, the requirements associated with 310.15(B)(7) have historically been limited to single-phase, 120/240-volt systems. For the 2017 *NEC*, single-phase, 208Y/120-volt systems will be eligible for these dwelling unit service and feeder conductor reductions as well. This change is most likely to affect large multi-family dwelling projects that are frequently served by three-phase systems with single-phase, 208Y/120-volt feeders to individual dwelling units.

In previous revision cycles of the *Code*, one major concern when single-phase, 208Y/120-volt systems were considered was current on the grounded (neutral) conductor. In a 208Y/120-volt system, the current is 120 degrees out-of-phase rather than 180 degrees as in a 120/240-volt system, which results in current always being present on the neutral conductor. In this manner, the neutral conductor would be considered a current-carrying conductor simply by definition.

In a single-phase 120/240 volt system, when the current is balanced, there will be no current flowing in the grounded conductor. If the ungrounded conductor currents are not identical, the grounded conductor only carries the imbalanced load, which is a very low amount of current. Because of this, the neutral conductor does not produce significant heat in the raceway or cabling encasing the feeder. However, if the grounded conductor conducts significant current, as it would in a 3-wire 208Y/120-volt system, heat will be generated in the neutral conductor. For this reason, these single-phase, 208Y/120-volt feeders are permitted to be sized in accordance with 310.15(B)(7)(1) through (3) only, and are not permitted to reduce the size of the grounded conductor as permitted by 310.15(B)(7)(4) if the requirements of 215.2 and 220.61 for feeder conductors are met. The requirements of 220.61(C)(1) state that "there shall be no reduction of the neutral or grounded conductor capacity of any portion of the 3-wire circuit consisting of 2 ungrounded conductors and the neutral conductor of a 4-wire, wye-connected 3-phase system."

Another change that occurred at 310.15(B)(7) was the addition of *Code* text that clarifies where correction or adjustment factors are required by 310.15(B)(2) or (3); they are permitted to be applied to the ampacity associated with the temperature rating of the conductor. There have been questions from installers and inspectors alike as to whether the temperature and correction factors should, or even could, be applied to the ampacity in the temperature column associated with the equipment termination values or the conductor temperature rating when the ampacity values permitted by 310.15(B)(7) were already applied to a dwelling unit service or feeder. This added text at 310.15(B)(7) will make it clear that they are permitted to be applied to the conductor temperature rating column ampacity when necessary due to temperature correction and adjustment factors. This provision was indicated in an informational note in the 2014 *NEC* but is now mandatory language in the 2017 *NEC*. Service and feeder conductors in residential applications are subject to the same environmental conditions as other types of installations.

The last change to report at 310.15(B)(7) involves the addition of a new Informational Note No. 1, which states that "the service or feeder ratings addressed by this section are based on the standard ampacity ratings from 240.6(A)." There is confusion in the installer and inspection communities as to how to apply this 83 percent adjustment factor that took the place of the previous values found in Table 310.15(B)(7) prior to the 2014 *NEC*.

A careful reading of the language at 310.15(B)(7) clearly states that this 83 percent adjustment would need to be applied to the "service rating" or the "feeder

310.15(B)(7)

rating." In other words, if the calculated load at a dwelling unit came out to be 251 amperes, this would make the service rating for this dwelling unit service a 300-ampere "service rating" based on the standard ampacity ratings found at 240.6(A). The 83 percent adjustment factor would be applied to the 300 amperes (300 amperes x .83 = 249 amperes). Several installers, inspectors, instructors, etc., will be applying the 83 percent adjustment factor to the 251 amperes (calculated load) rather than the "service rating" (300 amperes). This results in a very different outcome (251 amperes x 83 = 208 amperes), resulting in a different conductor size from Table 310.15(B)(16). Using the 75 degree column from Table 310.15(B)(16) would result in a 250 kcmil copper conductor for 249 amperes versus a 4/0 AWG copper conductor for a 208-ampere value. The ampacity values found at Table 310.15(B)(7) (now located in Informative Annex D) are based on the standard ampacity ratings of 240.6(A). The 175 amperes service rating currently being used in Informative Annex D, Example D7 is derived from the standard ampacity ratings of 240.6(A).

Without this new informational note directing users of the *Code* toward 240.6(A), there was not a good connection between the "service rating" or "feeder rating" and the standard ampacity ratings of 240.6(A), other than experience in working with the *NEC*. This new informational note will bridge this gap when applying the 83 percent adjustment factors of 310.15(B)(7).

310.15(B)(7)

First Revisions: FR 1504
Second Revisions: SR 1505
Public Inputs: 4807, PI 3669, PI 4739, PI 1169, PI 3786, PI 3477
Public Comments: PC 1159

312.5(C), Exception, Item (g)
Cable Raceway

312.5(C)

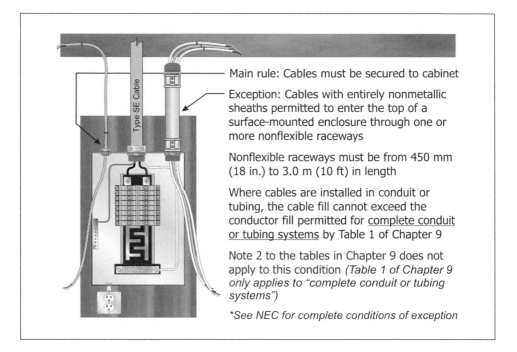

Main rule: Cables must be secured to cabinet

Exception: Cables with entirely nonmetallic sheaths permitted to enter the top of a surface-mounted enclosure through one or more nonflexible raceways

Nonflexible raceways must be from 450 mm (18 in.) to 3.0 m (10 ft) in length

Where cables are installed in conduit or tubing, the cable fill cannot exceed the conductor fill permitted for <u>complete conduit or tubing systems</u> by Table 1 of Chapter 9

Note 2 to the tables in Chapter 9 does not apply to this condition *(Table 1 of Chapter 9 only applies to "complete conduit or tubing systems")*

*See NEC for complete conditions of exception

312.5(C), Exception, Item (g) Cabinets, Cutout Boxes, and Meter Socket Enclosures.

- **Type of Change:** New

- **Change at a Glance:** Note 2 to the tables in Chapter 9 does not apply to the limited length of raceway required in 312.5(C), Exception, and the conductor fill limits of Chapter 9, Table 1 do apply.

- **Code Language: 312.5 Cabinets, Cutout Boxes, and Meter Socket Enclosures.**
Conductors entering enclosures within the scope of this article shall be protected from abrasion and shall comply with 312.5(A) through (C).

(C) Cables. Where cable is used, each cable shall be secured to the cabinet, cutout box, or meter socket enclosure.

Exception: *Cables with entirely nonmetallic sheaths shall be permitted to enter the top of a surface-mounted enclosure through one or more nonflexible raceways not less than 450 mm (18 in.) and not more than 3.0 m (10 ft) in length, provided all of the following conditions are met:*

(a) Each cable is fastened within 300 mm (12 in.), measured along the sheath, of the outer end of the raceway.

(b) The raceway extends directly above the enclosure and does not penetrate a structural ceiling.

(c) A fitting is provided on each end of the raceway to protect the cable(s) from abrasion, and the fittings remain accessible after installation.

(d) The raceway is sealed or plugged at the outer end using approved means so as to prevent access to the enclosure through the raceway.

(e) The cable sheath is continuous through the raceway and extends into the enclosure beyond the fitting not less than 6 mm (¼ in.).

(f) The raceway is fastened at its outer end and at other points in accordance with the applicable article.

(g) Where installed as conduit or tubing, the cable fill does not exceed the amount that would be permitted for complete conduit or tubing systems by Table 1 of Chapter 9 of this Code and all applicable notes thereto. Note 2 to the tables in Chapter 9 does not apply to this condition.

Informational Note: See Table 1 in Chapter 9, including Note 9, for allowable cable fill in circular raceways. See 310.15(B)(3)(a) for required ampacity reductions for multiple cables installed in a common raceway.

312.5(C)

■ **2014 *NEC* Requirement**
For conductor fill requirements for the "sleeve" of conduit or tubing required by 312.5(C), Exception, List Item (g) of this exception states that where installed as conduit or tubing, the cable fill cannot exceed the amount that would be permitted for complete conduit or tubing systems by Table 1 of Chapter 9. This requirement went on to indicate that "all applicable notes thereto" applied to the section of raceway.

■ **2017 *NEC* Change**
A new sentence was added to 312.5(C), Exception, Item (g) to indicate that Note 2 to the tables in Chapter 9 does not apply to this "sleeve" of conduit or tubing required if 312.5(C), Exception is employed.

Analysis of the Change:
Section 312.5 requires that whenever conductors enter a cabinet or meter socket enclosure, the conductors are required to be protected from abrasion. All openings through which conductors enter must be adequately closed. Where a cable is used, 312.5(C) generally requires each cable assembly to be secured to the cabinet with fittings and connectors specifically listed for the wiring method used.

An exception to this securing rule applies only to cables with entirely nonmetallic sheaths. This exception permits such cables to enter the top of a surface-mounted enclosure through one or more nonflexible raceways. The raceway is required to have a minimum length of 450 mm (18 in.) and a maximum length of 3.0 m (10 ft). This exception has seven conditions that all must be met in order to apply this exception without securing the individual cables to the enclosure (*see Code text for all conditions*).

The last of these conditions is located at List Item (g) of the exception to 312.5(C), which states that "where installed as conduit or tubing, the cable fill does not exceed the amount that would be permitted for complete conduit or tubing systems by Table 1 of Chapter 9 of this *Code* and all applicable notes thereto." For the 2017 *NEC*, a new sentence was added to this list item to indicate that "Note 2 to the tables in Chapter 9 does not apply to this condition."

There are ten notes to the tables in Chapter 9. The information relayed in Note 2 to the tables in Chapter 9 declares that "Table 1 applies only to complete conduit or tubing systems and is not intended to apply to sections of conduit or tubing used to protect exposed wiring from physical damage." Table 1 of Chapter 9 limits the percent of conductor fill of a conduit or tubing to 53 percent of the cross-sectional area of the conduit or tubing for one conductor, 31 percent for two conductors, and 40 percent for over 2 conductors.

312.5(C)

The added language in 312.5(C), Exception, Item (g) tells the user of the *Code* to treat the 450 mm (18 in.) to 3.0 m (10 ft) "sleeve" of conduit or tubing required for this exception as a "complete conduit or tubing system" as far as conductor fill is concerned. Prior to this revision at 312.5(C), Exception, Item (g), this appeared to be in conflict with Note 2 to the tables in Chapter 9. Once again, Note (2) specifies that Table 1 applies only to "complete conduit or tubing systems" and is not intended to apply to "sections of conduit or tubing" used to protect exposed wiring from physical damage or that provide a chase to enclosures.

First Revisions: FR 2403
Second Revisions: SR 2402
Public Inputs: PI 2576, PI 2575
Public Comments: PC 376

Table 312.6(A)

Minimum Wire-Bending Space at Terminals and Minimum Width of Wiring Gutters

Wire Size (AWG or kcmil)		Wires per Terminal									
		1		2		3		4		5	
All Other Conductors	Compact Stranded AA-8000 Aluminum Alloy Conductors (see Note 2)	mm	in.	mm	in.	mm	in.	mm	in.	mm	in.
14-10	12-8	Not Specified		—	—	—	—	—	—	—	—
8-6	6-4	38.1	1½	—	—	—	—	—	—	—	—
4-3	2-1	50.8	2	—	—	—	—	—	—	—	—
2	1/0	63.5	2½	—	—	—	—			—	—
1	2/0	76.2	3	—	—	—	—	—	—	—	—
1/0-2/0	3/0-4/0	88.9	3½	127	5	178	7	—	—	—	—
3/0-4/0	250-300	102	4	152	6	203	8	—	—	—	—
250	350	114	4½	152	6	230	8	254	10	—	—
300-350	400-500	127	5	203	8	254	10	305	12	—	—
400-500	600-750	152	6	203	8	254	10	305	12	356	14
600-700	800-1000	203	8	254	10	305	12	356	14	406	16
750-900	—	203	8	305	12	356	14	406	16	457	18
1000-1250	—	254	10	—	—	—	—	—	—	—	—
1500-2000	—	305	12	—	—	—	—	—	—	—	—

Note 1: Bending space at terminals shall be measured in a straight line from the end of the lug or wire connector *(in the direction that the wire leaves the terminal)* to the wall, barrier, or obstruction.

Note 2: This column shall be permitted to be used to determine the minimum wire-bending space for compact stranded aluminum conductors in sizes up to 1000 kcmil and manufactured using AA-8000 series electrical grade aluminum alloy conductor material in accordance with 310.106(B). The minimum width of the wire gutter space shall be determined using the all other conductors value in this table.

312.6(A)

312.6(A) Deflection of Conductors

- **Type of Change:** Revision

- **Change at a Glance:** New minimum wire-bending spaces for AA-8000 series compact stranded aluminum conductors have been added to Table 310.6(A).

- **Code Language: 312.6 Deflection of Conductors.**
  Conductors at terminals or conductors entering or leaving cabinets or cutout boxes and the like shall comply with 312.6(A) through (C).

  Exception: *Wire-bending space in enclosures for motor controllers with provisions for one or two wires per terminal shall comply with 430.10(B).*

  (A) Width of Wiring Gutters. Conductors shall not be deflected within a cabinet or cutout box unless a gutter having a width in accordance with Table 312.6(A) is provided. Conductors in parallel in accordance with 310.10(H) shall be judged on the basis of the number of conductors in parallel.

  Table 312.6(A) Minimum Wire-Bending Space at Terminals and Minimum Width of Wiring Gutters
  (See *NEC* for complete table content).

Notes [to Table 312.6(A)]:

1. Bending space at terminals shall be measured in a straight line from the end of the lug or wire connector (in the direction that the wire leaves the terminal) to the wall, barrier, or obstruction.

2. This column shall be permitted to be used to determine the minimum wire-bending space for compact stranded aluminum conductors in sizes up to 1000 kcmil and manufactured using AA-8000 series electrical grade aluminum alloy conductor material in accordance with 310.106(B). The minimum width of the wire gutter space shall be determined using all other conductors' value in this table.

312.6(A)

- **2014 *NEC* Requirement**

  For wire-bending space at terminals, the conductors must comply with either Table 312.6(A) or Table 312.6(B), depending on the conditions involved. Table 312.6(A) applies where the conductor *does not* enter or leave the enclosure through the wall opposite its terminal. Table 312.6(B) applies where the conductor *does* enter or leave the enclosure through the wall opposite its terminal. While Table 312.6(B) entertained compact stranded AA-8000 aluminum alloy conductors, Table 312.6(A) did not.

- **2017 *NEC* Change**

  The requirements for wire-bending space at terminals and the use of Table 312.6(A) or Table 312.6(B) remained the same. A new column was added to Table 312.6(A) addressing wire-bending space for compact stranded AA-8000 aluminum alloy conductors for consistency.

Analysis of the Change:

During the 2002 *NEC* revision cycle, a new column was added to Table 312.6(B) addressing wire-bending space for compact stranded AA-8000 aluminum alloy conductors. This addition to Table 312.6(B) was based on a 1999 fact-finding investigation that was performed to test the bending space requirements for the aluminum series AA-8000 compact stranded conductors. This 2002 *NEC* revision and the substantiating investigation were based on minimum wire-bending spaces for conductors entering or leaving an enclosure through the wall opposite its terminal. The 1999 investigation did not address the minimum wire-bending space for conductors that do not enter or leave an enclosure through the opposite wall, which is what Table 312.6(A) deals with. With a need for consistency between the two Article 312 tables, a new, updated fact-finding investigation was launched in 2015 to provide data for proposed changes to Table 312.6(A). This investigation resulted in a similar new column in Table 312.6(A) for wire-bending space for compact stranded AA-8000 aluminum alloy conductors.

The testing consisted of forming 90-degree bends in various samples of Type XHHW-2 aluminum alloy conductors and then terminating these conductors in a manner consistent with accepted electrical installation standards. The conductor and insulation were then inspected for potential damage. For consistency and comparison, several samples of the same size copper conductors were also tested. The evaluation of the conductors and the insulation revealed no apparent damage caused by bending the conductors to the minimum wire-bending measurements for compact stranded AA-8000 aluminum alloy conductors added to Table 312.6(A).

In reviewing the report, CMP 9 had some concerns related to the fact that the study set-up did not involve actual electrical enclosures. These concerns were put to rest as Table 314.6(A), unlike Table 314.6(B), generally covers bends that are made outside the enclosure and then set into place. Based on the results obtained from the fact-finding investigation, the spaces provided in Table 312.6(A) for compact stranded AA-8000 aluminum alloy conductors should be viable in actual field installations. It should be noted that these added values are minimum values. In no case was the wire bending radii exceeded for the minimum values set by the manufacturer. The dimensions added for aluminum conductors are consistent with minimum safety standards and provide a useful correlation with comparable material in Table 312.6(B).

The new fact-finding investigation was titled, "Conductor Bending Evaluation Report for Aluminum AA-8000 Series Conductors for Inclusion in Table 312.6(A)." This study was prepared for the National Electrical Manufacturers Association (NEMA) and performed at the facilities of Cogburn Bros., Inc. in Jacksonville, FL. The testing was witnessed by Intertek, a nationally recognized testing laboratory (NRTL).

First Revisions: FR 2435
Second Revisions: SR 2403
Public Comments: PC 1040, PC 1791

312.8(B)

312.8(B)

Switch and Overcurrent Device Enclosures

312.8(B) Switch and Overcurrent Device Enclosures

- **Type of Change:** New

- **Change at a Glance:** Power monitoring equipment is now required to be listed for the application when installed in free spaces of cabinets and cutout boxes.

- **Code Language: 312.8 Switch and Overcurrent Device Enclosures ~~with Splices, Taps, and Feed-Through Conductors.~~** The wiring space within enclosures for switches and overcurrent devices shall be permitted for other wiring and equipment subject to limitations for specific equipment as provided in (A) and (B).

  (A) Splices, Taps, and Feed-Through Conductors. The wiring space of enclosures for switches or overcurrent devices shall be permitted for conductors feeding through, spliced, or tapping off to other enclosures, switches, or overcurrent devices where all of the following conditions are met:

  (1) The total of all conductors installed at any cross section of the wiring space does not exceed 40 percent of the cross-sectional area of that space.

  (2) The total area of all conductors, splices, and taps installed at any cross section of the wiring space does not exceed 75 percent of the cross-sectional area of that space.

  (3) A warning label complying with 110.21(B) is applied to the enclosure that identifies the closest disconnecting means for any feed-through conductors.

  (B) Power Monitoring Equipment. The wiring space of enclosures for switches or overcurrent devices shall be permitted to contain power monitoring equipment where all of the following conditions are met:

  (1) The power monitoring equipment is identified as a field-installable accessory as part of the listed equipment, or is a listed kit evaluated for field installation in switch or overcurrent device enclosures.

  (2) The total area of all conductors, splices, taps, and equipment at any cross section of the wiring space does not exceed 75 percent of the cross-sectional area of that space.

- **2014 *NEC* Requirement**
  Section 312.8 contained information and regulations pertaining to conductors feeding through, spliced, or tapping off to other enclosures, switches, or overcurrent devices permitted in the wiring space of enclosures for switches or overcurrent devices. This section did not address other types of equipment such as power monitoring equipment being installed in these wiring spaces.

312.8(B)

■ **2017 *NEC* Change**

A new 312.8(B) was added to allow power monitoring equipment within the wiring space of enclosures for switches or overcurrent devices with specific conditions.

Analysis of the Change:

The wiring space within enclosures, such as a panelboard cabinet for switches or overcurrent devices, has been permitted to contain "other wiring and equipment" for a limited percentage (40% and 75%) of the cross-sectional area of the space as far back as the 1971 *NEC*. Before the 1971 *NEC*, in order for enclosures that contain switches or overcurrent devices to be used as a junction box, etc., the enclosure had to be "designed as suitable for the purpose" and provide "adequate space" for this purpose. The electrical industry has seen an increase over past few years in the proliferation of devices and equipment intended to be installed in cabinet enclosures containing switches or overcurrent devices.

These devices are typically manufactured by someone other than the manufacturer of the cabinet or panelboard and are not evaluated for that particular panelboard cabinet. These devices would include such things as equipment intended for measuring, monitoring, and controlling circuits as part of load monitoring or energy management system. Energy-monitoring current transformers (*UL White Book category XOBA*) is a specific example of this type of equipment.

To answer the demand for such equipment being installed in a cabinet containing switches or overcurrent devices, the the 2017 *NEC* adopted new text at 312.8(B) to allow power monitoring equipment within the wiring space of enclosures for switches or overcurrent devices with specific conditions. This additional text limits the inclusion of devices and equipment in a wiring space to power monitoring equipment that is identified as field installable accessories as part of the listed equipment, or as a listed kit evaluated for field installation in the specific equipment. This new wording also retains the limit on the amount of space occupied by all conductors, splices, taps, devices, and equipment to the same 75 percent fill requirement previously located at 312.8(2) [*now 312.8(A)(2)*].

CMP-9 rejected a proposal for the 2011 *NEC*, which would have allowed any and all types of utilization equipment to be installed in such things as a panelboard cabinet (see 2011 ROP 9-31). This proposal was rejected because these types of installations would result in obstructions within cabinets that could not be evaluated by qualified testing laboratories. This new provision will provide guidance to the installer and inspector as to when the addition of power monitoring equipment is allowed within a cabinet space.

312.8(B)

First Revisions: FR 2404
Second Revisions: SR 2401
Public Inputs: PI 3091
Public Comments: PC 1178, (29 total PCs,
see Second Draft Report for complete list of PCs)

314.16(A) and (B)

Number of Conductors in Outlet, Device, and Junction Boxes, and Conduit Bodies

314.16(A) & (B)

314.16(A) and (B) Number of Conductors in Outlet, Device, and Junction Boxes, and Conduit Bodies

- **Type of Change:** New

- **Change at a Glance:** New text was added to accommodate boxes with internal barriers for box volume and box fill calculations.

- **Code Language: 314.16 Number of Conductors in Outlet, Device, and Junction Boxes, and Conduit Bodies.**
  Boxes and conduit bodies shall be of an approved size to provide free space for all enclosed conductors. In no case shall the volume of the box, as calculated in 314.16(A), be less than the fill calculation as calculated in 314.16(B). The minimum volume for conduit bodies shall be as calculated in 314.16(C).

  The provisions of this section shall not apply to terminal housings supplied with motors or generators.

  Informational Note: For volume requirements of motor or generator terminal housings, see 430.12.

Boxes and conduit bodies enclosing conductors 4 AWG or larger shall also comply with the provisions of 314.28.

(A) Box Volume Calculations. The volume of a wiring enclosure (box) shall be the total volume of the assembled sections and, where used, the space provided by plaster rings, domed covers, extension rings, and so forth, that are marked with their volume or are made from boxes the dimensions of which are listed in Table 314.16(A). Where a box is provided with one or more securely installed barriers, the volume shall be apportioned to each of the resulting spaces. Each barrier, if not marked with its volume, shall be considered to take up 8.2 cm³ (½ in.³) if metal and 16.4 cm³ (1 in.³) if nonmetallic.

(1) Standard Boxes. (No change to *Code* text; see *NEC* for complete text)

(2) Other Boxes. (No change to *Code* text; see *NEC* for complete text)

(B) Box Fill Calculations. The volumes in paragraphs 314.16(B)(1) through (B)(5), as applicable, shall be added together. No allowance shall be required for small fittings such as locknuts and bushings. Each space within a box installed with a barrier shall be calculated separately.

(B)(1) through (B)(5) (No change to *Code text*; see *NEC* for complete text)

■ **2014 *NEC* Requirement**
The permitted number of conductors in an outlet, device, or junction boxes, along with conduit bodies is addressed at 314.16. The total volume (space) within a box or enclosure is calculated at 314.16(A) with box fill calculations covered at 314.16(B). A box fill calculation based on the 2014 *NEC* had to take into consideration conductor fill, internal clamps, support fittings, devices (switches and receptacles), and equipment grounding conductors when determining the minimum volume of space needed inside a box or enclosure.

■ **2017 *NEC* Change**
The volume or space that is occupied by an internal barrier in a box or enclosure was added to the items previously addressed for preforming a box fill calculation.

Analysis of the Change:

The *NEC* includes general rules for boxes such as sizing and support provisions. All boxes (enclosures) must be large enough to provide sufficient free space for all conductors and devices that will be enclosed within them to prevent overcrowding and possible physical damage when the devices or conductors are installed. The rules for the number of conductors permitted in an outlet, device, or junction boxes, along with conduit bodies are found at 314.16.

The volume of a box is the total volume in cubic centimeters or cubic inches of the assembled sections. This total volume (space) determines the number and

314.16(A) & (B)

size of conductors and wiring devices permitted to be contained in the box. Conductors, internal clamps, support fittings, and devices such as switches and receptacles take up space within the box, so the *Code* assigns to each conductor, clamp, support fitting, device, and equipment grounding conductor an associated volume allowance. This volume allowance is listed in cubic inches or cubic centimeters. Table 314.16(B) lists the volume allowance as a function of conductor size. When performing a box fill calculation, the volume allowance for each conductor, clamp, support fitting, device, and equipment grounding conductor is added together. The box must have a volume that equals or exceeds the total volume required for the contained items.

Table 314.16(A) provides box dimension and trade size in inches for standard metal boxes. The minimum cubic centimeter (cubic inch) capacity for each standard size metal box is given along with the maximum number of conductors of sizes 18 AWG through 6 AWG permitted in the box. As shown in the table, the number of conductors permitted applies only where all conductors are the same size. Where a box contains conductors of different sizes, the required volume of the box must be calculated.

314.16(A) & (B)

The volume or space that is occupied by an internal barrier in a box has not been addressed by these box-fill calculations until changes at 314.16(A) and (B) occurred in the 2017 *NEC*. Where a box is provided with one or more securely installed interior barriers, the *Code* will now require the volume of that barrier to be allocated to each of the resulting spaces. Each barrier, if not marked with its volume, will need to be considered to take up 8.2 cm³ (½ in.³) of space if metal and 16.4 cm³ (1 in.³) if nonmetallic. CMP-9 based this volume allowance on a simple volume calculation of 100 mm x 50 mm x 1.6 mm (4 in. x 2 in. x 1/16 in.) for metal, and double that volume for nonmetallic barriers.

Nonmetallic box barriers are provided with volume markings, but metal barriers for metal boxes are not currently marked with their volume consumption. With or without their volume markings, no mandatory text existed in previous editions of the *Code* for a requirement to consider these interior barriers when performing a box fill calculation. A newly added sentence at 314.16(B) will also make it clear that each space within a box installed with an interior barrier will need to be calculated separately.

Another change that was addressed by CMP-9 was removing the term "gang" in six locations under the column "Box Trade Size" in Table 314.16(A), which deals with metal boxes. Metal device boxes are supplied as individual boxes and then ganged in the field. The current text at 314.16(A) makes it clear that wiring volumes after ganging are not to be applied box by box but rather to the "assembled section." Table 314.16(A) was considered to be inconsistent by some users of the *Code* in that some of the existing rows such as "FS-single cover/gang (1¾)" reflect multi-gang box availability whereas other rows for device boxes do not reflect common availability as multi-gang boxes.

First Revisions: FR 2406
Public Inputs: PI 2692

314.17(B)
Type NM Cable Entering Metal Boxes

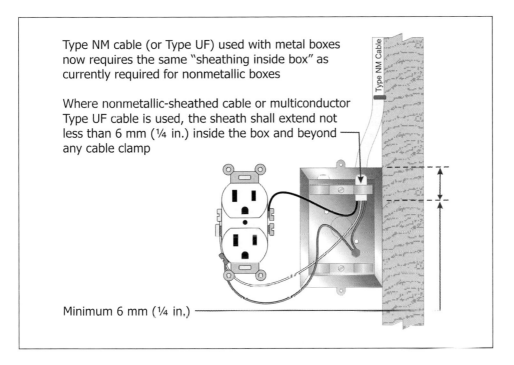

Type NM cable (or Type UF) used with metal boxes now requires the same "sheathing inside box" as currently required for nonmetallic boxes

Where nonmetallic-sheathed cable or multiconductor Type UF cable is used, the sheath shall extend not less than 6 mm (¼ in.) inside the box and beyond any cable clamp

Type NM Cable

Minimum 6 mm (¼ in.)

314.17(B)

314.17(B) Conductors Entering Boxes, Conduit Bodies, or Fittings

- **Type of Change:** New

- **Change at a Glance:** The outside sheath of Type NM or Type UF cable used with a metal box must now extend not less than 6 mm (¼ in.) inside the box as currently required for nonmetallic boxes.

- **Code Language: 314.17 Conductors Entering Boxes, Conduit Bodies, or Fittings.**
  Conductors entering boxes, conduit bodies, or fittings shall be protected from abrasion and shall comply with 314.17(A) through (D).

  (B) Metal Boxes and Conduit Bodies. Where metal boxes or conduit bodies are installed with messenger-supported wiring, open wiring on insulators, or concealed knob-and-tube wiring, conductors shall enter through insulating bushings or, in dry locations, through flexible tubing extending from the last insulating support to not less than 6 mm (¼ in.) inside the box and beyond any cable clamps. Where nonmetallic-sheathed cable or multiconductor Type UF cable is used, the sheath shall extend not less than 6 mm (¼ in.) inside the box and beyond any cable clamp. Except as provided in 300.15(C), the wiring shall be firmly secured to the box or conduit body. Where raceway or cable is installed with metal boxes or conduit bodies, the raceway or cable shall be secured to such boxes and conduit bodies.

■ **2014 *NEC* Requirement**
Provisions located at 314.17(C) mandate that the sheath of nonmetallic-sheathed (Type NM) cable or multiconductor Type UF cable is used with nonmetallic boxes or nonmetallic conduit bodies extend not less than 6 mm (¼ in.) inside the box or conduit body and beyond any cable clamp. No similar requirement exists for Type NM cable or multiconductor Type UF cables used with metal boxes or metal conduit bodies.

■ **2017 *NEC* Change**
New text added at 314.17(B) will now require nonmetallic-sheathed (Type NM) cable or multiconductor Type UF cable used with metal boxes or conduit bodies to have its sheath extend not less than 6 mm (¼ in.) inside the box and beyond any cable clamp.

Analysis of the Change:

In situations where nonmetallic-sheathed (Type NM) cable or multiconductor Type UF cable is the wiring method of choice and is installed in conjunction with nonmetallic boxes and/or nonmetallic conduit bodies, the sheath of the cables is required to extend not less than 6 mm (¼ in.) inside the box and beyond any cable clamp. This requirement is addressed at 314.17(C). While this requirement is specific to nonmetallic boxes and conduit bodies, the same protection for these cables and their associated conductors is needed when entering a metal box or conduit body as well.

This inconsistency was eliminated with identical text currently found at 314.17(C) being added to 314.17(B) for nonmetallic-sheathed cable or multiconductor Type UF cable being installed in a metal box or conduit body. This added text will provide a comparable requirement and assure that the cable clamp of a metal box will not be tightened down upon an exposed insulated conductor of a Type NM or Type UF cable. As with a nonmetallic box, the sheath of these cables should extend into the box and beyond the clamp to better protect the insulated conductors.

First Revisions: FR 2407
Public Inputs: PI 1329, PI 1717

314.17(B)

314.27(E)

Separable Attachment Fittings

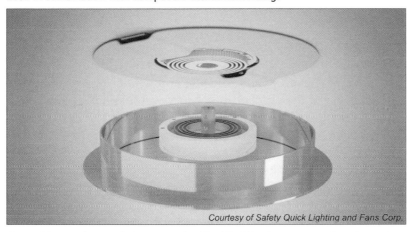

Outlet boxes permitted to support listed locking support and mounting receptacles used in combination with compatible attachment fittings

Courtesy of Safety Quick Lighting and Fans Corp.

Separable attachment fittings must be identified for the support of equipment within the weight and mounting orientation limits of the listing

Supporting receptacle installed within a box must be included in box fill calculation

314.27(E)

314.27(E) Outlet Boxes

- **Type of Change:** New

- **Change at a Glance:** Outlet boxes are permitted to support listed locking support and mounting receptacles used in combination with compatible attachment fittings.

- **Code Language: 314.27 Outlet Boxes**

  (E) Separable Attachment Fittings. Outlet boxes required in 314.27 shall be permitted to support listed locking support and mounting receptacles used in combination with compatible attachment fittings. The combination shall be identified for the support of equipment within the weight and mounting orientation limits of the listing. Where the supporting receptacle is installed within a box, it shall be included in the fill calculation covered in 314.16(B)(4).

- **2014 *NEC* Requirement**
  As required by 314.27(A), a box listed for the support of a luminaire or lampholder in a ceiling is required to be designed for the purpose and is required to support a luminaire weighing a minimum of 23 kg (50 lb.). Boxes used at luminaire, or lampholder outlets are required to be designed for the purpose and are required to be marked on the interior

of the box itself to indicate the maximum weight of the luminaire that is permitted to be supported by that box [if other than 23 kg (50 lb.)]. Vertical surface or wall-mounted device boxes are permitted to support luminaires that weigh not more than 3 kg (6 lb.). These device boxes may not be marked as being suitable for luminaire support since that is not their primary purpose. The luminaire or its supporting yoke must be secured to the box with at least two 6-32 screws.

A box used at ceiling fan outlets is not permitted to be used as the sole support for ceiling-suspended (paddle) fans unless it is specifically listed for the application and for the weight of the fan to be supported. This requirement applies to both metal and nonmetallic boxes. Outlet boxes or outlet box systems used as the sole support for a ceiling-suspended (paddle) fan must be listed, marked by the manufacturer as suitable for ceiling-suspended paddle fan support, and cannot support fans that weigh more than 32 kg (70 lb.). This box or system must be rigidly supported from a structural member of the building [see 314.27(C)].

314.27(E)

■ **2017 *NEC* Change**
In addition to the previous requirements at 314.27(A) through (D) for a box supporting a luminaire, lampholder, ceiling-suspended (paddle) fan, or other types of utilization equipment, 314.27(E) will now permit listed locking support and mounting receptacles and support means for supporting a luminaire, lampholder, or ceiling-suspended (paddle) fan.

Analysis of the Change:
From a historical standpoint, the *NEC* has typically required a box listed for the support of a luminaire or lampholder in a ceiling or on a vertical surface (such as a wall) when mounting a luminaire, lampholder, ceiling-suspended (paddle) fan, or other types of utilization equipment. A new 314.27(E) has been added to address new technology incorporating listed power supply devices and listed locking support and mounting receptacles and supporting means for luminaires, lampholders, and ceiling-suspended (paddle) fans. This listed locking support and matching mounting receptacle are designed to be installed in or to boxes designed for this purpose.

This new subsection in 314.27 recognizes newly listed technology designed to power and support luminaires and or ceiling suspended (paddle) fans from a receptacle and mounting means located in or mounted directly to the box. These listed fittings may now be used to support and power the luminaire or ceiling-suspended (paddle) fan directly, thus facilitating safe and efficient replacement of the luminaire or ceiling-suspended (paddle) fan.

The new provision for listed locking support and mounting receptacles for luminaires coincides with the revised definition of a "receptacle" in Article 100. A receptacle is now defined as "a contact device installed at the outlet for the connection of an attachment plug, or for the direct connection of electrical utilization equipment designed to mate with the corresponding contact device." This revised definition was necessary to correlate with these new provisions in

314.27(E) and to recognize the existence of equipment such as direct plug-in transformers, and other devices that do not employ a traditional receptacle and attachment plug cap.

It should be noted that this new language concerning locking support and mounting receptacles for luminaires is an option and not a requirement for mounting luminaires and ceiling-suspended (paddle) fans. CMP 9 has rejected this type of application in past *Code* cycles largely based on the belief that the subject belonged to either CMP-18 for luminaires or CMP-17 for ceiling-suspended (paddle) fans. This thought process was altered by the revised definition of "receptacle" in Article 100. Previous attempts to recognize these devices also sought to make these listed locking supports and mounting receptacles a requirement rather than an option for mounting luminaires, lampholders, etc. (see 2011 ROP 9-75 and the 2011 ROC 9-31).

In conjunction with this change in 314.27(E), similar *Code* language was added at 422.18 by CMP-17 for support of ceiling-suspended (paddle) fans (see SR 4806 and PC 662).

First Revisions: FR 2411
Second Revisions: SR 2406
Public Inputs: PI 4443, PI 4665
Public Comments: PC 669, PC 831, PC 1793

320.6

320.6

Listing Requirements. (Armored Cable: Type AC)

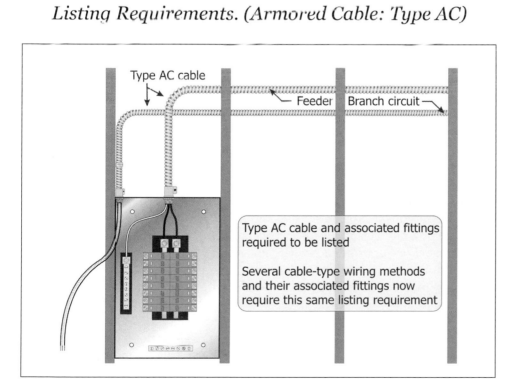

Type AC cable

Feeder | Branch circuit

Type AC cable and associated fittings required to be listed

Several cable-type wiring methods and their associated fittings now require this same listing requirement

320.6 Listing Requirements. (Armored Cable: Type AC)

- **Type of Change:** New

- **Change at a Glance:** Cable-type wiring methods and associated fittings are required to be listed.

- **Code Language: 320.6 Listing Requirements. (Armored Cable: Type AC).**
  Type AC cable and associated fittings shall be listed.

- **2014 *NEC* Requirement**
  Section 110.3(B) requires listed or labeled equipment to be installed and used in accordance with any instructions included in the listing or labeling, but there was no specific listing requirement for many of the cable-type wiring methods and their associated fittings.

- **2017 *NEC* Change**
  New listing requirements were added in a number of the cable-type wiring method articles that will require the wiring method (cable) and associated fittings to be listed.

320.6

Analysis of the Change:

Several public inputs were submitted during the 2017 *NEC* revision process which resulted in new listing requirements being incorporated into a number of the cable-type wiring method articles that will require the wiring method (cable) and associated fittings to be listed. Equipment used in electrical installations should be listed or labeled by a qualified third-party electrical products testing laboratory. Listed equipment is required to bear a listing label, and listed or labeled equipment is required be installed and used in accordance with any instructions included in the listing or labeling [see 110.3(B)]. The *Code* also requires electrical installations and equipment to be approved (110.2). The enforcement community is required to approve installations and generally base this approval on the use of listed products. The *NEC* provides additional guidance at 90.7, in that factory-installed internal wiring or the construction of equipment that is listed by a qualified electrical products testing laboratory need not be inspected at the time of installation, except to detect alterations or damage.

Many electrical inspection authorities rely heavily on labeling of equipment under the program of a qualified electrical testing laboratory. Some jurisdictions operate under law or ordinance where it is required that only listed and labeled equipment be used in a project. Other jurisdictions require listing or labeling only where such requirements are contained in the *Code* for a specific product. One of the primary roles of the inspector is to ensure that listed products are installed in accordance with the manner the product has been tested or evaluated and to ensure proper installation and use. This expectation is reason enough for the new listing requirements for several cable-type wiring methods and their associated fittings.

Listing is based on compliance with recognized product standards. Non-listed cables and associated fittings may not have been evaluated for compliance with such requirements; and in some cases, lack of such compliance may make it difficult to determine acceptance in the field. A non-listed cable-type wiring method may not function correctly with listed termination fittings. This new requirement in several cable-type wiring method articles will ensure that the cable installed in the field has been evaluated to the appropriate product standard and listed for use in accordance with *NEC* regulations.

In support of these new listing requirements, a new 110.3(C) was added in Article 110 requiring the listing process to be executed by a qualified third-party electrical testing laboratory, and that the product testing and certification process be in accordance with appropriate product standards. A new informational note was also added at 110.3(C) providing users of the *Code* with direction to the Occupational Safety and Health Administration (OSHA) website which provides a list of nationally recognized testing laboratories (NRTL).

For the 2017 *NEC*, the requirement that the wiring method (cable) and associated fittings be listed occurred at the following locations:

320.6	Type AC cable	(FR 1808, PI 1332)
322.6	Type FC cable	(FR 1801, PI 1334)
328.6	Type MV cable	(FR 1814, PI 1336)
330.6	Type MC cable	(FR 1816, PI 1337)
332.6	Type MI cable	(FR 1806, PI 1338)
334.6	Type NM, NMC, and NMS cable	(FR 1824, PI 886)
336.6	Type TC cable	(FR 1833, PI 1339)
338.6	Type SE cable	(FR 1827, PI 1341)
340.6	Type UF cable	(FR 1829, PI 887)

Type NM, NMC, NMS, and UF cable were already required to be listed, but the term "and associated fittings" was added to the listing requirements. These collective changes in the cable wiring method articles will leave only one wiring method, and its associated fittings are not required to be listed; that would be integrated gas spacer cable (Type IGS). Type IGS was intentionally excluded from the listing requirements since no product standard or methodology exists for listing this wiring method.

> First Revisions: FR 1808
> Public Inputs: PI 1332

320.6

324.12(5)

Uses Not Permitted. (Flat Conductor Cable: Type FCC)

324.12(5)

324.12(5) Uses Not Permitted. (Flat Conductor Cable: Type FCC)

- **Type of Change:** Revision

- **Change at a Glance:** Type FCC cable will now be permitted in administrative office areas of hospitals and school buildings.

- **Code Language: 324.12 Uses Not Permitted. (Flat Conductor Cable: Type FCC)**

  FCC systems shall not be used in the following locations:
  (1) Outdoors or in wet locations
  (2) Where subject to corrosive vapors
  (3) In any hazardous (classified) location
  (4) In residential, school, and hospital buildings
  (5) In school, and hospital buildings, other than administrative office areas

- **2014 *NEC* Requirement**
  Type FCC cable systems are not permitted to be used in outdoor or in wet locations, where subject to corrosive vapors, in any hazardous (classified) location or residential, school, or hospital buildings.

■ **2017 *NEC* Change**

Type FCC cable systems are still prohibited in outdoor or in wet locations, where subject to corrosive vapors, in any hazardous (classified) location, or in residential buildings. Type FCC cable is still prohibited in school and hospital buildings, but not in the "administrative office areas" of a school or hospital building.

Analysis of the Change:

Flat conductor cable (Type FCC) has been recognized as an acceptable *NEC* wiring method since the 1981 *NEC*. Type FCC cable is defined at 324.2 as "three or more flat copper conductors placed edge-to-edge and separated and enclosed within an insulating assembly." A flat conductor cable system is designed to provide a completely accessible, flexible wiring system. This type of wiring system is also designed for installation under carpet squares where the carpet squares adhere to the floor with release-type adhesives.

In previous editions of the *Code*, Type FCC cable was prohibited for use in "residential, school, and hospital buildings." While this type of wiring method is still prohibited in a residential building, revisions were made to 324.12 to continue to prohibit Type FCC cable in school and hospital buildings, but not in the "administrative office areas" of a school or hospital building.

Type FCC cable systems have been proven to be safe and reliable when installed and maintained in accordance their product specifications. Areas in a school building such as computer laboratories, administration offices, teacher lounges, reception workstations, and media centers do not present safety risks that would deter the use of Type FCC cable. Nor do non-patient care areas and non-treatment type rooms in hospitals and emergency care centers.

Today's modern workplaces encourage more collaborative interactions, which has driven design changes to the workspaces. These workspace environments required flexibility in the design of these spaces, often resulting in open room environments and using tables and desks for work surfaces. These open room designs typically have little to no access to the building's perimeter wall receptacle outlets. Providing electrical power to these spaces with Type FCC cable systems has been proven to be safe and reliable when installed and maintained in accordance with the *NEC* regulations.

Second Revisions: SR 1804
Public Input: PI 3753
Public Comments: PC 1655

324.12(5)

336.10(9)

Uses Permitted for Type TC Cable

336.10(9)

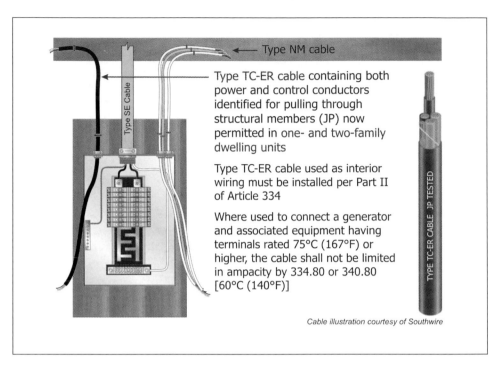

← Type NM cable

Type TC-ER cable containing both power and control conductors identified for pulling through structural members (JP) now permitted in one- and two-family dwelling units

Type TC-ER cable used as interior wiring must be installed per Part II of Article 334

Where used to connect a generator and associated equipment having terminals rated 75°C (167°F) or higher, the cable shall not be limited in ampacity by 334.80 or 340.80 [60°C (140°F)]

Type SE Cable

TYPE TC-ER CABLE JP TESTED

Cable illustration courtesy of Southwire

336.10(9) Uses Permitted. (Power and Control Tray Cable: Type TC)

- **Type of Change:** Revision and New

- **Change at a Glance:** Type TC-ER cable with a designation of "JP" will now be allowed to be installed without a raceway at dwelling units.

- **Code Language: 336.10 Uses Permitted. (Power and Control Tray Cable: Type TC)**
  Type TC cable shall be permitted to be used as follows:
  (1) For power, lighting, control, and signal circuits.
  (2) In cable trays, including those with mechanically discontinuous segments up to 300 mm (1 ft).
  (3) In raceways.
  (4) In outdoor locations supported by a messenger wire.
  (5) For Class 1 circuits as permitted in Parts II and III of Article 725.
  (6) For non–power-limited fire alarm circuits if conductors comply with the requirements of 760.49.
  (7) Between a cable tray and the utilization equipment or device(s), provided all of the following apply:
      (a) The cable is Type TC-ER.
      (b) The cable is installed in industrial establishments where the conditions of maintenance and supervision ensure that only qualified persons service the installation.

(c) The cable is continuously supported and protected against physical damage using mechanical protection such as struts, angles, or channels.

(d) The cable that complies with the crush and impact requirements of Type MC cable and is identified with the marking "TC-ER."

(e) The cable is secured at intervals not exceeding 1.8 m (6 ft).

(f) Equipment grounding for the utilization equipment ~~shall be~~ is provided by an equipment grounding conductor within the cable. In cables containing conductors sized 6 AWG or smaller, the equipment grounding conductor ~~shall~~ must be provided within the cable or, at the time of installation, one or more insulated conductors shall be permanently identified as an equipment grounding conductor in accordance with 250.119(B).

Exception to (7): Where not subject to physical damage, Type TC-ER shall be permitted to transition between cable trays and between cable trays and utilization equipment or devices for a distance not to exceed 1.8 m (6 ft) without continuous support. The cable shall be mechanically supported where exiting the cable tray to ensure that the minimum bending radius is not exceeded.

(8) Where installed in wet locations, Type TC cable shall also be resistant to moisture and corrosive agents.

(9) In one- and two-family dwelling units, Type TC-ER cable containing both power and control conductors that is identified for pulling through structural members shall be permitted. Type TC-ER cable used as interior wiring shall be installed per the requirements of Part II of Article 334.

Exception: *Where used to connect a generator and associated equipment having terminals rated 75°C (167°F) or higher, the cable shall not be limited in ampacity by 334.80 or 340.80.*

Informational Note No. 1: TC-ER cable that is suitable for pulling through structural members is marked "JP."

Informational Note No. 2: See 725.136 for limitations on Class 2 or 3 circuits contained within the same cable with conductors of electric light, power, or Class 1 circuits.

(10) Direct buried, ~~unless~~ where identified for such use. (*was located in "Uses Not Permitted"*)

Informational Note: See 310.15(A)(3) for temperature limitation of conductors

336.10(9)

■ **2014 *NEC* Requirement**
There were 7 different list items under "Uses Permitted" for Type TC cables in Article 336. None of these included permission to use Type TC or Type TC-ER as a wiring method at one- and two-family dwelling units.

■ **2017 *NEC* Change**

There are now 11 different list items under "Uses Permitted" for Type TC cable. New List Item (9) now permits Type TC-ER cable containing both power and control conductors that are identified for pulling through structural members to be installed in one- and two-family dwelling units.

Analysis of the Change:

Section 336.2 defines Power and Control Tray Cable (Type TC) as "a factory assembly of two or more insulated conductors, with or without associated bare or covered grounding conductors, under a nonmetallic jacket." This type of wiring method has been recognized since the 1975 *NEC*. Type TC cable is typically used to supply power to motors or loads in industrial settings. A typical installation for Type TC cable might include installation in cable trays, raceways, and outdoor locations where supported by a messenger wire. Type TC cable can be listed and identified for direct burial and used in Class 1, Division 2 hazardous locations and Class 1 control circuits.

For the 2017 *NEC*, Type TC-ER cable containing both power and control conductors that are identified for pulling through structural members has been added to "Uses Permitted" for installations in one- and two-family dwelling units. Type TC-ER cable used as interior wiring would have to be installed in accordance with the requirements of Part II of Article 334 for nonmetallic-sheathed cable (Type NM cable).

The "-ER" suffix stands for "Exposed Run." If Type TC cable meets certain additional crush and impact test requirements, the product standard (UL 1277) permits the manufacturer to add an "-ER" suffix to the basic listing printed on the cable, i.e., TC-ER. Once a Type TC cable is marked with this "-ER" rating, it is deemed durable enough to be used as exposed wiring. This rating means that Type TC-ER cable is allowed additional flexibility of installation, including certain allowances for use outside cable tray in industrial settings and the new allowance for installation in residential applications. Type TC-ER cable that is used in these residential applications must be identified for pulling through structural members and be marked "JP" (Joist Pull).

Type TC-ER cable meets the construction specifications in Part III of Article 334.100, 334.108, 334.112, and 334.116 for nonmetallic-sheathed cable (Type NM cable). Type TC-ER cable meets or exceeds the UL product standard crush and impact ratings for Type NM cable and Types SE and SER cable. Type TC-ER cable has to pass the same UL crush and impact tests as Type MC cable. This type of cable has gained popularity when installing a standby power generator at a dwelling unit. By allowing Type TC-ER cable to be installed exposed in a dwelling unit, the installer can secure the cable to the lower side of joists in unfinished basements or crawl spaces without installing a raceway for the cable.

A new exception will allow connection to a generator and associated equipment having terminals rated 75°C (167°F) or higher without being limited to the 60°C (140°F) limitations of ampacity by 334.80 or 340.80.

336.10(9)

First Revisions: FR 1840
Second Revisions: SR 1808
Public Input: PI 1116, PI 4359
Public Comments: PC 12, PC 1739, PC 763, PC 1796

344.14

Dissimilar Metals: Type RMC

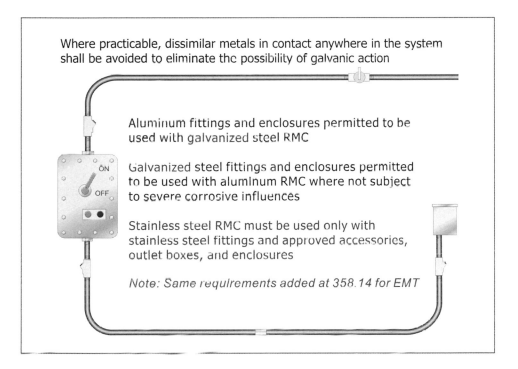

Where practicable, dissimilar metals in contact anywhere in the system shall be avoided to eliminate the possibility of galvanic action

Aluminum fittings and enclosures permitted to be used with galvanized steel RMC

Galvanized steel fittings and enclosures permitted to be used with aluminum RMC where not subject to severe corrosive influences

Stainless steel RMC must be used only with stainless steel fittings and approved accessories, outlet boxes, and enclosures

Note: Same requirements added at 358.14 for EMT

344.14

344.14 Dissimilar Metals. (Rigid Metal Conduit: Type RMC)

- **Type of Change:** Revision

- **Change at a Glance:** Stainless steel RMC must be used only with stainless steel fittings, approved accessories, outlet boxes, and enclosures.

- **Code Language: 344.14 Dissimilar Metals. (Rigid Metal Conduit: Type RMC)**
  Where practicable, dissimilar metals in contact anywhere in the system shall be avoided to eliminate the possibility of galvanic action. Aluminum fittings and enclosures shall be permitted to be used with galvanized steel RMC, and galvanized steel fittings and enclosures shall be permitted to be used with aluminum RMC where not subject to severe corrosive influences. Stainless steel RMC shall only be used with stainless steel fittings and approved accessories, outlet boxes, and enclosures.

- **2014 *NEC* Requirement**

  Where dissimilar metals and metallic raceways are concerned, contact between dissimilar metals anywhere in the system should be avoided to eliminate the possibility of galvanic action. Aluminum fittings and enclosures are permitted to be used with steel RMC, and steel fittings and enclosures are permitted to be used with aluminum RMC where not subject to severe corrosive influences. Stainless steel RMC was not mentioned at 344.14.

- **2017 *NEC* Change**

  Revisions occurred at 344.14 to clarify the acceptable fittings that can be used with different types of RMC, based on galvanic compatibility. With this revision, stainless steel RMC can only be used with stainless steel fittings, approved accessories, stainless steel outlet boxes, and stainless steel enclosures.

344.14

Analysis of the Change:

Dissimilar metals and alloys have different electrode potentials. When two or more dissimilar metals come into contact in an electrolyte, one metal acts as the anode (an electrode through which conventional current flows into a polarized electrical device) and the other as a cathode (the electrode from which a conventional current leaves a polarized electrical device). The electro-potential difference between the dissimilar metals is the driving force for an accelerated attack on the anodic member of the galvanic couple. The anode metal dissolves into the electrolyte and deposit collects on the cathodic metal. A galvanic action or corrosion is an electrochemical process in which one metal corrodes preferentially to another when both metals are in electrical contact, in the presence of an electrolyte. This same galvanic reaction is exploited in primary batteries to generate an electrical voltage.

344.14 was revised for the 2017 *NEC* to address dissimilar metals with rigid metal conduit (RMC) and to clarify the acceptable fittings that can be used with different types of RMC, based on galvanic compatibility. With this revision, stainless steel RMC can only be used with stainless steel fittings, approved accessories, stainless steel outlet boxes, and stainless steel enclosures.

Stainless steel RMC is more self-sacrificing (or cathodic) than aluminum RMC, and it is considerably more susceptible to the galvanic effect than steel and zinc (galvanized steel) RMC. Stainless steel RMC is subject to a more aggressive galvanic attack in the presence of an electrolyte. Stainless steel RMC used with aluminum or galvanized fittings, accessories, outlet boxes and enclosures could result in galvanic action, leading to corrosion.

It should be noted that these same revisions occurred at 358.14 for electrical metallic tubing (EMT) (see FR 2142, PI 2877).

First Revision: FR 2137
Public Inputs: PI 2875

350.28

Trimming of LFMC

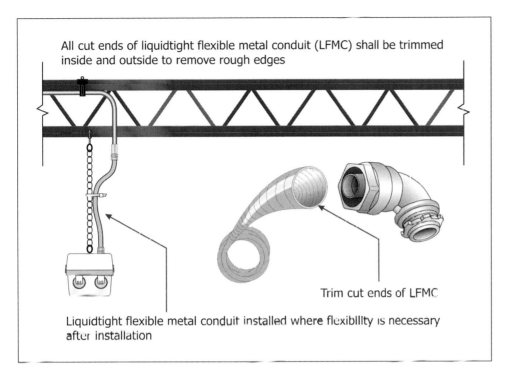

All cut ends of liquidtight flexible metal conduit (LFMC) shall be trimmed inside and outside to remove rough edges

Trim cut ends of LFMC

Liquidtight flexible metal conduit installed where flexibility is necessary after installation

350.28

350.28 Trimming. (Liquidtight Flexible Metal Conduit. Type LFMC)

- **Type of Change:** New

- **Change at a Glance:** Cut ends of LFMC shall be trimmed inside and outside to remove rough edges. This requirement will provide consistency between Article 350 and Article 356 (LFNC).

- **Code Language: 350.28 Trimming. (Liquidtight Flexible Metal Conduit: Type LFMC)**
  All cut ends of conduit shall be trimmed inside and outside to remove rough edges.

- **2014 *NEC* Requirement**
  Requirements were in place at ".28" of seven different articles, requiring that all cut ends of conduits be trimmed inside and outside to remove rough edges. This requirement was absent in Article 350 for liquidtight flexible metal conduit (Type LFMC).

- **2017 *NEC* Change**
  Language was added at 350.28 requiring cut ends of LFMC to be trimmed inside and outside to remove rough edges.

Analysis of the Change:

A new provision was added to Article 350 for liquidtight flexible metal conduit (Type LFMC) that will require all cut ends of LFMC to be trimmed inside and outside to remove rough edges. This new requirement for trimming can be found at 350.28 and is meant to provide consistency between Article 350 and Article 356 [Liquidtight Flexible Nonmetallic Conduit (Type LFMC)]. Trimming of Type LFMC is necessary to allow the proper installation of the steel grounding ferrule, which is important to maintain ground continuity of the steel sheath of Type LFMC.

Let's take a historical look at this 2017 *NEC* requirement. In the 1999 *NEC* and earlier, the installation requirements and construction specifications for Type LFMC and Type LFNC were both located in Article 351. During the 2002 *NEC* revision cycle, a proposal was submitted and accepted that would put this same trimming requirement (word for word) in the combined article for Type LFMC and Type LFNC (see 2001 ROC 8-362). At the same time, a proposal was submitted and accepted to give each of these two different wiring methods individual articles in the 2002 *NEC* (see 2001 ROP 8-327). This new proposed requirement for trimming conduits followed the existing requirements for Type LFNC to their new home in Article 356. Even though this trimming of the ends of cut conduits requirement would have applied (as intended) to both wiring methods, no similar trimming requirement joined the requirements for Type LFMC at its new home at Article 350. Fifteen years and five *Code* cycles later, this unintended oversight will be rectified.

Also interesting is the substantiation for the original proposal during the 2002 *NEC Code* cycle, which stated (in part), "Cut ends should be trimmed to prevent chafing of pulled conductors. Also, this article should be consistent with the requirements of articles covering similar raceways (e.g., Article 331)." This same trimming requirement is currently located at:

348.28 (Flexible Metal Conduit: Type FMC)
352.28 (Rigid Polyvinyl Chloride Conduit: Type PVC)
353.28 (High Density Polyethylene Conduit: Type HDPE Conduit)
354.28 (Nonmetallic Underground Conduit with Conductors: Type NUCC)
355.28 (Reinforced Thermosetting Resin Conduit: Type RTRC)
356.28 (Liquidtight Flexible Nonmetallic Conduit: Type LFNC), and
362.28 (Electrical Nonmetallic Tubing: Type ENT).

A very similar requirement for "reaming" of a metal conduit is located at 342.28 (Intermediate Metal Conduit: Type IMC), 344.28 (Rigid Metal Conduit: Type RMC), and 358.28(A) (Electrical Metallic Tubing: Type EMT).

First Revisions: FR 2169
Public Inputs: PI 2482

350.28

358.10

Uses Permitted. (Electrical Metallic Tubing: Type EMT)

358.10 Uses Permitted. (Electrical Metallic Tubing: Type EMT)

- ■ **Type of Change:** Revision

- ■ **Change at a Glance:** The "Uses Permitted" for EMT have been revised for consistency with other steel conduit articles (Type IMC and RMC).

- ■ **Code Language: 358.10 Uses Permitted. (Electrical Metallic Tubing: Type EMT)**

  (A) Exposed and Concealed. The use of EMT shall be permitted for both exposed and concealed work for the following:
  (1) In concrete, in direct contact with the earth or in areas subject to severe corrosive influences where installed in accordance with 358.10(B)
  (2) In dry, damp, and wet locations
  (3) In any hazardous (classified) location ~~except~~ as permitted by other articles in this *Code* (Was in "Uses Not Permitted")

  (B) Corrosion ~~Protection~~ Environments.
  (1) Galvanized Steel and Stainless Steel EMT, Elbows, and Fittings. ~~Ferrous or nonferrous~~ Galvanized steel and stainless steel EMT, elbows, ~~couplings~~, and fittings shall be permitted to be installed in concrete, in direct contact with the earth, or in areas subject to severe corro-

sive influences where protected by corrosion protection and approved as suitable for the condition.

(2) Supplementary Protection of Aluminum EMT. Aluminum EMT shall be provided with approved supplementary corrosion protection where encased in concrete or in direct contact with the earth.

(C) Cinder Fill. Galvanized steel and stainless steel EMT shall be permitted to be installed in cinder concrete or cinder fill where subject to permanent moisture ~~unless~~ when protected on all sides by a layer of non-cinder concrete at least 50 mm (2 in.) thick or when ~~unless~~ the tubing is installed at least 450 mm (18 in.) under the fill. (Was in "Uses Not Permitted")

(D) Wet Locations. All supports, bolts, straps, screws, and so forth shall be of corrosion-resistant materials or protected against corrosion by corrosion-resistant materials.

Informational Note: See 300.6 for protection against corrosion.

358.10

- **2014 *NEC* Requirement**
  "Uses Permitted" for EMT permitted the use of EMT in both exposed and concealed locations. Ferrous (steel) or nonferrous (aluminum) EMT, elbows, couplings, and fittings were permitted to be installed in concrete, in direct contact with the earth, or in areas subject to severe corrosive influences where protected by corrosion protection and approved as suitable for the condition. All supports, bolts, straps, screws, etc., had to be made of corrosion-resistant materials or protected against corrosion by corrosion-resistant materials when installed in a wet location. Under the banner of "Uses Not Permitted," EMT was permitted to be installed in cinder concrete or cinder fill where subject to permanent moisture when it was protected on all sides by a layer of non-cinder concrete at least 50 mm (2 in.) thick or if the tubing was at least 450 mm (18 in.) under the fill. EMT was prohibited to be installed in any hazardous (classified) location "except as permitted by other articles in the *NEC*."

- **2017 *NEC* Change**
  Section 358.10 for "Uses Permitted" for EMT was revised for consistency with other steel conduit articles. The requirements for installations in cinder concrete and hazardous (classified) locations for EMT were moved from 358.12 for "Uses Not Permitted" for EMT and reworded into positive text. Provisions for stainless steel EMT were also added to 358.10.

Analysis of the Change:

Electrical metallic tubing (EMT) is an unthreaded, thin-wall raceway of circular cross section designed for the physical protection and routing of conductors and cables and use as an equipment grounding conductor when installed utilizing appropriate fittings. EMT is made of steel (ferrous) with protective coatings or aluminum (nonferrous).

As for as the permitted uses for EMT, 358.10 (Uses Permitted) has been revised for consistency with other steel conduit articles such as Article 342 (Intermediate Metal Conduit: Type IMC) and Article 344 (Rigid Metal Conduit: Type RMC). Some requirements or "uses" for EMT were moved from 358.12 (Uses Not Permitted) and reworded using positive language. Provisions for stainless steel EMT were also added to 358.10 as stainless steel EMT is covered by UL797 (Electrical Metallic Tubing – Steel), the EMT product standard.

New text was added to (B)(1) and (2) to clarify the use of galvanized steel, stainless steel, and aluminum EMT in corrosive environments and installations in concrete, similar to the text allowed for RMC. According to UL 797, "EMT is provided with zinc, zinc-based, nonmetallic, or other alternate corrosion-resistant exterior coating and an organic or zinc interior coating. It is the users' responsibility to determine the appropriate product for their application." The UL Directory (White Book) states the following for EMT: "Galvanized steel electrical metallic tubing installed in concrete on grade or above generally requires no supplementary corrosion protection. Galvanized steel electrical metallic tubing in concrete slab below grade level may require supplementary corrosion protection."

Manufacturers of steel conduit apply a zinc coating to galvanized steel RMC, IMC, and EMT. With the zinc coating, these products are "protected by corrosion protection" as required by the *NEC*. In severe corrosive environments, the designer or AHJ may decide to require additional or supplementary protection. If supplementary corrosion protection is required or desired, it can be provided by a factory-applied PVC coating, paint approved for the purpose, or tape wraps approved for the application. When steel conduit/EMT emerges from concrete into soil, the Steel Tube Institute recommends that supplementary corrosion protection is applied a minimum of 100 mm (4 in.) on each side of the point where the conduit or EMT emerges.

358.10

First Revisions: FR 2144
Second Revisions: SR 2102
Public Inputs: PI 2975
Public Comments: PC 445

366.20

Parallel Conductors in Auxiliary Gutters

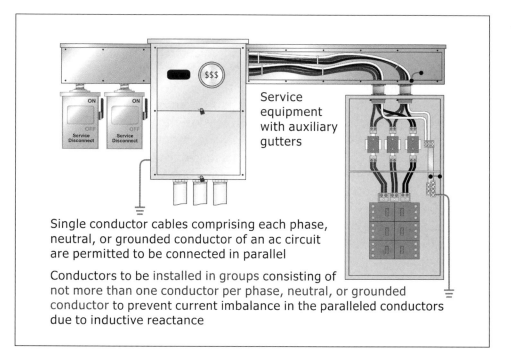

Service equipment with auxiliary gutters

Single conductor cables comprising each phase, neutral, or grounded conductor of an ac circuit are permitted to be connected in parallel

Conductors to be installed in groups consisting of not more than one conductor per phase, neutral, or grounded conductor to prevent current imbalance in the paralleled conductors due to inductive reactance

366.20 in left margin box.

366.20 Conductors Connected in Parallel

- **Type of Change:** New

- **Change at a Glance:** Language was added to address how to install conductors in parallel in an auxiliary gutter.

- **Code Language: 366.20 Conductors Connected in Parallel.**
  Where single conductor cables comprising each phase, neutral, or grounded conductor of an alternating-current circuit are connected in parallel as permitted in 310.10(H), the conductors shall be installed in groups consisting of not more than one conductor per phase, neutral, or grounded conductor to prevent current imbalance in the paralleled conductors due to inductive reactance.

- **2014 *NEC* Requirement**
  No provisions or guidance was given for the installation of parallel conductors in an auxiliary gutter. Parallel conductor installation requirement for conduits and raceways is found at 310.10(H) and for a cable tray at 392.20(C).

- **2017 *NEC* Change**
  The new requirements were added at 366.20 for the safe and proper installation of parallel conductors in an auxiliary gutter.

Analysis of the Change:

An auxiliary gutter is defined as a sheet metal enclosure (metallic auxiliary gutter) or a flame-retardant, nonmetallic enclosure (nonmetallic auxiliary gutter) used to supplement wiring spaces at meter centers, distribution centers, switchgear, switchboards, and similar points of wiring systems. These enclosures have hinged or removable covers for housing and protecting electrical wires, cable, and busbars. An auxiliary gutter is designed for conductors to be laid or set in place after the enclosures have been installed as a complete system (see 366.2).

Prior to the 2017 *NEC*, there were no provisions in Article 366 (which covers auxiliary gutters) pertaining to the proper procedures for installing conductors in parallel in an auxiliary gutter. Documented failures of paralleled conductors have occurred when these conductors were installed in wireways and auxiliary gutters and were not grouped together; this led to overheating and insulation breakdown due to the induction process. Induction heating is the process of heating an electrically conducting object (in this case, a conductor) by electromagnetic induction, through heat generated in the object by eddy currents (also called Foucault currents). Electromagnetic induction is the production of an electromotive force across a conductor exposed to time varying magnetic fields.

One of the primary concerns when installing conductors in parallel is ensuring that each conductor in the paralleled set has the same electrical characteristics as the others in the same set. The requirements for installing conductors in parallel can be found at 310.10(H), which states in part that all of the paralleled conductors in each phase and the neutral (or grounded conductor) set must be the same length and be made from the same conductor material. These paralleled conductors must be the same circular mil area and have the same type of insulation. All parallel conductors must be terminated in the same manner as well. This process ensures that each conductor in the parallel set will carry the same amount of current.

If parallel conductors are installed with different characteristics, some of the conductors are going to carry more or different current than the other conductors. Some of these conductors with different characteristics will offer more impedance than the other conductors. The conductors with higher current would result in possible overheating of the conductor and insulation damage.

The new requirements at 366.20 for installing parallel conductors in an auxiliary gutter will result in each paralleled phase conductor being the same length and the proper grouping of the different phases in relation to one another, which can reduce inductive overheating and result in a more balanced load between each conductor of a paralleled phase. This new requirement will result in single conductors from each phase, neutral or grounded conductor in a paralleled configuration installed in groups consisting of not more than one conductor per phase, neutral or grounded conductor. Each of these groups should have a single conductor from each phase (such as Phase A, B, C) and one from the neutral (or grounded) conductor. Each group of conductors should be installed with sufficient air gaps between each bundled group to ensure proper air circulation and subsequent cooling.

366.20

These parallel conductor requirements for auxiliary gutters added at 366.20 already exist for cable trays and can be found at 392.20(C). This same parallel conductor requirement is also being added at 376.20 for metal wireways (see FR 2182 and PI 4497) and at 378.20 for nonmetallic wireways (see FR 2106 and PI 4503).

First Revisions: FR 2179
Public Input: PI 4490

370.80

Ampacity of Conductors. (Cablebus)

370.80

This change is subject to a decision by NFPA's Standard Council.

See Appeal No. 70-13

Photo Courtesy of Power Bus Way

370.80 Ampacity of Conductors. (Cablebus)

- **Type of Change:** Revision and New

- **Change at a Glance:** Additional information was added to provide clarity for the allowable ampacities for cables installed in cablebus assemblies (Article 370) and align ampacities with cable tray installations (Article 392).

- **Code Language: 370.80 Ampacity of Conductors. (Cablebus)**

(A) Ampacity of Single Insulated Conductors. The ampacity of conductors in cablebus shall be in accordance with Table 310.15(B)(17) and Table 310.15(B)(19) for installations up to and including 2000 volts, or with Table 310.60(C)(69) and Table 310.60(C)(70) for installations 2001 to 35,000 volts.

(B) Ampacity of Cables Rated 2000 Volts or Less. In cablebus that terminates at equipment with conductor temperature limitations, the allowable ampacity of single-conductor cables shall be as permitted by 310.15(A)(2). The adjustment factors of 310.15(B)(3) (a) shall not apply to the ampacity of cables in cablebus. The ampacity of single-conductor cables, nominally rated 2000 volts or less, shall comply with the following:

(1) The ampacities for 600 kcmil and larger single conductor cables in ventilated cablebus shall not exceed 75 percent of the allowable ampacities in Table 310.15(B)(17) and Table 310.15(B)(19).

(2) Where cablebus are continuously covered for more than 1.8 m (6 ft) with solid unventilated covers, the ampacities for 600 kcmil and larger cables shall not exceed 70 percent of the allowable ampacities in Table 310.15(B)(17) and Table 310.15(B)(19).

(3) The ampacities for 1/0 AWG through 500 kcmil single conductor cables in ventilated cablebus shall not exceed 65 percent of the allowable ampacities in Table 310.15(B)(17) and Table 310.15(B)(19).

(4) Where cablebus are continuously covered for more than 1.8 m (6 ft) with solid unventilated covers, the ampacities for 1/0 AWG through 500 kcmil cables shall not exceed 60 percent of the allowable ampacities in Table 310.15(B)(17) and Table 310.15(B)(19).

(C) Ampacity of Type MV and Type MC Cables Rated 2001 Volts or Over. The ampacity of Type MV and Type MC cables, nominally rated 2001 volts or over, in cablebus shall comply with the following.

(1) The ampacities for 1/0 AWG and larger single-conductor cables in ventilated cablebus shall not exceed 75 percent of the allowable ampacities in Table 310.60(C)(69) and Table 310.60(C)(70).

(2) Where the cablebus are covered for more than 1.8 m (6 ft) with solid unventilated covers, the ampacities for 1/0 AWG and larger single-conductor cables shall not exceed 70 percent of the allowable ampacities in Table 310.60(C)(69) and Table 310.60(C)(70).

Informational Note No. 1: See 110.14(C) for conductor temperature limitations due to termination provisions for installations up to and including 2000 volts.

Informational Note No. 2: See 110.40 for conductor temperature limitations due to termination provisions for installations 2001 to 35,000 volts.

370.80

■ **2014 *NEC* Requirement**
Under the requirements of 370.80, the ampacity of conductors in cablebus comply with Table 310.15(B)(17) and Table 310.15(B)(19) for installations up to and including 2000 volts, or with Table 310.60(C)(69) and

Table 310.60(C)(70) for installations 2001 to 35,000 volts. Without a thorough knowledge of the *NEC*, no link was provided in Article 370 to the conductor termination provisions found in Article 110. No allowances were found in Article 370 for temperature and ampacity correction factors for conductors installed in a cablebus.

■ **2017 *NEC* Change**
With the same requirements for ampacity tables to use with cablebus remaining, new requirements have been added for ampacities of typical cablebus that align with the same requirements for single conductors installed in a cable tray. New informational notes will direct users of Article 370 back to the conductor termination requirements of 110.14(C) and 110.40.

370.80

Analysis of the Change:

A cablebus is defined as "an assembly of units or sections with insulated conductors having associated fittings forming a structural system used to fasten securely or support conductors and conductor terminations in a completely enclosed, ventilated, protective metal housing. This assembly is designed to carry fault current and to withstand the magnetic forces of such current" (see 370.2). Typical uses for cablebus would be in conjunction with things like service entrance applications, primary and secondary feeders, large generators and/or transformers, switchgear, motor control centers and large motors.

A cablebus system is typically assembled at the installation site from components supplied by the manufacturer in accordance with installation drawings and specifications provided for the specific project. Components for a complete cablebus system can include items such as straight sections, fittings, support blocks, covers, splice plates, hardware, equipment/environmental seals, tap boxes, single conductor cables, electrical compression connectors, termination kits, and other required accessories.

When installing, designing, and utilizing cablebus and applying the requirement of 370.80, users of the *Code* often don't realize or know that the requirements in 110.14(C) (electrical connection temperature limitations) and 110.40 (temperature limitations at terminals for over 1000 volts, nominal) apply to these installations. These termination limitations can and often do result in a requirement for larger conductors. An example of this would be when 90°C (194°F) conductors terminate on equipment with a temperature limitation of 75°C (167°F).

Revisions and new text have been incorporated into the requirements at 370.80 that will align ampacities of typical cablebus with the same requirements located at 392.80 for single conductors installed in a cable tray and removes any inconsistencies between the two wiring methods.

First Revisions: FR 2154
Second Revisions: SR 2110
Public Inputs: PI 1593
Public Comments: PC 635

Equipment For

Chapter 4

General Use

Articles 404 – 480

404.2(C)

Switch Connections

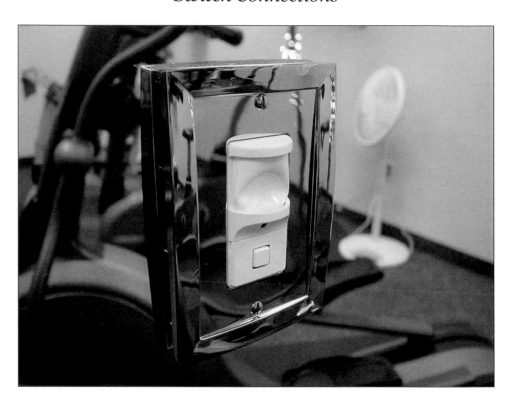

404.2(C) **Switch Connections**

- **Type of Change:** Revision

- **Change at a Glance:** Revisions clarified that a grounded conductor of the lighting circuit at switch locations shall be connected to the electronic device.

- **Code Language: 210.6 Branch-Circuit Voltage Limitations**.

  (C) Switches Controlling Lighting Loads. The grounded circuit conductor for the controlled lighting circuit shall be ~~provided~~ installed at the location where switches control lighting loads that are supplied by a grounded general-purpose branch circuit serving bathrooms, hallways, stairways, or rooms suitable for human habitation or occupancy as defined in the applicable building code. Where multiple switch locations control the same lighting load such that the entire floor area of the room or space is visible from the single or combined switch locations, the grounded circuit conductor shall only be required at one location. ~~for other than the following~~ A grounded conductor shall not be required to be installed at lighting switch locations under any of the following conditions:

(1) Where conductors enter the box enclosing the switch through a raceway, provided that the raceway is large enough for all contained conductors, including a grounded conductor

(2) Where the box enclosing the switch is accessible for the installation of an additional or replacement cable without removing finish materials

(3) Where snap switches with integral enclosures comply with 300.15(E)

(4) Where a switch does not serve a habitable room or bathroom [moved to parent text of 404.2(C)]

(5) Where multiple switch locations control the same lighting load such that the entire floor area of the room or space is visible from the single or combined switch locations [moved to parent text of 404.2(C)]

(6) (4) Where lighting in the area is controlled by automatic means

(7) (5) Where a switch controls a receptacle load
The grounded conductor shall be extended to any switch location as necessary and shall be connected to switching devices that require line-to-neutral voltage to operate the electronics of the switch in the standby mode and shall meet the requirements of 404.22.

Exception: The connection requirement shall become effective on January 1, 2020. It shall not apply to replacement or retrofit switches installed in locations prior to local adoption of 404.2(C) and where the grounded conductor cannot be extended without removing finish materials. The number of electronic lighting control switches on a branch circuit shall not exceed five, and the number connected to any feeder on the load side of a system or main bonding jumper shall not exceed 25. For the purpose of this exception, a neutral busbar, in compliance with 200.2(B) and to which a main or system bonding jumper is connected shall not be limited as to the number of electronic lighting control switches connected.

Informational Note: The provision for a (future) grounded conductor is to complete a circuit path for electronic lighting control devices.

■ **2014 *NEC* Requirement**
A grounded conductor is required at every location where switches control lighting loads supplied by a grounded general purpose branch circuit. This main rule was followed by seven specific conditions by which a grounded conductor was not required to be installed at a switch location.

The first condition permitted the grounded circuit conductor to be omitted from the switch enclosure where the wiring method employed was a raceway system with sufficient cross-sectional area that would allow the grounded conductor to be added to the switch location at a later date when and if needed.

404.2(C)

The second condition dealt with cable assemblies entering the switch box through a framing cavity that allowed for the installation of an additional or replacement cable without removing finish materials.

The third condition referenced snap switches with integral enclosures that comply with 300.15(E) where the enclosure itself would only accept the associated snap switch.

The fourth condition exempted rooms other than habitable rooms or bathrooms.

The fifth condition limited the presence of the grounded conductor to only one switch location where multiple switch locations control the same lighting load such that the entire floor area of the room or space is visible from the single or combined switch locations.

The sixth condition dealt with switch locations where lighting in the area is controlled by automatic means as an occupancy sensor switching device would be redundant.

404.2(C)

The seventh condition involved a switch controlling a receptacle load as no occupancy sensor will likely ever be listed for use with receptacle outlets, there is no need for a grounded conductor at this switch location.

■ **2017 *NEC* Change**
The previous seven conditions in which a grounded conductor was not required to be installed at lighting switch locations has been revised and reduced to only five conditions.

Previous conditions (4) and (5) were moved to the parent text of 404.2(C) and reworded into positive language. Enforceable language was added to require the grounded conductor to be connected and used by the switching device rather than simply be "present" at the switch enclosure.

A new exception was also added to exclude replacement or retrofit switches installed in locations before the local adoption of 404.2(C) where the grounded conductor cannot be extended without removing finish materials. This new exception also puts a limit to the number of electronic lighting control switches on a branch circuit or feeder.

Analysis of the Change:
The odyssey of requiring a grounded conductor at every switch location where switches control lighting loads supplied by a grounded general purpose branch circuit (with conditions and exception) began with the 2011 edition of the *NEC*. The concept from the beginning for requiring the presence and use of the grounded conductor at switch locations was due primarily to the increased demand for electronic lighting control devices (such as an occupancy sensor). These electronic lighting control devices require a standby current to maintain a ready state of detection for the function of these devices. These devices typically require standby

current even when they are in the "off" position. When the grounded conductor is not present, installers have been known to employ the equipment grounding conductor for the standby current of these control devices.

There are existing listed electronic lighting control devices readily available on the market that direct the installer to utilize the "green" or bare equipment-grounding conductor for connection to the device to act as the grounded conductor to power the electronics with 120 volts. This information is included in the manufacturer's instructions for these devices. This direction puts inspectors and electrical contractors alike in a dilemma when electronic lighting control devices are still being supplied that not only permit but require the equipment grounding conductor to be connected to the device to power the electronics with line voltage. From the inception of 404.2(C), CMP-9 intended to begin a process that would ultimately result in no current being introduced intentionally onto the equipment grounding conductor system due to the installation of electronic switching devices, such as an occupancy sensor. The equipment-grounding conductor should not be used to complete this circuit under any circumstance.

The latest attempt to eliminate this intentionally introduced current onto the equipment grounding conductor resulted in further revisions to 404.2(C) for the 2017 *NEC*. One of the first changes was in response to the indication that 404.2(C) required a grounding conductor to be "present" at switch locations, but did not demand that the supplied grounded conductor be used or "connected" to the switching device. To that end, the first sentence at 404.2(C) was revised to state that the grounded circuit conductor be "installed" at the switch locations rather than simply "provided." New more direct text was added further down in the requirement to state, "the grounded conductor shall be extended to any switch location as necessary and shall be connected to switching devices that require line-to-neutral voltage to operate the electronics of the switch in the standby mode."

404.2(C)

This requirement references 404.22, which is a new section under Part II of Article 404 for the "Construction Specifications" for a switching device. This new section addresses the fact that electronic lighting control switches must be listed and "shall not introduce current on the equipment grounding conductor during normal operation." This requirement has a future effective date of January 1, 2020. This requirement at 404.22 will be discussed in further detail in an analysis report later in this periodical.

The previously discussed grounded conductor connection requirement has an added exception that will delay enforcement until January 1, 2020. This exception further relieves this connection requirement from "replacement or retrofit switches installed in locations prior to local adoption of 404.2(C) and where the grounded conductor cannot be extended without removing finish materials." This exception will allow some continuation of older designs, which is warranted for replacement or retrofit installations in existing or previous applications.

This new exception goes on to limit the actual number of electronic lighting control switches on a branch circuit to "not exceed 5," and the number connected to any feeder on the load side of a system or main bonding jumper to "not exceed 25." Neutral current of 0.5 mA is the acceptable amount of current tolerance allowed by manufacturers of devices such as an appliance that can be allowed to flow over an equipment grounding return path and continue to be used safely. Using this 0.5 mA value, five electronic lighting control switches (listed to permit the equipment grounding conductor for neutral load connection) would be limited to the worst-case neutral current that the equipment grounding system would be expected to carry to 2.5 mA on branch circuit conductors, and 12.5 mA on feeder conductors. These electronic lighting control switches have been used for decades with no reported loss experience, but as they continue to increase in demand, ever-increasing neutral current loading will be imposed on an equipment grounding conductor system that is not, and never will be, designed for routing neutral load current.

Finally, the previous seven "conditions" in which a grounded conductor was not required to be installed at lighting switch locations have been revised and reduced to only five conditions. Two of the previous conditions were moved to the parent text of 404.2(C) and reworded into positive language. This revision clarifies where the grounded conductor is required or not required to be included. A grounded conductor is required at switch locations where general-purpose branch circuits serve "bathrooms, hallways, stairways, or rooms suitable for human habitation or occupancy as defined in the applicable building code." A *habitable space* is defined in both structural and residential building codes as: "A space in a building for living, sleeping, eating or cooking." This definition should make it clear that a grounded conductor is not required at switch locations, such a snap switch or "door-jam" switch for closet lighting since a closet is not considered "habitable space," and an electronic lighting control device such as an occupancy sensor is extremely unlikely, if not impossible, to be installed in those locations.

Office spaces are typically described as "occupancies" in the applicable building codes and not as "habitable space." The revised wording will clarify that these commercial occupancies are also under the umbrella of this grounded conductor at switch location requirement. While applying to both, the limitation on the actual number of electronic lighting control switches on a branch circuit or feeder previously discussed is geared more toward a commercial occupancy than a dwelling unit.

First Revisions: FR 2416
Second Revisions: SR 2408, SCR 54
Public Inputs: PI 4648, PI 4363, PI 449, PI 1375, PI 4000
Public Comments: PC 463, PC 948, PC 504

404.2(C)

404.22

Branch-Circuit Voltage Limitations

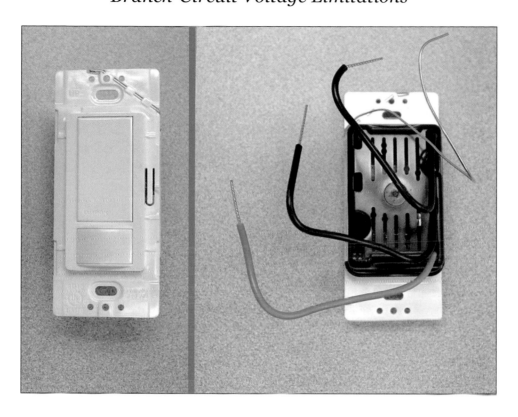

404.22

404.22 Branch-Circuit Voltage Limitations

- **Type of Change:** New

- **Change at a Glance:** New provisions were added for "Electronic Lighting Controlled Switches" prohibiting current on the equipment grounding conductor with a future effective date.

- **Code Language: 404.22 Electronic Lighting Control Switches.** Electronic lighting control switches shall be listed. Electronic lighting control switches shall not introduce current on the equipment grounding conductor during normal operation. The requirement to not introduce current on the equipment grounding conductor shall take effect on January 1, 2020.

  Exception: Electronic lighting control switches that introduce current on the equipment grounding conductor shall be permitted for applications covered by 404.2(C), Exception. Electronic lighting control switches that introduce current on the equipment grounding conductor shall be listed and marked for use in replacement or retrofit applications only.

- **2014 *NEC* Requirement**
  This provision did not exist in the 2014 *NEC*. A grounded conductor was required to be installed at switching locations where switches control lighting loads supplied by a grounded general-purpose branch circuit by the requirements of 404.2(C). This rule had seven conditions where the grounded conductor did not have to be present, but had no requirement for the switching device to be listed or prohibit intentionally introduced current onto the equipment grounding system as a result of the installation of electronic switching devices such as an occupancy sensor.

- **2017 *NEC* Change**
  In conjunction with revisions to 404.2(C), new text was added at 404.22 stating that electronic lighting control switching devices are required to be listed and "shall not introduce current on the equipment grounding conductor during normal operation." This prohibition on introducing current on the equipment grounding conductor has a future effective date of January 1, 2020.

Analysis of the Change:

A new section for electronic lighting control switching devices was added to Article 404, Part II, "Construction Specifications." This section is a companion piece to 404.2(C), which requires the grounded circuit conductor for the controlled lighting circuit to be installed at the location where switches control lighting loads that are supplied by a grounded general-purpose branch circuit. This new section at 404.22 addresses the fact that electronic lighting control switches must be listed and "shall not introduce current on the equipment grounding conductor during normal operation." This requirement has a future effective date of January 1, 2020, as well.

When CMP-9 initiated 404.2(C) in the 2011 *NEC*, the intent was to begin a process that would ultimately result in no current being introduced intentionally onto the equipment grounding system as a result of the installation of electronic switching devices such as an occupancy sensor.

Currently, readily available existing listed electronic lighting control switching devices come with two (2) "black" power leads (one for the ungrounded or "hot" supply conductor, and one for the "switch leg" conductor for the lighting load). These switching devices also come with one bare lead intended to be connected to the supply equipment grounding conductor, and one "green" lead conductor for connecting to the grounded (neutral) supply conductor. If no grounded or neutral conductor is present in the box or enclosure, per the manufacturer's instructions, the installer is directed to connect the "green" conductor from the switching device to the equipment grounding conductor. The "green" conductor from the switching device is the neutral conductor that provides 120-volt power to the electronic controls of the device itself. The equipment-grounding conductor should not be used to complete this circuit under any circumstance.

One of the main reasons that 250.4(A)(5) prohibits a grounded conductor from being connected to normally non-current-carrying metal parts of equipment

404.22

grounding conductor(s), or to be reconnected to ground on the load side of the service disconnecting means is to eliminate circulating currents from being introduced into the equipment grounding conductor path.

This new language at 404.22 will require the insulated grounded supply conductor to be installed and used with the proper listed electronic device. The future effective date provides the manufacturers a reasonable time frame to produce these switching devices with grounded conductor compatibility while being able to use existing inventory.

The new exception will recognize a retrofit installation or replacement situation in an existing situation where the grounded conductor is not installed. Electronic control switching devices that utilize the equipment grounding conductor for powering the device would still be permitted, but only in these retrofit applications. These products have been listed and in use for years. The product standard for these devices controls the amount of current permitted to be introduced on the equipment grounding conductor to no more than 0.5 mA. This exception will require devices that permit the use of the equipment grounding conductor for powering the electronics of the device to be listed and labeled for use in retrofit installations only where the grounded conductor is not provided in the switch device box or enclosure. Immediately eliminating these switching devices altogether from the marketplace (without a future effective date) would severely impact the installation of important energy saving controls in existing buildings.

404.22

First Revisions: FR 2423
Second Revisions: SR 2409, SCR 55
Public Inputs: PI 1375
Public Comments: PC 485, PC 832, PC 1256, PC 1797

406.2

Receptacles, Cord Connectors, and Attachment Plugs (Caps)

406.2

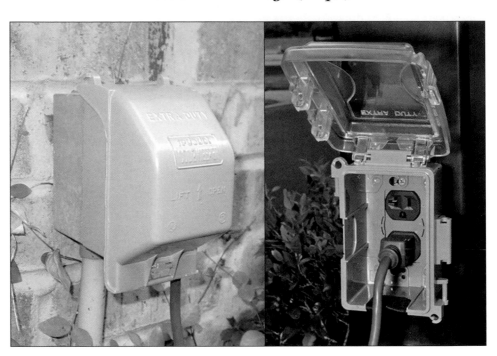

406.2 Receptacles, Cord Connectors, and Attachment Plugs (Caps)

- **Type of Change:** New

- **Change at a Glance:** A new definition for "Outlet Box Hood" was added at 406.2.

- **Code Language:** 406.2 Definitions. [Receptacles, Cord Connectors, and Attachment Plugs (Caps)]
  Outlet Box Hood. A housing shield intended to fit over a faceplate for flush-mounted wiring devices, or an integral component of an outlet box, or a faceplate for flush-mounted wiring devices. The hood does not serve to complete the electrical enclosure; it reduces the risk of water coming in contact with electrical components within the hood, such as attachment plugs, current taps, surge protective devices, direct plug-in transformer units, or wiring devices.

- **2014 *NEC* Requirement**
  While the term "outlet box hood" appeared and was used at two locations [314.15 and 406.9(B)(1)], no definition existed for this term.

- **2017 *NEC* Change**
  A clear and expressive definition for the term "outlet box hood" was added at 406.2.

Analysis of the Change:

The term "outlet box hood" was introduced to the *NEC* at 406.9(B)(1) during the 2011 *NEC* revision process. This section required, and still does today, all 15- and 20-ampere, 125- and 250-volt receptacles installed in a wet location to have an enclosure that is weatherproof, whether or not the attachment plug cap is inserted. This section also calls for all 15- and 20-ampere, 125- and 250-volt nonlocking-type receptacles to be listed as "weather-resistant." For the 2011 NEC, the *Code* required an "outlet box hood" installed for this purpose to be listed when installed at other than one- or two-family dwellings. The 2011 *NEC* also required the outlet box hood to be identified as "extra duty" where installed on an enclosure or conduits supported from grade.

For the 2014 *NEC*, a revision began the process of requiring all enclosures and covers installed in wet locations for 15- and 20-ampere, 125- and 250-volt receptacles to be listed and of the "extra duty" type, not just boxes supported from grade. This same revision also began requiring extra-duty-type outlet box hood covers at dwelling unit, as well as non-dwelling unit, installations. All outlet box hood covers should be required to be listed for use in a wet location when installed in a wet location, as they are relied upon to provide environmental protection for enclosed devices such as GFCI receptacle outlet devices. Outlet box hood covers are also used as a component of a weatherproof enclosure to protect other types of wiring devices, not just 15- and 20-ampere, 125- and 250-volt receptacles installed in a wet location covered by the requirements at 406.9(B)(1).

From the beginning, the missing piece of the puzzle for these "outlet box hoods" was determining exactly what they were, as no *NEC* definition existed for these devices. The 2017 *NEC* filled this gap by providing a clear definition at 406.2 for the term "outlet box hood." These outlet box hoods are commonly referred to in the field as "in-use" covers or "bubble" covers.

Requirements for extra-duty outlet box hoods can be found in ANSI/UL Product Standard 514D–2013, *Cover Plates for Flush-Mounted Wiring Devices*. Outlet box hood covers are available in extra duty, nonmetallic or metal designs. They are designed for use on decks, patios, porches, on the side of a building and at similar locations, and are built to withstand a variety of weather conditions. The nonmetallic outlet box hoods are typically constructed of UV resistant polycarbonate while the metal enclosures are typically made of powder-coated cast zinc.

It should be noted that the term "outlet box hood" appears in two separate articles of the *NEC* [see 314.15 and 406.9(B)(1)]. As the 2015 *NEC Style Manual* suggests (see 2.2.2.1), perhaps this new definition at 406.2 will be better placed in Article 100 in future editions of the *Code*.

406.2

First Revisions: FR 5111
Second Revisions: SCR 56

406.3(E)

Controlled Receptacle Marking

All nonlocking-type, 125-volt, 15- and 20-ampere receptacles controlled by an automatic control device, energy management, or building automation shall be marked with the "Controlled Receptacle Marking Symbol" from Figure 406.3(E) and the word "CONTROLLED"

Energy Management

Figure 406.3(E)

For receptacles controlled by an automatic control device, the marking shall be located on the receptacle face and visible after installation

406.3(E) Receptacle Rating and Type

- **Type of Change:** Revision

- **Change at a Glance:** Receptacles that are controlled by an automatic control device must be permanently marked with the symbol shown in Figure 406.3(E) and the word "Controlled." Required marking must be on the receptacle face (not the cover plate) and be visible after installation.

- **Code Language: 406.3 Receptacle Rating and Type. (E) Controlled Receptacle Marking.** All nonlocking-type, 125-volt, 15- and 20-ampere receptacles that are controlled by an automatic control device, or that incorporate control features that remove power from the receptacle outlet for the purpose of energy management or building automation, shall be marked with the symbol shown in Figure 406.3(E) and the word "controlled." For receptacles controlled by an automatic control device, the marking shall be located on the controlled receptacle outlet face where and visible after installation. In both cases where a multiple receptacle device is used, the required marking of the word "controlled" and symbol shall denote which contact device(s) are automatically controlled.

Figure 406.3(E) Controlled Receptacle Marking Symbol. (see *NEC* for actual symbol)

Exception: *The marking is not required for receptacles controlled by a wall switch that provide the required room lighting outlets as permitted by 210.70.*

■ **2014 *NEC* Requirement**

Receptacle outlets that are under an automatic control device or an automatic energy management system were required to be marked as indicated at 406.3(E), Controlled Receptacle Marking. This subsection required a marking symbol for receptacle outlets controlled by an automatic control device or by an automatic energy management system. The controlled receptacle marking symbol was displayed at Figure 406.3(E). An exception follows this rule to indicate that this marking is not required for receptacle outlets controlled by a wall switch to provide the required room lighting outlet(s) as permitted by 210.70(A)(1) Ex. No. 1.

■ **2017 *NEC* Change**

The word "Controlled" is now required to be placed on the controlled receptacle along with the previous symbol. The word "Controlled" was also added to Figure 406.3(E). The controlled receptacle symbol and the word "Controlled" are to be placed on the controlled receptacle face (not the faceplate or cover) and visible after installation.

406.3(E)

Analysis of the Change:

Energy management has become a common practice in today's electrical infrastructure through the control of utilization equipment, energy storage, and power production. Installation codes currently establish requirements for utilization equipment, energy storage, and power production that serves to address facility and personnel safety. Using an energy management system to control of certain receptacle outlets throughout buildings such as office buildings and educational facilities is an essential component of conserving energy.

For the 2014 *NEC*, requirements were put in place at 406.3(E) requiring a new marking symbol for receptacle outlets controlled by an automatic control device or by an automatic energy management system. These controlled receptacle outlets are often installed in places like an office building with energy management systems in place that shed load or deactivate these receptacle outlets by an automatic means at night when the building is, for the most part, unoccupied. Unfortunately, in a place like an office building, the end user of these controlled receptacles are typically unfamiliar with the controlled receptacle symbol (see symbol in illustration).

While the concept of 406.3(E) for marking controlled receptacles was a noble effort for the 2014 *NEC*, it fell short of its intended goal of informing and educating the end user of the presence of a controlled receptacle. This failure is because the general public, including office workers, receptionists, teachers, and students, had no idea as to what this simple symbol represented. At this early stage, a good number of electrical installers and inspectors would be hard-pressed to recognize the meaning behind this controlled receptacle symbol.

For the 2017 *NEC*, 406.3(E) was revised to provide additional information that will hopefully help the end user understand that the receptacle is controlled by an energy management system. One of these revisions requires that the word "Controlled" be placed on the controlled receptacle along with the previous symbol. The word "Controlled" was also added to Figure 406.3(E). Marking the receptacle with the word "Controlled" will help the end user better understand which receptacle is controlled, even if the end user is not familiar with electrical symbols.

Another change that occurred at 406.3(E) deals with the exact location where the marking of the controlled receptacle is to be placed. For the 2017 NEC, the symbol and the word "Controlled" are to be placed on the face of the controlled receptacle and be visible after installation. The 2014 *NEC* provisions allowed the symbol to be placed on the receptacle face or the faceplate. If the controlled receptacle marking only appeared on the faceplate, the controlled receptacle itself and its original intended faceplate could be easily separated. An example of this is when the walls are repainted. What happens to the receptacle faceplates during this painting process? They are typically tossed in a common container or box, and after the walls are dry, the painter will grab the first faceplate and install it on any receptacle, not necessarily its intended companion receptacle. The result could be confusing, especially in the case of a controlled receptacle that is split-wired with only one of the receptacles of a duplex receptacle controlled. It is important to indicate the *specific* controlled receptacle.

406.3(E)

Second Revisions: SR 5111
Public Inputs: PI 2805
Public Comments: PC 943

406.3(F)

Receptacle Rating and Type

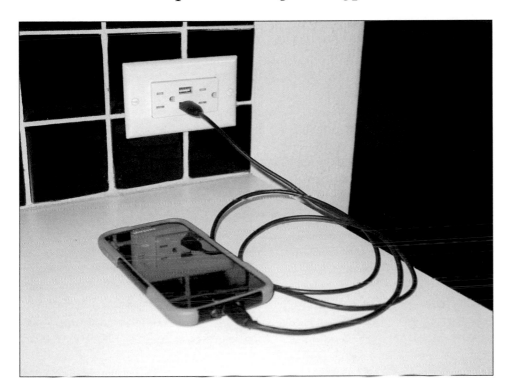

406.3 Receptacle Rating and Type

- **Type of Change:** New

- **Change at a Glance:** New requirements were added for receptacle outlets with USB charger(s).

- **Code Language:** 406.3 Receptacle Rating and Type.

  (F) Receptacle with USB Charger. A 125-volt 15- or 20-ampere receptacle that additionally provides Class 2 power shall be listed and constructed such that the Class 2 circuitry is integral with the receptacle.

- **2014 *NEC* Requirement**
  No provisions existed requiring a receptacle providing power to Class 2 equipment to be listed or that the Class 2 circuitry be an integral part of the receptacle.

- **2017 *NEC* Change**
  New provisions were added pertaining to 125-volt 15- or 20-ampere receptacle that additionally provides Class 2 power in the form of a USB charger. These new provisions require these devices to be listed and constructed such that the Class 2 circuitry is integral with the receptacle.

Analysis of the Change:

The use of USB (Universal Serial Bus) chargers has become commonplace in our electronic media driven society. USB is an industry standard developed in the 1990s that defines the cables, connectors, and communications protocols used in a bus for connection, communication, and power supply between computers and electronic devices. USB was designed to standardize the connection of computer peripherals, including keyboards, pointers, digital cameras, printers, portable media players, disk drives and network adapters. USB is often used with PCs (Personal Computers), both to communicate and to supply electric power. USB connections and charging has become routine on other devices, such as smartphones, PDAs (Personal Digital Assistant), handheld PCs, and video game consoles. USB has effectively replaced a variety of earlier interfaces, such as parallel ports, as well as separate power chargers for portable devices.

A new requirement has been added to Article 406 at 406.3(F) pertaining to 125-volt 15- or 20-ampere receptacle that additionally provides Class 2 power in the form of an USB charger. These new provisions require these devices to be listed and constructed such that the Class 2 circuitry is integral with the receptacle. For the 2014 NEC, Article 406 contained requirements for an assortment of different types of receptacles such as an isolated ground type receptacle, weather-resistant and tamper-resistant type receptacles, but no provisions exist requiring a receptacle providing power to Class 2 equipment to be listed.

Outlet devices consisting of a Class 2 power supply and Class 2 output connector(s) are presently readily available to the public. Some of these assemblies are intended to be secured and directly connected to a duplex receptacle. The combination of the Class 2 assembly and duplex receptacle has not been investigated to national standards. The product standard for receptacles, ANSI/UL 498 (*Attachment Plugs and Receptacles*), contains requirements that correspond to the required construction as well as the performance requirements to evaluate the suitability of a receptacle with integral power supply with Class 2 output connectors. Requiring the use of a listed receptacle with integral power supply with Class 2 output connectors will confirm that the installed device complies with the appropriate product standard

.

First Revisions: FR 5101
Public Inputs: PI 1371

406.3(F)

406.4(D)(4), Ex. No. 1 and Ex. No. 2
Replacement Receptacles (AFCI)

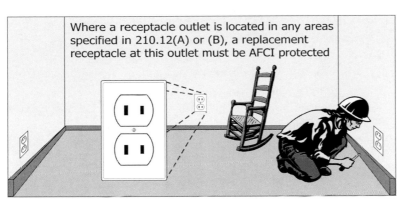

Where a receptacle outlet is located in any areas specified in 210.12(A) or (B), a replacement receptacle at this outlet must be AFCI protected

Ex. No. 1: AFCI protection not required where all of the following apply:

(1) Replacement complies with 406.4(D)(2)(b) *(two-wire system-GFCI)*

(2) Impracticable to provide an EGC as provided by 250.130(C)

(3) Listed combination type AFCI circuit breaker not commercially available

(4) GFCI/AFCI dual function receptacles not commercially available

Ex. No. 2: Exception at 210.12(B) shall not apply to replacement of receptacles

---

406.4(D)(4)

406.4(D)(4), Ex. No. 1 and Ex. No. 2 General Installation Requirements

- **Type of Change:** New

- **Change at a Glance:** Two new exceptions were added for AFCI requirements for replacement of existing receptacles.

- **Code Language: 406.4 General Installation Requirements.**
  Receptacle outlets shall be located in branch circuits in accordance with Part III of Article 210. General installation requirements shall be in accordance with 406.4(A) through (F).

  (D) Replacements. Replacement of receptacles shall comply with 406.4(D)(1) through (D)(6), as applicable. Arc-fault circuit-interrupter type and ground-fault circuit-interrupter type receptacles shall be installed in a readily accessible location.

  (4) Arc-Fault Circuit-Interrupter Protection. Where a receptacle outlet is ~~supplied by a branch circuit that requires arc-fault circuit-interrupter protection as specified elsewhere in this Code~~ located in any areas specified in 210.12(A) or (B), a replacement receptacle at this outlet shall be one of the following:

(1) A listed outlet branch-circuit type arc-fault circuit-interrupter receptacle
(2) A receptacle protected by a listed outlet branch-circuit type arc-fault circuit-interrupter type receptacle
(3) A receptacle protected by a listed combination type arc-fault circuit-interrupter type circuit breaker

Exception No. 1: *Arc-fault circuit-interrupter protection shall not be required where all of the following apply:*
(1) The replacement complies with 406.4(D)(2)(b).
(2) It is impracticable to provide an equipment grounding conductor as provided by 250.130(C).
(3) A listed combination type arc-fault circuit-interrupter circuit breaker is not commercially available.
(4) GFCI/AFCI dual function receptacles are not commercially available.

Exception No. 2: *Section 210.12(B), Exception shall not apply to re-placement of receptacles.*
~~This requirement becomes effective January 1, 2014.~~

406.4(D)(4)

- **2014 *NEC* Requirement**
  Where existing receptacles were replaced and that receptacle outlet was supplied by a branch circuit that under the most current edition of the *Code* would require AFCI protection, that replacement receptacle would have to be AFCI-protected either at the receptacle outlet itself by a listed outlet branch-circuit (OBC) type AFCI receptacle, or at the origin of the branch circuit by a listed combination AFCI overcurrent device.

- **2017 *NEC* Change**
  The main requirement of AFCI protection at replacement receptacles as described in the 2014 *NEC* holds true with two new exceptions added. The first new exception recognizes applications where an existing two-wire receptacle is replaced and no equipment grounding conductor can be installed. The second new exception stipulates that the exception to 210.12(B) does not apply when replacing existing receptacles.

Analysis of the Change:

Arc-fault circuit interrupter (AFCI) protection for replacement receptacle outlets was first added to the *Code* in the 2011 edition of the *NEC* whenever the replace-ment receptacle was supplied by a branch circuit that requires AFCI protection elsewhere in the *Code*. This change brought much needed AFCI protection to older, existing dwelling units. At the time of this 2011 change, Consumer Prod-uct Safety Commission data indicated that over 90 percent of fires of electrical origin were in homes over ten years of age.

The parent text of 406.4(D)(4) was revised by removing text concerning the branch circuit providing power to the replaced receptacle, and replacing that text with a reference to 210.12(A) or (B). This revision will clarify where AFCI protection is required, which is at the receptacle outlet being replaced and not at receptacles located downstream of the replaced receptacle. If a receptacle is being replaced in a bedroom and that branch circuit serves not only that bedroom but a receptacle located outdoors at the front porch, this outdoor receptacle need not be AFCI-protected simply because a bedroom receptacle was being replaced. A literal reading of the previous text could have been interpreted in that way.

Two new exceptions were added for the 2017 *NEC* following this main rule that requires AFCI protection for replacement of existing receptacles. The first exception recognizes applications where an existing two-wire receptacle (no equipment grounding conductor) is replaced, and no equipment grounding conductor can be installed. In this situation, if the panelboard where the branch circuit originates does not provide the option of a listed AFCI combination type overcurrent device, no method exists for meeting the requirement for AFCI protection for replacement receptacles (without this new exception). A GFCI receptacle is required for compliance with 406.4(D)(2)(b) and 406.4(D)(3) when replacing a non-grounding-type receptacle. At the same time, 406.4(D)(4)(1) would require a listed outlet branch circuit (OBC) type AFCI receptacle. Without this new exception, the installer was in conflict as to which *Code* rule to satisfy. The new Exception No. 1 to 406.4(D)(4) provides a resolution for this potential conflict until a receptacle that provides both GFCI and AFCI (dual function) protection simultaneously is commercially available. At the time of this writing, one manufacturer has a dual function GFCI/AFCI receptacle commercially available. Other device manufacturers have their product submitted for listing requirements.

406.4(D)(4)

The second exception clarifies that the exception to 210.12(B) does not apply when replacing existing receptacles. The requirements of 210.12(B) concern AFCI protection for branch-circuit wiring in areas specified at 210.12(A) when said wiring is modified, replaced, or extended at existing dwelling units. The exception to 210.12(B) permits existing branch-circuit conductors to be modified or extended up to 1.8 m (6 ft) without AFCI protection where no additional outlets or devices are installed. In a liberal interpretation, some users of the Code have claimed the exception to 210.12(B) to mean that if one were simply "to extend the conductors in an existing receptacle outlet box" [less than 1.8 m (6 ft)], that AFCI protection could be eliminated at that particular receptacle outlet. Adding this new Ex. No. 2 to 406.4(D)(4) should make it exceedingly evident that this erroneous interpretation has no validity.

Finally, the implementation date of January 1, 2014, for AFCI protection for replacement receptacles has long passed. This date requirement was in the 2011 *NEC*. Therefore, the statement addressing the 2014 effective date is unnecessary and has been removed.

First Revisions: FR 5105
Second Revisions: SR 5105, SCR 47
Public Input: PI 4267, PI 2024
Public Comments: PC 908, PC 1231, PC 632

406.4(D)(5)

Receptacle Replacement Tamper-Resistant Receptacles

Existing outlet to be replaced

Listed tamper-resistant receptacles are required for replacement receptacles where a receptacle outlet is required to be tamper-resistant elsewhere in the *Code* "except where a non-grounding receptacle is replaced with another non-grounding receptacle"

406.4(D)(5)

406.4(D)(5) General Installation Requirements

- **Type of Change:** Revision

- **Change at a Glance:** Tamper-resistant receptacles are required for replacement receptacles "except where a non-grounding receptacle is replaced with another non-grounding receptacle."

- **Code Language: 406.4 General Installation Requirements.** Receptacle outlets shall be located in branch circuits in accordance with Part III of Article 210. General installation requirements shall be in accordance with 406.4(A) through (F).

  (D) Replacements. Replacement of receptacles shall comply with 406.4(D)(1) through (D)(6), as applicable. Arc-fault circuit-interrupter type and ground-fault circuit-interrupter type receptacles shall be installed in a readily accessible location.

  (5) Tamper-Resistant Receptacles. Listed tamper-resistant receptacles shall be provided where replacements are made at receptacle outlets that are required to be tamper-resistant elsewhere in this *Code*, except where a non-grounding receptacle is replaced with another non-grounding receptacle.

- **2014 *NEC* Requirement**
  Listed tamper-resistant receptacles are required to be provided where replacements are made at receptacle outlets that are required to be tamper-resistant elsewhere in the *Code*. Non-grounding receptacles used as a replacement for another non-grounding receptacle as permitted in 406.4(D)(2)(a) are not required to be tamper-resistant by the requirements of 406.12, Exception to (A), (B), and (C), List Item (4).

- **2017 *NEC* Change**
  406.4(D)(5) still requires listed tamper-resistant receptacles where replacements are made at receptacle outlets that are required to be tamper-resistant elsewhere in the *Code* "except where a non-grounding receptacle is replaced with another non-grounding receptacle." The tamper-resistant receptacle requirements at 406.12 remained basically the same for dwelling units, guest rooms and guest suites of hotels and motels, and for a child care facility (see complete change report for 406.12 in this periodical).

Analysis of the Change:

Listed tamper-resistant receptacles are required to be provided where receptacles are replaced at outlets that are required to be tamper-resistant elsewhere in this *Code*. In other words, if an older existing receptacle in a dwelling unit or child care facility were to be replaced with a new receptacle, and this receptacle outlet is located in an area that would call for a listed tamper-resistant receptacle under today's *Code*, that new replacement receptacle would be required to be tamper-resistant as well. This requirement is found at 406.4(D)(5).

406.4(D)(5)

There appeared to be a contradiction to some *Code* users between the replacement receptacle requirements found in the 2014 *NEC* in 406.4(D)(5) and the tamper-resistant receptacle requirements found in 406.12, specifically in List Item (4) of the exception to 406.12(A), (B) and (C). A closer examination of these two Article 406 requirements reveals that there is no contradiction. Section 406.4(D)(5) calls for listed tamper-resistant receptacles where replacements are made at receptacle outlets that are required to be tamper-resistant "elsewhere in the *Code*." Section 406.12 is certainly one of those places that requires tamper-resistant receptacles "elsewhere in the *Code*." However, as stated in 406.12, Exception to (A), (B), and (C), List Item (4), nongrounding receptacles used for replacements as permitted in 406.4(D)(2)(a) are clearly exempted from tamper-resistant receptacle requirements as nongrounding, two-prong receptacles are not available in a tamper-resistant form.

To drive this point home and to remove any doubt concerning tamper-resistant receptacle requirements for nongrounding-type receptacles, CMP-18 revised 406.4(D)(5) by adding the phrase, "except where a non-grounding receptacle is replaced with another non-grounding receptacle."

Listed tamper-resistant receptacles were introduced into the *Code* in the 2008 edition of the *NEC*. These receptacles are manufactured in several styles that offer other features as well, such as GFCI protection, AFCI protection, and weather-resistant safeguarding. Listed tamper-resistant receptacles are not manufactured or available in a nongrounding, two-prong receptacle style. When it comes to replacement of receptacles, 406.4(D)(2)(a) permits a non-grounding-type receptacle as a replacement for another non-grounding-type receptacle. This revision at 406.4(D)(5) will provide a clean link between all of these tamper-resistant receptacle requirements.

First Revisions: FR 5107
Public Inputs: PI 1365

406.6(D)

Receptacle Faceplates (Cover Plates) with Integral Night Light and/or USB Charger

406.6(D)

Receptacle faceplates shall be installed so as to completely cover the opening and seat against the mounting surface

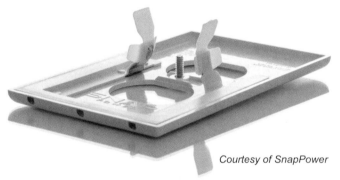

Courtesy of SnapPower

A flush device cover plate that additionally provides a night light and/or Class 2 output connector(s) shall be listed

The night light and/or Class 2 circuitry must be integral with the flush device cover plate

406.6(D) Receptacle Faceplates (Cover Plates)

- **Type of Change:** New

- **Change at a Glance:** New requirements were added for receptacle faceplates with integral night lights and/or USB chargers.

- **Code Language: 406.6 Receptacle Faceplates (Cover Plates).** Receptacle faceplates shall be installed so as to completely cover the opening and seat against the mounting surface. Receptacle faceplates mounted inside a box having a recess-mounted receptacle shall effectively close the opening and seat against the mounting surface.

(D) Receptacle Faceplate (Cover Plates) with Integral Night Light and/or USB Charger. A flush device cover plate that additionally provides a night light and/or Class 2 output connector(s) shall be listed and constructed such that the night light and/or Class 2 circuitry is integral with the flush device cover plate.

- **2014 *NEC* Requirement**
  There were no provisions included for receptacle faceplates with integral night lights and/or USB chargers.

- **2017 *NEC* Change**
  New requirements were added at 406.6(D) about receptacle faceplates with integral night lights and/or USB chargers. These faceplates must be listed and constructed such that the night light and/or Class 2 circuitry is "integral with the flush device cover plate."

Analysis of the Change:

Listed flush receptacle cover plates with an integral night light and/or Class 2 power supply with Class 2 output connector(s) are currently readily available to the public. These receptacle faceplates, typically embedded with three LED lights, are designed to look like traditional receptacle outlet cover plates and can be installed quickly by simply replacing the exiting receptacle cover plate. These cover plates are typically designed to slide into the electrical box and around the outlet receptacle making contact with the screw terminals located on the sides of the existing receptacle outlet, providing illumination while keeping both of the duplex receptacle outlets free for use at all times

A plug-in night light that is not "integral with the flush device cover plate," but simply designated to be plugged directly into a receptacle outlet presents a problem. The ease in removing these night light-type covers from the receptacle outlet increases its safety hazard. Small children are attracted to lighted objects, particularly objects accessible at their eye level near the floor. These plug-in night lights/covers provide a large gripping surface for small children to partially remove the plug-in night light from the receptacle outlet and potentially make contact with the energized insertion blades, exposing themselves to an electric shock hazard.

For the 2017 *NEC*, provisions were added to 406.6 about receptacle faceplates with integral night lights and/or USB chargers. These faceplates must be listed and constructed such that the night light and/or Class 2 circuitry is "integral with the flush device cover plate." The product standard for Class 2 power outlets, ANSI/UL 1310 (*Standard for Class 2 Power Units*) contains requirements that correspond to the required construction as well as the performance requirements to evaluate the suitability of a faceplate with an integral night light and/or Class 2 power supply with Class 2 output connector(s). Requiring the use of a listed flush device cover plate with an integral night light and/or Class 2 power supply with Class 2 output connector(s) will ensure that the installed device complies with the required characteristics of new 406.6(D).

First Revisions: FR 5109

406.6(D)

406.9(B)(1)

Extra-Duty Outlet Box Hoods

An outlet box hood installed at an enclosure for 15 and 20 amperes, 125 and 250 volt receptacles in a wet location to provide weatherproof protection whether or not an attachment plug cap is inserted or not must be listed and identified as "extra duty"

Must be Marked "Extra Duty"

"Extra Duty" Not Required

Other listed products, enclosures, or assemblies providing weatherproof protection that do not utilize an outlet box hood need not be marked "extra duty"

406.9(B)(1)

406.9(B)(1) Receptacles in Damp or Wet Locations

- **Type of Change:** Revision

- **Change at a Glance:** New provisions allowing "other listed products," enclosures, or assemblies providing weatherproof protection that do not utilize an outlet box hood need not be marked "extra duty" as required for the outlet box hoods.

- **Code Language: 406.9 Receptacles in Damp or Wet Locations. (B) Wet Locations.**
  (1) Receptacles of 15 and 20 Amperes in a Wet Location. Receptacles of 15 and 20 amperes, 125 and 250 volts installed in a wet location shall have an enclosure that is weatherproof whether or not the attachment plug cap is inserted. An outlet box hood installed for this purpose shall be listed and shall be identified as "extra duty." Other listed products, enclosures, or assemblies providing weatherproof protection that do not utilize an outlet box hood need not be marked "extra duty."

  Informational Note No. 1: Requirements for extra-duty outlet box hoods are found in ANSI/UL 514D-~~2000~~ 2013, Cover Plates for Flush-Mounted Wiring Devices. "Extra duty" identification and requirements are not applicable to listed receptacles, faceplates, outlet boxes, enclosures, or assemblies that are identified as either being suitable for wet locations or rated as one of the outdoor enclosure–type numbers of Table 110.28 that does not utilize an outlet box hood.

Exception: 15- and 20-ampere, 125- through 250-volt receptacles installed in a wet location and subject to routine high-pressure spray washing shall be permitted to have an enclosure that is weatherproof when the attachment plug is removed.

All 15- and 20-ampere, 125- and 250-volt nonlocking-type receptacles shall be listed and so identified as the weather-resistant type.

Informational Note No. 2: The ~~types~~ configuration of weather-resistant receptacles covered by this requirement are identified as 5-15, 5-20, 6-15, and 6-20 in ANSI/NEMA WD 6-~~2002~~ 2012, ~~Standard for Dimensions of Attachment Plugs and Receptacles~~ Wiring Devices — Dimensional Specifications.

- **2014 *NEC* Requirement**
  All 15- and 20-ampere, 125- and 250-volt receptacles installed in a wet location must have an enclosure and covers that are weatherproof whether an attachment plug cap is inserted or not. For all types of occupancies, all outlet box hood covers installed in wet locations for 15- and 20-ampere, 125- and 250-volt receptacles must be listed and of the "extra duty" type. All 15- and 20-ampere, 125- and 250-volt nonlocking-type receptacles must be listed as the weather-resistant type.

- **2017 *NEC* Change**
  The previous requirements for 15- and 20-ampere, 125- and 250-volt receptacles installed in a wet location still holds true with language added to indicate that other listed products, enclosures, or assemblies providing weatherproof protection that do not utilize an outlet box hood need not be marked "extra duty."

Analysis of the Change:

For the 2011 edition of the *NEC*, requirements were added to 406.9(B)(1) calling for in-use covers for non-dwelling unit receptacles installed in wet locations on an enclosure supported from grade to have hood covers of the "extra-duty" type. Revisions in the 2014 *NEC* to 406.9(B)(1) modified this initial requirement, making "extra duty" hood covers mandatory at all 15- and 20-ampere, 125- and 250-volt receptacles installed in a wet location (not just those supported from grade). These same 2014 *NEC* revisions removed the "for other than one- or two-family dwellings" requirement, making this "extra duty" outlet box hood requirement mandatory for all occupancies (including dwelling units).

For the 2014 *NEC*, this "extra duty" outlet box hood cover was problematic as listed equipment often incorporates receptacles that are protected by means other than an outlet box hood. An example of this would be a power outlet as covered by UL Product Standard 231 (Standard for Power Outlets). These power outlets typically locate a receptacle behind a hinged steel cover, which is not

406.9(B)(1)

an outlet box hood, and is not identified as "extra duty." This configuration has caused some confusion over the lack of "extra duty" identification on these types of listed assemblies.

For the 2017 *NEC*, in an effort to remedy this confusion or misapplication, 406.9(B)(1) was once again revised by adding an extra sentence to indicate that other listed products, enclosures, or assemblies providing weatherproof protection that do not utilize an outlet box hood need not be marked "extra duty." Language was also added to a 406.9(B)(1) informational note that further stresses the fact that "extra duty" identification and requirements are not applicable to listed receptacles, faceplates, outlet boxes, enclosures, or assemblies that are identified as either being suitable for wet locations or rated as one of the outdoor enclosure-type numbers of Table 110.28 (Enclosure Selection) that does not utilize an outlet box hood. Table 110.28 is used for selecting enclosures for use in specific locations (such as a damp or wet location) other than hazardous (classified) locations.

Other housekeeping revisions occurred with 406.9(B)(1) to make sure the informational notes and exception "immediately follow the main rule to which they apply" for compliance with the *NEC Style Manual*.

406.9(B)(1)

First Revisions: FR 5110
Second Revisions: SR 5102
Public Inputs: PI 759, PI 2304

406.12

Tamper-Resistant Receptacles

All 15- and 20-ampere, 125- and 250-volt nonlocking-type receptacles in areas specified in 406.12(1) through (7) must be listed tamper-resistant receptacles: (1) Dwelling units in all areas specified in 210.52 and 550.13; (2) Guest rooms and guest suites of hotels and motels; (3) Child care facilities

(4) Preschools/elementary educational facilities; (5) Waiting rooms, etc. in medical/dental offices; (6) Places of waiting-transportation, gymnasiums, etc.; (7) Dormitories

406.12

406.12 Tamper-Resistant Receptacles

- **Type of Change:** Revision/New

- **Change at a Glance:** Requirements for tamper-resistant receptacles were expanded to mobile homes, preschools and elementary education facilities, as well as other locations where small children are likely to congregate. TR receptacles were expanded to 250-volt receptacles as well as 125-volt receptacles.

- **Code Language: 406.12 Tamper-Resistant Receptacles.**
  ~~Tamper-resistant receptacles shall be installed as~~ All 15- and 20-ampere, 125- and 250-volt nonlocking-type receptacles in the areas specified in ~~406.12(A) through (C)~~ 406.12(1) through (7) shall be listed tamper-resistant receptacles.
  (1) Dwelling units in all areas specified in 210.52 and 550.13
  (2) Guest rooms and guest suites of hotels and motels
  (3) Child care facilities
  (4) Preschools and elementary education facilities
  (5) Business offices, corridors, waiting rooms and the like in clinics, medical and dental offices and outpatient facilities
  (6) Subset of assembly occupancies described in Article 518.2 to include places of waiting transportation, gymnasiums, skating rinks, and auditoriums
  (7) Dormitories

Informational Note: This requirement would include receptacles identified as 5-15, 5-20, 6-15, and 6-20 in ANSI/NEMA WD 6-2016, Wiring Devices — Dimensional Specifications.

Exception to ~~(A), (B), and (C)~~ (1), (2), (3), (4), (5), (6), and (7): Receptacles in the following locations shall not be required to be tamper-resistant:

(1) Receptacles located more than 1.7 m (5½ ft) above the floor

(2) Receptacles that are part of a luminaire or appliance

(3) A single receptacle or a duplex receptacle for two appliances located within the dedicated space for each appliance that, in normal use, is not easily moved from one place to another and that is cord-and-plug-connected in accordance with 400.10(A)(6), (A)(7), or (A)(8)

(4) Nongrounding receptacles used for replacements as permitted in 406.4(D)(2)(a)

406.12

- **2014 *NEC* Requirement**
  In all areas specified in 210.52 (which is the majority, but not all, areas of a dwelling unit), all nonlocking-type 125-volt, 15- and 20-ampere receptacles were required to be listed tamper-resistant receptacles, with an exception for four specific locations or areas. All nonlocking-type 125-volt, 15- and 20-ampere receptacles located in guest rooms and guest suites of hotels and motels, and in child care facilities were required to be listed tamper-resistant receptacles. The same exception applied for four specific locations or areas in dwelling units. Receptacles exempted from the tamper-resistant requirement are those located more than 1.7 m (5 ½ ft) above the floor, receptacles that are part of a luminaire or appliance, receptacles located in a dedicated appliance space, and nongrounding-type replacement receptacles.

- **2017 *NEC* Change**
  Along with the tamper-resistant receptacle requirements of the 2014 *NEC*, tamper-resistant receptacle requirements were expanded to mobile and manufactured homes, preschools and elementary education facilities, dormitories, business offices, corridors, waiting rooms and the like in clinics, medical and dental offices and outpatient facilities, assembly occupancies including places of waiting, transportation, gymnasiums, skating rinks, and auditoriums. The voltage rating at which tamper-resistant receptacle requirements are applicable was expanded to include both 125 volts and 250 volts.

Analysis of the Change:
Tamper-resistant (TR) receptacles became a requirement at most dwelling unit receptacle outlet locations with the implementation of the 2008 *NEC*. When introduced, this TR receptacle requirement was required at all 15- and 20-ampere receptacles specified at 210.52 for dwelling units. The original substantiation for justification of TR receptacles came from the U.S. Consumer Product Safety Commission's (CPSC) National Electronic Injury Surveillance System (NEISS). This substantiation indicated that from 1991 to 2001 over 24,000 children were

injured when they inserted foreign objects (paper clips, keys, etc.) into energized electrical receptacles.

The 2011 *NEC* saw TR receptacle requirements expanded to guest rooms and guest suites of hotels and motels and child care facilities, as children in these facilities have the same potential hazard for electrical burns and shock from insertion of a foreign object into a receptacle as they do in their homes. The exception that exists today for TR receptacles was also added to the 2011 *NEC* for dwelling units. This exception has four conditions or locations where tamper-resistant receptacles are not required, even if the receptacle outlet is specified at 210.52. The exception deals with locations where it is extremely unlikely a small child would have ready access to the receptacle, such as behind a large appliance (refrigerator). The 2014 *NEC*, the exception for TR receptacles was expanded to guest rooms and guest suites of hotels and motels and child care facilities.

For the 2017 *NEC*, 406.12 underwent quite a few changes involving TR receptacles. The structure of 406.12 was reorganized to put the areas that require TR receptacles into a list format and to avoid repeating common text such as "15- and 20-ampere, 125- and 250-volt nonlocking-type receptacles" in each and every list item.

One of the first changes involved an expansion of the voltage rating to 250 volts for nonlocking-type receptacles in certain locations that will be required to be of the tamper-resistant type. Receptacles rated at 250 volts are commonly used for air-conditioning and heating units in dwelling units, guest rooms and guest suites of hotels and motels as well as other locations. These 250-volt receptacles present the same, if not greater, potential hazard for electrical burns and shock hazard from insertion of a foreign object into a receptacle as their 125-volt comrades. Expanding the TR receptacle requirements to 250 volts for the same locations as required by 125-volt rated receptacles will enhance and further reduce the number of shock and burn injuries to small children.

For dwelling units, all 15- and 20-ampere, 125- and 250-volt nonlocking-type receptacles in the areas specified at 550.13 were added to receptacles requiring tamper-resistant protection. This requirement was expanded to include areas specified at 550.13, along with areas specified at 210.52, to bring TR receptacle requirements to mobile and manufactured homes. Once again, small children who live in mobile or manufactured homes are exposed to the same hazards caused by inserting objects into a receptacle as small children who live in constructed dwelling units, attend child care facilities, etc.

Finally, the areas and locations where TR receptacles are now required was expanded to include areas such as preschools and elementary education facilities, dormitories, business offices, corridors, waiting rooms, and the like, in clinics, medical and dental offices and outpatient facilities. The areas now requiring TR receptacles would also include assembly occupancies including places of waiting, transportation, gymnasiums, skating rinks, and auditoriums. These are all areas where small children would be present and have ready access to energized receptacle outlets.

406.12

A new informational note was also added providing information from the National Electrical Manufacturers Association (NEMA) concerning dimensional requirements for receptacles rated up to 60 amperes and 600 volts as well as dimensions for wall plates. The informational note identifies certain receptacles that would be included in this expanded TR receptacle requirements (see NEMA Standards Publication ANSI/NEMA WD 6-2016). The TR receptacle requirements are aimed at common receptacles found in the locations specified in 406.12 and are not intended to apply to special configurations of receptacles that may be required for specific dedicated equipment where tamper-resistant receptacles are not produced or available.

First Revisions: FR 5112
Second Revisions: SR 5107, SCR 45
Public Inputs: PI 1258, PI 414, PI 1363, PI 1995, PI 1040
Public Comments: PC 849

406.15

406.15

Dimmer-Controlled Receptacles

406.15 ~~Dimmer-Controlled Receptacles~~

- **Type of Change:** Deletion

- **Change at a Glance:** Dimmer-controlled receptacle provisions have been deleted.

- **Code Language:** ~~406.15 Dimmer-Controlled Receptacles.~~ ~~A receptacle supplying lighting loads shall not be connected to a dimmer unless the plug/receptacle combination is a nonstandard configuration type that is specifically listed and identified for each such unique combination.~~

- **2014 *NEC* Requirement**

  A new section was added at 406.15 to permit specific receptacles to be controlled by a dimmer under specific conditions. A receptacle supplying lighting loads can be connected to a dimmer if the plug/receptacle combination is a nonstandard configuration type and specifically listed and identified for each such unique combination.

- **2017 *NEC* Change**

  The requirements for dimmer-controlled receptacles at 406.15 have been deleted. This section sought to correct incompatibilities between certain types of dimmers and certain cord-and-plug connected loads. Such incompatibilities are currently dealt with in the listing of specific load types and the listing of specific dimmer types.

Analysis of the Change:

During the last *Code* revision cycle, new rules were added at 406.15 permitting certain receptacles to be controlled by a dimmer under specific conditions. In conjunction with 404.15(E), dimmer switches are not permitted to control receptacle outlets. Dimmer switches are to be used only to control permanently installed incandescent luminaires, unless listed for the control of other loads and installed accordingly. This 2014 *NEC* addition at 406.15 allowed a receptacle supplying lighting loads to be connected to a dimmer if the plug/receptacle combination is a nonstandard configuration type and specifically listed and identified for each such unique combination.

This requirement was directed at 120-volt cord- and plug connected lighting, such as LED type rope lighting. A use for this type of lighting device that is becoming commonplace is an installation under shelving or under cabinets. This type of lighting typically comes with a built-in extension cord that simply plugs into a conventional 120-volt receptacle outlet. According to the substantiation for this 2014 *NEC* addition, some of the manufacturers of these lighting sources provide a dimming feature that is listed with their product. Clear, concise *Code* language was needed to ensure standard grade receptacles were not being controlled from any dimming or voltage dropping device.

For the 2017 *NEC*, 406.15 was deleted in its entirely. As referenced earlier, the objective of 406.15 all along was to control the use of a dimmer being applied to a cord-connected receptacle load and to make sure that when this situation did occur, it was done with a "nonstandard configuration type plug/receptacle combination and specifically listed and identified for each such unique combination." The substantiation for the deletion of 406.15 stated that this issue was better handled by the listing and product standards for these unique and specific products.

One of the issues surrounding the creation of previous 406.15 was the use of the term "nonstandard configuration." Nonstandard is not defined with regard to plug/receptacle combinations. Was this meant to apply to something like a "twist-lock" type connection or was it intended to apply to a plug-in connector that could not mate with any existing NEMA type configuration?

406.15

Another issue with this deleted section was with the requirement that a plug/receptacle combination be "specifically listed and identified for each unique combination." Did this mean that a different unique connector pair was needed for each combination of dimmer and dimmable load or load type that was compatible with that dimmer? There are too many combinations of dimmer types (forward phase control, reverse phase control, sine wave, etc.) and safely dimmable loads and load types (halogen, fluorescent, magnetic ballasts, electronic transformers, LED drivers etc.), and not enough unique listed NEMA-recognized plug/receptacle connector combinations available to satisfy this previous requirement.

406.15

Perhaps the rules of the deleted 406.15 were too broad in nature in specifying an undefined type of plug/receptacle connector pairing related to cord-and-plug connected load and dimmer incompatibility. The addition of this section in the 2014 *NEC* brought about two Tentative Interim Amendments (TIA) to two separate locations in the *NEC*. TIAs are issued between *Code* cycles to fix or address something that needs immediate attention in order to achieve enforcement and/or compliance with a *Code* section. A TIA is tentative because it has not been processed through the entire standards-making procedures. It is interim because it is effective only between editions of the *Code*. A TIA automatically becomes a proposal for the next edition of the standard; as such, it then is subject to all of the procedures of the Code-making process.

One of these TIAs occurred at 520.45 for receptacles for electrical equipment on stages at theaters, motion picture and television studios, etc. (see TIA 14-4 2014-70). The other TIA occurred at 530.21(A) for plugs and receptacles (including cord connectors and flanged surface devices) at motion picture and television studios (see TIA 14-5 2014-70). These two TIAs exempted 520.45 and 530.21(A) from the requirements of now deleted 406.15. Theaters and motion picture and television studios employ safe applications of cord- and plug-connected loads to dimmers on a regular basis. In these theatrical settings, receptacles may be connected to dimmers, relays, or directly to an overcurrent protective device, depending on the needs of a particular production. In a modern theatrical lighting system, the configuration of a receptacle (dimmed, switched, or constant power) may even be determined by the configuration settings of the control system feeding the receptacle. Personnel operating a theatre are trained in the management of dimmed, switched, and constant-power circuits and receptacles. This has been the practice for many years

The creation of 406.15 was an attempt to solve a specific problem associated with emerging and evolving new technology, such as LED. As noble as the concept might have been, the addition of 406.15 did not solve this problem. Once again, the solution is better found with the listing and product standards for these unique and specific products.

First Revisions: FR 5113
Public Inputs: PI 1876

408.3(A)(2)

Barriers at Service Panelboards

Barriers required in all service panelboards, switchboards, and switchgear such that no uninsulated, ungrounded service busbar or service terminal is exposed to inadvertent contact by persons or maintenance equipment while servicing load terminations

Courtesy of Schneider Electric

Exception: This requirement shall not apply to service panelboards with provisions for more than one service disconnect within a single enclosure as permitted in 408.36, Exceptions No. 1, 2, and 3

408.3(A)(2)

408.3(A)(2) Support and Arrangement of Busbars and Conductors. (Switchboards, Switchgear, and Panelboards)

- **Type of Change:** Revision/New

- **Change at a Glance:** New requirements were added for barriers to be placed in all service panelboards so that no uninsulated, ungrounded service busbar or service terminal will be exposed to inadvertent contact by persons.

- **Code Language: 408.3 Support and Arrangement of Busbars and Conductors. (Switchboards, Switchgear, and Panelboards)**

  (A) Conductors and Busbars on a Switchboard, Switchgear, or Panelboard. Conductors and busbars on a switchboard, switchgear, or panelboard shall comply with 408.3(A)(1), (A)(2), and (A)(3) as applicable.

  (2) Service Switchboards and Switchgear. Barriers shall be placed in all service panelboards, switchboards, and switchgear such that no uninsulated, ungrounded service busbar or service terminal is exposed to inadvertent contact by persons or maintenance equipment while servicing load terminations.

Exception: This requirement shall not apply to service panelboards with provisions for more than one service disconnect within a single enclosure as permitted in 408.36, Exceptions No. 1, 2, and 3.

■ **2014 *NEC* Requirement**
The requirement of 408.3(A)(2) insisted that barriers be in place for all service *switchboards and switchgear* so that that no uninsulated, ungrounded service busbar or service terminal was exposed to inadvertent contact by persons or maintenance equipment while servicing load terminations. No such barrier provision existed for *panelboards.*

■ **2017 *NEC* Change**
The barrier requirements of 408.3(A)(2) were expanded to all service panelboards as well as service switchboards and switchgear. An exception also was added eliminating the barriers at panelboards installed to comply with the requirements of 408.36, Ex. No. 1, 2, and 3.

Analysis of the Change:

A requirement for switchboards in the 1978 *NEC* at 384-3(a) [now 408.3(A)(2)] called for a barrier to be placed in all service switchboards that would isolate the service busbars and terminals from the remainder of the switchboard. During the 1999 *NEC* revision cycle, this section was updated with the current language calling for no "inadvertent contact by persons or maintenance equipment while servicing load terminations." The term "switchgear" was added to this requirement for the 2014 *NEC*, making this barrier requirement applicable to all service switchboards and switchgear.

Concerns for electrical workers' safety have been raised in situations such as working in cabinets or cutout boxes that contain a panelboard supplied by service-entrance conductors containing a single main service disconnecting means. While moving the main circuit breaker or switch to the open "off" position will de-energize the panelboard, supply terminals to this disconnecting means will remain energized and exposed. Should a metal fish tape, tool or a loose uninsulated conductor come in contact with these exposed terminals, the result would likely be a ground fault producing an arc flash that could be lethal to the worker or expose the worker to serious burn injury.

With these types of situations in mind, the 2017 *NEC* expanded this "barrier" requirement to all service panelboards, as well as service switchboards and switchgear. Concerns over access to uninsulated live parts on the line side of service disconnecting means within a panelboard has been identified as a safety concern by installers and proponents of electrical safety in the workplace going back several *Code* cycles, with proposals and comments submitted to CMP-9 to that effect. CMP-9 has historically maintained that panelboards should not be serviced while energized unless appropriate NFPA 70E precautions are taken.

In concert with the new construction requirements for panelboards in UL Product Standard 67 (*Standard for Panelboards*), and in an attempt to address the safety concern of access to ungrounded, uninsulated live parts in a service

408.3(A)(2)

panelboard, new barrier provisions were introduced providing a level of isolation from line-side uninsulated live parts in a manner similar to that afforded in switchboards at the previous text at 408.3(A)(2) and UL 891 (*Standard for Switchboards*).

One of the hurdles to be overcome concerning the barrier requirement for service panelboards was the fact that providing such protection is more achievable for those service panelboards with a single-service disconnect, but less practical for service panelboards with multiple-service disconnects within the same enclosure as permitted by 408.36, Exceptions No. 1, 2, and 3. Section 408.36 calls for individual overcurrent protection for a panelboard while the exceptions to 408.36 recognize the "six means of disconnect" rules of 230.71 and the old "split-bus" panelboards that could be present in existing panelboards. The new exception to 406.3(A)(2) clarifies this situation. This multiple disconnecting means within a single enclosure concern also was presented to the UL Standards Technical Panel (STP) with purview of UL 67. STP-67 agreed to require single-service disconnect panelboards to be constructed in such a way that, with the service disconnect in the off position, "no ungrounded uninsulated live part is exposed to inadvertent contact by persons while servicing any load terminals."

Many types of construction of panelboards are available in the marketplace and many panelboards identified as "Suitable for Use as Service Equipment" can be field-converted to either a service or non-service (feeder) application. With this in mind, inclusion of any "line-side service barriers" will ultimately be the responsibility of the installer as these barriers will be provided by the manufacturer in the form of a field-installable kit for these convertible (service or feeder) panelboards.

408.3(A)(2)

While proponents of the "barrier" requirement for service panelboards have pointed out that this requirement has been in the Canadian Electrical Code (CEC) for many years, it should be noted that the CEC does not contain the "six means of disconnect" rule. In actuality, the CEC does not include these requirements directly; rather the terminal isolation requirements are located in the CSA Standard for Panelboards (C22.2 No. 29-11). It should also be noted that a panelboard manufactured to meet the CEC requirements (referred to as a "service box") will typically have the entire top portion of the panelboard enclosed by barriers. When contemplating this type of panelboard for use in the United States under the *NEC*, concerns were raised as to how to get branch circuits and feeders in and out of the top of these completely barricaded areas of the panelboard.

The solution to this issue in Canada was to install the panelboard on its side rather than top to bottom as traditionally witnessed in the US. Once again, the difference in CEC rules versus the *NEC* rules allowed this application, as the CEC does not have the "indicating" rule of *NEC* 240.81 that calls for the "up position" of a circuit breaker to be the "on" position. This problem was overcome for *NEC* compliance as panelboards manufactured for installation in the US meeting this "barrier" provision will only barricade the line-side service-entrance conductor lugs, taking advantage of the insulating factor of the insulated service-entrance conductor itself rather than barricade the entire top portion of the panelboard.

With the construction hurdles of panelboards produced for installation in the United States addressed for barriers, the *NEC* should contain the same safety driven requirements for panelboards as previously required for switchboards and switchgear. This new requirement for barriers at service panelboards will allow an "electrically safe work condition" (as defined in NFPA 70E) to be established when installers perform work on any and all service equipment.

First Revisions: FR 2424
Second Revisions: SR 2410
Public Inputs: PI 1281, PI 1467
Public Comments: PC 168

409.22(B)

Short-Circuit Current Rating

409.22(B)

409.22(B) Short-Circuit Current Rating. (Industrial Control Panels)

- **Type of Change:** Revision/New

- **Change at a Glance:** New requirements were added for documentation of available short-circuit current at industrial control panels and the date the short-circuit current calculation was performed.

■ **Code Language: 409.22(B) Short-Circuit Current Rating. (Industrial Control Panels).**

(A) Installation. An industrial control panel shall not be installed where the available ~~fault~~ short-circuit current exceeds its short-circuit current rating as marked in accordance with 409.110(4).

(B) Documentation. If an industrial control panel is required to be marked with a short-circuit current rating in accordance with 409.110(4), the available short-circuit current at the industrial control panel, and the date the short-circuit current calculation was performed shall be documented and made available to those authorized to inspect the installation.

■ **2014 *NEC* Requirement**
An industrial control panel was required not to be installed where the available fault current (short-current) exceeded its short-circuit current rating marked on the equipment as required by 409.110(4). However, there was no companion requirement demanding the actual available short-circuit current be documented and available to the AHJ, in order for the AHJ to verify that the equipment installed was rated within its established short-circuit current rating.

409.22(B)

■ **2017 *NEC* Change**
The missing companion component for documentation of the available short-circuit current (fault current) at industrial control panels was added at 409.22(B). This new requirement also required documentation of the date the short-circuit current calculation was performed.

Analysis of the Change:

New requirements were added to 409.22(B) involving the documentation of the available short-circuit current (fault current) at industrial control panels. These new provisions require the available short-circuit current at the industrial control panel to be documented, along with the date the short-circuit current calculation was performed. This documentation is to be made available to the AHJ.

The enforcement community has a difficult time enforcing proper short-circuit current ratings of industrial control panels as required by previous 409.22 [now 409.22(A)] and 409.110(4). Listed industrial control panels are typically marked by the manufacturer with the short-circuit current rating required for the particular piece of equipment but without this *Code* change, there is typically no information on the job site as to the available short-circuit at the industrial control panel. If the industrial control panel were marked in the field [similar to the requirements in 110.24(A) for field marking of available fault current for services], it would be much easier for the AHJ to ensure that the industrial control panels was being properly protected in the event of a short circuit or ground fault. Whenever an industrial control panel is being installed without a marked short-circuit current rating, the AHJ is often turning these installations down and sending the installer and/or designer back to step one to provide the marked short-circuit current rating as required by 409.110(4).

The enforcement community feels a sense of responsibility (rightfully so) to the general public and the building owner to assist in making sure a building is provided with the utmost "practical safeguarding of persons and property from hazards arising from the use of electricity" (see 90.1). This new requirement for available short-circuit documentation provides much-needed information to aid the electrical inspector when enforcing 409.22(A) and will ensure that the industrial control panel complies with its established short-circuit current rating.

While the *NEC* previously required this documentation at several places in the *Code*, this requirement was added at nine locations throughout the 2017 *NEC* [including this one at 409.22(B)]. This available short-circuit current documentation was added for other equipment such as motor control centers, air conditioning equipment, elevator control panels and industrial machinery. Also included in these short-circuit rating requirements were emergency system transfer equipment for emergency systems, legally required standby systems, optional standby systems, and critical operations power systems (COPS).

First Revisions: FR 3002
Second Revisions: SR 3003, SCR 1
Public Inputs: PI 4421, PI 4733
Public Comments: PC 1800, PC 409

410.62(C)(1)

410.62(C)(1)
Cord-Connected Lampholders and Luminaires

410.62(C)(1) Cord-Connected Lampholders and Luminaires

- **Type of Change:** Revision

- **Change at a Glance:** Reorganization occurred to the requirements for cord-connected lampholders and luminaires of the electric-discharge and LED types.

- **Code Language: 410.62 Cord-Connected Lampholders and Luminaires.**
  (C) Electric-Discharge and LED Luminaires. Electric-discharge and LED luminaires shall comply with (1), (2), and (3) as applicable.

  (1) Cord-Connected Installation. A luminaire or a listed assembly in compliance with any of the conditions in (a) through (c) shall be permitted to be cord connected if the following conditions apply: provided the luminaire is located directly below the outlet or busway, the flexible cord meets all the following: is not subject to strain or physical damage, and the cord is visible over its entire length outside the luminaire except at terminations.
  (a) A luminaire shall be permitted to be connected with a cord terminating terminated in a grounding-type attachment plug or busway plug.

  (b) A luminaire assembly equipped with a strain relief and canopy shall be permitted to use a cord connection between the luminaire assembly and the canopy. The canopy shall be permitted to include a section of raceway having a maximum not over 152 mm 150 mm (6 in.) in length and intended to facilitate the connection to an outlet box mounted above a suspended ceiling.

  (c) Listed luminaires connected using listed assemblies that incorporate manufactured wiring system connectors in accordance with 604.6(C) 604.100(C) shall be permitted to be cord connected.

- **2014 *NEC* Requirement**
  Electric-discharge and LED luminaires are permitted to be cord connected when the following conditions apply: the luminaire is located directly below the outlet or busway, the flexible cord is visible for its entire length outside the luminaire, is not subject to strain or physical damage, and is terminated in a grounding-type attachment plug cap or busway plug, or is a part of a listed assembly incorporating a manufactured wiring system connector in accordance with 604.6(C), or has a luminaire assembly with a strain relief and canopy having a maximum 152 mm (6 in.) long section of raceway for attachment to an outlet box above a suspended ceiling.

- **2017 *NEC* Change**
  The same basic requirements still apply to cord-connected electric-discharge and LED luminaires with the information re-organized into an easier to understand list format that improves the clarity of the content.

410.62(C)(1)

Analysis of the Change:

The basic requirements for cord-connected electric-discharge luminaires were first included in the 1971 *NEC* at 410-14. Electric-discharge lighting is defined in Article 100 as "systems of illumination utilizing fluorescent lamps, high-intensity discharge (HID) lamps, or neon tubing." Light-emitting diode (LED) type luminaires were added to the cord-connected provisions in the 2011 *NEC* at 410.62(C), its present home.

The 2017 *NEC* encountered much-needed reorganization and revision at 410.62(C)(2) for cord-connected installations of electric-discharge and LED luminaires. No technical changes were introduced to these cord-connected requirements, but the new layout is much easier to follow and comprehend. The previous language at 410.62(C)(1) was one long sentence that was tough to follow. The *NEC Style Manual* (see 3.3.1), in part, directs the members of the different Code-Making Panels to "use simple declarative sentence structure, and keep sentences short. Writing rules in long sentences full of commas, dependent clauses, and parenthetical expressions often creates confusion and misunderstanding."

The new re-organized text provides improved clarity while retaining the core intent of these cord-connected requirements.

410.62(C)(1)

First Revisions: FR 5118

Second Revisions: SR 5109

Public Inputs: PI 4019

Public Comments: PC 469

Article 411

Low-Voltage Lighting

Article 411 Low-Voltage Lighting

- ■ **Type of Change:** Revision

- ■ **Change at a Glance:** Article 411 was re-organized and renamed.

- ■ **Code Language:** Article 411 **Low-Voltage** Lighting ~~Systems Operating at 30 Volts or Less and Lighting Equipment Connected to Class 2 Power Sources.~~

  411.1 Scope. This article covers lighting systems and their associated components operating at no more than 30 volts ~~or less and their associated components. This article also covers lighting equipment connected to a Class 2 power source~~ ac or 60 volts dc. Where wet contact is likely to occur, the limits are 15 volts ac or 30 volts dc.

  Informational Note: Refer to Article 680 for applications involving immersion.
  411.3 Low-Voltage Lighting Systems.
  411.4 Listing Required.
  411.5 Specific Location Requirements.
  411.6 Secondary Circuits.
  411.8 Hazardous (Classified) Locations.
  (See *NEC* for complete text of Article).

- **2014 *NEC* Requirement**

  Article 411 applied to lighting systems operating at 30 volts or less and their associated components. The article also covered lighting equipment connected to a Class 2 power source. These Class 2 power sources were basically limited to the low voltage power supplies of *NEC* Chapter 9, Tables 11(A) or Table 11(B).

- **2017 *NEC* Change**

  The limitations of 411.3(A) and (B) for low-voltage lighting systems operating at 30 volts or less and the limitations of Class 2 low-voltage lighting systems conforming to *NEC* Chapter 9, Table 11(A) or Table 11(B) was removed for the 2017 *NEC*. These low-voltage lighting systems addressed by Article 411 are now basically limited by the maximum rating of 25 amperes for the output circuits of the power supply under all load conditions.

Analysis of the Change:

Since the 1996 *NEC*, the *Code* has recognized low-voltage lighting systems operating at a maximum of 30 volts. Since its inception, Article 411 has been designed to specifically cover the installation of nonhazardous low-voltage wiring and equipment. These low-voltage wiring systems are required to be listed with a maximum voltage of 30 volts (42.4 volts peak) with an isolating transformer separating the typically 120-volt branch circuit from the secondary low voltage side of the transformer.

Low-voltage landscape lighting systems for gardens, walkways, patios, decks, and accent illumination has been in use for the last 50 years. The electrical safety of low-voltage lighting combined with the low cost of operation for these systems have resulted in a proliferation in both residential and commercial installations throughout North America. UL Product Standard 2108 (*Standard for Low Voltage Lighting Systems*) and UL Product Standard 1838 (*Standard for Low Voltage Landscape Lighting Systems*) are the two main product standards that established the specific requirements for low-voltage lighting systems and components intended for permanent installation and for use in locations addressed by Article 411.

For the 2017 *NEC*, Article 411 was revised and re-organized for clarity. One of these revisions concerned the type of low-voltage Class 2 lighting systems covered by Article 411. Revisions in the 2014 *NEC* acknowledged that the provisions of Article 411 should apply to Class 2 luminaires operating above 30 volts (42.4 volts peak). These 2014 *NEC* revisions permitted luminaires operating up to 60 volts dc to be installed without grounding per the requirements of 411.6(A). This was justified because grounding (connected to earth or some conductive body that extends the ground connection) is not a necessary safety measure for products operating from an isolating source, and especially where voltages are within Class 2 limits where the human body has inherent resistant to the flow of electrical current.

The limitations of 411.3(A) and (B) for low-voltage lighting systems operating at 30 volts or less and the limitations of Class 2 low-voltage lighting systems

Article 411

conforming to NEC Chapter 9, Table 11(A) or Table 11(B) was removed for the 2017 *NEC*. For the 2014 *NEC*, the added requirements of 411.3(B) limited the low voltage power supply to the Class 2 power limits of *NEC* Chapter 9, Tables 11(A) or Table 11(B). According to the substantiation for the 2017 *NEC* revisions for 411.3, there is no safety-based reason for this limitation.

At 60 volts dc, Chapter 9, Table 11(B) limits a Class 2 power supply to a name-plate rating of 100 VA (volt/amperes or watts), which converts to 1.67 amperes. A literal compliance with this limitation required many low-voltage lighting systems with multiple luminaires to include multiple power supplies. There is no benefit in either fire or electric shock risk reduction to requiring the use of multiple power supplies for these low-voltage lighting systems. The power supply, along with the luminaire(s) and fitting(s), are evaluated for fire risk and shock hazard regardless of their power/current rating. What distinguishes Article 411 from Article 410 is the voltage limitation and isolation requirement, both of which allow for a different scheme of protection against electric shock injury.

The 2017 *NEC* revisions retained the requirement of 411.4(A) that a low-voltage bare conductor system must be listed as a system. The phrase, "lighting systems operating at 30 volts or less" was deleted from 411.4(A) as this was overly restrictive and in conflict with 411.4(B). Other types of low-voltage lighting systems (those that do not include bare conductors) are permitted to consist of an assembly of listed parts according to 411.4(B). Additionally, the previous sentence following 411.4(B) was a duplication of the "system" requirements for bare conductor systems as stated in 411.4(A), so it was deleted as well.

Article 411

The word "exposed" was deleted from 411.6(D). The term "exposed" is appropriate for the bare conductors covered under 411.6(C) but the wiring options permitted under 411.6(D) can apply to both exposed and concealed secondary circuit wiring.

This re-organization and revision to Article 411 should add clarity and make the *Code* more user-friendly when installing and inspection low-voltage lighting systems.

First Revisions: FR 5147
Public Inputs: PI 1888

422.2

Definition. (Appliances)

422.2 Definition. (Appliances)

- **Type of Change:** Deletion

- **Change at a Glance:** Previous definition of "Vending Machine" has been deleted.

- **Code Language: 422.2 Definition. (Appliances)**
  ~~Vending Machine. Any self-service device that dispenses products or merchandise without the necessity of replenishing the device between each vending operation and is designed to require insertion of coin, paper currency, token, card, key, or receipt of payment by other means.~~

- **2014 *NEC* Requirement**
  Vending machines were required to be GFCI-protected by the provisions of 422.51. To lend assistance in the GFCI requirements of vending machines, a definition for "Vending Machine" was included at 422.2.

- **2017 *NEC* Change**
  Vending machines are still required to be GFCI-protected, but the requirement has been relocated to 422.5(A)(5). All appliances operating at 50 volts or more are now required be listed (see new 422.6). In determining what constitutes a vending machine, the user of the *Code* will need to rely on the listing and the product standards for vending machines.

Analysis of the Change:

During the 2005 *NEC* revision process, Article 422 (Appliances) added new ground-fault circuit interrupter (GFCI) requirement for vending machines at 422.51. The substantiation for this GFCI requirement reported incidents where people were subjected to shock hazards by coming into contact with energized conductive surfaces of vending machines (some resulting in fatal electrocutions). GFCI provisions for vending machines provides a significant level of increased safety for users of vending machines that are often found in locations (both indoors and outdoors) that are exposed to wet or damp environments.

There were no real arguments concerning the fact that a vending machine needed to be GFCI-protected, the arguments centered around what constituted a vending machine. What qualifies as a vending machine for appropriate application of this rule? Does a coin-operated children's amusement ride often located at the front of retail stores qualify as a vending machine? How about a casino slot machine? What about an ATM machine or an ice maker at a hotel?

To help answer these questions about what qualifies as a vending machine, which, in turn, answers the ultimate question concerning GFCI protection, a definition of a "vending machine" was added at 422.51 for the 2008 *NEC*. A vending machine was defined as "any self-service device that dispenses products or merchandise without the necessity of replenishing the device between each vending operation and is designed to require insertion of a coin, paper currency, token, card, key, or receipt of payment by other means." This definition was relocated to 422.2 for the 2011 *NEC* and remained at this location for the 2014 *NEC*.

422.2

For the 2017 *NEC*, this definition of a vending machine at 422.2 was deleted along with its companion requirement for vending machines at 422.51. Did this 2017 *NEC* action eliminate the requirement for GFCI protection for vending machines? No, it did not, as all requirements for GFCI protection for appliances were gathered into a common location in the new 422.5 and vending machines are included in the list of appliances demanding GFCI protection [see 422.5(A)(5)].

CMP-17 determined that the definition of a vending machine was no longer necessary as a new listing requirement, added to the 2017 *NEC* at 422.6, calls for all appliances operating at 50 volts or more to be listed. In deleting the previous definition of a vending machine, CMP-17 stated that "the revision to require all appliances to be listed eliminates the need for a definition of vending machine." According to the substantiation to require appliances to be listed, it was stated that requiring appliances to be listed ensures the requirements of Article 422 are applied to the correct equipment. Using the previous 422.2 definition for vending machines or using marketing information or marketplace terms for other appliances could result in misapplication of requirements from Article 422 (including GFCI protection). Listing of appliances will properly classify the equipment and that listing for that particular appliance will ensure application of proper installation requirements.

The previous 422.2 definition of a vending machine was very broad in nature and, more than likely, could have encompassed equipment not listed as an appliance, which was never considered in the development of the GFCI requirements for vending machines in previous 422.51. Time will tell the electrical industry if this definition of a vending machine was necessary or not for proper application of GFCI protection. Some will argue that without this previous definition, the application of GFCI protection to vending machines will be even broader as the AHJ will now be the deciding factor as to what constitutes a vending machine and what does not. Hopefully, the AHJ will make the link and consider the product standards for vending machines in the determination as to what a vending machine is or is not.

An informational note that pointed users of the *Code* to the product standards for vending machines was part of the deletion of previous 422.51. For further information on the product standards for vending machines, see UL 541 (*Standard for Refrigerated Vending Machines*) and UL 751 (*Standard for Vending Machines*).

First Revisions: FR 4875

422.5

GFCI Protection for Appliances

GFCI requirements for Appliances *(250 volts or less and 60 amperes or less, single- or 3-phase)* have been moved to one location in Article 422 *(Multiple GFCI devices are permitted but not required)*

(1) Automotive vacuum machines; (2) Drinking water coolers; (3) High-pressure spray washing machines *(cord-and-plug-connected)*; (4) Tire inflation machines; (5) Vending machines

422.5 Ground-Fault Circuit-Interrupter (GFCI) Protection for Personnel

- **Type of Change:** New/Revision

- **Change at a Glance:** GFCI requirements from 210.8 and throughout Article 422 are related to personnel hazards from specific equipment (contact with equipment with excessive leakage current) and provide those requirements in a single location in Article 422.

- **Code Language: 422.5 Ground-Fault Circuit-Interrupter (GFCI) Protection for Personnel.**
  ~~The device providing GFCI protection required in this article shall be readily accessible.~~

  (A) General. Appliances identified in 422.5(A)(1) through (5) rated 250 volts or less and 60 amperes or less, single- or 3-phase, shall be provided with GFCI protection for personnel. Multiple GFCI protective devices shall be permitted but shall not be required.
  (1) Automotive vacuum machines provided for public use
  (2) Drinking ~~fountains~~ water coolers
  (3) High-pressure spray washing machines — cord- and plug-connected
  (4) Tire inflation machines provided for public use
  (5) Vending machines

  (B) Type. The GFCI shall be readily accessible, listed, and located in one or more of the following locations:
  (1) Within the branch circuit overcurrent device
  (2) A device or outlet within the supply circuit
  (3) An integral part of the attachment plug
  (4) Within the supply cord not more than 300 mm (12 in.) from the attachment plug
  (5) Factory installed within the appliance

- **2014 *NEC* Requirement**
  GFCI protection was required for five specific appliances within Article 422. GFCI protection was required for tire inflation machines and automotive vacuum machines provided for public use at 422.23; cord- and plug-connected high-pressure spray washing machines at 422.49; cord- and plug-connected and hard-wired vending machines at 422.51; and electric drinking fountains at 422.52. Most of these GFCI provisions had specifics as to the location and type of GFCI protection delivery methods were required. The device providing the GFCI protection required throughout Article 422 was required to be readily accessible by the requirements of 422.5.

- **2017 *NEC* Change**
  The five appliances requiring GFCI protection in Article 422 were grouped together, and the GFCI requirements for these appliances were relocated to one location at 422.5(A). A new 422.5(B) was also added allowing five options for the location and type of GFCI protective device provided to deliver GFCI protection to the specific appliances listed at 422.5(A).

Analysis of the Change:
The requirements to have specific appliances provided with ground-fault circuit-interrupter (GFCI) protection have been gathered into one location within

422.5

Article 422 for the 2017 *NEC*. This relocation has resulted in the expansion and revision of existing 422.5. Previously, the GFCI requirements for protection of appliances were spread out over several parts of Article 422, which made finding these GFCI requirements more difficult for the user of the *Code*.

This revision incorporates GFCI requirements from throughout Article 422 that are related to personnel shock hazards from specific appliances (contact with equipment with excessive leakage current) into a single location. The shock hazards associated with specific appliances have been substantiated, in past *Code* cycles, as abnormal conditions in the equipment related to intentional or unintentional physical abuse, harsh environments such as weather conditions, or simply shock hazards created with the end of life of an appliance. Collecting these specific GFCI requirements into one central location will increase clarity and usability.

In order to re-locate some of the GFCI requirements for such things as a dwelling unit dishwasher (presently located in 210.8), public inputs and comments were submitted to have these appliance-related GFCI provisions located at 422.5 as well. However, because these GFCI provisions for general purpose receptacle outlets related to locations and environmental factors and not to specific equipment, they remain grouped in 210.8 for now.

422.5

Based on the voltage limitation of the product standard for GFCIs (UL 943), the "250 volts or less" value was included in 422.5. In reviewing UL 943, this product standard covers single and three-phase GFCI protective devices that operate at several voltage levels, all rated 250 volts or less. As stated earlier, personnel shock hazards are typically related to abnormal conditions for the specific equipment and do not change regardless of the voltage (250 volts or less), nor do these shock hazards change with regard to single or three-phase applications. While UL 943 does not limit applications to 60 amperes or less, that ampere rating was chosen for the ampacity value at 422.5 because 60 amperes or less covers the appliance applications addressed at 422.5 where GFCI protection is commercially available.

A new 422.5(B) gives five options for the location and type of GFCI protective device to deliver GFCI protection to the specific appliances listed at 422.5(A). The shock hazard surrounding these appliances is associated with a person coming in contact with the appliance while grounded (connected to earth) at the same time the appliance is in a condition that allows current to flow outside the intended path. In these cases, the location and type of GFCI protective device employed is not relevant to the safety of the person involved. The five options identified by 422.5(B) permits the GFCI protection to be provided by any GFCI protective device listed and identified from UL 943. The options at 422.5(B) also provide owners, designers, and installers the ability to select the location most suitable for the conditions involved.

Where the appliances specified at 422.5(A) include built-in GFCI protection in the supply cord, the text at 422.5(A) does not require additional GFCI protection but recognizes that multiple levels of GFCI protection are compatible and do not cause any safety or operational concerns. The determination as to whether an appliance incorporates built-in GFCI protection in the appliance itself is an issue best resolved within the specific product standard, rather than being dictated by the *NEC*.

Finally, revisions to 422.5(A) changed the previous 422.52 term of *electric drinking fountain* to *drinking water cooler*. This decision was based on the specific identified term used in the applicable product standard for drinking water coolers (UL 399).

First Revisions: FR 4801
Second Revisions: SR 39
Public Inputs: PI 101, PI 2425, PI 1939,
PI 2424, PI 3004, PI 1940, PI 2818,
PI 76, PI 410, PI 3342, PI 1456

422.6

Listing Required. (Appliances)

422.6 Listing Required. (Appliances)

- **Type of Change:** New

- **Change at a Glance:** New listing requirement enforced for all appliances operating at 50 volts or more.

- **Code Language: 422.6 Listing Required. (Appliances)**
  All appliances operating at 50 volts or more shall be listed.

■ **2014 *NEC* Requirement**

There was no specific requirement for specific appliances addressed in Article 422 to be listed. Listed equipment was referenced in eleven different locations in Article 422, but not any requirement for the equipment covered to be specifically listed.

■ **2017 *NEC* Change**

A new section has been added to Article 422 requiring that all appliances operating at 50 volts or more must be listed.

Analysis of the Change:

A new section has been added to Article 422 at 422.6 dealing with listing requirements for appliances. Beginning with the 2017 *NEC*, all appliances operating at 50 volts or more will be required to be listed. All appliances should be listed to help determine the appropriate classification of the equipment and to ensure application of product standard installation requirements. This labeling requirement for appliances will go a long way in ensuring that listed and labeled equipment is installed and used in accordance with any instructions included in the listing or labeling of that particular piece of equipment [see 110.3(B)].

Requirements throughout Article 422 are related to specific appliances. Requiring appliances to be listed will greatly aid in assuring the specific requirements for a specific appliance are applied to the correct type of appliance or equipment. Relying on nothing more than *NEC* definitions and industry terms or product marketing information can and often does result in misinterpretation and misapplication of requirements located in Article 422 for appliances. Furthermore, Article 422 includes requirements that must be included in the construction of certain appliances. The listing requirements for that particular appliance are the best place to address those construction requirements.

In an effort to be specific as to which appliances need to be listed, CMP-17 took their direction from the requirements in 110.27, which states in part, "...live parts of electrical equipment operating at 50 volts or more shall be guarded against accidental contact..." as the means to specify which appliances covered in Article 422 would be required to be listed. The term "appliance" is very broad in nature. Without the specific listing requirement pertaining only to "all appliances operating at 50 volts or more," this new listing requirement could have been interpreted as having application to appliances that have no special installation requirements, such as portable appliances (which have their own listing and product standard requirements).

First Revisions: FR 4802
Second Revisions: SR 4801
Public Input: PI 3026
Public Comments: PC 1517

422.6

422.14

Infrared Lamp Industrial Heating Appliances

422.14

422.14 Infrared Lamp Industrial Heating Appliances

- **Type of Change:** Deletion/Relocation

- **Change at a Glance:** Rules for industrial infrared lamp heating appliances have been deleted and relocated in new Article 425.

- **Code Language:** 422.14 Infrared Lamp Industrial Heating Appliances.
  In industrial occupancies, infrared heating appliance lampholders shall be permitted to be operated in series on circuits of over 150 volts to ground, provided the voltage rating of the lampholders is not less than the circuit voltage.

  Each section, panel, or strip carrying a number of infrared lampholders (including the internal wiring of such section, panel, or strip) shall be considered an appliance. The terminal connection block of each such assembly shall be considered an individual outlet.

- **2014 *NEC* Requirement**
  Requirements pertaining to industrial infrared lamp heating appliances were located in Article 422 for appliances at 422.14.

■ **2017** *NEC* **Change**
Section 422.14 titled, "Infrared Lamp Industrial Heating Appliances," was deleted and the information relocated to new Article 425 at 425.14.

Analysis of the Change:

A new article is being added to chapter 4 for the 2017 *NEC*. This new Article 425 titled, "Fixed Resistance and Electrode Industrial Process Heating Equipment" will apply to such things as boilers, electrode boilers, duct heaters, strip heaters, immersion heaters, process air heaters, or other approved fixed electric equipment used for industrial process heating (see the reported change for Article 425 for more detailed information).

Part of the reasons for the creation of this new article was to gather existing *NEC* requirements covering industrial heating equipment and to relocate that information to its new home in Article 425. This process began with the transfer of the requirements for industrial infrared lamp heating appliances formerly located at 422.14. Requirements for industrial infrared lamp heating appliances have been in Article 422 in some form or fashion since the 1947 *NEC*. For the 2017 *NEC*, this information was moved into new Article 425.

422.14

This relocation brings requirements for commercial and industrial fixed resistance and process heating equipment together while improving clarity and usability of the *NEC* requirements for the installers and inspectors of these types of industrial heating systems. These types of heating lamps are part of a larger group of commercial/industrial heating equipment that deserves its own article.

First Revisions: FR 4874
Public Input: PI 1025

422.16(B)(2)

Built-In Dishwashers

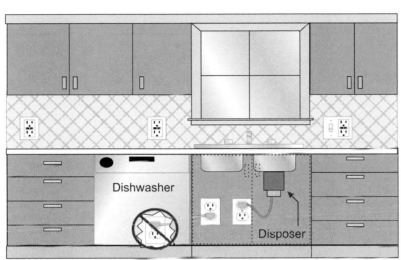

Receptacle outlet for cord-and-plug connected built-in dishwasher required to be located in the space adjacent to the space containing the dishwasher only with the length of a cord for a built-in dishwasher lengthened from 1.2 m (4 ft) to 2.0 m (6½ ft)

422.16(B)(2) Flexible Cords. (Appliances)

- **Type of Change:** Revision

- **Change at a Glance:** Maximum length of flexible cord for built-in dishwashers increased from 1.2 m (4 ft) to 2.0 m (6.5 ft) while the receptacle outlet for a built-in dishwasher can only be located in the space adjacent to the dishwasher.

- **Code Language: 422.16 Flexible Cords. (Appliances)**
  (B) Specific Appliances.
  (2) Built-in Dishwashers and Trash Compactors. Built-in dishwashers and trash compactors shall be permitted to be cord- and plug-connected with a flexible cord identified as suitable for the purpose in the installation instructions of the appliance manufacturer where all of the following conditions are met:

  (1) The flexible cord shall be terminated with a grounding-type attachment plug.
  Exception: *A listed dishwasher or trash compactor distinctly marked to identify it as protected by a system of double insulation, or its equivalent, shall not be required to be terminated with a grounding-type attachment plug.*
  (2) For a trash compactor, Tthe length of the cord shall be 0.9 m to 1.2 m

(3 ft to 4 ft) measured from the face of the attachment plug to the plane of the rear of the appliance.

(3) For a built-in dishwasher, the length of the cord shall be 0.9 m to 2.0 m (3 ft to 6.5 ft) measured from the face of the attachment plug to the plane of the rear of the appliance.

(4) Receptacles shall be located to ~~avoid~~ protect against physical damage to the flexible cord.

(5) The receptacle for a trash compactor shall be located in the space occupied by the appliance or adjacent thereto.

(6) The receptacle for a built-in dishwasher shall be located in the space adjacent to the space occupied by the dishwasher.

(7) The receptacle shall be accessible.

422.16(B)(2)

■ **2014 *NEC* Requirement**

A built-in dishwasher or a trash compactor is permitted to be cord- and plug-connected with a flexible cord identified for the purpose and terminated with a grounding-type attachment plug cap. The length of the flexible cord is permitted, for both a dishwasher and a trash compactor, to be 0.9 m to 1.2 m (3 ft to 4 ft) with the length measured from the face of the attachment plug to the plane created by the back of the appliance. The receptacles must be located so that the potential for physical damage to the flexible cord and attachment plug is minimized. The receptacle outlet for both a built-in dishwasher and a trash compactor could be located in the space occupied by the appliance or adjacent to it, and the receptacle must be accessible.

■ **2017 *NEC* Change**

Dishwashers are now only permitted to have the receptacle outlet for a cord- and plug-connected built-in dishwasher to be located in the space adjacent to the space occupied by the dishwasher. The maximum length of a cord for a built-in dishwasher was extended from the previous maximum length of 1.2 m (4 ft) to 2.0 m (6.5 ft) measured from the face of the attachment plug to the plane of the rear of the appliance. Other requirements for dishwashers and trash compactors remain the same as in the 2014 *NEC*.

Analysis of the Change:

Changes occurred for the 2017 *NEC* at 422.16(B)(2) which will only permit the receptacle outlet for a cord- and plug-connected built-in dishwasher to be located "in the space adjacent to the space occupied by the dishwasher." In previous editions of the *Code*, the receptacle outlet for a trash compactor or a built-in dishwasher could be located "in the space occupied by the appliance or adjacent thereto." This change corresponds with provisions in the product standard for household dishwashers, UL 749.

Section 8.3.3(a) of UL 749 states in part, "the power-supply receptacle for the appliance (dishwasher) shall be installed in a cabinet or on a wall adjacent to the under counter space in which the appliance is to be installed." In other words, UL 749 prohibits the installation of the power supply receptacle outlet for the dishwasher being installed in the same cabinet space as the dishwasher. This prohibition caused concern in the past as *NEC* 422.16(B)(2) allowed the power-supply receptacle outlet for the dishwasher to be located in the same space (behind the dishwasher). The dishwasher's product standard and the manufacturer's installation instructions did not, which was a violation of 110.3(B). This change occurred to align 422.16(B)(2) with the product standard for household dishwashers, UL 749.

To accommodate this potentially extended length of the cord for connection to a receptacle outlet in the adjacent cabinet space, the maximum length of a cord for a built-in dishwasher was extended from the previous length of 1.2 m (4 ft) to 2.0 m (6.5 ft), measured from the face of the attachment plug to the plane of the rear of the appliance. Some in the electrical community might argue that running a flexible cord through a drilled hole in a cabinet wall to the adjacent cabinet space will subject the flexible cord to physical damage and violate the uses not permitted for a flexible cord at 400.12(2) and (7). However, there are protective bushings that can be used in the drilled holes to protect the flexible cord.

First Revisions: FR 4804
Public Inputs: PI 1245

422.16(B)(4)

422.16(B)(4)

Range Hoods

Range hoods are permitted to be cord-and-plug connected where identified on installation instructions by manufacturer and meets the following:

Range hood/microwave oven combination→

Range

- Cord terminates in a grounding type plug
- Cord length is at least 450 mm (18 in.) and not more than 1.2 m (4 ft)
- Receptacle located to avoid physical damage to the cord
- Receptacle is accessible
- Receptacle is supplied by an individual branch circuit

Length of cord for cord-and-plug connected range hoods increased from 900 mm (36 in.) to 1.2 m (4 ft)

422.16(B)(4) Flexible Cords. (Appliances) Range Hoods

■ **Type of Change:** Revision

■ **Change at a Glance:** The maximum length of a flexible cord for a cord-and plug-connected range hood has been increased from 900 mm (36 in.) to 1.2 m (4 ft).

■ **Code Language: 422.16 Flexible Cords. (Appliances)**
(B) Specific Appliances.
(4) Range Hoods. Range hoods shall be permitted to be cord- and plug-connected with a flexible cord identified as suitable for use on range hoods in the installation instructions of the appliance manufacturer, where all of the following conditions are met:

(1) The flexible cord is terminated with a grounding-type attachment plug.

Exception: A listed range hood distinctly marked to identify it as protected by a system of double insulation, or its equivalent, shall not be required to be terminated with a grounding-type attachment plug.

(2) The length of the cord is not less than 450 mm (18 in.) and not over ~~900 mm (36 in.)~~ 1.2 m (4 ft).

(3) Receptacles are located to ~~avoid~~ protect against physical damage to the flexible cord.

(4) The receptacle is accessible.

(5) The receptacle is supplied by an individual branch circuit.

422.16(B)(4)

■ **2014 *NEC* Requirement**
Range hoods were permitted to be cord- and plug-connected with a flexible cord where the flexible cord was terminated with a grounding-type attachment plug (with an exception for system of double insulation); the length of the cord could not be less than 450 mm (18 in.) and not over 900 mm (36 in.); the receptacle had to be accessible, located to avoid physical damage to the flexible cord, and supplied by an individual branch circuit (in the event of the employment of a microwave oven).

■ **2017 *NEC* Change**
The requirements for a cord- and plug-connected range hood are much the same as the 2014 *NEC* with the length of the flexible cord expanded to 1.2 m (4 ft). The language pertaining to the receptacle needing to be located to "avoid" physical damage was changed to "protect against" physical damage to incorporate more enforceable language.

Analysis of the Change:

The length of a flexible cord used in conjunction with a range hood has historically been limited to a cord that is not less than 450 mm (18 in.) and not more than 900 mm (36 in.). For the 2017 *NEC*, the maximum length of a range hood flexible cord has been extended an extra foot to not more than 1.2 m (4 ft). The extra length was needed to accommodate larger range hoods that are currently available to the general public. This additional length will not impact the electrical safety of this installation.

With some of the designs of the newer range hoods, the previous maximum length of 900 mm (36 in.) was insufficient, putting undue stress and strain on the cord in order to reach the mating receptacle outlet. Some range hoods are now as wide as 1.2 m (48 in.) and, in some cases, even greater. The height (top to bottom) of some of the newer chimney-type range hoods is a concern for cord length as well.

UL Product Standard 507 (*Standard for Electric Fans*) at one time permitted a maximum length of flexible cord for a range hood to be up to 1.2 m (4 ft). During the 2005 *NEC* revision process, 422.16(B)(4) was incorporated into the *Code*. This 2005 *NEC* revision adopted the 450 mm (18 in.) to 900 mm (36 in.) length of range hood flexible cords. This 900 mm (36 in.) length was not really substantiated as a technical or safety reason for the limitation. The permission to use a cord- and plug-connection for a range hood provided ease in the ability to upgrade to a combination microwave/range hood. According to the CMP-17 Panel Statement, the additional requirements (length of cord, etc.) were added "to ensure a safe installation of a combined microwave/range hood" (see May 2004 ROP 17-21). UL 507 [which permitted up to 1.2 m (4 ft)] was subsequently revised to agree with the *NEC*, and now UL 507, Paragraph 9.16.5, requires the same length of flexible cord [450 mm (18 in.) and not more than 900 mm (36 in.)] for a range hood as does 422.16(B)(4).

It is likely that this revision to 422.16(B)(4) will once again spur changes to UL 507 for consistency between the two documents. Additionally, the product safety Standard (CSA C22.2 No. 113-12, Clause 5.4.2.15), for range hoods in Canada allows for a flexible cord length up to 1.2 m (4 ft). Permitting this same option in the United States would provide for more consistent requirements across North America. This would allow manufacturers to streamline production by not carrying two different cord lengths, one for the USA, and one for Canada.

First Revisions: FR 4805
Public Input: PI 4349

422.16(B)(4)

Article 424 Part V

Electric Space-Heating Cables

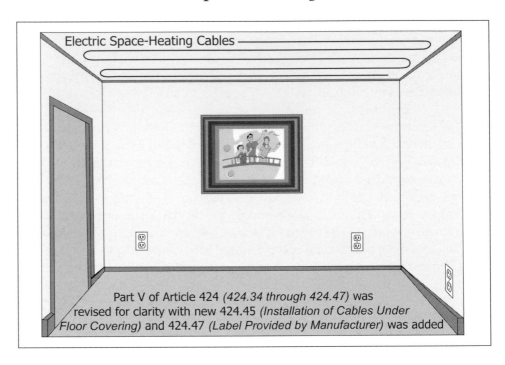

Electric Space-Heating Cables

Part V of Article 424 *(424.34 through 424.47)* was revised for clarity with new 424.45 *(Installation of Cables Under Floor Covering)* and 424.47 *(Label Provided by Manufacturer)* was added

424 Part V

Article 424 Part V Fixed Electric Space-Heating Equipment

- **Type of Change:** Revision

- **Change at a Glance:** Part V (424.34 through 424.47) of Article 424 was revised for clarity.

- **Code Language:** **Article 424 Fixed Electric Space-Heating Equipment**
  424.34 Heating Cable Construction.
  424.35 Marking of Heating Cables.
  424.36 Clearances of Wiring in Ceilings.
  424.38 Area Restrictions.
  424.39 Clearance from Other Objects and Openings.
  424.40 Splices.
  424.41 Ceiling Installation of Heating Cables on Dry Board, in Plaster, and on Concrete Ceilings.
  424.42 Finished Ceilings.
  424.43 Installation of Nonheating Leads of Cables.
  424.44 Installation of Cables in Concrete or Poured Masonry Floors.
  424.45 ~~**Inspection and Tests.**~~ **Installation of Cables Under Floor Covering.**
  424.46 Inspection and Test.
  424.47 Label Provided by Manufacturer.
  (See NEC for complete text)

- **2014 *NEC* Requirement**
  Part V of Article 424 addressed electric space-heating cables. These requirements encompassed sections 424.35 through 424.45.

- **2017 *NEC* Change**
  Part V of Article 424 was revised for simpler interpretation and application. Two new sections were added. These sections (424.45 and 424.47) address proper installations of cables under floor coverings and labels provided by the manufacturer. The previous edition of the *Code* did not properly address these added items in Part V.

Analysis of the Change:

For the proper installation of fixed electric space-heating equipment, users of the *Code* rely on Article 424 of the *NEC*. More specifically, Part V of Article 424 addresses electric space-heating cables, and for the 2017 *NEC*, has received significant revision and a few new additions.

One of the highlighted changes to Part V occurred at 424.35 for marking of heating cables. Each unit of heating cable is still required to be marked with an identifying name or identification symbol, catalog number, and ratings in volts and watts or volts and amperes, but the specific color identification marking of each cable has been removed. Each unit of fixed electric space-heating equipment (including heating cables) are required per 424.28(A) to be permanently marked with the rated voltage on the nameplate marking, which in turn identifies the voltage rating of the product. Additionally, 424.28(B) demands that the nameplate be located "so as to be visible or easily accessible after installation." This method of marking (nameplate label instead of color coded leads) is also allowed for heating panels. The previous requirements for color coding of heating cable leads was deemed unnecessary and was inconsistent with other heating products covered by Article 424.

The previous requirements of 424.38(A) limited heating cable installation to only the room or area in which they originated. Revisions to this section will now allow heating cables to extend beyond these rooms or areas. According to the substantiation for this revision, advances in technology, product designs, and product standards make it unnecessary to restrict heating cables to the room in which they originate, particularly for floor warming applications. When there is a path provided from one room to another, such as a doorway from the water closet area to the vanity area in a bathroom, the floor can be warmed with one heating cable circuit without creating safety concerns as long as the manufacturer's installation instructions are followed.

The title of 424.38(B) was changed from "Uses Prohibited" to Uses Not Permitted" to be more consistent with other articles of the *NEC*. This section received extensive revision as well. The previous restrictions for heating cables at this section seemed to pertain only to heating cables installed in or above ceiling areas. In addition to these ceiling restrictions, limitations for floor heating cables were added.

424 Part V

The word "Ceiling" was moved to the beginning (rather than the end) of the title of 424.41 to signify clearly that the entire section refers to ceiling installations only. Previously, some of the applications located in this section have been incorrectly used by some enforcers for application to heating cables located in floors or walls, where heating cables may be Code-compliant and acceptably installed up a vertical surface such as a step riser, bench front or similar.

The requirements and text of 424.44 for installations of heating cables in concrete or poured masonry floors was revised to eliminate prescriptive installation in that part of the heating cable design. The deleted installation criteria is part of UL 1673 (*Standard for Electric Space Heating Cables*) and is specified in the manufacturer's instructions for heating cables. These deleted instructions are already addressed as a part of the heating cable listing (see 424.6). Section 424.44(D) titled, "Spacing Between Heating Cable and Metal Embedded in the Floor" was deleted since heating cable is required to be listed, which requires a grounding component (braid or sheath) over the heated section of the cable. This requirement is also covered by UL 1673, but this product standard was not in existence when Article 424 and 424.44(D) were introduced into the *Code* in the 1968 edition of the *NEC*.

424 Part V

Two new sections were introduced to Part V of Article 424 with the inclusion of 424.45 (Installation of Cables Under Floor Coverings) and 424.47 (Label Provided by Manufacturer). These new sections will be discussed in greater detail with the next changes reported on in this manuscript.

The public inputs that lead to these revisions as new requirements in Part V of Article 424 were submitted by and represents the consensus of the Article 424 Electric Space Heating Working Task Group. This group was formed as an outcome of an industry Standards Technical Panel (STP) meeting for Electric Radiant Heating Panels and Cables.

First Revisions: FR 4815, FR 4823-29, FR 4831-34
Second Revisions: SR 4809
Public Inputs: PI 3515, PI 3517, PI 3527-29, PI 3533,
PI 3535, PI 3536, PI 3543-45, PI 4209, PI 4234
Public Comments: PC 945

424.45

Heating Cables Under Floor Coverings

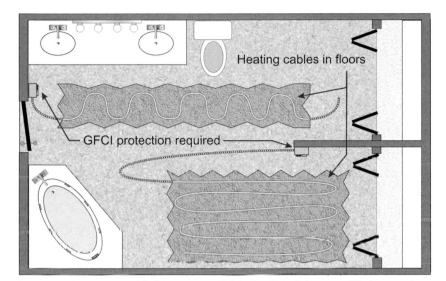

Heating cables in floors

GFCI protection required

New requirements added In Part V of Article 424 giving specific instruction for the installation of heating cables installed under floor coverings

424.45

424.45 Installation of Cables Under Floor Coverings

- **Type of Change:** New

- **Change at a Glance:** New requirements were added for the installation of heating cables installed under floor coverings.

- **Code Language: 424.45 Installation of Cables Under Floor Coverings.**

  (A) Identification. Heating cables for installation under floor covering shall be identified as suitable for installation under floor covering.

  (B) Expansion Joints. Heating cables shall not be installed where they bridge expansion joints unless provided with expansion and contraction fittings applicable to the manufacture of the cable.

  (C) Connection to Conductors. Heating cables shall be connected to branch-circuit and supply wiring by wiring methods described in the installation instructions or as recognized in Chapter 3.

  (D) Anchoring. Heating cables shall be positioned or secured in place under the floor covering, per the manufacturer's instructions.

  (E) Ground-Fault Circuit-Interrupter Protection. Ground-fault circuit-interrupter protection for personnel shall be provided.

(F) Grounding Braid or Sheath. Grounding means, such as copper braid, metal sheath, or other approved means, shall be provided as part of the heated length.

- **2014 *NEC* Requirement**
  Requirements found in Part IX of Article 424—specifically, 424.99—are explicit for the installation of electric heating panels and heating panel sets installed under floor coverings. There were no such requirements in Part V of Article 424 for electric space-heating cables.

- **2017 *NEC* Change**
  New requirements were added at 424.45 (Part V of Article 424) to give direction for the installation of heating cables installed under floor coverings.

Analysis of the Change:

A new 424.45 with prescriptive language for the installation of heating cables under floor coverings was added. This practice is not new to the electrical industry, but installation requirements for these under flooring heating cables is new for Article 424. By the provisions of 424.44(G), these types of heating cables were and are required to be GFCI protected where they are installed in electrically heated concrete or poured masonry floors of bathrooms, kitchens, and in hydromassage bathtub locations.

424.45

Heating cables and heating panels have become very similar in terms of installation and use. In previous editions of the *Code*, 424.99 has specifically permitted heating panels installed under floor coverings for several *Code* cycles. These rules are located under Part IX for electric radiant heating panels and heating panel sets. Heating panels, as well as heating cables, are being installed under floor coverings such as ceramic tile in bathroom and showers, under laminate flooring, and sometimes even under carpet. It is critical that these installations comply with the listing, product standard, and the manufacturer's instructions. Before the 2017 *NEC*, Part V of Article 424, which deals with electric space-heating cables, did not specifically mention under floor coverings for heating cables. According to some users of the *Code*, this left it unclear whether or not heating cables installed under a floor covering was permitted. To clear up this confusion and to make it clear that this type of installation is permitted by the *NEC*, the new text of 424.45 has been added, which is similar to the text of 424.99 for electric radiant heating panels and heating panel sets.

The public inputs that led to this new requirement in Part V were submitted by and represent the consensus of the Article 424 Electric Space Heating Working Task Group. This group was formed as an outcome of an industry Standards Technical Panel (STP) meeting for Electric Radiant Heating Panels and Cables. The UL product standards for these are UL 1693 (*Standard for Electric Radiant Heating Panels and Heating Panel Sets*) and UL 1673 (*Standard for Electric Space Heating Cables*).

First Revisions: FR 4834
Public Inputs: PI 3545

424.47

Label Provided by Manufacturer

Manufacturers of electric space-heating cables are to provide marking labels that indicate electric space-heating cables present and instructions that the labels be affixed to panelboards identifying branch circuits supply heating cables

⚠ CAUTION

RISK OF ELECTRICAL SHOCK-ELECTRICAL WIRING AND HEATING CABLES CONTAINED BELOW THE FLOOR. DO NOT PENETRATE FLOOR WITH NAILS, SCREWS, ETC.

Electric space-heating cables installed in this area. Avoid actions which may result in mechanical damage to these heating cables.

Room Name	Circuit Breaker	Volt Rating	Total Output	No. of Units
Master Bathroom	14	120 volts	2.55 A / Unit	3

If the electric space-heating cable installations are visible and distinguishable after installation, labels are not required to be provided and affixed to panelboards

424.47 Label Provided by Manufacturer

- **Type of Change:** New

- **Change at a Glance:** New provisions were added for manufacturers of electric space-heating cables to provide marking labels to be affixed to panelboards to identify which branch circuits supply the circuits to those space-heating installations.

- **Code Language: 424.47 Label Provided by Manufacturer.** The manufacturers of electric space-heating cables shall provide marking labels that indicate that the space-heating installation incorporates electric space-heating cables, and instructions that the labels shall be affixed to the panelboards to identify which branch circuits supply the circuits to those space-heating installations. If the electric space-heating cable installations are visible and distinguishable after installation, the labels shall not be required to be provided and affixed to the panelboards.

- **2014 *NEC* Requirement**
  Manufacturer's label requirements for the marking of heating panels and panel sets are located at 424.92(D). These requirements call for the manufacturer to provide marking labels that indicate that heating panels and panel sets are part of the space-heating installation. These labels must

424.47

also provide instruction for applying these labels to the supply panel-boards, and the label must further identify which branch circuits supply the heating panels and panel sets. This label requirement is located in Part IX of Article 424 with application for heating panels and panel sets. There were no such requirements in Part V of Article 424 for electric space-heating cables.

■ **2017 *NEC* Change**
New requirements for manufacturer's labels were added at 424.47 in Part V of Article 424 for application to electric space-heating cables. The manufacturer's label requirements for heating panels and panel sets at 424.92(D) remained the same.

Analysis of the Change:

New requirements for manufacturer's labels were added to the provisions for electric space-heating cables located in Part V of Article 424. These new require-ments, located at 424.47, instruct the manufacturer of electric space-heating cables to provide marking labels that indicate that electric space-heating cables are part of the space-heating installation. These labels must also give the install-er instructions to apply these labels to the supply panelboard, and the label must further identify which branch circuits supply the space-heating cables. This labeling requirement provides a bit of relief if the electric space-heating cable installations are visible and distinguishable after installation. In these cases, the labels are not required to be provided and affixed to the panelboards.

This manufacturer's label requirement is very similar to and correlates the requirements for the marking of heating panels and panel sets at 424.92(D). Previously, with this label requirement located only in Part IX for electric radi-ant heating panels and heating panel sets, it was often not possible to apply this requirement to electric space-heating cables.

The public inputs and First Revision that lead to this new requirement in Part V were submitted by and represents the consensus of the Article 424 Electric Space Heating Working Task Group. This group was formed as an outcome of an industry Standards Technical Panel (STP) meeting for Electric Radiant Heat-ing Panels and Cables. The UL product standards for these heating cables is UL 1673 (*Standard for Electric Space Heating Cables*).

First Revisions: FR 4823

424.47

Article 424 Part X

Fixed Electric Space-Heating Equipment

424 Part X

Article 424 Part X Fixed Electric Space-Heating Equipment

- **Type of Change:** New

- **Change at a Glance:** A new Part X was added to Article 424 for low-voltage fixed electric space-heating equipment.

- **Code Language:** Article 424 Fixed Electric Space-Heating Equipment.
  Part X. Low-Voltage Fixed Electric Space-Heating Equipment
  424.100 Scope. Low-voltage fixed electric space-heating equipment shall consist of an isolating power supply, low-voltage heaters, and associated equipment that are all identified for use in dry locations.

  424.101 Energy Source.
  (A) Power Unit. The power unit shall be an isolating type with a rated output not exceeding 25 amperes, 30 volts (42.4 volts peak) ac, or 60 volts dc under all load conditions.

  (B) Alternate Energy Sources. Listed low-voltage fixed electric space-heating equipment shall be permitted to be supplied directly from an alternate energy source such as solar photovoltaic (PV) or wind power. When supplied from such a source, the source and any power conversion equipment between the source and the heating equipment and its supply shall be listed and comply with the applicable section of the *NEC* for the source used. The output of the source shall meet the limits of 424.101(A).

424.102 Listed Equipment. Low-voltage fixed electric space-heating equipment shall be listed as a complete system.

424.103 Installation.
(A) General. Equipment shall be installed per the manufacturer's installation instructions.

(B) Ground. Secondary circuits shall not be grounded.

(C) Ground-Fault Protection. Ground-fault protection shall not be required.

424.104 Branch Circuit.
(A) Equipment shall be permitted to be supplied from branch circuits rated not over 30 amperes.

(B) The equipment shall be considered a continuous duty load.

- **2014 *NEC* Requirement**
  The 2014 *NEC* did not address low-voltage fixed electric space-heating equipment in Article 424.

- **2017 *NEC* Change**
  To address products identified as low-voltage fixed electric space-heating equipment, a new Part X was added to Article 424 for the 2017 *NEC*.

Analysis of the Change:

A new Part X was added to Article 424 for the 2017 *NEC*. This new Part X will cover low-voltage fixed electric space-heating equipment. While previous editions of the *NEC* did not exclude these low-voltage heating products, they did not address provisions for the relatively new technology low-voltage heating cables or heating panel products. Without these new requirements, essentially a low-voltage piece of equipment would have to meet all the same requirements as 120-volt or 240-volt rated equipment.

Low-voltage fixed electric space-heating equipment is readily available to the public, and it operates on a low voltage source such as 30-volts ac or less. The power for these low-voltage products typically originates from a 120-volt branch circuit, then uses an isolating transformer to drop the voltage to the desired level. Additionally, the power source may be a stand-alone system such as a photovoltaic (PV) system or other similar source. Low-voltage equipment does not pose the same level of risk of shock or fire hazard as a higher voltage product; therefore, it is appropriate to apply different or modified requirements for low-voltage systems and equipment. Lack of specific requirements in the *NEC*

424 Part X

for these low-voltage products can result in confusion and inconsistency in installation requirements applied to them.

The new requirements incorporated in Part X of Article 424 are very similar to provisions already in place in the *NEC* in Article 411 for low-voltage lighting systems. Requirements that specifically address low-voltage fixed, electric space-heating equipment will be beneficial to manufacturers, installers, and inspectors. Understanding the power sources for this low-voltage equipment, as well as the operating principles of such equipment, will better define the risk involved (fire, shock hazard, etc.) that may be present or that may be reduced with low-voltage fixed, electric space-heating equipment.

For the purpose of the low-voltage fixed electric space-heating equipment addressed in Part X of Article 424, the rated output does not exceed 25 amperes, 30 volts (42.4 volts peak) ac, or 60 volts dc under all load conditions. The 30-volt ac and 60-volt dc levels were chosen to correlate with accepted levels considered by many to be a threshold of reduction in risk of electric shock. It also aligns with the voltage levels for Class 2 ac and Class 2 dc voltage levels in Chapter 9, Tables 11(A) and 11(B), respectively. The 25-ampere maximum output current was added to limit secondary current levels to levels associated with most low-voltage fixed electric space-heating equipment. Without this 25 ampere limit, secondary current would be unlimited.

424 Part X

Adding specific provisions for low-voltage fixed electric space-heating equipment will improve the consistency of installations and facilitate application of the prescriptive requirements for these devices.

The public inputs that led to this new requirement in Part V were submitted by and represent the consensus of the Article 424 Electric Space-Heating Working Task Group. This group was formed as an outcome of an industry Standards Technical Panel (STP) meeting for Electric Radiant Heating Panels and Cables. The UL product standards for these are UL 1693 (*Standard for Electric Radiant Heating Panels and Heating Panel Sets*) and UL 1673 (*Standard for Electric Space Heating Cables*).

First Revisions: FR 4843
Public Inputs: PI 3565

Article 425

Fixed Resistance and Electrode Industrial Process Heating Equipment

425

Article 425 Fixed Resistance and Electrode Industrial Process Heating Equipment

- **Type of Change:** New

- **Change at a Glance:** New Article: Fixed Resistance and Electrode Industrial Process Heating Equipment.

- **Code Language:** **Article 425 Fixed Resistance and Electrode Industrial Process Heating Equipment**
  Part I. General
  425.1 Scope. This article covers fixed industrial process heating employing electric resistance or electrode heating technology. For the purpose of this article, heating equipment shall include boilers, electrode boilers, duct heaters, strip heaters, immersion heaters, process air heaters, or other approved fixed electric equipment used for industrial process heating. This article shall not apply to heating and room air conditioning for personnel spaces covered by Article 424, fixed heating equipment for pipelines and vessels covered by Article 427, and induction and dielectric heating equipment covered by Article 665, and industrial furnaces incorporating silicon carbide, molybdenum, or graphite process heating elements.

425

425.28 Nameplate.
(A) Marking Required.
(B) Location.

425.29 Marking of Heating Elements.

425.45 Concealed Fixed Industrial Heating Equipment – Inspection and Tests.

Part V. Fixed Industrial Process Duct Heaters
425.57 General.
425.58 Identification.
425.59 Airflow.
425.60 Elevated Inlet Temperature.
425.63 Fan Circuit Interlock.
425.64 Limit Controls.
425.65 Location of Disconnecting Means.

Part VI. Fixed Industrial Process Resistance-Type Boilers
425.70 Scope.

425.71 Identification.

425.72 Overcurrent Protection.
(A) Boiler Employing Resistance-Type Immersion Heating Elements in an ASME-Rated and Stamped   Vessel.
(B) Boiler Employing Resistance-Type Heating Elements Rated More Than 48 Amperes and Not   Contained in an ASME-Rated and Stamped Vessel.
(C) Supplementary Overcurrent Protective Devices.
(D) Suitable for Branch-Circuit Protection.
(E) Conductors Supplying Supplementary Overcurrent Protective Devices.
(F) Conductors for Subdivided Loads.

425.73 Overtemperature Limit Control.

425.74 Overpressure Limit Control.

Part VII. Fixed Industrial Process Electrode-Type Boilers
425.80 Scope.
425.81 Identification.
425.82 Branch-Circuit Requirements.
425.83 Overtemperature Limit Control.
425.84 Overpressure Limit Control.
425.85 Grounding.
425.86 Markings.
(*See NEC for complete text*)

425

■ **2014 *NEC* Requirement**

The 2014 *NEC* did not completely address requirements for industrial process heating equipment. Section 422.14 covered some requirements for infrared heat lamps.

■ **2017 *NEC* Change**

New Article 425 (Fixed Resistance and Electrode Industrial Process Heating Equipment) has been incorporated into the 2017 *NEC*. In previous editions, the *NEC* did not adequately address requirements for industrial process heating equipment. Section 422.14, which covered appliances with infrared heat lamps, has been relocated to new Article 425 at 425.14.

Analysis of the Change:

A new article has been introduced for the 2017 *NEC* in Chapter 4; it is titled, "Fixed Resistance and Electrode Industrial Process Heating Equipment." In previous editions, the *NEC* did not adequately address requirements for industrial process heating equipment. Article 422 for appliances, had some requirements for infrared heat lamps, but those requirements have been relocated to new Article 425.

Article 425 will apply to such things as boilers, electrode boilers, duct heaters, strip heaters, immersion heaters, process air heaters, or other approved fixed electric equipment used for industrial process heating. This article will not apply to heating and room air-conditioning for personnel or personnel spaces covered by Article 424; fixed heating equipment for pipelines and vessels covered by Article 427; induction and dielectric heating equipment covered by Article 665; and industrial furnaces incorporating silicon carbide, molybdenum, or graphite process heating elements.

Article 425 will provide clear requirements for installation and enforcement for industrial process heating equipment, including working space, listing requirements, marking of equipment, overcurrent protection, protection from physical damage, installation in damp or wet locations, and spacing from combustible materials. Relevant NFPA standards that would apply to this article would be NFPA 86, *Standard for Ovens and Furnaces* and NFPA 79, *Electrical Standard for Industrial Machinery*.

First Revisions: FR 4841
Second Revisions: SR 4813, SR 7509, SCR 119
Public Input: PI 879
Public Comments: PC 422

425

426.32

Impedance Heating Voltage Limitation Fixed Outdoor Electric Deicing and Snow Melting Equipment

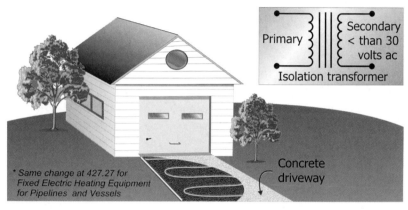

Secondary winding of an isolation transformer connected to the impedance heating elements shall not have an output voltage greater than 30 volts ac

Primary | Secondary < than 30 volts ac
Isolation transformer

* Same change at 427.27 for Fixed Electric Heating Equipment for Pipelines and Vessels

Concrete driveway

The allowance for voltage output greater than 30 volts ac if an impedance heating system for fixed outdoor electric deicing and snow-melting equipment is provided with Class A GFCI protection has been deleted

426.32 Voltage Limitations. (Fixed Outdoor Electric Deicing and Snow-Melting Equipment)

■ **Type of Change:** Revision

■ **Change at a Glance:** The allowance for voltage output greater than 30 volts ac if an impedance heating system for fixed outdoor electric deicing and snow-melting equipment is provided with Class A GFCI protection has been deleted.

■ **Code Language: 426.32 Voltage Limitations. (Fixed Outdoor Electric Deicing and Snow-Melting Equipment)**

~~Unless protected by ground-fault circuit-interrupter protection for personnel, the~~ The secondary winding of the isolation transformer connected to the impedance heating elements shall not have an output voltage greater than 30 volts ac. ~~Where ground-fault circuit-interrupter protection for personnel is provided, the voltage shall be permitted to be greater than 30 but not more than 80 volts.~~

■ **2014 *NEC* Requirement**
The secondary winding of an isolation transformer connected to an impedance heating element for fixed outdoor electric deicing and snow-

melting equipment could not have an output voltage greater than 30 volts ac unless it was protected by ground-fault circuit-interrupter (GFCI) for personnel. With GFCI protection of personnel, the voltage was permitted to be greater than 30 volts, but not more than 80 volts.

■ **2017 *NEC* Change**
The secondary winding of an isolation transformer connected to an impedance heating element cannot have an output voltage greater than 30 volts ac. The allowance for voltage output greater than 30 volts ac if the system is provided with Class A GFCI protection has been deleted.

Analysis of the Change:

Changes occurred at 426.32 to limit the output voltage of the secondary winding of an isolation transformer connected to impedance heating elements to not more than 30 volts ac. Previous editions of the *Code* allowed the voltage output to exceed 30 volts (but not more than 80 volts) where ground-fault circuit-interrupter (GFCI) protection for personnel was provided. This GFCI protection option was eliminated for the 2017 *NEC*.

This voltage limitation (with an exception for GFCI protection) has been in the *Code* since Article 426 went through an extensive reorganization for the 1981 *NEC*. When this rule was implemented in the 1981 *NEC*, GFCI protection for personnel was not defined or limited to the current Class A GFCI device of 4 to 6 mA. The definition of a ground-fault circuit interrupter added the inclusion of "when a current to ground exceeds the values established for a Class A device" and the fine print note that denoted the 4 to 6 mA tripping value for a Class A GFCI device during the 2002 edition of the *NEC*.

According to the submitter of the public input for this revision, the higher operating current levels of electrical impedance heating systems are not compatible with a Class A type GFCI protective device. An impedance heating system cannot be designed to have a leakage under 5 mA, which makes the Class A GFCI protection impractical. Allowing a Class A GFCI type protection system will only create a safety hazard due to a false expectation of the level of expected GFCI protection.

The original intent of the allowance of GFCI protection at 426.32 was to prevent arcing faults that could cause equipment damage and/or shock hazards for personnel. For this application, a problem was created when the definition of GFCI protection for personnel was defined beginning in the 2002 *NEC* as "not exceeding 4 to 6 mA." Since that occurrence (according to the submitter of the Public Input), the *Code* has allowed a protection system that simply does not function as intended.

This revision will result in increased safety for the user and these impedance heating systems. If left as previously written, an unsafe and misunderstood system may be supplied that could result in injury or death due to users expecting a level of protection that will not be functional.

426.32

This same revision occurred in Article 427 for impedance heating system for fixed electric heating equipment for pipelines and vessels at 427.27. See FR 4849 and PI 2239.

First Revisions: FR 4846
Public Input: PI 2240

430.2 and 430.4

Definitions: Part-Winding Motors

430.2 & .4

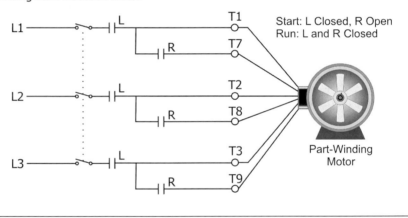

Part-Winding Motors. A part-winding start induction or synchronous motor is one that is arranged for starting by first energizing part of its primary (armature) winding and, subsequently, energizing the remainder of this winding in one or more steps. A standard part-winding start induction motor is arranged so that one-half of its primary winding can be energized initially, and, subsequently, the remaining half can be energized, both halves then carrying equal current. A hermetic refrigerant compressor motor shall not be considered a standard part-winding start induction motor.

Start: L Closed, R Open
Run: L and R Closed

Part-Winding Motor

430.2 and 430.4 Definitions. (Motors, Motor Circuits, and Controllers)

- **Type of Change:** Relocation/New

- **Change at a Glance:** A new definition was added at 430.2 for "Part-Winding Motors."

- **Code Language: 430.2 Definitions. (Motors, Motor Circuits, and Controllers)**
  430.2 Part-Winding Motors. A part-winding start induction or synchronous motor is one that is arranged for starting by first energizing part of its primary (armature) winding and, subsequently, energizing the remainder of this winding in one or more steps. A standard part-winding start induction motor is arranged so that one-half of its primary winding can be energized initially, and, subsequently, the remaining half can be energized, both halves then carrying equal current. A hermetic refrigerant

compressor motor shall not be considered a standard part-winding start induction motor.

430.4 Part-Winding Motors. ~~A part-winding start induction or synchronous motor is one that is arranged for starting by first energizing part of its primary (armature) winding and, subsequently, energizing the remainder of this winding in one or more steps. A standard part-winding start induction motor is arranged so that one-half of its primary winding can be energized initially, and, subsequently, the remaining half can be energized, both halves then carrying equal current. A hermetic refrigerant compressor motor shall not be considered a standard part-winding start induction motor.~~

Where separate overload devices are used with a standard part-winding start induction motor, each half of the motor winding shall be individually protected in accordance with 430.32 and 430.37 with a trip current one-half that specified.

Each motor-winding connection shall have branch-circuit short-circuit and ground-fault protection rated at not more than one-half that specified by 430.52.

Exception: A short-circuit and ground-fault protective device shall be permitted for both windings if the device will allow the motor to start. Where time-delay (dual-element) fuses are used, they shall be permitted to have a rating not exceeding 150 percent of the motor full load current.

- **2014 *NEC* Requirement**
  The definition of a part-winding motor was located at the beginning of 430.4.

- **2017 *NEC* Change**
  The definition of a part-winding motor was moved from 430.4 to its proper location at 430.2.

Analysis of the Change:

When looking at previous editions of the *Code*, 430.4 contained provisions for part-winding motors. The first paragraph seemed to be the definition of a part-winding motor. According to the *NEC Manual of Style*, Section 2.2.2.2 states that "if an article contains one or more definitions, the definition(s) shall be in the second section." To comply with the *NEC Style Manual*, this definition of a part-winding motor was moved from 430.4 to its proper location at 430.2. Provisions for part-winding motors were first introduced to the *NEC* at 430-3 during the 1965 edition of the *NEC*.

A part-winding or soft start motor is any system that is used to reduce inrush current, as well as strain on electrical circuits that supply power to motors. Inrush current is the initial surge of current into the windings when the motor is started. For a part-winding start, the winding in the motor must be split, so only a portion of it is connected when the motor is started. Dual voltage motors

430.2 & .4

typically have split windings, but they can only be started on the lower voltage. For example, a 240/480-volt motor will have the 240-volt winding powered initially. Typically, one-half of the winding will be powered initially, but it could be as much as two-thirds. The rest of the winding is added in with a relay or a timer when the motor has achieved a certain speed.

A part-winding motor will initially draw full voltage, but typically, only 65% of full current, and will rise to full current when the rest of the winding is added into the system. This process means that one of the contactors will be carrying 65% of the current during start-up. While the motor is running, each contactor will carry half the voltage. If load torque exceeds the torque provided by the part winding at a given speed, then the motor will lock in at that speed until the second part of the winding is connected. The motor will then develop full torque at that speed. The lower that speed is, the larger the surge of current the motor will experience when the second part of the winding is introduced into the system. A pumping action is a common application for part-winding motors.

First Revisions: FR 3010
Public Inputs: PI 487

430.2 & .4

430.53(D)(4)

Single Motor Taps on One Branch Circuit

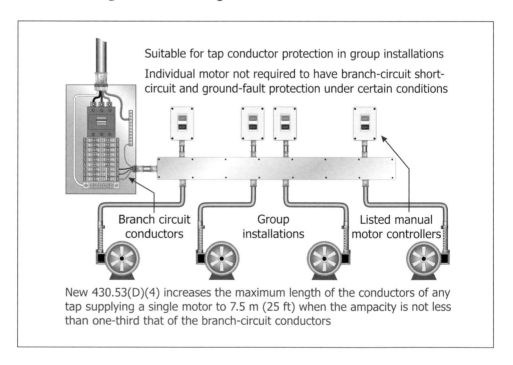

Suitable for tap conductor protection in group installations

Individual motor not required to have branch-circuit short-circuit and ground-fault protection under certain conditions

Branch circuit conductors

Group installations

Listed manual motor controllers

New 430.53(D)(4) increases the maximum length of the conductors of any tap supplying a single motor to 7.5 m (25 ft) when the ampacity is not less than one-third that of the branch-circuit conductors

430.53(D)(4) Several Motors or Loads on One Branch Circuit

- **Type of Change:** New

- **Change at a Glance:** New tap rule for a single motor allows 7.5 m (25 ft) taps with the same conditions as is allowed in other areas of the *NEC*.

■ **Code Language: 430.53 Several Motors or Loads on One Branch Circuit.**

Two or more motors or one or more motors and other loads shall be permitted to be connected to the same branch circuit under conditions specified in 430.53(D) and 430.53(A), (B), or (C). The branch-circuit protective device shall be fuses or inverse time circuit breakers.

(D) Single Motor Taps. For group installations described above, the conductors of any tap supplying a single motor shall not be required to have an individual branch-circuit short-circuit and ground-fault protective device, provided they comply with one of the following:

(1) No conductor to the motor shall have an ampacity less than that of the branch-circuit conductors.

(2) No conductor to the motor shall have an ampacity less than one-third that of the branch-circuit conductors, with a minimum in accordance with 430.22. The conductors from the point of the tap to the motor overload device shall be not more than 7.5 m (25 ft) long and be protected from physical damage by being enclosed in an approved raceway or by use of other approved means.

430.53(D)(4)

(3) Conductors from the ~~point of the tap from the~~ branch circuit ~~short-circuit and ground-fault protective device~~ to a listed manual motor controller additionally marked "Suitable for Tap Conductor Protection in Group Installations," or to a branch-circuit protective device, shall be permitted to have an ampacity not less than one-tenth the rating or setting of the branch-circuit short-circuit and ground-fault protective device. The conductors from the controller to the motor shall have an ampacity in accordance with 430.22. The conductors from the point of the tap to the controller(s) shall (1) be suitably protected from physical damage and enclosed either by an enclosed controller or by a raceway and be not more than 3 m (10 ft) long or (2) have an ampacity not less than that of the branch-circuit conductors.

(4) Conductors from the point of the tap from the branch circuit to a listed manual motor controller additionally marked "Suitable for Tap Conductor Protection in Group Installations," or to a branch-circuit protective device, shall be permitted to have an ampacity not less than one-third that of the branch-circuit conductors. The conductors from the controller to the motor shall have an ampacity in accordance with 430.22. The conductors from the point of the tap to the controller(s) shall (1) be suitably protected from physical damage and enclosed either by an enclosed controller or by a raceway and be not more than 7.5 m (25 ft) long or (2) have an ampacity not less than that of the branch-circuit conductors.

■ **2014 *NEC* Requirement**

Single motor taps for group installations were limited to a 3 m (10 ft) length by the provisions of 430.53(D)(3). Feeder tap conductors for motors were allowed as much as a 7.5 m (25 ft) tap length by the requirements found at 430.28(2).

■ **2017 *NEC* Change**
New 430.53(D)(4) increases the maximum length of the conductors of any tap supplying a single motor to 7.5 m (25 ft) when the ampacity is not less than one-third that of the branch-circuit conductors.

Analysis of the Change:

Two or more motors, or one or more motors and other loads, are permitted to be connected to the same branch circuit as specified in 430.53(D). This same section allows the conductors of any tap supplying a single motor not to have an individual branch-circuit short-circuit and ground-fault protective device for these group installations.

To comply with these group installations, the existing conditions described at 430.53(D)(3) allow these taps to have an ampacity not less than one-tenth the rating or setting of the branch-circuit short-circuit and ground-fault protective device. However, the maximum length of these reduced-ampacity tap conductors is limited to only 3 m (10 ft). This limited 3 m (10 ft) tap length applied in all reduced-ampacity applications, even those where the one-tenth reduction was not necessary or did not apply.

A new List Item (4) was added to 430.53(D) for the 2017 *NEC* that will increase the maximum length of the conductors of any tap supplying a single motor to 7.5 m (25 ft) when the ampacity is not less than one-third that of the branch-circuit conductors. This new 7.5 m (25 ft) tap provision merges the allowances of 430.28(2) for feeder taps with these single motor tap provisions at 430.53(D). Taps in lengths of up to 7.5 m (25 ft) have been a recognized part of the *NEC* for many *Code* cycles. The same 7.5 m (25 ft) tap allowance for single motor taps is a natural progression for the *NEC*.

First Revisions: FR 3014
Public Inputs: PI 1355, PI 1354

430.53(D)(4)

430.99

Available Fault Current for Motor Control Centers

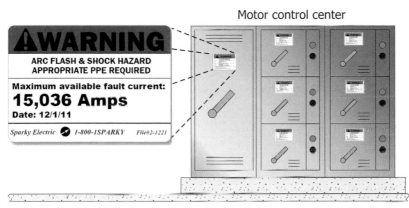

The available short circuit current at the motor control center and the date the short circuit current calculation was performed shall be documented and made available to those authorized to inspect the installation

Motor control center

⚠WARNING
ARC FLASH & SHOCK HAZARD
APPROPRIATE PPE REQUIRED
Maximum available fault current:
15,036 Amps
Date: 12/1/11
Sparky Electric 1-800-1SPARKY   File#2-1221

New requirements added for available short circuit current at motor control centers and the date the short circuit current calculation was performed

210.7 Available Fault Current. (Motors, Motor Circuits, and Controllers)

- **Type of Change:** New

- **Change at a Glance:** New requirements were added for available short-circuit current at the motor control center and the date the short-circuit current calculation was performed.

- **Code Language: 430.99 Available Fault Current. (Motors, Motor Circuits, and Controllers)**
  The available short- circuit current at the motor control center and the date the short-circuit current calculation was performed shall be documented and made available to those authorized to inspect the installation.

- **2014 *NEC* Requirement**
  Nondwelling unit service equipment is required to have the maximum available fault current legibly marked in the field with the date the fault-current calculation was performed on service equipment. There was no such available fault current documentation required for a motor control center.

- **2017 *NEC* Change**
  New provisions were added at 430.99 requiring documentation of the available short-circuit current (fault current) at motor control centers along with the date the short-circuit current calculation was performed.

430.99

Analysis of the Change:

Nondwelling unit service equipment is required by 110.24(A) to have the maximum available fault current legibly marked in the field on the service equipment. This field marking(s) is required to include the date the fault-current calculation was performed and be of sufficient durability to withstand the environment involved. While this available fault current (or short-circuit) marking requirement is mandated for service equipment, what about other types of electrical equipment that depend on a fault current rating as well?

A new requirement added at 430.99 for the 2017 *NEC* will necessitate documentation of the available short-circuit current (fault current) at motor control centers and the date the short-circuit current calculation was performed. This new fault current documentation will also require that this information be made available to those authorized to inspect the installation (the AHJ).

Electrical inspectors typically have a difficult time enforcing proper short-circuit current ratings (required by 110.9 and 110.10) on such things as a motor control center without this available fault current documentation. Motor control centers are required to be marked with the short-circuit current rating by the requirements of 430.98. The equipment is usually properly marked with the short-circuit current rating by the manufacturer, but there is typically no information on the job site as to the available short-circuit current (or fault current) at the equipment (for other than service equipment). This new requirement for documentation of the available short-circuit current will make it much easier for the installer and enforcement community to assure that the motor control center is being properly protected from fault currents.

Proper installation according to the equipment's short-circuit current rating and documentation of the available fault circuit current (and the date it was performed) will increase electrical safety. Documentation with a date the available fault current calculation was performed can reduce liability for contractors, inspectors, and manufacturers, by identifying that the equipment was installed originally with the correct short-circuit current rating.

While the *NEC* currently requires this available fault current documentation at many places in the *Code*, this same requirement was added at five locations throughout the 2017 *NEC*. This available short-circuit current (or fault current) documentation was added to the 2017 *NEC* for the following items:

430.99

NEC Section	Equipment	FR	SR	PI	PC
409.22(B)	Industrial control panels	FR 3002	SR 3003, SCR 1	PI 4421 PI 4733	PC 1800, PC 409
430.99	Motor control centers	FR 3016		PI 4437 PI 4712	
440.10	Air conditioning equipment	FR 3006	SR 3005	PI 4432 PI 4438 PI 4697 PI 4729	PC 1808
620.51(D)(2)	Elevator control panels	FR 3393	SR 3334		
670.5	Industrial machinery	FR 3336	SR 3336	PI 4709 PI 4427	PC 1301

First Revisions: FR 3016
Public Inputs: PI 4437, PI 4712

440.9

440.9

Grounding and Bonding—Rooftop Equipment

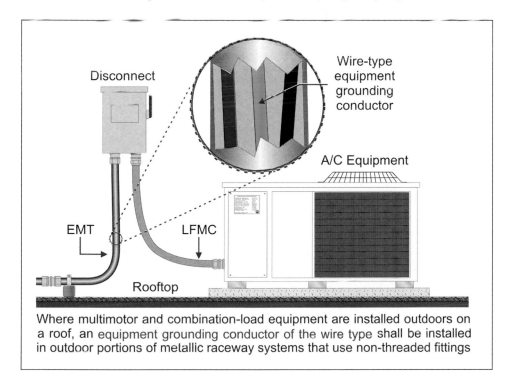

Where multimotor and combination-load equipment are installed outdoors on a roof, an equipment grounding conductor of the wire type shall be installed in outdoor portions of metallic raceway systems that use non-threaded fittings

440.9 Grounding and Bonding. (Air-Conditioning and Refrigerating Equipment)

- **Type of Change:** New

- **Change at a Glance:** A new requirement was added requiring a wire-type equipment grounding conductor for non-threaded conduit systems on rooftops supplying such things as HVAC equipment.

- **Code Language: 440.9 Grounding and Bonding. (Air-Conditioning and Refrigerating Equipment)**

  Where multimotor and combination-load equipment is installed outdoors on a roof, an equipment grounding conductor of the wire type shall be installed in outdoor portions of metallic raceway systems that use non-threaded fittings.

- **2014 *NEC* Requirement**
  By their respective articles, metallic raceway systems—such as liquidtight flexible metal conduit (LFMC) (Article 350) and electrical metallic tubing (EMT) (Article 358)—are permitted as acceptable wiring methods for outdoor multimotor and combination-load equipment such as heating and air-conditioning equipment. For the 2014 *NEC*, these two wiring methods were also permitted as their equipment grounding conductor (EGC) in outdoor portions of these metallic raceway systems installed on a roof in accordance with 250.118. No wire-type EGC was required in addition to these wiring methods.

- **2017 *NEC* Change**
  The outdoor portions of metallic raceway systems that use non-threaded fittings are now required to contain a wire-type equipment grounding conductor when installed outdoors on a roof to supply multimotor and combination-load equipment.

Analysis of the Change:

The outdoor portions of metallic raceway systems that use non-threaded fittings are now required to contain a wire-type equipment grounding conductor when installed outdoors on a roof to supply multimotor and combination-load equipment.

Concerns have been raised about metallic raceway systems that use non-threaded fittings installed outdoors on a rooftop and their ability to maintain continuity as the EGC. Steel electrical conduit and tubing has been shown to be an effective ground fault path in many installations when installed and maintained properly. However, when installed on a rooftop to supply such things as rooftop HVAC equipment, some metallic raceway systems installations become compromised from activities such as snow removal or roof repair/replacement. These activities can result in the metallic raceway systems on rooftops being subject to movement and damage that can separate their non-threaded conduit or tubing fittings, thereby losing effectiveness as an equipment grounding conductor.

440.9

To combat these activities, a new 440.9 has been added to the 2017 *NEC* requiring an equipment grounding conductor of the wire type to be installed in outdoor portions of metallic raceway systems that use non-threaded fittings where the metallic raceway systems supply multimotor and combination-load equipment installed outdoors on a roof. This new rule would not apply to metallic raceway systems that utilize threaded connections at couplings and conduits, such as RMC and IMC, as these fittings are unlikely to separate even under slight abuse or movement.

Previous proposals and comments have been submitted and accepted in both the 2011 *NEC* and the 2014 *NEC* seeking very similar requirements for a wire-type EGC associated with metallic raceway systems that use non-threaded fittings, only to be reversed at the last minute. In fact, it took a Certified Amending Motion (CAM) presented at the NFPA Annual Meeting in Chicago, IL, in June 2013, to deny a similar provision for the 2014 *NEC* (see CAM 70-19). This CAM sought to accept 2014 ROC 11-28 to remove a similar requirement at 440.9 and return to the 2011 *NEC* provisions. This CAM was accepted by the voting body by a vote of 137 to 136.

It should be noted that metallic raceway systems, such as EMT, are still recognized as quality ground-fault return paths and an effective equipment grounding conductor by the provisions of 250.118. The key to their effectiveness as their own EGC is proper installation and maintenance. At present, this "supplemental" wire-type EGC is required only for metallic raceway systems that use non-threaded fittings in this very specific condition installed outdoors on a rooftop.

First Revisions: FR 3005
Public Inputs: PI 1325, PI 4312, PI 836

440.9

440.65

Protection Devices for Room AC Units

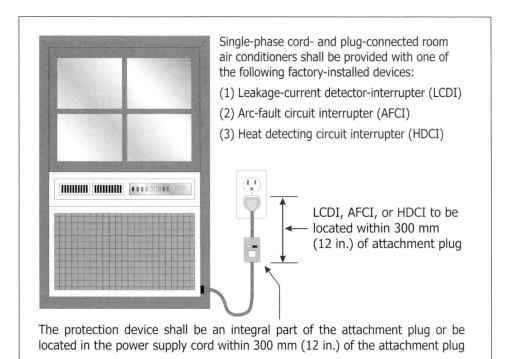

Single-phase cord- and plug-connected room air conditioners shall be provided with one of the following factory-installed devices:

(1) Leakage-current detector-interrupter (LCDI)

(2) Arc-fault circuit interrupter (AFCI)

(3) Heat detecting circuit interrupter (HDCI)

LCDI, AFCI, or HDCI to be located within 300 mm (12 in.) of attachment plug

The protection device shall be an integral part of the attachment plug or be located in the power supply cord within 300 mm (12 in.) of the attachment plug

440.65 Branch-Circuit Receptacle Requirements

- **Type of Change:** Revision and Deletion

- **Change at a Glance:** Heat detecting circuit interrupter (HDCI) was added to a list of devices for protection of single-phase room air conditioners.

- **Code Language: 440.65** ~~Leakage-Current Detector-Interrupter (LCDI) and Arc-Fault Circuit Interrupter (AFCI)~~ **Protection Devices.**

  Single-phase cord- and plug-connected room air conditioners shall be provided with one of the following factory-installed ~~LCDI or AFCI protection~~ devices:
  (1) Leakage-current detector-interrupter (LCDI)
  (2) Arc-fault circuit interrupter (AFCI)
  (3) Heat detecting circuit interrupter (HDCI)

  The ~~LCDI or AFCI~~ protection device shall be an integral part of the attachment plug or be located in the power supply cord within 300 mm (12 in.) of the attachment plug.

- **2014 *NEC* Requirement**
  Single-phase, cord- and plug-connected room air conditioners were re-

quired to be provided with factory installed leakage-current detector-interrupter (LCDI) or arc-fault circuit interrupter (AFCI) protection. This protection is required to be located within 300 mm (12 in.) of the attachment plug or an integral part of the attachment plug.

■ **2017 *NEC* Change**
In addition to the previously allowed protection for single-phase, cord- and plug-connected room air conditioners of LCDI or AFCI protection, a new form of protection was introduced at 440.65 allowing heat detecting circuit interrupter (HDCI) protection for room air conditioners. These three forms of protection for room air conditioners were placed in a list format for better clarity to the user of the *Code*.

Analysis of the Change:

Single-phase cord- and plug-connected room air conditioners have a known history of damaged power cords due to abuse or overheating that have resulted in shock hazards and been the source of occasional electrical fires. Seasonal use of portable room air conditioners contributes to potential abuse or damage to these cords as well.

To combat these safety issues, the use of leakage-current detector-interrupter (LCDI) or arc-fault circuit interrupter (AFCI) protection with room air conditioners was implemented at 440.65 during the 2002 *NEC* code cycle. Both of these types of protection devices will sense low levels of leakage of current due to insulation failure and provide greater protection against a potential fire than what would be provided by a standard overcurrent protective device. The energy levels detected by an LCDI or AFCI device are often too low to be recognized by standard circuit breakers or fuses.

440.65

For the 2017 *NEC*, 440.65 was revised into a list format and a new option for the protection of single-phase and cord- and plug-connected room air conditioners was added in the form of heat detecting circuit interrupter (HDCI) protection. HDCI is a relatively new technology in the field of protective devices. The basic requirements used to investigate HDCI protection products are contained in UL 2872 (*Outline of Investigation for Heat Detecting Circuit Interrupters*).

HDCI technology is intended for use in dehumidifiers, room air conditioners, and other refrigeration equipment. They incorporate the functionality of a leakage current detector interrupter and are intended to interrupt power to the protected device when an overheating condition occurs where the HDCI temperature sensor is mounted, or when leakage currents flowing from the conductors of the product's power-supply cord exceed a predetermined level. HDCI protection will also detect if an open circuit occurs in one of the temperature sensor leads of the HDCI temperature sensor. These HDCI devices have a maximum rating of 40 amperes and are intended for use on circuits rated 250 volts (ac) maximum. According to UL 2872, the requirements for HDCI protection are to be used with those of UL 1699 (*Standard for Arc-Fault Circuit-Interrupters*), as these requirements modify and supplement those of UL 1699.

Considering that HDCI technology incorporates all of the protection functions of an LCDI and more, adding HDCI protection as an alternative to LCDI or AFCI protection was a logical change.

First Revisions: FR 3021
Public Inputs: PI 1195

445.11

Marking. (Generators)

445.11

445.11 Marking. (Generators)

- **Type of Change:** Revision/New

- **Change at a Glance:** Nameplate marking requirements for generators have been revised and put into a list format.

- **Code Language: 445.11 Marking. (Generators)**
  Each generator shall be provided with a nameplate giving the manufacturer's name, the rated frequency, the number of phases if of ac, the rating in kilowatts or kilovolt-amperes, the power factor, the normal volts and amperes corresponding to the rating, ~~the rated revolutions per minute, and~~ the rated ambient temperature, ~~or~~ and rated temperature rise.

  Nameplates or manufacturer's instructions shall provide the following information for all stationary generators and portable generators rated more than 15 kW: ~~shall also give the power factor, the subtransient and transient impedances, the insulation system class, and the time rating.~~

(1) Subtransient, ~~and~~ transient, synchronous, and zero sequence ~~impedances~~ reactances

(2) Power ~~time~~ rating category

(3) Insulation system class

(4) Indication if the generator is protected against overload by inherent design, an overcurrent protective relay, circuit breaker, or fuse

(5) Maximum short-circuit current for inverter-based generators, in lieu of the synchronous, subtransient, and transient reactances
Marking shall be provided by the manufacturer to indicate whether or not the generator neutral is bonded to the generator frame. Where the bonding ~~of a generator~~ is modified in the field, additional marking shall be required to indicate whether the generator neutral is bonded to the ~~generator~~ frame.

445.11

- **2014 *NEC* Requirement**
  Marking requirements for generators required each generator to be provided with a nameplate. This nameplate was to indicate the manufacturer's name, the rated frequency, number of phases if of alternating current, the rating in kilowatts or kilovolt amperes, the normal volts and amperes corresponding to the rating, rated revolutions per minute, and rated ambient temperature or rated temperature rise. The power factor, the subtransient and transient impedances, the insulation system class, and the time rating markings are required for stationary and portable generators rated more than 15 kW. Manufacturer's marking provision requires indication of whether or not the generator neutral is bonded to the generator frame. This neutral bonding provision goes further to require additional marking to indicate whether the generator neutral is bonded to the generator frame whenever the bonding of a generator is modified in the field.

- **2017 *NEC* Change**
  This section involving a generator's nameplate marking was revised into a list format for stationary and portable generators rated more than 15 kW. The word "impedance" was replaced with the word "reactance." Generators rated more than 15 kW are now also required to be marked with the maximum short-circuit current for inverter-based generators. The requirement for the nameplate to provide the "power factor" for all stationary and portable generators rated more than 15 kW has been moved to the first sentence of 445.11 so as to apply to all sizes of generators. For stationary and portable generators rated more than 15 kW, the term "time rating" was replaced with "power rating category."

445.11

Analysis of the Change:

The required nameplate for a generator and the information provided by this nameplate gives the installer and the inspector alike much-needed information in determining compliance with *NEC* regulations concerning generators. These generator nameplates, as mandated by 445.11 will yield a wide variety of information as described in the *NEC* requirements above. For the 2017 *NEC*, this section was extensively revised to clarify the distinctions between generators and generator sets and to more clearly organize the requirements in a more user-friendly and technically precise manner. This revised information will assist the AHJ in determining compliance with 445.13 (ampacity of conductors for generators).

Previous editions of the *Code* described "subtransient and transient impedances" at 445.11. This phrase has been changed to "subtransient, transient, synchronous, and zero sequence reactances" when describing part of the information required on the nameplate (and now either the nameplate or the manufacturer's instructions) for all stationary and portable generators rated more than 15 kW. With the word "impedance" used rather that the correct term "reactance" being used at 445.11, this caused confusion for the manufacturer as well as the AHJ. "Impedance" was in conflict with the nationally recognized standard that is used to obtain subtransient, transient, synchronous, and zero sequence values for an alternator (generator). This standard is IEEE 115 – (*IEEE Guide for Test Procedures for Synchronous Machines:* Part I—Acceptance and Performance; Testing Part II—Test Procedures and Parameter Determination for Dynamic Analysis). *Reactance* is the proper term used throughout this document rather than impedance. *Impedance* is the total opposition to the flow of current. It is the combined effect of the resistance and the reactance of a circuit.

Generators rated more than 15 kW are now also required to be marked with the maximum short-circuit current for inverter-based generators to assist the installer and inspector when verifying proper overcurrent protection in the field. Newer generators are being manufactured with inverter based designs. Determining fault current ratings for a generator is difficult without the maximum short-circuit current marked on the generator by the manufacturer. Marking on the generator will now also be required to indicate whether the generator is inherently designed to prevent overload or whether an overcurrent protective relay, circuit breaker or fuse is provided.

The requirement for the nameplate to provide the "power factor" for all stationary and portable generators rated more than 15 kW has been moved to the first sentence of 445.11 so as to apply to all sizes of generators since this is a current practice for most manufacturers, and providing this power factor information is common across a very broad range of generator products. Language was also added to the nameplate requirements for all stationary and portable generators rated more than 15 kW to allow the necessary information to be part of the manufacturer's instructions or the nameplate where the previous provisions of 445.11 required the information to be part of the nameplate only.

For stationary and portable generators rated more than 15 kW, the term "time rating" was replaced with "power rating category." This change was necessary for generator sets to clarify if the generator set is intended for prime, continuous, limited time running, or emergency standby power use. Generators and generator sets are significantly different and, although their names are often used interchangeably, they have significantly different installation requirements. An example of a generator set, or "gen-set" for short, is a packaged combination of a diesel engine, a generator, and various ancillary devices (such as base, canopy, sound attenuation, control systems, circuit breakers, jacket water heaters and starting system).

First Revisions: FR 3602
Second Revisions: SR 3617
Public Inputs: PI 3015, PI 4460
Public Comments: PC 508, PC 252, PC 1215, PC 325

445.13(B)
Generator OCPD Provided

Ampacity of conductors between a generator and the first overcurrent protection device cannot be less than 115% of the nameplate current rating on the generator nameplate

An exception permits these conductors to have an ampacity of not less than 100% of the generators nameplate current rating if the generator is designed to operate to prevent overloading *[see 445.13(A) and exception]*

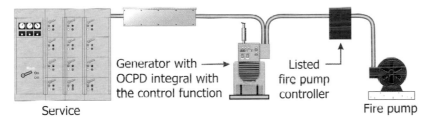

Generator with → OCPD integral with the control function

Listed → fire pump controller

Service

Fire pump

Feeder tap rules of 240.21(B) can be used if the generator or generator set is equipped with an overcurrent relay or other overcurrent device

Tapped conductors are not allowed for portable generators rated 15 kW or less where field wiring connection terminals are not accessible

445.13(B) Ampacity of Conductors. (Generators)

- **Type of Change:** New

- **Change at a Glance:** A new requirement clarifies that feeder taps can be used if the generator is equipped with an overcurrent relay or other overcurrent protective device.

- **Code Language: 445.13 Ampacity of Conductors. (Generators) (A) General.** The ampacity of the conductors from the generator output terminals to the first distribution device(s) containing overcurrent protection shall not be less than 115 percent of the nameplate current rating of the generator. It shall be permitted to size the neutral conductors in accordance with 220.61. Conductors that must carry ground-fault currents shall not be smaller than required by 250.30(A). Neutral conductors of dc generators that must carry ground-fault currents shall not be smaller than the minimum required size of the largest conductor.

Exception: *Where the design and operation of the generator prevent overloading, the ampacity of the conductors shall not be less than 100 percent of the nameplate current rating of the generator.*

(B) Overcurrent Protection Provided. Where the generator set is equipped with a listed overcurrent protective device, including or a combination of a current transformer and overcurrent relay, conductors shall be permitted to be tapped from the load side of the protected terminals in accordance with 240.21(B).

Tapped conductors shall not be permitted for portable generators rated 15 kW or less where field wiring connection terminals are not accessible.

445.13(B)

- **2014 *NEC* Requirement**
  The ampacity of conductors between a generator and the first overcurrent protection device cannot be less than 115 percent of the nameplate current rating on the generator's nameplate. An exception permits these conductors to have an ampacity of not less than 100 percent of the generator's nameplate current rating if the generator is designed to operate to prevent overloading. The neutral conductor(s) can be sized in accordance with 220.61. Conductors designed to transmit ground-fault currents cannot be smaller than required by 250.30(A) for grounding of a separately derived system. Neutral conductor(s) of dc generators designed to carry ground-fault currents are not permitted to be smaller than the minimum required size of the largest conductor.

- **2017 *NEC* Change**
  The existing provisions of the 2014 *NEC* for ampacity of conductors for generators were carried forward for the 2017 *NEC* and reassigned to 445.13(A) and exception. New provisions were added at 445.13(B) to clarify that the feeder tap rules of 240.21(B) can be used if the generator or generator set is equipped with an overcurrent relay or other overcurrent device, unless the tapped conductors are for portable generators rated 15 kW or less where field wiring connection terminals are not accessible.

Analysis of the Change:

The general rules of 445.13(A) [was 445.13] stipulate that the ampacity of the conductors between a generator and the first overcurrent protection device cannot be less than 115 percent of the nameplate current rating on the generator nameplate. This stipulation is required as these conductors have no overcurrent protection. The first overcurrent device does provide overload protection, but it does not provide overcurrent protection because it is not located in front of these conductors. An exception to these general rules permit these generator-feeding conductors to have an ampacity of not less than 100 percent of the generator's nameplate current rating if the generator is designed to operate to prevent overloading.

New for the 2017 *NEC* is 445.13(B). This subsection has been added to clarify that the feeder tap rules of 240.21(B) can be used if the generator or generator set is equipped with an overcurrent relay or other overcurrent device. This new provision goes on to clarify that tapped conductors are not allowed for portable generators rated 15 kW or less where field wiring connection terminals are not accessible.

Generators and generator sets powering multiple feeders for special loads, such as fire pumps through individual overcurrent protective devices, have been a common and fully accepted practice for several *Code* cycles. The 2011 *NEC* contained provisions at 445.19 that permitted a generator(s) to supply more than one load (multiple loads) where individual enclosures with overcurrent protection tapped from a single feeder if a generator(s) was provided with overcurrent protection. This section was deleted for the 2014 *NEC*. In deleting 445.19, CMP-13 stated that "a generator may be used for emergency, legally required standby, and optional standby circuits. The text of 445.19 closely aligns with 700.10(B)(5)(a), and although written in permissive format, may lead the reader to thinking that all generators must be connected to systems as described in 700.10(B)(5)(a)."

445.13(B)

The removal of 445.19 in the 2014 *NEC* revision cycle caused confusion among some users of the *Code* about the conditions under which tap conductors for generators were acceptable. The new provisions of 445.13(B) will clarify requirements for these tap conductors for generators and establish when they are suitable for use.

First Revisions: FR 3603
Second Revisions: SR 3618
Public Inputs: PI 3411
Public Comments: PC 509

445.18

Disconnecting Means and Shutdown of Prime Mover

445.18

445.18 Disconnecting Means and Shutdown of Prime Mover

- **Type of Change:** Revision/New

- **Change at a Glance:** Generator disconnecting means have been reorganized. Provisions for disconnecting means, shut down of the prime mover, and provisions for generators installed in parallel have been added.

- **Code Language:** 445.18 Disconnecting Means ~~Required for Generators~~ and Shutdown of Prime Mover.
  ~~Generators shall be equipped with a disconnect(s), lockable in the open position by means of which the generator and all protective devices and control apparatus are able to be disconnected entirely from the circuits supplied by the generator except where the following conditions apply:~~
  ~~(1) Portable generators are cord- and plug-connected, or~~
  ~~(2) Both of the following conditions apply:~~
  ~~a. The driving means for the generator can be readily shut down, is rendered incapable of restarting, and is lockable in the OFF position in accordance with 110.25.~~
  ~~b. The generator is not arranged to operate in parallel with another generator or other source of voltage.~~
  ~~**Informational Note:** See UL 2200-2012, Standard for Safety of Stationary Engine Generator Assemblies.~~

(A) Disconnecting Means. Generators other than cord- and plug-connected portable shall have one or more disconnecting means. Each disconnecting means shall simultaneously open all associated ungrounded conductors. Each disconnecting means shall be lockable in the open position in accordance with 110.25.

(B) Shutdown of Prime Mover. Generators shall have provisions to shut down the prime mover. The means of shutdown shall comply with all of the following:

(1) Be equipped with provisions to disable all prime mover start control circuits to render the prime mover incapable of starting

(2) Initiate a shutdown mechanism that requires a mechanical reset

The provisions to shut down the prime mover shall be permitted to satisfy the requirements of 445.18(A) where it is capable of being locked in the open position in accordance with 110.25.

Generators with greater than 15 kW rating shall be provided with an additional requirement to shut down the prime mover. This additional shutdown means shall be located outside the equipment room or generator enclosure and shall also meet the requirements of 445.18(B)(1) and (B)(2).

(C) Generators Installed in Parallel. Where a generator is installed in parallel with other generators, the provisions of 445.18(A) shall be capable of isolating the generator output terminals from the paralleling equipment. The disconnecting means shall not be required to be located at the generator.

445.18

- **2014 *NEC* Requirement**
Generators are required to be equipped with disconnect(s) that are lockable in the open position. This lockable disconnecting means must be able to disconnect the generator and all protective devices and control apparatus entirely from the circuits supplied by the generator. A couple of conditions existed that permit the disconnecting means requirements for generators to be omitted. (1) For portable generators that supply power from a self-contained receptacle outlet, which would accept a cord-and-plug connection, the cord and plug can serve as the disconnecting means. (2) For generators where the driving means can be readily shut down, they must also be rendered incapable of restarting and lockable in the off or "open" position in accordance with the locking provisions of 110.25, and the generator is not arranged to operate in parallel with another generator or with other source of voltage.

- **2017 *NEC* Change**
Revisions and new requirements were incorporated into 445.18 by installing three subsections for disconnecting means for a generator. The provisions of 445.18(A) retain the existing requirements, with revisions, for a disconnecting means for a generator. New 445.18(B) adds requirements

for the shutdown of the prime mover for a generator or generator set.

New 445.18(C) was added to clarify that when generators are installed in parallel, it is not necessary to provide a disconnecting means at each generator and the paralleling equipment as long as the generator is capable of isolating the generator output terminals from the paralleling equipment.

Analysis of the Change:

Generators are generally required to be equipped with an appropriate disconnecting means; these requirements are at 445.18. Historically, Article 445 has not listed requirements for the shutdown of the prime mover for a generator. Typically, a generator is the combination of an electrical generator and an engine (*prime mover*) mounted together to form a single piece of equipment. This combination is called a generator set or a "gen-set." In general, the engine is taken for granted and the combined unit is simply called a generator.

This lack of information and regulations for a "prime mover" is addressed for the 2017 *NEC* with the addition of 445.18(B), Shutdown of Prime Mover. This new requirement was added to require shutdown of the prime mover for generators and, in particular, generators rated greater than 15kW. A new sentence was also added to 445.18(B) to clarify that the general provisions to shut down the prime mover may also satisfy the requirements in 445.18(A) for a disconnecting means for the generator (or generator set) under specific conditions.

This additional requirement was necessary to provide a remote shutdown means in the event of an emergency. This shutdown means for the prime mover is needed to prevent the generator set from unexpectedly starting and running while the generator is shut down for such things as undergoing service. An effective means of stopping the generator set and preventing its operation also prevents the generator set from energizing downstream circuits while the system is shut down intentionally, as well.

A new 445.18(C), Generators Installed in Parallel, was added. This subsection clarifies that where generators are installed in parallel, it is not necessary to provide a disconnecting means at each generator and the paralleling equipment as long as the generator is capable of isolating the generator output terminals from the paralleling equipment. Arranging generators to operate in parallel is becoming usual practice for hospitals, data centers, and large buildings requiring onsite backup power. Generators installed in parallel are not exempt from requiring a disconnecting means to disconnect the control circuit, the fuel supply, and to render the generator incapable of restarting. For the generator to safely receive scheduled maintenance, paralleled applications require prevention of the generator from operation and the bus from energizing the generator. This requirement does not remove the requirement for identified overload protection at the generator, per the requirements of 445.12(A).

First Revisions: FR 3661
Second Revisions: SR 3620, SCR 82
Public Inputs: PI 1515, PI 1681, PI 1382
Public Comments: PC 1200

445.18

445.20

Ground-Fault Circuit-Interrupter Protection for Receptacles on 15-kW or Smaller Portable Generators

Receptacle outlets that are a part of a 15-kW or smaller portable generator shall have listed GFCI for personnel integral to the generator or receptacle

(A) Unbonded (Floating Neutral) Generators

(B) Bonded Neutral Generators

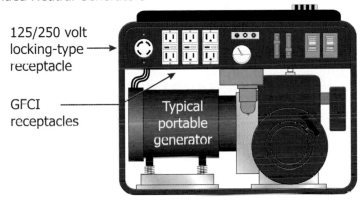

125/250 volt locking-type receptacle →

GFCI receptacles

Typical portable generator

If the generator was manufactured or remanufactured prior to January 1, 2015, listed cord sets or devices incorporating listed GFCI protection for personnel identified for portable use shall be permitted

445.20

445.20 Ground-Fault Circuit-Interrupter Protection for Receptacles on 15-kW or Smaller Portable Generators

- **Type of Change:** Revision/New

- **Change at a Glance:** Listed cord sets incorporating GFCI protection for portable generators manufactured or rebuilt prior to January 1, 2015, are now permitted. GFCI requirements have been separated into unbonded (floating neutral) generators versus bonded neutral generators.

- **Code Language: 445.20 Ground-Fault Circuit-Interrupter Protection for Receptacles on 15-kW or Smaller Portable Generators.** All 125-volt, single-phase, 15- and 20-ampere rReceptacle outlets that are a part of a 15-kW or smaller portable generator either shall have listed ground-fault circuit-interrupter protection (GFCI) for personnel integral to the generator or receptacle or shall not be available for use when the 125/250-volt locking-type receptacle is in use. If the generator does not have a 125/250-volt locking-type receptacle, this requirement shall not apply. as indicated in either (A) or (B):

  (A) Unbonded (Floating Neutral) Generators. Unbonded generators with both 125-volt and 125/250-volt receptacle outlets shall have listed GFCI protection for personnel integral to the generator or receptacle on all 125-volt and 15- and 20-ampere receptacle outlets.

Exception: *GFCI protection shall not be required where the 125-volt receptacle outlets(s) is interlocked such that it is not available for use when any 125/250-volt receptacle(s) is in use.*

(B) Bonded Neutral Generators. Bonded generators shall be provided with GFCI protection on all 125-volt and 15- and 20-ampere receptacle outlets.

Informational Note: Refer to 590.6(A)(3) for GFCI requirements for 15-kW or smaller portable generators used for temporary electric power and lighting.

Exception to (A) and (B): *If the generator was manufactured or remanufactured prior to January 1, 2015, listed cord sets or devices incorporating listed ~~ground-fault circuit-interrupter~~ GFCI protection for personnel identified for portable use shall be permitted. (See 2014 NEC TIA 14-2)*

■ **2014 *NEC* Requirement**
A new 445.20 titled, "Ground-Fault Circuit-Interrupter Protection for Receptacles on 15-kW or Smaller, Portable Generators" was added to Article 445. This section required all 125-volt, single-phase, 15- and 20- ampere receptacle outlets that are a part of a 15 kW or smaller portable generator to be equipped either with GFCI protection integral to the generator or receptacle or the generator had to be capable of rendering the 125-volt, single-phase, 15-and 20 ampere receptacle outlets unavailable for use when the 125/250-volt locking-type receptacles were in use. This requirement also indicated that if the generator did not have a 125/250-volt locking-type receptacle, this GFCI requirement was not applicable.

■ **2017 *NEC* Change**
The requirements of 445.20 were revised to separate GFCI requirements for unbonded (floating neutral) generators at 445.20(A) and bonded neutral generators at 445.20(B). Unbonded (floating neutral) generators requires GFCI protection at all 125-volt, 15- and 20-ampere receptacles, but only where both 125-volt and 125/250-volt receptacles exist on the generator. An exception to 445.20(A) eliminates GFCI protection where the 125-volt receptacle outlets(s) is interlocked such that it is not available for use when any 125/250-volt receptacle(s) is in use.

New 445.20(B) requires all 125-volt, 15- and 20-ampere receptacles on bonded neutral generators to be provided with GFCI protection. An exception to 445.20(A) and (B) permits GFCI protection in the form of listed cord sets or devices incorporating listed GFCI protection if the generator was manufactured or remanufactured prior to January 1, 2015.

445.20

Analysis of the Change:

Small portable generators sized 15 kW or smaller are used for many different applications. Portable generators are used extensively for temporary power at construction sites, but other applications apply as well, such as on camping trips, temporary connection of electrical circuits in a home or for small commercial buildings during power outages, and for power during emergency situations for all different types of installations due to natural disasters, such as hurricanes. In all of these applications, there are many potential hazards that can be associated with these temporary installations. Accidental cuts and abraded wire and cable, standing water, and wet locations are just a few examples of these potentially hazardous applications. During power outages from storms and other natural disasters, personnel who may not be familiar with adequate safety procedures often use these small portable generators to supply power in less than optimal conditions.

Article 445 was revised for the 2014 *NEC* by the addition of 445.20, which required all 125-volt, single-phase, 15- and 20-ampere receptacles on 15 kW or smaller generators to be integrally GFCI-protected to help eliminate the possibilities of shock hazards from damaged circuits, damaged equipment, or use of equipment in wet locations in situations described above.

445.20

After the 2014 *NEC* was published, Tentative Interim Amendment (TIA) 14-2 was issued pertaining to 445.20. This TIA was processed by CMP-13 and the *NEC* Correlating Committee and was issued by the Standards Council on October 22, 2013, with an effective date of November 11, 2013. A TIA is tentative because it has not been processed through the entire standards-making procedures. It is interim because it is effective only between editions of the standard (the *NEC*). A TIA automatically becomes a public input of the proponent for the next edition of the *NEC*; as such, it is then subject to all of the procedures of the standards-making process.

This TIA limited the GFCI requirement to 15 kW or smaller portable generators that were manufactured or remanufactured after January 1, 2015. According to the substantiation submitted with the TIA, without this limitation, this GFCI provision would apply to the use of any 15 kW or smaller portable generator, regardless of its date of manufacture, and would effectively ban the use of millions of portable generators that have been, and continue to be, used safely on a daily basis. The TIA allowed listed cord sets or devices incorporating listed GFCI protection for personnel identified for portable use to be used with older 15 kW or less portable generators. This concept is already permitted in temporary installations at 590.6(A)(3). The results of this TIA for the 2014 *NEC* have been incorporated into the 2017 *NEC* in the form of a new exception to 445.20(A) and (B).

The revision of 445.20 for the 2017 *NEC* also witnessed a separation of GFCI requirements for unbonded (floating neutral) generators versus bonded neutral generators as these requirements are not the same. Needed clarity is provided at new 445.20(A) for unbonded (floating neutral) generators to clearly require GFCI protection at all 125-volt, 15- and 20-ampere receptacles, but only where both 125-volt and 125/250-volt receptacles exist on the generator. Previous text at 445.20 is now incorporated into a new exception to 445.20(A) omitting GFCI protection where the 125-volt receptacle outlets(s) is interlocked such that it is not available for use when any 125/250-volt receptacle(s) is in use.

Clarity is also provided at new 445.20(B) by requiring all 125-volt, 15- and 20-ampere receptacles on bonded neutral generators to always be provided with GFCI protection. A new informational note directs users of the *Code* to 590.6(A)(3) for GFCI requirements for 15-kW or smaller portable generators used for temporary electric power and lighting.

First Revisions: FR 3604
Second Revisions: SR 3621
Public Inputs: PI 4194, PI 22, PI 2572, PI 4122
Public Comments: PC 956

480.3

Equipment. (Storage Batteries)

480.3 Equipment. (Storage Batteries)

- **Type of Change:** New

- **Change at a Glance:** Storage batteries and battery management equipment are now required to be listed (other than lead-acid batteries).

- **Code Language: 480.3 Equipment. (Storage Batteries)**
  Storage batteries and battery management equipment shall be listed. This requirement shall not apply to lead-acid batteries.

- **2014 *NEC* Requirement**
  Article 480 contained requirements and information for storage batteries, but there was no listing requirement for these storage batteries in this article.

- **2017 *NEC* Change**
  New listing requirement was added at 480.3, which will require storage batteries and battery management equipment to be listed. This listing requirement does not apply to lead-acid batteries.

Analysis of the Change:

As the scope of Article 480 indicates, this *NEC* article applies to all stationary installations of storage batteries. The safe installation and maintenance of many traditional installations of storage batteries, such as lead-acid or lead-calcium batteries, have been adequately addressed with the previous requirements contained in Article 480. However, as new battery chemistries and technologies (such as lithium-ion batteries) have been developed and introduced, different types of potential hazards have emerged.

Through the use of new technologies, energy density for storage batteries has significantly increased and continues to do so. Energy density is the amount of energy stored in a given system or region of space per unit volume or mass. As a case in point, lithium-ion battery energy density has been increasing at approximately 10 percent annually through technological advances such as reduced separator thicknesses. The principal functions of these separators are to prevent electronic conduction (i.e., short circuits or direct contact) between the anode and cathode while permitting ionic conduction via the electrolyte. These new battery technologies are quite different from their lead-acid battery counterparts. These differences have produced both new functional benefits along with challenges that have caused some notable safety incidents involving significant fires and explosions.

To combat some of these challenges with new battery storage technologies, a new listing requirement was added to the 2017 *NEC* at 480.3, which will require storage batteries and battery management equipment to be listed. This new listing provision recognizes the need for third party evaluation of storage batteries and battery management equipment by a third-party testing laboratory. This assessment and management are necessary to provide the installer, maintainer, and AHJ with necessary information and instructions for the safe application of storage batteries. It should be noted that these listing requirements do not apply to lead-acid batteries.

Product standards have been developed to address battery safety. These standards include UL 1642 (*Standard for Lithium Batteries*) and UL 1973 [*Standard for Batteries for Use in Light Electric Rail (LER) Applications and Stationary Applications*] for stationary batteries of all chemistries. These standards contain

480.3

fundamental safety requirements to assess proper measures of mitigation of the inherent hazards presented by batteries. Leveraging the safety afforded by compliance with these established standards is a reasonable and appropriate safety measure.

As large-scale development and deployment of energy storage is increased over the next few years for such things as photovoltaic (PV) systems, it is critical that the *NEC* promote the safe installation and maintenance of stationary battery equipment by leveraging the benefits afforded by proper listing requirements.

Second Revisions: SR 3629
Public Inputs: PI 3550
Public Comments: PC 1490

480.3

Special

Chapter 5

Occupancies

Articles 500 – 590

500.2

500.2 Article 100 — Definitions

Fourteen definitions that resided at 500.2 in previous editions of the *Code* have been relocated to Article 100 of the *NEC*

- **Combustible Dust**
- **Combustible Gas Detection System**
- **Control Drawing**
- **Dust-Ignitionproof**
- **Dusttight**
- **Hermetically Sealed**
- **Nonincendive Circuit**

- **Nonincendive Component**
- **Nonincendive Equipment**
- **Nonincendive Field Wiring**
- **Nonincendive Field Wiring Apparatus**
- **Oil Immersion**
- **Purged and Pressurized**
- **Unclassified Locations**

These relocated hazardous (classified) location definitions will include the phrase "[as applied to Hazardous (Classified) Locations]" at each of these Article 100 definitions

---

500.2 500.2 **Article 100 — Definitions**

- **Type of Change:** Relocation

- **Change at a Glance:** Fourteen existing definitions have been relocated to Article 100 from 500.2.

- **Code Language:** 500.2 Definitions Article 100 Definitions

  Combustible Dust [as applied to Hazardous (Classified) Locations].
  Combustible Gas Detection System [as applied to Hazardous (Classified) Locations].
  Control Drawing [as applied to Hazardous (Classified) Locations].
  Dust-Ignitionproof [as applied to Hazardous (Classified) Locations].
  Dusttight [as applied to Hazardous (Classified) Locations].
  Hermetically Sealed [as applied to Hazardous (Classified) Locations].
  Nonincendive Circuit [as applied to Hazardous (Classified) Locations].
  Nonincendive Component [as applied to Hazardous (Classified) Locations].
  Nonincendive Equipment [as applied to Hazardous (Classified) Locations].
  Nonincendive Field Wiring [as applied to Hazardous (Classified) Locations].
  Nonincendive Field Wiring Apparatus [as applied to Hazardous (Classified) Locations].

Oil Immersion [as applied to Hazardous (Classified) Locations].
Purged and Pressurized [as applied to Hazardous (Classified) Locations].
Unclassified Locations [as applied to Hazardous (Classified) Locations].
(*See NEC text in Article 100 for complete definition*).

- **2014 *NEC* Requirement**
  Fourteen definitions existed at 500.2 that applied to Articles 500 through 504 and Articles 510 through 516.

- **2017 *NEC* Change**
  The fourteen definitions that resided at 500.2 in previous editions of the *Code* have been relocated to Article 100 of the *NEC*.

Analysis of the Change:

From a historical perspective, CMP-14 has found Article 500, and in particular 500.2, a safe "landing spot" for any definition that applied to more than one hazardous (classified) location article rather than locate these multi-article definitions in Article 100 (as prescribed by the *NEC Style Manual*). Before the 2008 *NEC*, any definition located in Article 100 was under the preview of CMP-1 and any CMP sending a definition to Article 100 "lost control" or responsibility of that particular definition. This procedure changed with the 2008 *NEC* when the responsibility of a definition located in Article 100 and its technical meaning remained with the CMP most associated with a specific definition. For example, CMP-5 has responsibility over definitions pertaining to grounding and bonding, such as the definition of "Bonded," "Grounding Electrode," and so forth.

To comply with the *NEC Style Manual*, fourteen definitions that were located at 500.2 have been relocated to Article 100 of the *NEC*. Section 2.2.2.1 of the 2015 *NEC Style Manual* states, "In general, Article 100 shall contain definitions of terms that appear in two or more other articles of the *NEC*." Even though these definitions will be located in Article 100, they will still be defined by and under the control of CMP-14. To assist users of the *Code*, and in particular users of the Chapter 5 hazardous (classified) location articles, these relocated hazardous (classified) location definitions will include the term "[as applied to Hazardous (Classified) Locations]" immediately following the identification of the defined term prior to the actual definition.

Identifying these hazardous (classified) location definitions with the phrase "[as applied to Hazardous (Classified) Locations]" will provide a cross reference for hazardous (classified) location article users, assisting them in to "following the path" from previous 500.2 to Article 100. Using this phrase at the relocated definitions will also help users of the *Code* understand that these definitions only apply to hazardous (classified) location articles in Chapter 5.

First Revisions: FR 3918
Public Input: PI 1862

500.2

500.5(A)

~~Classifications of Locations~~ General

500.5(A)

The title of 500.5(A) was changed to "General" as it applies to all of 500.5

Refrigerant machinery rooms containing ammonia refrigeration may be classified as "unclassified" locations based on the use of gas detection and adequate ventilation *(concentration not exceeding 150 ppm)*

Class I, II, and III Locations and Groups

Substance	Gas	Dust	Fibers/Flyings
Class	Class I [500.5(B)]	Class II [500.5(C)]	Class III [500.5(D)]
Division 1 (Normally Hazardous)	Flammable or combustible concentrations exist under normal operating conditions	Group E, Groups F & G Normally in air in ignitible concentrations	Where they are manufactured
Division 2 (Normally Hazardous)	Confined within closed systems and closed containers	Groups F & G Not normally in air in ignitible quantities	Where they are stored
Groups	A, B, C, and D *NEC* 500.6(A)	E, F, and G *NEC* 500.6(B)	No Groups
NEC Article	501	502	503

500.5(A) Classifications of Locations

- **Type of Change:** New

- **Change at a Glance:** The title of 500.5(A) was changed to "General" as it applies to all of 500.5. Refrigerant machinery rooms containing ammonia refrigeration may be classified as "unclassified" locations based on the use of gas detection and adequate ventilation.

- **Code Language: 500.5 Classifications of Locations.**

  (A) ~~Classifications of Locations~~ **General.** Locations shall be classified depending on the properties of the flammable gas, flammable liquid-produced vapor, combustible liquid-produced vapors, combustible dusts, or fibers/flyings that ~~may~~ could be present, and the likelihood that a flammable or combustible concentration or quantity is present. Each room, section, or area shall be considered individually in determining its classification. Where pyrophoric materials are the only materials used or handled, these locations are outside the scope of this article.

  Informational Note No. 1: Through the exercise of ingenuity in the layout of electrical installations for hazardous (classified) locations, it is frequently possible to locate much of the equipment in a reduced level of classification or an unclassified location and, thus, to reduce the amount of special equipment required.

Refrigerant machinery rooms ~~and areas containing~~ that contain ammonia refrigeration systems ~~that~~ and are equipped with adequate mechanical ventilation that operates continuously or is initiated by a detection system at a concentration not exceeding 150 ppm shall be permitted to ~~may~~ be classified as "unclassified" locations.

Informational Note No. 2: For further information regarding classification and ventilation of areas involving closed-circuit ammonia refrigeration systems, see ANSI/ASHRAE 15-~~1994~~ 2013, Safety ~~Code for Mechanical Refrigeration~~ Standard for Refrigeration Systems, and ANSI/~~CGA G2.1-1989~~ IIAR 2–2014, ~~Safety Requirements for the Storage and Handling of Anhydrous Ammonia~~ Standard for Safe Design of Closed-Circuit Ammonia Refrigeration Systems.

- **2014 *NEC* Requirement**
  Section 500.5(A) titled "Classifications of Locations" indicates that locations are to be classified depending on the properties of the flammable gas, flammable liquid-produced vapor, combustible liquid-produced vapors, combustible dusts, or fibers/flyings that could be present. This section goes on to state that each room, section, or area is to be considered individually in determining its classification. Locations where pyrophoric materials are the only materials used or handled are considered outside the scope of Article 500. Rooms and areas containing ammonia refrigeration systems equipped with "adequate mechanical ventilation" may be classified as "unclassified" locations.

- **2017 *NEC* Change**
  The title of 500.5(A) was changed from "Classifications of Locations" to "General" as 500.5(A) applies to all of 500.5, including 500.5(B), (C), and (D). Revisions to the text of 500.5(A) clarify that "refrigerant machinery rooms" containing ammonia refrigeration may be classified as "unclassified" locations based on the use of gas detection and adequate ventilation with this "adequate ventilation" being defined as "continuous or initiated by a detection system at a concentration not exceeding 150 ppm (parts per million)."

500.5(A)

Analysis of the Change:
For classification of locations in a hazardous (classified) location, one of the first stops for the user of the *Code* would be 500.5, which gives a "roadmap" or description of the hazardous (classified) locations covered in the first four articles of Chapter 5 of the *NEC*. Class I locations are described at 500.5(B) as "those areas in which flammable gasses, flammable liquid-produced vapors, or combustible liquid-produced vapors are or may be present in the air in quantities sufficient to produce explosive or ignitible mixtures." Class II locations are described at 500.5(C) as "those areas that are hazardous because of the presence of combustible dust." According to 505.5(D), Class III locations are "those areas that are hazardous because of the presence of easily ignitible fibers or where materials producing combustible flyings are handled, manufactured, or used, but in which such fibers/flyings are not likely to be in suspension in the air in quantities sufficient to produce ignitible mixtures."

In determining classification of locations, 500.5(A) states that locations are to be classified depending on the properties of the flammable gas, flammable liquid-produced vapor, combustible liquid-produced vapors, combustible dusts, or fibers/flyings that could be present. This section also states that each room, section, or area is to be considered individually in determining its classification. For the 2017 *NEC*, the title of 500.5(A) was changed from "Classifications of Locations" to "General" as 500.5(A) applies to all of 500.5, including 500.5(B), (C), and (D). The previous title, which was a repeat of the title of 500.5 itself was confusing to some users of the *Code* and left doubt as to its application to the remainder of 500.5.

Another revision occurred at the last sentence of 500.5(A) (located between the two informational notes). It was revised to clarify that the refrigerant machinery rooms that contain ammonia refrigeration systems must be equipped with ventilation, not the refrigeration system itself when attempting to classify a location as "unclassified." This revision clarifies that "refrigerant machinery rooms" containing ammonia refrigeration may be classified as "unclassified" locations based on the use of gas detection and adequate ventilation, in order to harmonize with applicable ANSI standards that govern ammonia refrigeration systems (ANSI/IIAR 2 and ANSI/ASHRAE 15).

Referenced standards in the informational notes were updated for accuracy as well. A reference to ANSI/CGA G2.1-1989, Safety Requirements for the Storage and Handling of Anhydrous Ammonia in Informational Note No. 2 was removed as it is not applicable to ammonia systems described at 500.5(A).

First Revisions: FR 3934
Second Revisions: SR 3916, SCR 2
Public Inputs: PI 70
Public Comments: PC 1580

500.5(A)

Table 500.8(D)(2)

Equipment

Previous Table 500.8(D)(2) has been deleted as the table is no longer applicable

Fixed ignition temperature limits referenced in the table are no longer used to evaluate Class II temperature limitations on equipment

Table 500.8(D)(2) - Class II Temperatures

| Class II Group | Equipment Not Subject to Overloading | | Equipment (Such as Motors, Power Transformers) that may be overloaded | | | |
| | | | Normal Operation | | Abnormal Operation | |
	°C	°F	°C	°F	°C	°F
E	200	392	200	392	200	392
F	200	392	150	302	200	392
G	165	329	120	248	165	329

Table 500.8(D)(2) Equipment

- **Type of Change:** Deletion

- **Change at a Glance:** Previous Table 500.8(D)(2) Class II Temperatures has been deleted.

- **Code Language: 500.8 Equipment.**

  Articles 500 through 504 require equipment construction and installation that ensure safe performance under conditions of proper use and maintenance.

  (D) Temperature.
  (2) Class II Temperature. The temperature marking specified in 500.8(C) shall be less than the ignition temperature of the specific dust to be encountered. For organic dusts that may dehydrate or carbonize, the temperature marking shall not exceed the lower of either the ignition temperature or 165°C (329°F).

  Informational Note: See NFPA 499-2013, *Recommended Practice for the Classification of Combustible Dusts and of Hazardous (Classified) Locations for Electrical Installations in Chemical Process Areas*, for minimum ignition temperatures of specific dusts.

500.8(D)(2)

~~The ignition temperature for which equipment was approved prior to this requirement shall be assumed to be as shown in Table 500.8(D)(2).~~
Table 500.8(D)(2) Class II Temperatures
[Table 500.8(D)(2) has been deleted]

■ **2014 *NEC* Requirement**
The provisions of 500.8(D)(2) stated that the ignition temperature for which equipment was approved prior to the requirements of 500.8(D)(2) were to be assumed to be as shown in Table 500.8(D)(2). This table was based on fixed ignition temperature limits.

■ **2017 *NEC* Change**
Previous Table 500.8(D)(2) has been deleted as the table is no longer applicable because the fixed ignition temperature limits referenced in the table are no longer used to evaluate Class II temperature limitations on equipment.

Analysis of the Change:
Equipment used and installed in hazardous (classified) locations must be constructed and installed to ensure safe performance under conditions of proper use and maintenance. This equipment must be marked to show the environment for which it has been evaluated. For equipment installed in Class II locations, the temperature markings must be less than the ignition temperature of the specific dust that will be present. For organic dusts that may dehydrate or carbonize, the temperature marking cannot exceed the lower of either the ignition temperature or 165°C (329°F).

In previous editions of the *Code*, 500.8(D)(2) indicated that the ignition temperature for which equipment was approved prior to this requirement shall be assumed to be as shown in Table 500.8(D)(2). For the 2017 *NEC*, this table has been deleted. This previous Table 500.8(D)(2) and the sentence referencing the table were no longer relevant as the fixed ignition temperature limits referenced in the table are no longer applicable to Class II temperature limitations on equipment. A comparable reference for Class I locations for gasses and vapors was removed during the 2002 *NEC* revision process. The requirement for maximum surface temperature for Class II dust locations was changed from the fixed limits to the temperature class numbers during the same 2002 *NEC* revision cycle.

First Revisions: FR 3982
Public Input: PI 1621

500.8(D)(2)

501.10(B)(1)

Class I, Division 2

Rigid metal conduit (RMC) and intermediate metal conduit (IMC) with listed threadless fittings have been added to the allowable wiring methods in a Class I, Division 2 location

Cablebus also added to permitted wiring methods in a Class I, Division 2 location

Cablebus

RMC and IMC with listed threadless fittings

Class I, Division 2 location

501.10(B)(1)

501.10(B)(1) Wiring Methods. (Class I Locations)

- **Type of Change:** Revision

- **Change at a Glance:** RMC and IMC with threadless fittings and cablebus were added as acceptable wiring methods in Class I, Division 2 locations.

- **Code Language: 501.10 Wiring Methods. (Class I Locations)**
  Wiring methods shall comply with 501.10(A) or (B).

  (B) Class I, Division 2.
  (1) General. In Class I, Division 2 locations, all wiring methods permitted in 501.10(A) and the following wiring methods shall be permitted:
  (1) ~~All wiring methods permitted in 501.10(A)~~ Rigid metal conduit (RMC) and intermediate metal conduit (IMC) with listed threadless fittings.
  (2) Enclosed gasketed busways and enclosed gasketed wireways.
  (3) Type PLTC and Type PLTC-ER cable
  (4) Type ITC and Type ITC-ER cable
  (5) Type MC, MV, TC, or TC-ER cable
  (6) Listed reinforced thermosetting resin conduit (RTRC) and Schedule 80 PVC conduit (in industrial establishments with restricted public access with specific conditions).
  (7) Optical fiber cable

(8) Cablebus
(See NEC for complete text)

Where seals are required for boundary conditions as defined in 501.15(A)(4), the Division 1 wiring method shall extend into the Division 2 area to the seal, which shall be located on the Division 2 side of the Division 1–Division 2 boundary. [This sentence was located under List Item (6)]

- **2014 *NEC* Requirement**
  Acceptable wiring methods for Class I Division 2 locations are identified at 501.10(B). There were six list items under 501.10(B)(1) that included ten general wiring methods for Class I Division 2 locations, in addition to the wiring methods permitted in 501.10(A) for Class I Division 1 locations.

- **2017 *NEC* Change**
  Besides the wiring methods permitted in the previous *Code*, the wiring methods permitted for Class I, Division 2 locations have been expanded to include rigid metal conduit (RMC) and intermediate metal conduit (IMC) with listed threadless fittings, as well as cablebus.

501.10(B)(1)

Analysis of the Change:

A Class I, Division 2 location is where volatile flammable gasses, flammable liquid-produced vapors, or combustible liquid-produced vapors are handled, processed, or used, but will normally be confined within closed containers or closed systems unless accidental rupture, breakdown, or abnormal operation of equipment occurs. Positive mechanical ventilation can reduce locations to a Class I, Division 2 location as well.

The allowable wiring methods for a Class I, Division 2 location are found in 501.10(B). Several wiring methods are identified in this section, some with specific conditions attached to their acceptance as a Class I, Division 2 wiring method. The wiring methods permitted for Class I, Division 2 locations have been expanded to include rigid metal conduit (RMC) and intermediate metal conduit (IMC) with listed threadless fittings at 501.10(B)(1)(1). These added wiring methods provide an appropriate level of safety for a Class I, Division 2 location.

There seems to be little validation for requiring only threaded couplings and fittings for RMC and IMC in Class I, Division 2 locations since the previous and present *Code* requirements permit cables with threadless fittings to be installed in Class I, Division 2 locations. These threadless fittings will be allowed in the Class I, Division 2 area, but not at a Class I, Division 2 boundary, as sealing with threaded connections at the Class I, Division 2 boundaries is already addressed at 501.15(B)(2).

Cablebus was also added as it provides a level of safety equivalent to the other wiring methods permitted for Class I, Division 2 locations. Cablebus is similar to installed cable tray with spacing on the conductors. With cable tray already allowed in a Class I, Division 2 location, it would only be natural that cablebus with insulated cables be an allowed wiring method in Class I, Division 2 locations as well. The same change for the addition of "cablebus" occurred at

502.10(B)(1) (Class II, Division 1) (FR 3943, PI 3451);
503.10(A)(1) (Class III, Division 1) (FR 3944, PI 3449);
505.15(C)(1) (Class I, Zone 2) (FR 3946, PI 3447); and
506.15(C)   (Zone 22) (FR 3947, PI 3446).

The existing sentence referencing seals required for boundary conditions, which was located after 510.10(B)(1)(6) has been relocated below all the allowable wiring methods for a Class I, Division 2 location to clarify that this boundary seal requirement applies to the entire list of wiring methods [not just List Item (6)].

First Revisions: FR 3941
Second Revisions: SR 3901
Public Input: PI 2591, PI 3427
Public Comments: PC 564

501.15(D)(1)

Cable Seals — Class I Division 1

Seals for cables entering enclosures shall be installed within 450 mm (18 in.) of the enclosure or as required by the enclosure marking

 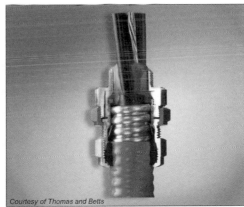

Courtesy of Thomas and Betts

Only explosionproof unions, couplings, reducers, elbows, and capped elbows that are not larger than the trade size of the enclosure entry are permitted between the sealing fitting and the enclosure

501.15(D)(1) Sealing and Drainage. (Class I Locations)

- **Type of Change:** New

- **Change at a Glance:** Text was added identifying the explosionproof fittings that can be installed between a cable seal and an enclosure in Class I, Division 1 locations.

■ **Code Language: 501.15 Sealing and Drainage. (Class I Locations)**
Seals in conduit and cable systems shall comply with 501.15(A) through (F). Sealing compound shall be used in Type MI cable termination fittings to exclude moisture and other fluids from the cable insulation.

(D) Cable Seals, Class I, Division 1. In Division 1 locations, cable seals shall be located according to 501.15(D)(1) through (D)(3).

(1) At Terminations. Cables shall be sealed with sealing fittings that comply with 501.15(C) at all terminations. Type MC-HL cables with a gas/vaportight continuous corrugated metallic sheath and an overall jacket of suitable polymeric material shall be sealed with a listed fitting after the jacket and any other covering have been removed so that the sealing compound can surround each individual insulated conductor in such a manner as to minimize the passage of gases and vapors.

Seals for cables entering enclosures shall be installed within 450 mm (18 in.) of the enclosure or as required by the enclosure marking. Only explosionproof unions, couplings, reducers, elbows, and capped elbows that are not larger than the trade size of the enclosure entry shall be permitted between the sealing fitting and the enclosure.

Exception: Shielded cables and twisted pair cables shall not require the removal of the shielding material or separation of the twisted pairs, provided the termination is sealed by an approved means to minimize the entrance of gasses or vapors and prevent propagation of flame into the cable core.

501.15(D)(1)

■ **2014 *NEC* Requirement**
The process for the installation of a cable seal in Class I, Division 1 location was detailed at 501.15(D)(1). The explosionproof fittings that can be installed between a cable seal and an enclosure in Class I, Division 1 location was not addressed.

■ **2017 *NEC* Change**
A new sentence was added to 501.15(D)(1) identifying that only explosionproof unions, couplings, reducers, elbows, and capped elbows that are not larger than the trade size of the enclosure entry are permitted between the cable sealing fitting and the enclosure in a Class I, Division 1 location.

Analysis of the Change:
Conduit and cable seals are required in hazardous (classified) locations. These seals serve two primary purposes. First, to contain explosions in explosionproof enclosures and thereby prevent the exploding gasses and flames from migrating into the conduit system during such events. These seals are intended to prevent the passage of flames from one portion of the electrical installation to another. Secondly, sealing is required to minimize the passage of gasses or vapors from a Class I, Division 1 location to a Division 2 location or one that is unclassified.

Sealing fittings are available in vertical installation types, and in types suitable for either vertical or horizontal installations.

The purpose of cable sealing is to prevent the spread of flame and to minimize the passage of gasses or vapors through the cable core. Where cables are connected to explosionproof enclosures, sealing fittings meeting the requirements in 501.15(D)(1) are required for all cable entries to such enclosures. In Class I, Division 1 locations, cable seals must be located and provided as required in 501.15(D)(1) through (D)(3).

Cables must be sealed at all terminations, or the cable and the sealing fitting are required to meet all of the rules in 501.15(C). An example of this would be Type MC-HL cables with multiple conductors that include a gas/vaportight continuous corrugated metallic sheath and an overall jacket of suitable polymeric material. This cable must be sealed with a listed fitting. The jacket, armor, and any other covering must be removed, so the sealing compound surrounds each individual insulated conductor to create a seal that minimizes the passage of flammable gasses, flammable liquid-produced vapors, or combustible liquid-produced vapors

501.15(D)(1)

In previous editions of the *Code*, the part that was missing from 501.15(D)(1) was guidance on the possible fittings that can or cannot be installed between the cable seal and the enclosure. For the 2017 *NEC*, a new sentence was added to 501.15(D)(1) identifying that only explosionproof unions, couplings, reducers, elbows, and capped elbows that are not larger than the trade size of the enclosure entry are permitted between the cable sealing fitting and the enclosure. Some explosionproof enclosures require seal fittings to be located as much as 450 mm (18 in.) away and are so marked. This situation would lend itself to fittings being installed between the enclosure and a cable seal.

First Revisions: FR 3973
Public Inputs: PI 1625

Table 511.3(C) and Table 511.3(D)

Area Classification, General. (Commercial Garages, Repair, and Storage)

Table 511.3(C) and Table 511.3(D) Area Classification, General. (Commercial Garages, Repair, and Storage)

- **Type of Change:** New

- **Change at a Glance:** Two new tables were added at 511.3 for clarification of area classification of major and minor commercial repair garages.

- **Code Language: 511.3 Area Classification, General. (Commercial Garages, Repair, and Storage)**

Where Class I liquids or gaseous fuels are stored, handled, or transferred, electrical wiring and electrical utilization equipment shall be designed in accordance with the requirements for Class I, Division 1 or 2 hazardous (classified) locations as classified in accordance with 500.5 and 500.6, and this article. A Class I location shall not extend beyond an unpierced wall, roof, or other solid partition that has no openings. [30A:8.3.5 1, 8.3.2 3]

(C) ~~Major~~ **Repair Garages, Major and Minor.** ~~Where flammable liquids having a flash point below 38°C (100°F) such as gasoline, or gaseous fuels such as natural gas, hydrogen, or LPG, will not be dispensed, but repair activities that involve the transfer of such fluids or gases are~~

~~performed, the classification rules in (1), (2), and (3) shall apply.~~ Where vehicles using Class I liquids or heavier-than-air gaseous fuels (such as LPG) are repaired, hazardous area classification guidance is found in Table 511.3(C).

Informational Note: For additional information, see NFPA 30A-2015, *Code for Motor Fuel Dispensing Facilities and Repair Garages*, Table 8.3.2.
~~(1) Floor Areas.~~
~~(a) Ventilation Provided.~~
~~(b) Ventilation Not Provided.~~
~~(2) Ceiling Areas.~~
~~(a) Ventilation Provided.~~
~~(b) Ventilation Not Provided.~~
~~(3) Pit Areas in Lubrication or Service Room.~~
~~(a) Ventilation Provided.~~
~~(b) Ventilation Not Provided.~~

Table 511.3(C) Extent of Classified Locations for Major and Minor Repair Garages with Heavier-Than-Air Fuel
[See *NEC* and *Analysis of Changes* illustration of Table 511.3(C) for complete *Code* text.]

511.3(C)&(D)

(D) ~~Minor~~ Repair Garages, **Major.** ~~Where flammable liquids having a flash point below 38°C (100°F) such as gasoline, or gaseous fuels such as natural gas or hydrogen, will not be dispensed or transferred, the classification rules in (D)(1), (D)(2), and (D)(3) shall apply to~~ the lubrication ~~and service rooms.~~ Where vehicles using lighter-than-air gaseous fuels (such as hydrogen and natural gas) are repaired or stored, hazardous area classification guidance is found in Table 511.3(D).

Informational Note: For additional information see NFPA 30A-2015, *Code for Motor Fuel Dispensing Facilities and Repair Garages*, Table 8.3.2.
~~(1) Floor Areas.~~
~~(a) Ventilation Provided.~~
~~(b) Ventilation Not Provided.~~
~~(2) Ceiling Areas.~~
~~(3) Pit Areas in Lubrication or Service Room.~~
~~(a) Ventilation Provided.~~
~~(b) Ventilation Not Provided.~~

Table 511.3(D) Extent of Classified Locations for Major Repair Garages with Lighter-than-Air Fuel
[See *NEC* and *Analysis of Changes* illustrations of Table 511.3(C) and Table 511.3(D) for complete *Code* text.]

[The existing *Code* language that appears to be deleted has been re-located to new Table 511.3(C) and new Table 511.3(D). See *NEC* and *Analysis of Changes* illustrations for complete *Code* text.]

Table 511.3(C) Extent of Classified Locations for Major and Minor Repair Garages with Heavier-Than-Air Fuel

Location	Class I		Extent of Classified Locations
	Division (Group D)	Zone (Group IIA)	
Repair garage, major (where Class I liquids or gaseous fuels are transferred or dispensed*)	1	1	Entire space within any pit, below-grade work area, or subfloor work area that is not ventilated
	2	2	Entire space within any pit, below-grade work area, or subfloor work area that is provided with ventilation of at least 0.3 m³/min/m² (1 ft³/min/ft²) of floor area, with suction taken from a point within 300 mm (12 in.) of floor level
	2	2	Up to 450 mm (18 in.) above floor level of the room, except as noted below, for entire floor area
	Unclassified	Unclassified	Up to 450 mm (18 in.) above floor level of the room where room is provided with ventilation of at least 0.3 m³/min/m² (1 ft³/min/ft²) of floor area, with suction taken from a point within 300 mm (12 in.) of floor level
	2	2	Within 0.9 m (3 ft) of any fill or dispensing point, extending in all directions
Specific areas adjacent to classified locations	Unclassified	Unclassified	Areas adjacent to classified locations where flammable vapors are not likely to be released, such as stock rooms, switchboard rooms, and other similar locations, where mechanically ventilated at a rate of four or more air changes per hour or designed with positive air pressure or where effectively cut off by walls or partitions
Repair garage, minor (where Class I liquids or gaseous fuels are transferred or dispensed*)	2	2	Entire space within any pit, below-grade work area, or subfloor work area that is not ventilated
	2	2	Up to 450 mm (18 in.) above floor level, extending 0.9 m (3 ft) horizontally in all directions from opening to any pit, below-grade work area, or subfloor work area that is not ventilated
	Unclassified	Unclassified	Entire space within any pit, below-grade work area, or subfloor work area that is provided with ventilation of at least 0.3 m³/min/m² (1 ft³/min/ft²) of floor area, with suction taken from a point within 300 mm (12 in.) of floor level
Specific areas adjacent to classified locations	Unclassified	Unclassified	Areas adjacent to classified locations where flammable vapors are not likely to be released, such as stock rooms, switchboard rooms, and other similar locations, where mechanically ventilated at a rate of four or more air changes per hour or designed with positive air pressure or where effectively cut off by walls or partitions

Includes draining of Class I liquids from vehicles.

511.3(C)&(D)

Table 511.3(D) Extent of Classified Locations for Major Repair Garages with Lighter-Than-Air Fuel

| Location | Class I | | Extent of Classified Locations |
	Division[2]	Zone[3]	
Repair garage, major (where lighter-than-air gaseous fueled[1] vehicles are repaired or stored)	2	2	Within 450 mm (18 in.) of ceiling, except as noted below
	Unclassified	Unclassified	Within 450 mm (18 in.) of ceiling where ventilation of at least 0.3 m³/min/m² (1 ft³/min/ft²) of floor area, with suction taken from a point within 450 mm (18 in.) of the highest point in the ceiling
Specific areas adjacent to classified locations	Unclassified	Unclassified	Areas adjacent to classified locations where flammable vapors are not likely to be released, such as stock rooms, switchboard rooms, and other similar locations, where mechanically ventilated at a rate of four or more air changes per hour or designed with positive air pressure or where effectively cut off by walls or partitions

[1]Includes fuels such as hydrogen and natural gas, but not LPG.
[2]For hydrogen (lighter than air) Group B, or natural gas Group D.
[3]For hydrogen (lighter than air) Group IIC or IIB+H2, or natural gas Group IIA.

511.3(C)&(D)

- **2014 NEC Requirement**

  Classification of areas where electrical wiring and electrical utilization equipment are used where Class I liquids or gaseous fuels are stored, handled, or transferred is addressed in the *NEC* at 511.3. Major repair garages for commercial use were addressed at 511.3(C). This subsection covered floor areas as well as ceiling areas of these major repair garages. Minor repair garages for commercial use were dealt with at 511.3(D) covering floor areas, ceiling areas, and pit areas in lubrication or service rooms. This information was delivered in a paragraph text format.

- **2017 NEC Change**

  The text provisions of 511.3(C) and (D) were revised into a table format and moved to two new tables in 511.3. The previous requirements of 511.3(C) and (D) were replaced with a new Table 511.3(C) covering both major and minor repair garages where heavier than air gaseous Class I liquids are transferred or dispensed. New Table 511.3(D) covers major repair garages where vehicles using lighter than air gaseous fuels are repaired or stored.

Analysis of the Change:

A major repair garage is defined at 511.2 as "a building or portions of a building where major repairs, such as engine overhauls, painting, body and fender work, and repairs that require draining of the motor vehicle fuel tank are performed on motor vehicles, including associated floor space used for offices, parking, or showrooms." A minor repair garage is defined as "a building or portions of a building used for lubrication, inspection, and minor automotive maintenance work, such as engine tune-ups, replacement of parts, fluid changes (e.g., oil, antifreeze, transmission fluid, brake fluid, air-conditioning refrigerants), brake system repairs, tire rotation, and similar routine maintenance work, including associated floor space used for offices, parking, or showrooms."

These definitions were added to the 2011 *NEC* at 511.2 to clearly describe what constitutes a major repair garage and what qualifies as a minor repair garage. These definitions are extracted material from NFPA 30A (*Code for Motor Fuel Dispensing Facilities and Repair Garages*). They were added the 2011 *NEC* to provide consistent and practical correlation between the *NEC* and the standard from which many of the requirements at 511.3 for area classification of commercial repair garages have been derived.

For the 2017 *NEC*, further revision to 511.3 resulted in the majority of the area classification text provisions that were covered at 511.3 being moved to two new tables in 511.3. These new table additions further align with NFPA 30A. The previous requirements of 511.3(C) and (D) were replaced with a new Table 511.3(C) covering both major and minor repair garages where heavier than air gaseous Class I liquids are transferred or dispensed. New Table 511.3(D) covers major repair garages where vehicles using lighter-than-air gaseous fuels are repaired or stored. Both of these new *NEC* Article 511 tables are derived from Table 8.3.2 from NFPA 30A. An informational note was added after the parent text of both 511.3(C) and (D) referring to the origin of these tables in NFPA 30A. Notes were added at the bottom of Table 511.3(D) to give guidance in applying the correct groups for hydrogen applications.

The addition of these tables will increase usability by providing a ready, easy-to-use reference to area classifications and differences between requirements where minor repairs and major repair operations and services for fuel consuming vehicles are performed. The reformatted layout of Table 511.3(C) and Table 511.3(D) retains all previous requirements of 511.3(C) and (D) but presents the information in a far more user-friendly fashion. These tables provide clear and concise rules regarding the relationship between areas that are classified without ventilation and those that are either reduced in classification or deemed unclassified as a result of providing appropriate amounts of ventilation.

First Revisions: FR 3954, FR 3955

511.3(C)&(D)

511.8

Underground Wiring

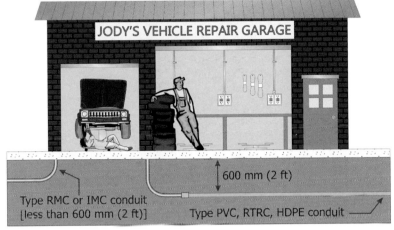

Underground wiring method for a commercial repair garage to be installed in threaded RMC conduit or threaded steel IMC conduit

JODY'S VEHICLE REPAIR GARAGE

600 mm (2 ft)

Type RMC or IMC conduit [less than 600 mm (2 ft)]

Type PVC, RTRC, HDPE conduit

Type PVC, RTRC, and HDPE conduit are permitted to be used where buried under not less than 600 mm (2 ft) of cover

511.8

511.8 Underground Wiring. (Commercial Garages, Repair and Storage)

- **Type of Change:** New

- **Change at a Glance:** New section was added to address the acceptable wiring methods for an underground installation at a commercial repair garage.

- **Code Language:** **511.8 Underground Wiring. (Commercial Garages, Repair and Storage)**

Underground wiring shall be installed in threaded rigid metal conduit or intermediate metal conduit.

Exception: *Type PVC conduit, Type RTRC conduit, and Type HDPE conduit shall be permitted where buried under not less than 600 mm (2 ft) of cover. Where Type PVC conduit, Type RTRC conduit, or Type HDPE conduit is used, threaded rigid metal conduit or threaded steel intermediate metal conduit shall be used for the last 600 mm (2 ft) of the underground run to emergence or to the point of connection to the aboveground raceway, and an equipment grounding conductor shall be included to provide electrical continuity of the raceway system and for grounding of non–current-carrying metal parts.*

■ **2014 *NEC* Requirement**

For an underground raceway installation under a commercial repair garage, Article 511 offered little guidance. Depending on what the area is classified, wiring methods described in 501.10(A) (for a Class I Division 1 location) would apply. Some users of the *Code* would migrate to 514.8 for an underground wiring method below a commercial garage, but 514.8 applies only if motor fuel dispensing facilities are involved.

■ **2017 *NEC* Change**

A new section (511.8) was added to Article 511 requiring the underground wiring method for a commercial repair garage to be installed in threaded rigid metal conduit (RMC) or threaded steel intermediate metal conduit (IMC). A new exception at 511.8 permits PVC conduit, RTRC conduit, and high-density polyethylene (HDPE) conduit to be used where buried under not less than 600 mm (2 ft) of cover.

Analysis of the Change:

For wiring methods installed under a commercial repair garage, where would one go in the *NEC* for guidance? In previous editions of the *Code*, nothing was mentioned about this underground location in Article 511, which addresses the electrical provisions of commercial repair garages. Wiring methods in the floor (slab), under the slab, or underground must be suitable for Class I Division 1 in accordance with 501.10(A). This requirement also applies to uninterrupted underground raceways, even where they extend above or below the slab according to *NEC* sections like 514.8.

Is this area below a commercial repair garage a Class I Division 1 location? Examination of 500.5(B) states that Class I locations are "those in which flammable gases, flammable liquid-produced vapors, or combustible liquid-produced vapors are or may be present in the air in quantities sufficient to produce explosive or ignitible mixtures." According to the "fire triangle" theory, three elements are needed to ignite a fire or explosion: heat, fuel, and an oxidizing agent (usually oxygen). How much air or oxygen is present in the earth below a concrete slab or structure? These questions were addressed in the 2005 *NEC* with revisions to 514.8 (motor fuel dispensing facilities) and other locations in the hazardous (classified) location articles in Chapter 5 of the *NEC*.

The added language at 514.8 in the 2005 *NEC* required underground wiring for motor fuel dispensing facilities to be installed in threaded rigid metal conduit (RMC) or threaded steel intermediate metal conduit (IMC). However, an exception to this rule was also revised that allowed rigid polyvinyl chloride conduit (PVC) conduit and reinforced thermosetting resin conduit (RTRC) where buried under not less than 600 mm (2 ft) of cover. This exception was in recognition of the fact that the "fire triangle" was not possible in this underground installations leaving this underground area "unclassified." Prior to the 2005 *NEC*, the underground area below items such as motor fuel dispensing facilities were considered a Class I Division 1 location.

511.8

In an effort to fill a void in Article 511 concerning underground wiring at a commercial repair garage, a new 511.8 titled "Underground Wiring" was added for the 2017 *NEC*. The added text at 511.8 was patterned after similar underground wiring provisions, such as 514.8 and 515.8(A). As with these other underground wiring sections, the main rule at 511.8 called for threaded RMC or IMC to be employed. The new exception permits PVC conduit, RTRC conduit, and high-density polyethylene (HDPE) conduit to be used where buried under not less than 600 mm (2 ft) of cover. Where PVC, RTRC, or HDPE conduit is used, threaded RMC or threaded steel IMC shall be used for the last 600 mm (2 ft) of the underground run to emergence, or the point of connection to the aboveground raceway. As properly required with any nonmetallic raceway, an equipment grounding conductor is required to be included to provide electrical continuity of the raceway system and for grounding of non-current-carrying metal parts.

First Revisions: FR 3994
Public Inputs: PI 1575

514.3(B)(3)

Classification of Location.
(Motor Fuel Dispensing Facilities)

514.3(B)(3) Classification of Location

- **Type of Change:** New

- **Change at a Glance:** Section 514.3(B)(2) and Table 514.3(B)(2) contain information concerning area classification for compressed natural gas, liquefied natural gas, and liquefied petroleum gas for dispensing devices. No detailed information existed at this section for area classification of fuel storage of these gases.

- **Code Language: 514.3 Classification of Location. (Motor Fuel Dispensing Facilities)**
[See Figure 514.3.]

(A) Unclassified Locations. (See *NEC* for complete text)

(B) Classified Locations. [See Figure 514.3(B).]
(1) Class I Locations. (See *NEC* for complete text)

(2) Compressed Natural Gas, Liquefied Natural Gas, and Liquefied Petroleum Gas Areas. (See *NEC* for complete text)

(3) Fuel Storage.
(a) Aboveground tanks storing CNG or LNG shall be separated from any adjacent property line that is or can be built upon, any public way, and the nearest important building on the same property. [30A: 12.3.1]

Informational Note: The relevant distances are given in Section 8.4 of NFPA 52-2013, Vehicular Gaseous Fuel Systems Code.

(b) Aboveground tanks storing hydrogen shall be separated from any adjacent property line that is or can be built upon, any public way, and the nearest important building on the same property. [30A: 12.3.2]

Informational Note: The relevant distances given in NFPA 2-2011, Hydrogen Technologies Code.

(c) Aboveground tanks storing LP-Gas shall be separated from any adjacent property line that is or can be built upon, any public way, and the nearest important building on the same property. [30A: 12.3.3]

Informational Note: The relevant distances are given in Section 6.3 of NFPA 58-2014, Liquefied Petroleum Gas Code.

(d) Aboveground tanks storing CNG, LNG, or LP-Gas shall be separated from each other by at least 6 m (20 ft) and from dispensing devices that dispense liquid or gaseous motor vehicle fuels by at least 6 m (20 ft). [30A: 12.3.3]

Exception No. 1: The required separation shall not apply to tanks or dispensers storing or handling fuels of the same chemical composition.

Exception No. 2: The required separation shall not apply when both the

514.3(B)(3)

gaseous fuel storage and dispensing equipment are at least 15 m (50 ft) from any other aboveground motor fuel storage or dispensing equipment.

Informational Note: For further information, see NFPA 52-2013, Vehicular Gaseous Fuel Systems Code, or NFPA 58-2014, Liquefied Petroleum Gas Code, as applicable.

(e) Dispenser Installations Beneath Canopies. Where CNG or LNG dispensers are installed beneath a canopy or enclosure, either the canopy or enclosure shall be designed to prevent accumulation or entrapment of ignitible vapors or all electrical equipment installed beneath the canopy or enclosure shall be suitable for Class I, Division 2 hazardous (classified) locations. [30A: 12.4]

(f) Specific Requirements for LP-Gas Dispensing Devices. [30A: 12.5] Dispensing devices for LP-Gas shall be located as follows:
(1) At least 3 m (10 ft) from any dispensing device for Class I liquids
(2) At least 1.5 m (5 ft) from any dispensing device for Class I liquids where the following conditions exist:
   a. The LP-Gas deliver nozzle and filler valve release no more than 4 cm3 (0.1 oz) of liquid upon disconnection.
   b. The fixed maximum liquid level gauge remains closed during the entire refueling process. [30A:12.5.2]
Table 514.3(B)(2) shall be used to delineate and classify areas for the purpose of installation of electrical wiring and electrical utilization equipment.

514.3(B)(3)

- **2014 *NEC* Requirement**
  Section 514.3(B)(2) and Table 514.3(B)(2) contain information concerning area classification for compressed natural gas, liquefied natural gas, and liquefied petroleum gas for dispensing devices. No detailed information existed at this section for area classification of fuel storage of these gases.

- **2017 *NEC* Change**
  Specific requirements for fuel storage of compressed natural gas, liquefied natural gas, and liquefied petroleum gas were put in place, along with references to other NFPA documents that offer further detail were added to the 2017 *NEC*.

Analysis of the Change:

Compressed natural gas (CNG) is a clean, low-cost, domestically available alternative fuel that can be used for such things as powering CNG vehicles. CNG is a non-toxic gas that is lighter than air, so it does not puddle (like gasoline) or sink to the ground like propane, which is heavier than air. Instead, CNG will rise and dissipate in the atmosphere. CNG also has a higher ignition temperature, which means that it is much harder to ignite than fuels like gasoline.

Liquefied natural gas (LNG) is natural gas (predominantly methane) that has been converted to liquid form for ease of storage or transport. It takes up about

1/600th the volume of natural gas in the gaseous state. It is odorless, colorless, non-toxic and non-corrosive. Hazards include flammability after vaporization into a gaseous state, freezing and asphyxia. Liquefied petroleum gas (LPG) is composed mainly of propane and butane while natural gas is composed of the lighter methane and ethane. LPG, also referred to as simply propane or butane, are flammable mixtures of hydrocarbon gasses used as fuel in heating appliances, cooking equipment, and vehicles.

The advantages to using these gases include the diminished energy dependence on foreign oil imports, the reduced cost compared to gasoline, and less emissions. All fuel sources contain energy that is released through combustion, and any fuel can be potentially dangerous if not properly handled. To combat these potential hazards, specific requirements for storage of these gases were put in place, along with references to other NFPA documents that offer further detail were added to the 2017 *NEC*.

514.3(B)(3)

Modern storage tanks for these gases are typically full containment type, which has a pre-stressed concrete outer wall and a high-nickel steel inner tank, with extremely efficient insulation between the walls. Large tanks are low aspect ratio (height to width) and cylindrical in design with a domed steel or concrete roof. Even with these construction precautions, care must still be top priority to insure electrical safety with proper distances maintained between these storage tanks and potential ignition sources. A new 514.3(B)(3) was added to the 2017 *NEC* with area classification information for compressed natural gas, liquefied natural gas, and liquefied petroleum gas fuel storage tanks.

The information is contained in 514.3(B)(3) and is extracted material from NFPA 30A (*Code for Motor Fuel Dispensing Facilities and Repair Garages*).

First Revisions: FR 4002

514.8 Ex. No. 2

Underground Wiring.
(Motor Fuel Dispensing Facilities)

Photos Courtesy of Carlon

514.8 Ex. No. 2 Underground Wiring. (Motor Fuel Dispensing Facilities)

- **Type of Change:** Revision

- **Change at a Glance:** Type HDPE conduit was added as an acceptable underground wiring methods for motor fuel dispensing facilities.

- **Code Language: 514.8 Underground Wiring. (Motor Fuel Dispensing Facilities)**

Underground wiring shall be installed in threaded rigid metal conduit or threaded steel intermediate metal conduit. Any portion of electrical wiring that is below the surface of a Class I, Division 1, or a Class I, Division 2, location [as classified in Table 514.3(B)(1) and Table 514.3(B)(2)] shall be sealed within 3.05 m (10 ft) of the point of emergence above grade. Except for listed explosionproof reducers at the conduit seal, there shall be no union, coupling, box, or fitting between the conduit seal and the point of emergence above grade. Refer to Table 300.5.

Exception No. 1: Type MI cable shall be permitted where it is installed in accordance with Article 332.

Exception No. 2: Type PVC conduit, ~~and~~ Type RTRC conduit, and Type HDPE conduit shall be permitted where buried under not less than 600 mm (2 ft) of cover. Where Type PVC conduit, ~~or~~ Type RTRC conduit, or

Type HDPE conduit is used, threaded rigid metal conduit or threaded steel intermediate metal conduit shall be used for the last 600 mm (2 ft) of the underground run to emergence or the point of connection to the aboveground raceway, and an equipment grounding conductor shall be included to provide electrical continuity of the raceway system and for grounding of non-current-carrying metal parts.

514.8

- **2014 *NEC* Requirement**
  Underground wiring for motor fuel dispensing facilities is required to be installed in threaded rigid metal conduit (RMC) or threaded steel intermediate metal conduit (IMC). Mineral-insulated, metal-sheathed (Type MI) cable is permitted where it is installed in accordance with Article 332. Rigid polyvinyl chloride conduit (PVC) conduit and reinforced thermosetting resin conduit (RTRC) where buried under not less than 600 mm (2 ft) of cover is also permitted as a wiring method under motor fuel dispensing facilities.

- **2017 *NEC* Change**
  In addition to the permitted wiring methods allowed in the 2014 *NEC*, high density polyethylene (HDPE) conduit was added to 514.8, Ex. No. 2 as an acceptable wiring method for underground installations for motor fuel dispensing facilities where buried under not less than 600 mm (2 ft) of cover.

Analysis of the Change:

Underground wiring methods for motor fuel dispensing facilities are described at 514.8. This section, which began with the 1968 *NEC*, was revised during the 2005 *NEC* process. Historically, underground wiring for motor fuel dispensing facilities has been required to be installed in threaded rigid metal conduit (RMC) or threaded steel intermediate metal conduit (IMC). Per exception, mineral-insulated, metal-sheathed (Type MI) cable is permitted where it is installed in accordance with Article 332. Another exception to this rule permitted rigid polyvinyl chloride conduit (PVC) conduit and reinforced thermosetting resin conduit (RTRC) where buried under not less than 600 mm (2 ft) of cover as a wiring method under motor fuel dispensing facilities.

For the 2017 *NEC*, high density polyethylene (HDPE) conduit was added to 514.8, Ex. No. 2 as an acceptable wiring method for underground installations for motor fuel dispensing facilities where buried under not less than 600 mm (2 ft) of cover. As with Type PVC and RTRC, whenever Type HDPE conduit is used, threaded RMC or threaded steel IMC must be used for the last 600 mm (2 ft) of the underground run to emergence from the ground or the point of connection to the aboveground raceway. As required with any nonmetallic raceway, an equipment grounding conductor is also required to be included to provide electrical continuity of the raceway system and for grounding of non-current-carrying metal parts.

Type HDPE provides at least the same level of protection and is an equivalent wiring method to that of Type PVC or Type RTRC when installed underground under not less than 600 mm (2 ft) of cover. Type HDPE is permitted in direct burial installations by 353.10(4). No issues exist concerning hazardous (classified) locations as this underground area under not less than 600 mm (2 ft) of cover is considered an "unclassified" location.

Type HDPE conduit was recognized as an *NEC* wiring method with the creation of Article 353 for the 2005 *NEC*. This conduit system is a nonmetallic flexible raceway manufactured from high density polyethylene for use in underground and innerduct applications.

First Revisions: FR 3993
Public Inputs: PI 2802

514.11(A), (B), and (C)
Emergency Controls for Fuel Dispensers

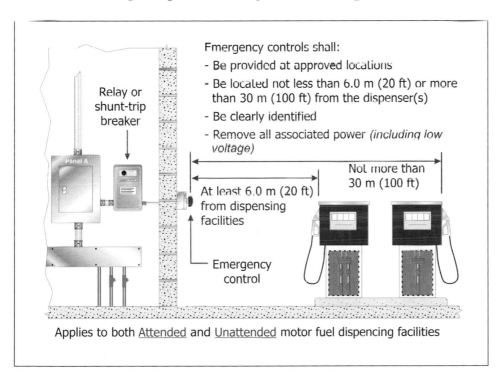

Emergency controls shall:
- Be provided at approved locations
- Be located not less than 6.0 m (20 ft) or more than 30 m (100 ft) from the dispenser(s)
- Be clearly identified
- Remove all associated power *(including low voltage)*

Relay or shunt-trip breaker

Panel A

At least 6.0 m (20 ft) from dispensing facilities

Not more than 30 m (100 ft)

Emergency control

Applies to both Attended and Unattended motor fuel dispencing facilities

514.11(A), (B), and (C) Circuit Disconnects. (Motor Fuel Dispensing Facilities)

- **Type of Change:** Revision

- **Change at a Glance:** Emergency shutoff device requirements for motor fuel dispensing facilities were revised to reflect the requirements of NFPA 30A and for clarity.

■ **Code Language: 514.11 Circuit Disconnects. (Motor Fuel Dispensing Facilities)**

(A) General. ~~Each circuit leading to or through dispensing equipment, including all associated power, communications, data, and video circuits, and equipment for remote pumping systems, shall be provided with a clearly identified and readily accessible switch or other approved means, located remote from the dispensing devices, to disconnect simultaneously from the source of supply, all conductors of the circuits, including the grounded conductor, if any.~~ Fuel dispensing systems shall be provided with one or more clearly identified emergency shutoff devices or electrical disconnects. Such devices or disconnects shall be installed in approved locations but not less than 6 m (20 ft) or more than 30 m (100 ft) from the fuel dispensing devices that they serve. Emergency shutoff devices or electrical disconnects shall disconnect power to all dispensing devices; to all remote pumps serving the dispensing devices; to all associated power, control, and signal circuits; and to all other electrical equipment in the hazardous (classified) locations surrounding the fuel dispensing devices. When more than one emergency shutoff device or electrical disconnect is provided, all devices shall be interconnected. Resetting from an emergency shutoff condition shall require manual intervention and the manner of resetting shall be approved by the authority having jurisdiction. [**30A**: 6.7]

~~Single-pole breakers utilizing handle ties shall not be permitted.~~
Exception: Intrinsically safe electrical equipment need not meet this requirement. [30A: 6.7]

(B) Attended Self-Service Motor Fuel Dispensing Facilities.
~~Emergency controls as specified in 514.11(A) shall be installed at a location acceptable to the authority having jurisdiction, but controls shall not be more than 30 m (100 ft) from dispensers.~~ At attended motor fuel dispensing facilities, the devices or disconnects shall be readily accessible to the attendant. [30A:6.7.1]

(C) Unattended Self-Service Motor Fuel Dispensing Facilities.
~~Emergency controls as specified in 514.11(A) shall be installed at a location acceptable to the authority having jurisdiction, but the control shall be more than 6 m (20 ft) but less than 30 m (100 ft) from the dispensers. Additional emergency controls shall be installed on each group of dispensers or the outdoor equipment used to control the dispensers. Emergency controls shall shut off all power to all dispensing equipment at the station. Controls shall be manually reset only in a manner approved by the authority having jurisdiction.~~ At unattended motor fuel dispensing facilities, the devices or disconnects shall be readily accessible to patrons and at least one additional device or disconnect shall be readily accessible to each group of dispensing devices on an individual island. [30A:6.7.2]
~~**Informational Note:** For additional information, see 6.7.1 and 6.7.2 of NFPA 30A-2012, Code for Motor Fuel Dispensing Facilities and Repair Garages.~~

514.11

- **2014 *NEC* Requirement**
  Each circuit leading to or through motor fuel dispensing facility equipment, including all associated power, communications, data, and video circuits, and equipment for remote pumping systems was required to be provided with a clearly identified and readily accessible switch or other approved means. This switching device was required to be located remote from the dispensing devices. This switching device was also required to provide simultaneous disconnection from the source of supply power for all conductors of the circuits, including the grounded conductor. Single-pole breakers utilizing handle ties were not permitted to be utilized as this switching device.

  Emergency controls for attended self-service facilities were required to be installed at a location acceptable to the authority having jurisdiction, but not more than 30 m (100 ft) from the dispensers. Emergency controls for unattended self-service facilities were required to be installed at a location acceptable to the authority having jurisdiction, more than 6 m (20 ft) but less than 30 m (100 ft) from the dispensers.

- **2017 *NEC* Change**
  The same basic requirements for the emergency shutoff devices still exist for the 2017 *NEC*. Fuel dispensing systems are required to be provided with one or more clearly identified emergency shutoff devices or electrical disconnects. Such devices or disconnects shall be installed in approved locations but not less than 6 m (20 ft) or more than 30 m (100 ft) from the fuel dispensing devices that they serve. Language was revised at 514.11 to clearly indicate that these minimum and maximum distances hold true at both attended and unattended motor fuel dispensing facilities.

514.11

Analysis of the Change:

Article 514 of the *NEC* gives instruction for the safe installation of electrical wiring and equipment in and around motor fuel dispensing facilities. The provisions for emergency shutoff controls at 514.11 provide the necessary means to safely remove power from the motor fuel dispensing facilities during an emergency situation. These emergency shutoff devices for attended or unattended self-service facilities have been in the *Code* since the 1993 *NEC*. Prior to the 2011 edition of the *NEC*, these emergency shutoff devices were only instituted for nominal power circuits. Low-voltage and power-limited circuits were not specifically addressed and are not part of the emergency shutoff provisions. These Class 2 circuits are capable of delivering enough of an energized spark to easily ignite fuel such as gasoline. For the 2011 *NEC*, both 514.11 and 514.13 were revised to specifically state that each dispensing device must have a means to remove all external voltage sources, regardless of type.

For the 2017 *NEC*, 514.11(A), (B), and (C) were revised to align with the requirements in NFPA 30A (*Code for Motor Fuel Dispensing Facilities and Repair Garages*) and to clarify what is required for an emergency shutoff device at both attended and unattended self-service motor fuel dispensing facilities. The 2017 *NEC* requirements at 514.11 are basically the same as those required in the previous *Code*, but the text was revised to an easier-to-understand format.

Larger fuel stations, which are very common along our interstate highway systems, may have several islands of dispensers located several hundreds of feet away from the main building. As previously written, the emergency shutoff devices for some of these fuel dispensing pumps could end up being installed further than 30 m (100 ft) from the dispenser itself. The previous *Code* language at 514.11 was being interpreted by some users of the *Code* as requiring the emergency controls to be within 30 m (100 ft) of the closest dispenser of a group while allowing the other dispensers to be located further than 30 m (100 ft) from an emergency control device. According to CMP-14, with their actions at 514.11 for the 2017 *NEC*, this was never the intent of 514.11.

The revised language at 514.11 now requires the emergency shutoff device to be not less than 6 m (20 ft) from and not more than 30 m (100 ft) from the fuel dispensing devices they serve. During an emergency situation, this reasonable distance will allow the attendant, or anyone using the dispensing pumps, the ability to quickly shut off all external power to a dispenser, from a safe distance away from the potential problem area.

514.11

First Revisions: FR 3996
Public Inputs: PI 1156, PI 1157

Article 516

Spray Application, Dipping, Coating, and Printing Processes Using Flammable or Combustible Materials

Article 516 was extensively revised for clarity and to align with NFPA 33 *Standard for Spray Application Using Flammable and Combustible Materials* and NFPA 34 *Standard for Dipping, Coating, and Printing Processes Using Flammable or Combustible Liquids*

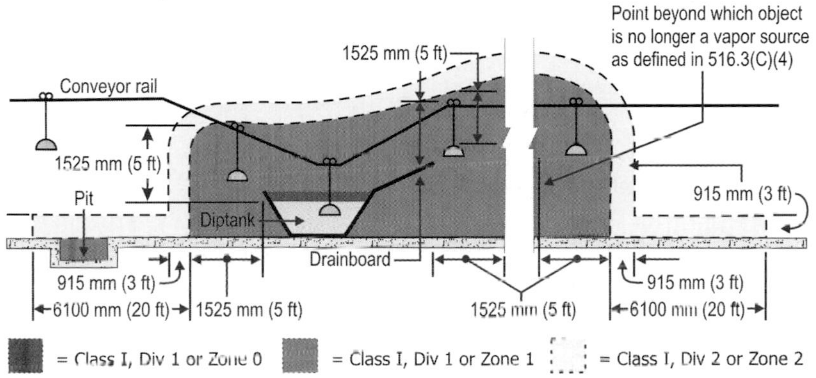

Figure 516.29(a) Electrical Area Classification for Open Dipping and Coating Processes Without Vapor Containment or Ventilation

516

Article 516 Spray Application, Dipping, Coating, and Printing Processes Using Flammable or Combustible Materials

- **Type of Change:** Revision

- **Change at a Glance:** Article 516 was extensively revised for clarity and to align with NFPA 33 and NFPA 34.

- **Code Language: Article 516 Spray Application, Dipping, Coating, and Printing Processes Using Flammable or Combustible Materials**

Part I. General

516.1 Scope. This article covers the regular or frequent application of flammable liquids, combustible liquids, and combustible powders by spray operations and the application of flammable liquids, or combustible liquids at temperatures above their flashpoint, by spraying, dipping, coating, printing, or other means.

516.2 Definitions.

Part II. Open Containers

516.3 ~~Classification of Locations.~~

516.4 ~~Wiring and Equipment in Class I Locations~~ Area Classification.

(See NEC for complete Code text)

516

- **2014 *NEC* Requirement**
  Article 516 covered spray application, dipping, coating, and printing processes using flammable or combustible materials. There were no parts to the article.

- **2017 *NEC* Change**
  Article 516 was re-arranged and revised to give the article a clearer outline. Four individual parts were added to the article. The requirements now align with the requirements of NFPA 33 and NFPA 34.

Analysis of the Change:

Article 516 covers the regular or frequent application of flammable liquids, combustible liquids, and combustible powders by spray operations and the application of flammable liquids, or combustible liquids at temperatures above their flashpoint, by spraying, dipping, coating, printing, or other means (see 516.1). This article provides requirements for proper location, design, and construction of spraying, dipping, coating, and printing equipment. This article also covers the installation, protection, and maintenance of electrical systems and equipment, control of ignition sources, ventilation, storage, handling, and distribution of flammable and combustible liquids.

This article has been part of the *Code* in some form since the 1953 edition of the *NEC*. At that time, it was titled, "Finishing Processes" and was located at Section 5130 as part of Article 510 for "Specific Occupancies." For the 2017 *NEC*, this article received an extensive overhaul and revision. The revision was intended to align Article 516 with NFPA 33, *Standard for Spray Application Using Flammable and Combustible Materials*, and NFPA 34, *Standard for Dipping, Coating, and Printing Processes Using Flammable or Combustible Liquids*.

The public input that lead to this extensive revision was developed by a Task Group consisting of the NFPA Committee on Finishing Processes and selected members of CMP-14. The public input originated from a tentative interim amendment (TIA 70-14-1) issued by the NFPA Standards Council on August 1, 2013. The TIA was issued due to changes to Article 516 for the 2014 *NEC* with provisions that were non-compliant with the *NEC Style Manual*. These 2014 *NEC* changes or revisions contained "major conflicts with other NFPA standards" as well. The task group formed between the Finishing Processes Committee and CMP-14 rewrote Article 516 in its entirety in order to include the correct extracted text and to reflect major revisions in both of the referenced NFPA standards (NFPA 33 and 34).

The previously defined terms at 516.2 for *Flash-Off Area* and *Resin Application Area* were deleted as these terms are not used anywhere in the *Code* other than the definition itself. A new definition of *Outdoor Spray Area* was added at 516.2 covering spray areas that are located outside the confines of a building.

First Revisions: FR 3956
Second Revisions: SR 3914
Public Inputs: PI 4242, PI 21, PI 4266, PI 1811, PI 1810, PI 4238
Public Comments: PC 176, PC 1811

517.2

517.2

Definition: Health Care Facilities — Governing Body

Governing Body. The person or persons who have the overall legal responsibility for the operation of a health care facility.

517.2 Definitions. (Health Care Facilities)

- **Type of Change:** New

- **Change at a Glance:** A new definition for *Governing Body* has been added to Article 517.

- **Code Language: 517.2 Definitions. (Health Care Facilities)**

  Governing Body. The person or persons who have the overall legal responsibility for the operation of a health care facility. [**99**: 3.3.62]

- **2014 *NEC* Requirement**
  The term *governing body* appeared in Informational Note No. 1 and Informational Note No. 5 following the definition of "patient care space," but the term was not defined in Article 517 or Article 100.

- **2017 *NEC* Change**
  The term "governing body" appears at seven different locations in Article 517 for the 2017 *NEC* and a new definition has been added at 517.2.

517.2

Analysis of the Change:

A new definition for *governing body* was added to 517.2 pertaining to health care facilities. This term appeared in a couple of informational notes in Article 517 in the 2014 *NEC*. Besides this new definition at 517.2, governing body has been added in five other locations throughout Article 517. For example, 517.18(C) will now say, "receptacles that are located within the patient rooms, bathrooms, playrooms, and activity rooms of pediatric units, or spaces with similar risk *as determined by the governing body*, other than nurseries, shall be listed tamper-resistant or shall employ a listed tamper-resistant cover." As this term is now used several times in Article 517, it needs to be defined.

Governing body will be defined as "the person or persons who have the overall legal responsibility for the operation of a health care facility." This new definition will be followed by the reference number "[99: 3.3.62]" as this is extracted material from NFPA 99 (*Healthcare Facilities Code*). This addition correlates information between the *NEC* and NFPA 99 as required by the *NEC Style Manual* at Section 4.3.2.

This new definition will eliminate some of the confusion that may exist for users of the *Code* when trying to determine who has responsibility for making decisions on certain matters in a health care facility.

First Revisions: FR 4255
Public Inputs: PI 2786, PI 2787

517.2

Definition: Health Care Facility

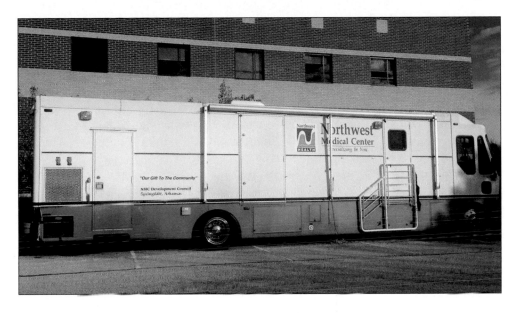

517.2 Definitions. (Health Care Facilities)

- **Type of Change:** Revision

- **Change at a Glance:** Definition of *Health Care Facility* was revised to include *mobile enclosures*.

- **Code Language: 517.2 Definitions. (Health Care Facilities)**

  Health Care Facilities. Buildings, or portions of buildings, or mobile enclosures in which human medical, dental, psychiatric, nursing, obstetrical, or surgical care are provided. [99: 3.3.67]

  Informational Note: Examples of health care facilities include, but are not limited to, hospitals, nursing homes, limited care facilities, clinics, medical and dental offices, and ambulatory care centers, whether permanent or movable.

- **2014 *NEC* Requirement**
  The term *Health Care Facility* was defined at 517.2 in the 2014 *NEC*. Though it did not exclude a mobile facility, it did not include this term in the definition. Examples of health care facilities were included in the definition.

- **2017 *NEC* Change**
  The definition of a *Health Care Facility* was revised for the 2017 *NEC* and now includes the term "mobile enclosures." The examples of a health care facility that were included in the definition in the previous edition of the *Code* are now found in an informational note below the revised definition.

517.2

Analysis of the Change:

The scope at the very beginning of Article 517 states that the provisions of Article 517 are to be applied to electrical construction and installation criteria in "health care facilities that provide services to human beings." That leads to the obvious question as to "What is a health care facility?" A stated definition of a health care facility located at 517.2 is the starting point to answer this question.

The definition of a *Health Care Facility* was revised for the 2017 *NEC* to give the user of the *Code* further explanation as to what constitutes these places of care and recovery. A health care facility is now defined as "buildings, portions of buildings, or mobile enclosures in which human medical, dental, psychiatric, nursing, obstetrical, or surgical care are provided." This definition is extracted material from NFPA 99 (*Healthcare Facilities Code*). The previous definition in both the *NEC* and NFPA 99 included examples of what a health care facility could encompass. Those examples were removed in the latest revision to NFPA 99. CMP-15 felt that these examples of health care facilities were important to the users of the *NEC* and retained them in an informational note following the revised *NEC* definition.

On careful examination of the revised definition of a health care facility, one of the first observations is the inclusion of the phrase "mobile enclosures" into the definition. This inclusion should make it abundantly clear that a health care facility is not limited to a traditional brick and mortar permanently constructed building. A health care facility can include a mobile or portable facility, such as a mobile blood bank, or mobile facilities as seen at sporting events. These facilities offer some of the same benefits as well as some of the same potential hazards to the electrical system as a traditional health care facility.

First Revisions: FR 4238
Public Inputs: PI 2801

517.2

517.2

Definition: Health Care Facilities — Medical Office (Dental Office)

Medical Office (Dental Office). A building or part thereof in which the following occur:

(1) Examinations and minor treatments or procedures are performed under the continuous supervision of a medical or dental professional;

(2) Only sedation or local anesthesia is Involved and treatment or procedures do not render the patient incapable of self-preservation under emergency conditions; and

(3) Overnight stays for patients or 24-hour operation are not provided. [99: 3.3.98]

517.2 Definitions. (Health Care Facilities)

517.2

517.2 Definitions. (Health Care Facilities)

- **Type of Change:** New

- **Change at a Glance:** A new definition for *Medical Office (Dental Office)* was added to 517.2.

- **Code Language: 517.2 Definitions. (Health Care Facilities)**

  Medical Office (Dental Office). A building or part thereof in which the following occur: (1) examinations and minor treatments or procedures are performed under the continuous supervision of a medical or dental professional; (2) only sedation or local anesthesia is involved and treatment or procedures do not render the patient incapable of self-preservation under emergency conditions; and (3) overnight stays for patients or 24-hour operation are not provided. [**99**: 3.3.98]

- **2014 *NEC* Requirement**
  The term, *medical and dental offices* was used at six different locations throughout Article 517 in the 2014 *NEC*, but the term was not defined.

- **2017 *NEC* Change**
  To define a well-used term in Article 517, a new definition for *Medical Office (Dental Office)* was added at 517.2 for the 2017 *NEC*.

Analysis of the Change:

A new definition for *Medical Office (Dental Office)* was added to 517.2 for the 2017 *NEC*. The terms, "medical and dental offices," business office, medical office, or dental office appear some ten times in Article 517 for the 2017 *NEC*. This fact alone would indicate a need for this term to be defined in Article 517. Inclusion of this definition will provide needed clarity when determining health care facility requirements, such as branch circuit requirements at patient bed locations. Some confusion may have existed in the past for users of the *Code* when using this term for electrical installations and the determination of Article 517 requirements for medical and dental offices.

This new definition will clarify that overnight stays for patients or 24-hour operation facilities do not encompass a medical or dental office. Only sedation or local anesthesia is involved in minor treatment or procedures under the continuous supervision of a medical or dental professional would be involved at a medical or dental office. Along with the category designations at the definition of *Patient Care Space*, this new definition will help provide installers and the enforcement community more information about these health care facility occupancies.

This new definition is extracted from NFPA 99 (Health Care Facilities Code). A parenthetic format was added to this definition to be consistent with the *NEC Style Manual*, Sections 2.2.2 and 3.2.3.

First Revisions: FR 4244

Public Inputs: PI 2835

517.2

517.2

Definition: Health Care Facilities — Patient Care Space

Definition for "**Patient Care Space**" was revised for clarity and to align with definitions in NFPA 99

Basic Care (Category 3) Space:
- Examination or treatment rooms in clinics
- Medical and dental offices
- Nursing homes
- Limited care facilities

General Care (Category 2) Space:
- Inpatient bedrooms
- Dialysis rooms
- In vitro fertilization rooms
- Procedural rooms
- Similar rooms

Critical Care (Category 1) Space:
- Special care units patient rooms used for critical care
- Intensive care
- Special care treatment rooms
 - Angiography laboratories
 - Cardiac catheterization labs
 - Delivery rooms
 - Operating rooms
 - Post-anesthesia care units
 - Trauma rooms

Support (Category 4) Space:
- Anesthesia work rooms
- Sterile supply
- Laboratories
- Morgues
- Waiting rooms
- Utility rooms
- Lounges

517.2

517.2 Definitions. (Health Care Facilities)

- **Type of Change:** Revision

- **Change at a Glance:** Revised definition of *Patient Care Space* will include four categories: Basic Care (Category 3) Space; General Care (Category 2) Space; Critical Care (Category 1) Space; and Support (Category 4) Space.

- **Code Language: 517.2 Definitions. (Health Care Facilities)**
Patient Care Space. Any space of ~~within~~ a health care facility wherein patients are intended to be examined or treated. [**99:** 3.3.127]

Informational Note No. 1: The governing body of the facility designates patient care space in accordance with the type of patient care anticipated ~~and with the definitions of the area classification~~. [**99:** 1.3.4.1]

Informational Note No. 2: Business offices, corridors, lounges, day rooms, dining rooms, or similar areas typically are not classified as patient care space. [**99:** A.3.3.127]

Basic Care (Category 3) Space. Space in which failure of equipment or a system is not likely to cause injury to the patients, staff, or visitors ~~caregivers~~ but ~~can~~ may cause patient discomfort. [99: 3.3.127.3]

Informational Note ~~No. 2~~: [Category 3] spaces, formerly known as basic care rooms [(spaces)] ~~is~~ are typically ~~a location~~ where basic medical or dental care, treatment, or examinations are performed. Examples include, but are not limited to, examination or treatment rooms in clinics, medical and dental offices, nursing homes, and limited care facilities. [**99**: A.3.3.127.3]

General Care (Category 2) Space. Space in which failure of equipment or a system is likely to cause minor injury to patients, staff, or visitors ~~caregivers~~. [99: 3.3.127.2]

Informational Note ~~No. 3~~: [Category 2] spaces were formerly known as general care rooms [(spaces)]. Examples include, ~~includes~~ but are not limited to ~~areas such as patient~~ inpatient bedrooms, ~~examining~~ dialysis rooms, ~~treatment~~ in vitro fertilization rooms, ~~clinics~~ procedural rooms, and similar rooms ~~areas where the patient may come into contact with electromedical devices or ordinary appliances such as a nurse call system, electric beds, examining lamps, telephones, and entertainment devices~~. [**99**: A.3.3.127.2]

Critical Care (Category 1) Space. Space in which failure of equipment or a system is likely to cause major injury or death to patients, staff, or visitors ~~caregivers~~. [99: 3.3.127.1]

Informational Note ~~No. 4~~: [Category 1] spaces, formerly known as critical care rooms [(spaces)], are typically where patients are intended to be subjected to invasive procedures and connected to line-operated, patient care–related appliances. Examples ~~includes~~ include, but are not limited to, special care ~~units~~ patient rooms used for critical care, intensive care ~~units~~, and special care treatment rooms such as ~~coronary care units,~~ angiography laboratories, cardiac catheterization laboratories, delivery rooms, operating rooms, post-anesthesia care units, trauma rooms, and other similar rooms ~~areas in which are patients are intended to be subjected to invasive procedures and are connected to line-operated, electromedical devices~~. [**99**: A.3.3.127.1]

Support (Category 4) Space. Space in which failure of equipment or a system is not likely to have a physical impact on patient care ~~patients or caregivers~~. [99: 3.3.127.4]

Informational Note ~~No. 5~~: [Category 4] spaces were formerly known as support rooms [(spaces)]. ~~where a procedure is performed that subjects patients or staff to wet conditions are considered as wet procedure areas. Wet conditions include standing fluids on the floor or drenching of the work area. Routine housekeeping procedures and incidental spillage of liquids do not define wet procedure areas. It is the responsibility of the governing body of the health care facility to designate the wet procedure areas.~~ Examples of support spaces include, but are not limited to, anesthesia work rooms, sterile supply, laboratories, morgues, waiting rooms, utility rooms, and lounges. [**99**: A.3.3.127.4]

517.2

- **2014 *NEC* Requirement**
  The definition of a *Patient Care Space* was located at 517.2. The four types of patient care spaces were described following the definition of a patient care space. This description was followed by five informational notes.

- **2017 *NEC* Change**
  The four types of patient care spaces were revised to include NFPA 99 numbered categories assigned to each of these types of patient care spaces. Bracketed NFPA 99s were was added after each description and informational note. Informational notes were relocated after each definition, and these informational notes contain examples of each of the different categories

Analysis of the Change:

A patient care space of a health care facility can be divided into four basic types: basic care, general care, critical care and support spaces. These four different patient care space groups were introduced into the 2014 *NEC*. Prior to the 2014 *NEC*, there were three basic types: general care, critical care, and wet procedure locations. The definition for *Patient Care Space* has gone through another extensive revision for the 2017 *NEC*. Numbered categories were assigned to each of these types of patient care spaces. These categories come from NFPA 99 (*Health Care Facilities Code*).

517.2

The 2012 edition of NFPA 99 underwent some major modification, one of which eliminated all occupancy chapters within the document and adopted a risk-based approach as far as the patient is concerned. At that time, a new process detailing building systems categories in healthcare facilities was introduced.

Category 1 covered facility systems in which failure of such equipment or system is likely to cause major injury or death of patients or caregivers (caregivers now replaced with staff, or visitors).

Category 2 is facility systems in which failure of such equipment is likely to cause minor injury to patients, staff or visitors.

Category 3 is facility systems in which failure of such equipment is not likely to cause injury to patients or caregivers but can cause patient discomfort.

Category 4 is facility systems in which failure of such equipment would have no impact on patient care. These categories are determined by documenting a defined risk-assessment procedure found in NFPA 99.

To correspond to the *NEC*, Category 1 was assigned to a critical care space, Category 2 is equivalent to a general care space, Category 3 is a basic care space, and Category 4 is a support space. The informational notes that were located together at the end of the patient care space definition and the descriptions of the four types of spaces have been relocated following each of the types or categories of patient care spaces. These informational notes contain examples of each of the different categories. With the categories and the informational notes being extracted material from NFPA 99, the bracketed NFPA 99 reference follows each description and informational note. The previous Informational Note No. 5 was relocated to the definition of *Wet Procedure Location*.

CMP-15 plans on a transition to reference only these NFPA 99 numbered patient care space categories by the 2023 *NEC*. For example, the 2017 *NEC* will reference a *Critical Care (Category 1) Space*, with the 2020 *NEC* identifying this space as a *Category 1 Space (Critical Care Space)* and, finally, the 2023 *NEC* referencing a *Category 1 Space*. This transition is similar to the one that took place in the *NEC* with the metric system becoming the dominant unit of measure in the *NEC*.

These revised definitions and the related informational notes will help clarify the meaning and use of these spaces for designers, installers, inspectors, and maintenance personnel alike. The relocation of the informational notes improves readability by immediately following the requirement to which each informational note applies.

517.16

First Revisions: FR 4247
Second Reivisions: SR 4215
Public Inputs: PI 4507, PI 2838, PI 4488
Public Comments: PC 1175, PC 1813, PC 470

517.16

Use of Isolated Ground Receptacles

New provisions were added to 517.16 pertaining to the proper installation of isolated ground receptacles located outside of a patient care vicinity

(1) Metal raceway that qualifies as EGC [517.13(A)]

(2) Redundant ground EGC [517.13(B)(1)]

(3) Isolated ground EGC [517.16(B)(1)]

Isolated grounding type receptacles are not permitted in a patient care vicinity

The probation of isolated ground receptacle inside a patient care vicinity are addressed at 517.16(A) and isolated ground receptacles installed outside a patient care vicinity are addressed at 517.16(B)

517.16

517.16 Use of Isolated Ground Receptacles. (Health Care Facilities)

- **Type of Change:** Revision and Relocation of Text

- **Change at a Glance:** Revisions to 517.16 were divided into two subdivisions for prohibition of isolated ground receptacle inside a patient care vicinity and isolated ground receptacles installed outside a patient care vicinity.

- **Code Language: 517.16 Use of Isolated Ground Receptacles. (Health Care Facilities)**
  (A) Inside of a Patient Care Vicinity. An isolated ground receptacle shall not be installed within a patient care vicinity. [99:6.3.2.2.7.1(B)]

  (B) Outside of a Patient Care Vicinity. Isolated ground receptacle(s) installed in patient care spaces outside of a patient care vicinity(s) shall comply with 517.16(B)(1) and (2).

  (1) The grounding terminals of isolated ground receptacles installed in branch circuits for patient care spaces shall be connected to an insulated equipment grounding conductor in accordance with 250.146(D) in addition to the equipment grounding conductor path required in 517.13(A).

The equipment grounding conductor connected to the grounding terminals of isolated ground receptacles in patient care spaces shall be clearly identified along the equipment grounding conductor's entire length by green insulation with one or more yellow stripes.

(2) The insulated equipment grounding conductor required in 517.13(B)(1) shall be clearly identified along its entire length by green insulation, with no yellow stripes, and shall not be connected to the grounding terminals of isolated ground receptacles but shall be connected to the box or enclosure indicated in 517.13(B)(1)(2) and to non-current-carrying conductive surfaces of fixed electrical equipment indicated in 517.13(B)(1)(3).

Informational Note No. 1: This type of installation is typically used where a reduction of electrical noise (electromagnetic interference) is necessary, and parallel grounding paths are to be avoided.

Informational Note No. 2: Care should be taken in specifying a system containing isolated ground receptacles, because the grounding impedance is controlled only by the grounding wires and does not benefit from any conduit or building structure in parallel with the grounding path. [**99:** A.6.3.2.2.7.1]

517.16

- **2014 *NEC* Requirement**
  Isolated ground receptacles were not permitted to be installed within a patient care vicinity of a health care facility by the provisions of 517.16. Provisions for installing an isolated ground receptacle outside of a patient care vicinity were not addressed in Article 517.

- **2017 *NEC* Change**
  New provisions were added to 517.16 pertaining to the proper installation of isolated ground receptacles located outside of a patient care vicinity. The prohibition of isolated ground receptacle inside a patient care vicinity are addressed at 517.16(A) and isolated ground receptacles installed outside a patient care vicinity are addressed at 517.16(B).

Analysis of the Change:

Isolated ground receptacles are permitted to have their grounding terminal purposely insulated from the receptacle mounting means for the reduction of electrical noise (electromagnetic interference) on the grounding circuit [see 250.146(D)]. The isolated ground receptacle grounding terminal is to be connected to an insulated equipment grounding conductor run with the circuit conductors. Once again, for the sake of the reduction of electrical noise, this isolated ground equipment grounding conductor is permitted to pass through one or more panelboards without a connection to the panelboard grounding terminal bar as well as pass through boxes, wireways, or other enclosures without being connected to such enclosures. The requirements of 406.3(D) calls for isolated ground receptacles to be identified by an orange triangle located on the face of the receptacle.

Changes were made to 517.16 for the 2014 *NEC* to make it clear that isolated ground receptacles were not permitted to be installed within a patient care vicinity of a health care facility. Changes to the 2011 *NEC* at 517.16 prohibited the use of isolated ground receptacles in the entire health care facility. This was a problem as NFPA 99 (Health Care Facilities Code) allows the use of isolated ground receptacles in health care facilities while forbidding their use within patient care vicinities only [see NFPA 99 6.3.2.2.7.1(A) and 6.3.2.2.7.1(B)].

The concern with isolated ground receptacles within a patient care vicinity is the assurance of the equipment grounding conductor redundancy requirement of 517.13(A) and (B) for wiring methods at a patient care vicinity. This *redundant grounding* provision in a patient care space requires two equipment grounding paths to always ensure one is functioning at all times. This is usually accomplished with a wire-type equipment grounding conductor within a metallic wiring method that meets the equipment grounding conductor provisions of 250.118. This redundant grounding provision cannot and should not be accomplished with an isolated ground receptacle equipment grounding conductor as this conductor should not be connected to the metal enclosure. Therefore, such a connection would negate the isolated grounding of an isolated ground receptacle established by 250.146(D).

Listed cord- and plug-connected medical instrumentation used in health care facilities outside of patient care vicinities (typically at nurses' monitoring stations) often require connection to isolated ground receptacles to ensure measurement accuracy by mitigating electrical noise or interference, which is essential to patient medical safety. Allowing isolated ground receptacles away from a patient care vicinity allows this mitigation against equipment interference without affecting patient safety.

517.16

For the third consecutive *Code* cycle, 517.16 experienced revisions regarding isolated ground receptacles and the number of equipment grounding conductors that must be installed for isolated ground receptacles installed outside the patient care vicinity or space of a health care facility. This change adds clarity to 517.16 and provides requirements for branch circuits serving spaces where isolated ground equipment grounding conductors and isolated ground receptacles are specified outside of a patient care vicinity. The new structure of 517.16 was divided into two subdivisions for prohibition of isolated ground receptacle inside a patient care vicinity and isolated ground receptacles installed outside a patient care vicinity.

Apparently, confusion still existed regarding the number of equipment grounding conductors that must be installed for isolated ground receptacles installed outside the patient care vicinity. To meet the requirements of 517.13(A) and (B) for redundant grounding provisions, it is not uncommon to find a wiring method of electrical metallic tubing (EMT) with a separate 12 AWG copper insulated equipment grounding conductor in spaces outside of a patient care vicinity. The problem comes in when this redundant grounding equipment grounding conductor is incorrectly utilized to serve double-duty as the isolated ground equipment grounding conductor where isolated ground receptacles are installed outside of a patient care vicinity. This type of installation is in violation of 250.146(D) and 517.13.

The new provisions of 517.16(B) will clearly identify the requirement of **three** grounding paths when isolated ground receptacles are required [*metal raceway or cable armor equipment grounding path, green wire type equipment grounding conductor for the 517.13 redundant grounding requirements, and a separate isolated ground equipment grounding conductor to comply with 250.146(D)*]. The new provisions of 517.16(B)(1) will demand a color designation of green with one of more yellow stripes for the isolated ground equipment grounding conductor. This color designation was chosen to provide a color pattern typically used as an industry standard for isolated ground equipment grounding conductors.

First Revisions: FR 4260

Second Reivisions: SR 4228, SR 4217

Public Inputs: PI 3059

Public Comments: PC 62, PC 1815, PC 746, PC 765, PC 848

517.30

Sources of Power. (Health Care Facilities)

517.30

517.30 Sources of Power. (Health Care Facilities)

- **Type of Change:** Revision/New

- **Change at a Glance:** Requirements for two independent sources of power and an alternate source of power for the essential electrical system for hospitals and other health care facilities were revised and relocated to

517.30. Fuel cell systems will now be permitted to serve as the alternate source for all or part of an essential electrical system.

■ **Code Language:** ~~517.35~~ 517.30 **Sources of Power. (Health Care Facilities)**

(A) Two Independent Sources of Power. Essential electrical systems shall have a minimum of the following two independent sources of power: a normal source generally supplying the entire electrical system and one or more alternate source(s) for use when the normal source is interrupted. [99: 6.4.1.1.4]

(B) ~~Alternate Source~~ Types of Power Sources. ~~The alternate source of power shall be one of the following:~~

(1) Generating Units. ~~Generator(s) driven by some form of prime mover(s) and located on the premises~~ Where the normal source consists of generating units on the premises, the alternate source shall be either another generating set or an external utility service. [**99**:6.4.1.1.5]
~~(2) Another generating unit(s) where the normal source consists of a generating unit(s) located on the premises~~
~~(3) An external utility service when the normal source consists of a generating unit(s)~~ located ~~on the premises~~
~~(4) A battery system located on the premises [99:6.4.1.2]~~

(2) Fuel Cell Systems. Fuel cell systems shall be permitted to serve as the alternate source for all or part of an essential electrical system, provided the following conditions apply:
　(1) Installation of fuel cells shall comply with the requirements in Parts I through VII of Article 692 for 1000 volts or less and Part VIII for over 1000 volts.

Informational Note: For information on installation of stationary fuel cells, see NFPA 853-2015, Standard for Installation of Stationary Fuel Cell Power Systems. [**99**:6.4.1.1.7]
　(2) N + 1 units shall be provided where N units have sufficient capacity to supply the demand loads of the portion of the system served. [**99**:6.4.1.7.2]
　(3) System shall be able to assume loads within 10 seconds of loss of normal power source.
　(4) System shall have a continuing source of fuel supply, together with sufficient on-site fuel storage for the essential system type.
　(5) A connection shall be provided for a portable diesel generator to supply life safety and critical portions of the distribution system. [**99**: 6.4.1.7.5(1) through (5)]
　(6) Fuel cell systems shall be listed for emergency system use.

(C) Location of Essential Electrical System Components. ~~Careful consideration shall be given to the location of the spaces housing the components of the~~ Essential electrical system components shall be located

517.30

517.30

to minimize interruptions caused by natural forces common to the area (e.g., storms, floods, earthquakes, or hazards created by adjoining structures or activities). ~~Consideration shall also be given to the~~ Installations of electrical services shall be located to reduce possible interruption of normal electrical services resulting from similar causes as well as possible disruption of normal electrical service due to internal wiring and equipment failures. ~~Consideration shall be given to the~~ Feeders shall be located to provide physical separation of the ~~main~~ feeders of the alternate source from the ~~main~~ feeders of the normal electrical source to prevent possible simultaneous interruption.

Informational Note: Facilities in which the normal source of power is supplied by two or more separate central station-fed services experience greater than normal electrical service reliability than those with only a single feed. Such a dual source of normal power consists of two or more electrical services fed from separate generator sets or a utility distribution network that has multiple power input sources and is arranged to provide mechanical and electrical separation so that a fault between the facility and the generating sources is not likely to cause an interruption of more than one of the facility service feeders.

■ **2014 *NEC* Requirement**

The requirements for Sources of Power for essential electrical system of a health care facility was located at 517.35. Two independent sources of power were required with one being the normal power source and one or more alternate power sources for use when the normal power source is interrupted. The alternate power source can be and is typically one or more generator sets or battery systems where permitted, intended to provide power during the interruption of the normal electrical services, or a second public utility electrical service intended to provide power during interruption of service normally provided by the generating facilities on the premises.

■ **2017 *NEC* Change**

The same basic provisions that were located at 517.35 were relocated to 517.30. Fuel cell systems will now be permitted to serve as the alternate source for all or part of an essential electrical system as any reference to a battery system has been deleted.

Analysis of the Change:

When reviewing the requirements of 517.35 from the 2014 *NEC*, the electrical power sources for the essential electrical system of a health care facility must be supplied by a minimum of two independent sources; a normal power source and one or more alternate power sources for use when the normal power source is interrupted. The normal power source is generally made up of a source supplied by the local electric utility power company and an on-site power generator(s), which can be a private on-site power generator unit(s) or another electric utility-supplied source. The alternate power source was permitted to be one of several options.

Typically, the alternate sources of power are supplied to the loads through a series of automatic and/or manual transfer switches. The transfer switches can be non-delayed automatic, delayed automatic, or manual transfer depending on the requirements of the specific branch of the essential electrical system that they are feeding. It is permissible to feed multiple branches or systems of the essential electrical system from a single automatic transfer switch provided that the maximum demand on the essential electrical system not exceed 150 kVA.

For the 2017 *NEC*, these requirements for two independent sources of power and an alternate source of power for the essential electrical system for hospitals and other health care facilities were revised and relocated to 517.30. Previous provisions for "Applicability" of the essential electrical system for hospitals was moved from 517.30(A) to its new location at 517.29(A). The provisions for the three separate branches of the essential electrical system (life safety, critical, and equipment branch) that were located at 517.30(B)(1) are now located at 517.31(A) while the *Code* text for transfer switches for the essential electrical system has been relocated to 517.31(B) from 517.30(B)(2). All these moves were to accommodate the move of previous 517.35 (Sources of Power) to 517.30.

This relocation and revision of Sources of Power requirements from 517.35 to 517.30 provides a more logical sequence and flow of the text while providing added clarity for users of the *Code*. The revised text at 517.29 makes it clear that the requirements of 517.29 through 517.30 in Part III (Essential Electrical System) apply to critical care (Category 1) and general care (Category 2) hospitals and other health care facilities using Type 1 essential electrical systems where patients are sustained by electrical life-support equipment.

517.30

One of the most noticeable changes to the requirements for the types of allowed power sources for these essential electrical systems was the added language at 517.30(B)(2) for fuel cell systems. Fuel cell systems will now be permitted to serve as the alternate source for all or part of an essential electrical system, with six specific conditions involved [see 517.30(B)(2)(1) through (6)]. Fuel cells provide a high level of reliability and have a proven reliability track record in data centers and other mission-critical facilities. There is no reason hospitals and other health care facilities should not be able to take advantage of this new technology as well. Other advantages to fuel cells include the fact that a failed fuel cell can be isolated and replaced without shutting down the entire string, and they have fuel flexibility from natural gas to diesel.

First Revisions: FR 4276

Second Reivisions: SR 4225, SCR 12

Public Inputs: PI 4171, PI 1295, PI 3257, PI 4289, PI 1487

Public Comments: PC 1501, PC 1817

517.34(B)

Critical Branch. (Essential Electrical System-Health Care Facilities)

517.34(B)

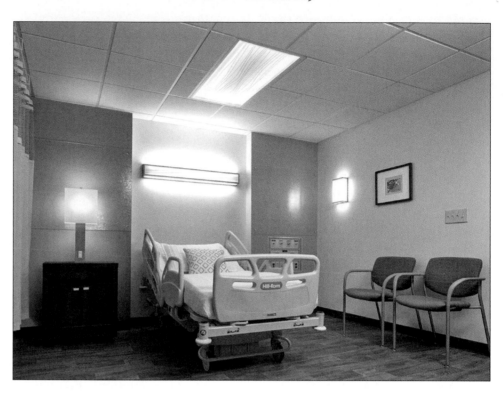

517.34(B) Critical Branch. (Essential Electrical System-Health Care Facilities)

- **Type of Change:** New

- **Change at a Glance:** New language was added to specifically allow the control of task illumination on the critical branch.

- **Code Language:** ~~517.33~~ 517.34 Critical Branch. (Essential Electrical System-Health Care Facilities)

  (A) Task Illumination and Selected Receptacles. The critical branch of the essential electrical system shall supply power for task illumination, fixed equipment, selected receptacles, and special power circuits serving the following areas and functions related to patient care: (*See NEC for complete Code text*)

  (B) Switching. It shall be permitted to control task illumination on the critical branch.

  (B) (C) Subdivision of the Critical Branch. It shall be permitted to subdivide the critical branch into two or more branches.

Informational Note: It is important to analyze the consequences of supplying an area with only critical care branch power when failure occurs between the area and the transfer switch. Some proportion of normal and critical power or critical power from separate transfer switches may be appropriate.

- **2014 *NEC* Requirement**
  Task illumination lighting was permitted to be controlled and supplied from the critical branch of the essential electrical system, but to some users of the *Code*, this was not specifically stated.

- **2017 *NEC* Change**
  Positive language was added at 517.34(B) to specifically permit the control of task illumination on the critical branch of the essential electrical system.

Analysis of the Change:

A new provision was added at 517.34 to make it crystal clear that task illumination and its control [switch(es)] are permitted to be supplied from the critical branch of the essential electrical system at a health care facility. What is task illumination? According to the definition at 517.2, task illumination is the "provision for the minimum lighting required to carry out necessary tasks in the described areas, including safe access to supplies and equipment, and access to exits." This definition could include a night light, an alcove or a lavatory mirror luminaire, the lighting at a prefabricated bedside patient unit (PBPU), or if available, a bathroom luminaire.

In the 2014 *NEC*, some doubt existed that the language permitted this application. Some would argue that the text at 517.33(A) [now 517.34(A)] gave this permission with the text stating that "the critical branch of the essential electrical system shall supply power for *task illumination*, fixed equipment, selected receptacles, and special power circuits serving the following areas and functions related to patient care" (with over two dozen health care locations being identified). The very definition of the "Critical Branch" states that a critical branch is "A system of feeders and branch circuits supplying power for *task illumination*, fixed equipment, select receptacles, and select power circuits serving areas and functions related to patient care and that is automatically connected to alternate power sources by one or more transfer switches during interruption of normal power source."

With the addition of 517.34(B) for the 2017 *NEC*, the new language clearly states that "It shall be permitted to control task illumination on the critical branch." This "task illumination" adventure started with a proposal for the 2014 *NEC* (see 2014 ROP 15-71 and ROC 15-68a). This 2014 *NEC* proposal sought to gain permission to "switch critical branch task illumination with single-pole, 3- and 4-way switches, motion sensors, automatic load control relays, dimming systems and low-voltage control systems." This proposal was accepted by CMP-15 at the 2014 *NEC* proposal stage, but was removed at the comment stage from the 2014 *NEC* with the following statement from CMP-15: "Based on the action taken on Proposals 15-52 and 15-48, the added language in 517.33(B) is

517.34(B)

no longer required because Article 700 no longer applies to the Critical Branch. Therefore, switching of task illumination is permitted."

What CMP-15 was referring to in their statement was the removal of references to the emergency system in Article 517 for the 2014 *NEC*. To correlate the requirements of the *NEC* and, in particular, Article 517 with NFP*A 99 (Health Care Facilities Code)*, 517.30(B) was re-organized for the 2014 *NEC* concerning the make-up of the essential system of a hospital. This action eliminated references to the Emergency System as this is not addressed in NFPA 99. By incorporating the changes made to correlate with NFPA 99, the term *Emergency System* was and is no longer used in Article 517, this removed major confusion resulting from the previous use of the word "emergency" in similar, yet sometimes quite different, ways in Article 517 and Article 700.

Critical task illumination lighting is provided in part for the comfort and convenience of the patient. This lighting should be allowed to be controlled by the patient at his or her discretion.

First Revisions: FR 4274
Public Inputs: PI 4203, PI 4211, PI 3255

520.2

520.2

Definitions: Adapter

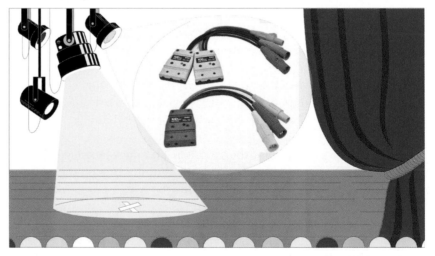

Adapter. A device used to adapt a circuit from one configuration of an attachment plug or receptacle to another configuration with the same current rating.

520.2 Definitions. (Theaters, Audience Areas of Motion Picture and Television Studios, Performance Areas, and Similar Locations): Adapter

- **Type of Change:** New

- **Change at a Glance:** A new definition for *Adapter* was added to Article 520.

- **Code Language: 520.2 Definitions. (Theaters, Audience Areas of Motion Picture and Television Studios, Performance Areas, and Similar Locations)**

  Adapter. A device used to adapt a circuit from one configuration of an attachment plug or receptacle to another configuration with the same current rating.

- **2014 *NEC* Requirement**
  The term *Adapter* was used several times in Article 520 but was not defined.

- **2017 *NEC* Change**
  A new definition of *Adapter* was added at 520.2 to address misapplication of this term in Article 520.

520.2

Analysis of the Change:

Article 520 of the *NEC* addresses the use of flexible conductors, including cable extensions, used to supply portable stage equipment for the entertainment industry, including theaters, television studios, and similar locations. Adapters are often used in these entertainment environments to connect multiple devices together or to a single source. These adapters may be constructed using individual wires inside of a fiberglass sleeve or a 3-conductor cable assembly. In some situations, it may be desirable to connect an Edison-equipped device to a stage-pin source, such as when using a household lighting source as an on-stage prop.

The *Code* previously addressed theater or stage adapter-type devices at a few locations such as the definition of a "Breakout Assembly" with this being defined as "an *adapter* used to connect a multipole connector containing two or more branch circuits to multiple individual branch-circuit connectors." The definition of a "Two-Fer" is described as "an *adapter* cable containing one male plug and two female cord connectors used to connect two loads to one branch circuit." Section 520.69, titled "Adapters" details the performance of two-fers, and other single- and multiple-circuit outlet devices used as adapters. This section states that each receptacle and its corresponding cable shall have the same current and voltage rating as the plug supplying it, and it shall not be utilized in a stage circuit with a greater current rating [see 520.69(A)].

For the 2014 *NEC*, 520.69(C) states that conductors for adapters and two-fers must be constructed with listed extra-hard usage or listed hard usage (junior hard service) cord, with this hard usage cord restricted in overall length to 1.0 m (3.3 ft). This overall length was changed to 2.0 m (6.6 ft) for the 2017 *NEC* as this length was intended to be limited to 1.0 m (3.3 ft) between connectors, which would mean 2.0 m (6.6 ft) total length of hard usage cord in a two-fer assembly.

What is an "adapter?" This term was and is used several times in Article 520, but it was not defined. This situation was remedied for the 2017 *NEC* with an added definition for "Adapter." This term is now defined as "a device used to adapt a circuit from one configuration of an attachment plug or receptacle to another configuration with the same current rating." This definition was needed to correct field misapplication of adapters. The rules for adapters have sometimes been misapplied in the entertainment industry to portable extension cords in Article 520 applications. The addition of a clear definition for an "Adapter" should help resolve this situation.

First Revisions: FR 4212
Public Inputs: PI 758

520.2

Definitions: Stage Switchboard, Portable

Stage Switchboard. A permanently installed switchboard, panelboard, or rack containing dimmers or relays with associated overcurrent protective devices, or overcurrent protective devices alone, used primarily to feed stage equipment.

Stage Switchboard, Portable. A portable rack or pack containing dimmers or relays with associated overcurrent protective devices, or overcurrent protective devices alone that are used to feed stage equipment.

520.2 Definitions. (Theaters, Audience Areas of Motion Picture and Television Studios, Performance Areas, and Similar Locations)

- **Type of Change:** Revision/New

- **Change at a Glance:** A new definition for *Stage Switchboard, Portable* was added to Article 520. The phrase "permanently installed" was added to the definition of Stage Switchboard.

■ **Code Language: 520.2 Definitions. (Theaters, Audience Areas of Motion Picture and Television Studios, Performance Areas, and Similar Locations)**

Stage Switchboard. A permanently installed switchboard, panelboard, or rack containing dimmers or relays with associated overcurrent protective devices, or overcurrent protective devices alone, used primarily to feed stage equipment.

Stage Switchboard, Portable. A portable rack or pack containing dimmers or relays with associated overcurrent protective devices, or overcurrent protective devices alone that are used to feed stage equipment.

■ **2014 *NEC* Requirement**
The 2014 *NEC* contained a definition for "Stage Switchboard." This definition was broad in nature and did not distinguish between permanently installed stage switchboards and stage switchboards of the portable type.

■ **2017 *NEC* Change**
A new definition for "Stage Switchboard, Portable" was added to Article 520 and the phrase "permanently installed" was added to the existing definition of "Stage Switchboard."

520.2

Analysis of the Change:
A definition of "Stage Switchboard" was added the Article 520 for the 2014 *NEC*. Stage switchboards are required to supply a wide variety of production-related equipment, not just lighting equipment. Clarification is needed on the differences between portable and permanent stage switchboards. For the 2017 *NEC*, a new definition for "Stage Switchboard, Portable" was added to Article 520 and the phrase "permanently installed" was added to the existing definition of "Stage Switchboard." This new definition for a portable stage switchboard clarifies that these devices can only feed stage equipment while a permanent stage switchboard can feed both stage and non-stage equipment.

Today in the entertainment and theatrical industry, the term "switchboard" is not used that often anymore. Apparently, "switchboard" is a holdover in the *Code* that no longer reflects common jargon. However, this new set of definitions are well understood in the entertainment industry, and the intent of these definitions is clear. Some of the more common terms used for "switchboard" are "dimmer rack," or a "relay rack/panel" depending on its function. Typically, this "switchboard" or "dimmer rack" equipment is listed and fits these definitions. It is entirely possible to encounter older versions of these products that were custom built for each job without a listing, but they still fit these definitions.

First Revisions: FR 4213, FR 4214
Public Inputs: PI 758, PI 982

525.23(D)

GFCI Protection for Carnivals, Circuses, Fairs, and Similar Events

525.23(D) Ground-Fault Circuit-Interrupter (GFCI) Protection. (Carnivals, Circuses, Fairs, and Similar Events)

- **Type of Change:** New

- **Change at a Glance:** New requirement for listed, labeled, and identification of portable GFCI protection for branch circuits fed by flexible cords.

- **Code Language:** 525.23 Ground-Fault Circuit-Interrupter (GFCI) Protection. (Carnivals, Circuses, Fairs, and Similar Events)

  (A) Where GFCI Protection Is Required. GFCI protection for personnel shall be provided for the following:
  (1) All 125-volt, single-phase, 15- and 20-ampere non-locking-type receptacles used for disassembly and reassembly or readily accessible to the general public
  (2) Equipment that is readily accessible to the general public and supplied from a 125-volt, single-phase, 15- or 20-ampere branch circuit

  The ~~ground-fault circuit-interrupter~~ GFCI shall be permitted to be an integral part of the attachment plug or located in the power-supply cord within 300 mm (12 in.) of the attachment plug. Listed cord sets incorporating ~~ground-fault circuit-interrupter~~ GFCI for personnel shall be permitted.

(B) Where GFCI Protection Is Not Required. Receptacles that are not accessible from grade level and that only facilitate quick disconnecting and reconnecting of electrical equipment shall not be required to be provided with GFCI protection. These receptacles shall be of the locking type.

(C) Where GFCI Protection Is Not Permitted. Egress lighting shall not be protected by a GFCI.

(D) Receptacles Supplied by Portable Cords. Where GFCI protection is provided through the use of GFCI receptacles, and the branch circuits supplying receptacles utilize flexible cord, the GFCI protection shall be listed, labeled, and identified for portable use.

■ **2014 *NEC* Requirement**
GFCI protection requirements for carnivals, circuses, fairs, and similar events were addressed at 525.23(A) through (C). The use of a standard GFCI receptacle supplied by a flexible cord was limited by 110.3(B), but there was no language in Article 525 prohibiting this application at carnivals, circuses, fairs, and similar events.

525.23(D)

■ **2017 *NEC* Change**
New requirements were imposed at 525.23(D) requiring GFCI protection to be listed, labeled, and identified for portable use when said GFCI protection is provided through the use of GFCI receptacles, and the branch circuits supplying these receptacles utilize a flexible cord.

Analysis of the Change:

For wiring at carnivals, circuses, fairs, and similar events, ground-fault circuit-interrupter (GFCI) protection is required at all 125-volt, single-phase, 15- and 20-ampere non-locking-type receptacles used for disassembly and reassembly of rides and equipment and at all 125-volt, single-phase, 15- and 20-ampere non-locking-type receptacles that are readily accessible to the general public. GFCI protection is also required at equipment that is readily accessible to the general public and supplied from 125-volt, single-phase, 15- or 20-ampere branch circuits.

Frequently, this required GFCI protection is delivered through a standard GFCI receptacle device installed at the end of a flexible cord. This installation can result in a potential hazard as an open neutral situation can easily develop in the field with this flexible cord arrangement due to wear-and-tear on the cord and plug connections. When this happens, the GFCI device does not and cannot function properly because this GFCI device no longer sees 120 volts needed to function properly, and fails to open (trip) properly. Under the UL product category (KCXS), standard GFCI receptacles are described as "flush receptacles and are intended to be installed in an outlet box for *fixed installation* on a branch circuit similar to a conventional receptacle."

To combat this situation, a new 525.23(D) was incorporated into the 2017 *NEC* calling for GFCI protection to be listed, labeled, and identified for portable use when any GFCI protection is provided through the use of GFCI receptacles, with the branch circuits supplying these receptacles utilize flexible cords. Portable GFCIs are plug-in type GFCIs provided with male blades or an integral power-supply cord for connection to a receptacle outlet. Portable GFCIs are also provided with one or more receptacle outlets located on the GFCI or a cord-connector body at the end of a length of flexible cord. These portable GFCI devices also interrupt power to the load when any single supply conductor (including the neutral conductor) is opened.

Even though the prohibition of a standard GFCI receptacle used in this manner at the end of a flexible cord could be enforced with its listing requirements [see 110.3(B)], the lack of an explicit rule in Article 525 has resulted in extensive application of these temporary GFCI set-ups at fairs and carnivals throughout the country for a number of years. This same type of temporary GFCI installation has resulted in a number of documented fatalities on construction sites, which resulted in a comparable restriction at 590.6(A)(2). Portable GFCIs with open neutral protection provide the protection needed to deal with worn cord and plug connections.

525.23(D)

It is important to point out that this new portable GFCI requirement at 525.23(D) incorporates a requirement for identified portable GFCI receptacles, but only on branch circuits fed by flexible cords. This provision does not apply to GFCI protection for portable structures or rides even though such structures and rides may be fed by flexible cord feeders. This portable GFCI provision for carnivals, circuses, fairs, and similar events introduces an additional desirable safety feature afforded by open-neutral sensing in listed, labeled, and identified portable GFCIs in specific applications, without extending that requirement to GFCI receptacles permanently installed in structures or rides, which would be impractical.

First Revisions: FR 4225
Second Revisions: SR 4208, SCR 120
Public Inputs: PI 2558
Public Comments: PC 1821

547.5(F)

Separate EGC (Agricultural Buildings)

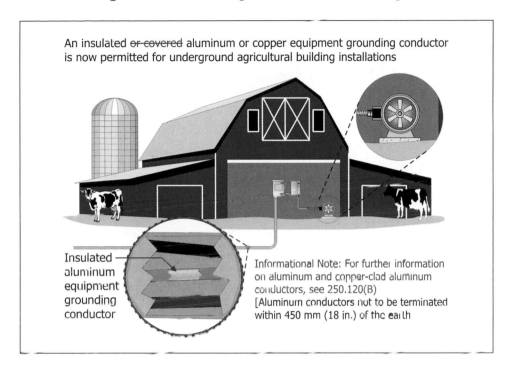

An insulated ~~or covered~~ aluminum or copper equipment grounding conductor is now permitted for underground agricultural building installations

Insulated aluminum equipment grounding conductor

Informational Note: For further information on aluminum and copper-clad aluminum conductors, see 250.120(B) [Aluminum conductors not to be terminated within 450 mm (18 in.) of the earth

547.5(F)

547.5(F) Wiring Methods. (Agricultural Buildings)

■ **Type of Change:** Revision/New

■ **Change at a Glance:** A separate equipment grounding conductor for an underground installation at an agricultural building must be insulated (covered conductor removed).

■ **Code Language: 547.5 Wiring Methods. (Agricultural Buildings)**

(F) Separate Equipment Grounding Conductor. Where an equipment grounding conductor is installed underground within a location falling under the scope of Article 547, it shall be insulated ~~or covered~~.

Informational Note: For further information on aluminum and copper-clad aluminum conductors, see 250.120(B).

■ **2014 *NEC* Requirement**
Provisions at 547.5(F) permitted an equipment grounding conductor installed underground at an agricultural building location to be an insulated or covered aluminum or copper conductor.

■ **2017 *NEC* Change**
A revision at 547.5(F) eliminated the permission to use a "covered" equipment grounding conductor for an underground installation at agricultural buildings.

Analysis of the Change:

Changes were introduced to 547.5(F) for the 2014 *NEC* permitting the use of an aluminum equipment grounding conductor, as well as copper, for underground installations at agricultural buildings or structures falling under the scope of Article 547. Previously *Code* language only permitted a copper equipment grounding conductor due to considerations regarding corrosion and oxidation, and exposure to the many contaminates present in and around livestock facilities. The use of aluminum conductors was allowed in this underground application since aluminum is highly corrosion resistant. Additionally, the equipment grounding conductors discussed in 547.5(F) for underground use were required to be "insulated or covered." This would make the metal used inside the insulated material irrelevant since the conductor is protected by this required insulation or covering.

For the 2017 *NEC*, 547.5(F) was further revised by removing the allowance of a "covered" conductor for these underground applications at agricultural buildings. A "covered conductor" is defined in Article 100 as "a conductor encased within material of composition or thickness that is not recognized by [the *NEC*] as electrical insulation." There is no *NEC*-required safety standard, product standard, evaluation or testing of this type of material placed on a conductor, so it is considered "covered." A "covered" conductor has no *NEC*-specified rating for any environment, particularly that of agricultural buildings. Additionally, there are no splicing mechanisms that are specifically rated for the harsh environments present in agricultural premises.

A new informational note was added at 547.5(F) with a reference to 250.120(B) to provide further information pertaining to the installation of equipment grounding conductors. This referenced subsection in Article 250 informs users of the *Code* that equipment grounding conductors of bare or insulated aluminum or copper-clad aluminum are permitted. Section 250.120(B) goes on to state that bare conductors cannot be in direct contact with masonry or the earth or where subject to corrosive conditions and that aluminum or copper-clad aluminum conductors cannot be terminated within 450 mm (18 in.) of the earth.

First Revisions: FR 5442
Public Inputs: PI 4336

547.5(F)

550.2

Definitions: Manufactured Home

550.2 Definitions. (Mobile Homes, Manufactured Homes, and Mobile Home Parks)

- ■ **Type of Change:** Revision

- ■ **Change at a Glance:** Existing definition of "Manufactured Home" was revised and excludes park trailers.

- ■ **Code Language: 550.2 Definitions. (Mobile Homes, Manufactured Homes, and Mobile Home Parks)**

Manufactured Home. A structure, transportable in one or more sections, ~~that,~~ which in the traveling mode is 2.4 m (8 ~~body~~-ft) or more in width or 12.2 m (40-ft) or more in length, or when erected on site, is 29.77 m² (320 ft²) or more ~~and that~~ is built on a permanent chassis and designed to be used as a dwelling with or without a permanent foundation, whether or not connected to the utilities, and includes plumbing, heating, air conditioning, and electrical systems contained ~~when connected~~ therein. The term manufactured home includes any structure that meets all the ~~provisions~~ requirements of this paragraph except the size requirements and with respect to which the manufacturer voluntarily files a certification required by the regulatory agency~~, and except that such term does not include any self-propelled recreational vehicle~~. Calculations used to determine the number of square meters (square feet) in a structure are based on the structure's exterior dimensions~~, measured at the largest horizontal projections when erected on site. These dimensions~~ and include all expandable rooms, cabinets, and other projections containing interior space, but do not include bay windows [501: 1.2.14].

For the purpose of this *Code* and unless otherwise indicated, the term *mobile home* includes manufactured homes and excludes park trailers defined in 552.4.

Informational Note No. 1: See the applicable building code for definition of the term permanent foundation.

Informational Note No. 2: See 24 CFR Part 3280, *Manufactured Home Construction and Safety Standards, of the Federal Department of Housing and Urban Development,* for additional information on the definition.

550.2

- ■ **2014 *NEC* Requirement**
  A manufactured home was defined at 550.2.

- ■ **2017 *NEC* Change**
  The existing definition for a "manufactured home" was revised for consistency with the definition of a "manufactured home" found in NFPA 501 (*Standard on Manufactured Housing*). The last sentence of the definition was revised to exclude park trailers.

Analysis of the Change:

A manufactured home is a type of prefabricated housing that is largely assembled in factories and then transported to sites of use. Manufactured homes are built as dwelling units of at least 29.77 m² (320 square feet) or more in size with a permanent chassis to assure the initial and continued transportability of the home. The requirement to have a wheeled chassis permanently attached differentiates "manufactured housing" from other types of prefabricated homes, such as modular homes. Since 1976, the Federal Government [Department of Housing and Urban Development (HUD)] has regulated the construction of all manufactured and prefabricated homes. Previously, standards and codes were voluntary. Today, quality manufactured homes are regularly built that meet or exceed all local, municipal or federal codes.

The existing definition for a "manufactured home" was revised for the 2017 *NEC* to be consistent with the same definition found in NFPA 501 (*Standard on Manufactured Housing*). To avoid conflicts, it is important to have the same definitions for items covered in multiple NFPA Standards. The last sentence of the definition for a manufactured home was revised to exclude park trailers. A park trailer is defined as "a unit that is built on a single chassis mounted on wheels and has a gross trailer area not exceeding 37 m² (400 ft²) in the set-up mode" (see 552.2). A park trailer is intended for seasonal use. It is not intended as a permanent dwelling unit or for commercial uses such as banks, clinics, offices, or similar uses.

First Revisions: FR 5401
Second Revisions: SR 5406
Public Inputs: PI 2462
Public Comments: PC 1822

550.13(B)

GFCI Protection Required for Mobile and Manufactured Homes

All 125-volt, single-phase, 15- and 20-ampere receptacle outlets installed in the following locations shall be provided with GFCI protection:

(1) Outdoors, including compartments accessible from outside the unit
(2) Bathrooms (including receptacles in luminaires)
(3) Kitchens, where receptacles are installed to serve countertop surfaces
(4) Sinks, where receptacle are installed within 1.8 m (6 ft) of the outside edge of a sink *(any sink)*
(5) Dishwashers

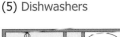 – Required GFCI protected receptacles

Dishwasher now requires GFCI protection

Overhead cut-away view of mobile or manufactured home

550.13(B)

550.13(B) Receptacle Outlets. (Mobile Homes, Manufactured Homes, and Mobile Home Parks)

- **Type of Change:** Revision

- **Change at a Glance:** GFCI protection for mobile homes was revised to reflect GFCI coverage for all sinks, dishwashers, and other locations similarly found at 210.8(A).

- **Code Language: 550.13 Receptacle Outlets. (Mobile Homes, Manufactured Homes, and Mobile Home Parks)**

  (B) Ground-Fault Circuit Interrupters (GFCI). All 125-volt, single-phase, 15- and 20-ampere receptacle outlets installed ~~outdoors, in compartments accessible from outside the unit, or in bathrooms, including receptacles in luminaires,~~ in the locations specified in 550.13(B)(1) through (5) shall have GFCI protection for personnel. ~~GFCI protection shall be provided for receptacle outlets serving countertops in kitchens and receptacle outlets located within 1.8 m (6 ft) of a wet bar sink. The exceptions in 210.8(A) shall be permitted.~~
  (1) Outdoors, ~~including in~~ compartments accessible from outside the unit
  (2) Bathrooms, including receptacles in luminaires
  (3) Kitchens, where receptacles are installed to serve countertop surfaces

(4) Sinks, where receptacles are installed within 1.8 m (6 ft) of the outer edge of the ~~a wet bar~~ sink

(5) Dishwashers

~~Feeders supplying branch circuits shall be permitted to be protected by a ground-fault circuit-interrupter in lieu of the provision for such interrupters specified herein.~~

Informational Note: For information on protection of dishwashers, see 422.5.

(Note to Reader: The GFCI requirements for dwelling unit dishwashers remained at 210.8(D) and not at 422.5 as indicated in the added informational note above.)

■ **2014 *NEC* Requirement**

GFCI requirements for mobile and manufactured homes were found at 550.13(B) and consisted of a long paragraph with several sentences. These provisions called for GFCI protection for outlets installed outdoors, and those outdoor outlets installed "in compartments accessible from outside the unit." GFCI protection was demanded for receptacle outlets serving bathrooms (including receptacles in luminaires), kitchen countertops, and receptacle outlets located within 1.8 m (6 ft) of a wet bar sink (not all sinks, just wet bar sinks). The GFCI protection could be delivered in a feeder supplying the associated branch circuits for these receptacle outlets.

■ **2017 *NEC* Change**

The GFCI provisions for mobile and manufactured homes were revised into a list format. Along with the previous GFCI requirements, GFCI requirements for all sinks (not just wet bar sinks), dishwashers and other locations similarly found at 210.8(A) were incorporated into 550.13(B). Clarification was added to the GFCI provisions for outdoor receptacle outlets to include all outdoor receptacle outlets including (but not limited to) outdoor receptacle outlets located in compartments accessible from outside the unit. The option of delivering the required GFCI protection through a feeder that supplied the branch circuits associated with the receptacle outlets requiring GFCI protection was removed.

Analysis of the Change:

Ground-fault circuit interrupter (GFCI) protection requirements for dwelling units have constantly changed and been updated from one *Code* cycle to the next since GFCI protection was first introduced at dwelling units for outdoor receptacle outlets in the 1971 *NEC*. Unfortunately, the GFCI requirements for mobile and manufactured homes have not always kept pace with the same GFCI requirements for conventional dwelling units. With that in mind, revisions and updates were made to 550.13(B) for the 2017 *NEC* related to GFCI requirements for mobile and manufactured homes.

The GFCI provisions for mobile and manufactured homes needed to be updated to reflect similar GFCI requirements at conventional dwelling units. Several changes have been incorporated into dwelling unit GFCI requirements at 210.8(A) (such as GFCI protection for all sinks, not just wet bar sinks) without

550.13(B)

these same GFCI provisions being implemented at mobile and manufactured homes as well. Does a person deserve less GFCI protection at a mobile or manufactured home than he deserves at conventional dwelling unit construction? The obvious answer to that question is "No!" Equal GFCI protection is warranted at all dwelling unit locations regardless of the type of dwelling unit involved.

The sentence, "The exceptions in 210.8(A) shall be permitted" was added at 550.13(B) in the 2011 *NEC* with the majority of exceptions previously located at 210.8(A) being removed for the 2008 edition of the *NEC*, leaving only two exceptions currently in 210.8(A). Only one could apply to a mobile or manufactured home (outdoor de-icing, snow-melting equipment) and that one requires GFCI protection by 426.28. The exception to 210.8(A)(5) deals with a permanently installed burglar or fire alarm system installed in an unfinished basement. Mobile and manufactured homes typically do not include a basement of any type, leaving this exception irrelevant to mobile or manufactured homes.

The option of delivering the required GFCI protection through a feeder that supplied the branch circuits associated with the receptacle outlets requiring GFCI protection was eliminated with the revisions of 550.13(B) for the 2017 *NEC*. No explanation was given for this feeder option being deleted. Perhaps it was felt that this option was implied with the provisions of 215.9 which states that "feeders supplying 15- and 20-ampere receptacle branch circuits shall be permitted to be protected by a ground-fault circuit interrupter in lieu of the provisions for such interrupters as specified in 210.8 and 590.6(A)." If that is the case, many users of the *Code* would argue that a direct link is needed between 550.13(B) and 215.9 as the provisions of 90.3 state that "Chapters 5, 6, and 7 apply to special occupancies, special equipment, or other special conditions and may supplement or modify the requirements in Chapters 1 through 7."

550.13(B)

The GFCI requirements for mobile and manufactured homes at 550.13(B) were reformatted into a list format for usability. These revisions and formatting will add enforceability and clarity while bringing needed consistency between mobile and manufactured homes and conventional dwelling units concerning GFCI requirements.

First Revisions: FR 5402
Second Revisions: SR 5414
Public Inputs: PI 580
Public Comments: PC 1823

550.25(B)

AFCI Protection at Mobile and Manufactured Homes

550.25(B)

AFCI protection at mobile and manufactured homes was revised by eliminating the specific "laundry list" of rooms and areas requiring AFCI protection at mobile and manufactured homes and simply requiring compliance with 210.12

Red = Outlets requiring AFCI protected branch circuits

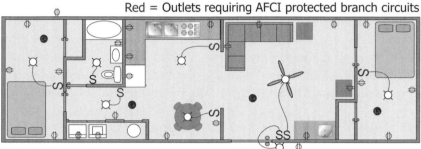

Overhead cut-away view of mobile or manufactured home

All 120-volt branch circuits that supply 15- and 20-ampere outlets shall comply with 210.12

550.25(B) Arc-Fault Circuit-Interrupter Protection. (Mobile Homes, Manufactured Homes, and Mobile Home Parks)

- **Type of Change:** Revision/Deletion

- **Change at a Glance:** AFCI requirements for mobile homes were expanded to reference AFCI requirements of 210.12.

- **Code Language:** **550.25 Arc-Fault Circuit-Interrupter Protection. (Mobile Homes, Manufactured Homes, and Mobile Home Parks)**
  (A) Definition. Arc-fault circuit interrupters are defined in Article 100.

  (B) Mobile Homes and Manufactured Homes. All 120-volt branch circuits that supply 15- and 20-ampere outlets ~~installed in family rooms, dining rooms, living rooms, parlors, libraries, dens, bedrooms, sunrooms, recreation rooms, closets, hallways, or similar rooms or areas of mobile homes and manufactured homes~~ shall comply with 210.12.

- **2014 *NEC* Requirement**
  For mobile and manufactured homes, AFCI protection was required by 550.25(B) at all 120-volt branch circuits that supply 15- and 20-ampere outlets installed in family rooms, dining rooms, living rooms, parlors, libraries, dens, bedrooms, sunrooms, recreation rooms, closets, hallways, or similar rooms.

■ **2017 *NEC* Change**
AFCI protection at mobile and manufactured homes was revised by eliminating the specific list of rooms and areas requiring AFCI protection at mobile and manufactured homes and simply requiring compliance with 210.12.

Analysis of the Change:

Arc-fault circuit interrupter (AFCI) protection for dwelling units has been a part of the *Code* since the 1999 *NEC*. AFCI protection was first required for mobile and manufactured homes at 550.25(B) for bedroom outlets in the 2002 edition of the *NEC*. The 2011 *NEC* witnessed AFCI protection expansion to family rooms, dining rooms, living rooms, parlors, libraries, dens, bedrooms, sunrooms, recreation rooms, closets, hallways, or similar rooms or areas.

Similar to GFCI requirements, AFCI protection at mobile and manufactured homes has not kept pace with the expansion of AFCI protection at conventional dwelling units. This omission leaves the user of the *Code* asking the same question concerning AFCI protection at mobile and manufactured homes that were asked concerning GFCI protection. Does a person deserve less AFCI protection in a mobile or manufactured home than he or she deserves in conventional dwelling unit construction? The obvious answer to that question is, of course, "No!" Equal AFCI protection is warranted at all dwelling unit locations regardless of the type of dwelling unit that is involved.

To that end, the provisions for AFCI protection at mobile and manufactured homes were revised at 550.25(B) by eliminating the "laundry list" of rooms and locations requiring AFCI protection at mobile and manufactured homes and simply requiring "all 120-volt branch circuits that supply 15- and 20-ampere outlets to comply with 210.12." With this reference to 210.12, any future changes to AFCI protection for conventional dwelling units will have the same effect at mobile and manufactured homes without CMP-19 having to keep up with the actions of CMP-2 (who has responsibility over 210.12 in Chapter 2).

By the time the 2017 edition of the *NEC* is published, the electrical industry will have over 15 years of experience with the manufacture and installation of AFCI protection devices and over nine years of experience with the combination-type AFCI protection devices. This calibration of AFCI protection requirements for conventional dwelling units as well as mobile and manufactured homes will make the installation and enforcement of these rules uniform while providing equally deserved AFCI protection at all dwelling units, no matter the type of construction.

First Revisions: FR 5404
Second Revisions: SR 5403
Public Inputs: PI 2432, PI 2878
Public Comments: PC 776

550.25(B)

551.2

Definition: Recreational Vehicle (RV) Park

551.2

Recreational Vehicle Park. Any parcel or tract of land under the control of any person, organization, or governmental entity wherein two or more RV, recreational park trailer, and/or other camping sites are offered for use by the public or members of an organization for overnight stays.

The definition of "Recreational Vehicle Park" was revised to make the definition consistent with that in NFPA 1194 *(Standard for RV Parks and Campgrounds)*

551.2 Definitions. (Recreational Vehicles and Recreational Vehicle Parks)

- **Type of Change:** Revision

- **Change at a Glance:** The definition of "Recreational Vehicle Park" was revised to make the definition consistent with that in NFPA 1194.

- **Code Language: 551.2 Definitions. (Recreational Vehicles and Recreational Vehicle Parks)**

  Recreational Vehicle Park. ~~A plot of land upon which~~ Any parcel or tract of land under the control of any person, organization, or governmental entity wherein two or more recreational vehicle ~~sites are located, established, or maintained for occupancy by recreational vehicles of the general public as temporary living quarters for recreation or vacation purposes~~, recreational park trailer, and/or other camping sites are offered for use by the public or members of an organization for overnight stays.

- **2014 *NEC* Requirement**
  The definition of "Recreational Vehicle Park" stated that an RV park was "a plot of land upon which two or more recreational vehicle sites are located, established, or maintained for occupancy by recreational vehicles of the general public as temporary living quarters for recreation or vacation purposes."

- **2017 *NEC* Change**
  The definition of "Recreational Vehicle Park" was revised to correlate with the same definition in NFPA 1194 (*Standard for Recreational Vehicle Parks and Campgrounds*).

Analysis of the Change:

A recreational vehicle park (RV park) can be as small as a just a few sites to large booming resorts with hundreds of sites, catering to RVs of every type and size. Some RV parks offer the simple solitude of campgrounds that provide merely the basics of electricity and fresh water at the site, while others provide full-service options with electricity, water and sewer hookups for each RV site. Electronically savvy *RVers* appreciate the Wi-Fi service provided at many of today's RV sites and campgrounds. RV parks can offer an overnight stay or longer in assigned RV "sites." Many RV parks also offer tent camping or cabins with limited facilities.

The *NEC* offers a definition for a *Recreational Vehicle Park* at 551.2. This same basic definition has been in Article 551 since the 1978 *NEC*. At that time, this definition was located at 551-41. It was moved to its current home at 551.2 during the 1990 *NEC* revision process. For the 2017 *NEC*, the definition of Recreational Vehicle Park was revised to correlate with the same definition in NFPA 1194 (*Standard for Recreational Vehicle Parks and Campgrounds*). This standard provides minimum construction requirements for safety and health for occupants using facilities supplied by RV parks and campgrounds offering temporary living sites for use by recreational vehicles, recreational park trailers, and other camping units.

These changes to this definition were needed to make the definition of recreational vehicle parks less specific and limiting and more encompassing, such as the definition of *Mobile Home Park* at 550.2. This revised definition correctly excludes locations such as RV sales lots and storage areas for RVs.

First Revisions: FR 5407
Public Inputs: PI 3957

551.2

551.71

Type Receptacles Provided at RV Parks

Every RV site (with electrical power provided) must be equipped with a certain number and type of receptacles *[see 551.71(A) through (F)]*

20-A, 125-V,
2-pole, 3-wire,
grounding type

30-A, 125-V,
2-pole, 3-wire,
grounding type

50-A, 125/250-V,
3-pole, 4-wire,
grounding type

551.71 has been broken into six separate first level subdivisions with titles

The number of RV sites required to be equipped with 50-ampere, 125/250-volt receptacles has increased from 20 percent to 40 percent for all new RV sites

GFCI devices used in RV site electrical equipment not required to be weather or tamper resistant in accordance with 406.9 and 406.12

551.71 Type Receptacles Provided. (Recreational Vehicle Parks)

- **Type of Change:** Revision

- **Change at a Glance:** Type of receptacle required to be provided at RV parks was increased to 40 percent of new sites for 50-ampere rated receptacle. Section 551.71 was reorganized into a list format for clarity.

- **Code Language: 551.71 Type Receptacles Provided. (Recreational Vehicle Parks)**

(A) 20-Ampere. Every recreational vehicle site with electrical supply shall be equipped with recreational vehicle site supply equipment with at least one 20-ampere, 125-volt receptacle.

(B) 30-Ampere. A minimum of 70 percent of all recreational vehicle sites with electrical supply shall each be equipped with a 30-ampere, 125-volt receptacle conforming to Figure 551.46(C)(1). This supply shall be permitted to include additional receptacle configurations conforming to 551.81. The remainder of all recreational vehicle sites with electrical supply shall be equipped with one or more of the receptacle configurations conforming to 551.81.

(C) 50-Ampere. A minimum of 20 percent of existing and 40 percent of all new recreational vehicle sites, with electrical supply, shall each be equipped with a 50-ampere, 125/250-volt receptacle conforming to the configuration as identified in Figure 551.46(C)(1). Every recreational vehicle site equipped with a 50-ampere receptacle shall also be equipped with a 30-ampere, 125-volt receptacle conforming to Figure 551.46(C)(1). These electrical supplies shall be permitted to include additional receptacles that have configurations in accordance with 551.81.

(D) Tent Sites. Dedicated tent sites with a 15- or 20-ampere electrical supply shall be permitted to be excluded when determining the percentage of recreational vehicle sites with 30- or 50-ampere receptacles.

(E) Additional Receptacles. Additional receptacles shall be permitted for the connection of electrical equipment outside the recreational vehicle within the recreational vehicle park.

(F) GFCI Protection. All 125-volt, single-phase, 15- and 20-ampere receptacles shall have listed ground-fault circuit-interrupter protection for personnel. The GFCI devices used in RV site electrical equipment shall not be required to be weather or tamper resistant in accordance with 406.9 and 406.12.

Informational Note: The percentage of 50 ampere sites required by 551.71 ~~may~~ could be inadequate for seasonal recreational vehicle sites serving a higher percentage of recreational vehicles with 50 ampere electrical systems. In that type of recreational vehicle park, the percentage of 50 ampere sites could approach 100 percent.

■ **2014 *NEC* Requirement**
Every RV site (with electrical power provided) must be equipped with a certain number and type of receptacles (see *Code* language above). For the 2014 *NEC*, language was added to require every recreational vehicle site equipped with a 50-ampere receptacle to also be equipped with a 30-ampere, 125-volt receptacle. All of the information concerning the type of receptacles required at an RV park was delivered in a long paragraph with multiple requirements involved.

■ **2017 *NEC* Change**
The section has been broken into six separate first level subdivisions with titles. The number of RV sites required to be equipped with 50-ampere, 125/250-volt receptacles has increased from 20 percent to 40 percent for all new recreational vehicle sites. GFCI devices used in RV site electrical equipment are not required to be weather- or tamper-resistant in accordance with 406.9 and 406.12.

Analysis of the Change:
The demands for the type and rating of receptacles provided at recreational vehicle (RV) parks continue to grow and expand. A 30-ampere rated system is the most common type of electrical system provided on RVs. In fact, last *Code* cycle, a new requirement was added at 551.71 requiring every RV site equipped with

551.71

a 50-ampere receptacle to also be equipped with a 30-ampere, 125-volt receptacle. This requirement was an attempt to stop or slow down the increasing use of a "cheater cord" at RV sites supplied with only a 50-ampere receptacle. These "cheater cords" are a 50-ampere to 30-ampere short cord being sold to connect a 30-ampere RV supply cord to a 50-ampere receptacle. Proper connection of the grounding and bonding connections is only one concern with these "cheater cords" being employed along with improper overcurrent protection for the RV itself.

For the 2017 *NEC*, the number of RV sites required to be equipped with 50-ampere, 125/250-volt receptacles at RV parks has increased from 20 percent to 40 percent of all new recreational vehicle sites. A minimum of 20 percent of existing RV sites equipped with a 50-ampere, 125/250-volt receptacle remains sufficient. The evolution of the RV industry continues to provide for the demands of the RV consumer who desires more and more service from the 120-volt electrical system by building more and more units with 50-ampere power supplies. The Recreation Vehicle Industry Association (RVIA) conducted a survey of its RV original equipment manufacturer (OEM) members that indicated over 30 percent of new RV production currently are being equipped with 50-ampere power supplies installed. These percentages will continue to increase year after year. As the industry increases the number of RVs equipped with 50-ampere supply cords, it is important to ensure that RV parks and campgrounds can safely accommodate these power supplies so that"cheater cord" adapters are not a viable option.

One of the first changes noticed at 551.71 for the 2017 *NEC* is the restructuring of the entire section. This section was one long paragraph containing multiple requirements. The section has been broken into six separate first level subdivisions with titles, which enhances readability and usability for this entire section.

Another change initiated at 551.71 was the use of the term *recreational vehicle site supply equipment*. This term is defined at 551.2 (necessary equipment intended to constitute the disconnecting means for the supply to that site) but is not mentioned in previous editions of the *Code* at 551.71.

Lastly, a new sentence was added at 551.71(F) specifying that "GFCI devices used in RV site electrical equipment shall not be required to be weather- or tamper-resistant in accordance with 406.9 and 406.12." In their Committee Statement, CMP-19 indicated that RV site electrical equipment listed for use in RV parks is NEMA 3R rated, weather-resistant rated equipment and the weather-resistant receptacle requirements of 406.9 are not needed. This statement went on to say that RV site electric equipment is not for use in a dwelling, so the tamper-resistant receptacle requirements of 406.12 is not necessary. Some users of the *Code* will be quick to point out that tamper-resistant receptacles are required at more places than just dwelling units (child care facilities, waiting areas at medical and office buildings, etc.). Tamper-resistant receptacles are required at locations where small children are likely to be present and have the opportunity to insert foreign objects into receptacle outlets. RV parks are certainly among the locations where this combination could occur. It will be interesting to

551.71

monitor any changing developments to this particular provision in future *Code* cycles.

First Revisions: FR 5411
Second Revisions: SR 5408
Public Inputs: PI 1179, PI 744
Public Comments: PC 371, PC 968

551.73(A)

Calculated load for RV parks

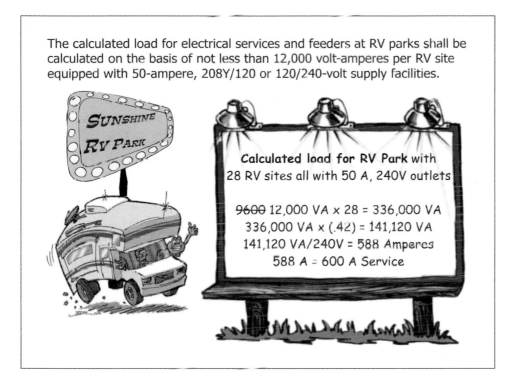

The calculated load for electrical services and feeders at RV parks shall be calculated on the basis of not less than 12,000 volt-amperes per RV site equipped with 50-ampere, 208Y/120 or 120/240-volt supply facilities.

SUNSHINE RV PARK

Calculated load for RV Park with 28 RV sites all with 50 A, 240V outlets

9600 12,000 VA x 28 = 336,000 VA
336,000 VA x (.42) = 141,120 VA
141,120 VA/240V = 588 Amperes
588 A = 600 A Service

551.73(A) Calculated Load. (Recreational Vehicle Parks)

- **Type of Change:** Revision

- **Change at a Glance:** The calculated load for electrical services and feeders at RV parks shall be calculated on the basis of not less than 12,000 volt-amperes per RV site equipped with 50-ampere, 208Y/120 or 120/240-volt supply facilities.

- **Code Language:** **551.73 Calculated Load. (Recreational Vehicle Parks)**

    (A) Basis of Calculations. Electrical services and feeders shall be calculated on the basis of not less than 9600 12,000 volt-amperes per

551.73(A)

site equipped with 50-ampere, 208Y/120 or 120/240-volt supply facilities; 3600 volt-amperes per site equipped with both 20-ampere and 30-ampere supply facilities; 2400 volt-amperes per site equipped with only 20-ampere supply facilities; and 600 volt-amperes per site equipped with only 20-ampere supply facilities that are dedicated to tent sites. The demand factors set forth in Table 551.73(A) shall be the minimum allowable demand factors that shall be permitted in calculating load for service and feeders. Where the electrical supply for a recreational vehicle site has more than one receptacle, the calculated load shall be calculated only for the highest rated receptacle.

Where the electrical supply is in a location that serves two recreational vehicles, the equipment for both sites shall comply with 551.77, and the calculated load shall only be calculated for the two receptacles with the highest rating.

■ **2014 *NEC* Requirement**
Electrical services and feeders for RV parks were required to be calculated on the basis of not less than 9600 volt-amperes per site equipped with 50-ampere, 208Y/120 or 120/240-volt supply facilities; 3600 volt-amperes per site equipped with both 20-ampere and 30-ampere supply facilities; 2400 volt-amperes per site equipped with only 20-ampere supply facilities; and 600 volt-amperes per site equipped with only 20-ampere supply facilities that are dedicated to tent sites.

■ **2017 *NEC* Change**
The minimum calculated load for RV parks sites equipped with 50-ampere, 208Y/120 or 120/240-volt supply facilities has increased from 9600 volt-amperes to 12,000 volt-amperes per site. The calculated loads for 20-ampere and 30-ampere supply facilities remained the same.

Analysis of the Change:

The electrical demands at recreational vehicle (RV) parks continues to increase as recreational vehicles become larger and consume more and more power. To that end, minimum calculated load for RV parks sites equipped with 50-ampere, 208Y/120 or 120/240-volt supply facilities has increased from 9600 volt-amperes to 12,000 volt-amperes per site for the 2017 *NEC*. In doing some research into the origin of the 9600 volt-ampere (or watts) calculated load, some interesting facts surfaced.

The calculated load requirements for RV parks was first instituted during the 1971 *NEC* at 551-41(a). At that time, only the 3600 volt-amperes per site equipped with both 20-ampere and 30-ampere supply facilities and the 2400 volt-amperes per site equipped with only 20-ampere supply facilities were recognized. The 9600 volt-amperes per site equipped with 50-ampere, 120/240-volt (no 208Y/120-volt then) supply facilities was added for the 1990 *NEC*. The original proposal (see 1990 ROP 19-92) for this 9600-volt-ampere rating recommended the 12,000 volt-amperes that is being instituted for the 2017 NEC. Part of the substantiation for the 1990 *NEC* proposed 12,000 volt-amperes stated that "the number chosen, 12,000 VA, is figured on the same basis as the other values starting, in this case, at 50 amperes, 240 volts. Whether the load is 40 or 50 amperes, the receptacle will have a 50-ampere configuration, and this is all that is known at the time of installation and inspection." The CMP-19 Panel Statement indicated that "12,000 volt-amperes for multiple 30-ampere receptacles is excessive."

A submitted comment resulted in a reduction from the proposed 12,000 volt-amperes to the 9600-volt-ampere value that remained in the *Code* until the 2017 *NEC*. The comment (see 1990 ROC 19-42) stated in part, "This value (9600 VA) comes from 80 percent or 40 amperes of the maximum rating. 40 amperes are the maximum that should be drawn thru a normal 50-ampere overcurrent protection device without chancing a trip. 80 percent is also a *NEC* limit used in various sections to define circuit full load."

As recreational vehicles become larger and demand more electrical power consumption, RV site feeders should be more realistically sized to meet the actual load served. 9600 VA was based on 40 amperes at 240 volts. 12,000 VA is based on 50 amperes and 240 volts. This change will serve to require larger service or feeder conductors to properly serve the load or fewer RV sites supplied by a service to an RV park.

First Revisions: FR 5413
Public Inputs: PI 745

551.73(A)

551.75(B)
Grounding Electrodes at RV Parks

551.75(B) Grounding. (RV Parks)

- **Type of Change:** New/Revision

- **Change at a Glance:** Grounding at RV Park pedestals (equipment): Grounding electrode systems are not required to be established at RV pedestal (equipment) that is not considered a service.

- **Code Language: 551.75 Grounding. (RV Parks)**
  (A) General. All electrical equipment and installations in recreational vehicle parks shall be grounded as required by Article 250.

  ~~Informational Note: See 250.32(A), Exception, for single branch circuits.~~

  (B) Grounding Electrode. Power outlets or recreational vehicle site supply equipment, other than those used as service equipment, shall not be required to have a grounding electrode. An auxiliary grounding electrode(s) in accordance with 250.54 shall be permitted to be installed.

- **2014 *NEC* Requirement**
  This section simply stated that all electrical equipment and installations in RV parks were required to be grounded as required by Article 250. This reference to the entirety of Article 250 was too broad in nature and left a wide variety of interpretation.

- **2017 *NEC* Change**
  A new 551.75(B) was added indicating that power outlets or RV site supply equipment (other than those used as service equipment) are not required to have a grounding electrode established at RV site electrical equipment.

Analysis of the Change:

Consider this scenario. You have a recreational vehicle (RV) pedestal sticking up in the middle of nowhere in an RV park. This particular RV pedestal is dedicated to serving a particular RV site with electrical power. Is this RV pedestal considered a structure? Is it equipment? If it is a structure, does it now require a grounding electrode system to be established at this location? Is this a service or is it a feeder? All you really wanted to do is hook up your RV in time to watch the big baseball game, and now you have such a headache from trying to figure out all these questions about a simple RV pedestal that you have to go lie down, and you miss the big game! A series of revisions occurred at a few locations for the 2017 *NEC* in an attempt to answer some of these questions from a *Code* standpoint.

A new structure was implemented for 551.75 by adding a new 551.75(B) which now states that power outlets or RV site supply equipment (other than those used as service equipment) are not required to have a grounding electrode established at that specific location. This new requirement directly correlates with the revised definitions for a *building* and a *structure* found in Article 100. A building is now defined as "a structure that stands alone or that is separat-

551.75(B)

ed from adjoining structures by fire walls." A structure is now defined as "that which is built or constructed, other than equipment."

These two related definitions were revised for the 2017 *NEC* as a result of a Task Group assigned by the *NEC* Correlating Committee to address structures (including RV pedestals) and to resolve issues with actions taken by CMP-19 on proposals and comments during the 2014 *NEC Code* cycle relative to comparing the definitions of structure" and building.

The addition of the phrase "other than equipment" at the end of the definition of Structure clarifies that structures do not include equipment. Part of the conclusion of the Task Group was to establish a difference between structures and equipment for the purpose of establishing a grounding electrode system as compared to installing optional or auxiliary electrodes at something like an RV pedestal. There was confusion for users of the *Code* as to what is considered "equipment" versus what is considered a "structure." Based on the previous definition of a structure, everything that is built or constructed is a structure, including equipment. With the revised definition of structure, equipment can be mounted on a structure, but the equipment itself is not a structure. Our RV pedestal described above is a perfect example of this situation.

551.75(B)

Over the last few *Code* cycles, this issue has been heavily debated by CMP-19 and the discussion always seemed to come down to whether the RV site equipment (RV pedestal) was considered a structure. If it is considered a structure, that would require the enforcement of 250.32(A) for establishing a grounding electrode system for buildings or structures supplied by a feeder(s) or branch circuit(s). This new provision at 551.75(B) will clarify that a grounding electrode system will not be required for feeders supplying RV site equipment, and will be consistent with the direction of CMP-1 concerning the revised definitions for a building or structure.

The previous informational note that directed users of the *Code* to 250.32(A) has been deleted, because this reference added to the confusion and implied that the installation of grounding electrode was required at the RV site electrical equipment such as an RV pedestal.

This change at 551.75(B) and the resulting direction that a grounding electrode system need not be established at RV site electrical equipment had a related effect that led to the deletion of 551.73(B). This section of the *Code* stated in part that "where the (RV) park service exceeds 240 volts, transformers, and secondary panelboards shall be treated as services." This sub-section was deleted as it is not in alignment with the rest of the *Code*. Transformers and panelboards that are downstream from the service are separately derived systems and should be treated as such (not as services). To treat these load-side separately derived systems as a service violates the definition of a *Service* in Article 100. Doing so would also generate circulating currents due to the bonding of the transformer and the bonding of the first disconnecting means. See SR 5409, PI 4028, PI 1877, and PC 850 for more information.

First Revisions: FR 5414
Public Inputs: PI 4642, PI 1532

Article 555

Marinas, Boatyards, and Commercial and Noncommerical Docking Facilities

551.75(B)

Article 555 Marinas, Boatyards, and Commercial and Noncommerical Docking Facilities

- **Type of Change:** Revision

- **Change at a Glance:** Revisions to Article 555 will now make this article applicable to commercial as well as dwelling unit docking facilities.

- **Code Language:** **Article 555 Marinas, Boatyards, and Commercial and Noncommerical Docking Facilities**

555.1 Scope. This article covers the installation of wiring and equipment in the areas comprising fixed or floating piers, wharves, docks, and other areas in marinas, boatyards, boat basins, boathouses, yacht clubs, boat condominiums, docking facilities associated with one-family dwellings, two-family dwellings, multifamily dwellings, and residential condominiums, any multiple docking facility, or similar occupancies, and facilities that are used, or intended for use, for the purpose of repair, berthing, launching, storage, or fueling of small craft and the moorage of floating buildings.
~~Private, noncommercial docking facilities constructed or occupied for the use of the owner or residents of the associated single-family dwelling are not covered by this article.~~

Informational Note: See NFPA 303-2011, *Fire Protection Standard for Marinas and Boatyards*, for additional information.

- **2014 *NEC* Requirement**
  The requirements for boatyards and marinas are found in Article 555. For the 2014 *NEC*, private, noncommercial docking facilities constructed or occupied for the use of the owner or residents of the associated single-family dwelling were not covered by this article.

- **2017 *NEC* Change**
  The title of Article 555 was changed from "Marinas and Boatyards" to "Marinas, Boatyards, and Commercial and Noncommercial Docking Facilities." Revisions to 555.1 make Article 555 relevant to dwelling unit docking facilities as well as commercial docking facilities.

Analysis of the Change:

Does Article 555 for marinas and boatyards apply to a privately owned, non-commercial docking facility associated with a dwelling unit? Well, the answer would depend on which edition of the *Code* is being enforced in the location of said docking facility. Prior to the 2002 *NEC*, residential docking facilities were covered by Article 555. During the 2002 *NEC* revision cycle, a total rewrite of Article 555 was completed that incorporated the physical installation rules contained in NFPA 303, *Fire Protection Standard for Marinas and Boatyards*. Included in this rewrite, a sentence was added to the scope of Article 555 that stated, "private, noncommercial docking facilities constructed or occupied for the use of the owner or residents of the associated single-family dwelling *are not covered* by this article" (see 2002 NEC ROP 19-135 and 2002 NEC ROC 19-71). This revision removed any residential docking facility from obligation of compliance with the requirements of Article 555. During this time, a designer, installer, or homeowner could certainly apply Article 555 rules to a particular residential docking facility installation if he or she so desired, but the requirements were not mandated by the *Code*.

For the 2017 *NEC*, changes to the scope of Article 555 will again place residential boat docks back under the compliance provisions of Article 555. Ground-fault circuit-interrupter (GFCI) protection is called for at 210.8(C) for outlets not exceeding 240 volts that supply boat hoists installed in dwelling unit locations. Public inputs were submitted during the 2017 *NEC* revision cycle requesting relocation of this GFCI rule. Great debate ensued among CMP-2 members, not so much about the merit of such a move, but about where to relocate this GFCI requirement for a residential boat hoist outlet if moved from Article 210. The logical new home for this boat hoist requirement would have been Article 555 if this article covered residential docking facilities.

As previously written, the *NEC* rules in Article 555 would not apply to residential boat docking facilities, yet the majority of the rules in Article 555 would be necessary at residential boat docks associated with single-family and multifamily dwelling occupancies. An electrical hazard is not smart enough to know if it is occurring at a dwelling unit or non-dwelling unit docking facility, and the

555

hazards are the same in these associated aquatic environments. This revision will resolve this issue by providing users of the *Code* with the ability to apply Article 555 requirements to all wiring, equipment, and electrical systems installed at boat docking facilities regardless of its location, be it residential, commercial, or industrial application.

The alternative to this revision to Article 555 for inclusion of residential docking facilities would be the creation of a new article for boat docking facilities associated with dwelling units. Creating a new separate article for residential docking facilities would result in unnecessary redundancy in the *NEC* as the rules would be repetitive since these environments present the same electrical hazards. Article 555 closely follows the provisions of NFPA 303.

The scope of NFPA 303 excludes boat docking facilities for single-family dwelling and multi-family dwelling occupancies, yet the purpose of the standard appears to address fire and electrical hazards that are present in any boat docking facility associated with any occupancy. Section 1.2 of NFPA 303 states the following: "This standard is intended to provide a minimum acceptable level of safety to life and property from fire, and electrical hazards at marinas and related facilities." The same purpose and reasons for requiring this protection are not different when applied to a dwelling unit docking facility. For correlation purposes, a companion public input was submitted to NFPA 303 for inclusion of noncommercial docking facilities.

First Revisions: FR 5438, FR 5435
Second Revisions: SR 5412
Public Inputs: PI 1374, PI 349, PI 1373
Public Comments: PC 1741

555

555.3

Ground-Fault Protection

The ~~main~~ overcurrent protective devices that supply the marina, boatyards, and commercial and noncommercial docking facilities shall have ground fault protection not exceeding 30 mA

GFP protection required for OCPDs for marinas, and now boatyards, and commercial and noncommercial docking facilities as well was reduced to a maximum of 30 mA rather than 100 mA

This GFP protection is required on all supply OCPDs *(not necessarily the main OCPD)*

555.3 Ground-Fault Protection. (Marinas, Boatyards and Commercial and Noncommercial Docking Facilities)

- **Type of Change:** Revision

- **Change at a Glance:** The ground-fault protection required for overcurrent protective devices for marinas, boatyards, and commercial and noncommercial docking facilities cannot exceed 30 mA (rather than 100 mA).

- **Code Language: 555.3 Ground-Fault Protection. (Marinas, Boatyards and Commercial and Noncommercial Docking Facilities)**

  The ~~main~~ overcurrent protective devices that ~~feeds~~ supply the marina, boatyards, and commercial and noncommercial docking facilities shall have ground fault protection not exceeding ~~100 mA~~ 30 mA. ~~Ground-fault protection of each individual branch or feeder circuit shall be permitted as a suitable alternative.~~

- **2014 *NEC* Requirement**
  Ground-fault protection (GFP) was required for the main overcurrent protective device (OCPD) for a marina. This GFP protection could not exceed 100 mA. Individual GFCI protection of each individual branch or feeder was permitted in lieu of the maximum 100 mA GFP protection at the main OCPD.

■ **2017 *NEC* Change**

The ground-fault protection required for overcurrent protective devices for marinas, and now boatyards, and commercial and noncommercial docking facilities as well was reduced to a maximum of 30 mA rather than 100 mA. This GFP protection is required in all supply overcurrent protective devices, not necessarily in the main OCPD. The allowance of GFCI protection in each individual branch or feeder was deleted as this 30 mA GFP protection is required in all supply OCPDs. GFCI protection is still required for 15- and 20-ampere, single-phase, 125-volt receptacles by the requirements of 555.19(B)(1).

Analysis of the Change:

A new 555.3 was added to Article 555 for the 2011 *NEC*. At the time, this section was calling for "ground-fault protection" on the main overcurrent protective device serving a marina or boatyard. This ground-fault protection was to have a maximum 100 milliamperes (mA) capacity. In lieu of this ground-fault protection on the main, individual GFCI protection on each branch circuit or feeder was permitted. Confusion existed with this provision before the ink dried on the 2011 *NEC* as this new requirement was aimed at "protection for personnel," not ground-fault protection (GFP) for equipment, yet the title and the *Code* language referenced ground-fault protection.

555.3

This added GFP requirement was proposed as a result of numerous fatalities occurring in and around marinas due to human contact with stray currents in contact with the water in these wet environments. Part of the substantiation noted several deaths as a result of drowning where the victims lost function of their limbs and the ability to react or swim. This 2011 *NEC* 100 mA GFP protection supplying a main service or feeder for a marina almost surely provided some degree of protection; however, there were issues that still needed to be addressed if the concern was with protection of personnel.

A Class A GFCI is intended to minimize electric shock hazards for the protection of people. This is a protective device that will open a circuit within a current range of 4-6 mA as required by UL 943 (*Ground-Fault Circuit-Interrupters*). It will function to de-energize a circuit or portion of a circuit, within an established period of time, where a current to ground exceeds a predetermined trip value of 4-6 mA. This 4-6 mA value is considered the let-go-threshold for humans. Any GFCI device with a predetermined trip value of greater than 4-6 mA is not providing true GFCI protection for personnel.

For the 2017 *NEC*, this maximum 100 mA capacity has been reduced to a maximum of 30 mA. This 30 mA ground-fault limit is consistent with that recommended in a report titled "Assessment of Hazardous Voltage/Current in Marinas, Boatyards and Floating Buildings" that was commissioned by NFPA's Fire Protection Research Foundation. This report was conducted by the American Boat and Yacht Council (ABYC) Foundation, Inc. This report stated in part:

"ABYC Standards recommend a device that interrupts the source of power feeding a fault within 100 milliseconds from the moment stray current exceeds

30 mA. While 30 mA through the body is more than enough to kill a swimmer (above the "let-go" threshold established for a Class A GFCI device), it is not sufficient to assume that all of the 30 mA leaking into the water will actually go through the swimmer. Rather, U. S. Coast Guard studies have shown that due to hemispherical 'spreading' of the electric field, only a portion of the leakage current will go thru the swimmer. The main exception to this occurs when the swimmer comes into direct contact with the voltage source itself, for example by grabbing a metallic ladder that has become energized. 30 mA represents an acceptable level that ABYC expects to prevent a majority of electric shock drowning (ESD) incidents while remaining practical enough to minimize unnecessary tripping."

The substantiation for this reduction to 30 mA went on to state, "It should also be noted that ABYC standards, since December 31, 2012, have required 30 mA equipment leakage circuit interrupters (ELCI) on water crafts. While boats are not subject to *NEC* requirements, boats are connected to electrical branch circuits that are."

Some users of the *Code* will argue that true protection for personnel (people) is only be achieved with Class A GFCI protection (maximum 4 to 6 mA current levels). This let-go level of protection would prove to be too sensitive for the wet environments encountered at marinas and docking facilities, resulting in continual "nuisance" tripping. The substantiation and reasoning for the 30 mA values is logical and has merit. Time will tell the marina industry, as well as the electrical industry, if this 30 mA value is sufficient. Let's hope the theories are correct. Who wants to be the first to jump in the water at your local marina and find out?

It should be noted that a related change occurred at 555.24 that calls for posting of signage to alert personnel coming into the vicinity of marinas and boatyards of the potential for shock hazards in the water in and around these nautical areas. See the *Analysis of Changes* report for 555.24 in this publication for more information.

555.3

First Revisions: FR 5436
Second Revisions: SR 5413
Public Inputs: PI 3152, PI 3258

555.19(B)(1)

GFCI Protection for Personnel

GFCI protection required for all 125-volt, single-phase, 15- and 20-ampere receptacles installed outdoors, in boathouses, and in buildings or structures used for storage, maintenance, or repair regardless of the intended use

The term, "where portable electrical hand tools, electrical diagnostic equipment, or portable lighting equipment are to be used" was deleted

The removal of this portable electrical hand tool, etc. conditional language will aid the AHJ in enforcement of the GFCI requirements at these locations

555.3

555.19(B)(1) Receptacles. (Marinas, Boatyards, and Commercial and Noncommercial Docking Facilities)

- **Type of Change:** Deletion

- **Change at a Glance:** GFCI protection for personnel is required for all 125-volt, single-phase, 15- and 20-ampere receptacles installed outdoors, in boathouses, and in buildings or structures used for storage, maintenance, or repair, without consideration of whether "electrical diagnostic equipment, electrical hand tools, or portable lighting equipment" is being used.

- **Code Language: 555.19 Receptacles. (Marinas, Boatyards, and Commercial and Noncommercial Docking Facilities)**
  Receptacles shall be mounted not less than 305 mm (12 in.) above the deck surface of the pier and not below the electrical datum plane on a fixed pier.

  (B) Other Than Shore Power.
  (1) Ground-Fault Circuit-Interrupter (GFCI) Protection for Personnel. Fifteen- and 20-ampere, single-phase, 125-volt receptacles installed outdoors, in boathouses, in buildings or structures used for storage, maintenance, or repair ~~where portable electrical hand tools, electrical diagnostic equipment, or portable lighting equipment are to be used~~ shall be provided with GFCI protection for personnel. Receptacles in other locations shall be protected in accordance with 210.8(B).

- **2014 *NEC* Requirement**

  GFCI protection for personnel was required for all 125-volt, single-phase, 15- and 20-ampere receptacles installed outdoors, in boathouses, and in buildings or structures used for storage, maintenance, or repair, but only in areas where electrical diagnostic equipment, electrical hand tools, or portable lighting equipment were to be used.

- **2017 *NEC* Change**

  The statement, "where portable electrical hand tools, electrical diagnostic equipment, or portable lighting equipment are to be used" was deleted. GFCI protection for personnel will now be required for all 125-volt, single-phase, 15- and 20-ampere receptacles installed outdoors, in boathouses, and in buildings or structures used for storage, maintenance, or repair regardless of the intended use of these receptacles.

Analysis of the Change:

The previous language at 555.19(B) required ground-fault circuit-interrupter (GFCI) protection for personnel at all 15- and 20-ampere, single-phase, 125-volt receptacles at marinas, boatyards, and commercial and noncommercial docking facilities that are installed outdoors, in boathouses, and in buildings or structures used for storage, maintenance, or repair. However, this GFCI protection was only called for "where portable electrical hand tools, electrical diagnostic equipment, or portable lighting equipment was to be used" at these locations.

For the enforcement community, it is extremely difficult for the AHJ to determine which receptacles will employ "portable electrical hand tools, electrical diagnostic equipment, or portable lighting equipment" and which receptacles will not. This determination is made even more difficult for the AHJ since this determination is typically required to be made on the final inspection with the marinas, docking facilities, buildings or structures, etc., unoccupied.

To this end, the 2017 *NEC* witnessed the deletion of the condition that the receptacles involved must supply "portable electrical hand tools, electrical diagnostic equipment, or portable lighting equipment" in order for GFCI protection to be required. For the 2017 *NEC*, all 15- and 20-ampere, single-phase, 125-volt receptacles at marinas, boatyards, and commercial and noncommercial docking facilities that are installed outdoors, in boathouses, and in buildings or structures used for storage, maintenance, or repair will require GFCI protection regardless of their end use.

The removal of this portable electrical hand tool, etc., conditional language will greatly aid the AHJ to enforce the GFCI requirements at these locations without debate from the installer, builder, or homeowner as to whether or not portable tools, portable lighting, and such will be used.

This exact same scenario and deletion of the same condition played out during the 2014 *NEC* revision process at 210.8(B)(8) for non-dwelling unit garages, service bays, and similar areas.

First Revisions: FR 5440
Public Inputs: PI 4669

555.19(B)(1)

555.24

Signage at Marinas, Boatyards, etc.

New requirements added for permanent safety signs to be installed to give notice of electrical shock hazard risks to persons using or swimming near a boat dock or marina

WARNING - POTENTIAL SHOCK HAZARD - ELECTRICAL CURRENTS MAY BE PRESENT IN THE WATER

The signs shall be clearly visible from all approaches to a marina or boatyard facility

Lunkerville Marina

555.19(B)(1)

555.24 Signage. (Marinas, Boatyards and Commercial and Noncommercial Docking Facilities)

- **Type of Change:** New

- **Change at a Glance:** New signage requirement at 555.24 for precautionary signage related to electric shock hazard in water around marinas and boatyards.

- **Code Language: 555.24 Signage. (Marinas, Boatyards and Commercial and Noncommercial Docking Facilities)**

  Permanent safety signs shall be installed to give notice of electrical shock hazard risks to persons using or swimming near a boat dock or marina and shall comply with all of the following:
  (1) The signage shall comply with 110.21(B)(1) and be of sufficient durability to withstand the environment.
  (2) The signs shall be clearly visible from all approaches to a marina or boatyard facility.
  (3) The signs shall state "WARNING — POTENTIAL SHOCK HAZARD — ELECTRICAL CURRENTS MAY BE PRESENT IN THE WATER."

- **2014 *NEC* Requirement**
  There were no requirements in the *NEC* or Article 555 requiring electrical shock hazard risk signage at marinas and boatyards.

- **2017 *NEC* Change**
  New requirements were added for permanent safety signs to be installed
  to give notice of electrical shock hazard risks to persons using or swimming near a boat dock or marina. The signage must comply with 110.21(B)
  (1) and be clearly visible from all approaches to a marina or boatyard facility. The signs shall state "WARNING — POTENTIAL SHOCK HAZARD
  — ELECTRICAL CURRENTS MAY BE PRESENT IN THE WATER."

Analysis of the Change:

Due in part to stray circulating currents in the water, swimming at marinas and
boatyards presents a significant danger of electric shock drowning (ESD) to people engaging in such aquatic activities. Eliminating recreational swimming in
the immediate vicinity of boats and docks using alternating current (ac) electrical power will help protect the public against the dangers associated with stray
currents associated with electrical use at marinas and boatyards.

To that end, a new 555.24 was added to the 2017 *NEC*. This new section will
require posting of signage to alert personnel coming into the vicinity of marinas
and boatyards of the potential for shock hazards in the water in and around
these nautical areas. Numerous ESD deaths and injuries (including electrocution in the water) at marinas and boatyards have been documented and investigated over the last decade. In all cases, these accidents would have been prevented if the victims had not swum in the water around boats and docks using ac
electrical power. The warnings provided by signage, along with enforcement by
marina and boatyard operators, will save lives and prevent injuries to the public.

In an NFPA report released in November of 2014, titled, "*Assessment of Hazardous Voltage/Current in Marinas, Boatyard, and Floating Buildings*," the
following was noted: "The American Boat and Yacht Council (ABYC) recommends that no recreational swimming at any time take place in a marina environment. Part of an effective plan against ESD will include a no swimming
policy and 'NO SWIMMING' signs posted throughout the facility. This plan will
also prevent possible injury due to boat traffic, harmful marine life, etc."

It is recognized that inspection and regular maintenance activities will still be
required in these marinas and boatyards. Actions such as disconnecting shore
connections to boats at and near the work location, securing power to docks or
sections of docks, and wearing protective equipment (such as wet suits) can be
used to provide adequate protection for maintenance personnel. The general
public does not have an understanding of the potential electrical dangers present within the confines of marinas and boatyards. Marina and boatyard operators clearly have a responsibility to provide protection from electrical hazards as
is stated in NFPA 303 (*Fire Protection Standard for Marinas and Boatyards*).

It should be noted that a related change occurred at 555.3 for ground-fault
protection. The ground-fault protection required for overcurrent protective
devices for marinas, and now boatyards, and commercial and noncommercial
docking facilities, as well, was reduced to a maximum of 30 mA rather than 100
mA. This GFP protection is required in all supply overcurrent protective devices,
not necessarily in the main OCPD. GFCI protection is still required for 15- and

555.24

20-ampere, single-phase, 125-volt receptacles by the requirements of 555.19(B)(1). See the *Analysis of Changes* report for 555.3 in this publication for more information. This safety enhancement should be viewed as protection for those who accidentally enter the water, and not as a "green light" for recreational swimming activities in marinas and boatyards.

Second Revisions: SR 5411
Public Inputs: PI 4565
Public Comments: PC 453, PC 733

590.4

Feeders (Temporary Installations)

555.24

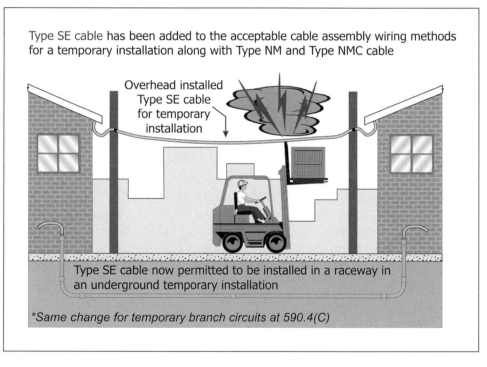

Type SE cable has been added to the acceptable cable assembly wiring methods for a temporary installation along with Type NM and Type NMC cable

Overhead installed Type SE cable for temporary installation

Type SE cable now permitted to be installed in a raceway in an underground temporary installation

Same change for temporary branch circuits at 590.4(C)

590.4 General. (Temporary Installations)

- **Type of Change:** Revision

- **Change at a Glance:** Type SE cable has been added to the acceptable cable assembly wiring methods for a temporary installation along with Type NM and Type NMC cable.

- **Code Language: 590.4 General. (Temporary Installations)**

    (B) Feeders. Overcurrent protection shall be provided in accordance with 240.4, 240.5, 240.100, and 240.101. Conductors shall be permitted within cable assemblies or within multiconductor cords or cables of a type identified in Table 400.4 for hard usage or extra-hard usage. For the purpose of this section, the following wiring methods shall be permitted:

(1) Type NM, ~~and~~ Type NMC, and Type SE cables shall be permitted to be used in any dwelling, building, or structure without any height limitation or limitation by building construction type and without concealment within walls, floors, or ceilings.

(2) Type SE cable shall be permitted to be installed in a raceway in an underground installation.

Exception: Single insulated conductors shall be permitted where installed for the purpose(s) specified in 590.3(C), where accessible only to qualified persons.

- **2014 *NEC* Requirement**
  The only permitted cable assembly wiring methods for temporary installations for branch circuits and feeders were Type NM and Type NMC cables.

- **2017 *NEC* Change**
  Along with Type NM and Type NMC cables, Type SE cable has been added to the acceptable cable assembly wiring methods for temporary installations. Type SE cable is now permitted to be installed in a raceway in a temporary underground installation as well.

590.4

Analysis of the Change:

For temporary installations, particularly at construction sites, the *Code* permits temporary branch circuits or feeders to be installed within cable assemblies or within multiconductor cords or cables of a type identified for hard usage or extra-hard usage [see 590.4(B) and (C)]. For the previous editions of the *Code*, a closer look at these rules for temporary installations of branch circuits and feeders delivered in a cable assembly will reveal that the only permitted cable assemblies were Type NM and Type NMC (nonmetallic-sheathed) cables.

Having established the two permitted cable assemblies for these temporary installations, it is very common to see Type SE (service-entrance) cable used for temporary power, particularly for temporary feeders. For the 2017 *NEC*, 590.4(B) will now permit Type SE cables as an acceptable wiring method for a temporary feeder along with Type NM and Type NMC cables. Type SE (including Types SEU and SER) cables have proven themselves to be more than adequate for this type of temporary installation. While the *NEC* should continue to prohibit such use in a permanent manner, it is necessary to modify the general rules for the installation of Type SE cable for temporary installations.

Another change involving Type SE cable was the addition of new 590.4(B)(2), which states, "Type SE cable shall be permitted to be installed in a raceway in an underground installation." The hustle and bustle of an active construction site does not lend itself to the safe installation of an overhead installation of feeders and branch circuits outside of a building or structure under construction.

During construction, there are many scenarios that require feeders and branch circuits to be run between buildings, structures, and job-site trailers. Installing these temporary feeders or branch circuits overhead is sometimes not feasible due to the constant aerial maneuvers by cranes, forklifts, etc. This type of overhead machinery is frequently moving construction material from one location to another. To prevent overhead feeders and branch circuits from constantly losing the match between these overhead conductors and cranes and forklifts when contact is made, it is common to see Type SEU and SER cable installed underground in PVC conduit as that is the most feasible way to get the job done without creating a possible hazardous overhead encounter.

Even though this underground installation is a safe and viable alternative for temporary installations, it was a *Code* violation by the restrictions of 338.12(A)(2), which indicates that Type SE cable is not permitted to be installed underground, with or without a raceway. Type SE cable is listed only for aboveground use. This new provision at 590.4(B)(2) will allow this type of underground installation on a temporary basis while still prohibiting this type of underground use for Type SE cable on a permanent basis.

This same allowance of Type SE cable as an acceptable cable assembly wiring method for temporary installations was installed at 590.4(C) for branch circuits while 590.4(B) deals with feeders.

590.4

First Revisions: FR 615
Public Inputs: PI 2846

590.6(A)(1)

GFCI Protection for Personnel in Temporary Installations

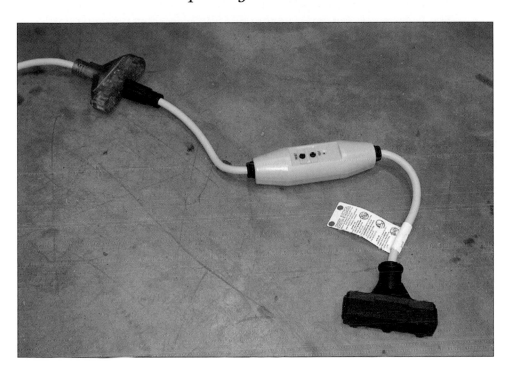

590.6(A)(1) Ground-Fault Protection for Personnel. (Temporary Installations)

- ■ **Type of Change:** Revision

- ■ **Change at a Glance:** GFCI protection is permitted in the form of portable GFCI cord sets in addition to GFCI protection required for all 125-volt, single-phase, 15-, 20-, and 30-ampere receptacle outlets that are not a part of the permanent wiring of the building or structure.

- ■ **Code Language: 590.6 Ground-Fault Protection for Personnel. (Temporary Installations)**
  Ground-fault protection for personnel for all temporary wiring installations shall be provided to comply with 590.6(A) and (B). This section shall apply only to temporary wiring installations used to supply temporary power to equipment used by personnel during construction, remodeling, maintenance, repair, or demolition of buildings, structures, equipment, or similar activities. This section shall apply to power derived from an electric utility company or from an on-site-generated power source.

  (A) Receptacle Outlets. Temporary receptacle installations used to supply temporary power to equipment used by personnel during construction, remodeling, maintenance, repair, or demolition of buildings, struc-

590.4

tures, equipment, or similar activities shall comply with the requirements of 590.6(A)(1) through (A)(3), as applicable.

Exception: In industrial establishments only, where conditions of maintenance and supervision ensure that only qualified personnel are involved, an assured equipment grounding conductor program as specified in 590.6(B)(2) shall be permitted for only those receptacle outlets used to supply equipment that would create a greater hazard if power were interrupted or having a design that is not compatible with GFCI protection.

(1) Receptacle Outlets Not Part of Permanent Wiring. All 125-volt, single-phase, 15-, 20-, and 30-ampere receptacle outlets that are not a part of the permanent wiring of the building or structure and that are in use by personnel shall have ground-fault circuit-interrupter protection for personnel. In addition to this required ground-fault circuit-interrupter protection for personnel, listed cord sets or devices incorporating listed ground-fault circuit-interrupter protection for personnel identified for portable use shall be permitted.

590.6(A)(1)

■ **2014 *NEC* Requirement**
All 125-volt, single-phase, 15-, 20-, and 30-ampere receptacle outlets that are not a part of the permanent wiring of the building or structure and that are in use by personnel are required to have GFCI protection for personnel. Listed cord sets or devices incorporating listed GFCI protection for personnel identified for portable use were permitted as well.

■ **2017 *NEC* Change**
The phrase "In addition to this required ground-fault circuit-interrupter protection for personnel," was added in front of "listed cord sets or devices incorporating listed ground-fault circuit-interrupter protection for personnel identified for portable use shall be permitted." This added language was to clarify that these portable GFCI cord sets or devices are permitted *in addition to* the GFCI protection required for all 125-volt, single-phase, 15-, 20-, and 30-ampere receptacle outlets that are not a part of the permanent wiring of the building or structure.

Analysis of the Change:

The provisions of 590.6 calls for ground-fault circuit interrupter (GFCI) protection for personnel for all temporary wiring installations. This section applies to temporary wiring installations used by personnel during construction, remodeling, maintenance, repair, or demolition of buildings, structures, equipment, or similar activities. This section also applies regardless if the temporary power is derived from an electric utility company or from an on-site-generated power source.

During the 2011 *NEC* revision cycle, the current structure of 590.6(A) was put in place with the addition of three second-level subdivisions, 590.6(A)(1) for receptacle outlets that are not part of permanent wiring, (A)(2) for receptacle outlets that are existing or installed as permanent wiring, and (A)(3) for receptacle outlets as part of a 15-kW or less portable generator. The reformatting was an effort to provide ease of use and "user-friendliness" to this section. In addition, this reformatting attempted to recognize the use of portable GFCI cord sets or devices and to continue to permit such portable GFCI devices during construction, remodeling, maintenance, repair, or demolition of buildings. The intent was to be able to allow these portable GFCI cord sets in addition to the required GFCI protection at the source of the circuit, not at the end of the circuit with these portable GFCI cord sets alone. On a construction site for temporary power, it is very common to see a cable or cord installed from the source of supply for the temporary branch circuit to a "spider box" or some other splitting device. If the GFCI protection were permitted to be provided at the splitting device rather than at the source, there would be no GFCI protection for the temporary cable leading to the splitting device where damage often occurs. The portable GFCI cord set device cannot be used as a substitute for protecting temporary wiring, thus protecting the worker on the construction site from damaged supply cables.

During this 2011 *NEC* rewrite, the phrase "Listed cord sets or devices incorporating listed ground-fault circuit-interrupter protection for personnel identified for portable use shall be permitted" was incorporated into 590.6(A)(2) and (A)(3), but not at 590.6(A)(1), leaving the erroneous impression that these portable GFCI cord sets could not be used with receptacle outlets that are not part of permanent wiring. In an effort to eradicate this misconception, a proposal and comment were submitted to CMP-3 and accepted to add this same listed cord set phrase to 590.6(A)(1) as was already present at 590.6(A)(2) and (A)(3) (see 2014 ROP 3-107a and ROC 3-38). All seemed right with this section until a literal reading of 590.6(A)(1) appeared to allow the listed cord sets or devices incorporating listed GFCI protection for personnel identified for portable use as a substitute for GFCI protection at the origin of the temporary branch circuit rather than as an additional level of GFCI protection as intended.

On August 14, 2014, a Tentative Interim Amendment (TIA 70-14-6) was issued by the Standards Council for 590.6(A)(1). Once a TIA is issued, it is as enforceable as the *Code* itself, but it is tentative because it has not been processed through the entire standards-making procedures. It is interim because it is effective only between editions of the standard. A TIA automatically becomes a public input of the proponent for the next edition of the standard; as such, it then is subject to all of the procedures of the standards-making process.

For the 2017 *NEC*, the phrase "In addition to this required ground-fault circuit-interrupter protection for personnel," was added in front of "listed cord sets or devices incorporating listed ground-fault circuit-interrupter protection for personnel identified for portable use shall be permitted." This added language mirrors the text added by TIA 70-14-6. This added language makes it clear that these portable GFCI cord sets or devices are permitted *in addition to* the GFCI protection afforded by the GFCI protection required at the origin of the temporary branch circuit.

First Revisions: FR 618
Public Inputs: PI 4827

590.6(A)(1)

Special

Chapter 6 Equipment

Articles 600 – 695

600.4(B)

Signs with a Retrofitted Illumination System

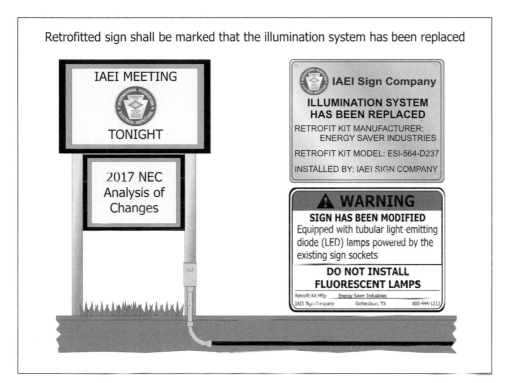

600.4(B) Signs with a Retrofitted Illumination System

- **Type of Change:** New

- **Change at a Glance:** New requirement calls for electric signs that have been retrofitted to be marked to indicate that it is a retrofit kit.

- **Code Language: 600.4 Markings. (Electric Signs and Outline Lighting)**

  (B) Signs with a Retrofitted Illumination System.

  (1) The retrofitted sign shall be marked that the illumination system has been replaced.

  (2) The marking shall include the kit providers and installer's name, logo, or unique identifier.

  (3) Signs equipped with tubular light-emitting diode lamps powered by the existing sign sockets shall require an additional warning label include a label alerting the service personnel that the sign has been modified. The label shall meet the requirements of 110.21(B). The label shall also include a warning not to install fluorescent lamps and shall also be visible during relamping.

600.4

- **2014 *NEC* Requirement**
  Article 100 defines a *Retrofit Kit*. Retrofit kits are required to be listed by the provisions of 600.3. Installation instructions are required by 600.4(E). In 600.12, field-installed secondary circuit wiring for retrofit kits is required to be installed according to the installation instructions. No marking or label is required for a sign with a retrofit kit installed.

- **2017 *NEC* Change**
  A new marking requirement was added to 600.4(B) to indicate that the illumination system has been replaced with a listed retrofit kit.

Analysis of the Change:

A *Retrofit Kit* is defined in Article 100 as "a general term for a complete subassembly of parts and devices for field conversion of utilization equipment." The sign and lighting industries have experienced an extensive movement toward the use of retrofit kits to achieve greater energy efficiency in signs and luminaires by replacing the in-place illumination systems with more energy efficient technology, such as light-emitting diodes (LED). To ensure that the parts are compatible with the field modification, a qualified nationally recognized testing laboratory (NRTL), such as UL, requires all the parts for luminaire and sign conversions to be assembled into a kit that the NRTL evaluates and labels as "Classified."

To that end, existing electric signs that have been retrofitted need to be marked, and the authority having jurisdiction (AHJ) will inspect the retrofit based on the installation instructions provided as part of the kits' listing. The installer and/or serving company needs to be notified that the sign has a retrofitted lighting system as a safety measure for future maintenance activities involving the sign. To greatly assist with these activities, a new marking requirement was added to 600.4 for the 2017 *NEC*.

This new marking requirement for retrofit kits will clarify that replacement of such things as fluorescent lamps is prohibited after a retrofit kit with tubular LEDs has been installed. This type of retrofit will require additional marking to alert service personnel that the sign has been modified. A reference to 110.21(B) will require the label to address the hazard involved with words and/or symbols. It also addresses the location of the required label. These markings must include the kit providers and installer's name, logo, or unique identifier. The installer of the kit needs to be identified since the installation company may not be the manufacturer of the retrofit kit or the original sign. This marking provides the AHJ with a means of identifying the installer of the field conversion.

First Revisions: FR 5135
Second Revisions: SR 5120
Public Inputs: PI 4553
Public Comments: PC 1465, PC 472, PC 399

600.6(A)(1), Ex. No. 2

Disconnects (Electric Signs and Outline Lighting)

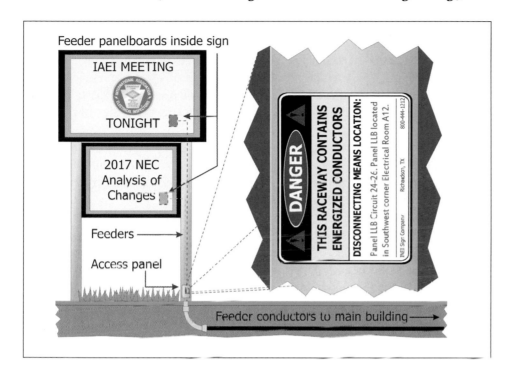

600.6(A)(1)

600.6(A)(1), Ex. No. 2 Disconnects (Electric Signs and Outline Lighting)

- **Type of Change:** New

- **Change at a Glance:** A new exception was added permitting energized conductors (with warning label) in a Chapter 3 raceway or metal-jacketed cable identified for the location to be run through a sign body or enclosure to a feeder panelboard(s) located within the sign body or enclosure.

- **Code Language: 210.6 Branch-Circuit Voltage Limitations**. Each sign and outline lighting system, feeder ~~circuit~~ conductor(s), or branch circuit(s) supplying a sign, outline lighting system, or skeleton tubing shall be controlled by an externally operable switch or circuit breaker that opens all ungrounded conductors and controls no other load. The switch or circuit breaker shall open all ungrounded conductors simultaneously on multi-wire branch circuits in accordance with 210.4(B). Signs and outline lighting systems located within fountains shall have the disconnect located in accordance with ~~680.12~~ 680.13.

  Exception No. 1: A disconnecting means shall not be required for an exit directional sign located within a building.

  Exception No. 2: A disconnecting means shall not be required for cord-connected signs with an attachment plug.

Informational Note: The location of the disconnect is intended to allow service or maintenance personnel complete and local control of the disconnecting means.

(A) Location.
(1) At Point of Entry to a Sign ~~Enclosure~~. The disconnect shall be located at the point the feeder circuit or branch circuit(s) supplying a sign or outline lighting system enters a sign enclosure, a sign body, or a pole in accordance with 600.5(C)(3) ~~and~~. The disconnect shall ~~disconnect~~ open all ~~wiring~~ ungrounded conductors where it enters the enclosure of the sign or pole.

Exception No. 1: *A disconnect shall not be required for branch cir-cuit(s) or feeder ~~circuits~~ conductor(s) passing through the sign where enclosed in a Chapter 3 listed raceway or metal-jacketed cable identified for the location.*

Exception No. 2: *A disconnect shall not be required at the point of entry to a sign enclosure or sign body for branch circuit(s) or feeder conductor(s) that supply an internal panelboard(s) in a sign enclosure or sign body. The conductors shall be enclosed in a Chapter 3 listed race-way or metal-jacketed cable identified for the location. A field-applied permanent warning label that is visible during servicing shall be applied to the raceway at or near the point of entry into the sign enclosure or sign body. The warning label shall comply with 110.21(B) and state the following: "Danger. This raceway contains energized conductors." The marking shall include the location of the disconnecting means for the en-ergized conductor(s). The disconnecting means shall be capable of being locked in the open position in accordance with 110.25.*

■ **2014 *NEC* Requirement**
A new 600.6(A)(1) titled, "At Point of Entry to a Sign Enclosure," was added to this subsection. This addition required the sign disconnect to be located at the point the feeder(s) or branch circuit(s) supplying a sign or outline lighting system enters a sign enclosure or pole. This new 2014 *NEC* provision also required disconnection of all wiring where it entered the enclosure of the sign or pole. The previous provisions for the disconnecting means to be within sight of the sign and the controller were pushed to 600.6(A)(2) and (A)(3) respectively.

■ **2017 *NEC* Change**
A new exception was added to specifically address a sign enclosure or sign body that supplies an internal panelboard(s) in that same sign enclosure or sign body. A field-applied permanent warning label that is visible during servicing is required to be applied to the raceway containing these energized conductors at or near the point of entry into the sign enclosure or sign body complying with 110.21(B). The marking on the warning label must include the location of the disconnecting means for the energized conductor(s), with the disconnecting means being capable of being locked in the open position in accordance with 110.25.

600.6(A)(1)

Analysis of the Change:

It is not uncommon at all in the electrical sign industry to attach or install a sign disconnecting means on a sign body or sign enclosure. It is also common practice and code-compliant to install exposed insulated conductors in sign sections and sign poles. Sections 600.5(C)(3) and 410.30(B) both permit metal or nonmetallic poles to be used as a raceway to enclose supply conductors. Installing these disconnecting means on or at the sign body or enclosure can sometimes create a false sense of security for service personnel. It is easy to assume the disconnect(s) de-energizes all conductors within the sign enclosure once the disconnecting means has been put in the open or "OFF" position.

For the 2014 *NEC*, a new 600.6(A)(1) titled, "At Point of Entry to a Sign Enclosure," was added requiring the sign disconnect to be located at the point the feeder(s) or branch circuit(s) supplying a sign or outline lighting system enters a sign enclosure or pole. An exception to this rule was also added allowing a branch circuit or feeder to pass through a sign where enclosed in a *NEC* Chapter 3 listed raceway allowing the disconnecting means at each section of a large sign. Did this provision go far enough to take into consideration such things as large Las Vegas-type signs that incorporate feeder panelboards inside the sign itself at each separate section of the sign?

To ensure that this is the case, a new Exception No. 2 was added to 600.6(A)(1) for the 2017 *NEC*. This exception specifically addresses a sign enclosure or sign body that supplies an internal panelboard(s) in that same sign enclosure or sign body. As with the existing exception (now Ex. No. 1), the conductors shall be enclosed in a Chapter 3 listed raceway the newly allowed metal-jacketed cable identified for the location. Where this new exception goes beyond the previous exception is a requirement for a "field applied permanent warning label" that is visible during servicing. This warning label is required to be applied to the raceway at or near the point of entry into the sign enclosure or sign body and to comply with 110.21(B). The warning label shall state the following:

"DANGER – THIS RACEWAY CONTAINS ENERGIZED CONDUCTORS"

The marking on the warning label must include the location of the disconnecting means for the energized conductor(s) with this disconnecting means being capable of being locked in the open position in accordance with 110.25.

The provisions at 600.6(A)(1) and the exceptions allow energized circuit conductors in a Chapter 3 raceway to be run through the sign body to a feeder panelboard(s) located within the sign body. This provision is not going to have much effect on the sign in front of the local car wash, but it will have a great effect on extremely large, multi-section signs that are built more like a multi-story building than a conventional sign. These Las Vegas-type signs are typically supplied from feeders originating at the premises service equipment and terminating at these feeder panelboards within the sign. For example, each of these feeders could be rated as much as 800 or 1,200 amperes. Due to the size and location of these signs, it is desirable and/or necessary to control multiple lighting loads at or from within the sign body or enclosure to facilitate servicing of

600.6(A)(1)

the sign. These feeder panelboards are located on different levels (stories) within the sign bodies or enclosures at different sections of the sign. It is impractical to de-energize the entire sign, much the same as it would be impractical to de-energize an entire multi-story building. Service personnel use the circuit breakers in the feeder panelboard(s) as a disconnecting means for branch circuits on the different levels (stories) where they are working.

Electrical safety dictates that these raceways be identified to prevent accidental or deliberate exposure to energized conductors. OSHA 1910.335(b)(1) requires the use of safety signs, safety symbols or accident-prevention tags to warn about potential electrical hazards. Warning labels and markings with similar warning of energized conductors are found in other places in the *Code*, such as 404.6(C) Ex.; 620.52(B); 690.5(C), etc. Equally as important, in the event of an emergency requiring de-energizing the live feeders or branch circuits passing through the sign body, the location of the disconnecting means, which is out of the line of sight and at a location other than the sign, must be known and accessible to service personnel or emergency responders. Providing a field-applied label with the location of the disconnecting means will contribute to electrical safety for service personnel as well as emergency first responders.

600.6(A)(1)

First Revisions: FR 5137
Second Reivisions: SR 5127, SCR 46
Public Inputs: PI 3225, PI 3532, PI 3546, PI 4571
Public Comments: PC 473, PC 757, PC 1230

600.33

Class 2 Sign Illumination Systems, Secondary Wiring

600.33 Class 2 Sign Illumination Systems, Secondary Wiring.

- **Type of Change:** New/Revision

- **Change at a Glance:** The title of 600.33 was changed and the section was expanded to cover all types of Class 2 systems, not just LED lighting systems.

- **Code Language: 600.33 ~~LED~~ Class 2 Sign Illumination Systems, Secondary Wiring.**
  The wiring methods and materials used shall be installed in accordance with the sign manufacturer's installation instructions using any applicable wiring methods from Chapter 3, Wiring Methods, and the requirements for Class 2 circuits contained in ~~Part III of Article 725, as applicable~~ 600.12(C), 600.24, and 600.33(A), (B), (C), and (D).

  (A) Insulation and Sizing of Class 2 Conductors. ~~Listed~~ Class 2 cable listed for the application that complies with Table ~~725.154~~ 600.33(A)(1) or Table 600.33(A)(2) for substitutions shall be installed on the load side of the Class 2 power source. The conductors shall have an ampacity not less than the load to be supplied and shall not be sized smaller than ~~22~~ 18 AWG.

Table 600.33(A)(1) Applications of Power Limited Cable in Signs and Outline Lighting
(See *NEC* and illustrations provided for complete *NEC Code* text)

Table 600.33(A)(2) Class 2 Cable Substitutions
(See *NEC* and illustrations provided for complete *NEC Code* text)

(1) General Use. CL2 or CL3, PLTC, or any listed applicable cable for general use shall be installed within and on buildings or structures.

(2) Other Building Locations. In other locations, any listed applicable cable permitted in 600.33(A)(1), (A)(2), (A)(3), and (A)(4) and Table 600.33(A)(1) and (A)(2) shall be permitted to be used as follows:
(1) CL2P or CL3P — Ducts, plenums, or other spaces used for environmental air
(2) CL2R or CL3R — Vertical shafts and risers
(3) Substitutions from Table 600.33(A)(2)

(3) Wet Locations. Class 2 cable used in a wet location shall be listed and marked ~~identified~~ suitable for use in a wet locations ~~or have a moisture-impervious metal sheath~~.

(4) Other Locations. ~~In other locations, any applicable cable permitted in Table 725.154 shall be permitted to be used~~ Class 2 cable exposed to sunlight shall be listed and marked sunlight resistant suitable for outdoor use.

(B) Installation. Secondary wiring shall be installed in accordance with (B)(1) and (B)(2).

(1) ~~Support~~ Wiring shall be installed and supported in a neat and workmanlike manner. Cables and conductors installed exposed on the surface of ceilings and sidewalls shall be supported by the building structure in such a manner that the cable is not ~~be~~ damaged by normal building use. The cable shall be supported and secured at intervals not exceeding 1.8 m (6 ft). Such cables shall be supported by straps, staples, hangers, cable ties, or similar fittings designed and installed so as not to damage the cable. The installation shall also comply with 300.4(D).

(2) Connections in cable and conductors shall be made with listed insulating devices and be accessible after installation. Where made in a wall, connections shall be enclosed in a listed box.

(C) Protection Against Physical Damage. Where subject to physical damage, the conductors shall be protected and installed in accordance with 300.4.

(D) Grounding and Bonding. Grounding and bonding shall be in accordance with 600.7.

600.33

■ **2014 *NEC* Requirement**
The title of 600.33 was "LED Sign Illumination Systems, Secondary Wiring." This section governed the wiring method and materials for light-emitting diode (LED) type sign systems.

■ **2017 *NEC* Change**
The title of 600.33 was changed to "Class 2 Sign Illumination Systems, Secondary Wiring," and the section was expanded to cover all types of Class 2 lighting systems, not just LED lighting systems.

Analysis of the Change:

As with any other type of electrical system, clear and concise requirements are needed for Class 2 circuits when used for electric signs and outline lighting. During the 2011 *NEC* revision cycle, 600.33 was added to the *Code*. This provided new provisions governing the wiring method and materials for light-emitting diode (LED) type sign systems. At the time, this was much needed and this new section was titled, "LED Sign Illumination Systems, Secondary Wiring." LED lighting systems have become an increasingly popular light source over the past decade or so, but LED technology is not the only Class 2 lighting source.

For the 2017 *NEC*, the title of 600.33 was changed to "Class 2 Sign Illumination Systems, Secondary Wiring," and the section was expanded to cover all types of Class 2 systems, not just LED systems. The previous title and content of this section limited the rules for use of Class 2 to LED systems, thus leaving other light sources powered by Class 2 sources outside the scope of the section. Revisions to Article 411 (Lighting Systems Operating at 30 Volts or Less and Lighting Equipment Connected to Class 2 Power Sources) in the 2014 *NEC* provided the model for the necessary changes to 600.33 by generically referring to "low-voltage lighting and equipment connected to a Class 2 power source" without specifying any particular illumination type such an LED lighting system. This same structure has been applied to sign illumination systems at 600.33 to make it clear that illumination systems other than LED systems with Class 2 circuits are permitted.

The previous provisions of 600.33 required wiring methods and materials to be installed in accordance with the sign manufacturer's installation instructions using any applicable wiring methods from Chapter 3 and the requirements for Class 2 circuits contained in Part III of Article 725. This reference to Part III of Article 725 (Class 2 and Class 3 Circuits) has been removed and replaced with appropriate Article 600 references [600.12(C), 600.24, and 600.33(A), (B), (C), and (D)] as these references now contain relevant *Code* rules for Class 2 electric signs. Section 600.33 now has all the requirements needed for Class 2 secondary wiring and removes the need to refer to Part III of Article 725, which does not refer to specific utilization equipment and does not separate Class 2 and Class 3 wiring methods.

Finally, for the insulation and sizing of Class 2 conductors for secondary wiring of sign illumination systems, the minimum size conductor is not to be sized smaller than 18 AWG (rather than 22 AWG). Typically, Class 2 conductors

600.33

referred to in UL product standards relating to secondary wiring for signs and outline lighting all refer to 18 AWG as the minimum size.

First Revisions: FR 5139
Second Revisions: SR 5124, SR 5123
Public Inputs: PI 4653, PI 4682, PI 4604, PI 3598
Public Comments: PC 1325, PC 1364

Table 600.33(A)(1) and Table 600.33(A)(2)

Signs and Outline Lighting

600.33

Table 600.33(A)(1) Applications of Power Limited Cable in Signs and Outline Lighting
Table 600.33(A)(2) Class 2 Cable Substitutions

- **Type of Change:** New

- **Change at a Glance:** A new table was added detailing the applications of power limited cable in signs and outline lighting and a companion table was added detailing Class 2 cable substitutions.

Table 600.33(A)(1) Applications of Power Limited Cable in Signs and Outline Lighting

Location	CL2	CL3	CL2R	CL3R	CL2P	CL3P	PLTC
Non-concealed spaces inside buildings	Y	Y	Y	Y	Y	Y	Y
Concealed spaces inside buildings that are not used as plenums or risers	Y	Y	Y	Y	Y	Y	Y
Environmental air spaces plenums- or risers	N	N	N	N	Y	Y	N
Wet locations	N	N	N	N	N	N	Y

Y = Permitted. N = Not Permitted.   *Reproduction of NEC Table 600.33(A)(1)*

Table 600.33(A)(2) Class 2 Cable Substitutions

Cable Type	Permitted Substitutions
CL3P	CMP
CL2P	CMP, CL3P
CL3R	CMP, CL3P, CMR
CL2R	CMP, CL3P, CL2P, CMR, CL3R
Cl3	CMP, CL3P, CMR, CL3R, CMG, CM, PLTC
CL2	CMP, CL3P, CL2P, CMR, CL3R, CL2R, CMG CM, PLTC, CL3
CL3X	CMP, CL3P, CMR, CL3R, CMG, CM, PLTC, CL3, CMX
CL2X	CMP, CL3P, CL2P, CMR, CL3R, CL2R, CMG, CM, PLTC, CL3, Cl2, CMX, CL3X

Reproduction of NEC Table 600.33(A)(2)

600.33

■ **Code Language:** **Table 600.33(A)(1) Applications of Power Limited Cable in Signs and Outline Lighting and Table 600.33(A)(2) Class 2 Cable Substitutions**

600.33 ~~LED~~ **Class 2 Sign Illumination Systems, Secondary Wiring.** The wiring methods and materials used shall be installed in accordance with the sign manufacturer's installation instructions using any applicable wiring methods from Chapter 3, Wiring Methods, and the requirements for Class 2 circuits contained in ~~Part III of Article 725, as applicable~~ 600.12(C), 600.24, and 600.33(A), (B), (C), and (D).

(A) Insulation and Sizing of Class 2 Conductors. ~~Listed~~ Class 2 cable listed for the application that complies with Table ~~725.154~~ 600.33(A)(1) or Table 600.33(A)(2) for substitutions shall be installed on the load side of the Class 2 power source. The conductors shall have an ampacity not less than the load to be supplied and shall not be sized smaller than ~~22~~ 18 AWG.

Table 600.33(A)(1) Applications of Power Limited Cable in Signs and Outline Lighting
(See *NEC* and illustrations provided for complete *NEC Code* text)

Table 600.33(A)(2) Class 2 Cable Substitutions
(See *NEC* and illustrations provided for complete *NEC Code* text)

- **2014 *NEC* Requirement**
  Listed Class 2 cable that complied with Table 725.154 was required to be installed on the load side of the Class 2 power source.

- **2017 *NEC* Change**
  Two new tables were added to 600.33(A). Table 600.33(A)(1) provides a list of acceptable Class 2 cables listed for the application in signs and outline lighting. Table 600.33(A)(2) provides a list of permitted cable substitutions in these sign applications.

600.33

Analysis of the Change:

Two new tables were added to 600.33(A) for the 2017 *NEC*. Table 600.33(A)(1) titled, "Applications of Power Limited Cable in Signs and Outline Lighting," details the requirements for Class 2 circuits listed for the application in signs and outline lighting. Table 600.33(A)(2) titled, "Class 2 Cable Substitutions," provides directions for ascertaining permitted cable substitutions in these sign applications.

The previous language at 600.33(A) referred to Table 725.154 "Applications of Listed Class 2, Class 3, and PLTC Cables in Buildings" and required that "listed Class 2 cable that complies with Table 725.154 shall be installed on the load side of the Class 2 power source." The permitted Class 2 cables for electric signs 600 not readily identifiable in Table 725.154, making it difficult or impossible to determine the permitted cable types for Class 2 sign wiring. Having this new Table 600.33(A)(1) located in Article 600 solves the difficulty and uncertainty of searching a table in Article 725 that does not incorporate a specific reference to types of power limited cable for signs. The locations and primary listed cable types found in new Table 600.33(A)(1) were extracted from Article 725 and UL's *Guide Information for Electrical Equipment* (*UL White Book*) under the category Power-Limited Circuit Cable (QPTZ).

New Table 600.33(A)(2) provides the necessary information and directions for ascertaining permitted cable substitutions. In addition to referencing new Tables 600.33(A)(1) and 600.33(A)(2), the text revision in 600.33(A) facilitates the use of Class 2 conductors that are acceptable for use in listed electric signs.

The conditions of use will be contained in UL's *Sign Component Manual* and in the sign installation instructions furnished with the Class 2 wired sign.

First Revisions: FR 5139
Second Revisions: SR 5124
Public Inputs: PI 3600
Public Comments: PC 1325, PC 1364

600.34, 600.2
Photovoltaic (PV) Powered Signs

600.34

600.34, 600.2 Photovoltaic (PV) Powered Sign

- **Type of Change:** New

- **Change at a Glance:** A new definition for *Photovoltaic (PV Powered) Sign* was added to 600.2 and new provisions for PV powered signs were added to Article 600 at 600.34.

- **Code Language:** **600.34 Photovoltaic (PV) Powered Sign. (Electric Signs and Outline Lighting)**

  600.2 Definitions.
  Photovoltaic (PV) Powered Sign. A complete sign powered by solar energy consisting of all components and subassemblies for installation either as an off-grid stand-alone, on-grid interactive, or non-grid interactive system.

600.34 Photovoltaic (PV) Powered Sign. All field wiring of components and subassemblies for an off-grid stand-alone, on-grid interactive, or non-grid interactive PV installation shall be installed in accordance with Article 690, as applicable, 600.34, and the PV powered sign installation instructions.

(A) Equipment. Inverters, motor generators, PV modules, PV panels, ac PV modules, dc combiners, dc-ac converters, and charge controllers intended for use in PV powered sign systems shall be listed for PV application.

(B) Wiring. Wiring from a photovoltaic panel or wiring external to the PV sign body shall be:
(1) Listed, labeled, and suitable for photovoltaic applications
(2) Routed to closely follow the sign body or enclosure
(3) As short as possible and secured at intervals not exceeding 0.91 m (3 ft)
(4) Protected where subject to physical damage

(C) Flexible Cords and Cables. Flexible cords and cables shall comply with Article 400 and be identified as extra hard usage, rated for outdoor use, and water and sunlight resistant.

(D) Grounding. Grounding a PV powered sign shall comply with Article 690, Part V and 600.7.

(E) Disconnecting Means. The disconnecting means for a PV powered sign shall comply with Article 690, Part III and 600.6.

(F) Battery Compartments. Battery compartments shall require a tool to open.

■ **2014 *NEC* Requirement**
There were no provisions in Article 600 for PV powered signs.

■ **2017 *NEC* Change**
Along with this new definition for a *Photovoltaic (PV Powered) Sign*, a new 600.34 titled "Photovoltaic (PV Powered) Sign," was added to Article 600 covering field wiring and installation of PV powered signs.

Analysis of the Change:
A Photovoltaic (PV) System is defined in Article 100 as "the total components and subsystem that, in combination, convert solar energy into electric energy suitable for connection to a utilization load." The installation rules for a PV system are found in Article 690. The sign and the PV industry are starting to see more and more PV powered signs. These PV powered signs are a special application of PV equipment that is described and covered by UL 48 (*Standard for Electric Signs*), specifically Section 4.4.4.12. With requirements for these PV powered signs located in Article 600, a new 600.34 was added for the 2017 *NEC* pertaining to field wiring and installations of PV powered signs.

600.34

In conjunction with these new requirements for PV powered signs, a new definition for a Photovoltaic (PV Powered) Sign was added to 600.2 in Article 600. This new definition provides the basis for new 600.34 with field wiring rules for installation and electrically safe usage. Signs powered by a PV system will require special installation instructions and a new 600.34 will provide these installation instructions in addition to the appropriate application rules of Article 690.

Along with this new definition, a new 600.34, Photovoltaic (PV Powered) Sign, was added to Article 600 covering field wiring and installation of PV powered signs. PV powered signs listed to UL 48 are to be used in accordance with *Code* requirements relative to general PV usage in Article 690 and specific rules for PV powered sign installations are covered in UL 48. The rules in 600.34 are intended to harmonize with Article 600, Article 690, and the end use of PV powered signs constructed in accordance with UL 48. Self-contained, stand-alone PV powered signs operating at or below Class 2 voltages are considered safe from electrical shock the same as any other Class 2 circuits (see 725.2 for a definition of Class 2 circuits). UL 48 does not require bonding or grounding for self-contained off-grid PV powered signs operating within the limits of Class 2 voltages. A self-contained off-grid PV powered sign having the photovoltaic panel as part of the sign housing and having all circuits operating at 30-volt dc or less is not required to be grounded or to comply with the bonding requirements [see 600.7(B)(1) Exception and UL 48. 4.4.12.19].

600.34

First Revisions: FR 5133, FR 5145
Second Revisions: SR 5122, SR 5121
Public Inputs: PI 1574, PI 3607
Public Comments: PC 474, PC 475

605.9(C)

Freestanding-Type Office Furnishings, Cord- and Plug-Connected

An individual office furnishing or groups of interconnected individual office furnishings shall not contain more than (13) 15-ampere, 125-volt receptacles

For purposes of this requirement, a receptacle is considered:
(1) Up to two (simplex) receptacles provided within a single enclosure and that are within 0.3 m (1 ft) of each other or...
(2) One duplex receptacle

605.9(C)

605.9(C) Freestanding-Type Office Furnishings, Cord- and Plug-Connected

- **Type of Change:** Revision

- **Change at a Glance:** Revision clarifies that thirteen duplex receptacles are the maximum number of receptacles permitted in office furnishings.

- **Code Language: 605.9 Freestanding-Type Office Furnishings, Cord- and Plug-Connected.**
  Individual office furnishings of the freestanding type, or groups of individual office furnishings that are electrically connected, are mechanically contiguous, and do not exceed 9.0 m (30 ft) when assembled, shall be permitted to be connected to the building electrical system by a single flexible cord and plug, provided that all of the conditions of 605.9(A) through (D) are met.

  (C) Receptacle ~~Outlets~~, Maximum. An individual office furnishing or groups of interconnected individual office furnishings shall not contain more than 13 15-ampere, 125-volt ~~receptacle outlets~~ receptacles. For purposes of this requirement, a receptacle is considered (1) up to two (simplex) receptacles provided within a single enclosure and that are within 0.3 m (1 ft) of each other or (2) one duplex receptacle.

- **2014** *NEC* **Requirement**
  An individual office furnishing or groups of interconnected individual office furnishings cannot contain more than thirteen 15-ampere, 125-volt receptacle outlets. Receptacle outlets can have "one or more receptacles installed."

- **2017** *NEC* **Change**
  An individual office furnishing or groups of interconnected individual office furnishings now cannot contain more than thirteen 15-ampere, 125-volt receptacles. For purposes of this requirement, a receptacle is considered up to two (simplex) receptacles provided within a single enclosure and that are within 0.3 m (1 ft) of each other, or one duplex receptacle.

Analysis of the Change:

Article 605 of the *NEC* covers "Office Furnishings." This coverage includes electrical equipment, lighting accessories, and wiring systems used to connect, contained within, or installed on office furnishings. *Office furnishings* are defined at 605.2 as "cubicle panels, partitions, study carrels, workstations, desks, shelving systems, and storage units that may be mechanically and electrically interconnected to form an office furnishing system."

The previous requirements located at 605.9(C) required that an individual office furnishing or groups of interconnected individual office furnishings not contain more than thirteen 15-ampere, 125-volt receptacle outlets. Article 100 defines a *receptacle outlet* is "an outlet where one or more receptacles are installed." So, how many individual contact device points can be installed at an office furnishing outlet for the connection of an attachment plug and maintain *Code* compliance? A literal reading of this *Code* requirement, along with a little math would reveal that receptacle outlets in the quadruplex configuration could involve as many as fifty-two individual contact points for the connection of an attachment plug at any one office furnishing.

This limitation of thirteen 15-ampere, 125-volt receptacle outlets at any one individual office furnishing has been in the *NEC* since Article 605 was introduced into the *Code* in the 1984 edition of the *NEC*. Looking back at that 1984 expansion reveals no explanation as to why "thirteen" became the magic number for the maximum number of receptacle outlets. One would suspect that this number was chosen based on the "not less than 90 volt-amperes per receptacle" requirement of 220.14(I) when it comes to calculating the minimum load for each outlet for general-use receptacles. If that is the case, 52 individual receptacle contact points would seem to be excessive when meeting the intent of this *Code* rule.

For clarification, a couple of changes were instituted at 605.9(C) for the 2017 *NEC*. First, the term *receptacle outlets* was changed to *receptacles*. This change moves the requirement away from the defined term of *receptacle outlet* where

605.9(C)

"one or more receptacles" can be installed. A new last sentence states that "For purposes of this requirement, a receptacle is considered (1) up to two (simplex) receptacles provided within a single enclosure and that are within 0.3 m (1 ft) of each other or (2) one duplex receptacle."

This change clarifies that twenty-six individual 15-ampere, 125-volt contact points (receptacles) is the maximum number of receptacles that can be installed at any individual office furnishing or groups of interconnected individual office furnishings. It also brings specific guidance to the maximum number of receptacles permitted in office furnishings.

First Revisions: FR 5131
Public Inputs: PI 4058

610.42(B)(3)
Branch-Circuit Short-Circuit and Ground-Fault Protection for Cranes and Hoists

610.42(B)(3)

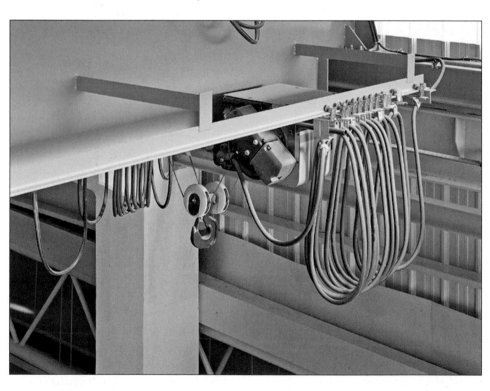

610.42(B)(3) Branch-Circuit Short-Circuit and Ground-Fault Protection. (Cranes and Hoists)

- **Type of Change:** Deletion

- **Change at a Glance:** Brake coils—branch circuit taps—have been deleted for cranes and hoists.

- **Code Language: 610.42 Branch-Circuit Short-Circuit and Ground-Fault Protection. (Cranes and Hoists)**
  Branch circuits shall be protected in accordance with 610.42(A). Branch-circuit taps, where made, shall comply with 610.42(B).

  (B) Taps.

  (1) Multiple Motors. Where two or more motors are connected to the same branch circuit, each tap conductor to an individual motor shall have an ampacity not less than one-third that of the branch circuit. Each motor shall be protected from overload according to 610.43.

  (2) Control Circuits. Where taps to control circuits originate on the load side of a branch-circuit protective device, each tap and piece of equipment shall be protected in accordance with 430.72.

  (3) Brake Coils. Taps without separate overcurrent protection shall be permitted to brake coils.

- **2014 *NEC* Requirement**
  Where two or more motors are connected to the same branch circuit, each tap conductor to an individual motor is required to have individual overcurrent protection. Where taps to control circuits originate on the load side of a branch-circuit protective device, each tap and piece of equipment is required to have overcurrent protection. Brake coil taps were permitted for cranes or hoists without separate overcurrent protection.

- **2017 *NEC* Change**
  Brake coil taps for cranes or hoists without separate overcurrent protection have been deleted.

610.42(B)(3)

Analysis of the Change:

Brake coils for cranes or hoists are passive devices designed to resist changes in current and to store energy in the form of a magnetic field. In their simplest form, they consist of a wire loop or coil. The inductance is directly proportional to the number of turns in the coil. Inductance also depends on the radius of the coil and on the type of material around which the coil is wound.

Previous language at 610.42(B)(3) permitted taps to crane or hoist brake coils without separate overcurrent protection. This provision has been deleted for the 2017 *NEC* as taps to brake coils should follow the same tap rules as every other installation. Traditionally, crane or hoist brakes were tapped from the motor leads with relatively short conductors, which was the genesis of this brake coil provision. However, with the advent of variable frequency drives and other electronic controls, typically a longer conductor is run between the control cabinet and the brake coil on most newly-installed cranes or hoist.

The risk of fire and more severe damage for new applications goes beyond the original intent of the previous *Code* language and warrants elimination of this brake coil provision. This elimination presents a hazard not only to the brake conductors but the other control and power conductors from the crane power bar electrification systems to the hoist (typically called a festoon in the crane and hoist industry).

First Revisions: FR 3303
Public Inputs: PI 3862

620.16

Short-Circuit Current Rating (Elevators, etc.)

Elevator control panel required to be marked with its short-circuit current rating and shall not be installed where the available short-circuit current exceeds its short-circuit current rating

Short-circuit current rating to be based on listing of assembly or established utilizing an approved method *(such as UL 508A)*

620.16 Short-Circuit Current Rating. (Elevators, Etc.)

- **Type of Change:** New

- **Change at a Glance:** Elevator control panels are required to be marked with a short-circuit current rating and shall not be installed where the available short-circuit current exceeds the marked short-circuit current rating.

- **Code Language:** 620.16 Short-Circuit Current Rating. (Elevators, Etc.)

  (A) Marking. Where an elevator control panel is installed, it shall be marked with its short-circuit current rating, based on one of the following:

(1) Short-circuit current rating of a listed assembly

(2) Short-circuit current rating established utilizing an approved method

Informational Note: UL 508A-2013, Supplement SB, is an example of an approved method.

(B) Installation. The elevator control panel shall not be installed where the available short-circuit current exceeds its short-circuit current rating, as marked in accordance with 620.16(A).

- **2014 *NEC* Requirement**
  There were no provisions in Article 620 pertaining to the short-circuit current rating or the available short-circuit current for elevators, dumbwaiters, escalators, moving walks, platform lifts, or stairway chairlifts.

- **2017 *NEC* Change**
  New short-circuit current rating marking requirements and installation restrictions for elevator control panels were added at 620.16.

620.16

Analysis of the Change:

A new marking requirement for short-circuit current ratings on elevator control panels was incorporated into 620.16 for the 2017 *NEC*. This new requirement also prohibits an elevator control panel from being installed where the available short-circuit current exceeds its short-circuit current rating. Elevator control panels are being misapplied in a large number of applications due to an inadequate short-circuit current rating for the equipment. These elevator control panels are often installed without being marked with a short-circuit current rating at all.

This new requirement establishes that the short-circuit current rating must be marked on the elevator control panel and that this short-circuit current rating is determined by its listing process or by an "approved method." An informational note was also added identifying UL 508A-2013 (*Standard for Industrial Control Panels*), Supplement SB, as an example of an approved method.

While the individual controllers within the elevator control panel often have their individual short-circuit current ratings marked on them (such as a motor controller marked per 430.8), the short-circuit current ratings can be almost impossible to read from outside the elevator control panel enclosure. Even if the short-circuit current rating of individual controllers can be read from outside the control panel, the short-circuit current rating for the entire elevator control panel takes into account more than just the ratings of the individual controllers. The short-circuit current rating marking requirement of 620.16(A) is patterned after other similar requirements in the *Code* such as 409.110(4), 440.4(B), and 670.3(A)(4). This new requirement will aid the AHJ greatly in determining whether the elevator control panel equipment is adequate for the available short-circuit current.

Marking the elevator control panel with its short-circuit current rating alone is not enough. The elevator control panel must also be used only within that marked short-circuit current rating. The new requirements of 620.16(B), which are similar to 409.22 and 670.5, increase electrical safety by ensuring that the elevator control panel is not installed where the available short-circuit current exceeds its short-circuit current rating.

First Revisions: FR 3331
Second Revisions: SR 3330
Public Inputs: PI 3842
Public Comments: PC 1840, PC 1304

Article 625

Electric Vehicle Charging System

Article 625

Article 625 Electric Vehicle Charging System

- **Type of Change:** Revision

- **Change at a Glance:** Article 625, Electric Vehicle Charging Systems, was reorganized

- **Code Language:** **Article 625 Electric Vehicle Charging System**
  I. General
  625.1 Scope.

625.2 Definitions.

625.4 Voltages.

625.5 Listed.
II. Equipment Construction
625.10 Electric Vehicle Coupler.
(A) Polarization.
(B) Noninterchangeability.
(A) Construction and Installation.
(B) Unintentional Disconnection.
(C) Grounding Pole.
(D) Grounding Pole Requirements.

625.15 Markings.
(A) General.
(B) Ventilation Not Required.
(C) Ventilation Required.

625.16 Means of Coupling.

Article 625

625.17 Cords and Cables.
(A) Power-Supply Cord.
(B) Output Cable
(1) Output Cable to the Electric Vehicle.
(2) Output Cable to the Primary Pad.
(C) Overall Cord and Cable Length.
(1) Not Fastened in Place
(2) Fastened in Place

625.18 Interlock.
625.19 Automatic De-Energization of Cable.
625.22 Personnel Protection System.

III. Installation
625.40 Electric Vehicle Branch Circuit
625.41 Overcurrent Protection.
625.42 Rating.
625.43 Disconnecting Means.

625.44 Electric Vehicle Supply Equipment Connection.
(A) Connections to 125-Volt, Single-Phase, 15- and 20-Ampere Receptacle Outlets Portable Equipment.
(B) Connections to Other Receptacle Outlets Stationary Equipment.
(C) Fixed Equipment.

625.46 Loss of Primary Source.
625.48 Interactive Systems.
625.50 Location.

625.52 Ventilation.
(A) Ventilation Not Required.
(B) Ventilation Required.
(1) Table Values.
Table 625.52(B)(1)(a) Minimum Ventilation Required in Cubic Meters per Minute (m3/min) for Each of the Total Number of Electric Vehicles That Can Be Charged at One Time

Table 625.52(B)(2)(1)(b) Minimum Ventilation Required in Cubic Feet per Minute (cfm) for Each of the Total Number of Electric Vehicles That Can Be Charged at One Time

(2) Other Values.
(3) Engineered Systems.
(4) Supply Circuits.

Part IV. Wireless Power Transfer Equipment
625.101 Grounding.

625.102 Construction.
(A) Type.
(B) Installation.
(C) Primary Pad.
(D) Protection of the Output Cable.
(E) Other Wiring Systems.
(See *NEC* for complete text)

■ **2014 *NEC* Requirement**
The requirements for Electric Vehicle Charging Systems were located in Article 625.

■ **2017 *NEC* Change**
Article 625 for Electric Vehicle Charging Systems was reformatted with provisions for wireless power transfer equipment being incorporated into the article.

Analysis of the Change:
Beginning with the 1996 edition, the *NEC* has included Article 625 for Electric Vehicle Charging Systems. This article has experienced extensive growth and change over the past twenty years since its inception. The 2017 *NEC* was no exception as far as revisions go. Wireless charging technology, as well as other changes, were incorporated into Article 625 for the 2017 edition of the *NEC*. The term *wireless power transfer* (*contactless inductive charging*) was added to the scope of Article 625 to address the use of this new technology.

Article 625

Some of the highlighted revisions to Article 625 include the deletion of requirements about polarization and non-interchangeability of EV couplers. Polarization is important for EV connectors and inlets so that they cannot be mated in any way that would allow the power contacts to mate with other contacts, thereby creating a potential hazard. Polarization is a construction feature that is evaluated as part of the product standard and involves a specific polarization test in UL 2251 (*Standard for Plugs, Receptacles, and Couplers for Electric Vehicles*). The pin configuration on this type of connector is not required to be marked to indicate which contact is associated with which circuit (power, pilot, communication, or ground). As this is a feature associated with a given configuration, it does not lend itself to easy verification or practical enforcement in the field. With this in mind, this deletion allows the listing of the equipment to verify these two coupler aspects as part of a listed system as required by 625.5.

A new provision was added at 625.40 calling for each outlet installed for the purpose of charging electric vehicles to be supplied by an individual branch circuit with no other outlets. This provision was a relocation of this EV branch circuit requirement from 210.17, as this requirement is better suited for a location within Article 625.

Requirements for equipment connection located at 625.44 were revised to facilitate provisions for a parallel construction method for portable, stationary, and fixed equipment. The overall intent of this revision is to establish requirements for the connection to the supply system for electric vehicle supply equipment. The previous wording at 625.44 was confusing and led to inconsistencies when one attempted to apply the requirements to electric vehicle supply equipment products.

Finally, a new Part IV entitled, "Wireless Power Transfer Equipment," was added to Article 625. Two new definitions, *Wireless Power Transfer (WPT)* and *Wireless Power Transfer Equipment (WPTE)* were added at 625.2. The technology behind wireless EV charging creates a connection between a *transmitting pad* on ground level (such as a garage floor) and a *receiving pad* integrated on the bottom of the electric vehicle. Wireless charging is viewed as an important technological evolution that help advance EV adoption due to its convenience and ease of use. Since it is automatic, EV charging is not as likely to be subject to "I forgot to charge my EV!" Wireless charging systems connect to the premises wiring like conductive systems; but unlike conductive or inductive, there is no physical connection to the vehicle. Instead, energy is safely transferred from the grid side to the vehicle through an alternating magnetic field.

> First Revisions: FR 3359-81, FR 3410-13, FCR 143
> Second Revisions: SR 3337, SR 3348
> Public Inputs: PI 1478, PI 3398
> Public Comments: Numerous PIs and PCs

Article 625

625.2

Electric Vehicle Charging System

625.2

625.2 Definitions. (Electric Vehicle Charging System)

- **Type of Change:** New

- **Change at a Glance:** Two new definitions were added: *Wireless Power Transfer (WPT)* and *Wireless Power Transfer Equipment (WPTE)*.

- **Code Language: 625.2 Definitions. (Electric Vehicle Charging System)**

  Wireless Power Transfer (WPT). The transfer of electrical energy from a power source to an electrical load via electric and magnetic fields or waves by a contactless inductive means between a primary and a secondary device.

  Wireless Power Transfer Equipment (WPTE). Equipment consisting of a charger power converter and a primary pad. The two devices are either separate units or contained within one enclosure.

- **2014 *NEC* Requirement**
  There were no requirements in Article 625 for wireless charging of electric vehicles.

■ **2017 *NEC* Change**

Two new definitions, *Wireless Power Transfer (WPT)* and *Wireless Power Transfer Equipment (WPTE)*, were added at 625.2 as well as a new Part IV of Article 625 entitled, "Wireless Power Transfer Equipment."

Analysis of the Change:

In anticipation of a growing trend in the charging of electric vehicles (EV), two new definitions were added to Article 625 for the 2017 *NEC*. Due to developing technologies, the definition of *Wireless Power Transfer (WPT)* and *Wireless Power Transfer Equipment (WPTE)* were added at 625.2 to cover upcoming charging systems. These definitions are derived from the terminology set forth in a Society of Automotive Engineers (SAE) standard, SAE J2954.

This standard, *Wireless Charging of Electric and Plug-in Hybrid Vehicles,* establishes minimum performance and safety criteria for wireless charging of electric and plug-in hybrid vehicles. This SAE International standard creates a technology matrix to evaluate multiple wireless charging technologies (inductive, magnetic resonance, etc.), identifiable charging locations such as residential or on-road (parking lot, roadway) locations, as well as Levels 1, 2, and 3 wireless charging stations.

Wireless charging of electric vehicles offers the advantage of charging without having to physically connect the electric vehicle to the electrical system. The new definitions support the new requirements added in the newly established Part IV of Article 625 titled, "Wireless Power Transfer Equipment."

625.2

First Revisions: FR 3413
Second Revisions: SR 3340
Public Comments: PC 1297

625.10

Electric Vehicle Coupler

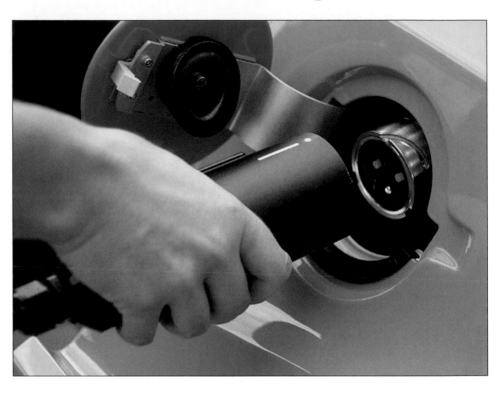

625.10 Electric Vehicle Coupler

- **Type of Change:** Deletion

- **Change at a Glance:** Provisions for polarization and non-interchange-ability of electric vehicle couplers were deleted.

- **Code Language: 625.10 Electric Vehicle Coupler.**
  The electric vehicle coupler shall comply with 625.10(A) through ~~(F)~~(D).

  ~~(A) Polarization. The electric vehicle coupler shall be polarized.~~
  ~~*Exception: A coupler that is part of a listed electric vehicle supply equipment.*~~

  ~~*(B) Noninterchangeability.* The electric vehicle coupler shall have a configuration that is noninterchangeable with wiring devices in other electrical systems. Nongroundingtype electric vehicle couplers shall not be interchangeable with grounding-type electric vehicle couplers.~~

  ~~(C)~~(A) Construction and Installation. The electric vehicle coupler shall be constructed and installed so as to guard against inadvertent contact by persons with parts made live from the electric vehicle supply equipment or the electric vehicle battery.

(D)(B) Unintentional Disconnection. The electric vehicle coupler shall be provided with a positive means to prevent unintentional disconnection.

(E)(C) Grounding Pole. The electric vehicle coupler shall be provided with a grounding pole, unless provided as part of a listed isolated electric vehicle supply equipment system.

(F)(D) Grounding Pole Requirements. If a grounding pole is provided, the electric vehicle coupler shall be so designed that the grounding pole connection is the first to make and the last to break contact.

■ **2014 *NEC* Requirement**
Electric vehicle couplers were required to comply with 625.10(A) through (F). This list included polarization requirements, non-interchangeability of electric vehicle couplers, construction and installation requirements. Provisions were provided to prevent unintentional disconnection and grounding pole requirements.

■ **2017 *NEC* Change**
The provisions for polarization and non-interchangeability of electric vehicle couplers were deleted for the 2017 *NEC* as this is a design issue addressed by the listing of the product.

625.10

Analysis of the Change:

An *electric vehicle coupler* is defined at 625.2 as "a mating electric vehicle inlet and electric vehicle connector set." Detailed provisions for an electric vehicle coupler are found at 625.10. An electric vehicle coupler connector with cable is designed to deliver a reliable interface for providing a charge to an electric vehicle. Electric vehicle couplers are built to UL Product Standard 2251 (*Standard for Safety of Plugs, Receptacles and Couplers for Electric Vehicles*) and comply with the Society of Automotive Engineers Standard SAE J1772 (*Electric Vehicle and Plug-in Hybrid Electric Vehicle Conductive Charge Coupler*).

A revision to 625.10 for the 2017 *NEC* included the deletion of requirements about polarization and non-interchangeability of EV couplers. Polarization is important for EV connectors and inlets so that they cannot be mated in any way that would allow the power contacts to mate with other contacts, thereby creating a potential hazard. This EV connector is a construction feature that is evaluated as part of the product standard and involves a specific polarization test in UL 2251. The pin configuration on this type of connector is not required to be marked to indicate which contact is associated with which circuit (power, pilot, communication, or ground). As this is a feature associated with a given configuration, it does not lend itself to easy verification or practical enforcement in the field.

Non-interchangeability of EV couplers is likewise associated with a given configuration and evaluated as part of the requirements of UL 2251. The ability or inability of these couplers to mate with other systems also does not lend itself to practical enforcement. With this in mind, this deletion allows the listing of the equipment to verify these two coupler aspects as part of a listed system, which is required by 625.5.

First Revisions: FR 3366
Public Inputs: PI 3937

Article 625, Part IV

Wireless Power Transfer Equipment

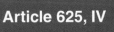

Photo courtesy of Oak Ridge National Laboratory

Researchers from Oak Ridge National Laboratory test a wireless charger on the fully-electric Toyota Scion iQ at a demonstration site.

Article 625, Part IV Wireless Power Transfer Equipment (Electric Vehicle Charging System)

- **Type of Change:** New

- **Change at a Glance:** New Part IV entitled, "Wireless Power Transfer Equipment," was added to Article 625.

- **Code Language:** **Part IV. Wireless Power Transfer Equipment (Electric Vehicle Charging System)**
  625.101 Grounding.

625.102 Construction.
(A) Type.
(B) Installation.
(C) Primary Pad.
(D) Protection of the Output Cable.
(E) Other Wiring Systems.
(See *NEC* for complete text)

- **2014 *NEC* Requirement**
  There were no requirements in Article 625 for wireless charging of electric vehicles.

- **2017 *NEC* Change**
  A new Part IV of Article 625 entitled, "Wireless Power Transfer Equipment" was added to Article 625, as well as two new definitions, *Wireless Power Transfer (WPT)* and *Wireless Power Transfer Equipment (WPTE)* were added at 625.2.

Analysis of the Change:
What if charging an electric vehicle (EV) was as easy as parking it! No need for cords or couplers. Just as Wi-Fi has freed consumers of wired devices when accessing the Internet, wireless EV charging technology may soon be as wide-spread. In anticipation of this wireless technology, a new Part IV of Article 625 was created for the 2017 *NEC* entitled, "Wireless Power Transfer Equipment."

The technology behind wireless EV charging creates a connection between a transmitting pad on ground level (such as a garage floor) and a receiving pad integrated on the bottom of the electric vehicle. The transmitting pad on the ground level is connected to a 240-volt source and generates a magnetic field of a certain frequency. When the coil in the EV receiving pad is tuned to oscillate at the same frequency, the magnetic field will generate a current in the receiving coil, charging the vehicle's battery.

New Part IV of Article 625 consists of two sections. New 625.101 includes requirements for grounding the non-ferrous metal primary pad base plate unless the listed wireless power transfer equipment employs a double-insulation system. The creation of new 625.102 provides construction requirements that are to be provided during the installation of wireless power transfer equipment.

First Revisions: FR 3378
Second Revisions: SR 3348
Public Inputs: PI 1346
Public Comments: PC 759, PC 760

Article 625, IV

645.3(B)

Information Technology Equipment

Other article and section references applying to wiring and cabling in plenums above an IT equipment rooms have been reformatted into a list format with appropriate titles added at each *Code* reference

The title was changed from "Plenums" to "Wiring and Cabling in Other Spaces Used for Environmental Air (Plenums)"

Environmental air space (plenum) above an IT equipment room

Return air   Ceiling above an IT equipment room

645.3(B)

645.3(B) Other Articles. (Information Technology Equipment)

- **Type of Change:** Revision

- **Change at a Glance:** References to other articles and sections applying to wiring and cabling in plenums above an IT equipment room were converted into a list format.

- **Code Language: 645.3 Other Articles. (Information Technology Equipment)**
  Circuits and equipment shall comply with 645.3(A) through ~~(G)~~(I), as applicable.

  (B) Wiring and Cabling in Other Spaces Used for Environmental Air (Plenums). The following sections and tables shall apply to wiring and cabling in a plenum other spaces used for environmental air (plenums) above an information technology equipment room:
  (1) Wiring methods: 300.22(C)(1)
  (2) Class 2, Class 3, and PLTC cables: 725.135(C) and Table 725.154
  (3) Fire alarm systems: 760.53(B)(2), 725.135(C) 760.135(C), and Table 760.154
  (4) Optical fiber cables: 770.113(C), and Table 770.154(a)
  (5) Communications circuits: 820.113(C) 800.113(C) and Table 800.154(a), (b), and (c)
  (6) CATV and radio distribution systems: 820.113(C) and Table 820.154(a)

■ **2014 *NEC* Requirement**
Wiring and cabling in a plenum above an information technology (IT)
equipment room had to comply with a list of other articles and sections
elsewhere in the *Code* other than the requirements of Article 645. This list
of twelve other *Code* references was identified at 645.3(B) in a long single
sentence.

■ **2017 *NEC* Change**
The information about other articles and sections applying to wiring and
cabling in plenums above an IT equipment room has been reformatted
into a list format with appropriate titles added at each *Code* reference. The
title of 645.3(B) was changed from "Plenums" to "Wiring and Cabling in
Other Spaces Used for Environmental Air (Plenums)."

Analysis of the Change:

Article 645 covers equipment, power-supply wiring, equipment interconnecting
wiring, and grounding of information technology (IT) equipment and systems
in an IT equipment room. Wiring methods in IT equipment rooms are allowed
to be installed and maintained per the requirements of Article 645 as long as
the room meets all the requirements of 645.4. To allow for quick and relatively easy interchange of wiring methods under raised floors in an IT equipment
room, some of the wiring method requirements (securing and supporting, etc.)
in Article 645 are not as stringent as in *NEC* Chapters 1–4. Because of these less
restrictive requirements in Article 645 for IT equipment rooms, all the requirements of 645.4 must be met for the room to be classified as an IT equipment
room.

645.3(B)

Other *NEC* articles that need to be applied to IT equipment rooms for specific conditions are addressed at 645.3. Some of these special conditions are fire
alarm circuits, communication circuits, and wiring in other spaces used for
environmental air (plenums) above an IT equipment room. The information at
645.3(B), simply titled "Plenums" in previous editions of the *Code*, was displayed in a single sentence with numerous *Code* references. This information
has been reformatted into a list format for the 2017 *NEC* with appropriate titles
added with each *Code* reference. The title of 645.3(B) was changed to "Wiring
and Cabling in Other Spaces Used for Environmental Air (Plenums)" to utilize
proper terminology for plenums and to correlate with other *Code* language such
as 300.22(C).

Conversion into a numbered list format improves both usability and readability
for this section. The revised text also corrects some of the *Code* references to
the plenum requirements in Articles 725, 760 and 820 due to changes that have
occurred in these articles.

First Revisions: FR 3341
Second Revisions: SR 3309
Public Inputs: PI 30, PI 526, PI 822
Public Comments: PC 45, PC 1837

645.5(E)

Wiring Methods and Cables Under a Raised Floor

Requirements for installing wiring methods and cables under a raised floor in an IT equipment room have been revised into a list format for clarity

Previous Table 645.5(E)(6) was deleted as it contained conflicting information about permitted cable types permitted under a raised floor and is no longer needed

Information technology equipment (typical) ⟶

645.5(E)

645.5(E) Supply Circuits and Interconnecting Cables. (Information Technology Equipment), Under Raised Floors

- **Type of Change:** Revision

- **Change at a Glance:** Requirements for installing wiring methods and cables under a raised floor in an IT equipment room have been revised for clarity.

- **Code Language: 645.5 Supply Circuits and Interconnecting Cables. (Information Technology Equipment)**

  (E) Under Raised Floors. Where the area under the floor is accessible and openings minimize the entrance of debris beneath the floor, power cables, communications cables, connecting cables, interconnecting cables, cord-and-plug connections, and receptacles associated with the information technology equipment shall be permitted under a raised floor of approved construction. The installation requirement shall comply with 645.5(E)(1) through (3)., provided the following conditions are met:
  (1) The raised floor is of approved construction, and the area under the floor is accessible.
  (2) The branch-circuit supply conductors to receptacles or field-wired equipment are in rigid metal conduit, rigid nonmetallic conduit, intermediate metal conduit, electrical metallic tubing, electrical nonmetallic tubing, metal wireway, nonmetallic wireway, surface metal raceway with

~~metal cover, surface nonmetallic raceway, flexible metal conduit, liquid-tight flexible metal conduit, or liquidtight flexible nonmetallic conduit, Type MI cable, Type MC cable, or Type AC cable and associated metallic and nonmetallic boxes or enclosures. These supply conductors shall be installed in accordance with the requirements of 300.11.~~

(1) Installation Requirements for Branch Circuit Supply Conductors Under a Raised Floor.
(a) ~~These~~ The supply conductors shall be installed in accordance with the requirements of 300.11.

(b) In addition to the wiring methods of 300.22(C), the following wiring methods shall also be permitted:
(1) Rigid metal conduit
(2) Rigid nonmetallic conduit
(3) Intermediate metal conduit
(4) Electrical metallic tubing
(5) Electrical nonmetallic tubing
(6) Metal wireway
(7) Nonmetallic wireway
(8) Surface metal raceway with metal cover
(9) Surface nonmetallic raceway
(10) Flexible metal conduit
(11) Liquidtight flexible metal conduit
(12) Liquidtight flexible nonmetallic conduit
(13) Type MI cable
(14) Type MC cable
(15) Type AC cable
(16) Associated metallic and nonmetallic boxes or enclosures
(17) Type TC power and control tray cable

(2) Installation Requirements for Electrical Supply Cords, Data Cables, Interconnecting Cables, and Grounding Conductors Under a Raised Floor. The following cords, cables, and conductors shall be permitted to be installed under a raised floor:
(1) Supply cords of listed information technology equipment in accordance with 645.5(B)
(2) Interconnecting cables enclosed in a raceway
(3) Equipment grounding conductors
(4) In addition to wiring installed in compliance with 725.135(C), Types CL2R, CL3R, CL2, and CL3 and substitute cables including CMP, CMR, CM, and CMG installed in accordance with 725.154(A), shall be permitted under raised floors.

Informational Note: Figure 725.154(A) illustrates the cable substitution hierarchy for Class 2 and Class 3 cables.

(5) Listed Type DP cable having adequate fire-resistant characteristics suitable for use under raised floors of an information technology equipment room

645.5(E)

Informational Note: One method of defining *fire resistance* is by establishing that the cables do not spread fire to the top of the tray in the "UL Flame Exposure, Vertical Tray Flame Test" in UL 1685-2011, *Standard for Safety for Vertical-Tray Fire-Propagation and Smoke-Release Test for Electrical and Optical-Fiber Cables*. The smoke measurements in the test method are not applicable.

Another method of defining fire resistance is for the damage (char length) not to exceed 1.5 m (4 ft 11 in.) when performing the CSA "Vertical Flame Test — Cables in Cable Trays," as described in CSA C22.2 No. 0.3- ~~M-2001~~ 09, *Test Methods for Electrical Wires and Cables*.

~~(3) Supply cords of listed information technology equipment are in accordance with 645.5(B).~~
~~(4) Ventilation in the underfloor area is used for the information technology equipment room only, except as provided in 645.4(2).~~
~~(5) Openings in raised floors for cords and cables protect cords and cables against abrasion and minimize the entrance of debris beneath the floor.~~
~~(6) Cables, other than those covered in 645.5(E)(2) and (E)(3), are one of the following:~~
~~a. Listed Type DP cable having adequate fire-resistant characteristics suitable for use under raised floors of an information technology equipment room~~
~~b. Interconnecting cables enclosed in a raceway~~
~~c. Cable type designations shown in Table 645.5(E)(6)~~
~~d. Equipment grounding conductors~~

(3) Installation Requirements for Optical Fiber Cables Under a Raised Floor. In addition to optical fiber cables installed in accordance with 770.113(C), Types OFNR, OFCR, OFN, and OFC shall be permitted under raised floors.

~~Table 645.5(E)(6) Cable Types Permitted Under Raised Floors~~
[Table 645.5(E)(6) has been deleted]

■ **2014 *NEC* Requirement**
The requirements for installing power cables, communications cables, connecting cables, interconnecting cables, cord-and-plug connections, and receptacles under a raised floor associated with the information technology equipment was (and is) addressed at 645.5(E). This information was delivered in long sentences and paragraphs. This information had a companion Table 645.5(E)(6) that contained several cable types permitted under a raised floor of an IT equipment room.

■ **2017 *NEC* Change**
First level subdivision 645.5(E) was revised and re-organized for usability and clarity. A list format was incorporated for usability as well. The previous Table 645.5(E)(6) was deleted as it is no longer needed.

645.5(E)

Analysis of the Change:

It is a very common sight to see wiring methods and interconnect cables in information technology (IT) equipment (computer) rooms located under a raised floor-type construction feature. This type of raised floor installation allows for more flexibility in routing the cables and for easier relocation of IT equipment within the IT equipment room when needed. It also reduces potential trip hazards to personnel working in the IT equipment room. For this wiring under a raised floor of an IT equipment room, installation requirements are modified. In some cases, a relaxed version of the general electrical wiring methods required by Chapters 1 through 4 of the *Code* is allowed, but only if the room complies with all the requirements at 645.4 and qualifies as an IT equipment room.

All power cables, communication cables, connecting cables and interconnecting cables are permitted under the IT equipment room raised floor provided that: the raised floor is of a suitable construction; the area under the floor is accessible; ventilation in the under-floor area is used for the computer room only; and any openings between the under- and above-floor areas minimize the entrance of debris and protect any cables routed through the opening against abrasion.

For the 2017 *NEC*, this entire first level subdivision at 645.5(E) has been revised and re-organized for usability and clarity. A list format was incorporated where possible. The new revised parent text at 645.5(E) organizes the conditions for using the underfloor area for wiring from an installation requirements standpoint. Three new second level subdivisions then lay out the requirements for branch-circuit wiring [645.5(E)(1)], data, cords, interconnection cables and grounding conductors [645.5(E)(2)], and optical fiber cabling [645.5(E)(3)]. The revised under-floor wiring method requirements are stated in a manner consistent with 645.4 by first referencing the general wiring methods (as applicable) in *NEC* Chapters 3, and Articles 725 (Class 1, Class 2, and Class 3 Remote-Control, Signaling, and Power-Limited Circuits) and Article 770 (Fire Alarm Systems) and then stating which alternate wiring methods are acceptable.

The previous Table 645.5(E)(6) has been deleted as it was no longer needed. This table also contained conflicting information pertaining to NPLFR, FPLR, NPLF, FPL, CATVR, and CATV cables as these cables are not permitted under a raised floor in a IT equipment room. These cables installed in IT equipment rooms are covered by 645.3(E) for fire alarm cables and 645.3(G) for community antenna television (CATV) and radio distribution systems equipment installed in an IT equipment room. Previous Table 645.5(E)(6) contained a list of acceptable cables permitted under a raised floor without a hint of how to choose the proper cable nor how to install it properly.

645.5(E)

First Revisions: FR 3354
Second Revisions: SR 3312
Public Inputs: PI 39, PI 362, PI 821
Public Comments: PC 70, PC 1839

645.18

Surge Protection for Critical Operations Data Systems

Surge protection is now required to be provided for critical operations data systems

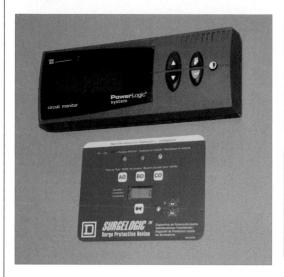

Surge arresters

Surge protective devices (SPD)

645.18

645.18 Surge Protection for Critical Operations Data Systems. (Information Technology Equipment)

- **Type of Change:** New

- **Change at a Glance:** A new requirement was added for surge protection for critical operations data systems.

- **Code Language: 645.18 Surge Protection for Critical Operations Data Systems. (Information Technology Equipment)** Surge protection shall be provided for critical operations data systems.

- **2014 *NEC* Requirement**
  Surge protection for critical operations data systems was not addressed in Article 645 in the 2014 *NEC*. Surge protection devices were, and are, required at all facility distribution voltage levels of a critical operations power system by the provisions of 708.20(D).

- **2017 *NEC* Change**
  Surge protection is now required for critical operations data systems by the provisions of new 645.18.

Analysis of the Change:

A *Critical Operations Data System* is defined at 645.2 as "an information technology equipment system that requires continuous operation for reasons of public safety, emergency management, national security, or business continuity." A new section was added at 645.18 demanding that surge protection be provided for critical operations data systems. Surge arresters and surge-protective devices (SPD) are typically the devices installed to a particular element of the electrical system to achieve the desired surge protection and ensure reliable electrical power.

This new surge protection requirement in Article 645 correlates with 708.20(D) for Critical Operations Power Systems. Section 708.20(D) calls for surge protection devices to be provided at all facility distribution voltage levels of a critical operations power system. This requirement often results in critical operations data centers including localized surge protection as part of the manufactured equipment. This requirement at 645.18 addresses an additional level of surge protection that is needed as close as possible to the incoming supply for the critical operations data system. For surge protection to be effective, multiple levels of surge protection typically must be provided.

Surge protection at utilization equipment is only one piece of the total surge protection package that is necessary to be effective. The definition of *Critical Operations Data System* substantiates the need for a complete and effective surge protection system. The purpose of the *NEC* as stated at 90.1(A) is "the practical safeguarding of persons and property from hazards that arise from the use of electricity." This new requirement at 645.18 for surge protection provisions for critical operation data systems supports this overall purpose. Critical operation data systems are essential in weather-related events, loss of utility power, or other catastrophic conditions.

This surge protection is not meant solely for protection against weather-related events such as lightning. This surge protection also addresses internal surges caused by localized switching within the power distribution system as well as utility switching which is a common occurrence.

645.18

First Revisions: FR 3356
Public Inputs: PI 2683, PI 1494

Article 650
Pipe Organs

Article 650 **Pipe Organs**

- **Type of Change:** New/Revision

- **Change at a Glance:** Article 650 covering pipe organs was revised for clarity.

- **Code Language:** **Article 650 Pipe Organs**
  650.1 Scope. This article covers those electrical circuits and parts of electrically operated pipe organs that are employed for the control of the keyboards and of the sounding apparatus, typically organ pipes ~~and keyboards~~.

  Informational Note: The typical pipe organ is a very large musical instrument that is built as part of a building or structure.

  650.2 Definitions.
  Electronic Organ. A musical instrument that imitates the sound of a pipe organ by producing sound electronically.

  Informational Note: Most new electronic organs produce sound digitally and are called digital organs.

Pipe Organ. A musical instrument that produces sound by driving pressurized air (called wind) through pipes selected via a keyboard.

Sounding Apparatus. The sound-producing part of a pipe organ, including, but not limited to, pipes, chimes, bells, the pressurized air (wind)-producing equipment (blower), associated controls, and power equipment.

Informational Note: The sounding apparatus is also referred to as the "pipe organ chamber."

650.3 Other Articles.
(A) Electronic Organ Equipment.
(B) Optical Fiber Cable.

650.4 Source of Energy.

650.5 Grounding or Double Insulation of the DC Power Supply.

650.6 Conductors.
(A) Size.
(B) Insulation.
(C) Conductors to Be Cabled.
(D) Cable Covering.

650.7 Installation of Conductors.

650.8 Overcurrent Protection.

650.9 Protection from Accidental Contact. The wiring of the sounding apparatus shall be within the lockable enclosure (organ chamber) where the exterior pipes shall be permitted to form part of the enclosure.

Informational Note: Access to the sounding apparatus and the associated circuitry is restricted by an enclosure. In most pipe organ installations, exterior pipes form part of the enclosure. In other installations, the pipes are covered by millwork that permits the passage of sound.

(See *NEC* for complete text of Article 650)

■ **2014 *NEC* Requirement**
Article 650 covers those electrical circuits and parts of electrically operated pipe organs that are employed for the control of the sounding apparatus and keyboards.

■ **2017 *NEC* Change**
Article 650 was revised by adding 650.2 for definitions pertaining to this article. A new 650.9 was added pertaining to protection against accidental contact with the sounding apparatus.

Article 650

Article 650

Analysis of the Change:

Article 650 covers electrical circuits and parts of electrically operated pipe organs that are employed for the control of the keyboards and of the sounding apparatus. Article 650 covers pipe organs that are typically large in nature and of an elaborate, one-of-a-kind design. The sounding apparatus, while typically organ pipes, can include other sound-producing mechanisms. This article has been a part of the *Code* since the 1930s.

The article experienced extensive revisions for the 2017 *NEC*, the first noticeable change being the addition of three definitions for *electronic organ*, *pipe organ*, and *sounding apparatus*. Previous editions of Article 650 had no definitions; these definitions are important terms for the application of this article.

Another noteworthy change was the addition of 650.9 titled, "Protection from Accidental Contact." Because the sounding apparatus has exposed circuits, its wiring is required to be located within a lockable enclosure (typically the organ chamber) where the exterior pipes form part of the enclosure. Access to the interior of the sounding apparatus should be limited to qualified personnel. Typically, the exterior pipes are tightly spaced so the combination of exterior pipes and walls of a room prevent unauthorized access. In other situations, the pipes are covered by decorative millwork that permits sound to pass through it.

First Revisions: FR 3318-26
Second Revisions: SR 3316
Public Inputs: Numerous PIs
Public Comments: PC 1844

660.5

Disconnecting Means for X-Ray Equipment

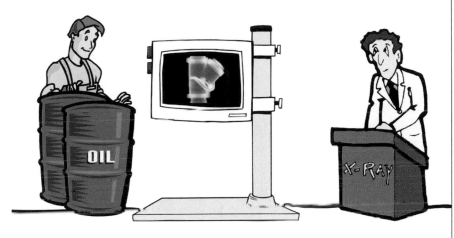

Disconnecting means for industrial-type x-ray equipment required to be located "within sight" of the X-ray controls and readily accessible

Previous language indicated that the disconnecting means could be placed anywhere (several rooms away) as long as the disconnecting means was "readily accessible" regardless of its location

660.5

660.5 Disconnecting Means. (X-Ray Equipment)

- **Type of Change:** Revision

- **Change at a Glance:** Disconnecting means for industrial-type x-ray equipment is required to be located "within sight" of the X-ray controls and readily accessible.

- **Code Language: 660.5 Disconnecting Means. (X-Ray Equipment)**
  A disconnecting means of adequate capacity for at least 50 percent of the input required for the momentary rating, or 100 percent of the input required for the long-time rating, of the X-ray equipment, whichever is greater, shall be provided in the supply circuit. The disconnecting means shall be ~~operable from a location readily accessible from~~ located within sight from the X-ray control and readily accessible. ~~For equipment connected to a 120-volt, nominal, branch circuit of 30 amperes or less, a grounding-type attachment plug cap and receptacle of proper rating shall be permitted to serve as a disconnecting means.~~

  Exception: The disconnecting means for the X-ray equipment shall not be required under either of the following conditions, provided that the controller disconnecting means is lockable in accordance with 110.25:

(1) Where such a location of the disconnecting means for the X-ray equipment is impracticable or introduces additional or increased hazards to persons or property

(2) In industrial installations, with written safety procedures, where conditions of maintenance and supervision ensure that only qualified persons service the equipment.

■ **2014 *NEC* Requirement**
The disconnecting means for X-ray equipment was required to be operable from a location readily accessible from the X-ray control.

■ **2017 *NEC* Change**
The disconnecting means for X-ray equipment is now required to be located within sight from the X-ray control and readily accessible.

660.5

Analysis of the Change:

The requirements of Article 660 cover all X-ray equipment operating at any frequency or voltage for industrial or other nonmedical or nondental use. X-ray equipment installed for use in a healthcare facility is covered by Article 517, Part V. Industrial X-ray equipment is required to have a disconnecting means of adequate capacity. In previous editions of the *NEC*, 660.5 required this disconnecting means to be "operable from a location readily accessible from the X-ray control." This disconnecting means requirement was intended to ensure the X-ray equipment operator has a means to quickly disconnect the X-ray equipment from its supply circuit. A literal reading of this previous language could be misinterpreted to mean that the disconnecting means could be placed anywhere (several rooms away from the X-ray control, on another floor, etc.) as long as the disconnecting means was "readily accessible" regardless of its location.

For the 2017 *NEC*, this disconnecting means requirement has been changed to read "the disconnecting means shall be located within sight from the X-ray control and readily accessible." This revised text will ensure the proper location of the disconnecting means, with the use of the defined term *within sight*.

A new exception to this disconnecting means rule was added for X-ray equipment in industrial locations where a disconnecting means would be impracticable or introduces additional or increased hazards to persons or property and in industrial installations (with written safety procedures) where conditions of maintenance and supervision ensure that only qualified persons service the equipment. These conditions are quite common in industrial applications.

First Revisions: FR 3333
Public Inputs: PI 2093

670.6

Surge Protection for Industrial Machinery

Industrial machinery with safety interlock circuits is now required to have surge protection installed

Photo Courtesy of Eaton

670.6

670.6 Surge Protection. (Industrial Machinery)

- **Type of Change:** New

- **Change at a Glance:** A new requirement was added for surge protection of industrial machinery with safety interlocking circuits.

- **Code Language: 670.6 Surge Protection. (Industrial Machinery)** Industrial machinery with safety interlock circuits shall have surge protection installed.

- **2014 *NEC* Requirement**
  There were no provisions in Article 670 for surge protection of industrial machinery with safety interlocking circuits.

- **2017 *NEC* Change**
  A new requirement was added at 670.6 requiring industrial machinery with safety interlock circuits to be provided with surge protection.

Analysis of the Change:

Industrial machinery is defined at 670.2 as "a power-driven machine (or a group of machines working together in a coordinated manner), not portable by hand while working, that is used to process material by cutting; forming; pressure; electrical, thermal, or optical techniques; lamination; or a combination of these processes." Industrial machinery can include associated equipment used to transfer material or tooling, including fixtures, to assemble/disassemble, to inspect or test, or to package. The associated electrical equipment, including the logic controller(s) and associated software or logic together with the machine actuators and sensors, are considered as part of the industrial machinery as well.

NFPA 79 (*Electrical Standard for Industrial Machinery*) is the standard used for industrial machinery. NFPA 79 provides safeguards for industrial machinery to protect operators, equipment, facilities, and work-in-progress from fire and electrical hazards. Requirements for industrial machinery apply to electrical/electronic equipment, apparatus, or systems supplied as part of industrial machines operating from a nominal voltage of 600 volts or less, and commencing at the point of connection of the supply to the electrical equipment of the machine.

A new requirement has been added to Article 670 applying to Industrial machinery with safety interlock circuits. These industrial machinery applications will now be required to be provided with surge protection. A study entitled, "Data Assessment for Electrical Surge Protective Devices," commissioned by the NFPA Fire Protection Research Foundation, provided results of a 2013 and 2014 survey of facility managers concerning surge damage. This survey shows that 26 percent of the responders had damage to safety interlocking systems on machines due to electrical surges. These safety interlocking systems are in place to protect workers from serious injuries and death due to interactions with the machinery.

By definition, a *safety interlock* is "a device or means that places a machine or machine component into a zero, or substantially reduced, danger-mode upon intent to access; or a device or means that will actively prevent access to a hazard upon intended access." A very simplistic example of a safety interlock is found on a household clothes dryer. Upon opening the clothes dryer door, the high-speed rotation of the dryer's drum will stop, and the drum will not operate with the dryer door open.

Protecting workers by protecting the industrial machinery safety interlocking systems from damage due to surges is a step forward in electrical safety.

First Revisions: FR 3357
Public Inputs: PI 4156

670.6

680.2 and Part VIII of Article 680

Swimming Pools, Fountains, and Similar Installations

Electrically Powered Pool Lift. An electrically powered lift that provides accessibility to and from a pool or spa for people with disabilities.

680.2

680.2 and Part VIII of Article 680 Definitions, Swimming Pools, Fountains, and Similar Installations

- **Type of Change:** New

- **Change at a Glance:** A new definition for *Electrically Powered Pool Lift* was added to 680.2 and a new Part VIII entitled, "Electrically Powered Pool Lifts," was added to Article 680.

- **Code Language: 680.2 Definitions. (Swimming Pools, Fountains, and Similar Installations)**
  Electrically Powered Pool Lift. An electrically powered lift that provides accessibility to and from a pool or spa for people with disabilities.

  Part VIII. Electrically Powered Pool Lifts
  680.80 General. Electrically powered pool lifts as defined in 680.2 shall comply with Part VIII of this article. They shall not be required to comply with other parts of this article.

  680.81 Equipment Approval. Lifts shall be listed and identified for swimming pool and spa use.

  Exception No. 1: Lifts where the battery is removed for charging at another location and the battery is rated less than or equal to the low-voltage contact limit shall not be required to be listed or labeled.

Exception No. 2: Solar-operated or -recharged lifts where the solar panel is attached to the lift and the battery is rated less than or equal to 24 volts shall not be required to be listed or labeled.

Exception No. 3: Lifts that are supplied from a source not exceeding the low-voltage contact limit and supplied by listed transformers or power supplies that comply with 680.23(A)(2) shall not be required to be listed.

680.82 Protection. Pool lifts connected to premises wiring and operated above the low-voltage contact limit shall be provided with GFCI protection for personnel.

680.83 Bonding. Lifts shall be bonded in accordance with 680.26(B)(5) and (B)(7).

680.84 Switching Devices. Switches and switching devices that are operated above the low-voltage contact limit shall comply with 680.22(C).

680.85 Nameplate Marking. Electrically powered pool lifts shall be provided with a nameplate giving the identifying name and model and rating in volts and amperes, or in volts and watts. If the lift is to be used on a specific frequency or frequencies, it shall be so marked. Battery-powered pool lifts shall indicate the type reference of the battery or battery pack to be used. Batteries and battery packs shall be provided with a battery type reference and voltage rating.

Exception: Nameplate ratings for battery-powered pool lifts shall only need to provide a rating in volts in addition to the identifying name and model.

■ **2014 *NEC* Requirement**
There were no requirements or a definition for an *Electrically Powered Pool Lift* anywhere in Article 680.

■ **2017 *NEC* Change**
A new definition for *Electrically Powered Pool Lift* along with a new Part VIII entitled, "Electrically Powered Pool Lifts," were added to Article 680.

Analysis of the Change:
If you have been around any public swimming pool over the past five years or so, be it at a hotel or wherever, you have undoubtedly seen a strange looking contraption constructed right beside the pool or spa water that resembles something like a mechanical arm from the space shuttle. What you have more than likely encountered is an electrically powered pool lift. These inventive pool lifts are required components at public aquatic facilities by the Department of Justice and the Americans with Disabilities Act (ADA).

A new definition for an *Electrically Powered Pool Lift* at 680.2 along with a new

680.2

Part VIII (680.80 through 680.85) were incorporated into Article 680 for the 2017 *NEC*. These lifts are defined as "an electrically powered lift that provides accessibility to and from a pool or spa for people with disabilities." These lifts allow persons with disabilities to have access to public swimming pools, spas, and hot tubs

Before the 2017 *NEC*, installation of these mandated powered pool lifts has been without compliance to any *NEC* requirements, in particular, requirements in Article 680. In Chapter 10 (Swimming Pools, Wading Pools, and Spas) of the Assessment of Benefits and Costs of Final Accessibility Guidelines for Recreation Facilities for the *Americans with Disabilities Act* (*ADA*), Section 15.8.2 states that "at least two accessible means of entry must be provided for each public use and common use swimming pool. Primary means must be a pool lift or sloped entry. Secondary means must be a pool lift, sloped entry, transfer wall, transfer system, or pool stairs."

This new definition is a companion to a new term now found in a new Part VIII of Article 680 pertaining to electrically powered pool lifts. Part VIII to Article 680 puts into place prescribed rules for the installation of these mandatory pool lifts with adequate safety requirements for all pool users. These new rules for electrically powered pool lifts include general requirements at 680.80, equipment approval (listing requirements) at 680.81, GFCI protection requirements at 680.82, bonding requirements at 680.83, switching device requirements at 680.84, and nameplate marking requirements at 680.85.

680.2

680.80 General. Electrically powered pool lifts as defined in 680.2 shall comply with Part VIII of Article 680

680.81 Equipment Approval.

680.82 Protection. (GFCI)

680.83 Bonding.

680.84 Switching Devices.

680.85 Nameplate Marking.

New definition for "Electrically Powered Pool Lift" was added to 680.2 and a new Part VIII titled, "Electrically Powered Pool Lifts" was added to Article 680

First Revisions: FR 4860, FR 4859

Second Revisions: SR 4830

Public Inputs: PI 4024

Public Comments: PC 1185

680.2

Swimming Pools, Fountains, and Similar Installations

680.2 Definitions. (Swimming Pools, Fountains, and Similar Installations)

- **Type of Change:** Revision

- **Change at a Glance:** Revised definition for *Storable Swimming, Wading, or Immersion Pools; or Storable/Portable Spas and Hot Tubs*. This revision clarifies this definition by adding "on or above the ground" for a pool, spa, or hot tub with nonmetallic, molded polymeric walls or inflatable fabric walls regardless of dimension, which is the basis for the requirements within this article.

- **Code Language: 680.2 Definitions. (Swimming Pools, Fountains, and Similar Installations)**

  Storable Swimming, Wading, or Immersion Pools; or Storable/Portable Spas and Hot Tubs. ~~Those~~ Swimming, wading, or immersion pools that are intended to be stored when not in use, constructed on or above the ground and are capable of holding water to a maximum depth of 1.0 m (42 in.), or a pool, spa, or hot tub constructed on or above the ground, with nonmetallic, molded polymeric walls or inflatable fabric walls regardless of dimension.

- **2014 *NEC* Requirement**
  The definition of *Storable Swimming, Wading, or Immersion Pools* added the term *or Storable/Portable Spas and Hot Tubs* in the definition.

This definition included storable swimming, wading, or immersion pools; or storable/portable spas and hot tubs that are constructed on or above the ground and are capable of holding water to a maximum depth of 1.0 m (42 in.). This definition also included any pool with nonmetallic, molded polymeric walls or inflatable fabric walls regardless of dimension.

- **2017 *NEC* Change**
  Further clarification was instituted with the phrase "constructed on or above the ground" added before storable/portable "nonmetallic, polymeric or inflatable tubs, spas, or pools regardless of the dimension." This addition clarifies that a storable/portable pool, spa, or hot tub with nonmetallic, molded polymeric walls or inflatable fabric walls regardless of dimension is always installed "on or above the ground."

Analysis of the Change:

The definition of *Storable Swimming, Wading, or Immersion Pools; or Storable/Portable Spas and Hot Tubs* has been revised once again for the 2017 *NEC*. This definition was revised for the 2014 *NEC* by adding "Storable/Portable Spas and Hot Tubs" to the already defined storable swimming, wading, or immersion pools. These portable spas and hot tub systems are very similar in design, structure and installation to storable pools. They bring the same concerns, such as location, ground-fault circuit-interrupter (GFCI) protection, listing requirements, etc., as storable pools. The 2014 *NEC* revision to this definition brought clarity to such things as the requirement at 680.42(C), which describes the need for underwater luminaires to comply with 680.23 and 680.33 for storable or portable spas and hot tubs, as well as for storable pools. Before this revised definition in 2014, it was difficult for the enforcement community to apply Article 680 safety regulations to storable or portable spas and hot tubs.

For the 2017 *NEC*, further clarification demonstrated that storable/portable nonmetallic, polymeric or inflatable tubs, spas, or pools regardless of the dimension would be installed "on or above the ground." The 2014 *NEC* language at this definition was interpreted by some users of the *Code* that the possibility existed for nonmetallic, polymeric or inflatable tubs, spas, or pools to be installed "in the ground." This interpretation was incorrect as any pool "constructed in the ground or partially in the ground, and all others capable of holding water in a depth greater than 1.0 m (42 in.)" are considered by definition to be a permanently installed swimming, wading, immersion, or therapeutic pool.

First Revisions: FR 4873
Public Inputs: PI 1310

680.2

680.7

Grounding and Bonding Terminals in Wet Environments

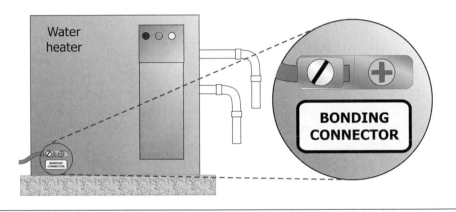

Grounding and bonding terminals shall be identified for use in wet and corrosive environments

Field-installed grounding and bonding connections in a damp, wet, or corrosive environment shall be composed of copper, copper alloy, or stainless steel

Grounding and bonding terminals shall be listed for direct burial use

680.7

680.7 Grounding and Bonding Terminals. (Swimming Pools, Fountains, and Similar Installations)

- **Type of Change:** New

- **Change at a Glance:** New requirements for grounding and bonding terminals to be identified for use in wet and corrosive environments were added. Grounding and bonding terminals at pools, spas, hot tubs, etc., are subjected to severe environmental conditions, including wet and corrosive conditions. This new text adds specific requirements to address those conditions.

- **Code Language: 680.7 Grounding and Bonding Terminals. (Swimming Pools, Fountains, and Similar Installations)** Grounding and bonding terminals shall be identified for use in wet and corrosive environments. Field-installed grounding and bonding connections in a damp, wet, or corrosive environment shall be composed of copper, copper alloy, or stainless steel. They shall be listed for direct burial use.

- **2014 *NEC* Requirement** There were no specifics for grounding and bonding terminations in Article 680. Specific means for terminating equipment grounding conductors, bonding jumpers, etc., to metal enclosures would be described at 250.8. This description would include listed pressure connectors, pressure connectors listed as grounding and bonding equipment, etc.

- **2017 *NEC* Change**
  A new grounding and bonding termination requirement was added at 680.7. This new requirement calls for grounding and bonding terminals to be identified for use in wet and corrosive environments and listed for direct burial applications as well.

Analysis of the Change:

Many grounding and bonding terminals are associated with swimming pool, spa, and similar aquatic locations. These bonding terminals are subjected to severe environmental conditions, including wet and corrosive environments. When installed in these wet or corrosive conditions, grounding and bonding lugs or terminations must be listed for the application.

For the 2017 *NEC*, a new grounding and bonding termination requirement was added at 680.7. This new requirement calls for grounding and bonding terminals to be identified for use in wet and corrosive environments. Field-installed grounding and bonding connections installed in a damp, wet, or corrosive environment will need to be composed of copper, copper alloy, or stainless steel. These grounding and bonding terminations must also be listed for direct burial applications as well.

The specification demanding that these terminations be made of copper, copper alloy or stainless steel will provide a more corrosion-resistant material for these applications. The specification of direct burial use is intended to mandate copper alloys of a minimum 80 percent copper. This alloy specification is in the listing requirements for connectors to be marked suitable for direct burial. Grounding and bonding terminations listed to UL 467 (*Grounding and Bonding Equipment*) with a rating for direct burial would mandate materials that have proven resistant to the corrosive environments around swimming pool equipment, such as stainless steel, copper, and high copper content copper alloys.

680.7

First Revisions: FR 4852
Second Revisions: SR 4816
Public Inputs: PI 3883
Public Comments: PC 1098

Table 680.10

Underground Wiring Location in Wet Locations

Previous 680.10 (Underground Wiring Location) moved to 680.11 and previous Table 680.10 Minimum Cover Depths was deleted

Table 680.10 was "kicked out" of the *Code*

Table 680.10 Minimum Cover Depths

Wiring Method	Minimum Burial	
	mm	in.
Rigid metal conduit	150	6
Intermediate metal conduit	150	6
Nonmetallic raceways listed for direct burial under minimum of 102 mm (4 in.) thick concrete exterior slab and extending not less than 162 mm (6 in.) beyond the underground installation	150	6
Nonmetallic raceways listed for direct burial without concrete encasement	150	18
Other approved raceways*	450	18

*Raceways approved for burial only where concrete encased shall require a concrete envelope not less than 50 mm (2 in.) thick

Table 300.5 burial depth requirements will now apply around swimming pools, spas, hot tubs, fountains, and similar installations

680.10

Table 680.10 Underground Wiring Location. (Swimming Pools, Fountains, and Similar Installations)

- **Type of Change:** Deletion

- **Change at a Glance:** Previous 680.10 (Underground Wiring Location) was moved to 680.11, and previous Table 680.10 was deleted. Table 300.5 burial depth requirements will now apply around pools.

- **Code Language: 680.~~10~~ 11 Underground Wiring Location. (Swimming Pools, Fountains, and Similar Installations)** Underground wiring shall ~~not be permitted under the pool or within the area extending 1.5 m (5 ft) horizontally from the inside wall of~~ be permitted where installed in rigid metal conduit, intermediate metal conduit, rigid polyvinyl chloride conduit, reinforced thermosetting resin conduit, or Type MC cable, suitable for the conditions subject to that location. Underground wiring shall not be permitted under the pool unless this wiring is necessary to supply pool equipment permitted by this article. ~~Where space limitations prevent wiring from being routed a distance 1.5 m (5 ft) or more from the pool, such wiring shall be permitted where installed in complete raceway systems of rigid metal conduit, intermediate metal conduit, or a nonmetallic raceway system. All metal conduit shall be corrosion resistant and suitable for the location. The~~ Minimum cover depth shall be as given in ~~Table 680.10~~ Table 300.5.
(Table 680.10 Minimum Cover Depths has been deleted)

■ **2014 *NEC* Requirement**

Underground wiring was not permitted under the pool or within an area extending 1.5 m (5 ft) horizontally from the inside wall of the pool unless this wiring was necessary to supply pool equipment. Where space limitations prevented wiring from being routed a distance 1.5 m (5 ft) or more from the pool, such wiring was permitted to be installed within 1.5 m (5 ft) of the pool where installed in complete raceway systems of rigid metal conduit, intermediate metal conduit, or a nonmetallic raceway system. All metal conduit was required to be corrosion-resistant and suitable for the location. The minimum cover depths for wiring installed within 1.5 m (5 ft) of the pool were dictated by Table 680.10.

■ **2017 *NEC* Change**

Underground wiring is now permitted to be installed in close proximity to the pool, and no consideration needs to be given as to whether this wiring is "necessary to supply pool equipment." The wiring methods employed are to be rigid metal conduit, intermediate metal conduit, rigid polyvinyl chloride conduit, reinforced thermosetting resin conduit, or Type MC cable, suitable for the conditions subject to that location. Underground wiring shall not be permitted to be installed *under* the pool unless this wiring is necessary to supply pool equipment permitted by Article 680. The minimum burial depth cover requirements will now be facilitated by Table 300.5, and Table 680.10 for minimum cover depths around pools has been deleted.

Analysis of the Change:

When dealing with the previous underground wiring provisions of 680.10 (now 680.11) and previous Table 680.10, do these restrictions for underground wiring related to swimming pools and similar locations apply only to the 1.5 m (5 ft) radius around the swimming pool or do these underground restrictions apply outside of this 1.5 m (5 ft) radius as well? What about the burial depth requirements described at 300.5 and Table 300.5, when do these provisions come into play, if at all?

These questions concerning burial depth requirements around a swimming pool have been asked by users of the *Code* for quite a while. To give a proper answer to these questions, a brief history of 680.10 is in order. Before the 1999 *NEC*, 680.10 was one simple sentence as follows: "Underground wiring shall not be permitted under the pool or within the area extending five ft (1.52 m) horizontally from the inside wall of the pool." At that time (1996 *NEC*), two exceptions existed for this main rule. The first exception was for the wiring necessary to supply pool equipment, and the other exception was for wiring being routed within five ft (1.52 m) because of space limitations. For this 1996 edition of the *NEC*, Table 680.10 was referenced and applied only to the Exception No. 2 for space limitation. It was clear that the burial depth requirements of Table 680.10 only applied (and could only apply) to the area within 1.5 m (5 ft) of the pool.

The exceptions to 680.10 were rewritten into positive language during the 1999 *NEC* revision process (see 1998 ROP 20-105). The substantiation simply stated,

"Clarifying the rule by rewriting the Exceptions in positive language." While most users of the *Code* would agree with rewriting exceptions into positive language when possible is a good thing, it could be easily argued that this intended clarification was not achieved with this 1999 revision

In an attempt to clarify these questions, 680.11 (that was previously located at 680.10) was revised for the 2017 *NEC*. These revisions clarify that the wiring methods underground near pools must be installed using a wiring method that can withstand the conditions unique to the pool environment (rigid metal conduit, intermediate metal conduit, rigid polyvinyl chloride conduit, etc.). Language was revised to insist that only wiring related to the swimming pool itself may be run under pools to feed such things as approved wet-niche luminaires, etc. This revision resolves the previously perceived conflicting language that stated only pool wiring could be within 1.5 m (5 ft), and then the next sentence permitted other wiring within the 1.5 m (5 ft) zone limited to pool wiring in the previous sentence. CMP-17 made a definitive statement by indicating that all underground wiring should be installed per Table 300.5, thus eliminating the need for and the requirements of previous Table 680.10.

This revised text at 680.11 (was 680.10) will allow something like a service lateral or an underground feeder to an accessory building to be routed within 1.5 m (5 ft) or in close proximity to the pool even though this service or feeder is not "necessary to supply pool equipment." The revised text will not allow this service or feeder that is not "necessary to supply pool equipment" to be run "under" the pool structure.

First Revisions: FR 4853

Public Inputs: PI 4762, PI 2670, PI 2769

680.10

680.12 and 680.14

Protection against Corrosive Environments
in Wet Locations

Photo courtesy of David Williams, Michigan

680.12 and 680.14 680.12 Equipment Rooms and Pits. (Swimming Pools, Fountains, and Similar Installations) and 680.14 Corrosive Environment

- **Type of Change:** Revision and New

- **Change at a Glance:** A new requirement for protection against a corrosive environment for electrical equipment installed in equipment rooms and pits was added at 680.12 and 680.14.

- **Code Language: 680.11 12 Equipment Rooms and Pits. (Swimming Pools, Fountains, and Similar Installations)**

Electrical equipment shall not be installed in rooms or pits that do not have drainage that prevents water accumulation during normal operation or filter maintenance. Equipment shall be suitable for the environment in accordance with 300.6.

Informational Note: Chemicals such as chlorine cause severe corrosive and deteriorating effects on electrical connections, equipment, and enclosures when stored and kept in the same vicinity. Adequate ventilation of indoor spaces such as equipment and storage rooms is addressed by ANSI/APSP-11, *Standard for Water Quality in Public Pools and Spas*, and can reduce the likelihood of the accumulation of corrosive vapors.

680.14 Corrosive Environment.

(A) General. Areas where pool sanitation chemicals are stored, as well as areas with circulation pumps, automatic chlorinators, filters, open areas under decks adjacent to or abutting the pool structure, and similar locations shall be considered to be a corrosive environment. The air in such areas shall be considered to be laden with acid, chlorine, and bromine vapors, or any combination of acid, chlorine, or bromine vapors, and any liquids or condensation in those areas shall be considered to be laden with acids, chlorine, and bromine vapors, or any combination of acid, chlorine, or bromine vapors.

(B) Wiring Methods. Wiring methods in the areas described in 680.14(A) shall be listed and identified for use in such areas. Rigid metal conduit, intermediate metal conduit, rigid polyvinyl chloride conduit, and reinforced thermosetting resin conduit shall be considered to be resistant to the corrosive environment specified in 680.14(A).

680.12/.14

- **2014 *NEC* Requirement**
  Electrical equipment cannot be installed in rooms or pits that do not have proper drainage for the prevention of water accumulation during normal operation or filter maintenance. Article 680 did not address the prevention of corrosion to electrical equipment in rooms or pits.

- **2017 *NEC* Change**
  In addition to proper drainage as required by previous 680.11, 680.12 now requires electrical equipment located in equipment rooms or pits to be suitable for the environment in accordance with 300.6, which calls for materials suitable for the environment in which they are to be installed. New requirements at 680.14 detail the corrosion resistance of wiring methods needed in swimming pool installations where chemicals are stored.

Analysis of the Change:

When installing electrical equipment in a room or pit, it is important to make sure that proper drainage is provided to prevent water accumulation at the electrical equipment during normal operation or maintenance. Another thing that needs to be part of the evaluation process for the installation of electrical equipment in a designated room or pit is the likelihood of corrosion. Electrical equipment should not be installed in areas where the electrical equipment and metal components are going to be subject to a corrosive environment without proper corrosion protection being implemented.

Quite a few places in Article 680 discuss things like metal conduits needing to be corrosion resistant and suitable for the location, but corrosion protection was not addressed in previous editions of the *Code* in Article 680 for electrical equipment in designated rooms or pits. This situation was rectified for the 2017

NEC with the revision of 680.12, which was 680.11 in the 2014 *NEC*, and the creation of new 680.14. *Code* language was added at 680.12 and 680.14 requiring electrical equipment located in equipment rooms or pits or areas where pool sanitation chemicals are stored to be suitable for the environment in accordance with 300.6. A look at 300.6 reveals that "raceways, cable trays, cablebus, auxiliary gutters, cable armor, boxes, cable sheathing, cabinets, elbows, couplings, fittings, supports, and support hardware shall be of materials suitable for the environment in which they are to be installed."

The new provisions at 680.14 identify areas where pool sanitation chemicals are stored, as well as areas with circulation pumps, automatic chlorinators, filters, open areas under decks adjacent to or abutting the pool structure, and similar locations as being considered to be a corrosive environment. The air in such areas is also considered to be laden with acid, chlorine, and bromine vapors, or any combination of acid, chlorine, or bromine vapors. This new section also requires wiring methods in these areas to be listed and identified for use in such areas.

Swimming pool and spa equipment is often subject to deteriorating chemicals, especially in rooms or pits. The equipment and wiring methods in these locations often fail due to exposure to these corrosive chemicals. Chlorine and other pool chemicals severely deteriorate electrical connections of conductors and accelerate rust and deterioration of metal parts of electrical equipment. These chemicals are often stored, mixed and dispensed in the same room or area as the electrical equipment. This new corrosion-resistance requirement at 680.12 addresses the suitability of the equipment for these locations and will allow the AHJ to address these issues from a *Code* standpoint.

A new informational note was also added at 680.12 to clarify the corrosive conditions that are of concern that led to this added text.

680.12/.14

> First Revisions: FR 4854
> Second Revisions: SR 4817, SCR 43
> Public Inputs: PI 3963, PI 4102

680.21(A)

Motors in Swimming Pools, Fountains, and Similar Installations

---

Where installed in noncorrosive environments, branch circuits wiring methods for permanently installed swimming pool pump motors are to comply with the general requirements of *NEC* Chapter 3 wiring methods

Restricted wiring methods will now only apply in areas where:

(1) protection from physical damage is needed

(2) protection from environmental conditions associated with wet, damp, and corrosive conditions are present

---

680.21(A) (Swimming Pools, Fountains, and Similar Installations)

- **Type of Change:** Revision/Deletion

- **Change at a Glance:** Provisions for wiring methods for a permanently installed swimming pool pump motor have been revised.

- **Code Language: 680.21 Motors. (Swimming Pools, Fountains, and Similar Installations)**

  (A) Wiring Methods. The wiring to a pool motor shall comply with (A)(1) unless modified for specific circumstances by (A)(2), (A)(3), (A)(4), or (A)(5).

  (1) General. ~~The branch circuits for pool-associated motors shall be installed in rigid metal conduit, intermediate metal conduit, rigid polyvinyl chloride conduit, reinforced thermosetting resin conduit,~~ Wiring methods installed in the corrosive environment described in 680.14 shall comply with 680.14(B) or shall be Type MC cable listed for ~~the~~ that location. Other wiring methods and materials shall be permitted in specific locations or applications as covered in this section. ~~Any~~ Wiring methods installed in these locations ~~employed~~ shall contain an insulated copper equipment grounding conductor sized in accordance with 250.122 but not smaller

680.21(A)

than 12 AWG.

Where installed in noncorrosive environments, branch circuits shall comply with the general requirements in Chapter 3.

~~**(2) On or Within Buildings.** Where installed on or within buildings, electrical metallic tubing shall be permitted.~~

~~**(3)**~~ **(2) Flexible Connections.** Where necessary to employ flexible connections at or adjacent to the motor, liquidtight flexible metal or liquidtight flexible nonmetallic conduit with approved fittings shall be permitted.

~~**(4) One-Family Dwellings.** In the interior of dwelling units, or in the interior of accessory buildings associated with a dwelling unit, any of the wiring methods recognized in Chapter 3 of this Code that comply with the provisions of this section shall be permitted. Where run in a cable assembly, the equipment grounding conductor shall be permitted to be uninsulated, but it shall be enclosed within the outer sheath of the cable assembly~~

~~**(5)**~~ **(3) Cord-and-Plug Connections.** Pool-associated motors shall be permitted to employ cord-and-plug connections. The flexible cord shall not exceed 900 mm (3 ft) in length. The flexible cord shall include a copper equipment grounding conductor sized in accordance with 250.122 but not smaller than 12 AWG. The cord shall terminate in a grounding-type attachment plug.

- **2014 *NEC* Requirement**
The wiring method for a permanently installed swimming pool pump motor was limited to rigid metal conduit, intermediate metal conduit, rigid polyvinyl chloride (PVC) conduit, reinforced thermosetting resin conduit, or Type MC metal-clad cable specifically listed for the location. Electrical metallic tubing (EMT) was permitted to be used on or within buildings. Where flexible connections are necessary at or adjacent to the motor, liquidtight flexible metal or liquidtight flexible nonmetallic conduit with approved fittings was permitted. Pool pump motors located in one-family dwellings were permitted to be supplied by any of the general wiring methods recognized in *NEC* Chapter 3 where the wiring method was located inside the dwelling unit or an accessory building. All motors associated with permanently installed pools were required to be connected to an insulated copper equipment-grounding conductor not to be smaller than 12 AWG.

- **2017 *NEC* Change**
The restricted wiring methods previously described in 680.21(A)(1) through (A)(5) will now only apply in areas where protection from physical damage is needed or where protection from environmental conditions associated with wet, damp, and corrosive conditions are present.

680.21(A)

Where installed in noncorrosive environments (such as in the interior of a dwelling unit), branch circuits wiring methods for permanently installed swimming pool pump motors only need to comply with the general requirements of wiring methods mentioned in Chapter 3 of the *NEC*.

Analysis of the Change:

The wiring methods for a branch circuit for a permanently installed swimming pool pump motor are addressed in 680.21(A). Historically, these wiring methods have been limited to rigid metal conduit, intermediate metal conduit, rigid polyvinyl chloride (PVC) conduit, reinforced thermosetting resin conduit, or Type MC metal-clad cable specifically listed for the location. Electrical metallic tubing (EMT) is permitted to be used on or within buildings. Where flexible connections are necessary at or adjacent to the motor, liquidtight flexible metal or liquidtight flexible nonmetallic conduit with approved fittings is permitted. From a historical perspective, pool pump motor circuits located in buildings used as, or associated with, one-family dwellings have been permitted to be any of the general wiring methods recognized in Chapter 3 of the *NEC*. Both Type NM cable and Type UF cable were permitted to be used, with noted conditions, inside a dwelling unit.

680.21(A)

All motors associated with permanently installed pools are required to be connected to an equipment-grounding conductor. The equipment grounding conductor is to be sized based on the rating of the overcurrent protective device (fuse or circuit breaker typically) ahead of the branch circuit supplying the motor in conjunction with Table 250.122. This equipment-grounding conductor must be an insulated copper conductor and is not permitted to be smaller than 12 AWG.

The previous restrictions at 680.21(A)(1) related to wiring methods for permanently installed swimming pool pump motors addressed concerns for two issues: (1) protection from physical damage, and (2) protection from environmental conditions associated with wet, damp, and corrosive conditions associated with swimming pools, spas, hot tubs, etc. The remaining requirements described portions of those branch circuit wiring methods installed in areas not likely to encounter either of these conditions described at 680.21(A)(1).

For the 2017 *NEC*, revisions and deletions occurred at what was 680.21(A)(1) through (A)(5) [now 680.21(A)(1) through (A)(3)] to revise the *Code* language so that the restricted wiring methods will only apply in areas where protection from physical damage is needed or where protection from environmental conditions associated with wet, damp, and corrosive conditions are present. Where installed in noncorrosive environments (such as in the interior of a dwelling unit), branch circuits wiring methods for permanently installed swimming pool pump motors will simply need to comply with the general wiring method requirements of Chapter 3 in the *NEC*.

The change also resulted in the deletion of 680.21(A)(2) [On or Within Buildings] and 680.21(A)(4) [One-Family Dwellings], as these distinctions for these noncorrosive environments no longer needed to be highlighted since the new text added at 680.21(A)(1) now indicates that "where installed in noncorrosive environments, branch circuits shall comply with the general requirements in Chapter 3."

First Revisions: FR 4855
Second Revisions: SR 4818, SCR 119
Public Inputs: PI 3443
Public Comments: PC 732

680.22(A)(2)
Pool Pump Motor Receptacles

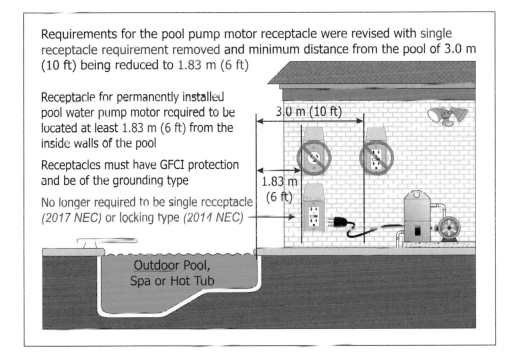

Requirements for the pool pump motor receptacle were revised with single receptacle requirement removed and minimum distance from the pool of 3.0 m (10 ft) being reduced to 1.83 m (6 ft)

Receptacle for permanently installed pool water pump motor required to be located at least 1.83 m (6 ft) from the inside walls of the pool

Receptacles must have GFCI protection and be of the grounding type

No longer required to be single receptacle (2017 NEC) or locking type (2014 NEC)

3.0 m (10 ft)

1.83 m (6 ft)

Outdoor Pool, Spa or Hot Tub

680.22(A)(2)

680.22(A)(2) Lighting, Receptacles, and Equipment. (Swimming Pools, Fountains, and Similar Installations)

- **Type of Change:** Revision/Deletion

- **Change at a Glance:** Requirements for the pool pump motor receptacle were revised with the single receptacle requirement removed and the minimum distance from the pool of 3.0 m (10 ft) being reduced to 1.83 m (6 ft).

- **Code Language: 680.22 Lighting, Receptacles, and Equipment. (Swimming Pools, Fountains, and Similar Installations)**

  (A) Receptacles.
  (2) Circulation and Sanitation System, Location. Receptacles that

provide power for water-pump motors or for other loads directly related to the circulation and sanitation system shall be located at least ~~3.0 m (10 ft)~~ 1.83 m (6 ft) from the inside walls of the pool.~~, or not less than 1.83 m (6 ft) from the inside walls of the pool if they meet all of the following conditions:~~ These receptacles shall have GFCI protection and be of the grounding type.
~~(1) Consist of single receptacles~~
~~(2) Are of the grounding type~~
~~(3) Have GFCI protection~~

680.22(A)(2)

- **2014 *NEC* Requirement**
  Receptacles that supply power for pool pump motors or other loads directly related to the circulation and sanitation system required the receptacle(s) to be located at least 3.0 m (10 ft) from the inside walls of the pool. Permission was granted at 680.22(A)(2) to allow the circulation and sanitation receptacle(s) to be located not less than 1.83 m (6 ft) from the inside walls of the pool if the receptacle(s) complied with all of the following conditions: consist of single receptacles; are of the grounding type; and are provided with GFCI protection.

- **2017 *NEC* Change**
  Receptacles that supply power for pool pump motors or other loads directly related to the circulation and sanitation system can now be located not less than 1.83 m (6 ft) from the inside walls of the pool, provided the receptacle(s) are of the grounding type and equipped with GFCI protection.

Analysis of the Change:

The requirements pertaining to a receptacle outlet that provides power to a water-pump motor or other loads directly related to the circulation and sanitation system of a permanently installed swimming pool have received extensive revision over the last four *Code* cycles.

In the 2005 *NEC*, 680.22(A)(1) called for these pool pump motor receptacles to be located at least 3.0 m (10 ft) from the inside walls of the pool. However, these receptacles were permitted to be located up to, but no closer than, 1.5 m (5 ft) from the inside walls of the pool if they consisted of a single receptacle configuration, employed a locking-type configuration, were of the grounding type and were provided with GFCI protection. This configuration was an attempt to eliminate the possibility of plugging in a portable 120-volt radio or similar appliance into the receptacle dedicated to the pool pump motor and having the ability to place portable equipment (such as a radio) right beside the pool's edge.

During the 2008 *NEC* revision cycle, CMP-17 decided that Article 680 needed a consistent measurement distance for the minimum or maximum distances mentioned for receptacle outlets referenced throughout Article 680. This decision resulted in the distance requirements for receptacle outlets required in the 2005 *NEC* [1.5 m (5 ft) to 3.0 m (10 ft)] being changed to a consistent 1.83 m (6 ft) distance. This action by CMP-17 was enacted in part due to the expanded GFCI protection requirements added throughout Article 680 during the same revision cycle. This resulted in 680.22(A)(1), in which the minimum distance that a pool-pump receptacle outlet could be located from the inside walls of the pool was changed from "not less than 1.5 m (5 ft) from the inside walls of the pool" to "not less than 1.83 m (6 ft) from the inside walls of the pool" if the four conditions mentioned earlier (single locking and grounding-type GFCI protected receptacle outlet) are met. This change created an unintentional problem because a regular convenience receptacle outlet that previously was required to be "3.0 m (10 ft) from the inside walls of the pool" was also changed and allowed to be located "1.83 m (6 ft) from the inside walls of the pool." With this consistent "1.83 m (6 ft)" distance now incorporated throughout Article 680, there was no advantage or need for this single locking and grounding type receptacle outlet for the pool pump motor.

In the last *Code* cycle, 680.22(A)(2) [previously 680.22(A)(1)] eliminated the need for a locking-type configuration. If the convenience receptacles of 680.22(A)(3) do not require a locking configuration, why would the circulation and sanitation receptacle need a locking configuration? This 1.83 m (6 ft) distance is considered sufficient based on the cord lengths [typically less than 1.83 m (6 ft)] of appliances and utilization equipment likely to be used around permanently installed swimming pools.

For the 2017 *NEC*, 680.22(A)(2) reduced the minimum distance of "3.0 m (10 ft) from the inside walls of the pool" for the pool pump receptacle outlet to "not less than 1.83 m (6 ft) from the inside walls of the pool." The requirement for the pool pump motor receptacle outlet to consist of a single receptacle configuration was also eliminated. Once again, why would the pool pump motor receptacle outlet need to be located 3.0 m (10 ft) from the inside walls of the pool or be a single receptacle configuration if any convenience receptacle outlet cannot be located less than 1.83 m (6 ft) from the inside walls of the pool and be of the duplex type configuration?

Pool pump motor receptacle outlets are still required to be GFCI-protected. GFCI receptacle devices commonly consist of the duplex configuration. The previous list format historically employed at 680.22(A)(1) was also eliminated as only two conditions remain for the pool pump motor and these remaining conditions were compiled into one sentence.

First Revisions: FR 4856
Public Inputs: PI 4351, PI 358

680.22(A)(2)

680.22(B)(7)

Low-Voltage Gas-Fired Luminaires, Decorative Fireplaces, Fire Pits, and Similar Equipment

680.22(B)(7)

New requirements added for low-voltage gas-fired luminaires, decorative fireplaces, fire pits, and similar equipment

Listed low-voltage gas-fired luminaires, decorative fireplaces, fire pits, and similar equipment using low-voltage ignitors with outputs that do not exceed the low-voltage contact limit shall be permitted to be located less than 1.5 m (5 ft) from the inside walls of a permanently installed pool

680.22(B)(7) Low-Voltage Gas-Fired Luminaires, Decorative Fireplaces, Fire Pits, and Similar Equipment

- **Type of Change:** New

- **Change at a Glance:** New requirements were added for low-voltage gas-fired luminaires, decorative fireplaces, fire pits, and similar equipment.

- **Code Language: 680.22 Lighting, Receptacles, and Equipment. (Swimming Pools, Fountains, and Similar Installations)**

  (B) Luminaires, Lighting Outlets, and Ceiling-Suspended (Paddle) Fans.

  (7) Low-Voltage Gas-Fired Luminaires, Decorative Fireplaces, Fire Pits, and Similar Equipment. Listed low-voltage gas-fired luminaires, decorative fireplaces, fire pits, and similar equipment using low-voltage ignitors that do not require grounding, and are supplied by listed transformers or power supplies that comply with 680.23(A)(2) with outputs that do not exceed the low-voltage contact limit shall be permitted to be located less than 1.5 m (5 ft) from the inside walls of the pool. Metallic equipment shall be bonded in accordance with the requirements in 680.26(B). Transformers or power supplies supplying this type of equipment shall be installed in accordance with the requirements in 680.24. Metallic gas piping shall be bonded in accordance with the requirements in 250.104(B) and 680.26(B)(7).

- **2014 *NEC* Requirement**
  Low-voltage luminaires around permanently installed pools were addressed in 680.22(B)(6). These provisions permitted specific low-voltage luminaires to be located less than 1.5 m (5 ft) from the inside walls of the pool under certain conditions. These luminaires must be of the type that does not require a grounding means and cannot exceed the voltage limitations defined in the definition of *Low Voltage Contact Limit* in 680.2. These luminaires must also be supplied by transformers or power supplies listed for swimming pool and spa use that comply with 680.23(A)(2).

- **2017 *NEC* Change**
  New provisions were added in 680.22(B)(7) to specifically address low-voltage gas-fired luminaires, decorative fireplaces, fire pits, and similar equipment. With the inclusion of electronic ignitors for these devices, *NEC* regulations were needed for this type of low-voltage, gas-fired equipment.

680.22(B)(7)

Analysis of the Change:
A new definition for *Low Voltage Contact Limit* was introduced in 680.2 during the 2011 *NEC* revision cycle. This definition pertains to low-voltage luminaires installed around swimming pools, fountains, and spas. Low-voltage lighting systems are referenced several times within Article 680 for requirements for low-voltage luminaires. This definition was needed to assist users of the *Code* in determining the voltage limitations for these applications.

For the 2017 *NEC*, a new 680.22(B)(7) titled, "Low-Voltage Gas-Fired Luminaires, Decorative Fireplaces, Fire Pits, and Similar Equipment," has been introduced into the *Code*. These features have become one of the most popular outdoor additions to a pool area, but they also require the coordination of several key elements such as masonry, gas and plumbing, stonework and now electrical with the introduction of electronic igniters to these units. These new provisions for low-voltage gas fire equipment were needed with the conversion of gas luminaire technology away from manual ignition and toward the use of low-voltage electronic ignitors, bringing formerly gas-only devices and appliances under the requirements of the *NEC* as pertaining to the electrical control and low-voltage ignitor equipment.

Clarification was needed to eliminate confusion as to the types of luminaires covered under 680.22(B). Some in the inspection community were interpreting the *Code* language to exclude and reject listed electronically ignited gas-fired decorative luminaires, fire pits, and other equipment that otherwise meet the requirements of 680.22(B)(6) for low-voltage luminaires. The definition of *luminaire* in Article 100 does not specify the type of light source, power source or fuel source. Therefore, gas-fired luminaires would be included in this definition, as are LED, incandescent, halogen, compact fluorescent, and other technologies not specifically mentioned in the definition of a luminaire.

In order for this low-voltage gas-fired equipment to be located less than 1.5 m (5 ft) from the inside walls of the pool, listed low-voltage gas-fired luminaires, decorative fireplaces, fire pits, and similar equipment using low-voltage ignitors, addressed in 680.22(B)(7), must not require grounding. This low-voltage gas-fired equipment is also required to be supplied by listed transformers or power supplies that comply with 680.23(A)(2) with outputs that do not exceed the low-voltage contact limit. Metallic equipment is required to be bonded in accordance with the requirements in 680.26(B) for equipotential bonding. Transformers or power supplies supplying this type of low-voltage gas-fired equipment is required to be installed in accordance with the requirements in 680.24. The metallic gas piping must be bonded in accordance with the requirements in 250.104(B) and 680.26(B)(7).

First Revisions: FR 4857
Second Revisions: SR 4819, SCR 119
Public Inputs: PI 530
Public Comments: PC 947

680.25

680.25

Swimming Pool Panelboard Feeders

Previous 680.25(B) for grounding of swimming pool panelboard feeders was deleted as grounding provisions for swimming pool panelboard feeders have been incorporated into the revised text at 680.25(A)

The revised text at 680.25(A) requires restricted wiring methods only in areas where harsh conditions *(physical damage, environmental conditions, corrosive conditions, etc.)* are present

In noncorrosive environments, Chapter 3 wiring methods permitted

680.25 Feeders. (Swimming Pools, Fountains, and Similar Installations)

■ **Type of Change:** Revision/Deletion

■ **Change at a Glance:** Wiring methods and grounding provisions for swimming pool panelboard feeders were revised.

■ **Code Language: 680.25 Feeders. (Swimming Pools, Fountains, and Similar Installations)**
These provisions shall apply to any feeder on the supply side of panelboards supplying branch circuits for pool equipment covered in Part II of this article and on the load side of the service equipment or the source of a separately derived system.

~~(A) Wiring Methods.~~
~~(1)~~ **(A) Feeders.** ~~Feeders shall be installed in rigid metal conduit or intermediate metal conduit. The~~ following ~~wiring methods shall be permitted if not subject to physical damage:~~ Where feeders are installed in corrosive environments as described in 680.14, the wiring method of that portion of the feeder shall be as required in 680.14(B) or shall be liquidtight flexible nonmetallic conduit. Wiring methods installed in corrosive environments as described in 680.14 shall contain an insulated copper equipment grounding conductor sized in accordance with Table 250.122, but not smaller than 12 AWG.

Where installed in noncorrosive environments, feeders shall comply with the general requirements in Chapter 3.

~~(1) Liquidtight flexible nonmetallic conduit~~
~~(2) Rigid polyvinyl chloride conduit~~
~~(3) Reinforced thermosetting resin conduit~~
~~(4) Electrical metallic tubing where installed on or within a building~~
~~(5) Electrical nonmetallic tubing where installed within a building~~
~~(6) Type MC cable where installed within a building and if not subject to corrosive environment~~
~~(2)~~ **(B) Aluminum Conduit.** Aluminum conduit shall not be permitted in the pool area where subject to corrosion.

~~(B) Grounding. An equipment grounding conductor shall be installed with the feeder conductors between the grounding terminal of the pool equipment panelboard and the grounding terminal of the applicable service equipment or source of a separately derived system. For other than feeders to separate buildings that do not utilize an insulated equipment grounding conductor in accordance with 680.25(B)(2), this equipment grounding conductor shall be insulated.~~
~~(1) Size. This conductor shall be sized in accordance with 250.122 but not smaller than 12 AWG. On separately derived systems, this conductor shall be sized in accordance with 250.30(A)(3) but not smaller than 8 AWG.~~
~~(2) Separate Buildings. A feeder to a separate building or structure shall be permitted to supply swimming pool equipment branch circuits, or feeders supplying swimming pool equipment branch circuits, if the grounding arrangements in the separate building meet the requirements in 250.32(B).~~

680.25

680.25

- **2014 *NEC* Requirement**

   The wiring methods for feeders on the supply side of panelboards supplying branch circuits for pool equipment were required to be installed in rigid metal conduit or intermediate metal conduit. Where not subject to physical damage, six specific wiring methods with conditions were permitted for this feeder installation including EMT and PVC. This feeder was required to include an insulated equipment grounding conductor.

- **2017 *NEC* Change**

   The previous 680.25(B) for grounding of swimming pool panelboard feeders was deleted in its entirety as grounding provisions for swimming pool panelboard feeders have been incorporated into the revised text at 680.25(A). The revised text at 680.25(A) requires restricted wiring methods only in areas where harsh conditions (such as physical damage, environmental conditions, corrosive conditions, etc.) are present. Chapter 3 wiring methods are now otherwise permitted.

Analysis of the Change:

The wiring methods and requirements for grounding of feeder(s) on the supply side of panelboards supplying branch circuits for pool equipment have experienced quite a bit of revision over the last three *Code* cycles. For the 2011 *NEC*, an exception to 680.25(A)(1) permitted an "existing" feeder between an "existing" remote panelboard and service equipment to be run in flexible metal conduit or an approved cable assembly that included an equipment grounding conductor (EGC) within its outer sheath. This permission was an exception to the requirement found at 680.25(B) that demanded a wiring method that included an insulated EGC for these swimming pool panelboard feeders.

Installers and inspectors alike struggled with the term "existing" in this exception. What did "existing" mean? Some would argue that a new feeder at new construction becomes "existing" the minute it is installed. To determine the wiring method for a feeder to a swimming pool panelboard, what difference should it make if the feeder and the remote panelboard are "existing" or not?

The exception for "existing" feeders allowing the installation of the feeder without an insulated EGC was deleted for the 2014 *NEC*. Under these revised provisions, nonmetallic-sheathed cable (Type NM cable) was no longer an acceptable wiring method for this feeder as Type NM cable typically does not employ an insulated EGC.

For the 2017 *NEC*, 680.25 as a whole received even more revision. Previous 680.25(B) for grounding of swimming pool panelboard feeders was deleted in its entirety as grounding provisions for swimming pool panelboard feeders have been incorporated into the revised text at 680.25(A). The revised text at 680.25(A) requires restricted wiring methods only in areas where harsh conditions are present. Chapter 3 wiring methods are now otherwise permitted.

References are made to the new 680.14, Corrosive Environment which will require wiring methods in any corrosive areas [as described in 680.14(A)] to be "listed and identified for use in such areas." The mentioned restrictions on wiring methods for swimming pool panelboard feeders are related to concerns for two issues: protection from physical damage and protection from environmental conditions (wet, damp, and corrosive conditions) associated with pools, spas, hot tubs, etc. The remaining text describes portions of those feeders installed in areas that are not likely to encounter those severe conditions.

The prohibition of aluminum conduit in the pool area where subject to corrosion was retained as it was moved to its new home in 680.25(B); it was previously located in 680.25(A)(2).

First Revisions: FR 4863, FR 4864
Second Revisions: SR 4829
Public Inputs: PI 3818, PI 3799
Public Comments: PC 731

680.27(B)(1), Ex. and 680.27(B)(2), Ex.
Specialized Pool Equipment

680.27

680.27(B)(1), Ex. and 680.27(B)(2), Ex. Specialized Pool Equipment. (Swimming Pools, Fountains, and Similar Installations)

■ **Type of Change:** New

- **Change at a Glance:** New exceptions were added for pool cover motors that allow motors not rated to exceed the low-voltage contact limit to be installed less than 1.5 m (5 ft) from the inside walls of the pool and omit GFCI protection.

- **Code Language: 680.27 Specialized Pool Equipment. (Swimming Pools, Fountains, and Similar Installations) (B) Electrically Operated Pool Covers.**

  (1) Motors and Controllers. The electric motors, controllers, and wiring shall be located not less than 1.5 m (5 ft) from the inside wall of the pool unless separated from the pool by a wall, cover, or other permanent barrier. Electric motors installed below grade level shall be of the totally enclosed type. The device that controls the operation of the motor for an electrically operated pool cover shall be located such that the operator has full view of the pool.

  Informational Note No. 1: For cabinets installed in damp and wet locations, see 312.2.
  Informational Note No. 2: For switches or circuit breakers installed in wet locations, see 404.4.
  Informational Note No. 3: For protection against liquids, see 430.11.

  Exception: *Motors that are part of listed systems with ratings not exceeding the low-voltage contact limit that are supplied by listed transformers or power supplies that comply with 680.23(A)(2) shall be permitted to be located less than 1.5 m (5 ft) from the inside walls of the pool.*

  (2) Protection. The electric motor and controller shall be connected to a branch circuit protected by a ground-fault circuit interrupter.

  Exception: *Motors that are part of listed systems with ratings not exceeding the low-voltage contact limit that are supplied by listed transformers or power supplies that comply with 680.23(A)(2).*

- **2014 *NEC* Requirement**
  The electric motors, controllers, and wiring for an electrically operated pool cover (regardless of the voltage rating) were required to be located not less than 1.5 m (5 ft) from the inside wall of the pool unless separated from the pool by a wall, cover, or other permanent barrier. Electric motors installed below grade level are required be of the totally enclosed type. The device that controls the operation of the pool cover motor is required to be located such that the operator has full view of the pool. The electric motor and controller were required to be connected to a branch circuit protected by a ground-fault circuit interrupter (GFCI).

- **2017 *NEC* Change**
  Two exceptions were added below the parent text of 680.27(B)(1) and 680.27(B)(2) recognizing pool cover motors that are part of a listed sys-

680.27

tem with ratings not exceeding the low-voltage contact limits, allowing such a low-voltage type motor to be installed within 1.5 m (5 ft) of the inside walls of the pool, and the omission of GFCI protection for said motor.

Analysis of the Change:

Electrically operated pool covers have advanced considerably in recent years. From hand crank models to fully low-voltage electronic, key-operated systems, today's automatic covers are more reliable, durable, and safer than ever before. Pool covers typically consist of a reinforced vinyl fabric running between a track on either side of the pool's length. An aluminum roller on one end typically houses the cover and the tension rope when the cover is stored. One end of the roller will be attached to an electric motor, which is wired to a two-direction switch (open or closed). These pool cover motors can have a voltage rating as much as 240 volts or a voltage rating not exceeding the low-voltage contact limit supplied by listed transformers or power supply. Electrically operated pool covers can have a direct impact on water, chemical, electrical and heat savings. These pool coverings have also been attributed to drowning prevention. Provisions for electrically operated pool covers have been a *Code* requirement since the 1984 edition of the *NEC*.

The parent text of 680.27(B)(1) and (B)(2) appears to assume that the electrically operated pool cover utilizes a motor running at nominal voltage. New designs in pool cover motors are becoming available that are powered by swimming pool transformers and operate at voltages not exceeding the low-voltage contact limit. For the 2017 *NEC*, exceptions have been added below the parent text of 680.27(B)(1) and 680.27(B)(2) recognizing these low-voltage designs and allowing such a low-voltage type motor to be installed within 1.5 m (5 ft) of the inside walls of the pool and the omission of GFCI protection.

The text for these added exceptions was fashioned from the existing text for low-voltage underwater luminaires not requiring grounding, described at 680.22(B)(6), as these low-voltage pool cover motors present the same risk of electric shock (or lack thereof).

First Revisions: FR 4877

680.27

680.28

Swimming Pools Gas-Fired Water Heater

680.28

680.28 Gas-Fired Water Heater. (Swimming Pools, Fountains, and Similar Installations)

- **Type of Change:** New

- **Change at a Glance:** New requirements were added for GFCI protection for swimming pool and spa gas-fired water heaters.

- **Code Language: 680.28 Gas-Fired Water Heater. (Swimming Pools, Fountains, and Similar Installations)**
  Circuits serving gas-fired swimming pool and spa water heaters operating at voltages above the low-voltage contact limit shall be provided with ground-fault circuit-interrupter protection for personnel.

- **2014 *NEC* Requirement**
  No provisions existed for GFCI protection for swimming pool and spa water heaters (gas or electric). The requirements of 680.22(A)(2) called for GFCI protection for receptacles that provide power for water-pump motors or other loads directly related to the circulation and sanitation system.

- **2017 *NEC* Change**
  New provisions were added requiring branch circuits serving gas-fired

swimming pool and spa water heaters operating at voltages above the low-voltage contact limit to be provided with GFCI protection for personnel.

Analysis of the Change:

Does a branch circuit for a swimming pool water heater require ground-fault circuit interrupter (GFCI) protection? What if the pool heater is an electric, 240-volt heater? What about a 125-volt rated electric pool heater? Is GFCI protection required then? What about a gas-fired swimming pool water heater with a 125-volt branch circuit for the electronic ignitor, etc.? For users of the *Code* prior to the 2017 *NEC*, the answer to all of the previous questions was that no GFCI protection was specifically or directly required for a swimming pool water heater.

GFCI protection for personnel is not required for electric water heater installations as the risk of electric shock is considered adequately mitigated through the use of proper grounding provisions [see 680.6(3)] and the listing installation requirement for the use of current collectors on the input and output side of the heater. These current collectors have proven reliable to prevent unacceptable levels of current in the pool in the event of corrosion of the immersed heating elements of an electric pool heater. However, these current collectors are not present with a gas-fired swimming pool heater. The 125-volt branch circuit to a gas-fired water heater is susceptible to a loss of current and a ground-fault condition as much as any other piece of electrical equipment.

680.28

To address this issue, branch circuits serving gas-fired swimming pool and spa water heaters operating at voltages above the low-voltage contact limit are required to provide GFCI protection for personnel beginning with the 2017 *NEC*. This requirement adds a measure of safety to the end user of the swimming pool in future installations.

Some within the electrical industry, including some enforcers of the *Code,* have relied on the requirements of 680.22(A)(2) to enforce GFCI protection for receptacle outlets that provide power to pool heaters of permanently installed pools. This particular provision required GFCI protection for "receptacles that provide power for water-pump motors or other loads directly related to the circulation and sanitation system." The argument being that a pool heater would fall into this category of "other loads directly related to the circulation and sanitation system." Regardless if this is a legitimate *Code* interpretation or not, this new GFCI requirement for gas-fired water heaters will give users of the *Code* a strong, direct requirement for GFCI protection for this one heating aspect of the aquatic environment moving forward.

First Revisions: FR 4869

Public Inputs: PI 2578

680.74

Bonding in Hydromassage Bathtubs

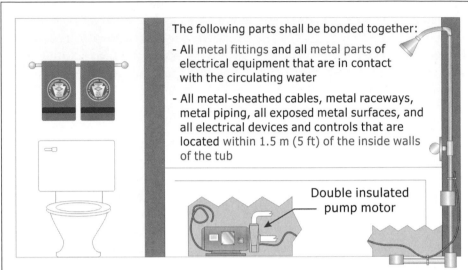

The following parts shall be bonded together:

- All metal fittings and all metal parts of electrical equipment that are in contact with the circulating water

- All metal-sheathed cables, metal raceways, metal piping, all exposed metal surfaces, and all electrical devices and controls that are located within 1.5 m (5 ft) of the inside walls of the tub

Double insulated pump motor

Bonding requirements for hydromassage bathtubs was reformatted into a list format

New exception was added to exempt "small conductive surfaces not likely to become energized" from hydromassage bathtub bonding requirements

680.74 Bonding. (Hydromassage Bathtubs)

- **Type of Change:** Revision/New

- **Change at a Glance:** Bonding requirements for hydromassage bathtubs were reformatted into a list format. A new exception was added to exempt bonding of small conductive surfaces.

- **Code Language: 680.74 Bonding. (Hydromassage Bathtubs)**
  ~~Both metal piping systems and grounded metal parts in contact with the circulating water shall be bonded together using a solid copper bonding jumper, insulated, covered, or bare, not smaller than 8 AWG. The bonding jumper shall be connected to the terminal on the circulating pump motor that is intended for this purpose. The bonding jumper shall not be required to be connected to a double insulated circulating pump motor. The 8 AWG or larger solid copper bonding jumper shall be required for equipotential bonding in the area of the hydromassage bathtub and shall not be required to be extended or attached to any remote panelboard, service equipment, or any electrode. The 8 AWG or larger solid copper bonding jumper shall be long enough to terminate on a replacement non-double-insulated pump motor and shall be terminated to the equipment grounding conductor of the branch circuit of the motor when a double-in-~~

sulated circulating pump motor is used.

(A) General. The following parts shall be bonded together:

(1) All metal fittings within or attached to the tub structure that are in contact with the circulating water

(2) Metal parts of electrical equipment associated with the tub water circulating system, including pump and blower motors

(3) Metal-sheathed cables and raceways and metal piping that are within 1.5 m (5 ft) of the inside walls of the tub and not separated from the tub by a permanent barrier

(4) All exposed metal surfaces that are within 1.5 m (5 ft) of the inside walls of the tub and not separated from the tub area by a permanent barrier

(5) Electrical devices and controls that are not associated with the hydromassage tubs and that are located within 1.5 m (5 ft) from such units

Exception No. 1: Small conductive surfaces not likely to become energized, such as air and water jets, supply valve assemblies, and drain fittings not connected to metallic piping, and towel bars, mirror frames, and similar nonelectrical equipment not connected to metal framing shall not be required to be bonded.

Exception No. 2: Double-insulated motors and blowers shall not be bonded

(B) All metal parts required to be bonded by this section shall be bonded together using a solid copper bonding jumper, insulated, covered, or bare, not smaller than 8 AWG. The bonding jumper(s) shall be required for equipotential bonding in the area of the hydromassage bathtub and shall not be required to be extended or attached to any remote panelboard, service equipment, or any electrode. In all installations a bonding jumper long enough to terminate on a replacement non-double-insulated pump or blower motor shall be provided and shall be terminated to the equipment grounding conductor of the branch circuit of the motor when a double-insulated circulating pump or blower motor is used.

■ **2014 *NEC* Requirement**
The requirements for equipotential bonding in the area of a hydro massage bathtub were incorporated into one long paragraph. These requirements indicated what needed to be bonded as well as the provisions for the bonding jumper(s) required to accomplish this equipotential bonding.

■ **2017 *NEC* Change**
The former requirements for equipotential bonding of a hydromassage bathtub were retained and placed into a list format. Section 680.74 now

680.74

has two first level subdivisions, (A) and (B), with two exceptions for 680.74(A). A list of metallic items located "within 1.5 m (5 ft) of the inside walls of the tub" were added to the items required to be bonded. A new exception now exempts bonding of "small conductive surfaces."

Analysis of the Change:

The requirements for equipotential bonding in the area of a hydromassage bathtub are covered by the provisions of 680.74. For the 2014 *NEC*, these equipotential bonding provisions were incorporated into one of the longest paragraphs in the *NEC*. The previous provisions found at 680.74 called for all metal piping associated with a hydromassage bathtub and all grounded metal parts in contact with the circulating water to be bonded together using an 8 AWG solid copper bonding jumper. This bonding jumper is required to be connected to the terminal on the hydromassage bathtub circulating pump motor.

The bonding jumper was not to be connected to a double insulated circulating pump motor. This section also required an 8 AWG or larger solid copper bonding jumper long enough to terminate on a replacement non-double insulated pump motor, with a termination to the equipment grounding conductor of the branch circuit of the motor when a double insulated circulating pump motor is used. The language clarified that the 8 AWG or larger solid copper bonding jumper(s) was not to be extended or attached to any remote panelboard, service equipment, or electrode. This bonding jumper is for equipotential bonding in the area of the hydromassage bathtub, not to establish a connection to the earth (grounding).

For the 2017 *NEC*, these former requirements were reformatted into a much easier to use list format. Section 680.74 now has two first level subdivisions, (A) and (B). The first subdivision at 680.74(A) describes the parts that are required to be bonded. Besides the metal parts of electrical equipment associated with the tub water circulating system, all metal fittings within or attached to the tub structure that are in contact with the circulating water are now required to be bonded together.

This subdivision now requires all metal-sheathed cables, metal raceways, metal piping, and exposed metal surfaces within 1.5 m (5 ft) of the inside walls of the tub to be bonded. It also requires that all electrical devices and controls not associated with the hydromassage tub that are located within 1.5 m (5 ft) from such units are to be bonded for equipotential bonding purposes. Bonding (connecting) is necessary for ensuring the same voltage potential on all conductive parts and no real harm can come from bonding conductive components together.

A new 680.74(A), Exception No. 1 was added this *Code* cycle to exempt "small conductive surfaces not likely to become energized" from hydromassage bathtub bonding requirements. This exception would include such things as isolated air and water jets, supply valve assemblies, and drain fittings not connected to metallic piping. Other items impacted by this new exception would include towel bars, mirror frames, and similar nonelectrical equipment not connected to metal framing. This "small conductive surfaces" exception is very similar to the

680.74

one in the parent text of 680.26(B)(5), which exempts small "isolated parts that are not over 100 mm (4 in.) in any dimension and do not penetrate into the pool structure more than 25 mm (1 in.)" from equipotential bonding for a permanently installed pool.

The requirements of 680.74(B) bring together the previous requirements associated with the 8 AWG solid copper bonding jumper(s) necessary to accomplish this equipotential bonding of the hydromassage bathtubs. The entirety of the revision and new provisions of 680.74(A) and (B) are intended to clarify the intent of the requirement for bonding in the area around hydromassage bathtubs.

First Revisions: FR 4870
Public Inputs: PI 151, PI 2129

682.15

GFCI Protection in Bodies of Water

682.15

682.15 Ground-Fault Circuit-Interrupter (GFCI) Protection. (Natural and Artificially Made Bodies of Water)

- **Type of Change:** Revision

- **Change at a Glance:** Section 628.12 now requires that all receptacles installed outdoors and in or on floating buildings or structures within the electrical datum plane area are to be provided with GFCI protection for personnel (not just in areas used for storage, maintenance, or repair where portable electric hand tools, electrical diagnostic equipment, or portable lighting equipment are to be used).

- **Code Language: 682.15 Ground-Fault Circuit-Interrupter (GFCI) Protection. (Natural and Artificially Made Bodies of Water)**

  Fifteen- and 20-ampere single-phase, 125-volt through 250-volt receptacles installed outdoors and in or on floating buildings or structures within the electrical datum plane area ~~that are used for storage, maintenance, or repair where portable electric hand tools, electrical diagnostic equipment, or portable lighting equipment are to be used~~ shall be provided with GFCI protection for personnel. The GFCI protection device shall be located not less than 300 mm (12 in.) above the established electrical datum plane.

- **2014 *NEC* Requirement**
  GFCI protection was required for 15- and 20-ampere, single-phase, 125-volt through 250-volt receptacles installed outdoors and in or on floating buildings or structures within the electrical datum plane area. Protection was required only in areas used for storage, maintenance, or repair where portable electric hand tools, electrical diagnostic equipment, or portable lighting equipment were used.

- **2017 *NEC* Change**
  GFCI protection for personnel is now required for all 15- and 20-ampere, single-phase, 125-volt through 250-volt receptacles installed outdoors and in or on floating buildings or structures within the electrical datum plane area, not just those receptacles in areas used for storage, maintenance, or repair where portable electric hand tools, electrical diagnostic equipment, or portable lighting equipment are to be used.

Analysis of the Change:
Many 15- and 20-ampere single-phase, 125-volt through 250-volt receptacles installed outdoors and in or on floating buildings or structures within the electrical datum plane area are installed for purposes other than the use of "portable electric hand tools, electrical diagnostic equipment, or portable lighting equipment." As previously written at 682.15, no receptacle in or on these floating buildings or structures require GFCI protection unless that receptacle is used for "portable electric hand tools, electrical diagnostic equipment, or portable lighting equipment."

For the 2017 *NEC*, the description, "areas that are used for storage, maintenance, or repair where portable electric hand tools, electrical diagnostic equipment, or portable lighting equipment are to be used" was deleted. GFCI protection for personnel is now required for all 15- and 20-ampere, single-phase, 125-volt through 250-volt receptacles installed outdoors and in or on floating buildings or structures within the electrical datum plane area without having to determine if portable electric hand tools, etc., will be used or not. The GFCI

682.15

protection device must be located not less than 300 mm (12 in.) above the established electrical datum plane.

By removing the qualifying language, it will be clear that GFCI protection for personnel is required under all situations encountered within the electrical datum plane area. This change will help eliminate the debate between installers and enforcers in these areas concerning whether portable tools, portable lighting, and the like, are being used or not. This deletion of text is similar to the changes that occurred last *Code* cycle at 210.8(B)(8) concerning GFCI protection for 125-volt, single-phase, 15- and 20-ampere receptacles installed in all non-dwelling unit garages, service bays, and similar areas.

First Revisions: FR 4871
Public Inputs: PI 4679

690.2

Functional Grounded PV System

682.15

Functional Grounded PV System. A PV system that has an electrical reference to ground that is not solidly grounded.

PV Modules Junction Box DC Disconnect Inverter Utility Service

ON

OFF

DC EGC AC GEC →

Combiner Box Grounding Electrode System

Informational Note: A functional grounded PV system is often connected to ground through a fuse, circuit breaker, resistance device, non-isolated grounded ac circuit, or electronic means that is part of a listed ground-fault protection system. Conductors in these systems that are normally at ground potential may have voltage to ground during fault conditions.

200.6 Definitions. [Solar Photovoltaic (PV) Systems]

- **Type of Change:** New

- **Change at a Glance:** A new definition for *Functional Grounded PV System* was added at 690.2.

- **Code Language: 690.2 Definitions. [Solar Photovoltaic (PV) Systems]**

  Functional Grounded PV System. A PV system that has an electrical reference to ground that is not solidly grounded.

  Informational Note: A functional grounded PV system is often connected to ground through a fuse, circuit breaker, resistance device, non-isolated grounded ac circuit, or electronic means that is part of a listed ground-fault protection system. Conductors in these systems that are normally at ground potential may have voltage to ground during fault conditions.

- **2014 *NEC* Requirement**

  There was no definition for *functional grounded PV system* in the 2014 *NEC*. The term was not used anywhere in Article 690. The term *reference (center tap) conductor* was used a couple of times in Article 690, but there was no definition. Most referenced or functional grounded PV systems were treated as if they were solidly grounded systems.

690.2

- **2017 *NEC* Change**

  A new definition for *Functional Grounded PV System* was added at 690.2. This term is now used in six different locations throughout Article 690.

Analysis of the Change:

A new definition for *Functional Grounded PV System* was added at 690.2 in the 2017 NEC. According to this new definition, a functional grounded PV system is "a PV system that has an electrical reference to ground that is not solidly grounded." An informational note added below the definition indicates that a functional grounded PV system is often connected to ground through a fuse, circuit breaker, resistance device, non-isolated grounded ac circuit, or electronic means that is part of a listed ground-fault protection system. This informational note goes on to inform users of the *Code* that conductors in these systems that are normally at ground potential may have voltage to ground during fault conditions.

This new definition clears up the confusion over the use of the terms *functional grounded PV systems* and *reference grounded PV systems* throughout Article 690 and the use of the term *solidly grounded systems*. Most PV systems are not solidly grounded; however, the installation requirements are written as if they were solidly grounded. This approach creates confusion for the AHJ, installer, and service personnel. By clearly delineating functional grounded PV systems from solidly-grounded PV systems, the safety requirements for installation become much clearer. *Solidly Grounded* is defined in Article 100 as "connected to ground without inserting any resistor or impedance device." This definition, and other references to a functional grounded PV system, allows for a single installation method for all PV systems rather than different requirements for grounded and ungrounded systems.

Previous versions of this *Code* treated referenced or functional grounded PV systems as if they were solidly grounded and then added warning labels for installers and maintenance personnel that the associated PV conductors that they might expect to be at ground voltage potential could actually be current-carrying conductors. This new definition at other sections of Article 690, such as 690.41, assumes that all conductors could have voltage whether or not they are intended to be at earth's voltage potential under normal operating conditions.

Most PV systems installed in the past decade are actually functional grounded systems rather than solidly grounded systems as defined in Article 100. For functional grounded PV systems with an interactive inverter output, the ac equipment grounding conductor is connected to associated grounded ac distribution equipment. This connection is often the connection to ground for ground-fault protection and equipment grounding of the PV array.

In system grounding, one of the ungrounded circuit (current-carrying) conductors is bonded (connected) to the equipment grounding system and also to earth. This is referred to as reference or functional grounding in most cases. The ungrounded conductor that has been connected to the equipment grounding system and to earth is known as the "grounded conductor." The connection between the grounded conductor and the equipment grounding system is known as the system bonding jumper per *NEC* terminology. With a non-isolated inverter, the lack of isolation to the grounded ac service conductors requires that the dc PV array be ungrounded for the inverter to work. While this type of system is operating, the dc PV array actually becomes referenced to ground through the ac output conductors. The PV industry often refers to this system configuration as "ungrounded," but in reality the PV array is only ungrounded when the inverter is not operating. As soon as the inverter begins producing power, the whole system becomes referenced to ground through the ac service conductors.

This definition was actually changed from *Reference Grounded PV System* to *Functional Grounded PV System* during the 2017 *NEC* revision process to avoid "reference ground" being confused with the concepts in Article 517, Health Care Facilities. The new term *Functional Grounded PV System* matches the International Electrotechnical Commission (IEC) use of the term as well.

690.2

First Revisions: FR 954
Second Revisions: SR 932
Public Inputs: PI 3757
Public Comments: PC 1018, PC 1847

690.7

Maximum Voltage in Solar Photovoltaic (PV) Systems

690.7

690.7 Maximum Voltage [Solar Photovoltaic (PV) Systems]

- **Type of Change:** New

- **Change at a Glance:** Maximum voltage requirements for PV systems were revised for clarity; three first level subdivisions remain.

- **Code Language: 690.7 Maximum Voltage [Solar Photovoltaic (PV) Systems]**
The maximum voltage of PV system dc circuits shall be the highest voltage between any two circuit conductors or any conductor and ground. PV system dc circuits on or in one- and two-family dwellings shall be permitted to have a maximum voltage of 600 volts or less. PV system dc circuits on or in other types of buildings shall be permitted to have a maximum voltage of 1000 volts or less. Where not located on or in buildings, listed dc PV equipment, rated at a maximum voltage of 1500 volts or less, shall not be required to comply with Parts II and III of Article 490.

(A) ~~Maximum~~ Photovoltaic ~~System Voltage~~ Source and Output Circuits.

Table 690.7(A) Voltage Correction Factors for Crystalline and Multicrystalline Silicon Modules

~~(B) Direct-Current Utilization Circuits.~~
(B) DC-to-DC Converter Source Output Circuits.

~~(C) Photovoltaic Source and Output Circuits.~~
~~(D) Circuits over 150 Volts to Ground.~~
~~(E)~~ **(C) Bipolar Source and Output Circuits.**
(See *NEC* for complete *Code* text)

■ **2014 *NEC* Requirement**
Requirements for maximum voltages for PV systems were found at 690.7. The section had five first level subdivisions. Table 690.7 was part of this section as well.

■ **2017 *NEC* Change**
Section 690.7 went through an extensive revision this cycle to simplify these maximum voltage requirements. Three first level subdivisions remain, and Table 690.7 was changed to Table 690.7(A), as this is where the reference to this table exists.

Analysis of the Change:
The requirements of 690.7 pertain to maximum voltages of PV systems while 690.8 relates to circuit sizing and maximum circuit current ratings of PV systems. Section 690.7 went through an extensive revision in the 2017 *NEC*, simplifying these maximum voltage requirements and addressing the use of the terms related to *maximum voltage* and *maximum current* used throughout Article 690. The revised 690.7 now has only three first level subdivisions: (A) Photovoltaic Source and Output Circuits [previous (A) Maximum Photovoltaic System Voltage and (C) Photovoltaic Source and Output Circuits combined together into one first level subdivision], (B) DC-To-DC Converter Source and Output Circuits (a new section to address this equipment); and (C) Bipolar Source and Output Circuits.

The previous text at 690.7(C) pertaining to the maximum voltage of PV system dc circuits on or in one- and two-family dwellings and other types of buildings has been relocated to 690.7. This places the maximum voltages allowed for these different occupancies up front for a more logical order. Previous provisions at 690.7(A) titled, "Maximum Photovoltaic System Voltage." only addressed PV source and output circuits, while previous 690.7(C) addressed basically the same issue. It was confusing to have two first level subdivisions dealing with the essentially the same subject.

The correction methods of Table 690.7(A) [was Table 690.7] survived the revision process and were brought forward for the 2017 *NEC* with a reference at 690.7(A)(2). This table was developed using the most severe temperature factors for crystalline silicon PV modules, meaning that the results of using the adjustment factors in Table 690.7(A) will be at least as conservative as using the actual correction factors. The simplicity of the table, and the complexity of properly applying the correction factors, suggest that Table 690.7(A) should be allowed to be used as an alternative, simple calculation for maximum voltage for PV systems.

The revised 690.7(A) simplifies the language of the three methods used to calculate maximum voltage. A new recognized method of determining the maximum

690.7

voltage for larger PV systems is addressed at 690.7(A)(3) for PV systems of 100 kW or larger. This method permits a documented and stamped PV system design, using an "industry standard method" and provided by a licensed professional electrical engineer for PV systems with a generating capacity of 100 kW or greater. A new informational note was also added at this point to point users of the *Code* to an example of an "industry standard method" for calculating maximum voltage of a PV system, such as SAND 2004-3535, *Photovoltaic Array Performance Model* published by Sandia National Laboratories. This industry standard method is a more complex method that has been developed and validated within the PV industry for a number of years and should be considered as an acceptable voltage calculation approach for large scale PV systems.

The previous 690.7(B) titled, "Direct-Current Utilization Circuits," was removed from 690.7 as it referred to the output of PV modules, which is not applicable for the output of dc-to-dc converters. These loads are not under the scope of Article 690 and did not belong in this article. New 690.7(B) titled, "DC-to-DC Converter Source and Output Circuits," provides guidance on how to properly calculate voltage on these dc circuits.

690.7

The previous provisions of 690.7(D), titled, "Circuits over 150 Volts to Ground," were removed as they dealt more with the wiring method itself and did not specifically deal with maximum voltage.

The previous text at 690.7(E) titled, "Bipolar Source and Output Circuits," has been relocated to 690.7(C) and revised to recognize the newly defined functional grounded PV systems. The previous text at this location had requirements for solidly grounded bipolar source and output circuits requiring one conductor from each monopole to be solidly grounded (connected to ground without inserting any resistor or impedance device).

First Revisions: FR 1020
Second Revisions: SR 935, SCR 62, SCR 63, SCR 64, SCR 938
Public Inputs: Numerous PIs
Public Comments: PC 1074, PC 477, PC 587, PC 1362, Numerous PCs, CPC 935, CPC 936, CPC 937

690.8(A)(1)

Circuit Sizing and Current of PV Systems

In addition to the 125 percent method permitted by 690.8(A)(1)(1), a second option was added for calculating the maximum current for a PV source circuit using an industry standard method provided by a licensed professional electrical engineer *[690.8(A)(1)(2)]*

Cannot be less than 70 percent of the value calculated using the 125 percent method

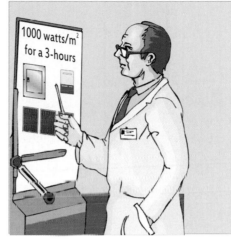

1000 watts/m² for a 3-hours

690.8(A)(1)

Applies to PV systems with a generating capacity of 100 kW or greater

690.8(A)(1) Circuit Sizing and Current. [Solar Photovoltaic (PV) Systems]

- **Type of Change:** Revision/New

- **Change at a Glance:** The revision allows for engineering supervision to be used in calculating source circuit maximum current.

- **Code Language: 690.8 Circuit Sizing and Current. [Solar Photovoltaic (PV) Systems]**

  (A) Calculation of Maximum Circuit Current. The maximum current for the specific circuit shall be calculated in accordance with 690.8(A)(1) through (A)~~(5)~~(6).

  Informational Note: Where the requirements of 690.8(A)(1) and (B)(1) are both applied, the resulting multiplication factor is 156 percent.

  (1) Photovoltaic Source Circuit Currents. The maximum current shall be ~~the sum of parallel module rated short-circuit currents multiplied by 125 percent.~~ calculated by one of the following methods:

(1) The sum of parallel-connected PV module–rated short-circuit currents multiplied by 125 percent

(2) For PV systems with a generating capacity of 100 kW or greater, a documented and stamped PV system design, using an industry standard method and provided by a licensed professional electrical engineer, shall be permitted. The calculated maximum current value shall be based on the highest 3-hour current average resulting from the simulated local irradiance on the PV array accounting for elevation and orientation. The current value used by this method shall not be less than 70 percent of the value calculated using 690.8(A)(1)(1).

Informational Note: One industry standard method for calculating maximum current of a PV system is available from Sandia National Laboratories, reference SAND 2004-3535, *Photovoltaic Array Performance Model*. This model is used by the System Advisor Model simulation program provided by the National Renewable Energy Laboratory.

690.8(A)(1)

- **2014 *NEC* Requirement**
  For calculating the maximum current for a PV source circuit, the sum of parallel module rated short-circuit currents multiplied by 125 percent was required.

- **2017 *NEC* Change**
  In addition to the 125 percent method permitted by previous editions of the *Code*, a second option was added for calculating the maximum current for a PV source circuit using an industry standard method provided by a licensed professional electrical engineer.

Analysis of the Change:

For PV circuit sizing and maximum circuit current ratings of PV systems, one would need to visit the provisions of 690.8. In previous editions of the *Code*, only one choice existed at 690.8(A)(1) for calculating the maximum current for a PV source circuit. The PV source circuit maximum current was the sum of parallel module rated short-circuit currents (Isc) multiplied by 125 percent. As an example, if a PV module has a rated short-circuit current of 9.2 amperes, this would calculate to 9.2 A × 1.25 = 11.5 amperes.

For the 2017 *NEC*, a second option was added for calculating the maximum current for a PV source circuit. This new permitted option involves using an "industry standard method" provided by a licensed professional electrical engineer. This engineering method would only apply to PV systems with a generating capacity of 100 kW or greater. Engineers who are experts in electrical system design are employed to perform all aspects of system design. An engineer qualified to design PV systems is capable of making the necessary calculations or running the necessary simulations to develop accurate maximum circuit currents of PV source circuits based on the specifics of an installation location. A new informational note was also added below 690.8(A)(1)(2) to point users of the *Code* to an example of an "industry standard method" for calculating maximum voltage of a

PV system, such as SAND 2004-3535, *Photovoltaic Array Performance Model*, published by Sandia National Laboratories.

The previous 125 percent calculation method in the 2014 *NEC* [and now at 690.8(A)(1)(1)] is conservative and based on PV systems without ground-fault protection and that are capable of operating in short-circuit conditions indefinitely. If the PV array were to be exposed to the rated solar irradiance of 1000 watts/m² for a 3-hour period, typical of tracking systems, the maximum dc circuit current in a PV source or output circuit will be approximately 70 percent of the value calculated in 690.8(A)(1)(1) using the 125 percent method. Solar irradiance is the power per unit area received from the sun in the form of electromagnetic radiation in the wavelength range of the measuring instrument. The SI unit of irradiance is watt per square meter (W/m²).

The 125 percent calculation method is fine for small systems as a simple calculation, but engineering supervision is now allowed for larger PV systems to use more accurate, less conservative calculations. Due to system location, orientation, and design parameters, the use of a "one-size-fits-all" 125 percent methodology results in overly conservative requirements that add significant and unnecessary costs to larger projects while adding no value from a safety or performance perspective. Computer software is readily available to engineers who can calculate the actual current generated on PV source circuits based on all the design parameters of a given location. The added engineering supervision language in this new calculation option allows for engineers to calculate the maximum current and apply that current to sizing of PV source circuit conductors.

690.8(A)(1)

First Revisions: FR 966
Second Revisions: SR 939
Public Inputs: PI 4089, PI 3220
Public Comments: PC 996, PC 493

690.11, Exception

Photovoltaic DC Arc-Fault Circuit Protection

PV AFCI protection requirements and 690.11 received extensive revision and a new exception was added

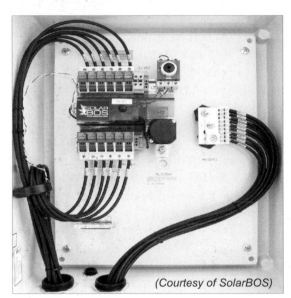

New exception added for PV systems allowing PV output circuits and dc-to-dc converter output circuits *(not installed on or in buildings)* that are direct buried, installed in metallic raceways, or installed in enclosed metallic cable trays to omitted PV AFCI protection

AFCI Combiner, 600 Volt (dc), 12 input circuits with NEMA-4X fiberglass enclosure

(Courtesy of SolarBOS)

690.11, Exception Arc-Fault Circuit Protection (Direct Current). [Solar Photovoltaic (PV) Systems]

- **Type of Change:** Revision/New

- **Change at a Glance:** A new exception that allows AFCI protection to be omitted was added for PV systems not installed on or in buildings with wiring methods that are direct buried, installed in metallic raceways, or installed in enclosed metallic cable trays.

- **Code Language: 690.11 Arc-Fault Circuit Protection (Direct Current). [Solar Photovoltaic (PV) Systems]**
  Photovoltaic systems ~~with dc source circuits, dc output circuits, or both,~~ operating at ~~a PV system maximum system voltage of~~ 80 volts dc or greater, shall be protected by a listed ~~(dc)~~ PV arc-fault circuit interrupter, ~~PV type,~~ or other system components listed to provide equivalent protection. ~~The PV arc-fault protection means shall comply with the following requirements:~~ The system shall detect and interrupt arcing faults resulting from a failure in the intended continuity of a conductor, connection, module, or other system component in the ~~dc~~ PV system ~~source and~~ dc ~~PV output~~ circuits.

(1) The system shall detect and interrupt arcing faults resulting from a failure in the intended continuity of a conductor, connection, module, or other system component in the dc PV source and dc PV output circuits.
(2) The system shall require that the disabled or disconnected equipment be manually restarted.
(3) The system shall have an annunciator that provides a visual indication that the circuit interrupter has operated. This indication shall not reset automatically.

Informational Note: Annex A includes the reference for the Photovoltaic DC Arc-Fault Circuit Protection product standard.

Exception: For PV systems not installed on or in buildings, PV output circuits and dc-to-dc converter output circuits that are direct buried, installed in metallic raceways, or installed in enclosed metallic cable trays are permitted without arc-fault circuit protection. Detached structures whose sole purpose is to house PV system equipment shall not be considered buildings according to this exception.

690.11

- **2014 *NEC* Requirement**
  The requirements for arc-fault circuit interrupter (AFCI) protection for PV systems is found at 690.11. This section called for listed (dc) arc-fault circuit interrupter, PV type, or other system components to provide equivalent protection for PV systems with dc source circuits, dc output circuits, or both, operating at a PV system maximum system voltage of 80 volts or greater. This PV AFCI protection is required to detect and interrupt arcing faults resulting from a failure in the intended continuity of a conductor, connection, module, or other system component in the dc PV source and dc PV output circuits. Two specific performance characteristics were included in these PV AFCI requirements.

- **2017 *NEC* Change**
  The requirement for PV AFCI protection at 690.11 was revised by removing the previous subsections 690.11(2) and (3). A new exception allows PV AFCI protection to be omitted for PV systems that are not installed on or in buildings where the output circuits and dc-to-dc converter output circuits are direct buried, installed in metallic raceways, or installed in enclosed metallic cable trays.

Analysis of the Change:

Arc-fault circuit interrupter (AFCI) protection (dc) was first introduced in 690.11 during the 2011 *NEC* revision process. This section required listed (PV) AFCI protection for PV systems with dc source circuits, dc output circuits, or both. PV AFCI protection requirements are limited to PV systems with a maximum system voltage of 80 volts dc or greater. PV systems can be subjected to environmental hazards such as wind, rain, snow, ice, and temperature extremes. These systems can deteriorate over time and develop insulation failures or internal PV module conductor arc-fault conditions. In PV systems, these arcing faults are direct current (dc) and are far more difficult to interrupt than ac faults because of the non-time varying (non-zero crossing) nature of dc currents. Series arcing faults resulting from a failure in the intended continuity of a conductor, connection, module, or other system component are most prevalent and may occur anywhere in the dc system. Fault currents to ground will be detected by the ground-fault protection required by 690.41(B) [was 690.5(A)].

For the 2017 *NEC*, PV AFCI protection and 690.11 received extensive revision. A new exception was also added for omission of PV AFCI protection for PV output circuits and dc-to-dc converter output circuits of PV systems not installed on or in buildings where the wiring method is direct buried, installed in metallic raceways, or installed in enclosed metallic cable trays.

One of the first revisions noticed is the deletion of 690.11(2) and (3). These items described the manner in which the PV AFCI protection acts to differentiate between a true arcing event and a false noise signature, as well as the action taken upon detecting an arc. CMP-4 determined that these topics are more appropriately addressed by the product standard for these PV AFCI devices (UL 1699B) rather than be included in the requirements of the *NEC*. The technical "how-docs-it-work" associated with dc arc-fault detection is still under investigation, and thus, the mitigation behavior should not be specified in the *Code*. The product standard for PV AFCI (dc) devices is UL 1699B (*Outline of Investigation for Photovoltaic (PV) DC Arc-Fault Circuit Protection*). UL 1699B covers dc PV AFCI protection devices intended for use in solar photovoltaic electrical energy systems as described in Article 690 of the *NEC*. PV AFCI protection is intended to mitigate the effects of arcing faults that may pose a risk of fire ignition under certain conditions if the arcing persists.

690.11

The terms *dc source circuits* and *dc output circuits* have been replaced by *PV system dc circuits*, which includes PV source circuits, dc-dc converter source circuits, PV output circuits, and dc-dc converter output circuits. The previous language implied that the required PV AFCI protection applied only to PV source and output circuits. The revision ensures that all dc-dc converter circuits are arc-fault protected as well.

The new exception eliminates PV output circuits and dc-to-dc converter output circuits for ground-mounted systems where the circuits are direct buried, installed in metallic raceways, or installed in enclosed metallic cable trays. These output circuits for larger PV systems are typically installed in raceways, directly buried, or otherwise protected from physical damage, posing a significantly lesser risk of an arc-related ignition event. On the other hand, PV source circuits are commonly installed in free air, exposed to environmental hazards and physical damage at the array structure resulting in degradation hence the need for PV AFCI protection.

It should be noted that this new exception does not apply to PV output circuits and dc-to-dc converter output circuits installed on or in buildings such as rooftop-mounted PV systems as these systems still need PV AFCI protection.

First Revisions: FR 971
Second Revisions: SR 945
Public Inputs: PI 2271, PI 3779, PI 939, PI 3885
Public Comments: PC 500, PC 1849, PC 890, PC 1318

690.12

Rapid Shutdown of PV Systems on Buildings

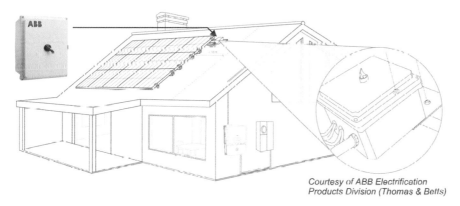

The rapid shutdown requirements for PV systems has been revised to emphasize the primary purpose of the rapid shutdown requirements is to reduced shock hazard for emergency responders and to answer questions regarding the functionality of the PV rapid shutdown device itself

Courtesy of ABB Electrification Products Division (Thomas & Betts)

The structure of 690.12 is now divided into four separate sub-sections titled, 690.12(A) Controlled Conductors, (B) Controlled Limits, (C) Initiation Device, and (D) Equipment

690.12 Rapid Shutdown of PV Systems on Buildings. [Solar Photovoltaic (PV) Systems]

- **Type of Change:** New/Revision

- **Change at a Glance:** The requirements for rapid shutdown for PV systems have been revised and divided into four subsections

- **Code Language: 690.12 Rapid Shutdown of PV Systems on Buildings. [Solar Photovoltaic (PV) Systems]**
  PV system circuits installed on or in buildings shall include a rapid shutdown function ~~that controls specific conductors~~ to reduce shock hazard for emergency responders in accordance with 690.12~~(1)~~(A) through ~~(5)~~(D) as ~~follows~~.

Exception: Ground mounted PV system circuits that enter buildings, of which the sole purpose is to house PV system equipment, shall not be required to comply with 690.12.

(1)(A) Controlled Conductors. Requirements for controlled conductors shall apply ~~only~~ to PV circuits supplied by the PV system ~~conductors of more than 1.5 m (5 ft) in length inside a building, or more than 3 m (10 ft) from a PV array~~.

(B) Controlled Limits. The use of the term array boundary in this section is defined as 305 mm (1 ft) from the array in all directions. Controlled conductors outside the array boundary shall comply with 690.12(B)(1) and inside the array boundary shall comply with 690.12(B)(2).

(2)(1) Outside the Array Boundary. Controlled conductors located outside the boundary or more than 1 m (3 ft) from the point of entry inside a building shall be limited to not more than 30 volts ~~and 240 volt-amperes~~ within ~~10~~ 30 seconds of rapid shutdown initiation. ~~(3)~~ Voltage ~~and power~~ shall be measured between any two conductors and between any conductor and ground.

(2) Inside the Array Boundary. The PV system shall comply with one of the following:

(1) The PV array shall be listed or field labeled as a rapid shutdown PV array. Such a PV array shall be installed and used in accordance with the instructions included with the rapid shutdown PV array listing or field labeling.

Informational Note: A listed or field labeled rapid shutdown PV array is evaluated as an assembly or system as defined in the installation instructions to reduce but not eliminate risk of electric shock hazard within a damaged PV array during fire-fighting procedures. These rapid shutdown PV arrays are designed to reduce shock hazards by methods such as limiting access to energized components, reducing the voltage difference between energized components, limiting the electric current that might flow in an electrical circuit involving personnel with increased resistance of the conductive circuit, or by a combination of such methods.

(2) Controlled conductors located inside the boundary or not more than 1 m (3 ft) from the point of penetration of the surface of the building shall be limited to not more than 80 volts within 30 seconds of rapid shutdown initiation. Voltage shall be measured between any two conductors and between any conductor and ground.

(3) PV arrays with no exposed wiring methods, no exposed conductive parts, and installed more than 2.5 m (8 ft) from exposed grounded conductive parts or ground shall not be required to comply with 690.12(B)(2).

690.12

The requirement of 690.12(B)(2) shall become effective January 1, 2019.

(C) Initiation Device. The initiation device(s) shall initiate the rapid shutdown function of all the PV system. The device "off" position shall indicate that the rapid shutdown function has been initiated for all PV systems connected to that device. For one-family and two-family dwellings, an initiation device(s) shall be located at a readily accessible location outside the building.

~~(4) The rapid shutdown initiation methods shall be labeled in accordance with 690.56(B).~~

The rapid shutdown initiation device(s) shall consist of at least one of the following:
(1) Service disconnecting means
(2) PV system disconnecting means
(3) Readily accessible switch that plainly indicates whether it is in the "off" or "on" position

Informational Note: One example of why an initiation device that complies with 690.12(C)(3) would be used is where a PV system is connected to an optional standby system that remains energized upon loss of utility voltage.

Where multiple PV systems are installed with rapid shutdown functions on a single service, the initiation device(s) shall consist of not more than six switches or six sets of circuit breakers, or a combination of not more than six switches and sets of circuit breakers, mounted in a single enclosure, or in a group of separate enclosures. These initiation device(s) shall initiate the rapid shutdown of all PV systems with rapid shutdown functions on that service. Where auxiliary initiation devices are installed, these auxiliary devices shall control all PV systems with rapid shutdown functions on that service.

~~(5)~~(D) Equipment. Equipment that performs the rapid shutdown functions, other than initiation devices such as listed disconnect switches, circuit breakers, or control switches, shall be listed ~~and identified~~ for providing rapid shutdown protection.

Informational Note: Inverter input circuit conductors often remain energized for up to 5 minutes with inverters not listed for rapid shutdown.

- **2014 *NEC* Requirement**
  A new 690.12 titled, "Rapid Shutdown of PV Systems on Buildings" was added to the 2014 *NEC*. This section applies to PV systems installed on or in buildings. This section required PV source circuits to be de-energized from all sources within 10 seconds of when the utility supply is de-energized or when the PV power source disconnecting means is opened.

690.12

■ **2017 *NEC* Change**

The rapid shutdown requirements of 690.12 were revised to emphasize the primary purpose of the rapid shutdown requirements, which is to reduce shock hazard for emergency responders, and to answer questions regarding the functionality of the PV rapid shutdown device itself. The structure of 690.12 is now subdivided into four separate subsections: (A) Controlled Conductors, (B) Controlled Limits, (C) Initiation Device, and (D) Equipment.

Analysis of the Change:

To increase the electrical and fire safety of photovoltaic (PV) systems on or in buildings, a new "rapid shutdown" requirement was added to Article 690 at 690.12 for the 2014 *NEC*. This new section was intended to incorporate a significant improvement in safety for rooftop PV systems based on the safety concerns for first responders during emergency conditions at PV-equipped buildings and structures.

The genesis of the rapid shutdown requirements of 690.12 began with the United States Department of Homeland Security (DHS) Assistance to Firefighters grant program. Under this program, Underwriters Laboratories (UL) examined concerns about PV systems and potential impacts on firefighting operations. Key concerns included firefighter vulnerability to electrical hazards and casualties when attempting to extinguish a fire involving a PV system. This research project by UL provided evidence of the need for the ability to de-energize PV-generated power sources in the event of an emergency. The use of PV systems is increasing at a rapid pace. As a result of greater utilization, traditional firefighter tactics for suppression, ventilation, and overhaul of a fire at PV-related buildings have been complicated, leaving firefighters vulnerable to severe hazards.

In the three-year time frame from the birth of the rapid shutdown requirements at 690.12, several questions related to the functionality of the PV rapid shutdown devices itself arose in the electrical industry for which 690.12 simply did not have answers. For the 2017 *NEC*, 690.12 experienced extensive revision in an effort to address these issues. The bulk of the revisions were instigated by CMP-4 based on a combination of public inputs and public comments provided by the International Association of Fire Fighters (IAFF) and the Solar Energy Industries Association (SEIA). The *NEC* Correlating Committee organized a Fire Fighter Safety and PV Systems Task Group with a goal that included recommended consensus language for the 2017 *NEC* requirements of 690.12. This task group and the resulting public inputs and public comments involved cooperation among many organizations and stakeholders impacted by the 690.12 rapid shutdown requirement.

The parent text of 690.12 received some revision to emphasize that the primary existence of the rapid shutdown requirements is to reduce shock hazard for emergency responders. Some users of the *Code* were under the impression that the rapid shutdown requirements of 690.12 were intended to provide electrical isolation for electrical worker safety. Electrical isolation and safe practices of NFPA 70E are covered by the disconnecting means requirements in Part III (Disconnecting Means) of Article 690. The rapid shutdown devices should not

690.12

be depended upon for electrical worker safety any more than the rapid shutdown devices should be considered the required disconnecting means for the PV system.

The structure of 690.12 was segmented into four separate sub-sections titled: (A) Controlled Conductors, (B) Controlled Limits, (C) Initiation Device, and (D) Equipment. One of the selected revisions to this rapid shutdown section occurred at what is now 690.12(A) [was 690.12(1)]. The previous text called for the rapid shutdown of controlled conductors to be applied "only to PV system conductors of more than 1.5 m (5 ft) in length inside a building, or more than 3 m (10 ft) from a PV array." The revision clarified that these controlled conductors would only include "PV circuits supplied by the PV system." The PV systems and the rapid shutdown can only control the ac output of PV inverters on the PV supply side of the circuit. The PV circuits connected to a utility-connected source or circuit breaker [which are likely located more than 3 m (10 ft) from a PV array] cannot be de-energized by the rapid shutdown system since the utility source will likely need to be turned off separately by the servicing utility company.

Quite a bit of new information and requirements were added at 690.12(B) for the limits of the controlled rapid shutdown conductors. The use of the term array boundary in this section has been defined as 305 mm (1 ft) from the array in all directions. Controlled rapid shutdown conductors outside the array boundary must comply with the new 690.12(B)(1) [was 690.12(2)]. This provision calls for the controlled conductors located outside the array boundary to be limited to not more than 30 volts within 30 seconds of rapid shutdown initiation. This shutdown limitation was initially a 10-second initiation in the 2014 NEC.

690.12

Controlled rapid shutdown conductors located inside the array boundary will be required to comply with the new 690.12(B)(2). This section offers three options or methods for compliance with the rapid shutdown regulations. The first method is a listing/performance requirement that the PV array be evaluated by a third-party testing agency as a rapid shutdown PV array. At issue here is the fact that there is currently no product standard by which these PV arrays can be evaluated. It is the hope of the electrical community, CMP-4, and, in particular, the PV industry that this new PV array listing requirement in the NEC will serve as the driving force in the development of this much-needed PV array product standard. It is further anticipated that once a PV array product standard is developed, many PV arrays will achieve these listing provisions. However, some PV array configurations will require field evaluation for proper third-party labeling, which is why the field labeling option was made available.

Controlled rapid shutdown conductors located inside the array boundary, or not more than 1 m (3 ft) from the point of penetration of the surface of the building, are limited to not more than 80 volts within 30 seconds of rapid shutdown initiation by 690.12(B)(2)(2). As indicated at 690.12(B)(2)(3), PV arrays with no exposed wiring methods, no exposed conductive parts, and installed more than 2.5 m (8 ft) from exposed grounded conductive parts or ground (such as on a rooftop) are not required to comply with the inside the array boundary requirements for controlled rapid shutdown conductors of 690.12(B)(2). It should also be noted that the requirements for controlled rapid shutdown conductors located inside the array boundary addressed at 690.12(B)(2) has a future effective date of January 1, 2019, and would not take effect upon the immediate adoption of the 2017 *NEC*.

A new 690.12(C), titled "Initiation Device", was added to clarify that the function of the initiation device is to (as the name indicates) initiate rapid shutdown. This new initiation device section clarifies that an initiation device in the "off" position puts the PV system in the rapid shutdown mode. Another provision is a requirement for the rapid shutdown initiator device to be located on the outside of the building for one- and two-family dwellings. This requirement was at the request of the fire service industry as many one- and two-family dwelling service disconnects may be located on the inside of the building, which can be difficult for firefighters to access during emergency situations.

Finally, provisions were included at 690.12(D) requiring that the equipment that performs the rapid shutdown functions (other than initiation devices such as listed disconnect switches, circuit breakers, or control switches) be listed for providing rapid shutdown protection. This requirement was located (in part) in the 2014 *NEC* at 690.12(5).

690.12

First Revisions: FR 1008
Second Revisions: SR 1002
Public Inputs: 9 total PIs
Public Comments: PC 1332, PC 502 (35 total PCs)

690.13

Photovoltaic System Disconnecting Means

690.12

690.13 Photovoltaic System Disconnecting Means. [Solar Photovoltaic (PV) Systems]

- **Type of Change:** Revision/New

- **Change at a Glance:** New interrupting rating and type of disconnect requirements were added to the PV disconnecting means requirements along with extensive revision to the existing requirements, including PV disconnecting means connected to the supply side of a service disconnecting means having to be "listed as suitable for use as service equipment."

- **Code Language: 690.13** ~~Building or Other Structure Supplied by a~~ **Photovoltaic System Disconnecting Means. [Solar Photovoltaic (PV) Systems]**
  Means shall be provided to disconnect ~~all ungrounded dc conductors of~~ the PV system from all ~~other conductors in a building or other structure~~ wiring systems including power systems, energy storage systems, and utilization equipment and its associated premises wiring.

  (A) Location. The PV system disconnecting means shall be installed at a readily accessible lo~~cation either on the outside of a building or structure or inside nearest the point of entrance of the system conductors.~~
  Exception: *Installations that comply with 690.31(F) shall be permitted*

~~to have the disconnecting means located remote from the point of entry of the system conductors. The PV system disconnecting means shall not be installed in bathrooms.~~

Informational Note: PV systems installed in accordance with 690.12 address the concerns related to energized conductors entering a building.

(B) Marking. Each PV system disconnecting means shall plainly indicate whether in the open (off) or closed (on) position and be permanently marked "PV SYSTEM DISCONNECT" or equivalent ~~to identify it as a PV system disconnect~~. Additional markings shall be permitted based upon the specific system configuration. For PV system disconnecting means where the line and load terminals may be energized in the open position, the device shall be marked with the following words or equivalent:

WARNING
ELECTRIC SHOCK HAZARD
TERMINALS ON THE LINE AND LOAD SIDES MAY BE ENERGIZED IN
THE OPEN POSITION

690.13

The warning sign(s) or label(s) shall comply with 110.21(B).

(C) Suitable for Use. ~~Each~~ If the PV system is connected to the supply side of the service disconnecting means as permitted in 230.82(6), the PV system disconnecting means shall ~~not be required to~~ be listed as suitable for use as service equipment.

(D) Maximum Number of Disconnects. ~~The~~ Each PV system disconnecting means shall consist of not more than six switches or six sets of circuit breakers, or a combination of not more than six switches and sets of circuit breakers, mounted in a single enclosure, or in a group of separate enclosures. A single PV system disconnecting means shall be permitted for the combined ac output of one or more inverters or ac modules in an interactive system.

Informational Note: This requirement does not limit the number of PV systems connected to a service as permitted in 690.4(D). This requirement allows up to six disconnecting means to disconnect a single PV system. For PV systems where all power is converted through interactive inverters, a dedicated circuit breaker, in 705.12(D)(1), is an example of a single PV system disconnecting means.

~~**(E) Grouping.** The PV system disconnecting means shall be grouped with other disconnecting means for the system in accordance with 690.13(D). A PV disconnecting means shall not be required at the PV module or array location.~~

(E) Ratings. The PV system disconnecting means shall have ratings sufficient for the maximum circuit current available short-circuit current, and voltage that is available at the terminals of the PV system disconnect.

(F) Type of Disconnect.
(1) Simultaneous Disconnection. The PV system disconnecting means shall simultaneously disconnect the PV system conductors of the circuit from all conductors of other wiring systems. The PV system disconnecting means shall be an externally operable general-use switch or circuit breaker, or other approved means. A dc PV system disconnecting means shall be marked for use in PV systems or be suitable for backfeed operation.

(2) Devices Marked "Line" and "Load." Devices marked with "line" and "load" shall not be permitted for backfeed or reverse current.

(3) DC-Rated Enclosed Switches, Open-Type Switches, and Low-Voltage Power Circuit Breakers. DC-rated, enclosed switches, open-type switches, and low-voltage power circuit breakers shall be permitted for backfeed operation.

- **2014 *NEC* Requirement**
  The disconnecting means for a building or other structure supplied by a PV system was covered by the requirements of 690.13. The section had five first level subdivisions: (A) Location, (B) Marking, (C) Suitable for Use, (D) Maximum Number of Disconnects, and (E) Grouping.

- **2017 *NEC* Change**
  The requirements for PV disconnecting means at 690.13 received extensive revisions along with a few new provisions added. This section now has six first level subdivisions: (A) Location, (B) Marking, (C) Suitable for Use, (D) Maximum Number of Disconnects, (E) Rating, and (F) Type of Disconnect.

690.13

Analysis of the Change:

For the specific disconnecting means requirements for the ungrounded dc conductors of a PV systems, a visit to 690.13 is in order. This section and the rules for the PV disconnecting means were extensively revised for the 2017 *NEC*.

The previous provisions of 690.13(A) indicated that the PV disconnecting means had to be installed at a "readily accessible location either on the outside of a building or structure or inside nearest the point of entrance" of the PV system conductors. A literal interpretation of this rule would necessitate practically all rooftop PV systems circuits conductors to be kept on the building exterior (along the rooftop and the side of the building) until they reach a readily accessible outside disconnect or one on the inside "nearest the point of entrance." By definition, rooftops or attic spaces directly below a rooftop are not considered to be "readily accessible locations nearest the point of entrance." The exception that followed 690.13(A) permitted the PV circuits to be run inside a building or structure, provided the PV circuit conductors are installed to meet 690.31(G). This section permits dc PV output circuit conductors to run inside any building, provided that they are installed in a metallic raceway, Type MC cable (that qualifies as an equipment grounding conductor), or a metal enclosure from the point of penetration of the surface of the building or structure to the first "readily accessible disconnecting means."

For the 2017 *NEC*, 690.13(A) was revised by removing the "nearest the point of entrance" language and the accompanying exception. This PV disconnecting means must meet the provisions of 690.12 for rapid shutdown and full compliance with this rule would satisfy the previous provisions of 690.13(A). The previous requirement of no PV disconnecting means located in bathrooms has been moved to the general requirements of 690.4(E) as it pertains to both equipment and disconnecting means.

The requirement at 690.13(B) for marking or identifying of PV disconnecting means has been expanded for the 2017 *NEC*. Previous marking requirements at 690.13(B) did not give any specific details as to these marking provisions. Instead, these details were provided at 690.17(E) and 690.53. These marking requirements have been moved to one location in 690.13(B) for this *Code* cycle.

The "Suitable for Use" requirements at 690.13(C) previously indicated that a PV system disconnecting means did not have to be identified as being "suitable for use as service equipment," which is a requirement for a service disconnecting means to a building or structure. This first level subdivision has been modified to require the PV disconnecting means connected to the supply side of a service disconnecting means [which is permitted by 230.82(6)] to be "listed as suitable for use as service equipment." If a PV system is being directly connected to a servicing utility, it is important that the first disconnecting means be "listed and marked as suitable for service equipment." This marking makes it clear that the grounded conductor can be properly bonded to enclosure, as well as to the grounding electrode conductor and the equipment grounding conductor. This revision will also ensure that the PV disconnecting means has an adequate available fault current rating. More and more PV systems are being connected as permitted by 705.12(A) [supply side connection of interconnected electric power production sources], which makes it even more important that these PV disconnecting means meet the requirements for service equipment.

The "Maximum Number of Disconnects" requirement at 690.13(D) remained the same with the exception that "the PV system disconnecting means" be revised to "each PV disconnecting means" to clearly indicate that it is permissible to have multiple PV systems on a building or structure and that each such system is permitted to have up to six means of disconnect as the PV system disconnecting means.

The grouping of PV disconnects requirements previously located at 690.13(E) provided a general statement that indicated that a PV disconnecting means was not required at the PV module or array location. This grouping was not so much a "grouping of disconnects" issue as a general statement and is now indicated in the parent text of 690.13. The grouping of PV disconnects is addressed at 690.13(D).

A new 690.13(E) requires the PV system disconnecting means to have interrupting and voltage ratings sufficient for the maximum available short-circuit

690.13

current ratings that are available at the terminals of the PV system disconnect. This requirement is an important safety aspect for any disconnecting means, including a PV disconnecting means. As stated at 110.9, "Equipment intended to interrupt current at fault levels shall have an interrupting rating sufficient for the nominal circuit voltage and the current that is available at the line terminals of the equipment." PV disconnecting means that are inadequately rated for either the system voltage or available fault current levels present a safety hazard, as there is no guarantee that they will be able to interrupt faults without damage either to themselves or other equipment in the PV system. Without proper interrupting ratings, this could present a significant fire hazard.

Last but not least, a new 690.13(F) was added to the PV disconnecting means provisions. This first level subdivision titled, "Type of Disconnect" details three aspects of the PV disconnecting means. Simultaneous disconnection is discussed at 690.13(F)(1) with the PV system disconnecting means required to simultaneously disconnect the PV system conductors of the circuit from all conductors of other wiring systems. This PV system disconnecting means can be an externally operable general-use switch or circuit breaker, or other means "approved" by the AHJ.

For "back-fed devices," 690.13(F)(1) now requires a dc PV system disconnecting means to be marked for use in PV systems or to be suitable for backfed operation. Section 690.13(F)(2) will now indicate that devices marked with "line" and "load" will not be permitted for backfeed or reverse current while dc-rated, enclosed switches, open-type switches, and low-voltage power circuit breakers will be permitted for backfeed operation by the provisions of 690.13(F)(3).

690.13

First Revisions: FR 1014
Second Revisions: SR 946, SR 947, SR 948, SR 103
Public Inputs: Numerous PIs
Public Comments: PC 1000, PC 924, PC 1692, PC 653

690.31(C)(1)

Single-Conductor Cable in PV Systems

690.31(C)(1)

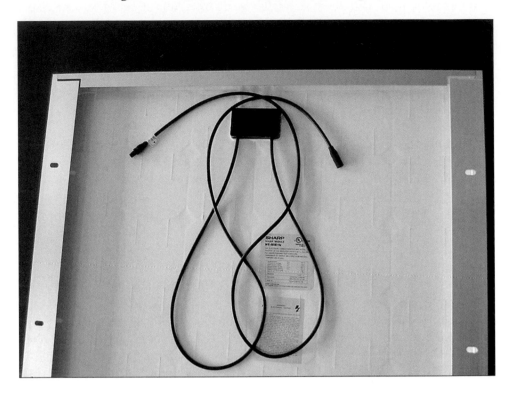

690.31(C)(1) 690.31 (Wiring) Methods Permitted. [Solar Photovoltaic (PV) Systems]

- **Type of Change:** Revision and Deletion

- **Change at a Glance:** The exception requiring raceways to be used when required by 690.31(A) was removed. The rule now limits exposed conductors to within the array footprint only. The section now permits Type USE-2 conductors to be installed in ungrounded as well as grounded systems.

- **Code Language:** 690.31 (Wiring) Methods Permitted. [Solar Photovoltaic (PV) Systems]

(C) Single-Conductor Cable.
(1) General. Single-conductor cable Type USE-2 and single-conductor cable listed and ~~labeled~~ identified as photovoltaic (PV) wire shall be permitted in exposed outdoor locations in PV source circuits ~~for PV module interconnections~~ within the PV array. PV wire shall be installed in accordance with 338.10(B)(4)(b) and 334.30.

~~**Exception:** Raceways shall be used when required by 690.31(A).~~

- **2014 *NEC* Requirement**

  Single-conductor Type USE-2 cable and single-conductor cable listed and labeled as photovoltaic (PV) wire were permitted in exposed outdoor locations in PV source circuits for PV module interconnections within a PV array. An exception to this rule required PV source and output circuits to be guarded or installed in a raceway, where operating at maximum system voltages greater than 30 volts and installed in a readily accessible location.

- **2017 *NEC* Change**

  The term *listed and labeled* was replaced with *listed and identified* when describing single-conductor PV wire. A new installation requirement and references to 338.10(B)(4)(b) and 334.30 have been added to 690.31(C)(1) for PV wiring in a PV array. The exception requiring a PV wire installed in a readily accessible location within a PV array be installed in a raceway was removed.

Analysis of the Change:

One of the provisions that makes PV installations unique from other installations in the *Code* is the allowance for PV systems to use exposed single-conductor cables for the circuits within a PV array as permitted by 690.31(C)(1). Single-conductor Type USE-2 cable and single-conductor cable listed as PV wire are permitted in exposed outdoor locations in PV source circuits within the PV array. PV wire typically has thicker insulation and jacketing, better sunlight resistance, flame resistance, and better flexibility at low temperatures than Type USE-2 conductors. Practically all PV modules installed today are shipped from the manufacturer with two single PV wire conductors pre-installed to the module's junction box. The PV cables typically have quick-connect plugs installed to facilitate easier field wiring associated with PV modules.

690.31(C)(1)

This allowance of exposed single-conductor cables for the circuits within a PV array had an exception in the previous edition of the *Code* which required raceways to be used "when required by 690.31(A)." A quick look at 690.31(A) in the 2014 *NEC* reveals a requirement to install PV source and output circuits in a raceway when operating at maximum system voltages greater than 30 volts and installed in a readily accessible location. This exception was removed for the 2017 *NEC* to continue to allow the use of exposed single-conductor cables for PV circuits as long as the wiring remains within the PV array footprint.

Another change to this single-conductor provision at 690.31(C)(1) was to replace the term *labeled* after "listed and" with the term *identified*, as PV cables are identified with the marking on the cable. The cable reel will have the listing label from the manufacturer, but this may not be available during an inspection process whereas the identified marking is required to be visible on the PV cable at 1.0 m (40 in.) intervals.

A new installation requirement and reference to 338.10(B)(4)(b) and 334.30 have been added to this requirement for PV wiring in the PV array as well. The requirements of 338.10(B)(4)(b) pertain to "Uses Permitted" for exterior installations of service-entrance cable used for feeders or branch circuits, and reference Part I of Article 225, which deals with support of open conductors. Securing and supporting requirements for nonmetallic-sheathed (Type NM) cable are found at 334.30.

Public inputs were submitted to CMP-4 seeking support requirements for exposed single-conductor cables for the circuits within a PV array at minimum intervals of 300 mm (12 in.) to prevent any movement and potential damage. The new supporting requirements for PV wiring from 334.30, which calls for support at intervals not exceeding 1.4 m (4½ ft) and within 300 mm (12 in.) of every outlet box, junction box, cabinet, or fitting, are practical and should provide sufficient protection of the PV conductors from the physical damage common to PV systems. A simple reference to 338.10(B)(4)(b) and 334.30 is appropriate for these exterior location installations and was preferred by CMP-4 rather than repeating these requirements in Article 690 that are already detailed in Chapter 3.

First Revisions: FR 976
Second Revisions: SR 955
Public Inputs: PI 875, PI 4768, PI 3803
Public Comments: PC 478, PC 1003, PC 1853

690.35

690.35

Ungrounded Photovoltaic Power Systems

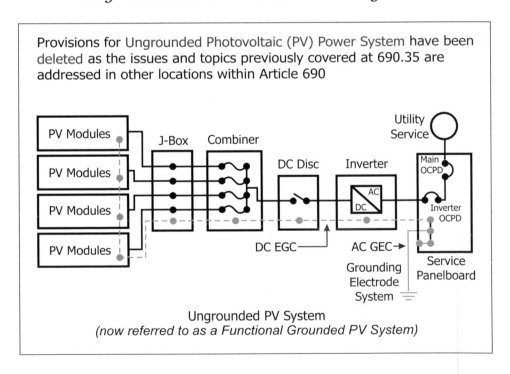

Provisions for Ungrounded Photovoltaic (PV) Power System have been deleted as the issues and topics previously covered at 690.35 are addressed in other locations within Article 690

Ungrounded PV System
(now referred to as a Functional Grounded PV System)

690.35 Ungrounded Photovoltaic Power Systems

- **Type of Change:** Deletion

- **Change at a Glance:** Section 690.35 for "Ungrounded Photovoltaic Power Systems" has been deleted in its entirety.

- **Code Language:** ~~690.35 Ungrounded Photovoltaic Power Systems.~~

  ~~Photovoltaic power systems shall be permitted to operate with ungrounded PV source and output circuits where the system complies with 690.35(A) through (G).~~
  ~~(A) Disconnects.~~
  ~~(B) Overcurrent Protection.~~
  ~~(C) Ground-Fault Protection.~~
  ~~(D) Conductors.~~
  ~~(E) Battery Systems.~~
  ~~(F) Marking.~~
  ~~(G) Equipment.~~

  (See 2014 *NEC* for complete *Code* text)

690.35

- **2014 *NEC* Requirement**
  The requirements for the installation of an ungrounded photovoltaic (PV) power system were located at 690.35(A) through (G).

- **2017 *NEC* Change**
  The requirements for an ungrounded photovoltaic (PV) power system at 690.35 have been deleted. Ungrounded systems are now defined as a functional grounded PV system.

Analysis of the Change:

The requirements at 690.35 pertaining to the installation of an ungrounded photovoltaic (PV) power system were first recognized by the *Code* during the 2005 *NEC* revision cycle. At that time, PV power systems were being installed and operated safely with none of the PV source circuits or PV output circuits grounded. As with any "ungrounded" system, it should be noted that the system is grounded (connected to earth) through an established grounding electrode system. What is missing in an "ungrounded" system is an intentionally grounded conductor. These provisions added at 690.35 allowed PV systems to operate with the PV source and output circuits ungrounded providing several conditions were met.

For the 2017 *NEC*, these requirements for an ungrounded photovoltaic (PV) power system have been deleted, as the issues and topics previously covered at 690.35 are addressed in other locations within Article 690. There is no longer any need to distinguish between the wiring methods of ungrounded systems, and what is now defined as a functional grounded PV system (see new definition at 690.2). The only distinction needed is between a solidly grounded PV systems and all other PV systems.

The previous requirements of 690.35(A) for disconnects for all PV sources and output circuit conductors are covered at Part III of Article 690 and, in particular, 690.13. Previous 690.35(B) and overcurrent protection is addressed at 690.9. Former provisions for ground-fault protection at 690.35(C) are now covered at 690.41(B). Provisions for PV system conductors formerly addressed at 690.35(D) are specified at 690.31. The former language at 690.35(E) permitted the use of a PV system with an ungrounded battery system. Removing this first level subdivision and 690.35 in its entirety do not delete the ability to continue such practices as 690.71 addresses.

The previous language at 690.35(F) for marking requirements for ungrounded PV systems is no longer needed and has been eliminated. Adequate marking provisions for PV systems are addressed at other places like 690.13(B) and 690.31(G)(3) and (G)(4). The prior language of 690.35(G) pertaining to equipment was covered quite well at 690.4(B).

First Revisions: FR 982
Public Inputs: PI 3814

690.41

690.41

PV System Grounding Configurations

The requirements for System Grounding of PV systems was revised to properly address the methods by which PV systems are grounded (six configurations)

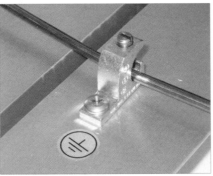 

690.41(A) PV System Grounding Configurations   **690.41(B) (GFP) Ground-Fault Protection**

The previous text of 690.5 for ground-fault protection of PV systems was moved to 690.41(B) to better coincide with grounding requirements

690.41 System Grounding. [Solar Photovoltaic (PV) Systems]

- **Type of Change:** Revision and Relocation of Text

- **Change at a Glance:** The requirements for "System Grounding" of PV systems was revised to properly address the methods by which PV systems are grounded. The previous text of 690.5 was moved to 690.41(B) to expand existing grounding requirements.

- **Code Language:** 690.41 System Grounding. [Solar Photovoltaic (PV) Systems]

(A) PV System Grounding Configurations. One or more of the following system grounding configurations shall be employed: ~~Photovoltaic systems shall comply with one of the following:~~

(1) ~~Ungrounded systems shall comply with 690.35.~~ 2-wire PV arrays with one functional grounded conductor

(2) ~~Grounded two-wire systems shall have one conductor grounded or be impedance grounded, and the system shall comply with 690.5.~~ Bipolar PV arrays according to 690.7(C) with a functional ground reference (center tap)

(3) ~~Grounded bipolar systems shall have the reference (center tap) conductor grounded or be impedance grounded, and the system shall comply with 690.5.~~ PV arrays not isolated from the grounded inverter output circuit

(4) ~~Other methods that accomplish equivalent system protection in accordance with 250.4(A) with equipment listed and identified for the use shall be permitted to be used.~~ Ungrounded PV arrays

(5) Solidly grounded PV arrays as permitted in 690.41(B) Exception

(6) PV systems that use other methods that accomplish equivalent system protection in accordance with 250.4(A) with equipment listed and identified for the use

(B) Ground-Fault Protection. ~~Grounded~~ dc PV arrays shall be provided with dc ground-fault protection meeting the requirements of 690.41(B)(1) and (2) to reduce fire hazards. (was 690.5)

Exception: ~~Ground-mounted or pole-mounted PV arrays with not more than two paralleled source circuits and with all dc source and dc output circuits isolated from buildings shall be permitted without ground-fault protection.~~ PV arrays with not more than two PV source circuits and with all PV system dc circuits not on or in buildings shall be permitted without ground-fault protection where solidly grounded. (was 690.5 Exception)

690.41

(1) Ground-Fault Detection. The ground fault ~~protection~~ protective device or system shall ~~be capable of detecting a~~ detect ground fault(s) in the PV array dc current-carrying conductors and components, including any ~~intentionally~~ functional grounded conductors, and be listed for providing PV ground-fault protection. [was 690.5(A)(1) and (A)(4)]

(2) Isolating Faulted Circuits. The faulted circuits shall be isolated by one of the following methods:

(1) The ~~ungrounded~~ current-carrying conductors of the faulted circuit shall be automatically disconnected.

(2) The inverter or charge controller fed by the faulted circuit shall automatically cease to supply power to output circuits and isolate the PV system dc circuits from the ground reference in a functional grounded system. [was 690.5(B)(1) and (B)(2)]

690.41

- **2014 *NEC* Requirement**
  The section for "System Grounding" was revised into a list format for clarity. A reference to "over 50" volts was deleted since the 2014 *NEC* revised list included all types of PV systems at any voltage. The term *solidly* grounded was removed for consistency. An allowance for impedance grounding and a reference to 690.5 (ground-fault protection) were also added for clarity when grounded 2-wire and bipolar PV systems were installed.

- **2017 *NEC* Change**
  The provisions of 690.41 were revised to properly address the methods by which PV systems are grounded. Two new first level subdivisions were added to 690.41 — 690.41(A) addresses "PV System Grounding Configurations," while 690.41(B) covers "Ground-Fault Protection" for PV systems. To cap off this revision, the former text of 690.5 was relocated to 690.41(B) to concur with the revised grounding requirements for PV systems.

Analysis of the Change:
The grounding of electrical circuits and systems and the bonding of conductive components of an electrical installation have remained the same from a technical basis for decades. Despite this, the subject of grounding and bonding remains one of most misunderstood and misinterpreted concepts in the electrical community. This misunderstanding worsens when these basic requirements are applied to the installation of a PV system. System grounding of PV systems is covered at 690.41.

This section allows both grounded and ungrounded PV array conductors. Both types of systems require ground-fault detection on the PV source and output circuit conductors with one very restrictive exception. The only PV system that does not require ground-fault protection is a small PV system, with no more than two source circuits where all the dc conductors are not installed on buildings [see previous 690.5 Exception, now 690.41(B) Exception]. The 2014 *NEC* clarified in 690.5 that ground-fault detection in grounded PV systems must detect ground faults in intentionally grounded conductors. Grounded PV inverters, to be compliant with the 2014 *NEC*, had to be either augmented with external ground-fault detection equipment that meets this 2014 *NEC* requirement or be certified to detect faults in the grounded conductor.

In the 2017 *NEC*, 690.41 now addresses the methods by which PV systems are grounded. Most existing PV systems are not solidly grounded, but rather grounded through fuses or circuit breakers. The grounding method is specific to the method of ground-fault protection implemented. Another part of this revision was to move the former text of 690.5 to its new home at 690.41(B) to better coincide with the revised grounding requirements for PV systems.

Ground-fault protection is related to system grounding and the issues that system grounding address. Rather than having these ground-fault detection requirements in a completely different section of 690, it is easier for users of the *Code* to have ground-fault protection grouped with the requirements for system ground. In fact, all ground-fault detection methods currently used in PV systems are a function of the system grounding method used. In most cases, the ground-fault detector either provides the reference to ground (earth) or makes measurements on the conductors relative to earth. By acknowledging how PV systems employ ground-fault protection and, in turn, employs system grounding, related disconnecting means and overcurrent protection methods can be correctly described in the *Code*.

690.41

Revisions to the 2014 *NEC* language at 690.41 expanded the list of system grounding methods to "impedance" grounded systems (sometimes referred to as a resistance grounded system). These 2014 *NEC* revisions used the term "grounded" which was interpreted by some users of the *Code* to mean "solidly grounded" in much of the provisions of Article 690. While the word "solidly" was removed from the 2014 *NEC* language, the related requirements about solidly grounded PV systems were not changed. The 2017 *NEC* revisions form a new 690.41(A) for "PV System Grounding Configurations" and use the newly defined term *functional grounded* (see new definition of *Functional Grounded PV System* at 690.2).

The first configuration described in 690.41(A)(1) is a functional grounded 2-wire PV system, which happens to be the most common PV systems installed in the United States. The second configuration described at 690.41(A)(2) is a functional grounded bipolar PV system. Bipolar systems [that meet the requirements of 690.7(C)] have addressed the main concern of bipolar PV systems, which is overvoltage. These bipolar systems cannot be solidly grounded to provide ground fault protection. By the new definition, they are functional grounded bipolar systems.

The third configuration at 690.41(A)(3) refers to functional grounded PV systems where the ac output is not isolated from the dc PV array. This configuration requires that the PV array circuits have no low resistance connection to earth in order to function properly. These non-isolated PV systems are able to very accurately detect ground faults and have been categorized by some users of the *Code* (somewhat erroneously) as "ungrounded" PV systems.

The fourth configuration at 690.41(A)(4) is for an ungrounded PV system. This type of system is currently quite rare in the United States in all but large-scale PV systems. This type of PV system operates with an ac isolation transformer and dc PV array that is floating with respect to grounding (connected to earth). Ground-fault protection for these systems is fairly simple in that an isolation monitor operates continuously on the array. The fifth configuration described at 690.41(A)(5) is for solidly grounded PV systems that meet the exception in 690.41(B). These are small systems that don't require ground-fault protection. The sixth configuration at 690.41(A)(6) is consistent with the previous fourth option in the 2014 *NEC*. Similar language has been part of 690.41 since the inception of Article 690 in the 1984 *NEC*.

A new 690.41(B) was created in conjunction with the relocation of ground-fault protection requirements for PV systems from 690.5 to 690.41(B). The previous text detailing requirements for ground-fault detectors has been removed as these requirements more appropriately belong in the product standard. These requirements have been in the ground-fault detection standard for over a decade and are no longer needed in the *NEC*. The basic product standard used to investigate ground-fault detection products is UL 1053 (*Ground-Fault Sensing and Relaying Equipment*). Some requirements are also found in UL 943 (*Ground-Fault Circuit-Interrupters*). The text of 690.5 was moved to 690.41(B) to better coincide with grounding requirements.

While the PV ground fault protection function is often a built-in feature of an inverter or charge controller, it may also be built into stand-alone products and other PV system products like PV combiners and dc/dc converters. This new text will better support the PV ground-fault protection functionality in equipment other than inverters and charge controllers.

690.41

First Revisions: FR 991
Second Revisions: SR 966
Public Inputs: PI 3768. PI 4681, PI 2563, PI 3761, PI 1077
Public Comments: PC 521, PC 1013, PC 1562, PC 671

690.47

Grounding Electrode System in PV Systems

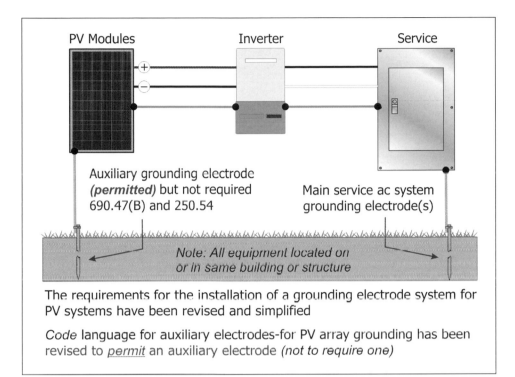

PV Modules   Inverter   Service

Auxiliary grounding electrode *(permitted)* but not required 690.47(B) and 250.54

Main service ac system grounding electrode(s)

Note: All equipment located on or in same building or structure

The requirements for the installation of a grounding electrode system for PV systems have been revised and simplified

Code language for auxiliary electrodes-for PV array grounding has been revised to *permit* an auxiliary electrode *(not to require one)*

690.47

690.47 Grounding Electrode System. [Solar Photovoltaic (PV) Systems]

- **Type of Change:** New/Revision

- **Change at a Glance:** The requirements for the installation of grounding electrodes and grounding electrode conductors for PV systems have been simplified. The text for auxiliary electrodes for PV array grounding has been revised to *permit* an auxiliary electrode rather than require one.

- **Code Language: 690.47 Grounding Electrode System. [Solar Photovoltaic (PV) Systems]**

  ~~(A) Alternating-Current Systems.~~
  ~~(B) Direct-Current Systems.~~
  ~~(C) Systems with Alternating-Current and Direct-Current Grounding Requirements.~~
  (See 2014 *NEC* language for complete *Code* text)

  (A) Buildings or Structures Supporting a PV Array. A building or structure supporting a PV array shall have a grounding electrode system installed in accordance with Part III of Article 250.

PV array equipment grounding conductors shall be connected to the grounding electrode system of the building or structure supporting the PV array in accordance with Part VII of Article 250. This connection shall be in addition to any other equipment grounding conductor requirements in 690.43(C). The PV array equipment grounding conductors shall be sized in accordance with 690.45.

For PV systems that are not solidly grounded, the equipment grounding conductor for the output of the PV system, connected to associated distribution equipment, shall be permitted to be the connection to ground for ground-fault protection and equipment grounding of the PV array.

For solidly grounded PV systems, as permitted in 690.41(A)(5), the grounded conductor shall be connected to a grounding electrode system by means of a grounding electrode conductor sized in accordance with 250.166.

Informational Note: Most PV systems installed in the past decade are actually functional grounded systems rather than solidly grounded systems as defined in this *Code*. For functional grounded PV systems with an interactive inverter output, the ac equipment grounding conductor is connected to associated grounded ac distribution equipment. This connection is often the connection to ground for ground-fault protection and equipment grounding of the PV array.

(B) (D) Additional Auxiliary Electrodes for Array Grounding. A Grounding electrodes shall be permitted to be installed in accordance with 250.52 and 250.54 at the location of all ground- and pole-mounted PV arrays and as close as practicable to the location of roof-mounted PV arrays. The electrodes shall be permitted to be connected directly to the array frame(s) or structure. The de grounding electrode conductor shall be sized according to 250.166 250.66. Additional electrodes are not permitted to be used as a substitute for equipment bonding or equipment grounding conductor requirements. The structure of a ground- or pole-mounted PV array shall be permitted to be considered a grounding electrode if it meets the requirements of 250.52. Roof-mounted PV arrays shall be permitted to use the metal frame of a building or structure if the requirements of 250.52(A)(2) are met.

■ **2014 *NEC* Requirement**
The requirements for grounding electrode systems for PV arrays and systems were addressed at 690.47 with four first level subdivisions. The provisions included: (A) for ac systems, (B) for dc systems, (C) for systems with ac and dc grounding requirements, and (D) for additional auxiliary electrodes for array grounding.

■ **2017 *NEC* Change**
For the 2017 *NEC*, the requirements for the installation of grounding electrodes and grounding electrode conductors have been greatly simplified, while maintaining the safety of PV systems. The provisions of former

690.47

690.47(A), (B), and (C) have been abridged and incorporated into the new 690.47(A). The provisions of former 690.47(D) [now 690.47(B)] pertaining to additional auxiliary electrodes for PV array grounding have been revised to clarify that these auxiliary electrodes are permitted but not required.

Analysis of the Change:

The requirements for a grounding electrode system for PV systems are addressed at 690.47. These requirements have experienced numerous changes over the past three decades since Article 690 was introduced in the 1984 *NEC*. When these requirements were first introduced into the *NEC* and implemented in the field, most PV systems were installed in remote locations where no utility service was available. The vast majority of PV systems installed today are connected with utility services. The grounding electrode system requirements of Article 250 govern how these electrode systems must be installed. Most grounded PV systems today install a grounding electrode conductor (GEC) from the PV inverter (location of the ground-fault protector) to the existing grounding electrode system for the building. Ungrounded PV systems do not require the installation of an additional GEC since the required ac equipment grounding conductor on the inverter output circuit meets these grounding requirements.

690.47

For the 2017 *NEC*, the requirements for the installation of grounding electrodes and grounding electrode conductors have been greatly simplified, while maintaining the safety of PV systems. Rather than give specifics for grounding requirements of PV systems, what remains of 690.47(A) merely refers to sections or parts of Article 250 without repeating the specific grounding electrode rules. These requirements were further simplified to require only a GEC to be attached to solidly grounded PV systems. Solidly grounded PV systems are becoming very rare since they do not have ground-fault detectors and, therefore, are restricted to one or two source circuits separate from the main building.

The previous requirements of 690.47(B) addressed dc systems and separately derived systems with dc branch circuits. This first level subdivision had been misinterpreted to apply to all PV systems. Over a couple of *Code* cycles, former 690.47(B) had become a mixture of confusing requirements for separately derived dc systems, ungrounded PV systems, and ac equipment grounding systems, which clearly did not belong in this first level subdivision titled, "Direct-Current Systems." The important safety provisions of former 690.47(B) were reworded and maintained in the parent text of 690.47(A) while 690.47(B) was deleted.

The former requirements of 690.47(C) were simplified and relocated to 690.47(A) to maintain the safety requirements for all PV system types and grounding configurations. Grounding electrode conductors are intended to be installed between a system grounded conductor and the grounding electrode (or a point on the grounding electrode system). As noted in the new definition of *Functional Grounded PV Systems*, the majority of PV systems are not solidly grounded systems that would require a grounding electrode conductor. Rather, they are functional-grounded systems as the grounded conductor is not directly connected to ground, it is referenced to ground by a fuse, circuit breaker, resistance device, non-isolated grounded ac circuit, or electronic means that is part of a listed ground-fault protection system. Throughout the *NEC*, grounding electrode conductors are only connected to the grounded current-carrying conductor for solidly grounded systems. Other systems can be safely installed using an equipment grounding conductor (EGC) to ground exposed non-current-carrying metal parts. The rewritten 690.47(A) requires PV array EGCs to be connected to the local grounding electrode system in addition to wherever else the EGC must be connected in order to comply with the newly rewritten rules of 690.43(C)

Another revision that needs to be pointed out with the rewrite of 690.47(A) is the requirement for a connection from the PV array equipment grounding conductor to the grounding electrode system of the building or structure supporting the PV array. The requirements of 250.50 for grounding electrodes generally requires each structure to have a grounding electrode system. This revision requires a grounding electrode system to be added for a PV system, but only if the building or structure does not already have one. In other words, a new ground-mounted PV system will require a new grounding electrode system, as will a building-mounted system, but only if that building did not previously have a grounding electrode system. An example would be a PV array, mounted on a detached garage that previously had no electrical service.

690.47

The new informational note after 690.47(A) was added to point users of the *Code* to the substantial addition of the newly defined "functional grounded PV system" as opposed to previous versions of the *NEC* that treated all grounded PV systems as solidly grounded PV systems. With this newly defined way of discussing how PV systems are grounded, it is clear that a dc grounding electrode conductor is no longer necessary to ground a PV system.

Finally, the previous previsions of 690.47(D) [now 690.47(B)] pertaining to additional auxiliary electrodes for PV array grounding have been revised to clarify that auxiliary electrodes are permitted but not required. For most PV systems installed on a rooftop, the large quantity of conductive material increases the likelihood of a lightning strike. An auxiliary grounding electrode system would help to minimize the effects of such a lightning strike. The primary purpose of an auxiliary grounding electrode is to maintain the frames of the PV array to as close to local earth voltage potential as possible. This potential can also be achieved through a properly installed equipment grounding conductor back to an established grounding electrode system for the building or structure. As indicated by the language of 250.54 for auxiliary grounding electrodes, the additional grounding electrodes are permitted to be installed but are never a requirement as implied by the previous language at 690.47(D) in the 2014 *NEC*.

First Revisions: FR 995
Second Revisions: SR 969, SCR 106
Public Inputs: PI 4024, PI 1081, PI 4373, PI 346
Public Comments: PC 936, PC 1363

690.56(C)
Identification of Power Sources

Two different labels are required on buildings depending on what type of rapid shutdown system is on the building

Systems with multiple rapid shutdown types will be required to have a detailed directory as simple sign will not be sufficient to clarify the levels of hazard

Plaque or directory required within 1 m (3 ft) of service

Revision requires any building with a rapid-shutdown PV system to have a plaque to indicate to first responders that rapid-shutdown is provided

SOLAR PV SYSTEM EQUIPPED WITH RAPID SHUTDOWN

TURN RAPID SHUTDOWN SWITCH TO THE "OFF" POSITION TO SHUTDOWN PV SYSTEM AND REDUCE SHOCK HAZARD IN ARRAY

SOLAR PV SYSTEM EQUIPPED WITH RAPID SHUTDOWN

TURN RAPID SHUTDOWN SWITCH TO THE "OFF" POSITION TO SHUTDOWN CONDUCTORS OUTSIDE THE ARRAY

CONDUCTOR WITHIN ARRAY REMAIN ENERGIZED IN SUNLIGHT

Figure 690.56(C)(1)(a): Label for PV Systems that Shut Down the Array and the Conductors Leaving the Array

Figure 690.56(C)(1)(b): Label for PV Systems that Shut Down the Conductors Leaving the Array Only

690.56(C) Identification of Power Sources

- **Type of Change:** New/Revision

- **Change at a Glance:** Provisions for identifying a PV "Rapid Shutdown System" have been extensively revised. Two new figures with illustrated labels have been added to indicate to first responders that rapid shutdown is provided.

- **Code Language: 690.56 Identification of Power Sources.**

  (A) Facilities with Stand-Alone Systems. Any structure or building with a PV power system that is not connected to a utility service source and is a stand-alone system shall have a permanent plaque or directory installed on the exterior of the building or structure at a readily visible location ~~acceptable to the authority having jurisdiction~~. The plaque or directory shall indicate the location of system disconnecting means and that the structure contains a stand-alone electrical power system. The marking shall be in accordance with 690.31(G).

  (B) Facilities with Utility Services and PV Systems. ~~Buildings or structures with both utility service and a PV system shall have a permanent plaque or directory providing the location of the service disconnecting means and the PV system disconnecting means if not located at the~~

same location. The warning sign(s) or label(s) shall comply with 110.21(B). Plaques or directories shall be installed in accordance with 705.10.

(C) ~~Facilities~~ **Buildings** with Rapid Shutdown. ~~Buildings or structures with both utility service and a PV system, complying with 690.12, shall have a permanent plaque or directory including the following wording: PHOTOVOLTAIC SYSTEM EQUIPPED WITH RAPID SHUTDOWN The plaque or directory shall be reflective, with all letters capitalized and having a minimum height of 9.5 mm (3/8 in.), in white on red background.~~

Buildings with PV systems shall have permanent plaques or directories as described in 690.56(C)(1) through (C)(3).

(1) Rapid Shutdown Type. The type of PV system rapid shutdown shall be labeled as described in 690.56(C)(1)(a) or (1)(b):
(a) For PV systems that shut down the array and conductors leaving the array:

SOLAR PV SYSTEM IS EQUIPPED WITH RAPID SHUTDOWN.

TURN RAPID SHUTDOWN SWITCH TO THE "OFF" POSITION TO SHUT DOWN PV SYSTEM AND REDUCE SHOCK HAZARD IN ARRAY.

The title "SOLAR PV SYSTEM IS EQUIPPED WITH RAPID SHUTDOWN" shall utilize capitalized characters with a minimum height of 9.5 mm (3/8 in.) in black on yellow background, and the remaining characters shall be capitalized with a minimum height of 4.8 mm (3/16 in.) in black on white background. [See Figure 690.56(C)(1)(a).]

(b) For PV systems that only shut down conductors leaving the array:
SOLAR PV SYSTEM IS EQUIPPED WITH RAPID SHUTDOWN

TURN RAPID SHUTDOWN SWITCH TO THE "OFF" POSITION TO SHUT DOWN

CONDUCTORS OUTSIDE THE ARRAY. CONDUCTORS IN ARRAY REMAIN

ENERGIZED IN SUNLIGHT.

The title "SOLAR PV SYSTEM IS EQUIPPED WITH RAPID SHUTDOWN" shall utilize capitalized characters with a minimum height of 9.5 mm (3/8 in.) in white on red background, and the remaining characters shall be capitalized with a minimum height of 4.8 mm (3/16 in.) in black on white background. [See Figure 690.56(C)(1)(b).]

Figure 690.56(C)(1)(a): Label for PV Systems that Shut Down the Array and the Conductors Leaving the Array.
(See *NEC* and illustration above for label)

690.56(C)

Figure 690.56(C)(1)(b): Label for PV Systems that Shut Down the Conductors Leaving the Array Only.
(See *NEC* and illustration above for label)

The labels in 690.56(C)(1)(a) and (b) shall include a simple diagram of a building with a roof. The diagram shall have sections in red to signify sections of the PV system that are not shut down when the rapid shutdown switch is operated.

The rapid shutdown label in 690.56(C)(1) shall be located on or no more than 1 m (3 ft) from the service disconnecting means to which the PV systems are connected and shall indicate the location of all identified rapid shutdown switches if not at the same location.

(2) Buildings with More Than One Rapid Shutdown Type. For buildings that have PV systems with both rapid shutdown types or a PV system with a rapid shutdown type and a PV system with no rapid shutdown, a detailed plan view diagram of the roof shall be provided showing each different PV system and a dotted line around areas that remain energized after the rapid shutdown switch is operated.

(3) Rapid Shutdown Switch. A rapid shutdown switch shall have a ~~plaque~~ or ~~directory~~ label located on or no more than 1 m (3 ft) from the ~~service disconnecting means~~ switch that includes the following wording:

RAPID SHUTDOWN SWITCH FOR SOLAR PV SYSTEM

The ~~plaque~~ or ~~directory~~ label shall be reflective, with all letters capitalized and having a minimum height of 9.5 mm (3⁄8 in.), in white on red background.

- **2014 *NEC* Requirement**
  In conjunction with the rapid shutdown provisions of 690.12, a new 690.56(C) was added during the 2014 *NEC* revision cycle that required buildings or structures with both utility service and a PV system to have a permanent plaque or directory that includes the verbiage "PHOTOVOLTAIC SYSTEM EQUIPPED WITH RAPID SHUTDOWN" when the building or structure is in compliance with 690.12 and a rapid shutdown system.

- **2017 *NEC* Change**
  Through an extensive revision process, 690.56(C) was divided into three list items: (C)(1) addresses rapid shutdown types; (C)(2) deals with buildings with more than one rapid shutdown type; and (C)(3) makes provisions for the rapid shutdown switch or rapid shutdown initiator (RSI). Two new figures were added in 690.56(C)(1) to illustrate new labels that are now required for the two different types of rapid shutdown systems for a PV installation [see Figure 690.56(C)(1)(a) and Figure 690.56(C)(1)(b)]. A detailed plan view diagram of the roof is required in certain situations

690.56(C)

by 690.56(C)(2) to provide illustrated guidance showing each different PV system and should include a "dotted line" around areas that remain energized after the rapid shutdown initiation switch is activated. The requirements of 690.56(C)(3) necessitate a rapid shutdown switch to have a label located directly on the RSI or no more than 1 m (3 ft) from the rapid shutdown switch that includes the words, "RAPID SHUTDOWN SWITCH FOR SOLAR PV SYSTEM."

Analysis of the Change:

One of the more significant changes to the 2014 *NEC* was the addition of the rapid shutdown provision for PV systems in 690.12. At the time this requirement was added to the 2014 *NEC*, 690.12 applied to PV systems installed on or in buildings and would require that PV source circuits be de-energized from all sources within 10 seconds of when the utility supply is de-energized or when the PV power source disconnecting means was placed in the open (off) position. List item (4) of this requirement stated that "the rapid shutdown initiation methods shall be labeled in accordance with 690.56(C)."

690.56(C)

Coinciding with the rapid shutdown provisions of 690.12, a new 690.56(C) was added during the 2014 *NEC* revision cycle that required buildings or structures with both utility service and a PV system to have a permanent plaque or directory that includes the verbiage "PHOTOVOLTAIC SYSTEM EQUIPPED WITH RAPID SHUTDOWN" (when the building or structure was in compliance with 690.12 and a rapid shutdown system).

Both of these sections received extensive revision during the 2017 *NEC* revision process (see the *Analysis of Changes* report at 690.12 earlier in this publication). The requirements for identification of power sources on "buildings" with rapid shutdown provisions began its revision process with a change to the title of 690.56(C) from "Facilities with Rapid Shutdown" to "Buildings with Rapid Shutdown" to make it very clear where these provision are to be implemented. Subsection (C) of 690.56 was further divided into three list items with 690.56(C)(1) addressing "Rapid Shutdown Types." The types of rapid shutdown were further divided into two categories: PV systems that shut down both the array and the conductors leaving the array; *and* PV systems that shut down the conductors leaving the array only.

Two new figures (illustrations) were added to this section to depict for the user of the *Code* new labels or signage now required for these two different types of rapid shutdown for PV systems [see Figure 690.56(C)(1)(a) and Figure 690.56(C)(1)(b)]. Detailed wording and instructions were given with these labels. The illustrated labels are provided so that users can visualize what the labels are intended to look like. These labels were designed with the firefighting community and first responders in mind. Technical terms were avoided in an attempt to make these labels understandable to non-technical, non-*NEC* personnel. These labels are intended to clearly convey to first responders that a rapid shutdown system is available and to give details as to its location as the rapid shutdown system may not be visible to first responders from the ground level.

For buildings that have either a PV system with both rapid shutdown types or a PV system with a rapid shutdown type and a PV system with no rapid shutdown, a detailed plan view diagram of the roof must be provided showing each different PV system. This diagram must include a dotted line around areas that remain energized after the rapid shutdown initiation switch is employed. This requirement is found at the newly created 690.56(C)(2).

Section 690.56(C)(3) requires that a rapid shutdown switch must have a label located on or no more than 1 m (3 ft) from the rapid shutdown switch that includes the words, "RAPID SHUTDOWN SWITCH FOR SOLAR PV SYSTEM." This label is loosely based on a requirement at the previous 690.56(C) for a "plaque or directory" located at the service disconnecting means. The location of this label corresponds with the location requirements for a plaque or directory for stand-alone or off-grid PV systems as described at 690.56(A).

Many of the revised new marking requirements for rapid shutdown of PV systems were developed by the NFPA Fire Fighter Safety and PV Systems Task Group that was reorganized in December of 2014. This collaborative Task Group worked on public inputs and comments for NFPA 1 (*Fire Code*), NFPA 70 (*NEC*), and other related documents. This Task Group is made up of over twenty participants from CMP-4, the solar industry, the fire service, the insurance industry, test laboratories, and other relevant stakeholders.

690.56(C)

The new revisions to 690.56(C) are intended to clearly communicate to the firefighting community (and anyone else for that matter) what is safe to touch and what is not safe to touch. Anything that is not safe to touch should be labeled as energized. The revisions also direct firefighters and first responders to the location of the rapid shutdown initiator switch, clearly identifying what equipment is still live after the system has been shut down. This change allows a firefighter or first responder to take proper precautions when responding to an emergency situation on a building or structure involving a PV system and a rapid shutdown device.

First Revisions: FR 989
Second Revisions: SR 1003
Public Inputs: PI 4713, PI 3728
Public Comments: PC 1355, PC 673, PC 997, PC 1658, PC 619

Article 690, Part VII

Branch-Circuit Receptacle Requirements

Article 690, VII

690.57 Connection to Other Sources. PV systems connected to other sources shall be installed in accordance with Parts I and II of Article 705.

Part VII of Article 690 was revised and replaced with a reference to Part I and Part II of Article 705 where interconnected electric power production source requirements are located

200.6 Article 690, Part VII

- **Type of Change:** New/Deletion

- **Change at a Glance:** Part VII of Article 690 was revised with a reference to Article 705 where interconnected electric power production source requirements are found.

- **Code Language: Part VII. Connection to Other Sources [Solar Photovoltaic (PV) Systems]**
  690.57 Load Disconnect. A load disconnect that has multiple sources of power shall disconnect all sources when in the off position.

  690.59 Connection to Other Sources. PV systems connected to other sources shall be installed in accordance with Parts I and II of Article 705.

  690.60 Identified Interactive Equipment. Only inverters and ac modules listed and identified as interactive shall be permitted in interactive systems.

  690.61 Loss of Interactive System Power. An inverter or an ac module in an interactive solar PV system shall automatically de-energize its output to the connected electrical production and distribution network

~~upon loss of voltage in that system and shall remain in that state until the electrical production and distribution network voltage has been restored. A normally interactive solar PV system shall be permitted to operate as a stand-alone system to supply loads that have been disconnected from electrical production and distribution network sources.~~

~~**690.63 Unbalanced Interconnections.** Unbalanced connections shall be in accordance with 705.100.~~

~~**690.64 Point of Connection.** Point of connection shall be in accordance with 705.12.~~

■ **2014 *NEC* Requirement**

Part VII of Article 690 contained five sections: 690.57, Load Disconnect; 690.60, Identified Interactive Equipment; 690.61, Loss of Interactive System Power; 690.63, Unbalanced Interconnections; and 690.64, Point of Connection. These requirements were duplicate requirements from Article 705 or referenced sections in Article 705.

■ **2017 *NEC* Change**

Revisions to Part VII of Article 690 removed the majority of Part VII and replaced it with one reference to Article 705 where interconnection requirements are covered in detail. Part VII of Article 690 now contains one section, 690.59, Connection to Other Sources.

Article 690, VII

Analysis of the Change:

Grid-connected or utility-interactive PV systems are designed to operate in parallel with the electric utility grid. The primary component in this interconnection process is the inverter, also known as a power conditioning unit (PCU) [see the definition of *Inverter* at 690.2]. The inverter is a device that changes dc input (produced by the PV array) to an ac output consistent with the voltage and power quality required by the local utility grid. The inverter will automatically stop delivering electrical energy to the utility grid when the grid is not energized in order to protect local electric utility personnel. A bi-directional interface is made between the PV system ac output circuits and the electric utility network, typically at an on-site distribution panel. This allows the power produced by the PV system to either supply on-site electrical loads or to backfeed back onto the grid when the PV system output is greater than the on-site load demand. This safety feature is required in all grid-connected PV systems.

Whenever one or more electric power-producing sources like a PV system are operating in parallel with a primary source(s) of electricity in the manner described above, rules need to be in place to regulate this interconnection. The rules can be found at Article 705 Interconnected Electric Power Production Sources. Previous editions of the *Code* contained rules for connection to other sources at Part VII (690.57 through 690.64) for Article 690. Many of these requirements previously found in Part VII of Article 690 were repetitive requirements from Article 705 or referenced sections in Article 705.

For the 2017 *NEC*, revisions to Part VII of Article 690 remove the content of Part VII and replace it with one simple reference to Article 705 where all these interconnection requirements are located. Former 690.57, Load Disconnect, was found to have antiquated language and was no longer relevant to PV systems. The language was removed along with the remainder of the previous language at Part VII of Article 690. What remains at Part VII of Article 690 is one simple new sentence at 690.59 which states, "PV systems connected to other sources shall be installed in accordance with Parts I and II of Article 705." Part I of Article 705 covers general requirements for interconnected electric power production sources while Part II of Article 705 concerns requirement for utility-interactive inverters.

The old saying, "Why reinvent the wheel?" is relevant here as this revision removes the duplicated language in Article 690 with language that is already contained in Article 705

.

First Revisions: FR 1004
Second Revisions: SR 972, SCR 108
Public Inputs: PI 1183, PI 4740
Public Comments: PC 905, PC 1158, PC 1290, PC 1337, PC 906

690.71

690.71

Energy Storage Systems for PV Installations

690.71 General. (Energy Storage Systems) [Solar Photovoltaic (PV) Systems]

- **Type of Change:** Revision and Relocation of Text

- **Change at a Glance:** Previous provisions for the installation of storage batteries for PV systems have been relocated to new Article 706.

- **Code Language:** 690.71 ~~Installation~~ General. (~~Energy~~ Storage ~~Batteries~~ Systems) [Solar Photovoltaic (PV) Systems]

  An energy storage system connected to a PV system shall be installed in accordance with Article 706.

  ~~(A) General. Storage batteries in a solar photovoltaic system shall be installed in accordance with the provisions of Article 480. The interconnected battery cells shall be considered grounded where the photovoltaic power source is installed in accordance with 690.41.~~
  ~~(B) Dwellings.~~
  ~~(C) Current Limiting.~~
  ~~(D) Battery Nonconductive Cases and Conductive Racks.~~
  ~~(E) Disconnection of Series Battery Circuits.~~
  ~~(F) Battery Maintenance Disconnecting Means.~~
  ~~(G) Battery Systems of More Than 48 Volts.~~
  ~~(H) Disconnects and Overcurrent Protection.~~
  ~~(See 2014 NEC text for complete Code language)~~

- **2014 *NEC* Requirement**
  Storage batteries in a solar photovoltaic (PV) system had to be installed in accordance with Article 480, Storage Batteries, and with Section 690.71. Section 690.71 contained eight first level subdivisions.

- **2017 *NEC* Change**
  The former provisions of 690.71 for installation of PV storage battery systems have been relocated to Part III of Article 706, leaving one reference to new Article 706 at 690.71.

Analysis of the Change:
The requirements of 690.71 for the installation of storage batteries of PV systems have been part of Article 690 since the 2002 *NEC*. Storage batteries for PV systems accumulate excess energy created by the PV system and store it to be used at night or when there is no other energy input. Battery capacity is listed in ampere hours at a given voltage, such as 220 ampere-hours at 6 volts. Manufacturers typically rate storage batteries at a 20-hour rate, so a 220 amp-hour battery will deliver 11 amperes for 20 hours. PV storage batteries are typically electrochemical devices sensitive to climate, charge/discharge cycle history, temperature, and age. The performance of these batteries also depends on such things as climate, location and usage patterns.

690.71

For the 2017 *NEC*, a new Article 706, Energy Storage System, has been introduced to the *Code*. This article applies to all permanently installed energy storage systems (ESS) operating at over 50 volts ac or 60 volts dc that may be stand-alone or interactive with other electric power production sources. In conjunction with this new article, the former provisions of 690.71 for installation of PV storage battery systems have been relocated to Part III of Article 706. Rather than have the identical language in two different articles and to coordinate these provisions, CMP-4 determined it would be much simpler for 690.71 to simply refer users to Article 706.

In previous editions of the *Code*, batteries were addressed in a few different locations, such as Article 480 for storage batteries and Article 690 for storage batteries for PV systems. This arrangement was appropriate with the requirements for storage batteries historically covering lead-acid batteries. Section 690.71 added provisions to address the application of batteries in general, not just lead acid to PV systems, and also addressed storage batteries. The current state of energy storage technology (including batteries) and the anticipated evolution of energy storage support the need for a singular set of requirements in the *NEC* covering such systems. This need has been accomplished with the creation of Article 706.

The NFPA dc Task group used Part VIII of Article 690 for storage batteries for PV systems as a basis for requirements in the new Article 706 for energy storage systems.

First Revisions: FR 1012
Second Revisions: SR 973, SCR 109
Public Inputs: PI 3194, Numerous (24) PI's
Public Comments: PC 1146

690.71

Article 691

Large-Scale Photovoltaic (PV) Electric Power Production Facility

Photo courtesy of Scott Humphrey

Article 691 Large-Scale Photovoltaic (PV) Electric Power Production Facility

- **Type of Change:** New

- **Change at a Glance:** New Article 691 for "Large-Scale Photovoltaic (PV) Electric Power Production Facility was added to the *NEC*.

- **Code Language:** **Article 691 Large-Scale Photovoltaic (PV) Electric Power Production Facility**

  691.1 Scope. This article covers the installation of large-scale PV electric power production facilities with a generating capacity of no less than 5000 kW, and not under exclusive utility control.

  Informational Note No. 1: Facilities covered by this article have specific design and safety features unique to large-scale PV facilities and are operated for the sole purpose of providing electric supply to a system operated by a regulated utility for the transfer of electric energy.

  Informational Note No. 2: Section 90.2(B)(5) includes information about utility-owned properties not covered under this *Code*. For additional information on electric supply stations, see ANSI/IEEE C2-2012, *National Electrical Safety Code.*

691.2 Definitions.

691.4 Special Requirements for Large-Scale PV Electric Supply Stations.

691.5 Equipment Approval.

691.6 Engineered Design.

691.7 Conformance of Construction to Engineered Design.

691.8 Direct Current Operating Voltage.

691.9 Disconnection of Photovoltaic Equipment.

691.10 Arc-Fault Mitigation.

Article 691

691.11 Fence Grounding.
(See 2017 *NEC* for complete *Code* text)

■ **2014 *NEC* Requirement**
The 2014 *NEC* did not include specific regulations for large-scale PV electric power production facilities. Any *NEC* requirements regulated on these large scale PV systems had to be gleaned out of Article 690, which covers solar photovoltaic (PV) systems.

■ **2017 *NEC* Change**
A new Article 691 for "Large-Scale Photovoltaic (PV) Electric Power Production Facility" was added to the 2017 *NEC*. This article covers the installation of large-scale PV electric power production facilities operated for the sole purpose of providing electric supply to the utility transmission or distribution system with a generating capacity of no less than 5,000 kW.

Analysis of the Change:
In the last few years, large-scale PV systems producing in excess of 5 megawatts have become commonplace in the United States. Some of these systems can produce upwards of 50 megawatts. A 50 megawatt PV system produces the equivalent energy of roughly 25,000 residential PV systems. While the number of large-scale PV systems is relatively small, the volume of electricity generated by these systems is greater than the combined output of all residential and commercial PV systems currently addressed in Article 690. The rapid increase in the number of large-scale PV electric supply stations presents new challenges to installers, but in particular to the AHJ when facing inspection and approval of a PV power plant within their geographical jurisdiction. These large-scale PV systems are difficult, if not impossible, to fit under the current scope of Article 690.

With this in mind, a new article has emerged in the 2017 *NEC* for larger-scaled PV systems. The article covers the installation of large-scale PV electric power production facilities operated for the sole purpose of providing electric supply to the utility transmission or distribution system with a generating capacity of no less than 5,000 kW. Facilities covered by this article have specific design and safety features unique to large-scale PV facilities. These large-scale PV systems are typically accessible only to qualified personnel rather than to the general public. Unlike smaller scale PV systems, large-scale PV electric power production facilities are designed and operated similarly to traditional utility power generating plants. Unqualified individuals are not allowed to access the system for their own safety and for protection of the system, which is crucial to grid stability. Access to large-scale PV electric supply stations must be restricted by a fencing structure to ensure that systems are adequately protected from the general public.

Photovoltaic technology has experienced rapid changes over the last decade. The pace of change has created challenges for nationally recognized testing laboratories (NRTL) responsible for listing electrical equipment and for the organizations responsible for writing standards and for the *NEC*. One of the keys in the determination of PV systems covered by Article 690 is that the PV system is connected on the customer's side of the meter and that the electricity generated is primarily used to offset the local facility's normal electrical loads. Backfeeding the electrical grid is allowed but is incidental to the purpose of the system. Large-scale PV systems typically connect to the grid on the utility side of the metering system rather than the customer side. They are typically connected at medium voltages (4.16 kV to 34.5 kV) or even transmission voltages (69 kV or higher) rather than at 480 volts or lower.

Article 691

This new article will assist the AHJ when assessing compliance of large-scale PV electric supply stations, while at the same time enabling system engineers to use engineering best practices in the design of large-scale PV electric supply stations.

This new article is the result of detailed work performed by the NFPA Large-Scale PV Task Group. Two groups of stakeholders — the Solar Energy Industries Association (SEIA) Codes and Standards Working Group and the Solar America Board of Codes and Standards (SolarABCs) PV Industry Forum — worked closely with this task group, and supported the work that was developed.

First Revisions: FR 7511
Second Revisions: SR 975-985, SCR 110, SCR 112
Public Inputs: PI 3289, PI 4087, PI 4088
Public Comments: Numerous (20) PCs, PC 624, PC 729

695.6(G)

Power Wiring. (Fire Pumps)

Ground-fault protection of equipment shall not be installed in any fire pump power circuit

Revision changed 695.6(G) from "ground-fault protection of equipment shall not be permitted for fire pumps" to "ground-fault protection of equipment shall not be installed in any fire pump power circuit"

695.6(G)

695.6(G) Power Wiring. (Fire Pumps)

- **Type of Change:** Revision

- **Change at a Glance:** The revision clarified that ground-fault protection of equipment is not permitted for fire pump power circuit(s).

- **Code Language: 695.6 Power Wiring. (Fire Pumps)**
  Power circuits and wiring methods shall comply with the requirements in 695.6(A) through (J), and as permitted in 230.90(A), Exception No. 4; 230.94, Exception No. 4; 240.13; 230.208; 240.4(A); and 430.31.

  (G) Ground-Fault Protection of Equipment. Ground-fault protection of equipment shall not be ~~permitted for fire pumps~~ installed in any fire pump power circuit. [**20**: 9.1.8.1]

- **2014 *NEC* Requirement**
  The language at 695.6(G) indicated that ground-fault protection (GFP) of equipment shall not be "permitted" for fire pumps.

- **2017 *NEC* Change**
  The text at 695.6(G) was changed to state that ground-fault protection of equipment "shall not be installed" in any fire pump power circuit.

Analysis of the Change:

A fire pump is part of a fire sprinkler system's water supply. In the event of a fire, feeders and wiring methods to fire pumps are required to have an extra measure of protection to allow the fire pump to do its job and to extinguish the fire. Fire pumps and their wiring methods are sacrificial by nature. The fire pump should run to protect people and property with the fire-quenching water that sprinkler systems and emergency crews need in order to do their jobs. The requirements in Article 695 for fire pumps are intended to protect life and property by providing requirements for the selection and installation of fire pumps, ensuring that fire suppression systems work as intended to deliver adequate and reliable water supplies in a fire emergency.

Because of this sacrificial nature, it should be made clear that fire pumps are not to be supplied with ground-fault protection (GFP). The language at 695.6(G) banning GFP for fire pumps has been in the *Code* since the 2005 *NEC*. The former language at 695.6(G) indicated that ground-fault protection of equipment shall not be "permitted" for fire pumps. The word "permitted" is typically associated with permissive language or an option in the *Code*. Some users of the *Code* have incorrectly interpreted this rule to mean that providing GFP for a fire pump is an option rather than a prohibition. While it should be apparent that GFP is not suitable for use with fire pumps because of the necessity for the fire pumps to continue to operate even under fault condition, it became necessary to change the language at 695.6(G) to make that point even clearer.

For the 2017 *NEC*, the text at 695.6(G) was changed from "ground-fault protection of equipment shall not be permitted for fire pumps" to "ground-fault protection of equipment shall not be installed in any fire pump power circuit." Hopefully, this will be clear enough language to prevent anyone from applying GFP to a fire pump. The new terminology is extracted material from NFPA 20 (*Standard for the Installation of Stationary Fire Pumps for Fire Protection*) as indicated with the bracketed text at the end of the new language at 695.6(G).

This revision should also make it clear that there may be GFP protection such as is often found at multi-tenant buildings with campus-style distribution systems, but GFP is not allowed in the fire pump power circuits of these buildings.

695.6(G)

Second Revisions: SR 3624
Public Comments: PC 211

695.15

Surge Protection (Fire Pumps)

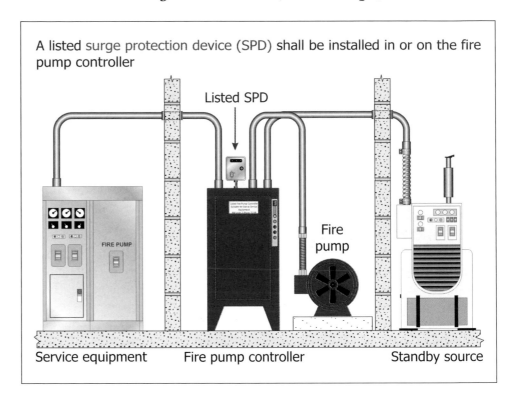

A listed surge protection device (SPD) shall be installed in or on the fire pump controller

Listed SPD

Fire pump

Service equipment   Fire pump controller   Standby source

695.15 695.15

695.15 Surge Protection. (Fire Pumps)

- **Type of Change:** New

- **Change at a Glance:** A listed surge protection device (SPD) is now required to be installed in or on fire pump controllers.

- **Code Language: 695.15 Surge Protection. (Fire Pumps)**
  A listed surge protection device shall be installed in or on the fire pump controller.

- **2014 *NEC* Requirement**
  Surge protection was not required for fire pumps or fire pump controllers.

- **2017 *NEC* Change**
  A new requirement was added to 695.15 demanding a listed surge protection device (SPD) be installed in or on all fire pump controllers.

Analysis of the Change:

A *surge protection device (SPD)* is defined in Article 100 as, "a protective device for limiting transient voltages by diverting or limiting surge current; it also prevents continued flow of follow current while remaining capable of repeating these functions." There are four types of SPDs that are described in the Article

100 definition as well. A spike or surge in current that goes un-arrested can cause significant damage to appliances and electronic equipment. This damage can result from such things as the starting and stopping of power electronic equipment, direct or indirect lightning strikes, and imposition of a higher voltage on a lower voltage system. SPDs have proven to provide protection for components and systems against the damages of voltage surges.

A listed SPD is required or permitted for such things as modular data centers, wind electric systems, and emergency systems. For the 2017 *NEC*, SPD protection is being added for items such as critical operations data systems and industrial machinery. Joining these crucial operations needing SPD protection for the 2017 *NEC* will be fire pump controllers. The location and type of SPD is a design issue and remains with the designer and/or installer. The SPDs for fire pump controllers are required to be listed devices as already required by former 285.5 (now 285.6).

A study titled, "Data Assessment for Electrical Surge Protective Devices," commissioned by the National Fire Protection Research Foundation, provided results of a 2013 and 2014 survey of facility managers concerning surge damage. This study shows that twelve percent of the fire pumps involved had damage due to voltage surges. Much of this damage could have been prevented with properly sized and listed surge protective devices. The new requirement for listed SPD for fire pump controllers is vitally important as fire pumps are so critical for life-safety.

First Revisions: FR 3658
Public Inputs: PI 2579

695.15

Special Conditions

Chapter 7

Conditions

Articles 700 – 770

700.2 and 700.25

Branch Circuit Emergency Lighting Transfer Switch

Branch Circuit Emergency Lighting Transfer Switch is allowed to be used to transfer emergency lighting loads supplied by branch circuits rated at 20 amperes or less from the normal branch circuit to an emergency branch circuit

Non-Emergency Lighting Circuits

Branch Circuit Emergency Lighting Transfer Switch

Utility Power Source

Normal Power Feed

Emergency Power Source

Dimmer Bank or Relay Panel

Lighting Circuits for Emergency Use

Emergency Input Power

Branch Circuit Emergency Lighting Transfer Switch. A device connected on the load side of a branch circuit overcurrent protective device that transfers only emergency lighting loads from the normal supply to an emergency supply.

700.2 & .25

700.2 and 700.25 Branch Circuit Emergency Lighting Transfer Switch

- **Type of Change:** New

- **Change at a Glance:** A new definition for *Branch Circuit Emergency Lighting Transfer Switch* along with provisions for the same at 700.25 have been added to the 2017 NEC.

- **Code Language: 700.2 Definitions. (Emergency Systems) Branch Circuit Emergency Lighting Transfer Switch.** A device connected on the load side of a branch circuit overcurrent protective device that transfers only emergency lighting loads from the normal supply to an emergency supply.

  Informational Note: See ANSI/UL 1008, *Transfer Switch Equipment*, for information covering branch circuit emergency lighting transfer switches.

  700.25 Branch Circuit Emergency Lighting Transfer Switch. Emergency lighting loads supplied by branch circuits rated at not greater than 20 amperes shall be permitted to be transferred from the normal branch circuit to an emergency branch circuit using a listed branch circuit emergency lighting transfer switch. The mechanically held requirement of 700.5(C) shall not apply to listed branch circuit emergency lighting transfer switches.

- **2014 *NEC* Requirement**
  The specifications of the device used to transfer emergency lighting loads from a normal branch circuit to an emergency branch circuit were not addressed in the 2014 *NEC*.

- **2017 *NEC* Change**
  A new 700.25 titled, "Branch Circuit Emergency Lighting Transfer Switch" was added to allow these devices to be used to transfer emergency lighting loads supplied by branch circuits rated at not greater than 20 amperes from the normal branch circuit to an emergency branch circuit. A new definition for *Branch Circuit Emergency Lighting Transfer Switch* was also added at 700.2.

700.2 & .25

Analysis of the Change:

Article 700, titled "Emergency Systems" applies to the electrical safety of the installation, operation, and maintenance of emergency systems. These emergency systems consist of circuits and equipment intended to supply, distribute, and control electricity for illumination, power, or both, to required facilities when the normal electrical supply or system is interrupted.

For the 2017 *NEC*, a new section was added to Article 700 at 700.25 titled, "Branch Circuit Emergency Lighting Transfer Switch." This section permits emergency lighting loads supplied by branch circuits rated at not greater than 20 amperes to be transferred from the normal branch circuit to an emergency branch circuit using a listed "branch circuit emergency lighting transfer switch." This addition will accommodate a new class of transfer switching devices intended for operation of individual branch circuits in an emergency lighting system. The product standard and the design requirements for these new devices can be found in UL 1008 (*Transfer Switch Equipment*).

To coincide with this new section and term used at 700.25, a new definition for *Branch Circuit Emergency Lighting Transfer Switch* was added at 700.2. This definition states that a branch circuit emergency lighting transfer switch is "a device connected on the load side of a branch circuit overcurrent protective device that transfers only emergency lighting loads from the normal supply to an emergency supply." This definition supports the provisions added at 700.25.

In some past situations, an automatic load control relay (ALCR) has been used to transfer emergency lighting loads from the normal supply to an emergency supply (even though this is a code violation of 700.26). During the 2011 *NEC*, 700.24 (now 700.26 in the 2017 *NEC*) was added to the *Code*. This section covers the requirements for ALCRs and specifically states, "the load control relay shall not be used as transfer equipment." UL 924 (*Standard for Emergency Lighting and Power Equipment*) transfer-capable ALCRs were never intended for use as general purpose transfer equipment. However, these devices fall within the *NEC* definition of transfer equipment because they can be used for transferring a load between two asynchronous power sources (normal and emergency). Even if they do meet the definition of transfer equipment, they do not meet the current requirements of Article 700 for emergency transfer switches. ALCRs have not undergone any evaluation as emergency transfer switches.

This is part of the reason it was necessary for these new branch-circuit emergency lighting transfer switches to be introduced into the 2017 *NEC*. These devices (and transfer-capable ALCRs that are re-evaluated as branch circuit emergency lighting transfer switches under UL 1008) will now be evaluated using performance and construction requirements comparable to those applied to traditional emergency transfer switches for use on branch circuits rated up to 20 amperes.

First Revisions: FR 3607, FR 3620
Public Inputs: PI 753, PI 752

700.3(F)

Temporary Source of Power for Maintenance or Repair of the Alternate Source of Power

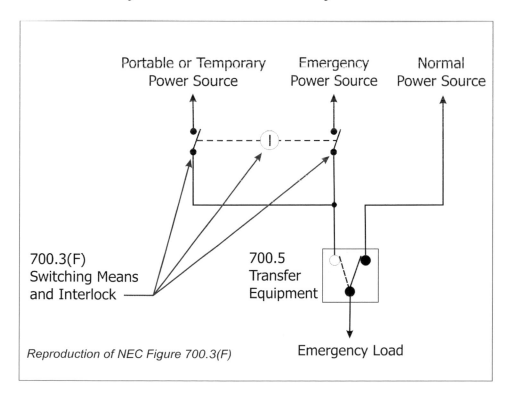

Reproduction of NEC Figure 700.3(F)

700.3(F) Temporary Source of Power for Maintenance or Repair of the Alternate Source of Power

- **Type of Change:** New

700.3(F)

■ **Change at a Glance:** New provisions were added at 700.3(F) providing performance-based requirements for a portable or temporary alternate source to be available whenever a single alternate source of power for emergency system is out of service for maintenance or repair.

■ **Code Language: 700.3 Tests and Maintenance**
(F) Temporary Source of Power for Maintenance or Repair of the Alternate Source of Power. If the emergency system relies on a single alternate source of power, which will be disabled for maintenance or repair, the emergency system shall include permanent switching means to connect a portable or temporary alternate source of power, which shall be available for the duration of the maintenance or repair. The permanent switching means to connect a portable or temporary alternate source of power shall comply with the following:

1. Connection to the portable or temporary alternate source of power shall not require modification of the permanent system wiring.

2. Transfer of power between the normal power source and the emergency power source shall be in accordance with 700.12.

3. The connection point for the portable or temporary alternate source shall be marked with the phase rotation and system bonding requirements.

4. Mechanical or electrical interlocking shall prevent inadvertent interconnection of power sources.

5. The switching means shall include a contact point that shall annunciate at a location remote from the generator or at another facility monitoring system to indicate that the permanent emergency source is disconnected from the emergency system.

It shall be permissible to utilize manual switching to switch from the permanent source of power to the portable or temporary alternate source of power and to utilize the switching means for connection of a load bank.

Informational Note: There are many possible methods to achieve the requirements of 700.3(F). See Figure 700.3(F) for one example.

Figure 700.3(F) (See *NEC* and illustration provided at this change for complete figure)

Exception: The permanent switching means to connect a portable or temporary alternate source of power, for the duration of the maintenance or repair, shall not be required where any of the following conditions exists:

1. All processes that rely on the emergency system source are capable of being disabled during maintenance or repair of the emergency source of power.

2. The building or structure is unoccupied and fire suppression systems are fully functional and do not require an alternate power source.

3. Other temporary means can be substituted for the emergency system.

4. A permanent alternate emergency source, such as, but not limited to, a second on-site standby generator or separate electric utility service connection, capable of supporting the emergency system, exists.

■ **2014 *NEC* Requirement**
Under the title of "Capacity" and "Selective Load Pickup, Load Shedding, and Peak Load Shaving," a sentence appeared at the end of 700.4(B) stating, "a portable or temporary alternate source shall be available whenever the emergency generator is out of service for major maintenance or repair." No prescriptive requirements existed for this requirement.

■ **2017 *NEC* Change**
A new first level subdivision is titled, "Temporary Source of Power for Maintenance or Repair of the Alternate Source of Power" was added at 700.3(F) calling for emergency systems that rely on a single alternate source of power to include a permanent switching means to connect a portable or temporary alternate source of power while the single alternate source of power is disabled for maintenance or repair. This permanent switching means must be available for the duration of the maintenance or repair. This new requirement comes with an exception with four conditions.

700.3(F)

Analysis of the Change:

As stated in the scope of Article 700, the emergency system of a building is critical to the electrical safety of said building. The emergency system consists of circuits and equipment intended to supply, distribute, and control electricity for illumination, power, or both, to required facilities when the normal electrical supply or system is interrupted. Does this critical operation dwindle in importance at all when the emergency system is disabled for maintenance or repair? CMP-13 answered this question with the addition of 700.3(F) for the 2017 *NEC*.

This new first level subdivision is titled, "Temporary Source of Power for Maintenance or Repair of the Alternate Source of Power." This new provision calls for emergency systems that rely on a single alternate source of power to include a permanent switching means to connect a portable or temporary alternate source of power while the single alternate source of power is disabled for maintenance or repair. This permanent switching means must be available for the duration of the maintenance or repair. This new requirement comes with an exception with four conditions. No prescriptive requirements existed prior to this change.

The former last sentence at 700.4(B) (which some users of the *Code* felt was improperly located in 700.4) provided the inspiration for the new 700.3(F) pertaining to the performance-based requirements for a portable or temporary alternate source to be available whenever the emergency generator is out of service for major maintenance or repair. With this one sentence, it was difficult to determine what would be considered "major" maintenance or repair. Oil changes are not considered a major maintenance item, but on a large generator, this can take several hours to perform. In the event of maintenance on a large generator where an outage is incurred, the emergency system will not be available to provide needed power to the facility during the maintenance procedure. This revision provides necessary clarity for the maintenance requirements of emergency systems.

A new Figure 700.3(F) has also been introduced to show one possible method to utilize manual switching from the single alternate source of power to the portable or temporary alternate source of power and to utilize the switching means for connection of a load bank.

First Revisions: FR 3616
Second Revisions: SR 3602, SCR 84
Public Inputs: PI 3005
Public Comments: PC 318, PC 317

700.5(E)

700.5(E)

Short-Circuit Current Rating Marked on Transfer Equipment of Emergency Systems

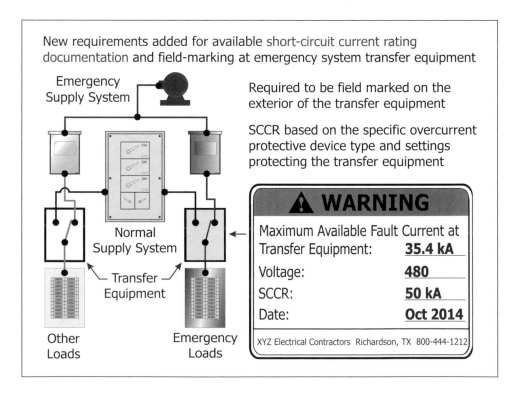

New requirements added for available short-circuit current rating documentation and field-marking at emergency system transfer equipment

Emergency Supply System

Required to be field marked on the exterior of the transfer equipment

SCCR based on the specific overcurrent protective device type and settings protecting the transfer equipment

Normal Supply System

Transfer Equipment

Other Loads

Emergency Loads

⚠ **WARNING**

Maximum Available Fault Current at Transfer Equipment:	**35.4 kA**
Voltage:	**480**
SCCR:	**50 kA**
Date:	**Oct 2014**

XYZ Electrical Contractors Richardson, TX 800-444-1212

700.5(E) Transfer Equipment (Emergency Systems)

- **Type of Change:** New

- **Change at a Glance:** New requirements were added for available short-circuit current rating documentation and field-marking at emergency system transfer equipment.

- **Code Language: 700.5 Transfer Equipment (Emergency Systems) (E) Documentation.** The short-circuit current rating of the transfer equipment, based on the specific overcurrent protective device type and settings protecting the transfer equipment, shall be field marked on the exterior of the transfer equipment.

- **2014 *NEC* Requirement**
  There was no requirement for a field marking of the short-circuit current rating of emergency system transfer equipment in Article 700 of the 2014 *NEC*.

- **2017 *NEC* Change**
  A new requirement was added at 700.5(E) that will now require the short-circuit current rating of the transfer equipment to be field marked on the exterior of the transfer equipment. This short-circuit current rating will be based on the specific overcurrent protective device type and settings protecting the transfer equipment.

700.5(E)

Analysis of the Change:

Emergency systems are designed to power exit lighting, fire detection and alarm systems, elevators, fire pumps, and public safety communications systems in buildings where artificial illumination is required for safe exiting and panic control. They might also power ventilation systems considered essential to preserving health and life, or industrial processes where power interruption would result in hazards to life or injury.

Transfer equipment for an emergency system must be automatic, identified for emergency use, supply only emergency loads, and approved by the AHJ. Automatic transfer switches must be electrically operated, mechanically held, and listed for emergency system use when rated 1000-volt ac and below. When transfer equipment is installed, it is required to be marked per UL 1008 (*Transfer Switch Equipment*) with the short-circuit current rating. UL 1008 contains many options for short-circuit protection.

For the 2017 *NEC*, a new requirement was added at 700.5(E) calling for the short-circuit current rating of the transfer equipment to be field marked on the exterior of the transfer equipment. This short-circuit current rating will be based on the specific overcurrent protective device type and settings protecting the transfer equipment.

This additional field marking on the transfer equipment was deemed necessary as a transfer switch of this nature is typically marked by the manufacturer with several different options resulting in numerous short-circuit current rating values. These manufacturer-marked short-circuit current rating values can vary based upon the overcurrent protective device type, ampere rating and settings. Without this new short-circuit current rating field marking, this can be confusing for the inspection community as it is not obvious which short-circuit current rating is being utilized. This new field marking of the short-circuit current rating value will be based on the specific type of overcurrent protective device, ampere rating, and installed settings, which are known factors for the designer and/or installer.

This is similar to the requirements in 110.24(A) for field marking of available fault current for services. The available fault current must be documented to verify compliance with 110.9, Interrupting Rating, and 110.10, Circuit Impedance, Short-Circuit Current Ratings, and Other Characteristics.

Note to Reader: This same new requirement for available short-circuit current rating documentation and field-marking occurred at the following locations:

701.5(D)	Legally Required Standby Systems	See FR 7519
702.5	Optional Standby Systems	See FR 7520
708.24(E)	Critical Operations Power Systems (COPS)	See FR 7521

First Revisions: FR 7518

700.5(E)

700.10(A)

Marking of Boxes and Enclosures for Emergency Circuits or Systems

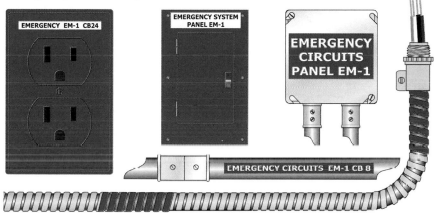

In addition to boxes and enclosures, exposed emergency system cables and raceway systems not associated with boxes or enclosures required to be permanently marked to be readily identified as a component of an emergency circuit or system

Receptacles supplied from the emergency system are now required to be identified by a "distinctive color or marking" on the receptacle cover plates or the receptacle

700.10(A) Wiring, Emergency System

- **Type of Change:** Revision/New

- **Change at a Glance:** Identification for emergency circuits has been expanded to include cables and raceways not associated with boxes or enclosures. Emergency system receptacles now require identification with a distinctive color or marking.

- **Code Language: 700.10 Wiring, Emergency System.**
  (A) Identification. Emergency circuits shall be permanently marked so they will be readily identified as a component of an emergency circuit or system by the following methods:

  (1) All boxes and enclosures (including transfer switches, generators, and power panels) for emergency circuits shall be permanently marked ~~so they will be readily identified~~ as a component of an emergency circuit or system.

  (2) Where boxes or enclosures are not encountered, exposed cable or raceway systems shall be permanently marked to be identified as a component of an emergency circuit or system, at intervals not to exceed 7.6 m (25 ft).

Receptacles supplied from the emergency system shall have a distinctive color or marking on the receptacle cover plates or the receptacles.

700.10(A)

- **2014 *NEC* Requirement**
  All boxes and enclosures for emergency circuits are required to be permanently marked so they will be readily identified as a component of an emergency circuit or system.

- **2017 *NEC* Change**
  In addition to boxes and enclosures, these identification requirements have been expanded to exposed emergency system cables and raceway systems not associated with junction boxes or enclosures. Receptacles supplied from the emergency system are now required to be identified by a "distinctive color or marking" on the receptacle cover plates or the receptacle.

Analysis of the Change:

When it comes to Article 700 emergency systems, the *Code* calls for all boxes and enclosures for emergency circuits to be permanently marked or identified. It is essential to the maintenance and integrity of these emergency circuits that they be readily identified as components of the emergency circuit or system. The emergency system enclosures required to be marked or readily identified would include such things as transfer switches, generators, and power panelboards. The *Code* is not specific as to the means of identification for the emergency systems. This identification could include color, signs, or a labeling system. A very common industry practice (not a *Code* requirement) is the use of the color "red" in identification of the emergency system. Again, this could be spray paint, labels, etc. It is common to see emergency system labels with white lettering on a red background.

For the 2017 *NEC*, the emergency system identification at 700.10(A) has been expanded to more than just boxes and enclosures. These requirements will now be mandated for exposed emergency system cables and raceway systems that might not be associated with junction boxes or enclosures. An example of this type of installation could be a metallic cable system daisy-chained from emergency luminaire to emergency luminaire without installing a junction box between luminaires. This process would leave the emergency system wiring method from luminaire to luminaire indistinguishable from the normal system. New provisions at 700.10(A)(2) will now require exposed emergency circuit or system cable or raceway systems to be permanently marked as a component of an emergency circuit or system, at intervals not to exceed 7.6 m (25 ft) where boxes or enclosures are not encountered.

It is an extremely difficult task for an inspector or installer to follow a cable or raceway in a ceiling where every cable or raceway in that same ceiling is identical and not identified as something other than the normal branch circuits or feeders. This expansion of identification should be beneficial to electricians and inspectors without causing undue hardship during the initial installation. Again, this means of identification method could be as simple as spray painting the cable or raceway every 7.6 m (25 ft) similar to identification of independent grid wires specific to support of wiring methods above a suspended ceiling as required by 300.11(A)(1) and (A)(2).

Another significant change occurred involving these emergency system identification requirements at 700.10(A). Receptacles supplied from the emergency system are now required to be identified by a "distinctive color or marking" on the receptacle cover plates or the receptacle itself. As with the boxes, enclosures, cables, and raceways, the *Code* is not specific as to the means or method to be used to accomplish the receptacle "distinctive color or marking" requirements. Red-colored receptacles and covers similar to what is commonly used in health care facilities would certainly be "distinctive," as would blue-colored receptacles.

It might be beneficial to future users of this emergency system to identify the identification means for emergency system receptacles (even though this is not a *Code* requirement). Marking or identification of receptacles supplied from an emergency system is necessary for the end user to identify emergency supplied devices for connection of equipment needed when there is a loss of normal power.

First Revisions: FR 3612
Second Revisions: SR 3603
Public Inputs: PI 2656
Public Comments: PC 1129

700.10(A)

700.10(D)

Fire Protection of Emergency System Feeders in Health Care Occupancies

700.10(D)

Occupancy areas requiring fire protection requirements for emergency system feeders was expanded for the 2017 *NEC*

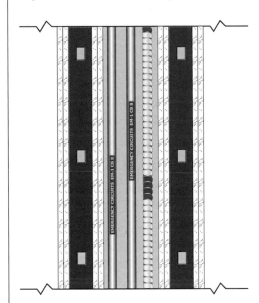

Fire protection provisions for emergency system feeders required for the following occupancies:

(1) Assembly occupancies for not less than 1000 persons

(2) Buildings above 23 m (75 ft) in height

(3) Health care occupancies where persons are not capable of self preservation

(4) Educational occupancies with more than 300 occupants

700.10(D) Wiring, Emergency System

- **Type of Change:** Revision/New

- **Change at a Glance:** Health care occupancies where persons are not capable of self-preservation and educational occupancies with more than 300 occupants have been added to the requirements for fire protection of emergency system feeders (in addition to high-rise buildings and those buildings with large occupancy loads).

- **Code Language: 700.10 Wiring, Emergency System.**
  (D) Fire Protection. Emergency systems shall meet the additional requirements in (D)(1) through (D)(3) in ~~assembly occupancies for not less than 1000 persons or in buildings above 23 m (75 ft) in height.~~ the following occupancies:

  (1) Assembly occupancies for not less than 1000 persons

  (2) Buildings above 23 m (75 ft) in height.

  (3) Health care occupancies where persons are not capable of self preservation

(4) Educational occupancies with more than 300 occupants

(1) Feeder-Circuit Wiring.
(2) Feeder-Circuit Equipment.
(3) Generator Control Wiring.
(See *NEC* for complete text)

■ **2014 *NEC* Requirement**
Fire protection measures had to be considered for emergency system feeders that were installed in assembly occupancies with an occupancy not less than 1000 persons or buildings with a height exceeding 23 m (75 ft).

■ **2017 *NEC* Change**
Fire protection provisions for emergency system feeders were expanded to also include health care occupancies where persons are not capable of self-preservation and educational occupancies with more than 300 occupants (in addition to high-rise buildings and those buildings with large occupancy loads).

700.10(D)

Analysis of the Change:
All efforts must be exhausted when it comes to the protection of emergency circuits in multi-occupancy and high-rise buildings from damage due to a fire. When combined with the spread of smoke and heat, such damage could result in far greater loss of life and destruction of property than would have otherwise occurred. To that end, fire protection is required for emergency feeder circuits by the provisions of 700.10(D). Meeting the fire protection requirements of 700.10(D) for emergency system feeders starts in the engineering, designing, and plan review stages of a project. The installation of these feeders in accordance with 700.10(D) is verified by on-site inspections and typically involves both the structural and electrical inspectors working together.

These fire protection methods include such things as automatic fire suppression systems, listed electrical circuit protective systems with a minimum 2-hour fire rating, cables or raceways listed as fire-restrictive cable systems, listed fire-rated assemblies that have a minimum fire rating of 2 hours and contain only emergency wiring circuits, or encasement in a minimum of 50 mm (2 in.) of concrete.

In previous editions of the *Code*, these fire protection requirements for emergency system feeders applied to emergency systems that were installed in assembly occupancies with an occupancy not less than 1000 persons or buildings with a height exceeding 23 m (75 ft) (high rise buildings). For the 2017 *NEC*, these fire protection requirements for emergency system feeders were expanded to also include health care occupancies where persons are not capable of self-preservation and educational occupancies with more than 300 occupants.

This 2017 expansion recognizes that areas such as schools, learning centers, universities, hospitals, and nursing homes could qualify as not being a high rise building or 1000-person assembly occupancy, yet the importance and the challenges of safe evacuation in the event of fire are similar and just as critical. During the 2017 *NEC* first draft public input stage, CMP-13 debated public inputs to include all buildings in these fire prevention requirements, but could not reach consensus as issues were raised concerning the financial impact this would have on small business occupancies. During the 2017 *NEC* second draft public comment stage, CMP-13 achieved enough support for health care occupancies where persons are not capable of self-preservation and educational occupancies with more than 300 occupants to be included in the fire protection provisions for emergency system feeders of 700.10(D).

The text at 700.10(D) has been reformatted into a more "user-friendly" list format. This revision/addition at 700.10(D) will result in additional safety to enhance the safe evacuation of the occupants in the event of a fire emergency at all building occupancies that fall under the requirements of the revised 700.10(D). Many schools and health care facilities that are not high-rise buildings or 1000-person assembly occupancies will now have their emergency systems protected from a fire for a minimum of two hours.

Note that this revision/addition at 700.10(D) required coordination with the provisions of 700.12 for the equipment for sources of power to an emergency system. The same basic revisions/additions of health care occupancies where persons are not capable of self-preservation and educational occupancies with more than 300 occupants were incorporated at 700.12 as well to provide correlation between 700.10(D) and 700.12.

Second Revisions: SR 3612, SR 3613
Public Inputs: PI 1246, PI 2564, PI 3895
Public Comments: PC 395, PC 563

700.10(D)

701.6(D)

Ground-Fault Sensors at Alternate Locations in Standby Systems

The sensor for ground-fault signal devices is generally required to be located at, or ahead of, the main system disconnecting means for the legally required standby source of a legally required standby system

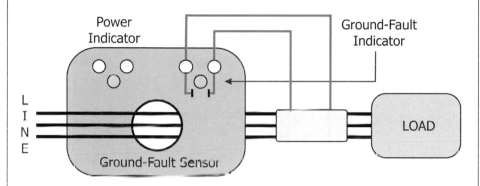

Code language was added at 701.6(D) to allow the ground fault sensor to be located at an alternate location for systems with multiple emergency sources connected to a paralleling bus

701.6(D)

701.6(D) Signals. (Legally Required Standby Systems)

- **Type of Change:** Revision/New

- **Change at a Glance:** New text was added to allow a ground-fault sensor to be located at an alternate location for legally required standby systems with multiple emergency sources connected to a paralleling bus.

- **Code Language: 701.6 Signals. (Legally Required Standby Systems)**
  Audible and visual signal devices shall be provided, where practicable, for the purposes described in 701.6(A), (B), (C), and (D).

  (D) Ground Fault. To indicate a ground fault in solidly grounded wye, legally required standby systems of more than 150 volts to ground and circuit-protective devices rated 1000 amperes or more. The sensor for the ground-fault signal devices shall be located at, or ahead of, the main system disconnecting means for the legally required standby source, and the maximum setting of the signal devices shall be for a ground-fault current of 1200 amperes. Instructions on the course of action to be taken in event of indicated ground fault shall be located at or near the sensor location.

For systems with multiple emergency sources connected to a paralleling bus, the ground fault sensor shall be permitted at an alternate location.

Informational Note: For signals for generator sets, see NFPA 110-2013, *Standard for Emergency and Standby Power Systems.*

■ **2014 *NEC* Requirement**
The sensor for the ground-fault signal devices was required to be located at, or ahead of, the main system disconnecting means for the legally required standby source. This sensor is designed to indicate a ground fault in solidly grounded wye, legally required standby systems of more than 150 volts to ground and circuit-protective devices rated 1000 amperes or more. The maximum setting of the signal devices must be set for a ground-fault current of 1200 amperes.

■ **2017 *NEC* Change**
Code language was added to allow the ground-fault sensor to be located at an "alternate location" for systems with multiple emergency sources connected to a paralleling bus.

701.6(D)

Analysis of the Change:

Ground-fault protection (GFP) of equipment is essential in protecting electrical equipment rated more than 150 volts to ground with circuit-protective devices rated 1000 amperes or more. A low-level arcing ground fault can destroy switchgear in seconds before the main service overcurrent protection can detect such ground-faults and open the circuit. In systems such as a 480/277 volt solidly grounded system, there is sufficient voltage to maintain an arc between one phase and ground but not enough current to cause a large main overcurrent device to trip and clear the fault quickly. The resulting arc is similar to an electric arc weld, consuming large amounts of metal in the seconds it takes the overcurrent device to operate. A properly installed and operating GFP system will detect and clear the fault in milliseconds, fast enough to limit damage to acceptable levels.

The *Code* is very specific in locations such as 701.6(D) as to the location of ground-fault protection equipment and devices to allow the GFP equipment to function properly. Situations such as neutrals grounded downstream, or neutrals bonded to ground in the wrong locations, can defeat ground-fault protection or cause inadequate tripping. Incorrect current sensor installation and wrong polarity can cause false tripping as well. A properly installed ground-fault sensor can provide a reliable and cost-effective method for sensing ground faults. With the current-carrying conductors routed through the sensing device, when the ground-fault current reaches the level set by the trip point adjustment, the sensing relay trips, illuminates the tripped LED indicator and provides an output signal.

The provisions of 701.6(D) for legally required standby systems call for the sensor for the ground-fault signal devices to be located at, or ahead of, the main system disconnecting means for the legally required standby source. This system works well if only one source is involved. For the 2017 *NEC*, language was added to allow the ground fault sensor to be located at an alternate location for systems with multiple emergency sources connected to a paralleling bus. For multiple emergency sources, ground fault sensing may be determined by zero sequence sensing, differential relaying of the paralleling bus in conjunction with residual ground fault sensing device of the feeders, or other equivalent means.

When generators are operated in parallel as a separately derived system like those often seen in legally required standby systems, there must be only one neutral to ground bond at the first means of disconnect in the system. However, when each generator is considered a source, the obvious (but incorrect) conclusion will be that each generator should have the neutral bonded at each disconnecting means. The consequence of this is often ineffective ground-fault protection for the system and a potential for nuisance tripping of the ground-fault system due to temporary imbalances in the load sharing control system.

If the source of the system is the bus, then the required GFP will be located on feeders connected to the bus, rather than the generator sets. In this manner, the GFP detection devices can more easily discriminate between more and less critical loads, and would not disable the system for a downstream fault and critical loads such as emergency circuits. Less critical circuits can be tripped, resulting in an overall better protection for less critical systems, and better reliability for critical circuits. In parallel applications, it is not uncommon for the generator paralleling breakers (the breaker or device that connects the generator to the common bus) to be smaller than some of the feeders on the bus. Technically, this makes selective coordination of the system impossible to attain.

The new language dealing with systems with multiple emergency sources connected to a paralleling bus will help to clarify the requirements for installing the ground fault sensor as this new language specifically permits the installation at an alternate location.

This same change occurred at 700.6(D) for Emergency Systems (see FR 3638 and PI 1530).

Second Revisions: SR 3608
Public Comments: PC 257

701.6(D)

702.12(C)

Power Inlets used with Optional Standby Generators

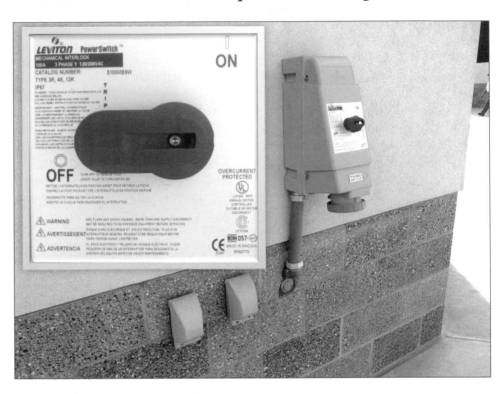

702.12(C)

702.12(C) Power Inlets Rated at 100 Amperes or Greater, for Portable Generators

■ **Type of Change:** New

■ **Change at a Glance:** New requirements were added for power inlets used with optional standby generators to ensure that disconnection of the power inlet does not occur under load.

■ **Code Language: 702.12 Outdoor Generator Sets. (Optional Standby Systems)**

(A) ~~Permanently Installed Generators and~~ **Portable Generators Greater Than 15 kW and Permanently Installed Generators.** (See *NEC* for complete text)

(B) Portable Generators 15 kW or Less. (See *NEC* for complete text)

(C) Power Inlets Rated at 100 Amperes or Greater, for Portable Generators. Equipment containing power inlets for the connection of a generator source shall be listed for the intended use. Systems with power inlets shall be equipped with an interlocked disconnecting means.

Exception No. 1: If the inlet device is rated as a disconnecting means.

Exception No. 2: Supervised industrial installations where permanent space is identified for the portable generator located within line of sight of the power inlets shall not be required to have interlocked disconnecting means nor inlets rated as disconnects.

- **2014 *NEC* Requirement**
  No provisions existed in Article 702 for interlocked disconnecting means or listing requirements of power inlets for the connection of a generator source of an optional standby system.

- **2017 *NEC* Change**
  New language was added requiring optional standby equipment containing power inlets rated 100 amperes or more for the connection of a generator source to be listed for the intended use and be equipped with an interlocked disconnecting means. Two exceptions have been added after this new language to address instances where the inlet has been rated as a disconnecting means and for supervised industrial installations where permanent space has been identified for the portable generator to be located within line of sight of the power inlets.

Analysis of the Change:

Optional standby systems are those backup systems that are utilized when normal power failure can cause physical discomfort, serious interruption of an industrial process, damage to process equipment, or disruption of business, but the power failure does not cause life threatening conditions or impose any safety hazards. Optional standby systems typically consist of one of two types of systems—those that are permanently installed in their entirety including prime movers, or those that are arranged for a connection to a premises wiring system from a portable alternate power supply.

Outdoor generator sets are often employed to serve as an optional standby system to continue supplying electricity during power outages. As stated above, these optional standby generators or generator sets can be permanently installed or of the portable type. Permanently installed generators can be installed indoors, but with an extensive exhaust system and change-of-air system in place. Portable generators are typically maintained outside the building or structure as they emit deadly carbon monoxide gas. Sometimes, half the trick is getting the electricity safely inside the building from these outside sources.

It is not uncommon to find power inlet boxes serving as a gateway between the inside need or desire for electricity and the outside supply source. With a power inlet box installed on the outside of the building, typically near the main service electrical panelboards, wiring from this power inlet box is installed to a manual transfer switch, which restores power to the entire main electrical panelboard or selected branch circuits inside the building.

For the 2017 *NEC*, *Code* language was added at 702.12(C) to ensure that optional standby equipment containing power inlets rated 100 amperes or more for the connection of a generator source be "listed for the intended use" and be

702.12(C)

equipped with an interlocked disconnecting means. This new provision will provide the necessary means to ensure that disconnection of the power inlet does not occur under load conditions. A portable generator can be located "not within sight" from the point at which it electrically connects to the building through a permanently installed power inlet. If a person cannot visibly see the generator to which it is connected, disconnecting under load can present a safety hazard if the inlet is not rated for load break or the "intended use."

Two new exceptions were also added following 702.12(C). The first exception gives an exemption from the requirements for being listed for the intended use and having an interlocked disconnecting means if the power inlet device is rated as a disconnecting means itself. Power inlet devices rated up to 60 amperes that are also rated as a disconnecting means are readily available. There are also load-break solutions available that possess load-break capabilities up to and above 100 amperes. The second exception pertains to supervised industrial installations where permanent space is identified for the portable generator to be located within line of sight of the power inlets. If a supervised industrial installation meets the conditions of this exception, the power inlet box or device is not required to be an interlocked disconnecting means nor be rated as a disconnecting means.

The new language at 702.12(C) is intended to require either that the power inlet devices used with portable outdoor generators be load break rated or that the power inlet be interlocked with a disconnecting means to ensure that the disconnect is opened before disconnecting the portable generator.

First Revisions: FR 3632
Public Inputs: PI 3589

702.12(C)

Article 705, Part IV
Microgrid Systems

A new Part IV was added to Article 705 recognizing "Microgrid Systems" as an interconnected electric power production source

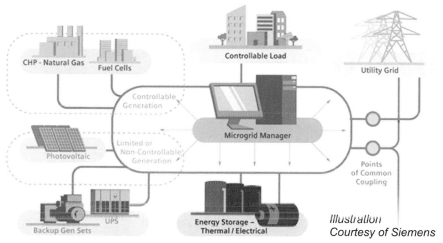

CHP - Natural Gas Fuel Cells

Controllable Load

Utility Grid

Controllable Generation

Microgrid Manager

Photovoltaic

Limited or Non-Controllable Generation

Points of Common Coupling

Backup Gen Sets UPS

Energy Storage – Thermal / Electrical

Illustration Courtesy of Siemens

Microgrid systems, sometimes referred to as "intentionally islanded systems" and "stand-alone systems" are a way to add resiliency against loss of power in premises wiring systems

Article 705, IV

Article 705, Part IV **Microgrid Systems**

- **Type of Change:** New

- **Change at a Glance:** New Part IV was added to Article 705 recognizing microgrid systems as an interconnected electric power production source.

- **Code Language:** **Part IV. Microgrid Systems (Interconnected Electric Power Production Sources)**

  705.150 System Operation. Microgrid systems shall be permitted to disconnect from the primary source of power or other interconnected electric power production sources and operate as a separate microgrid system.

  705.160 Primary Power Source Connection. Connections to primary power sources that are external to the microgrid system shall comply with the requirements of 705.12.

  705.165 Reconnection to Primary Power Source. Microgrid systems that reconnect to primary power sources shall be provided with the necessary equipment to establish a synchronous transition.

705.170 Microgrid Interconnect Devices (MID). Microgrid interconnect devices shall comply with the following:

(1) Be required for any connection between a microgrid system and a primary power source

(2) Be listed or field labeled for the application

(3) Have sufficient number of overcurrent devices located to provide overcurrent protection from all sources

Informational Note: MID functionality is often incorporated in an interactive or multimode inverter, energy storage system, or similar device identified for interactive operation.

- **2014 *NEC* Requirement**
  Article 705 did not address the installation of microgrid systems, intentionally islanded systems, or stand-alone systems as interconnected electric power production sources.

- **2017 *NEC* Change**
  A new Part IV was added to Article 705 titled, "Microgrid Systems." Microgrid systems are sometimes referred to as "intentionally islanded systems" and "stand-alone systems." Microgrids are a way to add resiliency against loss of power in premises wiring systems.

Article 705, IV

Analysis of the Change:

An interconnected electric power production source is an installation of one or more electric power production sources operating in parallel with a primary source(s) of electricity. An example of this type of primary sources includes a utility supply or an on-site electric power source(s). An example of an electric power production source operating in parallel with a primary source (and often used) is a microgrid system.

Microgrid systems are modern, localized, small-scale grids, contrary to the traditional, centralized electricity grid. Microgrids can disconnect from the centralized grid and operate autonomously, strengthen grid resilience, and help mitigate grid disturbances because they can continue operating while the main grid is down; and they can function as a grid resource for faster system response and recovery. They often use diesel generators and are installed by the community they serve. Microgrids increasingly employ a mixture of different distributed energy resources, such as solar hybrid power systems, which reduce the amount of emitted carbon significantly. Microgrids also support a flexible and efficient electric grid, by enabling the integration of growing deployments of renewable sources of energy such as solar and wind, and distributed energy resources such as combined heat and power, energy storage, and demand response. In addition, the use of local sources of energy to serve local loads helps reduce energy losses in transmission and distribution, further increasing efficiency of the electric delivery system.

For the 2017 *NEC*, CMP-4 recognized the need to incorporate microgrid systems into Article 705. This incorporation resulted in a new Part IV titled, "Microgrid

Systems," being added to the 2017 *NEC*. Microgrid systems are sometimes referred to as "intentionally islanded systems" and "stand-alone systems." As noted above, microgrids are getting recognition as a way to add resiliency against loss of power in premises wiring systems.

This new Part IV of Article 705 includes:

705.150 System Operations
705.160 Primary Power Source Connection
705.165 Reconnection to Primary Power Source and
705.170 Microgrid Interconnect Devices (MID)

The original structure of the new Part IV of Article 705 that was proposed in the 2017 *NEC* First Draft stage included a section on wiring methods for stand-alone systems operating in the stand-alone mode. By the time this new Part IV worked its way through the *NEC* revision process, CMP-4 recognized the information in this section was more appropriate to be included in a new Article 710 titled, "Stand-Alone Systems."

First Revisions: FR 1045
Second Revisions: SR 1005, SR 1000, SR 987
Public Comments: Numerous PCs

Article 705, IV

Article 706

Energy Storage Systems

Illustration Courtesy of A123 Systems

Article 706 Energy Storage Systems

- **Type of Change:** New

- **Change at a Glance:** The new article, "Energy Storage Systems," applies to all permanently installed energy storage systems (ESS) operating at over 50 volts ac or 60 volts dc that may be stand-alone or interactive with other electric power production sources.

- **Code Language:** Article 706 Energy Storage Systems
  Part I. General

706.1 Scope. This article applies to all permanently installed energy storage systems (ESS) operating at over 50 volts ac or 60 volts dc that may be stand-alone or interactive with other electric power production sources.

Informational Note: The following standards are frequently referenced for the installation of energy storage systems:

(1) NFPA 111-2013, *Standard on Stored Electrical Energy Emergency and Standby Systems*

(2) IEEE 484-2008, *Recommended Practice for Installation Design and Installation of Vented Lead-Acid Batteries for Stationary Applications*

(3) IEEE 485-1997, *Recommended Practice for Sizing Vented Lead-Acid Storage Batteries for Stationary Applications*

(4) IEEE 1145-2007, *Recommended Practice for Installation and Maintenance of Nickel-Cadmium Batteries for Photovoltaic (PV) Systems*

(5) IEEE 1187-2002, *Recommended Practice for Installation Design, and Installation of Valve-Regulated Lead-Acid Batteries for Stationary Applications*

(6) IEEE 1578-2007, *Recommended Practice for Stationary Battery Electrolyte Spill Containment and Management*

(7) IEEE 1635/ASHRAE 21-2012, *Guide for the Ventilation and Thermal Management of Stationary Battery Installations Batteries for Stationary Applications*

(8) UL 810A, *Electrochemical Capacitors*

(9) UL 1973, *Batteries for Use in Light Electric Rail (LER) Applications and Stationary Applications*

(10) UL 1989, *Standard for Standby Batteries*

Article 706

(11) UL Subject 2436, *Spill Containment for Stationary Lead Acid Battery Systems*

(12) UL Subject 9540, *Safety of Energy Storage Systems and Equipment*

(See *NEC* for complete text)

Article 706

- **2014 *NEC* Requirement**
  No article about energy storage systems existed. Rules for energy storage systems were discussed in Articles 480, 690, 692, and 694.

- **2017 *NEC* Change**
  A new Article 706 titled, "Energy Storage Systems," was added to the *NEC* pertaining to all permanently installed energy storage systems (ESS).

Analysis of the Change:

Article 706 applies to all permanently installed energy storage systems (ESS) that may be stand-alone or interactive with other electric power production sources. An ESS is defined as "one or more components assembled together capable of storing energy for use at a future time." An ESS can include but is not limited to batteries, capacitors, and kinetic energy devices (e.g., flywheels and compressed air). These systems can have ac or dc output for utilization and can include inverters and converters to change stored energy into electrical energy.

This article is primarily the result of the work developed by a 79-member DC Task Group formed by the *NEC* Correlating Committee. The DC Task Group had to combine input from many different sources and other working groups (including the IEEE battery group, and the Article 690 task group), and other organizations such as NEMA and many companies, including manufacturers of equipment covered by this new article. Twelve standards were referenced in the development of this new article. These standards are included in the informational note located after the Scope at 706.1. The developing DC Task Group also had to consider existing text concerning energy storage in articles such as Articles 480, 690, 692, and 694 and how those articles correlate with this new Article 706.

Energy storage is the capture of energy produced at one time for use at a later time. Energy storage involves converting energy from forms that are difficult to store to more conveniently or economically storable forms. Placing the rules that apply to energy storage systems in one article will provide clear direction to *Code* users.

Article 706

First Revisions: FR 3662
Second revisions: SR 3631-36, SR 3638-59
Public Inputs: PI 4219, PI 4276
Public Comments: Numerous PCs 48 total

708.10(A)(2)

Illuminated Faces or Indicator Lights on COPS Receptacles

In a building in which COPS are present with other types of power systems:

The receptacle cover plates or the receptacles themselves supplied from the COPS shall have a distinctive color or marking so as to be readily identifiable

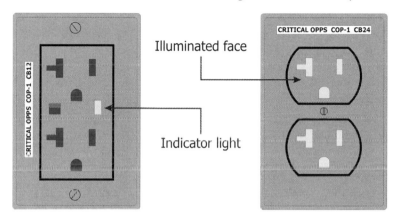

Illuminated face

Indicator light

Nonlocking-type, 125-volt, 15- and 20-ampere receptacles supplied from the COPS must have an illuminated face or an indicator light to indicate that there is power to the receptacle

708.10(A)(2) Receptacle Identification

- **Type of Change:** New

- **Change at a Glance:** In addition to a distinctive color or marking so as to be readily identifiable, nonlocking-type, 125-volt, 15- and 20-ampere receptacles supplied from the COPS shall also have an illuminated face or an indicator light to indicate that there is power to the receptacle.

- **Code Language: 708.10 Feeder and Branch Circuit Wiring. [Critical Operations Power Systems (COPS)] (A) Identification.**

   (1) Boxes and Enclosures. In a building or at a structure where a critical operations power system and any other type of power system are present, all boxes and enclosures (including transfer switches, generators, and power panels) for critical operations power system circuits shall be permanently marked so they will be readily identified as a component of the critical operations power system.

   (2) Receptacle Identification. In a building in which COPS are present with other types of power systems described in other sections in this article, the cover plates for the receptacles or the receptacles themselves supplied from the COPS shall have a distinctive color or marking so as to be readily identifiable. Nonlocking-type, 125-volt, 15- and 20-ampere receptacles supplied from the COPS shall have an illuminated face or an indicator light to indicate that there is power to the receptacle.

Exception: If the COPS supplies power to a DCOA that is a stand-alone building, receptacle cover plates or the receptacles themselves shall not be required to have distinctive marking.

- **2014 *NEC* Requirement**
  Cover plates for the receptacles, or the receptacles themselves, in COPS facilities are required to have a distinctive color or marking so as to be readily identifiable from other non-COPS receptacles. An exception states that receptacle marking and identification of the COPS system receptacles are not required at a designated critical operations area (DCOA) that is a stand-alone building.

- **2017 *NEC* Change**
  In addition to the distinctive color or marking requirement for COPS receptacles, all nonlocking-type, 125-volt, 15- and 20-ampere receptacles supplied from the COPS are now required to have an illuminated face or an indicator light to indicate that there is power to the receptacle.

708.10(A)(2)

Analysis of the Change:

Since the 2008 edition of the *NEC*, Article 708, Critical Operations Power Systems (COPS), has been a part of the *Code*. This article addresses homeland security issues for facilities that are "mission critical" in disastrous times such as terrorist attacks, flooding, hurricanes, etc. The requirements for COPS designated buildings go far beyond those of Article 700, Emergency Systems. These COPS electrical systems must continue to operate during the full duration of an emergency or disaster and beyond. Examples of facilities that might be designated as a COPS system include police stations, fire stations, and hospitals.

Cover plates for the receptacles or the receptacles themselves in these COPS facilities are required to have a "distinctive color or marking so as to be readily identifiable" from other receptacles in accordance with 708.10(A)(2). An exception states that receptacle marking and identification of the COPS system receptacles are not required at a designated critical operations area (DCOA) that is a stand-alone building, as all the receptacles would then be supplied from the COPS system. For the 2017 *NEC*, this COPS receptacle identification has been taken a step further by requiring all nonlocking-type, 125-volt, 15- and 20-ampere receptacles supplied from the COPS to have an "illuminated face or an indicator light" to indicate that there is power to the receptacle.

This new illuminator or indicator light provision provides for ready and continuous ability to identify energized receptacles that are part of the COPS system. It is essential that nonlocking-type 125-volt, 15- and 20-ampere receptacles have either an indicator light or an illuminated face so that users of the receptacles know that they are energized in an emergency when not all receptacles are working. It is not uncommon for receptacles fed from the COPS system to remain de-energized until called upon in an emergency system. Such receptacles that test out to be "un-energized" could suddenly become energized. The COPS receptacle itself also needed an additional identification means to alleviate issues arising from remodeling the room (such as painting) and the original COPS receptacle cover plate not being re-installed properly on its original COPS receptacle.

The ability of a person to distinguish receptacles supplied from the COPS becomes more critical as receptacles controlled for the purpose of energy management or building automation become more prevalent as well [see 406.3(E)].

First Revisions: FR 3634
Public Inputs: PI 2433

Article 710
Stand-Alone Systems

A new article for "Stand-Alone Systems" was added to address the operating parameters for electric power production sources in a stand-alone mode

Stand-alone power systems typically include one or more methods of electricity generation, energy storage, and regulation

Article 710 Stand-Alone Systems

- **Type of Change:** New

- **Change at a Glance:** A new article for "Stand-Alone Systems" was added to address the operating parameters for electric power production sources in a stand-alone mode.

- **Code Language: Article 710 Stand-Alone Systems.**
  710.1 Scope. This article covers electric power production sources operating in stand-alone mode.

  710.6 Equipment Approval. All equipment shall be listed and labeled or field labeled for the intended use.

  710.15 General. Premises wiring systems shall be adequate to meet the requirements of this *Code* for similar installations supplied by a feeder or service. The wiring on the supply side of the building or structure disconnecting means shall comply with the requirements of this *Code*, except as modified by 710.15(A) through (F).
  (A) Supply Output.
  (B) Sizing and Protection.
  (C) Single 120-Volt Supply.
  (D) Energy Storage or Backup Power System Requirements.
  (E) Back-Fed Circuit Breakers.
  (F) Voltage and Frequency Control.

  (See *NEC* for complete *Code* text)

- **2014 *NEC* Requirement**
  Requirements for stand-alone systems existed in Articles 690, 692 and 694, but not in one central location.

- **2017 *NEC* Change**
  The requirements of stand-alone systems were brought to one location and a new Article 710, Stand-Alone Systems, was created for the 2017 *NEC*.

Article 710

Analysis of the Change:

Article 710, Stand-Alone Systems, was added to the 2017 *NEC*. As indicated in its scope, the article covers electric power production sources operating in a stand-alone mode. A stand-alone power system, sometimes referred to as a remote area power supply, is an off-the-grid system for locations that are not connected to an electricity distribution system. Stand-alone power systems will typically include one or more methods of electricity generation, energy storage, and regulation.

This information was originally proposed to be a new Part IV of Article 705 (Interconnected Electric Power Production Sources) titled, "Intentionally Islanded and Stand-Alone Systems." The requirements for stand-alone systems simply did not fit well in Article 705 (interconnected systems). For stand-alone systems to remain at the end of Article 705, the scope and title of Article 705 would have had to be revised to encompass both interconnected and non-interconnected systems. During the Second Draft Meeting, CMP-4 decided a new article made more sense and were supported by the original submitter of the public input (which was the DC Task Group) and the *NEC* Correlating Committee.

A new article for stand-alone systems is important to the development of the *NEC*. While these safety requirements existed in Articles 690, 692 and 694 of the 2014 *NEC*, the requirements for a stand-alone system should apply to other power sources such as engine generators. The hazards of feeding multi-wire branch circuits with single-phase 120 volts are the same whether the source is a generator or an inverter. Stand-alone systems are becoming more prevalent due to emerging technology in energy storage and local generation. Unlike stand-alone systems, optional standby systems do not provide 24/7 power by definition. The lessons learned from tens of thousands of stand-alone PV systems should apply to any stand-alone power source.

Second Revisions: SR 987
Public Inputs: PI 4026
Public Comments: PC 349, PC 1015

Article 712

Direct Current Microgrids

DC Microgrid - A power distribution system consisting of more than one interconnected dc power sources, supplying dc dc converters(s), dc loads(s), and/or ac loads(s) powered by dc-ac inverters(s).

Article 712 **Direct Current Microgrids**

- **Type of Change:** New

■ **Change at a Glance:** Article 712 "Direct Current Microgrids" was added to the 2017 *NEC* for a power distribution system consisting of more than one interconnected dc power sources, supplying dc–dc converters(s), dc loads(s), and/or ac loads(s) powered by dc–ac inverters(s).

■ **Code Language:** Article 712 Direct Current Microgrids

Part I. General
712.1 Scope. This article applies to direct current microgrids.
712.2 Definitions.
712.3 Other Articles.
712.4 Listing and Labeling.
712.10 Directory.

Part II. Circuit Requirements
712.25 Identification of Circuit Conductors.
712.30 System Voltage.

Part III. Disconnecting Means
712.34 DC Source Disconnecting Means.
712.35 Disconnection of Ungrounded Conductors.
712.37 Directional Current Devices.

Part IV. Wiring Methods
712.52 System Grounding.
712.55 Ground Fault Detection Equipment.
712.57 Arc Fault Protection.

Part V. Marking
712.62 Distribution Equipment and Conductors.
712.65 Available DC Short Circuit Current.

Part VI. Protection
712.70 Overcurrent Protection.
712.72 Interrupting and Short-Circuit Ratings.

Part VII. Systems over 1000 Volts
712.80 General.
(See *NEC* for complete text)

■ **2014 *NEC* Requirement**
DC microgrids were not addressed specifically in the 2014 *NEC*.

■ **2017 *NEC* Change**
A new Article 712 for dc microgrids was added for a power distribution system consisting of more than one interconnected dc power sources, supplying dc–dc converters(s), dc loads(s), and/or ac loads(s) powered by dc–ac inverters(s).

Article 712

Analysis of the Change:

A new article has been developed for direct current (dc) microgrids. A dc microgrid is defined as a power distribution system consisting of more than one interconnected dc power sources, supplying dc–dc converters(s), dc loads(s), and/or ac loads(s) powered by dc–ac inverters(s). A dc microgrid is typically not directly connected to an ac primary source of electricity, but some dc microgrids interconnect via one or more dc–ac bidirectional converters or dc–ac inverters. DC microgrids allow the direct utilization of power from dc sources to dc loads such as LED lighting, communications equipment, computers, variable-speed motor drives, etc. Direct utilization of dc, whether generated by PV systems, fuel cells or other means (without intervening dc–ac and ac–dc conversion steps) leads to higher efficiencies and potentially smaller and lower-cost equipment than ac-coupled methods.

DC microgrids with energy storage also offer inherent resilience and security from failure of primary power sources. They also allow significantly simpler interconnection of power sources than ac microgrids, as no synchronization equipment is needed with dc. The need for higher efficiency in telecom and data centers has driven these industries to implement dc microgrids in hundreds of data centers around the world. It is a trend that will likely continue to grow. In addition to use in data centers, dc microgrids are being demonstrated in many government, academic and commercial facilities.

As with new Articles 706, Energy Storage Systems, and 710, Stand-Alone Systems, this new article was the result of the work of the DC Task Group of the *NEC* Correlating Committee. While the basic requirements for wiring methods, overcurrent protection, and grounding are specified in other articles of the *NEC*, they do not cover all of the issues involved when multiple dc sources and dc loads are interconnected. This alone justifies the need for this new DC Microgrid article as an important first step and as a place-holder for future requirements in this rapidly developing arena.

Some in the electrical industry feel that the word "microgrid" is jargon and non-specific. To some, "microgrid" infers utility owned conductors and equipment. To ensure fundamental separation between utility wiring and premises wiring, proper terminology needs to provide clear separation between the two systems. As this technology on "microgrids" continues to emerge, we need to ensure that the lines do not become blurred between utility wiring and premises wiring. Perhaps further movement in terminology will be seen in future editions of the *NEC*.

Article 712

First Revisions: FR 3663
Second Revisions: SR 3627
Public Inputs: PI 4027
Public Comments: PC 1016, PC 1017, PC 1019, PC 1021, PC 1174

725.3(M) and (N)

Cable Routing Assemblies and Communications Raceways for Class 2, Class 3, and PLTC Cables

---

New provisions were added to 725.3 (Other Articles) for cable routing assemblies and communications raceways used with Class 2, Class 3 and PLTC cables

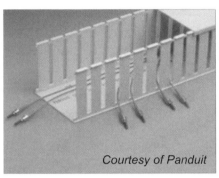

Courtesy of Panduit

Cable Routing Assembly

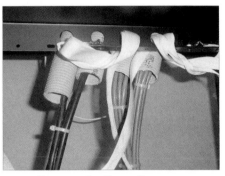

Communications Raceways

New 725.3(M) and (N) will provide guidance in the selection, listing and installation requirements for cable routing assemblies and communication raceways used for Class 2, Class 3 and PLTC cables

---

725.3 (sidebar)

725.3(M) and (N) Other Articles (Class 1, Class 2, and Class 3 Remote-Control, Signaling, and Power-Limited Circuits)

- **Type of Change:** New

- **Change at a Glance:** New requirements were added to 725.3 for cable routing assemblies and communications raceways for Class 2, Class 3 and PLTC cables.

- **Code Language: 725.3 Other Articles (Class 1, Class 2, and Class 3 Remote-Control, Signaling, and Power-Limited Circuits)** Circuits and equipment shall comply with the articles or sections listed in 725.3(A) through (L) (N). Only those sections of Article 300 referenced in this article shall apply to Class 1, Class 2, and Class 3 circuits.

  (M) Cable Routing Assemblies. Class 2, Class 3 and Type PLTC cables shall be permitted to be installed in plenum cable routing assemblies, riser cable routing assemblies, and general-purpose cable routing assemblies selected in accordance with the provisions of Table 800.154(c), listed in accordance with the provisions of 800.182, and installed in accordance with the provisions of 800.110(C) and 800.113.

  (N) Communications Raceways. Class 2, Class 3 and Type PLTC cables shall be permitted to be installed in plenum communications raceways, riser communications raceways and general-purpose communications raceways selected in accordance with the provisions of Table 800.154(b), listed in accordance with the provisions of 800.182, and installed in accordance with the provisions of 800.113 and 362.24 through 362.56, where the requirements applicable to electrical nonmetallic tubing (ENT) apply.

■ **2014 *NEC* Requirement**
Cable routing assemblies and communications raceways are both defined in Article 100. Both were addressed in Article 725 at 725.133 for the installation of conductors and equipment, 725.139 for installation of conductors of different circuits in the same cable routing assembly, 725.179 for listing and marking of Class 2, Class 3, and Type PLTC cables in communications raceways and cable routing assemblies, and Table 725.154 for the applications of listed Class 2, Class 3, and PLTC cables in buildings. Permission to apply other articles for the installation of cable routing assemblies and communications raceways was not granted at 725.3.

■ **2017 *NEC* Change**
New 725.3(M) and (N) were added for "Other Articles" to provide guidance in the selection, listing and installation requirements for cable routing assemblies and communication raceways used for Class 2, Class 3 and PLTC cables.

725.3

Analysis of the Change:

Article 725 applies to Class 1, Class 2, and Class 3 remote-control, signaling, and power-limited circuits that are not an integral part of a device or appliance. The circuits described in Article 725 are characterized by usage and electrical power limitations that differentiate them from electric light and power circuits. Article 725 describes alternative requirements for these circuits to those of Chapters 1 through 4 with regard to minimum wire sizes, ampacity adjustment and correction factors, overcurrent protection, insulation requirements, and wiring methods and materials. The requirements of 725.3 give a host of "Other Articles" that these Class 1, Class 2, and Class 3 circuits must comply with such as 300.17 for the number and size of conductors in a raceway, 300.21 for limitations of the spread of fire or products of combustion, 430.72(A) where tapped from the load side of the motor branch-circuit protective device(s), etc.

For the 2017 *NEC*, a new 725.3(M) has been added to provide consistency in the selection, listing and installation requirements for cable routing assemblies as referenced in Table 800.154(c), 800.182, 800.110(C) and 800.113. Additionally, 725.3(N) has been added to provide consistency in the selection, listing and installation requirements of communications raceways with references to Table 800.154(b), 800.182, 800.113 and 362.24 through 362.56 where the requirements applicable to electrical nonmetallic tubing (ENT) apply.

These new first level subdivisions were added to 725.3 not only to promote consistency in the use of cable routing assemblies and communications raceways throughout the *Code,* but also to align these requirements with the respective definitions in Article 100. The provisions for listing communications raceways and cable routing assemblies are addressed at 800.182 and did not need to be repeated in Article 725, but did need to be referenced. The new text at 725.3(M) and (N) limits the application of cable routing assemblies and communication raceways in Article 725 to Class 2, Class 3 and PLTC cables only.

These new first level subdivisions were the result of public inputs submitted by the Cable Routing Assembly and Communications Raceways Installation Issues Task Group formed by the *NEC* Correlating Committee. This same change occurred at 760.3(L) and (M) for fire alarm circuits (see FR 634, PI 200, PI 201, PI 304).

First Revisions: FR 622, FR 623
Public Inputs: PI 205, PI 305, PI 206, PI 317

725.135

725.135(K)(6), (L)(6) and (M)(6)

Type CMUC Undercarpet Communication Wiring and Cables under Modular Flooring and Planks

Type CMUC undercarpet communication wiring and cables is permitted to be installed under modular flooring and planks as well as under carpet

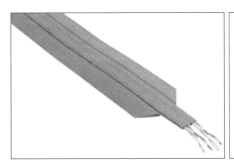 

Wiring methods for the installation of Class 2, Class 3, and power-limited tray cables (PLTC) at one- and two-family dwellings, multifamily dwellings, and other building locations is described at 725.135(K), (L), and (M)

This would include CL2P, CL3P, CL2R, CL3R, CL2, CL3, and PLTC cables as well as Type CMUC undercarpet communications wires and cables

725.135(K)(6), (L)(6) and (M)(6) Installation of Class 2, Class 3, and PLTC Cables

- **Type of Change:** Revision

- **Change at a Glance:** Type CMUC undercarpet communication wiring and cables are permitted to be installed under modular flooring and planks, as well as under carpet.

- **Code Language: 725.135 Installation of Class 2, Class 3, and PLTC Cables.**
  Installation of Class 2, Class 3, and PLTC cables shall comply with 725.135(A) through (M).

  (K) Other Building Locations. The following wires and cables shall be permitted to be installed in building locations other than the locations covered in 725.135(B) through (I):
  (See NEC text at 725.135(K)(1) through (6) for complete list of wiring methods)

  (6) Type CMUC undercarpet communications wires and cables installed under carpet, modular flooring, and planks

  (L) Multifamily Dwellings. The following wires and cables shall be permitted to be installed in multifamily dwellings in locations other than the locations covered in 725.135(B) through (I):
  (See NEC text at 725.135(L)(1) through (6) for complete list of wiring methods)

  (6) Type CMUC undercarpet communications wires and cables installed under carpet, modular flooring, and planks

  (M) One- and Two-Family Dwellings. The following wires and cables shall be permitted to be installed in one- and two-family dwellings in locations other than the locations covered in 725.135(B) through (I):
  (See NEC text at 725.135(M)(1) through (6) for complete list of wiring methods)

  (6) Type CMUC undercarpet communications wires and cables installed under carpet, modular flooring, and planks

- **2014 NEC Requirement**
  Type CMUC undercarpet communications wires and cables were permitted to be installed under carpet.

- **2017 NEC Change**
  New Code language was introduced at 725.135(K), (L), and (M) to clearly indicate that Type CMUC undercarpet communications wires and cables can be installed under modular flooring and planks, as well as under carpet.

Analysis of the Change:

According to the scope of Article 725, this article applies to Class 1, Class 2, and Class 3 remote-control, signaling, and power-limited circuits that are not an integral part of a device or appliance. For the installation of Class 2, Class 3, and According to the scope of Article 725, it applies to Class 1, Class 2, and Class 3 remote-control, signaling, and power-limited circuits that are not an integral part of a device or appliance. For the installation of Class 2, Class 3, and PLTC cables, the place to visit is 725.135. The appropriate wiring methods for the

725.135

installation of Class 2, Class 3, and power-limited tray cables (PLTC) at one- and two-family dwellings, multifamily dwellings, and other building locations are described at 725.135(K), (L), and (M). These first level subdivisions give a list of wires and cables permitted to be installed in these locations, such as Types CL2P, CL3P, CL2R, CL3R, CL2, CL3, and PLTC cables.

Another wiring method permitted at one- and two-family dwellings, multifamily dwellings, and other building locations is Type CMUC undercarpet communications wires and cables. Type CMUC is used for applications that require the cable to be run under carpet. This cable can be used in homes, offices, and retail applications. Robust enough to be used in high-traffic areas, Type CMUC is often used in areas that are not easily accessible by traditional cabling methods. Previous requirements at 725.135(K), (L), and (M) for Type CMUC undercarpet communications wires and cables indicated that this type of cabling could be "installed under carpet." For the 2017 *NEC*, new language was introduced at 725.135(K), (L), and (M) to further indicate that Type CMUC undercarpet communications wires and cables can be installed under "modular flooring, and planks" as well as under carpet.

725.135

The new text at 725.135(K), (L), and (M) introduces the use of additional floor coverings, other than carpet, for Type CMUC cabling. Commercial and retail building owners are rapidly adopting alternate floor covering for use in their facilities in addition to carpet squares, such as modular vinyl planks and tile, laminate, and hardwood. Type CMUC wire and cable is similar in nature to Type FCC (flat conductor cable) addressed at Article 324. Based on a UL fact-finding investigation, there were no additional heating effects caused by the alternate flooring when tested using type FCC cables. Type FCC cables carry more power than Type CMUC. Therefore, the results of the UL fact-finding report should also apply to Type CMUC. Based on testing, the type of flooring does not have an impact on the performance of the cables.

The product standard for Type CMUC (data) systems will not be required to be changed or modified due to the changes at 725.135(K), (L), and (M) allowing this wiring method to be used with alternate floor coverings. Manufacturers of Type CMUC will simply modify all of their manufacturer's specifications, instructions sheets, catalog information and other documentation to address these alternate floor coverings. Installation practices will be essentially the same when the cable is used with the newly allowed floor covering types.

This same change occurred at 800.113(K), (L) and (M) for the installation of communication wires, cables, and raceways, and cable routing assemblies (see PI 2616, FR 4671, FR 4272, FR 4273, PC 220, PC 221, PC 222, SCR 29, SCR 33, and SCR 34).

First Revisions: FR 621
Second Revisions: SR 620, SR 621, SR 622
Public Inputs: PI 2645
Public Comments: PC 223, PC 224, PC 225

725.144, Table 725.144

Transmission of Power and Data. (Class 1, Class 2, and Class 3 Remote-Control, Signaling, and Power-Limited Circuits)

Table 725.144 Ampacities of Each Conductor in Amperes in 4-Pair Class 2 or Class 3 Data Cables Based on Copper Conductors at an Ambient Temperature of 30°C (86° F) with All Conductors in All Cables Carrying Current, 60°C (140°F), 75°C (167°F), and 90°C (194°F) Rated Cables

AWG	Number of 4-Pair Cables in a Bundle																				
	1			2-7			8-19			20-37			38-61			62-91			92-192		
	Temperature Rating			Temperature Rating			Temperature Rating			Temperature Rating			Temperature Rating			Temperature Rating			Temperature Rating		
	60°C	75°C	90°C	60°C	75°C	90°C	60°C	75°C	90°C	60°C	75°C	90°C	60°C	75°C	90°C	60°C	75°C	90°C	60°C	75°C	90°C
26	1	1	1	1	1	1	0.7	0.8	1	0.5	0.6	0.7	0.4	0.5	0.6	0.4	0.5	0.6	NA	NA	NA
24	2	2	2	1	1.4	1.6	0.8	1	1.1	0.6	0.7	0.9	0.5	0.6	0.7	0.4	0.5	0.6	0.3	0.4	0.5
23	2.5	2.5	2.5	1.2	1.5	1.7	0.8	1.1	1.2	0.6	0.8	0.9	0.5	0.7	0.8	0.5	0.7	0.8	0.4	0.5	0.6
22	3	3	3	1.4	1.8	2.1	1	1.2	1.4	0.7	0.9	1.1	0.6	0.8	0.9	0.6	0.8	0.9	0.5	0.6	0.7

Note 1: For bundle sizes over 192 cables, or for conductor sizes smaller than 26 AWG, ampacities shall be permitted to be determined by qualified personnel under engineering supervision.

Note 2: Where only half of the conductors in each cable are carrying current, the values in the table shall be permitted to be increased by a factor of 1.4.

Informational Note: The conductor sizes in data cables in wide-spread use are typically 22–26 AWG.

725.144, Table 725.144 Transmission of Power and Data. (Class 1, Class 2, and Class 3 Remote-Control, Signaling, and Power-Limited Circuits)

- **Type of Change:** New

- **Change at a Glance:** New 725.144 language and an accompanying Table 725.144 were added introducing a new cable Type "LP" (Limited Power) with a marked current limitation, along with a table limiting the bundling of other communication cables used for transmitting power and data.

- **Code Language: 725.144 Transmission of Power and Data. (Class 1, Class 2, and Class 3 Remote-Control, Signaling, and Power-Limited Circuits)**

The requirements of 725.144(A) and (B) shall apply to Class 2 and Class 3 circuits that transmit power and data to a powered device. The requirements of Parts I and III of Article 725 and 300.11 shall apply to Class 2 and Class 3 circuits that transmit power and data. The conductors that

725.144

carry power for the data circuits shall be copper. The current in the power circuit shall not exceed the current limitation of the connectors.

Informational No. 1: One example of the use of cables that transmit power and data is the connection of closed-circuit TV cameras (CCTV).

Informational Note No. 2: The 8P8C connector is in widespread use with powered communications systems. These connectors are typically rated at 1.3 amperes maximum.

Table 725.144 Ampacities of Each Conductor in Amperes in 4-Pair Class 2 or Class 3 Data Cables Based on Copper Conductors at an Ambient Temperature of 30°C (86° F) with All Conductors in All Cables Carrying Current, 60°C (140°F), 75°C (167°F), and 90°C (194°F) Rated Cables
(See NEC and illustration provided for complete text of Table 725.144)

(A) Use of Class 2 or Class 3 Cables to Transmit Power and Data. Where Types CL3P, CL2P, CL3R, CL2R, CL3, or CL2 transmit power and data, the following shall apply, as applicable:
(1) The ampacity ratings in Table 725.144 shall apply at an ambient temperature of 30°C (86°F).
(2) For ambient temperatures above 30°C (86°F), the correction factors of 310.15(B)(2) shall apply.

Informational Note: One example of the use of Class 2 cables is a network of closed- circuit TV cameras using 24 AWG, 60°C rated, Type CL2R, Category 5e local area network (LAN) cables.

(B) Use of Class 2-LP or Class 3-LP Cables to Transmit Power and Data. Types CL3P-LP, CL2P-LP, CL3R-LP, CL2R-LP, CL3-LP, or CL2-LP shall be permitted to supply power to equipment at a current level up to the marked ampere limit located immediately following the suffix LP and shall be permitted to transmit data to the equipment. The Class 2-LP and Class 3-LP cables shall comply with the following, as applicable:

Informational Note 1: The "(xxA)" following the suffix -LP indicates the ampacity of each conductor in a cable.

Informational Note 2: An example of a limited power (LP) cable is a cable marked Type CL2-LP(0.5A), 23 AWG. A Type CL2-LP (0.5), 23 AWG could be used in any location where a Type CL2 could be used; however, the LP cable would be suitable for carrying up to 0.5 A per conductor, regardless of the number of cables in a bundle. If used in a 7-cable bundle, the same cable could carry up to 1.2 amperes per conductor.

(1) Cables with the suffix "-LP" shall be permitted to be installed in bun-

dles, raceways, cable trays, communications raceways, and cable routing assemblies.

(2) Cables with the suffix "-LP" and a marked ampere level shall follow the substitution hierarchy of Table 725.154 and Figure 725.154(A) for the cable type without the suffix "LP" and without the marked ampere level.

(3) System design shall be permitted by qualified persons under engineering supervision.

■ **2014 *NEC* Requirement**
Table 11(A) and Table 11(B) in Chapter 9 addresses power and current limitations on Class 2 and Class 3 circuits. These tables are referenced at 725.121. No references are found in the 2014 *NEC* for Type LP cables.

■ **2017 *NEC* Change**
New provisions were added at 725.144 and Table 725.144 pertaining to remote powering over local area networking (LAN) cable. Additional information was introduced concerning new Type LP cable.

Analysis of the Change:

Over the past decade or so, power-over-local area networking (LAN) cable technologies such as power-over-ethernet (PoE) have become a viable powering option for a broad range of applications. Device manufacturers are designing more sophisticated equipment that demands increased power. As this power is increased, the heat generated within the cable increases as well. This increase in heat is of particular concern when the cables are bundled. The additional heat generated by the increased current could push the cables beyond their rated temperatures.

To address this concern, a new type of "limited-power" cable has been introduced to simplify the cable choice and installation considerations. The "-LP" cable designation indicates that the cable has been evaluated to carry the marked current under reasonable worst-case installation scenarios without exceeding the temperature rating of the cable. The certification takes into account large bundle sizes, high ambient temperatures and other issues related to environmental effects, such as enclosed spaces or conduits. Typically, these cables are 4-pair "Category" type cables originally designed and intended for the transmission of data and communications. However, changes in technologies and equipment design have resulted in these cables increasingly being used to provide low voltage (less than 60 volts dc), limited power along with the data and communications signals.

The previous edition of the *Code* (2014 *NEC*) addressed data and communications circuits in Articles 725 and Chapter 8 respectively. Article 725 references Table 11(B), Class 2 and Class 3 Direct-Current Power Source Limitations, for power and current limitations on these circuits (see 725.121). Chapter 8 contained no specific requirements or references for power or current limitations on these circuits. Existing data from a number of sources have suggested that

725.144

the present current limits in the *NEC*, where they exist, are too high for these cabling systems and the way they are deployed.

For the 2017 *NEC*, provisions were added at new 725.144 related to remote powering over local area networking (LAN) cable. The public inputs and comments that lead to these new provisions suggested that the existing Class 2 limits in Table 11B of the *NEC* permitted maximum currents that could result in the overheating of cables and recommended adding ampacity limitations for these applications based on wire size (AWG) and bundle size. These new provisions introduce special cable designs developed for use as alternatives to more traditional cables with fewer restrictions on cable designs and the installations.

725.144

These new provisions include requirements for limiting the conductor ampacities for communications cable systems based on wire gauges and bundle sizes. Also, the new special cables ("LP" cables) were introduced. New language added at 725.179(I) indicates that limited power (LP) cables must be listed as suitable for carrying power and data up to a specified current limit for each conductor without exceeding the temperature rating of the cable where the cable is installed in cable bundles in free air or installed within a raceway, cable tray, or cable routing assembly. The cables must also be marked with the suffix "-LP" with the ampere limit located immediately following the suffix LP, where the current limit is in amperes per conductor. For example, a 1 ampere Class 2 limited-power cables could be marked "CL2-LP (1.0A)." The ampere limit located immediately following the suffix LP is the ampacity of each conductor in a cable.

The new 725.144 and accompanying table have been added to the 2017 *NEC* based upon the UL Fact Finding Report on Power over Local Area Network Type Cables (4-Pair Data / Communications Cables). Additionally, this language introduces the new cable Type LP that provides a current limitation to compensate for cable bundling and some other installation considerations for power over Ethernet. Bundling and bunching of cables for transmission of data and power results in heating. No conductor (or cable) should be used in such a manner that its operating temperature exceeds its rated maximum temperature.

Second Revisions: SR 611
Public Inputs: PI 1837
Public Comments: PC 692, PC 1689

727.4(5) Ex. to (5)

Type ITC-ER Between Cable Trays and Utilization Equipment

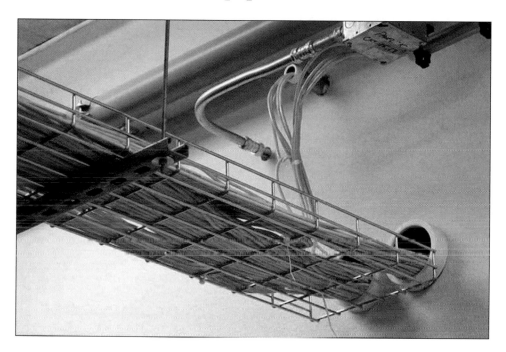

727.4(5)

727.4(5) Ex. to (5) Uses Permitted. (Instrumentation Tray Cable: Type ITC)

- **Type of Change:** New

- **Change at a Glance:** A new exception has been added for Type ITC-ER to allow transition between cable trays and between cable trays and utilization equipment or devices for a distance not to exceed 1.8 m (6 ft) without continuous support where not subject to physical damage.

- **Code Language: 727.4 Uses Permitted. (Instrumentation Tray Cable: Type ITC)**
  Type ITC cable shall be permitted to be used as follows in industrial establishments where the conditions of maintenance and supervision ensure that only qualified persons service the installation:

  (1) In cable trays.

  (2) In raceways.

  (3) In hazardous locations as permitted in 501.10, 502.10, 503.10, 504.20, 504.30, 504.80, and 505.15.

  (4) Enclosed in a smooth metallic sheath, continuous corrugated metallic sheath, or interlocking tape armor applied over the nonmetallic sheath in

accordance with 727.6. The cable shall be supported and secured at intervals not exceeding 1.8 m (6 ft).

(5) Cable, without a metallic sheath or armor, that complies with the crush and impact requirements of Type MC cable and is identified for such use with the marking ITC-ER shall be permitted to be installed exposed. The cable shall be continuously supported and protected against physical damage using mechanical protection such as dedicated struts, angles, or channels. The cable shall be secured at intervals not exceeding 1.8 m (6 ft).

Exception: Where not subject to physical damage, Type ITC-ER shall be permitted to transition between cable trays and between cable trays and utilization equipment or devices for a distance not to exceed 1.8 m (6 ft) without continuous support. The cable shall be mechanically supported where exiting the cable tray to ensure that the minimum bending radius is not exceeded.

(6) As aerial cable on a messenger.

727.4(5)

(7) Direct buried where identified for the use.

(8) Under raised floors in rooms containing industrial process control equipment and rack rooms where arranged to prevent damage to the cable.

(9) Under raised floors in information technology equipment rooms in accordance with 645.5(E)(5)(b).

- **2014 *NEC* Requirement**
  An exception exists at 336.10(7) for power and control tray cable permitting Type TC-ER cable to transition between cable trays and between cable trays and utilization equipment or devices for a distance not to exceed 1.8 m (6 ft) without continuous support (where not subject to physical damage). Under this new exception, TC-ER cable must be mechanically supported where exiting the cable tray to ensure that the minimum bending radius is not exceeded. This exception did not apply to instrumentation tray cable (Type ITC-ER).

- **2017 *NEC* Change**
  The same exception that exists for power and control tray cable (Type TC-ER) at 336.10(7) has been added at 727.4(5) for instrumentation tray cable (Type ITC-ER).

Analysis of the Change:

Since the 1996 *NEC*, instrumentation tray cable (Type ITC) has been a part of the *Code* and defined at 727.2 as "a factory assembly of two or more insulated conductors, with or without a grounding conductor(s), enclosed in a nonmetallic sheath." Article 727 is devoted to Type ITC cable, and the article covers the use, installation, and construction specifications of Type ITC cable for application to instrumentation and control circuits operating at 150 volts or less and 5 amperes or less.

According to 727.5 for "Uses Permitted," Type ITC cable is only to be used in industrial establishments where the conditions of maintenance and supervision ensure that only qualified persons will service the installation. This section goes on to describe nine conditions of use to Type ITC cable. One of the conditions of use is identified at 727.4(5) as Type ITC cable, without a metallic sheath or armor, that complies with the crush and impact requirements of Type MC cable. This subsection goes on to insist that the Type ITC cable installed exposed be identified for such use with the marking "ITC-ER." This cable must also be continuously supported and protected against physical damage using mechanical protection such as dedicated struts, angles, or channels as well as secured at intervals not exceeding 1.8 m (6 ft).

New for the 2017 *NEC*, an exception has been added for 727.4(5) permitting Type ITC-ER cable to transition between cable trays and between cable trays and utilization equipment or devices for a distance not to exceed 1.8 m (6 ft) without continuous support (where not subject to physical damage). Under this new exception, this ITC cable must be mechanically supported where exiting the cable tray to ensure that the minimum bending radius is not exceeded.

727.4(5)

An exception for "Uses Permitted" for power and control tray cable (Type TC-ER) currently exists at 336.10(7) which permits Type TC-ER cable "to transition between cable trays and between cable trays and utilization equipment or devices for a distance not to exceed 1.8 m (6 ft) without continuous support." The same allowance should be permitted for Type ITC-ER cables since the construction of these cables is very similar to Type TC-ER cables. Installers were typically installing Type ITC-ER cables with the same practices as Type TC-ER cable, unaware that the exception for Type TC-ER cable was not in place for Type ITC-ER cables in Article 727. This new exception [which is word-for-word to the existing exception at 336.10(7)] will equal out the playing field of these two similar tray cables.

First Revisions: FR 631
Public Inputs: PI 771

760.176(G) and 760.179(I)

Temperature Ratings and Conductor Size Markings on NPLFA and PLFA Cables

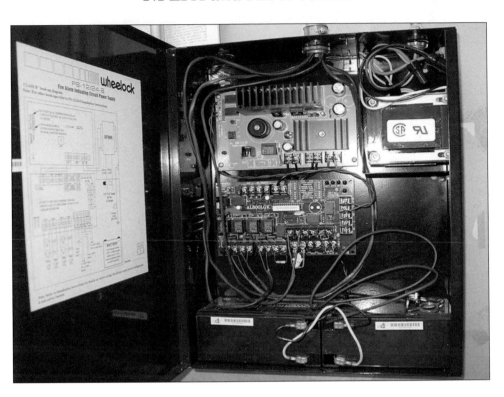

760.176(G) and 760.179(I) Listing and Marking of NPLFA Cables and Listing and Marking of PLFA Cables and Insulated Continuous Line-Type Fire Detectors

- **Type of Change:** Revision

- **Change at a Glance:** A new requirement was added for temperature ratings and conductor size to be marked on the jacket of NPLFA and PLFA cables when the temperature rating exceeds 60°C (140°F).

- **Code Language: Part IV. Listing Requirements (Fire Alarm Systems)**

760.176 Listing and Marking of NPLFA Cables. Non-power-limited fire alarm cables installed as wiring within buildings shall be listed in accordance with 760.176(A) and (B) and as being resistant to the spread of fire in accordance with 760.176(C) through (F), and shall be marked in accordance with 760.176(G). Cable used in a wet location shall be listed for use in wet locations or have a moisture-impervious metal sheath.

(G) NPLFA Cable Markings. Multiconductor non-power-limited fire alarm cables shall be marked in accordance with Table 760.176(G). Non–

power-limited fire alarm circuit cables shall be permitted to be marked with a maximum usage voltage rating of 150 volts. Cables that are listed for circuit integrity shall be identified with the suffix "CI" as defined in 760.176(F). Temperature rating shall be marked on the jacket of NPLFA cables that have a temperature rating exceeding 60°C (140°F). The jacket of NPLFA cables shall be marked with the conductor size.

Informational Note: Cable types are listed in descending order of fire resistance rating.

760.179 Listing and Marking of PLFA Cables and Insulated Continuous Line-Type Fire Detectors. PLFA cables installed as wiring within buildings shall be listed as being resistant to the spread of fire and other criteria in accordance with 760.179(A) through (H) and shall be marked in accordance with 760.179(I). Insulated continuous line-type fire detectors shall be listed in accordance with 760.179(J). Cable used in a wet location shall be listed for use in wet locations or have a moisture-impervious metal sheath.

(I) Cable Marking. The cable shall be marked in accordance with Table 760.179(I). The voltage rating shall not be marked on the cable. Cables that are listed for circuit integrity shall be identified with the suffix CI as defined in 760.179(G). Temperature rating shall be marked on the jacket of PLFA cables that have a temperature rating exceeding 60°C (140°F). The jacket of PLFA cables shall be marked with the conductor size.

Informational Note: Voltage ratings on cables may be misinterpreted to suggest that the cables may be suitable for Class 1, electric light, and power applications.

Exception: Voltage markings shall be permitted where the cable has multiple listings and voltage marking is required for one or more of the listings..

■ **2014 *NEC* Requirement**
Temperature ratings and conductor size markings were not required for the jacket of fire alarm circuits.

■ **2017 *NEC* Change**
New temperature rating marking requirements were added for fire alarm circuits requiring the jacket of NPLFA and PLFA cables that have a temperature rating exceeding 60°C (140°F) to be marked with the appropriate temperature rating. The jacket of these fire alarm cables must also be marked with the conductor size as well.

Analysis of the Change:

Article 760 covers the installation of wiring and equipment for fire alarm systems. This installation would include all circuits controlled and powered by the fire alarm system. These fire alarm circuits are defined at 760.2 as "the portion

760.176 & 9

of the wiring system between the load side of the overcurrent devices or the power-limited supply and the connected equipment of all circuits powered and controlled by the fire alarm system." Fire alarm circuits are classified as either non–power-limited fire alarm (NPLFA) circuits or power-limited fire alarm (PLFA) circuits.

The listing and marking requirements for fire alarms circuits are addressed at 760.176 for NPLFA circuits and 760.179 for PLFA circuits. These listing and marking requirements would include such things as conductor insulation and material requirements, conductor sizing, voltage ratings, plenum ratings, circuit integrity, wet location identification, etc. For the 2017 *NEC*, new marking requirements were added for fire alarm circuits requiring a temperature rating to be marked on the jacket of NPLFA and PLFA cables that have a temperature rating exceeding 60°C (140°F). This temperature rating reference of 60°C (140°F) is consistent with the product standard listing requirements for fire alarm cables. The jacket of these cables must now be marked with the conductor size as well.

760.176 & 9

This required temperature rating information is important for both the installer and inspector as well as the system designer when utilizing "power over Ethernet" (PoE) and other technologies where the fire alarm cable pairs carry data and power. The conductor size in fire alarm cables is typically in the range of 22 to 26 AWG. When several of these fire alarm cables (as well as other cables) are bundled together in a draft-free, insulated space, dissipating the heat generated by the fire alarm circuit conductors can be an issue. Current levels on these fire alarm circuits continue to increase (in some cases as much as 1 ampere). To design, install, and inspect these systems, obtainable, detailed information concerning these fire alarm cables is essential.

The jacket of both NPLFA and PLFA cables must be marked with the conductor size to identify the specific size of the conductor in the cables so that determination of maximum current for these fire alarm circuits can be properly evaluated.

First Revisions: FR 643, FR 642
Public Inputs: PI 330, PI 1596, PI 3064, PI 1608

770.44

Overhead (Aerial) Optical Fiber Cables

Overhead Electric Service Drop

Overhead (Aerial) Optical Fiber Cables

770.44

770.44 Overhead (Aerial) Optical Fiber Cables

- **Type of Change:** New

- **Change at a Glance:** New requirements were placed at 770.44 for overhead (aerial) optical fiber cables that enter a building.

- **Code Language: 770.44 Overhead (Aerial) Optical Fiber Cables.** Overhead optical fiber cables containing a non–current-carrying metallic member entering buildings shall comply with 840.44(A) and (B).

  (A) On Poles and In-Span. Where outside plant optical fiber cables and electric light or power conductors are supported by the same pole or are run parallel to each other in-span, the conditions described in 770.44(A)(1) through (A)(4) shall be met.

  (1) Relative Location. Where practicable, the outside plant optical fiber cables shall be located below the electric light or power conductors.

  (2) Attachment to Cross-Arms. Attachment of outside plant optical fiber cables to a cross-arm that carries electric light or power conductors shall not be permitted.

(3) Climbing Space. The climbing space through outside plant optical fiber cables shall comply with the requirements of 225.14(D).

(4) Clearance. Supply service drops and sets of overhead service conductors of 0 to 750 volts running above and parallel to optical fiber cable service drops shall have a minimum separation of 300 mm (12 in.) at any point in the span, including the point of their attachment to the building. Clearance of not less than 1.0 m (40 in.) shall be maintained between the two services at the pole.

(B) Above Roofs. Outside plant optical fiber cables shall have a vertical clearance of not less than 2.5 m (8 ft) from all points of roofs above which they pass.

Exception No. 1: The requirement of 770.44(B) shall not apply to auxiliary buildings such as garages and the like.

Exception No. 2: A reduction in clearance above only the overhanging portion of the roof to not less than 450 mm (18 in.) shall be permitted if (a) not more than 1.2 m (4 ft) of optical fiber cable service drop cable passes above the roof overhang, and (b) the cable is terminated at a through- or above-the-roof raceway or approved support.

Exception No. 3: Where the roof has a slope of not less than 100 mm in 300 mm (4 in. in 12 in.), a reduction in clearance to not less than 900 mm (3 ft) shall be permitted.

Informational Note: For additional information regarding overhead wires and cables, see ANSI/IEEE C2-2012, *National Electric Safety Code, Part 2, Safety Rules for Overhead Lines.*

770.44

- **2014 *NEC* Requirement**
  Part II of Article 770 did not contain information pertaining to optical fiber cables installed overhead to a building or structure. Section 840.44 for premises-powered optical fiber-based broadband communications systems contained information applying to overhead outside plant optical fiber cables, but there was no such information in Article 770.

- **2017 *NEC* Change**
  A new 770.44 was added under Part II of Article 770 titled, "Overhead (Aerial) Optical Fiber Cables." This section contains needed information for the installation of overhead (aerial) optical fiber cables to buildings directly for Article 770.

Analysis of the Change:
Over the last decade or so, optical fiber cable has become the preferred option for delivering applications like Internet service, telephone systems, and cable television. Fiber optic cabling is based on optical fibers, which are long, flexible, hair-width strands of ultra-pure glass. For the finished cable to transmit data signals, it needs to be connected to the two other main components of an optical

fiber system. The first of these is the optical transmitter, a device that converts electrical and analog signals into modulating light signals, then releases that data into the fiber optic cable. The cable then relays the data emitted by the optical transmitter to the optical receiver, which accepts the light signal and reformats the data into its original form. Optical fiber cable has advantages over standard copper coaxial cables, in that it can transmit larger quantities of data with far less loss, can maintain signals over long distances, carries little risk of corrosion, and is virtually free from interference.

In previous editions of the *Code*, under the title of "Cables Outside and Entering Buildings," Part II of Article 770 did not contain information about optical fiber cables installed overhead to a building or structure. That was rectified in the 2017 *NEC* with a new 770.44 being added under Part II titled, "Overhead (Aerial) Optical Fiber Cables." A section dealing with overhead outside plant optical fiber cables exists in Article 840 for premises-powered optical fiber-based broadband communications systems (see 840.44), but was not previously included in Article 770 for optical fiber cables.

This new language at 770.44 was structured based on the language for overhead (aerial) spans at 800.44 (Communications Circuits), 820.44 (Community Antenna Television and Radio Distribution Systems), 830.44 (Network-Powered Broadband Communications Systems), and 840.44 (Premises-Powered Broadband Communications Systems). The word "Aerial" was added to the title at 840.44 to parallel the new revision at 770.44 along with 800.44, 820.44 and 830.44; otherwise, this new 770.44 text is identical to existing language at 840.44.

First Revisions: FR 4519
Second revisions: SR 4510
Public Inputs: PI 1677
Public Comments: PC 47

770.44

770.48(A) and (B)
Optical Fiber Cables Entering Building

Unlisted conductive and nonconductive outside plant optical fiber cables are generally permitted to be installed in building spaces where the length of the cable within the building *(measured from its point of entrance)* does not exceed 15 m (50 ft) and the cable enters the building from the outside and is terminated in an enclosure

The point of entrance is now permitted to be extended from the penetration of the external wall or floor slab by continuously enclosing the entrance optical fiber cables in RMC or IMC to the point of emergence

Unlisted nonconductive outside plant optical fiber cables installed in PVC or EMT cannot be installed in risers, ducts, or plenums used for environmental air

Outside plant optical fiber cables

770.48

770.48(A) and (B) Optical Fiber Cables Entering Building

- **Type of Change:** Revision

- **Change at a Glance:** The point of entrance for optical fiber cables can now be extended when enclosed in rigid metal conduit (RMC) or intermediate metal conduit (IMC). Nonconductive outside plant optical fiber cables cannot be installed in PVC or EMT in risers, ducts and plenums for environmental air, and other places used for environmental air.

- **Code Language:** 770.48 Unlisted Cables and Raceways Entering Buildings. (Optical Fiber Cables and Raceways)

(A) Conductive and Nonconductive Cables. Unlisted conductive and nonconductive outside plant optical fiber cables shall be permitted to be installed in building spaces, other than risers, ducts used for environmental air, plenums used for environmental air, and other spaces used for environmental air, where the length of the cable within the building, measured from its point of entrance, does not exceed 15 m (50 ft) and the cable enters the building from the outside and is terminated in an enclosure.

The point of entrance shall be permitted to be extended from the penetration of the external wall or floor slab by continuously enclosing the entrance optical fiber cables in rigid metal conduit (RMC) or intermediate metal conduit (IMC) to the point of emergence.

Informational Note No. 1: Splice cases or terminal boxes, both metallic and plastic types, typically are used as enclosures for splicing or terminating optical fiber cables.

~~**Informational Note No. 2:** See 770.2 for the definition of Point of Entrance.~~

(B) Nonconductive Cables in Raceway. Unlisted nonconductive outside plant optical fiber cables shall be permitted to enter the building from the outside and shall be permitted to be installed in any of the following raceways:
(1) Intermediate metal conduit (IMC)
(2) Rigid metal conduit (RMC)
(3) Rigid polyvinyl chloride conduit (PVC)
(4) Electrical metallic tubing (EMT)

Unlisted nonconductive outside plant cables installed in rigid polyvinyl chloride conduit (PVC) or electrical metallic tubing (EMT) shall not be permitted to be installed in risers, ducts used for environmental air, plenums used for environmental air, and other spaces used for environmental air.

770.48

- **2014 *NEC* Requirement**
Unlisted conductive and nonconductive outside plant optical fiber cables are permitted to be installed in building spaces where the length of the cable within the building, measured from its point of entrance, does not exceed 15 m (50 ft) and the cable enters the building from the outside and is terminated in an enclosure. Unlisted nonconductive outside plant optical fiber cables are permitted to enter a building from the outside only while installed in four specific raceway wiring methods.

- **2017 *NEC* Change**
The point of entrance is now permitted to be extended from the penetration of the external wall or floor slab by continuously enclosing the entrance optical fiber cables in RMC or IMC to the point of emergence. *Code* language was also added to clarify that unlisted nonconductive outside plant optical fiber cables installed in PVC or EMT cannot be installed in risers, ducts used for environmental air, plenums used for environmental air, and other spaces used for environmental air.

Analysis of the Change:
The provisions of 770.48(A) permits unlisted conductive and nonconductive outside plant optical fiber cables to be installed in building spaces (other than risers, ducts used for environmental air, plenums used for environmental air, and other spaces used for environmental air). This outside plant optical fiber cable is only permitted to be installed in building spaces where the length of the cable within the building, measured from its point of entrance, does not exceed 15 m (50 ft) and the cable enters the building from the outside and is terminated in an enclosure. The term *outside plant* refers to all the cables, conduits, ducts, poles, towers, repeaters, repeater huts, and other equipment located between

a demarcation point in a switching facility and a demarcation point in another switching facility or the customer premises. Simply put, this is the portion of the optical fiber cable system or network that resides outside the facilities, connecting to the outside world.

For the 2017 *NEC*, a new sentence was added at the end of 770.48(A) permitting the *point of entrance* (which is the beginning measuring point for the entering outside plant optical fiber cable) to be extended from the penetration of the external wall or floor slab by continuously enclosing the entrance optical fiber cables in rigid metal conduit (RMC) or intermediate metal conduit (IMC) to the *point of emergence*. "Point of entrance" is defined at 770.2 as "the point within a building at which the optical fiber cable emerges from an external wall, or from a concrete floor slab." This new sentence allows the "point of entrance" for optical fiber cable to be extended anywhere within a building as long as the entering optical fiber cable is contained in rigid metal conduit (RMC) or intermediate metal conduit (IMC) and the "point of emergence" becomes the end of said conduit.

770.48

The provisions of 770.48(B) permit unlisted nonconductive outside plant optical fiber cables to enter the building from the outside while installed in (1) intermediate metal conduit (IMC), (2) rigid metal conduit (RMC), (3) rigid polyvinyl chloride conduit (PVC), or (4) electrical metallic tubing (EMT). A new last sentence was added to 770.48(B) clarifying that unlisted nonconductive outside plant optical fiber cables installed in PVC conduit EMT cannot be installed in risers, ducts used for environmental air, plenums used for environmental air, and other spaces used for environmental air.

This new sentence will provide consistency between the requirements of 770.48(A) and (B). While 770.48(A) permits the installation of unlisted optical fiber cables in plenums and risers only when enclosed in RMC or IMC, this first level subdivision does not permit rigid PVC conduit and EMT containing unlisted outside plant cable to be run in risers, air ducts or plenums. As stated previously, RMC and IMC are permitted to extend the "point of entrance" to any point in the building. The added text at 770.48(B) will agree with 770.48(A) and make it abundantly clear that rigid PVC conduit and EMT containing unlisted outside plant cable are not permitted to be installed in risers, air ducts or plenums.

The previous Informational Note No. 2 at 770.48(A) was deleted. This I-Note pointed users of the *Code* to the definition of "Point of Entrance" located at 770.2. The previous Informational Note No. 2 was found to be unnecessary due to this definition being located at 770.2.

This same basic change occurred at 800.48 (see FR 4654, SR 4524, PI 1566, PI 4539, PC 189, PC 190, PC 457, PC 1873) and 820.48 (see FR 4556, SR 4542, PI 1567, PC 202, PC 459). In the title of 770.48, the term *and Raceways* was deleted to make the Article 770 title consistent with the titles of 800.48 and 820.48.

First revisions: FR 4521
Second Revisions: SR 4511
Public Inputs: PI 128, PI 1561, PI 4525
Public Comments: PC 177, PC 455, PC 1870

770.49

Metallic Entrance Conduit Grounding

Metallic conduit containing optical fiber entrance cable shall be connected by a bonding conductor or grounding electrode conductor to a grounding electrode in accordance with 770.100(B)

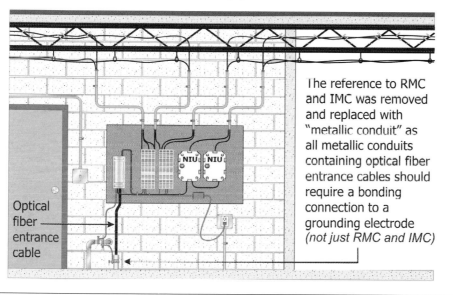

The reference to RMC and IMC was removed and replaced with "metallic conduit" as all metallic conduits containing optical fiber entrance cables should require a bonding connection to a grounding electrode *(not just RMC and IMC)*

Optical fiber entrance cable

770.49

770.49 Metallic Entrance Conduit Grounding

- **Type of Change:** Revision

- **Change at a Glance:** All metallic conduit (not just RMC and IMC) enclosing optical fiber entrance cable must be connected by a bonding conductor or grounding electrode conductor to a grounding electrode.

- **Code Language:** Code Language: **770.49 Metallic Entrance Conduit Grounding. (Optical Fiber Cables and Raceways)** ~~Rigid metal conduit (RMC) or intermediate metal conduit (IMC)~~ Metallic conduit containing optical fiber entrance cable shall be connected by a bonding conductor or grounding electrode conductor to a grounding electrode in accordance with 770.100(B).

■ **2014 *NEC* Requirement**
Rigid metal conduit (RMC) or intermediate metal conduit (IMC) containing optical fiber entrance cable had to be connected by a bonding conductor or grounding electrode conductor to a grounding electrode in accordance with 770.100(B).

■ **2017 *NEC* Change**
The reference to RMC and IMC was removed and replaced with "metallic conduit" as all metallic conduits containing optical fiber entrance cables should require a bonding connection to a grounding electrode (not just RMC and IMC).

Analysis of the Change:

Point of Entrance was defined in the 2011 *NEC* as "the point within a building at which the cable emerges from an external wall, from a concrete floor slab, or from a rigid metal conduit (Type RMC) or an intermediate metal conduit (Type IMC) connected by a grounding conductor to an electrode in accordance with 770.100(B)." For the 2014 *NEC*, this definition was revised to remove the references to the grounding requirements. In making this revision, CMP-16 was concerned that the definition could be construed to contain a requirement, which would be a violation of Section 2.2.2 of the *NEC Style Manual*.

For the 2014 *NEC*, this 2011 *NEC* grounding requirement was moved to a newly created 770.49, Metallic Entrance Conduit Grounding. As previously written, 770.49 required that only rigid metal conduit (RMC) or intermediate metal conduit (IMC) containing optical fiber entrance cable be connected by a bonding conductor or grounding electrode conductor to a grounding electrode in accordance with 770.100(B). For the 2017 *NEC*, the reference to RMC and IMC was removed and replaced with "metallic conduit" as all metallic conduits containing optical fiber entrance cables should require a bonding connection to a grounding electrode (not just RMC and IMC).

Electrical metallic tubing (EMT) as permitted in 770.48(B)(4) should also be grounded and bonded for electrical safety. It should be noted that EMT is only permitted for use with "nonconductive optical fiber cable" as this cable contains no electrical conductive members and is not subject to the hazards associated with electrical power contact or lightning events. Conductive optical fiber cable, paired-conductor telephone cable (Article 800) and COAX cable (Article 820) contain metallic components and may be subject to power and lightning influences therefore they are limited to installation in the more robust RMC or IMC.

The same change occurred at 800.49 for communications circuits (see FR 4655, PI 1563), 820.49 for community antenna television and radio distribution systems (see FR 44557, PI 1564), and 830.49 for network-powered broadband communications systems (see FR 46015, PI 1565).

First Revisions: FR 4522
Public Inputs: PI 1562, PI 561

770.49

770.100(B)(3)(2)
Lightning Protection Systems Conductors

770.100

770.100(B)(3)(2) **Lightning Protection Systems Conductors**

- **Type of Change:** Revision

- **Change at a Glance:** Revised language was added to clarify that lightning protection system conductors, (not just air terminal conductors), are not to be used as part of the grounding electrode conductor or as a grounding electrode for optical fiber systems or any communication system.

- **Code Language:** **770.100 Entrance Cable Bonding and Grounding. (Optical Fiber Cables and Raceways)**
  Where required, the non–current-carrying metallic members of optical fiber cables entering buildings shall be bonded or grounded as specified in 770.100(A) through (D).

  (B) Electrode. The bonding conductor and grounding electrode conductor shall be connected in accordance with 770.100(B)(1), (B)(2), or (B)(3).

  (1) In Buildings or Structures with an Intersystem Bonding Termination. If the building or structure served has an intersystem bonding termination as required by 250.94, the bonding conductor shall be connected to the intersystem bonding termination.
  ~~Informational Note: See Part I of Article 100 for the definition of Intersystem Bonding Termination.~~

(2) In Buildings or Structures with Grounding Means. If an intersystem bonding termination is established, 250.94(A) shall apply. If the building or structure served has no intersystem bonding termination, the bonding conductor or grounding electrode conductor shall be connected to the nearest accessible location on one of the following:

(1) The building or structure grounding electrode system as covered in 250.50

(2) The grounded interior metal water piping system, within 1.5 m (5 ft) from its point of entrance to the building, as covered in 250.52

(3) The power service accessible means external to enclosures using the options identified in 250.94(A), Exception as covered in 250.94

(4) The nonflexible metallic power service raceway

(5) The service equipment enclosure

(6) The grounding electrode conductor or the grounding electrode conductor metal enclosure of the power service, or

(7) The grounding electrode conductor or the grounding electrode of a building or structure disconnecting means that is grounded to an electrode as covered in 250.32

(3) In Buildings or Structures Without Intersystem Bonding Termination or Grounding Means. If the building or structure served has no intersystem bonding termination or grounding means, as described in 770.100(B)(2), the grounding electrode conductor shall be connected to either of the following:

(1) To any one of the individual grounding electrodes described in 250.52(A)(1), (A)(2), (A)(3), or (A)(4).

(2) If the building or structure served has no grounding means, as described in 770.100(B)(2) or (B)(3)(1), to any one of the individual grounding electrodes described in 250.52(A)(7) and (A)(8) or to a ground rod or pipe not less than 1.5 m (5 ft) in length and 12.7 mm (½ in.) in diameter, driven, where practicable, into permanently damp earth and separated from lightning protection system conductors as covered in 800.53 and at least 1.8 m (6 ft) from electrodes of other systems. Steam or hot water pipes or air terminal conductors (lightning-rod conductors) lightning protection system conductors shall not be employed as electrodes for non-current-carrying metallic members.

■ **2014 _NEC_ Requirement**
Revised language was added to clarify that lightning protection system conductors, (not just air terminal conductors), are not to be used as part

770.100

of the grounding electrode conductor or as a grounding electrode for optical fiber systems or any communication system.

- **2017 *NEC* Change**

  The term *air terminal conductors (lightning-rod conductors)* was replaced with the broader term *lightning protection system conductors* to clarify that no lightning protection system conductors should not be used as a part of the grounding electrode conductor or as a grounding electrode for optical fiber systems.

Analysis of the Change:

For grounding and bonding and connection to a grounding electrode system for optical fiber cable systems, 770.100(B) offers provisions for three different applications; (1) In buildings or structures with an intersystem bonding termination (IBT), (2) In buildings or structures without an intersystem bonding termination, but with a grounding means, or (3) In buildings or structures without an intersystem bonding termination or grounding means.

In applications where the building or structure served has no intersystem bonding termination or grounding means, the grounding electrode conductor (or bonding jumper) for the optical fiber cable system is required to be connected to an established grounding electrode consisting of either (1) a metal underground water pipe [250.52(A)(1)], (2) a metal in-ground support structure(s) [250.52(A)(2)], (3) a concrete-encased electrode [250.52(A)(3)], or (4) a ground ring grounding electrode system [250.52(A)(4)].

If the building or structure served has no grounding means, such as a nonflexible metallic power service raceway, service equipment enclosure, etc., or none of the grounding electrodes described above, the grounding electrode conductor (or bonding jumper) for the optical fiber cable system is required to be connected to either a plate electrode [250.52(A)(7)] or a local metal underground system or structure [250.52(A)(8)] or to a driven ground rod or pipe not less than 1.5 m (5 ft) in length and 12.7 mm (½ in.) in diameter. If this driven ground rod is employed, it needs to be driven into permanently damp earth (where practicable) and separated from lightning protection system conductors and electrodes of other systems by at least 1.8 m (6 ft).

In previous editions of the *Code* (beginning with the 2008 *NEC*), steam or hot water pipes or "air terminal conductors (lightning-rod conductors)" were not permitted to be used as electrodes for non–current-carrying metallic members. For the 2017 *NEC*, the term *air terminal conductors (lightning-rod conductors)* was replaced with the broader term *lightning protection system conductors*. All lightning protection system conductors (including but not only air terminal conductors) should not be used as a part of the grounding electrode conductor or as a grounding electrode for optical fiber systems or any communication system.

A lightning protection system is a complete system of rods, cables, and groundings designed to intercept a lightning strike and divert it safely to ground (the earth), avoiding structural damage to buildings and other vulnerable objects. A

770.100

complete lightning protection system consists of metallic rods, heavy-duty cable, and solid grounding air terminals. The lightning protection system conductors connect air terminals to grounded lightning rods (to ground). Air terminals do not attract lightning; they simply provide a safe path for the lightning current to flow to ground. Lightning protection system conductors consist of heavy cables that carry lightning current from the air terminals to the ground. These cables are run along the tops and around the edges of roofs, then down one or more corners of a building to the ground rod(s). Air terminal conductors are just a part of the complete lightning protection system conductors.

This same change occurred at 800.100(B)(3)(2) for communications circuits (see FR 4662, PI 4413); 820.100(B)(3)(2) for community antenna television and radio distribution systems (see FR 4562, PI 4428); and 830.100(B)(3)(2) for network-powered broadband communications systems (see FR 4606, PI 4433).

First Revisions: FR 4526
Public Inputs: PI 4401

770.100

Communication Systems

Chapter 8

810.15

Grounding of Radio and TV Equipment

Masts and metal structures supporting antennas shall be grounded in accordance with 810.21 unless...

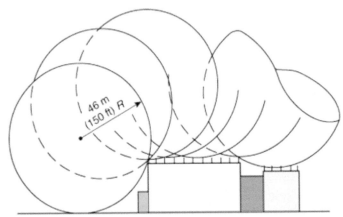

Zone of protection as determined by the "Rolling Sphere" method

the antenna and its related supporting mast or structure are within a zone of protection defined by a 46 m (150 ft) radius "rolling sphere"

810.15 **Grounding of Radio and TV Equipment**

- **Type of Change:** Revision/New

- **Change at a Glance:** Radio and television antennas are required to be grounded unless they are located within the zone of protection afforded by surrounding taller structures as determined by the "rolling sphere" theory of lightning protection.

- **Code Language: 810.15 Grounding. (Radio and Television Equipment)**
  Masts and metal structures supporting antennas shall be grounded in accordance with 810.21 unless the antenna and its related supporting mast or structure are within a zone of protection defined by a 46 m (150 ft) radius rolling sphere.

  Informational Note: See 4.8.3.1 of NFPA 780-2014, *Standard for the Installation of Lightning Protection Systems,* for the application of the term "rolling sphere."

- **2014 *NEC* Requirement**
  Masts and metal structures supporting radio and television antennas were required to be grounded using a bonding conductor or grounding electrode conductor as described at 810.21.

- **2017 *NEC* Change**

  Grounding of masts and metal supporting structures for radio and television antennas can be eliminated when the antenna and its related supporting mast or structure are within a zone of protection defined by a 46 m (150 ft) radius "rolling sphere" described in NFPA 780-2014, *Standard for the Installation of Lightning Protection Systems*.

Analysis of the Change:

Masts and metal structures supporting radio and television antennas are required to be grounded (*connected to earth*). This grounding is to be accomplished by the provisions of 810.21, which deals with materials used, installation of, support, physical protection, etc., of bonding conductors and grounding electrode conductors of receiving stations. Lightning, power contact, and static buildup can cause significant voltage levels on masts and towers, which can cause a ground fault condition when in contact with grounded objects or personnel. These masts, along with shielded cables, and antenna support structures must be properly grounded.

In previous editions of the *NEC*, there was no relief for these grounding requirements for masts and metal structures supporting radio and television antennas. For the 2017 *NEC*, 810.15 was revised to permit omission of grounding of masts and metal structures supporting radio and television antennas when the antenna and its related supporting mast or structure are within a zone of protection defined by a 46 m (150 ft) radius rolling sphere. A new informational note was also added to direct users of the *Code* to NFPA 780-2014, *Standard for the Installation of Lightning Protection Systems*, for the application of the term "rolling sphere."

Section 4.8.3.1 of the 2014 edition of NFPA 708 addresses what is known as the "Rolling Sphere Model" of lightning protection. This model of protection describes a zone of protection that includes the space not intruded by a rolling sphere having a radius of 46 m (150 ft). Where the sphere is tangent to earth and resting against a strike termination device(s), all space in the vertical plane between the two points of contact and under the sphere is considered to be in the "rolling sphere" zone of protection. According to this section of NFPA 708, all possible placements of the rolling sphere shall be considered when determining the zone of protection using the rolling sphere model.

This revision will bring the *Code* up to date with the technology surrounding smaller antennas where they are not likely to be impacted by transient voltages using the "rolling sphere" model of lightning protection. Data gathered from experience with this lightning protection model indicates that these small antennas have not been a safety risk to either life or property due to these "zones of protection." These antennas, when installed in protected areas, are highly unlikely to become energized, and there is no sound reason to require these protected antennas and mast to be grounded per 810.15 and 810.21.

This same change occurred at 820.100 and Informational Note for community antenna television (CATV) and radio distribution systems (see FR 4559, PI 3923).

810.15

First Revisions: FR 4546
Second Revisions: SR 4539
Public Input: PI 4141
Public Comment: PC 322

840.2

Network Terminals

840.2

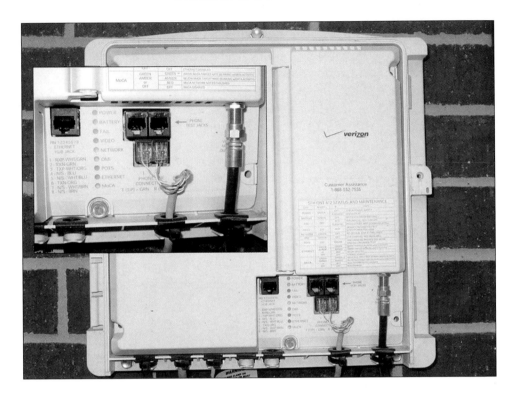

840.2 Network Terminals

- **Type of Change:** Revision

- **Change at a Glance:** The definition of *Optical Network Terminal (ONT)* was revised to *Network Terminal*.

- **Code Language: 840.2 Definitions (Premises-Powered Broadband Communications Systems)**
  ~~Optical~~ **Network Terminal ~~(ONT)~~.** A device that converts ~~an optical signal~~ network-provided signals (optical, electrical, or wireless) into component signals, including voice, audio, video, data, wireless, optical, and interactive ~~service electrical~~ services, and is considered ~~to be~~ a network ~~interface equipment~~ device on the premises that it is connected to a communications service provider and is powered at the premises.

■ **2014 *NEC* Requirement**

The scope of Article 840 indicated that the article covers premises-powered optical fiber-based broadband communications systems that provide any combination of voice, video, data, and interactive services through an optical network terminal (ONT). The term, *Optical Network Terminal (ONT)* was defined at 840.2..

■ **2017 *NEC* Change**

The scope of Article 840 now advises that the article covers premises-powered broadband communications systems that consist of an optical fiber, twisted pair, or coaxial cable to the premises supplying a broadband signal to a network terminal. The term *Network Terminal* is defined at 840.2 and replaces the term, *Optical Network Terminal (ONT)*.

Analysis of the Change:

The unique installation of premises-powered broadband communication systems is covered by Article 840 of the *NEC*. A basic premises-powered broadband communications system configuration typically consists of an optical fiber cable to the premises, which is referred to as "Fiber-to-the Premises" (FTTP). This FTTP will typically supply a broadband signal to a device called an "Optical Network Terminal" (ONT) that converts the broadband optical signal into component electrical signals such as traditional telephone, video, high-speed internet, and interactive services. Optical fiber based systems are not the only type of systems that can deliver these broadband signals to the premise.

For the 2017 *NEC*, revisions were incorporated throughout Article 840 to accommodate twisted pair-based and coaxial cable-based systems in addition to optical fiber-based systems for premises-powered broadband communication systems. This incorporation resulted in the existing definition of *Optical Network Terminal (ONT)* being replaced with the more generic term of *Network Terminal*. In order to expand the coverage of Article 840, a series of public inputs were accepted to recognize twisted-pair and coaxial cable based systems in addition to optical fiber-based systems.

Types of twisted-pair cable include unshielded twisted-pair (UTP) and shielded twisted-pair (STP). The historical foundation of the public telephone network was built upon twisted-pair based systems. Many companies today still have access to networks through a local loop built on a twisted-pair system. Although twisted-pair systems have contributed a great deal to the evolution of communications, advanced applications on the horizon require larger amounts of bandwidth than twisted-pair can deliver, so the future of twisted-pair is diminishing.

The other transmission medium that was recognized by these 2017 revisions was coaxial cable system. In the center of a coaxial cable is a copper wire that acts as the conductor, where the information travels. The copper wire in coaxial cable is thicker than that in twisted-pair, and it is also unaffected by surrounding wires so that it can provide a higher transmission rate than twisted-pair. The center conductor is surrounded by plastic insulation, which helps filter out extraneous interference. The insulation is covered by the return path, which is usually

840.2

braided-copper shielding or aluminum foil-type covering. Outer jackets form a protective covering for coaxial cable, with the number and type of outer jackets dependent on the intended use of the cable.

First Revision: FR 4586
Public Input: PI 1840

840.48

Unlisted Wires and Cables Entering Building

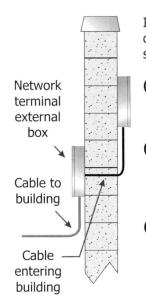

Installations of unlisted premises-powered broadband communication wires and cables entering buildings shall comply with 840.48(A), (B), or (C), as applicable

Network terminal external box

Cable to building

Cable entering building

(A) Optical Fiber Cables - Installations of unlisted optical fiber cables entering buildings shall comply with 770.48

(B) Communications Wires and Cables - Installations of unlisted communications wires and unlisted multipair communications cables entering buildings shall comply with 800.48

(C) Coaxial Cables - Installations of unlisted coaxial cables entering buildings shall comply with 820.48

840.48 Unlisted Wires and Cables Entering Building

- **Type of Change:** Revision

- **Change at a Glance:** Three new first-level subdivisions which outline specific requirements for unlisted optical fiber cables, communication wires and cables, and coaxial cables were added to 840.48.

- **Code Language:** **840.48 Unlisted Wires and Cables and ~~Raceways~~ Entering Buildings. (Premises-Powered Broadband Communications Systems)**
~~The requirements of 770.48 shall apply~~ Installations of unlisted cables entering buildings shall comply with 840.48(A), (B), or (C), as applicable.

(A) Optical Fiber Cables. Installations of unlisted optical fiber cables entering buildings shall comply with 770.48.

(B) Communications Wires and Cables. Installations of unlisted communications wires and unlisted multipair communications cables entering buildings shall comply with 800.48.

(C) Coaxial Cables. Installations of unlisted coaxial cables entering buildings shall comply with 820.48.

- **2014 *NEC* Requirement**
  For unlisted premises-powered broadband communications system cables entering a building, compliance with 770.48 was required.

- **2017 *NEC* Change**
  Premises-powered broadband communications system wires and cables will now be required to comply with 770.48 for unlisted optical fiber cables entering buildings, 800.48 for unlisted communications wires and unlisted multipair communications cables entering buildings, and 820.48 for unlisted coaxial cables entering buildings.

Analysis of the Change:

As noted with the explanatory text at 840.2 of this periodical, revisions were incorporated throughout Article 840 to accommodate twisted pair-based and coaxial cable-based systems in addition to optical fiber-based systems for premises-powered broadband communication systems. Previously, 840.48 dealt with unlisted premises-powered broadband communications cables entering a building. As Article 840 primarily dealt with optical-fiber-based systems, 840.48 simply advised users of the *Code* to comply with 770.48 (Unlisted Optical Fiber Cables and Raceways Entering Buildings).

For the 2017 *NEC*, 840.48 was revised to incorporate specific requirements for unlisted optical fiber cables, communication wires and cables, and coaxial cables. The title was changed to "Unlisted Wires and Cables Entering a Building" rather than "Unlisted Cables and Raceways Entering a Building" as this section deals with wires and cables. Raceways typically do not enter a building in conjunction with premises-powered broadband communications systems, therefore, "raceways" was deleted from the title.

Data and communications cabling installed in a building is typically required to be listed. Listing designations can be found throughout Articles 725, 770, 800, 820, and 830. Each article has listing requirements for such things as hazardous (classified) locations, mechanical execution of work, and the spread of fire or products of combustion and their intended use. Article 840 has references to these Articles 725, 770, 800, 820, and 830 listing references.

Articles 770, 800, and 820 each have paragraphs that describe how unlisted communication cables are permitted to be installed where the length of the cable within the building, measured from the point of entrance, does not exceed 15 m (50 ft), and the cable enters the building from the outside. These same rules will now apply to premises-powered broadband communications system wires and cables as the revisions to 840.48 now will reference 770.48 for unlisted op-

840.48

tical fiber cables entering buildings, 800.48 for unlisted communications wires and unlisted multipair communications cables entering buildings, and 820.48 for unlisted coaxial cables entering buildings.

First Revisions: FR 4633
Public Inputs: PI 1851, PI 254

840.160

Powering Circuits

New 840.160 (Powering Circuits) was added under new Part VI (Premises Powering of Communication Equipment over Communication Cables) with direction to new 725.144 for power delivery circuits that exceed 60 watts on communications cables

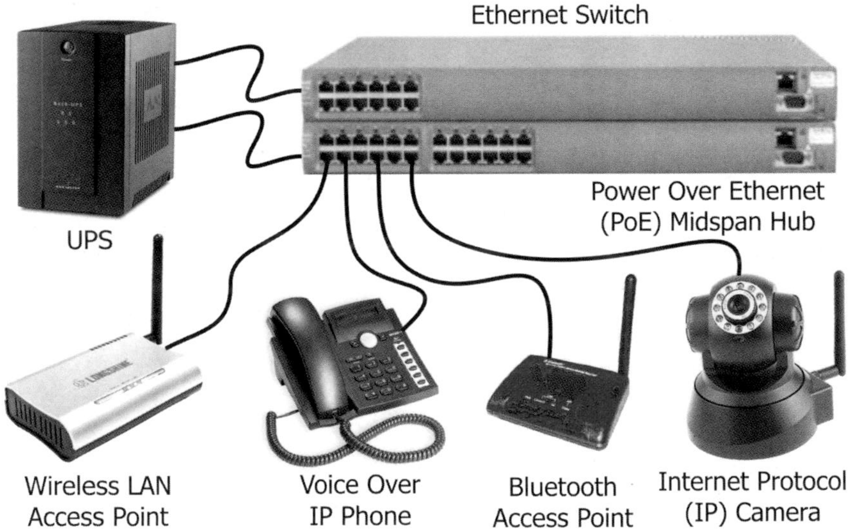

Ethernet Switch

Power Over Ethernet (PoE) Midspan Hub

UPS

Wireless LAN Access Point | Voice Over IP Phone | Bluetooth Access Point | Internet Protocol (IP) Camera

840.160 Powering Circuits

- **Type of Change:** New

- **Change at a Glance:** New 840.160 (Powering Circuits) was added under new Part VI (Premises Powering of Communication Equipment over Communication Cables) with direction to comply with the new 725.144 for power delivery circuits that exceed 60 watts on communications cables.

- **Code Language:** **Part VI. Premises Powering of Communications Equipment over Communications Cables (Premises-Powered Broadband Communications Systems)**

840.160 Powering Circuits. Communications cables, in addition to carrying the communications circuit, shall also be permitted to carry circuits for powering communications equipment. Where the power supplied over a communications cable to communications equipment is greater than 60 watts, communication cables and the power circuit shall comply with 725.144 where communications cables are used in place of Class 2 and Class 3 cables.

- **2014 *NEC* Requirement**
  There were no provisions in Article 840 for communication cables delivering power exceeding 60 watts.

- **2017 *NEC* Change**
  New requirements were added at 840.160 giving permission for communication cables to carry circuits for powering communications equipment. This section goes on to indicate that where the power supplied over a communications cable is greater than 60 watts, communication cables and the power circuit must comply with new 725.144 where communications cables are used in place of Class 2 and Class 3 cables.

Analysis of the Change:

Over the past decade or so, power-over-local area networking (LAN) cable technologies such as power-over-ethernet (PoE) have become a viable powering option for a wide range of applications including premises-powered broadband communications systems. PoE is being widely used today with data and communications circuits. Device manufacturers are designing more sophisticated equipment that demands increased power. As this power is increased, the heat generated within the cable increases as well. This is especially true when the cables are bundled. The additional heat generated by the increased current could push the cables beyond their rated temperatures.

To address this concern, a new type of "limited-power" cable has been introduced to simplify the cable choice and installation considerations. The "-LP" cable designation indicates that the cable has been evaluated to carry the marked current under reasonable worst-case installation scenarios without exceeding the temperature rating of the cable. The certification takes into account large bundle sizes, high ambient temperatures and other issues related to environmental effects, such as enclosed spaces or conduits.

No conductor (or cable) should be used in such a manner that its operating temperature exceeds its rated maximum temperature. Optical fiber cables and communications cables are required have a temperature rating of not less than 60°C (140°F) by sections 770.179 and 800.179. Where cables carrying communications and power are installed, cables rated for temperatures above 60°C (140°F) may be required.

For the 2017 *NEC*, provisions were added at new 725.144 for Class 1, Class 2, and Class 3 remote-control, signaling, and power-limited circuits related to remote powering over local area networking (LAN) cable. These new provi-

840.160

sions include requirements for limiting the power and conductor ampacities of powering over communications cable systems based on wire gauges and bundle sizes. In addition, the new special cables ("LP" cables) were introduced. In conjunction with these Article 725 changes, a new 840.160 was added under a new Part VI (Premises Powering of Communication Equipment over Communication Cables) of Article 840. Rather than repeat the information described in Article 725, this new wording directs the user of the *Code* to 725.144 for power delivery circuits that exceed 60 watts on communications cables.

The provisions of 725.144 (and by reference Part VI of Article 840 and 840.160) provide for the use of the new type of "limited-power" cable with properties chosen to be safe in worst-case installation conditions. The listing requirements for these cables are in 840.170. Similar to Type CMP-CI, Type CMR-CI and Type CM-CI cables, the new "LP" cables are marked Type CMP-LP, Type CMR-LP and Type CM-LP. These cables are listed to have adequate ampacity (wire gauge) and temperature rating for worst-case ambient thermal conditions, e.g., a hot attic, and worst case heating produced by the maximum permissible current being carried by the cables.

840.160

First Revisions: FR 4643
Second Revisions: SR 4564
Public Inputs: PI 1861
Public Comments: PC 638, PC 1181
[Numerous PCs (29) Involved]

Tables & Annex D

Tables

Annex D

Chapter 9

Notes to Tables, Note 9

A multiconductor cable, optical fiber cable, or flexible cord of two or more conductors shall be treated as a single conductor for calculating percentage conduit or tubing fill area

For cables that have elliptical cross sections, the cross-sectional area calculation shall be based on using the major diameter of the ellipse as a circle diameter

Assemblies of single insulated conductors without an overall covering shall not be considered a cable when determining conduit or tubing fill area

The conduit or tubing fill for the assemblies shall be calculated based upon the individual conductors

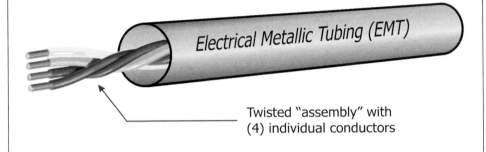

Electrical Metallic Tubing (EMT)

Twisted "assembly" with
(4) individual conductors

Tables

Chapter 9 Tables Chapter 9, Notes to Tables, Note 9

- **Type of Change:** Revision/New

- **Change at a Glance:** New language was added at Note 9 to specify that assemblies of single insulated conductors without an overall covering shall not be considered a cable when determining conduit and tubing fill area.

- **Code Language: Chapter 9 Tables**
  Notes to Tables
  (9) A multiconductor cable, optical fiber cable, or flexible cord of two or more conductors shall be treated as a single conductor for calculating percentage conduit or tubing fill area. For cables that have elliptical cross sections, the cross-sectional area calculation shall be based on using the major diameter of the ellipse as a circle diameter. Assemblies of single insulated conductors without an overall covering shall not be considered a cable when determining conduit or tubing fill area. The conduit or tubing fill for the assemblies shall be calculated based upon the individual conductors.

- **2014 *NEC* Requirement**
  Assemblies of single insulated conductors without an overall covering were not addressed in the notes to the Chapter 9 tables.

- **2017 *NEC* Change**
  New text was added to Note 9 of the Chapter 9 tables to clearly specify that assemblies of single insulated conductors without an overall covering are not to be considered a cable when determining conduit or tubing fill area. The conduit or tubing fill for the assemblies is to be calculated based upon the individual conductors.

Analysis of the Change:

Paying close attention to the tables and notes to the tables of Chapter 9 is the key to determining proper conductor fill for conduits, tubings, and raceways. Proper conductor fill will avoid conductor overheating and possible insulation damage due to excessive heat. Conductors enclosed in a conduit, tubing, or raceway must have proper space and free air around the conductors to properly dissipate heat from the loaded conductors.

Note 9 to the tables of Chapter 9 directs users of the *Code* to treat multiconductor cables, optical fiber cables, or flexible cords of two or more conductors as a single conductor for calculating percentage conduit or tubing fill area. If the cable is elliptical-shaped (such as nonmetallic-sheathed cable), the cross-sectional area calculation shall be based on using the major diameter of the ellipse as a circle diameter. This provision for conduit fill for cables is intended to allow the cable wiring methods in Chapter 3 to be considered a single entity when calculating conduit fill.

New for the 2017 *NEC*, text was added to Note 9 to indicate that assemblies of single insulated conductors without an overall covering are not to be considered a cable when determining conduit or tubing fill area as the conduit or tubing fill for the assemblies is to be calculated based upon the individual conductors.

In recent years, an industry practice developed that allowed twisting several single conductors together and placing the assembly on one reel for shipping and installation. As convenient as this twisting action might be for spooling and shipping, it does not change the essential nature of the pull or the product or change the conduit fill properties of the individual conductors. UL 44 (*Standard for Thermoset-Insulated Wires and Cables*) and UL 83 (*Standard for Thermoplastic-Insulated Wires and Cables*) consider these twisted conductors to be "assemblies," and they are specifically differentiated from multiple conductor cables in these UL standards. Without a definition for "cable" in the *NEC*, this new language at Note 9 to the Chapter 9 tables will clarify this misinterpreted cable application.

First Revisions: FR 2126
Public Inputs: PI 3511

Tables

Informative Annex D, Example D3
Example D3 Store Building

A store 50 ft by 60 ft, or 3000 ft2, has 30 ft of show window. There are a total of 80 duplex receptacles. The service is 120/240 V, single phase 3-wire service. Actual connected lighting load is 8500 VA.

Calculated Load *(see 220.40)*
Noncontinuous Loads

Receptacle Load *(see 220.44)* 80 receptacles at 180 VA		14,400 VA
10,000 VA at 100%		10,000 VA
14,400 VA − 10,000 VA = 4400 at 50%		2,200 VA
	Subtotal	12,200 VA

Continuous Loads

General Lighting*	3000 ft² at 3 VA/ft²	9,000 VA
Show Window Lighting Load	30 ft at 200 VA/ft *[see 220.14(G)]*	6,000 VA
Outside Sign Circuit *[see 220.14(F)]*		1,200 VA
	Subtotal	16,200 VA
	Subtotal from noncontinuous	12,200 VA
	Total noncontinuous loads + continuous loads =	28,400 VA

*In the example, ~~125% of~~ the actual connected lighting load (8500 VA ~~× 1.25 = 10,625 VA~~) is less than ~~125% of~~ the load from Table 220.12, so the minimum lighting load from Table 220.12 is used in the calculation. Had the actual lighting load been greater than the value calculated from Table 220.12, ~~125% of~~ the actual connected lighting load would have been used.

Informative Annex D Example D3 Store Building

- **Type of Change:** Revision

- **Change at a Glance:** Example D3 (Store Building) was revised to remove the "125%" for continuous loads for calculating the volt-amperes (VA) for the actual connected lighting loads.

- **Code Language: Informative Annex D, Example D3**
  A store 50 ft by 60 ft, or 3000 ft2, has 30 ft of show window. There are a total of 80 duplex receptacles. The service is 120/240 V, single phase 3-wire service. Actual connected lighting load is 8500 VA.
  (See *NEC* for complete calculated load and complete text)

  *In the example, ~~125% of~~ the actual connected lighting load (8500 VA ~~× 1.25 = 10,625 VA~~) is less than ~~125% of~~ the load from Table 220.12, so the minimum lighting load from Table 220.12 is used in the calculation. Had the actual lighting load been greater than the value calculated from Table 220.12, ~~125% of~~ the actual connected lighting load would have been used.

  Minimum Size Feeder (or Service) Overcurrent Protection
  [see 215.3 or 230.90]

Subtotal noncontinuous loads	12,200 VA
Subtotal continuous load at 125%	20,250 VA
(16,200 VA × 1.25)	
	_____
	Total 32,450 VA

32,450 VA ÷ 240 V = 135 A

The next higher standard size is 150 A (see 240.6).

■ **2014 *NEC* Requirement**
In the Informative Annex D3 example for a store building, the actual connected lighting load is calculated at "125% of the actual connected lighting load (8500 VA × 1.25 = 10,625 VA) and compared to 125% of the load from Table 220.12.

■ **2017 *NEC* Change**
The "125%" for the actual connected lighting load has been removed as continuous loads are calculated at 125% in the "Minimum Size Feeder (or Service) Overcurrent Protection."

Analysis of the Change:

Informative Annex D gives the user of the *Code* examples of some of the common calculations expressed throughout the *Code*. Informative Annex D is not a part of the requirements of the *NEC*, but is included for informational purposes only. Example D3 gives an example of calculating noncontinuous and continuous loads for a store building. This example includes calculations for such things as minimum number of branch circuits required, receptacle loads, and minimum size feeder (or service) overcurrent protection.

In previous editions of the *Code*, this example informs the user of the *Code* when determining the actual connected lighting load that "125% of the actual connected lighting load (8500 VA × 1.25 = 10,625 VA) is less than 125% of the load from Table 220.12, so the minimum lighting load from Table 220.12 is used in the calculation." For the 2017 *NEC*, this "125%" for the actual connected lighting load has been removed.

Factoring a continuous connected lighting load at 125% is not appropriate in the "Calculated Load" section of this example. There is no such "125%" factor in the 220.12 provision. Factoring for continuous loads at 125% is covered in the "Minimum Size Feeder (or Service) Overcurrent Protection" as required by 215.3 or 230.90 respectively.

First Revisions: FR 341
Public Inputs: PI 1181

Annex D

Informative Annex D, Example D7

Sizing of Service Conductors for Dwelling(s)

Example D7 for "Sizing of Service Conductors for Dwelling(s)" has been revised clarifying the use of temperature corrections and adjustment factors along with the 83% adjustment from 310.15(B)(7)

Service-entrance conductors: 310.15(B)(7) rating can be applied along with temperature and adjustment correction factors from 310.15(B)(2) or (3)

Previous Table 310.15(B)(7) was inserted after Example D7 for reference and use with sizing of dwelling unit service and main feeder conductors

Annex D

Informative Annex D, Example D7 Sizing of Service Conductors for Dwelling(s)

- **Type of Change:** Revision

- **Change at a Glance:** The example for "Sizing of Service Conductors for Dwelling(s)" has been revised clarifying the use of temperature corrections and adjustment factors. Previous Table 310.15(B)(7) was inserted after the example for reference and use.

- **Code Language: Example D7 Sizing of Service Conductors for Dwelling(s) [see 310.15(B)(7)]**
  Service conductors and feeders for certain dwellings are permitted to be sized in accordance with 310.15(B)(7).

  With No Required Adjustment or Correction Factors
  If a 175-ampere service rating is selected, a service conductor is then sized as follows:

  175 amperes × 0.83 = 145.25 amperes per 310.15(B)(7).

  If no other adjustments or corrections are required for the installation, then, in accordance with Table 310.15(B)(16), a 1/0 AWG Cu or a 3/0 AWG Al meets this rating at 75°C (167°F).

With Required Temperature Correction Factor

If a 175-ampere service rating is selected, a service conductor is then 175 amperes × 0.83 = 145.25 amperes per 310.15(B)(7).

If the conductors are installed in an ambient temperature of 40°C (104°F), the conductor ampacity must be multiplied by the appropriate correction factor in Table 310.15(B)(2)(a). In this case, we will use an XHHW-2 conductor, so we use a correction factor of 0.91 to find the minimum conductor ampacity and size:

145.25 x .91 – 159.6 amperes

In accordance with Table 310.15(B)(16), a 2/0 AWG CU or a 4/0 AWG AL would be required.

If no temperature correction or ampacity adjustment factors are required, the following table includes conductor sizes calculated using the requirements in 310.15(B)(7). This table is based on 75°C terminations and without any adjustment or correction factors.

(See NEC and illustration provided for complete table added at Example D7)

- **2014 NEC Requirement**
  Informative Annex Example D7 gave an example for sizing dwelling unit service conductors using the 83 percent allowable ampacity value adjustment from 310.15(B)(7). The example did not show any adjustment or temperature correction factors.

- **2017 NEC Change**
  Informative Annex Example D7 was revised to give two examples for sizing dwelling unit service conductors. The previous D7 is identified as an example with no required adjustment or correction factors, and a new example was added to illustrate the method used when temperature correction factors are involved. The new example calculates the size for dwelling unit service conductors with the allowed 310.15(B)(7) eighty-three percent adjustment along with a temperature correction factor from Table 310.15(B)(2)(a).

Annex D

Analysis of the Change:

From the publication of the 1956 *NEC*, residential service-entrance conductors have been permitted to be sized at slightly higher ampacity values than the normal limitations found in ampacity tables such as Table 310.15(B)(16). This higher ampacity allowance was permitted primarily due to the diversity loads associated with dwelling units. The 2011 *NEC* contained Table 310.15(B)(7) that listed these dwelling unit ampacity values for dwelling unit services or the main feeder rated from 100 to 400 amperes. The table, whose genesis could be traced to a note at the bottom of Table 1a of Chapter 10 of the 1956 *NEC*, was removed from the *Code* for the 2014 *NEC*. This dwelling unit ampacity table makes a triumphant return for the 2017 *NEC*, following Example D7 in Informative Annex

D. The table was added to show the correct dwelling unit service or feeder conductor sizes required if there are no adjustment or correction factors that must be applied. The conductor sizes shown in this table correspond to the 83 percent allowance permitted by the provisions of 310.15(B)(7) for dwelling unit service and feeder conductors.

When applying the 83 percent adjustments or the ampacity values from previous Table 310.15(B)(7) to dwelling unit service or feeder conductors, there has always been a "gray area," for installers and inspectors alike, as to whether temperature and correction factors should or even could be applied to these adjusted ampacity values. Were temperature and correction factors already built into the ampacity values of 310.15(B)(7) or previous Table 310.15(B)(7)? Language was added to 310.15(B)(7) to help clarify these questions. This new text at 310.15(B)(7) indicates that where correction or adjustment factors are required by 310.15(B)(2) or (3), they are permitted to be applied to the ampacity associated with the temperature rating of the conductor. This added text at 310.15(B)(7) will make it clear that they are permitted to be applied to the conductor temperature rating column ampacity when necessary due to temperature correction and adjustment factors. This provision was indicated in an informational note in the 2014 *NEC* but is now part of the enforceable language in the 2017 *NEC*. Service and feeder conductors sized in compliance with 310.15(B)(7) are subject to the same environmental conditions that apply to conductors that are not selected according to 310.15(B)(7).

Informative Annex Example D7 Sizing of Service Conductors for Dwelling(s) [Former Table 310.15(B)(7)]

Service or Feeder Rating (Amperes)	Conductor (AWG or kcmil)	
	Copper	Aluminum or Copper-Clad Aluminum
100	4	2
110	3	1
125	2	1/0
150	1	2/0
175	1/0	3/0
200	2/0	4/0
225	3/0	250
250	4/0	300
300	250	350
350	350	500
400	400	600

This same temperature and correction factor clarification was incorporated into

Example D7 for an example of sizing of service conductors for dwelling units. The previous D7 example is now under the banner of "With No Required Adjustment or Correction Factors." A new example with the title of "With Required Temperature Correction Factor" gives the sizing of dwelling unit service conductors with the allowed 310.15(B)(7) eighty-three percent adjustment along with a temperature correction factor from Table 310.15(B)(2)(a).

First Revisions: FR 1513
Public Inputs: PI 3922

Informative Annex D, Example D8
Feeder Short-Circuit and Ground-Fault Protection

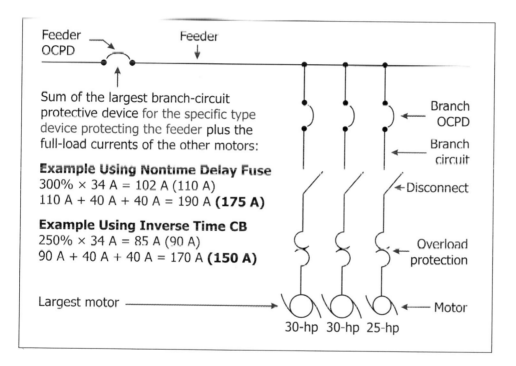

Informative Annex D, Example D8 Motor Circuit Conductors, Overload Protection, and Short-Circuit and Ground-Fault Protection

- **Type of Change:** Revision/New

- **Change at a Glance:** Example D8 was revised to provide an additional example using different types of protective devices for feeder short-circuit and ground-fault protection.

- **Code Language: Example D8 Motor Circuit Conductors, Overload Protection, and Short-Circuit and Ground-Fault Protection** (see 240.6, 430.6, 430.22, 430.23, 430.24, 430.32, 430.52, and 430.62, Table 430.52, and Table 430.250)

Determine the minimum required conductor ampacity, the motor overload protection, the branch-circuit short-circuit and ground-fault protection, and the feeder protection, for three induction-type motors on a 480-V, 3-phase feeder, as follows:

(a) One 25-hp, 460-V, 3-phase, squirrel-cage motor, nameplate full-load current 32 A, Design B, Service Factor 1.15

(b) Two 30-hp, 460-V, 3-phase, wound-rotor motors, nameplate primary full-load current 38 A, nameplate secondary full-load current 65 A, 40°C rise.

(See *NEC* for complete text for Example D8)

Feeder Short-Circuit and Ground-Fault Protection

(a) Example Using Nontime Delay Fuse. The rating of the feeder protective device is based on the sum of the largest branch-circuit protective device (example is 110 A) for the specific type of device protecting the feeder: 300% × 34 A = 102 A (therefore the next largest standard size, 110 A, would be used) plus the sum of the full-load currents of the other motors, or 110 A + 40 A + 40 A = 190 A. The nearest standard fuse that does not exceed this value is 175 A *[see 240.6 and 430.62(A)]*.

(b) Example Using Inverse Time Circuit Breaker. The largest branch-circuit protective device for the specific type of device protecting the feeder, 250% × 34 A = 85 A. The next larger standard size is 90 A, plus the sum of the full-load currents of the other motors, or 90 A + 40 A + 40 A = 170 A. The nearest standard inverse time circuit breaker that does not exceed this value is 150 A *[see 240.6 and 430.62(A)]*

- **2014 *NEC* Requirement**
  Example D8 might have led users of the *Code* to the assumption that only one type of protective device was used for feeder short-circuit and ground-fault protection.

- **2017 *NEC* Change**
  Example D8 has been revised for the "Feeder Short-Circuit and Ground-Fault Protection" portion to show (a) an example using non-time delay fuse and (b) an example using inverse time circuit breaker.

Analysis of the Change:

When it comes time to determine the short-circuit and ground-fault protection for a feeder supplying specific fixed motor load(s), 430.62(A) gives direction to determine which motor supplied by the feeder has the largest rated branch-circuit short circuit and ground-fault protective device. The next step is to add up the full-load currents (FLC) of the other motors in the group and then add this FLC sum of these other motors to the device rating of the largest rated branch-circuit short circuit and ground-fault protective device. The "round-up" rule for motor branch circuits [430.52(C)(1) Ex 1] does not apply to a motor feeder protection device rating; therefore, rounding down to the overcurrent protection device that does not exceed this calculated value is required.

An example of this complicated motor feeder short-circuit and ground-fault protection helps illustrate this point. That is where Example D8 in Informative Annex D comes in handy. This example experienced extensive revision under the "Feeder Short-Circuit and Ground-Fault Protection" banner for the 2017 *NEC*. The feeder portion of Example D8 was divided into two categories: (a) an example using a non-time delay fuse and (b) an example using an inverse time circuit breaker. The previous text in the example might have led the user of the *Code* to think that the size of the short-circuit and ground-fault protective device of the feeder was always based upon the type of protective device that had been chosen for the largest protective device of the branch circuits fed by the feeder, plus the sum of the other motors. An additional example using different types of devices was needed and, therefore, added for this *Code* cycle.

The previous Example D8 relating to motor feeder short-circuit and ground-fault protection calculations did not accurately reflect the requirements of 430.62(A). The new text in the example introduces the phrase "for the specific device protecting the feeder" to properly correspond with 430.62(A). The additional text in the revised example further clarifies the requirement where a different type of protective device is used.

Annex D

Second Revisions: SR 3007
Public Inputs: PI 440
Public Comments: PC 562, PC 309

Analysis of Changes, *NEC-2017*

Editor-in-Chief — David Clements

Director of Education — L. Keith Lofland

Technical Advisor, Education, Codes and Standards — Joseph Wages Jr.

Director of Publishing — Kathryn Ingley

Project Manager: Publishing, Research, & Data — Laura Hildreth

Creative Director / Cover Design — John Watson

Principal Author — L. Keith Lofland

Technical Review — Christel Hunter, L. Keith Lofland, Joseph Wages, Jr., Mark Earley, Mark Hilbert, Jeff Sargent, Donny Cook, James Rogers, David Williams, Paul Dobrowsky

IAEI representatives to 2017 Code-Making Panels:

- CMP-1 Paul Sood and Gary Jones
- CMP-2 Mark Hilbert and Jim Imlah
- CMP-3 Susan Newman-Scearce and Joseph Wages, Jr.
- CMP-4 James Rogers and Rhonda Parkhurst
- CMP-5 Charles Palmieri and William Pancake, III
- CMP-6 John Stacey and Borgia Noel
- CMP-7 David Williams and Allen Turner
- CMP-8 Pete Jackson and Grant Hammett
- CMP-9 David Humphrey and L. Keith Lofland
- CMP-10 Robert Kauer and Christopher Mark Jensen
- CMP-11 Robert Fahey and Rodney Jones
- CMP-12 Phil Clark and Phillip Yehl
- CMP-13 Steve Froemming and Barbara Jo Ann Mentzer
- CMP-14 Haywood C. Kines and Mitchell Feininger
- CMP-15 Joe Dupriest and Clinton Bret Stoddard
- CMP-16 Tom Moore and Larry Chan
- CMP-17 Donny Cook and Ira Lee Douglas
- CMP-18 Jack Jamison, Jr. and Rick Hollander
- CMP-19 Ron Chilton and Dean Hunter

Photographs by:

Companies
Allied Wire and Cable, Inc.
Belden Cable
Bender Incorporated
Bridgeport Fittings
Carlon
Copper Bussman
Cooper Lighting
Eaton Corporation
Erico International
Generac
Hubbell
Leviton
Littlefuse
NEMA
Oak Ridge National Laboratory
Panduit
Pass and Seymore/Legrand
Power Bus Way
RSCC Wire and Cable
Safety Quick Lighting and Fan Corp.
Seimens
Schneider Electric/ Square D Company
Shermco Industries
SnapPower
SolarBOS
Southwire Company, Inc.
Thomas and Betts
Underwriters Laboratories, Inc.

Individuals
IAEI Archives
James Conrad
Donny Cook
Steve Douglas
Jeff Fecteau
Darrell Hefley
Mark Hilbert
Scott Humphrey
Randy Hunter
Michael J. Johnston
David Kendall
Chad Kennedy
Jim LeFevre
L. Keith Lofland
Rick Maddox
Bill McGovern
Dale Missey
Dick Owen
Brian Rock
James Rogers
Joseph Wages, Jr.
John Wiles
Dave Williams

Composed at International Association of Electrical Inspectors in Georgia and Helvetica LT Std by Adobe®
Printed by Walsworth Print Group on 70# Gloss Text. Bound in 12 pt. Cover.